John Wren

To Helga, without whom this book, and so much else in my life, would have been impossible

JOHN WREN
a life reconsidered

James Griffin

Scribe Publications
Melbourne

Scribe Publications Pty Ltd
PO Box 523
Carlton North, Victoria Australia 3054
Email: scribe@bigpond.net.au

First published by Scribe Publications 2004

Edited by Jean Dunn
Jacket design by Miriam Rosenbloom
Typeset in 11 on 14.3 pt Minion by J&M Typesetting
Printed and bound in Australia by Griffin Press

National Library of Australia
Cataloguing-in-Publication data

Griffin, James, 1929- .
John Wren : a life reconsidered.

Bibliography.
Includes index.
ISBN 1 920769 11 0.

1. Wren, John 1871–1953. 2. Gamblers - Australia - Biography. 3. Sports promoters - Australia - Biography. I. Title.

795.092

www.scribepub.com.au

Contents

Illustrations

[*between pages 214 and 215*]

The family photographs and the David Low cartoon were kindly provided by Christopher Wren.

Preface

My interest in writing about John Wren was aroused when I was researching the entry on Archbishop Daniel Mannix for the *Australian Dictionary of Biography*. What had passed for biographies of this eminent prelate seemed inadequate and, overall, hagiographical, needing revision. The result was controversial, but a number of scholars were kind enough to believe that what I produced was, on the whole, more veracious than what had previously been written. There was a contrary problem in relation to Mannix's friend, John Wren; for political reasons he had been mercilessly vilified in Frank Hardy's best-seller, *Power Without Glory*, the research for which was clearly fraudulent.

Subsequently I wrote the entry on John Wren for the *ADB* and, together with Geoffrey Browne, delivered a paper, 'Some light in shady places?' at the sixth Irish-Australian Conference in Melbourne in July 1990 (published in P. Bull et al. (eds), *Irish-Australian Studies*, 1991). In that article I pointed out that the problem in writing more comprehensively about Wren was 'one of evidence':

> Documentary and reliably recorded oral testimony are in short supply. Wren kept no diaries; his business records are not preserved. His letters are scarce and brief. His activities and general career were rarely analytically scrutinised in spite of the Hardy trial [1951] and the various royal commissions that concerned themselves with interests in which he had a part. Only his oldest son, John F. Wren, has provided any reminiscences from among the Wren family ... Wren's secretaries and friends, even if they had had Boswellian aspirations, would have been stumped by their subject's taciturnity ...

As it turned out, there was much more to be extracted from the public record, even newspapers, than I envisaged in 1990. Then in 1992 Penny Wren, wife of John Wren's grandson, Christopher, discovered a basket full of letters and assorted documents, the most noteworthy of which were ten revealing letters to John Wren from Dr H. V. Evatt, former High Court Justice, president of the United Nations General Assembly and leader of the federal parliamentary Opposition. I publicised these letters in three issues of *Eureka Street* in 1992, but admirers of Evatt seemed reluctant to acknowledge them. Obviously, more comprehensive research was needed, and a more informative biography than hitherto was possible—one which would confront the legends surrounding Wren and examine the allegations made about him in *Power Without Glory.*

Scrutiny of my range of sources will explain why at my age and living in Canberra I needed a research assistant. I found an excellent professional one in Damien Cash, a younger member of a family with whom I had a lifelong friendship. Realising my problems, and themselves keen to know the truth about their forebear, five grandchildren of John Wren—Christopher Wren (Melbourne), Michael Wren (Sydney), John Wren (Brisbane), Gabrielle Pizzi (Melbourne) and Sue Wardlaw (Melbourne)—paid Damien Cash's research expenses. I had previously been acquainted with the three grandsons as a teacher at Xavier College, Kew, in the 1950s and 1960s. They were as keen to know about their grandfather as I was. No other subsidy has been necessary and no influence whatsoever has been brought to bear on me in the writing of this biography. In view of the breadth of John Wren's activities this research cannot be exhaustive, and further research may open up other veins of enquiry, fill out some of the incidents recounted here, and modify some judgments.

I would like to thank most particularly Damien Cash for his thorough, lucid and highly literate assistance and, going back further into the 1980s, Geoffrey Browne, who uncovered some recondite documents and was always a source of reliable information. Richard Stremski (*Kill for Collingwood*) was most generous in giving me access to research notes, as was Niall Brennan (*John Wren, Gambler*) in providing me with copies of informative correspondence to himself and newspaper articles on Wren's Tote. Michael Berry of Broad Oak Productions (Maleny, Queensland) made available two audio tapes of the late J. F. Wren. I am also grateful to the late J. F. Wren for several lengthy interviews. The late S. M. Keon MLA, MHR, was an occasional source. Ray Betts, a senior of Coopers & Lybrand (which incorporated Buckley & Hughes, Wren's accountants), and the late Pierce Cody were also generous with documents and recollections. I profited from conversations with and access to papers of the late Pauline Armstrong (*Frank Hardy and the Making of* Power Without Glory).

The late Les McCarthy of the Melbourne Diocesan Historical Commission was most helpful in the mid-1980s. Fr T. B. Boland gave me access to some Wren correspondence in the Brisbane Archdiocesan Archives. The manuscript rooms of the National Library of Australia (Canberra), Oxley Library (Brisbane), LaTrobe Library (Melbourne) and Baillieu Library (University of Melbourne) provided sources. The late Lady Barry and Joan Hardy gave me access to Mr Justice Barry's papers in the National Library of Australia. Other informants include Susan Aird, Frank Bongiorno, John Coburn SJ, Mimi Colligan, K. S. Inglis, Pat Kelly, Christopher Koch, Elizabeth Kwan, Michael McKernan, Robert Murray, Bede Nairn, Laurie Roberts, Bob Rose, Alf Sleigh, Bill Stutt, Ann Turner and Christopher Wren.

For constructive comments, encouragement and various assistance I would like to thank Bruce Armstrong, Dorothy and Pat Cash, Leo Cash, Michael Cash, Michael Kelly SJ, David Lovell, Georgina and Paul McSweeney, Kay and Tom Matthiesson, Sylvia and the late Jim Morrissey, Bede Nairn, Hank Nelson, Paul Ormonde, Jim and Eve Provan, the late Geoffrey Serle, Colin Thornton-Smith, Bill Tully, Ian Willis, Ian Wilson and Christopher and Penny Wren. My thanks also go to Jean Dunn as professional editor and Henry Rosenbloom as my expeditious and adventurous publisher. My deep gratitude to my wife Helga for her unflagging support in typing and editing and for her advice and tolerance is expressed implicitly in the dedication of this book. Our family has encouraged and assisted us in a variety of ways.

James Griffin

Sectarianism is an influence difficult to combat, because its propaganda is for the most part insidious and underground. Ir rarely comes out into the open. It performs its lethal work in the dark, with murderous innuendo and slanderous tongue. Sectarianism thrives on ignorance and prejudice and is responsible for more ill-will, hatred and rancour in the community than any single cause.

E. G. THEODORE
Labour Daily, 25 May 1925

Introduction

JOHN WREN, financial investor, sports impresario, political 'fixer' and philanthropist, may be the most maligned person in Australian literature.

Born into an Irish-Catholic family in working-class Collingwood in 1871, but already prosperous by his early twenties as a result of his illegal gambling activities, Wren moved in the early 1900s across the Yarra River to the elevated and elite Studley Park. There he overlooked his native suburb, where he was generally regarded as a benefactor. Beyond the inner suburbs of Melbourne, Wren was frequently seen as a corrupt, secretive 'godfather'. In 1950 he was sensationally denounced and defamed in Frank Hardy's best-selling novel *Power Without Glory* as Australia's Al Capone.

More than fifty years after Wren's death in 1953 the defamations are still current, even internationally. Australian expatriate and foundation editor of *Virago*, Carmen Callil, and noted Irish novelist Colm Toibin include *Power Without Glory* in their compilation, *The Modern Library: the Two Hundred Best Novels in English since 1950*. They justify their choice not on literary grounds or on the success of Wren's fictional characterisation of 'John West', but on what they believe to have been the real, the historical, John Wren:

> John Wren was the corrupt business magnate who *controlled Melbourne*—its sporting, gambling and political life, its police and

> its Catholic Church—in the decades before 1950 [emphasis added] It is in Hardy's understanding of the evil grandeur of the man and the tangled forces that explain him and bring him down that the value of this novel lies.[1]

Hardy levelled many charges against Wren's pseudonym, 'John West'—such as his involvement in homicides, terrorist bombing, thuggery, racketeering and blackmail; rigging of sporting events, and corruption of politicians, the judiciary, police and even clergy; and abuse of family—but he did not allege overall control of the metropolis. In fact, there is a passage in *Power Without Glory* where, to his chagrin, 'West' is reminded by a certain 'Baineton' (a scion of swindler William Baillieu, who became the so-called Money King of Australia) that ultimate power lies with the mining directors and bankers, not with an upstart from Collingwood.

But Callil and Toibin can take heart from two surveys jointly undertaken in 1999 by the Melbourne *Age* and the *Sydney Morning Herald.* Asked what was the 'most influential work published in Australia during the twentieth century', the 'opinion leaders' nominated *Power Without Glory*; the general readers placed it second. What did that mean and how was it understood by respondents?

The publication of *Power Without Glory* resulted in a highly publicised criminal-libel trial of Hardy in June 1951, and one can speculate about the political effects of that event on the August referendum on the dissolution of the Communist Party, for example. The former communist journalist Rupert Lockwood had a more fertile idea of what the book was about and whose interest Hardy was ultimately promoting:

> [*Power Without Glory* was] a damaging corruption of Australian economic and social history. By concentrating on Irish-Catholics the Hardy book shielded the real economic owners, the finance manipulators and rulers of Australia. The interest thus shielded welcomed *Power Without Glory* ... Irish conspiracies by Sinn Feiners and others, Catholic plans for control in vital fields and the rest, substituted in Australia for European anti-Semitism.[2]

Power Without Glory may have provided grist for Labor's leader, Dr H. V. Evatt, when in October 1954 he blamed Catholic Actionists in his party for his defeat in that year's federal elections. Reversing a maxim which Balzac inscribed under a bust of Napoleon, Evatt told Hardy, so the latter claimed, that what he had done in *Power Without Glory* with his pen, he (Evatt) intended to consummate with the sword.[3] In this sense, the book could have had a role in the Labor Split of 1954–5 and thus in the maintenance of Liberal-National (Country) Party governments for the next seventeen years.

But this is hardly what the opinion leaders or newspaper readers meant. Certainly, *Power Without Glory* had aggravated the anti-Catholic sectarianism which had been a feature of Australian society since its beginnings. But is this all that 'influential' meant? Or had Hardy's creation of a credible archetypal villain—an Al Capone, as he branded Wren—justified Australians' cynicism about politicians and the inequalities in our society?

Today it seems remarkable that such a crude *roman à clef* could have had such impact. But Wren's notoriety is still such that for many reputable writers it is almost *de rigueur* to preface even passing references to him with terms such as 'nefarious', 'shady', 'sleazy', 'criminal', 'racketeer' and 'gangster'.

Hardy's calumny has been perpetuated by Australia's most celebrated and controversial historian, C. Manning Clark, in the fifth volume of *A History of Australia.* He linked the personally austere and usually taciturn Wren with John Norton—the paranoid, dipsomaniac proprietor of the scandal-sheet *Truth*—as 'a preyer on humanity' who 'debauched society'. Their photographs are juxtaposed, and Clark read in Wren's face 'the loneliness of a man enslaved by the bitch goddess of success'. As for Wren's philanthropy, Clark saw him simply as 'a Father Christmas to the afflicted and the distressed'. Only someone bred and living in bourgeois comfort could fail to appreciate how vital were the handouts to the poor by people like Wren before the days of the welfare state, or how well-intentioned they might be. Clark was convinced that Wren made 'huge sums of money by roguery' and that he intimidated Labor politicians in particular:

> outwardly the purest of the pure, but inwardly ravening wolves in the presence of alcohol or women [they] cowered in the corridors of Parliament House when a hireling of John Wren whispered what might happen to them if they did not toe the line.[4]

How did Clark arrive at these opinions? His footnotes contain only one substantive source, an article in the first issue of the *Lone Hand* (1 May 1907), an offshoot of the often scurrilous Sydney *Bulletin.* His mentors were Hardy and *Power Without Glory*; Hardy boasted that the historian 'used to ring him to check the facts when he was researching the life and works of John Wren'.[5]

Wren legends have been plentiful, and live on. On the very weekend when John Wren's last surviving offspring, John Francis Wren, died, a local pagliaccio published a magazine article on 'monumental' buildings including The Tote, in Johnston Street, Collingwood:

> This lovely old working-class pub … steeped in history and … emblematic of the people and its neighbourhood …
>
> Many Melburnians have heard the stories about the infamous underworld figure John Wren, on whom Frank Hardy based his novel *Power Without Glory.* Between the wars and beyond, Wren used the tote as the centre of his activities. He was a feared man among the locals of Collingwood, or Carringbush, as it was then known.
>
> Sit in the front bar … and hear the regular drinkers tell stories about Wren and the secret tunnels under the road to his SP bookmaking office.[6]

How does one cram so many furphies into so small a space? In Wren's heyday there was no such hotel as The Tote, a name capitalising on Hardy's book. And 'Carringbush' was Hardy's pseudonym for Collingwood, although there are educated Melbourne people who assert that Carringbush was the original name of the area.[7] I have never heard of the teetotalling Wren frequenting such a hotel or any other. Wren's 'tote' was the totalisator (rather than SP, or starting price) betting that he notoriously worked in Collingwood. It closed in 1907. And those secret tunnels, like the ones under the road between the homes of Archbishop Mannix and John Wren, were fables.

A notable historian of Melbourne, Graeme Davison, believes that Wren 'would not have become a figure of history without the publication of [*Power Without Glory*].[8] Some readers of social history, however, may well be surprised at the amount of ink and indignation spilt over Wren in the early years of the past century, and at his significance as a focus for sectarianism. Aficionados of sport should at least admire Wren's initiative in providing so much public entertainment—in theatre and cinema, too: John Cain Jr. considers John Wren 'arguably the most innovative and audacious showman in Australia' during the first half of the twentieth century.[9] There will be differing opinions as to Wren's influence in politics, but since the discovery in 1992 of H. V. Evatt's letters to him, attesting friendship and asking for favours, it can hardly be dismissed as negligible or uninteresting. The Catholic Church certainly used Wren's 'good offices'—and substantial sums of his money. And his reputation stood high in the business world; he was no mere speculator or asset-stripper.

All this justifies a fresh biography, and the sources I have investigated yield, I believe, a significantly different characterisation of John Wren than the one which has been handed down to us.

CHAPTER ONE

Family and Character

JOHN WREN'S FATHER, described as a 'labourer' (later as a 'pitcher-setter'), emigrated from County Clare, Ireland, aged fifteen in 1848—three years before gold was discovered and Victoria was officially separated from New South Wales. The unwanted transportation of convicts to eastern Australia did not cease until 1853, but John Snr was not a 'ticket-of-leave' man.[1] A grandfather, James Wren, followed in 1852. Almost seventy years of age, he settled at first at Epping and then, after the death of his wife, née Catherine O'Brien, he married Catherine Smith, née Logie, and went to live in Gold Street, Collingwood, where he died. Wren's mother, Margaret née Nester, a 'domestic' aged fifteen and also from Clare, arrived in 1854.

John Snr and Margaret married in St Francis Church, Melbourne, on 5 August 1864, both signing the register with an X. Neither became literate but, in a land of brash opportunity, which offered male suffrage and equal common law and statutory rights, they managed to acquire a modest competency. They had, however, the disadvantages of being Irish, Catholic and working class.

Only one Christian name is registered on John Wren's certificate of birth (3 April 1871) at 35 Ballarat Street, Collingwood; 'Stephen' was added at his baptism (23 April) in St Patrick's Cathedral, the proximity of the two events indicating a strong Irish-Catholic affiliation.[2] His life was to span the foundation of the Australian Labor Party (1891), two great depressions (1890s, 1930s), federation of the Australian colonies (1901), two world wars (1914–18, 1939–45) and their aftermath, until his death in 1953.

Wren's parents were not indigent, nor their house a slum, as Hardy maintained. When his mother died in Collingwood in 1901, she left three single-fronted, four-roomed brick cottages in Gold Street, valued at £900, to her 'dear husband', who was 'joint tenant' with her of the double-fronted house in Ballarat Street. Wren's eldest son, John Francis, the custodian of family lore, said that while his grandfather had been 'a heavy drinker', the household reputedly was otherwise carefully run, frugal without luxuries, but certainly not sordid. Margaret was resourceful and hospitable. John Snr was a pro-unionist. Wren remembered being asked to accompany his father to the Melbourne Town Hall to hear Rev. Prior Butler appeal for funds on behalf of the London dockers during their long strike in the 1880s.[3]

Wren's birth certificate lists two older brothers, Joseph aged four and Edward Arthur aged two. There were no further children. After his rise to riches, Wren remained bonded to his brothers; obviously it was a 'loyal' family. Wren named his second son after the rather indolent but genial Joseph ('a binge drinker', said John Francis). Like Arthur he came to own substantial property (probate, £59,234) which, as he did not marry, he left entirely to Wren, who was no doubt the provenance. Wren's eldest daughter was named after his mother and another after his maternal grandmother, indicating some reverence for his forebears.

Family disgrace

The Wren family was disgraced when, on 27 February 1889, chief justice Higinbotham recorded sentences of death against four young men, one (Meredith) for criminally assaulting Emma Hamilton on the river bank near the Johnston Street Bridge, Collingwood, the other three (Batty, Arthur Wren and Minogue) for aiding and abetting, although Batty had also taken part in the assault. An associate was found not guilty and discharged. His Honour remarked:

> there were circumstances … that led him to think … the prisoners should be recommended to the prerogative of the royal mercy and should not suffer the extreme penalty of the law … they would be subject to a … very heavy and severe term of imprisonment.

Meredith and Batty who actually raped Emma Hamilton, and Arthur Wren who did not, had their sentences reduced to twelve years with two separate floggings of twelve lashes each. Thomas Minogue's sentence—he had 'turned dog' and blamed Arthur for the happening—was commuted to seven years with one flogging of fifteen lashes. His Honour, in his 'exhaustive summing up extending over two hours', said:

> The character of the prosecutrix was a matter that the jury would have to consider. She was a married woman living apart from her husband and cohabiting with a man named Riley in Collingwood [next door to the Wrens]. It also appeared she had been drinking with two of the prisoners [one of them Arthur Wren] on the day before the assault, and her testimony regarding the whole occurrence would not be worthy of credence were it not that it was corroborated by other evidence. He had hardly believed that the woman had sunk so low as to be a consenting party in the presence of others, as was suggested for the defence. The jury were all young men, having been chosen he supposed, because they were more likely to feel the same passions as would probably have actuated the prisoners, but he hoped that would not prevent them from fairly considering the merits of the case. He also reminded them that the feeling of disgust towards an immoral woman could be carried too far.

Obviously in this case, it was not. Constable Gleeson had said of the accused:

> the prisoners are all bad characters and have several times been before the Court for various offences. Prisoner Meredith only came out of Pentridge at 9.00 am on 23 January [the morning of the offence], after serving a sentence of two years for burglary. They are all companions.

Meredith (alias John Edwards) had three 'priors' as well as two years for burglary; Batty had three including assault and larceny; Minogue had ten. Arthur, barely twenty years old and the youngest, had three 'priors' for abusive language only, the last on the previous 10 December involving Emma Hamilton. He had done nothing serious enough to be sent to jail until he quite culpably abetted, even could be said to have provoked the rape.

John Francis Wren, born twenty years after the conviction, believed that his Uncle Arthur, whom he said was 'a nice, kindly man', had been harshly treated. The story as he had heard it—and it would probably not have been discussed with him in any detail—was that Hamilton, 'a lady of the night', had occupied at one time one of his parents' cottages, and that Arthur had had an altercation with her on one occasion over the rent. The suggestion was that she was paying him back by implicating him in her rape. The evidence showed that she was living with Riley next to Arthur's parents' house. In the previous December she had taken Arthur to court for abusive language and he was fined £10 or three months. After that, she said, she did not speak to him.

However, on Saturday 19 January, Emma Hamilton had left Riley. But then, she said, she was with Arthur 'nearly the whole of Tuesday' (22 February). She had pawned her ring to buy drinks. There are discrepancies between her deposition and her evidence, and it is obvious her memory was affected by drink. She had met a man whom she hardly knew called Ted Ivanhoe (actually Vinall), who squired her on Tuesday night after 11 pm when Arthur left. She met him next day (Wednesday 23 February), and went to the riverside. There they were approached by Arthur and Minogue. Arthur, she said, plucked a brooch from the neck of her dress and pocketed it. 'Ivanhoe' did nothing in response but soon moved some distance away with Hamilton. All the defendants then followed, with apparent menace. Meredith threw Hamilton to the ground; Batty held her legs. Meredith and then Batty 'had connection' with her. She screamed out, 'Arthur Wren, for God's sake go for a policeman'. He laughed, 'Serve you right, you bugger, I have my revenge. Do you remember Christmas time?' He then observed the rape from a distance. The gallant 'Ivanhoe' was 'also standing on the bank'.

There can be little doubt that Arthur took a lead at least in harassing Hamilton, but his family and others would have thought, in line with contemporary attitudes, that his punishment should have been less than Meredith's and Batty's. The original sentence seems draconian, and there is little doubt that it would have been less so for a youth with a similar petty record from 'Yarraside', as Manning Clark dubbed the affluent suburbs south of the river.

Arthur Wren's parents humbly petitioned His Excellency the Earl of Hopetoun, Governor of Victoria, in June 1891, for 'generous clemency'. They had 'by industry … acquired a little property and … to the best of their ability reared their children in a respectful and law-abiding way'. Arthur, 'a well conducted boy' who fell in with 'bad companions', was by then only twenty-two, and Hamilton was 'a woman of low character' who had 'a bad feeling' against him. Arthur 'could not be said to belong to a criminal class' and had undergone 'the worst part' of his sentence, the flogging. The petition was supported by Fr Aylward, W. D. Beazley MLA (Collingwood), William Keele (former mayor of Collingwood), Edgar Wilkins (city councillor, later MLA) and two other prominent citizens who attested to John and Margaret Wren's 'respectability'. Arthur's conduct in prison by 2 July 1891 was said to be 'good', but the Crown Law Office was 'unable to discover any grounds which would warrant … any interference with the decision' of 1889. Arthur must have remained of good behaviour because he was released on 2 April 1898, within two days of his eligibility under ordinary regulations governing remissions.[4]

Arthur seems to have been accepted back into the family without disruptive recriminations. The *Lone Hand* reported that he was employed at the Tote at least part-time, perhaps as 'a bodyguard', but the postal directories of 1905 have him listed as 'bootmaker', living at 140 Gold Street, Clifton Hill. As the 'informant' on his father's 1901 death certificate, he gave his address as 35 Ballarat Street. He married, had a child, Alice, whose debut at St John the Baptist parish ball in 1921 he attended as 'A Wren from Ascot Vale'. His wife predeceased him. The *Australian Leather Journal, Boot and Shoe Recorder* states that Arthur 'was a partner in the Artur (sic) Manufacturing Co Pty Ltd which went out of business some years ago' (c. 1931, it seems). Its first listing is in the *Victorian Postal Directory* in 1923. It is possible he was involved in other such companies before this. We know that he was nominally the major shareholder in Jacka, Edmonds and Co from 1920 to 1931. His will (dated 24 July 1934) shows him back at the double-fronted weatherboard at 35 Ballarat Street, the house then grandly called Claireville. He prospered, evidently owing to the support of his brother John. His estate, sworn to probate, amounted to £52,468. Of this, prime real estate at 27 Swanston Street in the heart of Melbourne accounts for £43,118 and is left (or returned) to John, as is £2,412 in shares, almost all in Maize Products Pty Ltd. There is a cash debt of £4,000 owing to Ellen

Wren, disbursed by her in two lots in 1924 and 1927 without interest. Arthur owns the Ballarat Street house and the Gold Street cottages and these are left to his daughter, Alice, with furniture and personal effects. John Wren is the sole executor, and a witness to the will is his ever-faithful secretary, Frank Lawrence.[5]

Arthur's obituary in the *Argus* (of all places, being no admirer of John Wren) describes him as 'a retired boot manufacturer' whose 'many unobtrusive acts of philanthropy won him a wide circle of friends. He was beloved by the poor of Collingwood'. The *Australian Leather Journal* referred to his 'wide circle of friends' and 'his philanthropy … well known in the poorer quarters'. *Australasian Footwear*, another trade journal, confirms that 'he was well known in the Collingwood district for his many kindly acts and … gifts to poor people'.[6] Perhaps his nephew, John Francis Wren, was not far from the mark in calling a reformed Arthur 'a helluva good chap'.[7]

Character

How profound the impact of this family disgrace was on John Wren, not quite eighteen, is unknowable, but the anguish and shaming would have intensified any ingrained grievance against authority and steeled a determination to 'get on'. He swore off smoking and drinking and set out to acquire investment capital. The *Australasian Typographical Journal* in 1904 derided Wren as illiterate, but what follows here will give the lie to that. He had left school at twelve, where he had been apt at mathematics or rather, at that level, 'sums'. He worked first in a woodyard for five shillings a week and then as a 'boot clicker' at Whybrow's factory. Apparently he broke his apprenticeship bonds. It would have affected him that his parents were illiterate even if respected; the elder of his brothers, Joseph, was probably already a binge drinker although a genial chap, while the other was in gaol for the foreseeable future.

Wren was short but not inordinately so. His statistics when he joined the army at forty-four were height 5 feet 4 inches (166 cms) and weight 10 stone 10 pounds (68 kilograms). His 'chest expansion' of 36–37 inches exceeded the 34 inches required.[8] Photographs show a trim, sturdy welterweight. He was regarded as bandy-legged, but this was the result of a poorly set fracture and not, as has been asserted,[9] malnutrition or rickets. He walked with hesitancy rather than a limp, said his son—until his later years, when he did limp.

He was a competent sportsman. Stremski records in his history of the Collingwood Football Club that in 1892 Wren had won a suit of clothes as best player in its second-best junior side. He was a member of its match committee and a potential recruit for the main club team. Quick reflexes probably compensated for his lack of speed. He was still playing cricket, his favourite sport, in 1902. (To play on Saturday afternoons with the Tote at full throttle suggests commitment). The *Bulletin* in 1899 had referred to him as 'a bit of an all-round phenomenon … teetotaller, non-smoker, good cricketer, tiger at football, no slouch of a pug'.[10]

His son, John Francis Wren, remembered an occasion at home one Saturday:

> there was a knock at the door and I went out. There was a big young fellow there and he said, 'Can I see your father?' Father said, 'Send him in', and he came into the dining room. Afterwards I saw my father taking him up the drive and suddenly there was a fight. Father beat him, cut him to pieces. He came back to the house with blood all over his hands—the veins on the back of his hands had burst during the fight. That happens to some people in a bare-knuckle fight. I asked him why he had gone up the drive for the fight and he said, 'I didn't want to worry your mother'.[11]

John Francis never learnt what the fight was about. Wren was then roughly fifty years old. When in 1951 Wren heard that Don Campbell KC had suggested in the court proceedings that he had driven his wife to adultery, he wrote out a challenge to a duel with fists or pistols, the former preferred. Campbell was in leg calipers; Wren could hardly walk. Nellie was 'petrified', but the note was never sent.[12]

Aside from not smoking or drinking, Wren was sexually puritanical: he detested smut and swearing. He was awkward with women, having had no sisters. His brother Joe did not marry; his binges may be related to that, in what was a common enough Irish Jansenist bachelor trait. Wren was thirty when he was married on 31 December 1901 at St Patrick's Cathedral by Fr Patrick Phelan, its administrator, who had been rector of St Joseph's, Collingwood, and would become Bishop of Sale. Phelan was a scholarly and highly esteemed priest—even the anti-Catholic *Vigilant* officially mourned his passing. But for the availability of Daniel Mannix in 1912, Phelan could possibly have become Archbishop of Melbourne. He was on a short-list of three. As parish priest he must have come to know a good deal about his wealthy and notorious parishioner, and was to acknowledge his life-long friendship with him.[13]

Wren married Ellen Mahon, who was twenty-six—a mature woman, not a convent ingenue as later portrayed. She was born in 1875 at Casterton in western Victoria, had been educated at Good Shepherd Convent in Abbotsford and was a devout Catholic. When Wren died, Nellie told Fr William Hackett SJ that Phelan had said to her at the nuptials, 'You've married not a man but a miracle'[14]—an indication of deep respect from both parties. Nellie's father had been a police constable and her mother a milliner at the time of their marriage in 1875 at Wickliffe near Ararat. The Mahons lived in Johnston Street near the Tote. Wren would have known Nellie for years before marriage, surely since adolescence. It was probably a long courtship.

It is consistent with what we know of Wren that he would choose to marry a woman of decorum and piety. He was frequently absent from home on business, but would hardly have been other than a conventional Edwardian husband, not much given to dalliance. They had nine children between 1903 and 1919, one dying at birth. John Francis, an urbane man himself, thought his father 'did not understand women'. He related how his father, noticing that his wife had no jewellery, told one of his staff to buy her some pearls, but that cultured pearls would do as she would not know the difference. Then, 'as if embarrassed by his own frugality', he added, 'better get three strings of whatever you choose'. Years after his father's death, John Francis discovered 'a magnificent old plumed hat stored at the back of the cupboard':

> When he asked [his mother] … about it she said she had bought the hat forty or fifty years before and had worn it proudly at some important race meeting. Her husband who was up in the public grandstand … saw her in the hat, promenading on the lawn below, and when they went home he told her he did not want her to wear it again because it was too showy. She never did.[15]

A clutch of polite postcards to 'Mrs [Sugar] Roberts' from 'Nellie Wren' or 'N W' (no first names, please) in 1930–1 during a grand tour of Europe shows Nellie in her fifties to have been an attentive if unimaginative traveller of her time. Literate, they are written in a clear correct hand as tutored by the nuns. With a friend from the Cody family, business partners of John, she disembarked from Toulon in the spring of 1930, stayed on the Seine in Paris ('the noisiest place on earth'), visited her eldest daughter in Bavaria and petted her infant grandchildren, toured Salzburg and Berlin, passed through the Kaiser's Gate, thence to London where she ran into a nurse who had tended her at Mt St Evin's Hospital, and who 'got quite excited'. In Ireland she needed her 'galoshes', an umbrella and 'hobnailed boots' as it was 'nearly always raining', but the flowers and scenery, especially in Killarney were splendid. She visited a Franciscan Abbey despoiled by Oliver Cromwell, where the monks had been martyred. On Palm Sunday 1931 (was this the same trip?) she was in Rome. She saw the Colosseum where Christian martyrs had been 'tortured for the faith', was 'thrilled' about an 'audience' with the Pope (with hundreds of others) and called on Cardinal Cerretti who had been Apostolic Delegate in Australia during the First World War and had received John in Melbourne in 1928. Mussolini had done 'wonderful work bringing his country out of disorder' and, judging by what she had read of doings in Australia, it needed a dictator too. Funds obviously were not unlimited; the pound sterling's losing its value kept them in London, where there was 'dreadful disorder' and 'a lot of misery among the very poor'. This, Nellie thought 'more due to ignorance than anything else' as 'soap and water seems to be a stranger to some very slatternly women about the streets who could do with a good dry clean'.

There was nothing unconventional about Nellie. Unlike Edna Everage, she moved unpretentiously though genteelly from Casterton and Collingwood to Kew, but mentally she had not left her Catholic mentors or suburban mores.[16] She died at Caritas Christi hospice in 1969, cherished by her family.

John did not accompany Nellie overseas. He had taken her to New Zealand for their honeymoon and, in spite of later announcements that he was going overseas, travelled only once to Fiji to see the gold mines. Even at home he cultivated self-sufficiency and was often remote. Following house renovations in 1917 he had bedded down in a sleep-out open on two sides for, he thought, his health. He rose at

6.30 am, shaved, showered in hot then cold water (as the health faddists counselled) and allowed the air to dry him. His suits were bought off the hook, three at a time; his hats were sporty. Only his overcoat made a concession to luxury; it had a fur collar. He wore a rimless pince-nez which often shattered on the floor when he bent down, as did the 'two-bob' pocket watches bought from Coles. A secretary was sent out immediately for new ones. He did not use the £500 gold watch which his long-time partner, Ben Nathan, bequeathed him in 1935. He detested swank. He frequently dined alone. His meals were spare, mainly vegetarian. Not only did he shun business lunches, he did without lunch altogether, drinking water or at most a glass of milk. He needed a clear head for business, he said, and could not understand *bon viveurisme.* He avoided snapshots, interviews and publicity, unless necessary.[17]

After his marriage, Wren moved across the Yarra to a double-storeyed Italianate mansion, Studley House, overlooking Collingwood. But it was not furnished with ostentation; nor did he collect pictures or antiques. The house had been built by John Hodgson, a pioneer of Studley Park and a Melbourne city councillor in the 1850s. Built of brick on a bluestone base, it was simple and symmetrical in design. It was surrounded by a wide, two-storey verandah supported by two tiers of pillars, in doric and ionic orders, plain in style:

> It looked like a Greek temple, apart from some restrained but characteristically Victorian decorations—a row of urns on the parapet and panels of cast-iron lace in a chaste design between the pillars. It had traditionally been painted white [and was popularly known as 'the White House'].

In 1916 Wren more than doubled the size of his house:

> The interiors of both sections were remodelled, with the most fashionable details of the time. All the ceilings were given new plaster mouldings, in a variety of modern motifs—acorns and oak leaves, for example. The new doors and woodwork were gold and maple with fretted panels above some doorways. All the old windows were replaced with new lead-lighted ones fitted with colored glass decoration.[18]

Since 1966 Studley House has been the property of Burke Hall, Xavier College Preparatory School.

A farmlet went with the mansion; the household was almost self-sufficient in food, except for most meat and basic groceries, there being poultry, a cow and vegetable gardens tended by a full-time hand. Until the Second World War there were several servants, but Fr Hackett in the late 1940s was surprised to find Nellie and daughter Angela doing the housework. Kathleen Murphy, who worked in the home for a year in the 1930s, found Wren to be 'a very kind and thoughtful man always ready to help anyone in need':

> He obtained work for my late husband and his brother and at least two other men in the year I was there. When I left to get married, he gave me a wedding present cheque of £5 [two weeks wages at that time] and girls who worked there longer were given £10.
>
> Mr Wren also instructed his cook, never to refuse a meal to any swagman who called for one. In those days they were quite numerous.
>
> Mr Wren did a lot of good and only the people concerned knew of it.[19]

Richard (Dick) Lean, manager of some of Wren's major enterprises for forty years, maintained that:

> JW never forgot an old servant. It was common for him to call on some one who had worked for him in the old days but had fallen on hard times, and needed help.
>
> He didn't care where or how they lived. He'd nose around the house, picking up ornaments here and there, asking questions as a blind. When he left, his old crony would find a wad of notes under or beside one of the ornaments JW had been admiring. He would never embarrass them by offering them money.

On very hot days he would sometimes instruct Lean to send ice-creams to the nurses at St Vincent's Hospital. Wren's solicitor and neighbour Bernard Nolan, who drove him to the Stadium on Saturday nights, recalled how he would often stop on the way and give money to 'down and outers' in Collingwood houses, often to people he remembered from early days. On one occasion, noticing that a paperboy was shivering with cold, Wren took him into a nearby shop and bought him a complete set of clothes.[20] It is easy for the affluent to mock such facile patronage but the needy rarely did so, especially in times when there was little social security and, for example, an accident at work did not generate automatic sick leave or workers' compensation.

Wren twice owned a Buick, but he did not drive and generally walked the four miles to the city. Frequently, before he left work, one of his staff would go to the tram terminus and take a seat, giving it up to him when he got on. His office was sparely furnished, with a few sporting photos and, later, religious pictures on the wall, and without evidence of elaborate filing systems. So much was kept in his head. He preferred to deal in cash (even large amounts) rather than cheques, but he did write them. His telephone calls were short, even abrupt, and not sociable. He did not entertain much at home, although there were rare festive occasions such as a visit from the Sistine Chapel Choir in 1921 and from Fritz Kreisler, the virtuoso violinist, in 1925. Kreisler wrote to Wren on 17 July 1925:

> May I call your kind attention to a young Australian violinist, Miss Gertrude Healy. I was greatly impressed with her talents and firmly believe that if her artistic faculties are developed in a proper way, she will ripen into an artist that will be a great credit to her native country.

Fifty years on Healy, by then a nun, Sister Catherine of Siena, recalled how Wren had summoned her immediately. She found him 'blunt, straight and a very fine man'. He offered to 'back' her. She had already studied in Europe and, for family reasons, declined to return. She taught, among others, Wren's eldest daughter Margaret, whom he sent overseas to study.[21] This was the 'debaucher' whom Manning Clark said was 'without culture … refinement'.[22]

Sport provided Wren's most enjoyable recreation. His Saturdays began with attendance at the office, on to the races if he had a horse running, or to the football to see Collingwood if at all possible, where he barracked fanatically. In the evening he would go to the Stadium. He had his own seat near the ringside, and a few for guests. He was enthusiastic about his gladiators, feinting left hooks and uppercuts and shouting encouragement. He disliked southpaws (boxers with a left-handed stance) because they were negative. He enjoyed it when they were 'flattened'. He also enjoyed the skills or antics of his wrestlers.[23]

Court jester

Wren had antics of his own, especially with his old mate, Robert 'Sugar' Roberts, the most farcical of Collingwood mayors. Would-be inventors who sought finance from Wren would be sent to Roberts to be sorted out. Sugar would occasionally refer a crackpot to Wren who once, for payback, sent a fellow with a novel fire extinguisher to the Roberts' home to give a demonstration. He was ejected just as he began to set fire to the curtains. On another occasion on his way to the racetrack for the dawn training gallops, Wren knocked up Roberts who emerged at the door, bleary-eyed, holding out the billy for the milkman. Wren snatched it and ran down the street with Roberts hollering after him. Horseplay rather than wit, but Wren was not just the forbidding runt with the piercing cold stare that his disparagers portray. John Francis Wren thought Roberts the most comical personality he had ever met, on a par with Hollywood's W. C. Fields. Wren delighted in him.

Roberts was Collingwood's quintessentially cheery, prospering larrikin. Born in 1870 in the goldmining town of Clunes, in which he retained a generous interest, he became an associate of Wren in the 1890s while working as a blacksmith's striker at the Newport railway workshop. A journalistic briefing of 1921 said that, after acquiring capital through Murmur's Caulfield Cup win in 1904, he was induced by Wren to field (operate as a bookmaker) on his pony courses. An attempt to keep Roberts off registered courses resulted in Wren's employing a King's Counsel to challenge the rule excluding those who had operated on unregistered ones. The rule was rescinded; Roberts went straight to the ring in the elite Paddock rather than graduating from the *hoi polloi* Flat or the second-class Hill. Living in Clifton Hill, Collingwood's most comfortable ward, he could be seen in his garden on Sunday mornings in pyjamas and dressing-gown with his signature drivelling cigar clamped in the centre of his mouth and doffing his otherwise irremovable bowler hat to any lady passing by. With this greeting graciously acknowledged, he would mutter archly to any cobber in earshot, 'There goes another bloody vote'.[24]

Roberts was Wren's lieutenant in local politics but by no means a mere stooge—although, according to John Francis Wren, he 'reported' goings-on to his putative 'boss' on Sundays. In his own right he became a patron of Catholic social clubs, donating trophies for inter-parish billiards competitions and raising funds for a parish hall, where in 1918 his wife was crowned Queen of Sports 'amid a blaze of lights and scenic effects'. He became inaugural president of the United Parish Men's Clubs, which merged with the Catholic Workers' Association. But neither philanthropy nor Wren could save him after his 1925 Fitzroy by-election debacle. He was expelled from the Labor Party, but meekly sought forgiveness; his 'heart and soul' had always been with Labor. He rose again, and in 1933 was elected mayor of Collingwood. In a dispute over the election of a non-Labor man as his successor, which he regarded as irregular, he seized and sat on the mayoral robes, defying other councillors to retrieve them. The *Sun*'s caption read: 'AMAZING SCENES MARK COLLINGWOOD MAYORAL ELECTION'. At the supper on his retirement as mayor, the Labor Leader of the Opposition, Tom Tunnecliffe, said that 'Cr Roberts was the best advertising medium Collingwood had had for years'.[25]

Progeny

John and Nellie Wren had nine children: Madeline Margaret (1903–82), John Joseph (1905, died aged four months), Elinor (1906–48), John Francis (1910–92), Mary Dorothea (1911–79), Anthony (1912–46), Joseph (1915–86), Angela (1916–57) and Francis Xavier (1919–22). Wren was neither a negligent, uncouth husband nor a tyrannical, abusive father with little regard for the autonomy of his children. To his sons he was a somewhat forbidding but not unapproachable patriarch, who was more indulgent to his daughters. He did not use corporal punishment, but John Francis recalled his father severely remonstrating after complaints about some negligence and an unfavourable report about his lack of progress at the university's Newman College.

The boys went to the elite Jesuit-run Xavier College. A contemporary recalled their not enjoying patched clothes,[26] evidently prescribed by their father so that they would experience some of the frugality of his Collingwood upbringing. He nurtured his sons' cricketing skills, as both John Francis (1927–8) and Anthony (1931) captained the Xavier XI. The girls went to posh Sacré Coeur. Elocution was prescriptive in both schools and even the boys called their parents 'Father' and 'Mother', not

Collingwood's 'Mum' and 'Dad'. Some affectation may have been obligatory, but Wren himself did not change his accent or his manners or tastes and was quite decidedly a Collingwood pleb all his life. The children were not unduly restricted, although as they became adult Wren frowned on, probably tried to forbid, alcoholic parties—but then he was so often away and Nellie seems to have been anything but stern.

The eldest child, Margaret, studied music overseas and became an accomplished violinist. She married a German piano salesman, Paul Andreas, whom she met in South America. It was an unhappy marriage and Andreas, back in Germany, became a Nazi supporter. After separating from her husband in 1933, she remained in Germany with her children, citizens of the Reich, and survived on a rural property throughout the war. A letter to Wren (dated 17 April 1947) exists, signed by the secretary of External Affairs, John W. Burton, under direct instruction from his minister H. V. Evatt, then a friend of Wren, informing him that the department had deposited his cheque of £300 in a State Bank in London for Margaret's exit from Germany.[27] She returned to Australia in the 1970s but did not find it congenial. She died in Dublin in 1982.

The second daughter, Elinor, attended Santa Sophia College at Sydney University, where she distinguished herself in student affairs and social life rather than study, so that her superiors suggested after a year that she return to Melbourne. She wrote a column for the Melbourne Catholic diocesan *Advocate* and a short hagiograph about a nun, which has not been traced. She was described by Peter Norris, a leading Melbourne solicitor,[28] as 'a most charming person':

> She and Mrs Wren had a wonderful rapport. With each of them, if you went to a party at the Wren's … you would go away thinking you were the only one there as far as Elinor or her mother were concerned. That was a tremendous gift.

Elinor was a spirited radical in politics, perhaps a member of the Communist Party. John Francis, the eldest boy and nearest sibling, confessed that she was the only member of the family whom he disliked. Old Wren, he said, made quite a scene when Elinor told him that she wanted to marry a prominent left-wing Melbourne University identity,

Sam White, a Ukrainian Jew by birth. He had come to Australia aged six and made headlines when he was dunked by ra-ra tory boys in the university lake in 1934 for his political views. A playboy, White was expelled from the Communist Party for 'bourgeois bohemianism', otherwise known as drunkenness. He became a journalist and war correspondent, and later a witty columnist on Parisian society for the London *Evening Standard.* He published a life of Charles de Gaulle and *Sam White's Paris* (1983). He was awarded the Legion of Honour. An item in the social columns in *Truth* has Elinor visiting Margaret on her estate in Bavaria in 1936 and writing home allegorically with 'a considerable amount of ingenuity' about the Nazi regime, to get 'past the eagle eyes' of the censor.[29]

In 1943 Elinor married Edward L. Jones in Chelsea, London. He had been a resident in Australia, was the son of a late bishop of Lewes and a great-grandson of General Sir John Jones who, as chief engineer during the Peninsular War with Napoleon, was responsible for the first fortifications of Gibraltar. There were no children. In 1948 she was afflicted with cancer. Wren had her X-rays flown to Melbourne to be inspected by his physician, Sir Hugh Devine. In her will of 1936, in which she left all to her mother, she described herself as a journalist.

The youngest daughter, Angela, less robust, but bright and witty according to Peter Norris, remained unmarried with no specified occupation. She had a nervous collapse over the *Power Without Glory* trial, lived mostly at home, seems to have been anorexic and died a lonely death in a flat in 1956, a few weeks after a serious operation. Contemporaries thought that she had contributed to her own death, but the coroner's pathologist found that it was due to an acute pulmonary oedema. There were no funeral notices. Her probate evaluation was £95,111, which excluded her share of her father's estate. It was distributed in equal shares among siblings and the children of Anthony.[30]

Both John Francis and Joseph were university educated and cultivated men. John was a business man and an art collector; Joseph a lawyer. John's reminiscences were respectful without any tinge of resentment. He reduced their cogency somewhat by disclosing that until Hardy's book was published he was not aware that his father had run the Collingwood Tote. This is probably true, as he was not born when the Tote closed. His elders would hardly have reported that his father had been a lawbreaker, while discretion probably silenced other intimates. Joseph was sociable, lived quietly and became a patron of the Amstell Golf Club.

The most problematic son was Anthony, on whom Hardy based the character 'John West' Jnr. He died after falling from his bedroom window onto the sandstone path below on 29 December 1945. Suffering from contusions of the brain, a fractured skull and shock, he died on New Year's Day. The coroner returned an open finding. It is not clear what happened. Anthony was a heavy drinker, given to throwing boisterous parties. He was a Sydney-based company director and shareholder in Morrison's Outdoor Catering, which serviced racecourses and sports grounds (for example, Randwick Racecourse, Sydney Cricket Ground). Letters from his widow, Nora, to his brothers reveal some 'transgression' by her and probably him, which caused his parents at least to snub her—so that the only provision in their wills for her was indirectly through her children. They were to receive their due only when the youngest of three turned thirty, which would have been around 1970. Meanwhile a competency was provided, but quite beneath Nora's expectations. It appears they were obliged to live in Tasmania. Old John had refused to buy them a Sydney house.[31]

Tragedy dogged the family when Anthony Jnr, aged 20, a talented poet but also a schizophrenic, fell from Taroona cliff near Hobart in October 1953.[32] Grandfather Wren lay dying in Melbourne and was not told of this latest family anguish. Novelist Christopher Koch, a close friend of Tony and a promising poet at the time, was thought to be diverting Tony from a legal career and encouraging scepticism about his religion. Their relationship was discouraged. Koch casts Tony Wren as 'Shane Noonan' in his novel, *The Boys in the Island*, and believes pressure was brought to bear (possibly by Mary?) on his London publisher in 1958 to excise certain passages, although he does not abuse his dramatic licence as Hardy did in *Power Without Glory*. Those passages were subsequently restored. A new complete edition is to be published.[33]

The titian beauty

Mary Dorothea was described in *Smith's Weekly* as 'Melbourne's Titian beauty'. A striking auburn-haired personality, she frequented left-wing circles in the 1930s. She aspired to be an actress and appeared in several of Gregan McMahon's productions, apparently shocking her father on one occasion by flamboyantly smoking on stage. With Elinor she was a member of the Barbusse Club, named after the French pacifist-communist novelist André Barbusse, also founder of the World Movement. A reminiscence of Mary Wren in A. F. ('Bluey') Howells, *Against The Stream The Memories of a Philosophical Anarchist 1927–1939*, contradicts her characterisation as 'Mary West', in *Power Without Glory*:

> It was said of Mary Wren that she was old John's favourite daughter ... she seemed able to twist him round her finger. Just how much of her father's character she inherited I would not guess as I never knew the old man, except by sight. I visited his home often but he never seemed to be at home. Mary had wit, charm and good looks, and she was one of the most amiable, easy-to-get-on-with women I have ever met ... there was almost a brother–sister relationship between us.
>
> For a man who did not drink, John Wren kept a very fine cellar, which Mary and Elinor and their friends made a very good use of.[34]

Paddy Kelly, Wren's former jockey and attendant, supports this opinion of the Wren menage: 'I have stayed in the home and no one could be nicer to each other or happier together'.[35] This may be too good to be true, but it is certainly not the picture in *Power Without Glory.* Les Barnes, the Communist Party's historian, recalled:

> The parts about the family in *PWG* didn't fit in with what I personally knew about John Wren. I knew Mary Wren; I worked with her in the peace movement. I also knew Elinor. Mary never said anything to suggest she was unhappy at home or that there was conflict with her father about her work. The peace movement could always get use of his stadium for meetings. Mary was also openly associated with it.[36]

Mary's posh manners caused at least one oaf to delight in making her squirm when the Left dined out, asking for 'scuffle' (*soufflé*), talking of 'bourgeois sorts', pinching her bottom and asking her if 'the bloody old man's got any tips for Saturday'. Howells confirms that it was Mary's influence with her father that procured the West Melbourne Stadium for the famous Defend Kisch Committee protest meeting on 18 November 1934. Some eight thousand people turned up to demonstrate against the deportations of the European 'revolutionary' Egon Kisch and the New Zealand communist Gerald Griffin; the principal speakers were leftists Maurice Blackburn and Frank Brennan.

Wren does not seem to have been outraged by his daughter's radicalism. On the contrary, conservative as he became over the years, he still enjoyed riling authority to please his favourite daughter. In the early phase of the Russian revolution he may even have been mildly sympathetic, as so many were before the new regime settled in. In any case, protest meetings would hardly have worried him. The communist author Edgar Ross claimed that Wren 'procured' a forged passport for the activist Paddy Lamb to attend the Third Communist International in 1921. The informant, says Ross, 'was Paddy Lamb himself', with whom Ross had boarded in the same household, and the 'contact' was the mysterious Dan Green. Recent research has failed to find corroboration for this improbable story, in which even a generous gesture by Wren has to be punctuated by a crime. 'Forged' could cover minor irregularity as well as serious illegality.[37]

In his history of the Communist Party, *The Reds*, Stuart Macintyre takes up gossip and has Mary eloping with Sam White. This furphy is repeated in White's entry in the *Monash Biogaphical Dictionary*. Prewar, she did go to England. The Wren–Evatt letters (see Chapter 15) show that contact with her father was sustained. Les Barnes said that he 'knew Mary and was not aware of any opposition from her father when she sought to go to Spain'. (She got only as far as England). In January 1944, with Elinor and her husband as witnesses, she married a war correspondent, Stanley Harrison, and worked firstly as a press publicity officer in Chelsea and then as a welfare worker. She divorced Harrison in 1957 on grounds of adultery. Later, according to Peter Norris, she lived in 'an unpretentious house in Hammersmith', and 'spent her life looking after the poor'. But he did not say or apparently even notice that she had an alcohol problem. As Margaret complained, her volatility had led her from communism back to Catholicism, the Labor Party and welfare, and then to antipathy to religion.[38] In London she retained some style. When her nephew, Christopher Wren, visited London in 1969 they were ushered to 'Miss Wren's table' at the Savoy Grill. She returned to Melbourne in 1979 and died in St Vincent's Hospital aged sixty-eight.[39]

While it is clear that the publication of *Power Without Glory* had a tragic effect on Angela, the prospect of scurrilous publicity must have been a deterrent to Margaret and Mary returning home permanently. Wren's family had its tragedies: four of the nine children predeceased John and five predeceased Nellie. Its spirited diversity indicates anything but domestic repression. Wren's strict impartiality in leaving equal shares in his estate to his seven adult children or their offspring reflects something admirable about his attitude towards them. Moreover, the execution of the wills of those who died is left in the hands of the brothers, John and Joseph, again indicating family trust rather than estrangement or alienation.

Largesse

John Wren's behaviour has often been stigmatised as shadowy, shady, sinister; as though he scarcely had a public personality. Events such as the Building Workers' Strike 1906–7 (Chapter 6) and the pro-Ireland rallies of 1917–22 (Chapter 10), show that this was far from true. Rather, some of his public involvements suggest, at least occasionally, something of an exhibitionist, even vulgarly so when splashing money about. When suspicion immediately fell on him after the bombing of Detective-Sergeant O'Donnell's house in 1906, Wren's reaction was to offer a supplementary reward to that promised by the police on the arrest of the perpetrator(s), and £1,000 if anything could be proved against himself. As a ploy, it did not convince the unfriendly; daring one's critics to *prove* some malfeasance can look suspicious. Wren did much the same forty years later, when S. M. Keon in 1948 accused him of corrupting the recent state election. 'A thousand nicker on the line' if anyone can prove anything against me, Wren virtually said, evoking a sub-culture where verbal arguments are characterised by absolute statements, arrant denials, and bets. These gestures jarred on genteel sensibilities: it was maladroit, larrikinish Collingwood repartee; ranting to be judged by the same criterion (innocent till proved guilty) as Yarraside.

In his vernacular way, Wren sincerely believed in putting his money where his mouth was. The noted English sporting journalist, Ben Bennison, did not see Wren's offer of £1,000 in 1942 to the two wartime air aces, squadron leaders Keith 'Bluey' Truscott DFC and Bar (Australian) and Brendan 'Paddy' Finucane (Irish), as a plutocrat's self-advertisement. (When the RAF refused to allow such gifts, about which Wren would have been quite obtuse, he gave the money to their mothers to be held in trust. In a letter of 31 May 1942 to Wren, Finucane's father said that 'Paddy' appreciated 'the motive which prompted you to make the gift' and hoped Wren was enjoying health and would continue to do so.) The gift was dated 15 May, the day before Truscott, who had shot down fourteen German planes in the Battle for Britain was allowed to lead his former Melbourne football team in a match at the Melbourne Cricket Ground before a crowd of twenty thousand. Bennison wrote:

> appreciation of gallantry and battles against incredible odds is characteristic of Wren, for ever he did have a heart (and pocket) for a fighter. He himself was born one and will remain one to the end of his days. Wren was bred big, without frills or flowers ... It is a man ready at all times to back his fancy as I best know him. We became acquainted as long ago as 1912, when he cabled from Sydney that he would bet £1,000 that Hughie Mehegan would beat Freddie Welch, a Pontypridd Welshman, over 20 rounds of the National Sports Club. When it was broadcast that Mehegan had the backing of so much money, noses took a quizzical shape, and small wonder, for in affairs of the Ring side-stakes oftener than not are just plain hokum-pokum ... We have long been familiar with the blather-skite—the fellow given to shouting the odds without having the least intention (or the wherewithal) to lay them ... Oh yes, Welch, together with Harry Marks, his sponsor, made no bones about covering Wren's thousands, and, although the Australian fought, as became a 'digger', to his last ounce, [Welch] won with a goodly number of points to spare. For his part, Wren was abundantly satisfied with a certainty that his man gave him a magnificent run for his money.[40]

This gift to the Spitfire aces reminded Bennison of A. E. Whitlaw's present of £1,000 to Don Bradman for his record 334 runs at Leeds in 1930. He sensed nothing exhibitionist there. Bradman did not disdain Wren's promise of £1 per run with a minimum of £200 for his testimonial game in December 1948. 'I hope he scores 500', said Wren. Although he saw only the last ten minutes of the master's 123 runs, he paid him £300. This was publicised contrary to his wishes. In 1946 Wren had offered to compensate the great Bill O'Reilly if he would continue to trundle his leg spinners for Australia. O'Reilly declined without suggesting that Wren's money was tainted. The time had come for him to retire.[41] But others sneered.

Wren enjoyed making money in a competitive but not, it would seem, in a niggardly way, although he disliked being bested even in small deals. He also enjoyed both gambling and giving money away—dispensing largesse, if you like—although it is not suggested here that he ever put his fortune in jeopardy. He made an extraordinary statement in September 1919 on the occasion of a presentation to him by Collingwood citizens:

> he held it to be a crime for a person of means to squander money. It was his duty to spend his money for the benefit of his fellow men. Neither did he believe in hoarding money. His idea was that a man should spend his means during his life time in the best way his judgement dictated.[42]

He told Fr Hackett in 1950 that he had given away some £2 million during his lifetime. This is credible. If so, most of it was given anonymously. John Mullins, a Labor politician who served on the Hospital and Charities Board for six years, estimated that Wren donated 'half-a-million pounds' during that period, 'always anonymous'.[43] His Stadium and race tracks were made available free of charge to both Catholic and other organisations, such as the Austin Hospital.

No doubt there was more than a dash of display when there was a public fundraising, but Wren genuinely thought wealth should be seen to set an example, and he acted that way. His patronage of Caritas Christi, the hospice for the dying opposite Studley House, was intimate and generally private. During the Second World War he financed two buildings. Sister Chrysogonous recalled how, if the plumbing burst during the night, the nuns would ring Mr Wren. He would have it fixed instantly. When the nuns were being harassed by derelicts camping on the river bank, Wren built a stone fence around the premises.

Wren did not, however, respond to Mannix's appeal in 1915–16 for funds to build Newman College at the University of Melbourne. In those days few of Collingwood's offspring were in tertiary education, and there was even narking resentment of those who attempted it and joined the elite. Wren himself had not needed it, although his attitude would change when his own children came of age. He refused to subscribe, and pointedly gave the archbishop a cheque for £100 towards a primary school being constructed nearby. Similarly, Fr Hackett, founder of the Catholic Central Library, failed to cadge any money from Wren for his brainchild, although he was an intimate of the household. He had the same frustration with Wren's business cobber, Pierce Cody, also an otherwise generous donor to the church. They were not bookish.[44] Wren's largest benefactions were to St Vincent's Hospital and Caritas Christi.

A number of people have testified to personal acts of generosity by Wren from which he could not have hoped to gain anything. Peter Norris acted for W. O'Donnell Pty Ltd, brass founders of West Melbourne. 'Billy' O'Donnell, the principal, also a bookmaker, used to relieve Richard Lean at the Stadium. Like Wren he did not drink or smoke; he arrived at his office at 7 am and left at 7 pm for most of eighty years. He died aged ninety-five. At one stage Wren found out that O'Donnell's business was under stress, and presented him with a brown paper bag with £10,000 in it; for whatever reason, he preferred not to write cheques. O'Donnell demurred because he was unable to say when he would pay it back. Wren's answer was: 'Take it, use it, pay it back when and if you can'. The debt was paid in due course. On another occasion O'Donnell wanted urgently to extend his overdraft. The bank manager refused, but Wren also had an account at that bank. O'Donnell said that Wren picked up the phone and rang the bank manager: 'Can you tell me what my balance is?' Then, 'Oh, Mr Billy O'Donnell tells me he wants to increase his overdraft limit to £5,000. Would that be alright?' 'Yes, Mr Wren.'[45]

Peter Norris also tells of someone Wren did not know, a man with whom Norris 'had been very friendly in the army' and who 'could see a commercial advantage in New Guinea recovering mattress fibre from coconuts':

> I told him that the only person I knew who might be interested in such a venture was Mr Wren and I arranged for him to interview my friend. I had a telephone call subsequently from Mr Wren who said 'Peter, is this man honest?' I told him I was certain the man was honest—I'd lived close with him in the army for about 12 months and in that time would have discovered any weaknesses in his moral

> outlook—at least I thought so anyway. Mr Wren said 'thank you' and that was the end of the conversation. He advanced £1,000 to my friend to carry on the work and the venture failed. At no stage did Mr Wren look for any interest in the project nor did he seek to recover the amount he had advanced.[46]

But Wren's patronage was not reserved for friends and clients. In response to an advertisement seeking information about Wren, Maryanne Sweeney, a freelance writer, wrote in about her grandmother's second husband who fell 'critically ill just after the war':

> it was difficult to get a bed in a nursing home (they had long waiting lists). Mum tried all over the place to get relief for Grandma ... In the end she rang John Wren, whom she had never spoken to, but believed he would help people in any way in his power ... She found him easy to talk to and in no time he rang back to say there was a bed waiting ... at Caritas Christi. Mum and Dad found it difficult to believe what Hardy wrote, after Wren had been so good to Mum—not knowing her, he never saw [her] or spoke to her again.[47]

A handwritten list compiled from Wren's bank statements within three years of his death shows 139 *ad hoc* monetary gifts. Of these 59 are for £50 or more. The list does not include the £33,000 publicly given in 1953 to the St Vincent's Hospital Appeal or the £7,000 cheque of the previous year to open the appeals's bank account and pay the wages of the organiser. Two donations of £5,000 went to St Vincent's. Three of £1,000 each were for the University of Melbourne (about which he must have mellowed since the Newman College foundation days), the Blessed Sacrament Fathers of St Francis Church, Melbourne (where his parents had married) and the Christian Brothers. Of five cheques for £500, two are for the Women's Hospital and the others for the Lord Mayor's Appeal, a new University Colleges' Appeal and a Ford Motors charity. Three of £200 were for the Christian Brothers, the St Vincent de Paul Society and the Ned Hanlon (Queensland Catholic Labor premier 1946–52) Memorial. Of forty-six cheques between £50 and £100, twelve were for non-Catholic institutions including the Methodist Home for Children and the Methodist Peace Memorial Homes. Wren did give preference to his own—they were not the most privileged in the community—but not exclusively so.[48]

Commentators have been cynical about Wren's published benefactions as though he were only expecting to buy secular respectability or sempiternal salvation.[49] Catholic Actionists such as Stan Keon liked to say that old Wren never did anything for nothing. Similar strictures do not appear to have been uttered about other philanthropists such as Wren's rival bookmaker, Solomon (Sol) Green, or the Chocolate King and Wren's sometime partner, Sir Macpherson Robertson, who endowed the 1934 Melbourne Centenary Air Race. Wren's disdain for Yarraside and its pretensions and for keeping a court to match his wealth elicited reciprocal feelings from the Melbourne Club and business cliques. But they did not disdain to do business with such a wealthy man who always kept his word.

Granny Foster

The story of Wren's refusal in 1913 to accept a large legacy (at that time, a small fortune) from Eliza 'Granny' Foster, who died in Clifton Hill on 22 July 1913, was drolly publicised in the *Age* (25 July) under this headline

A GIFT OF 20 000 POUNDS
Declined with Thanks

and in *Truth* (26 July) under this:

'ST JOHN WREN!'
Patron of Moral Principle
Great Object Lesson to Coin-Chasing Wowsers.

'Granny' Foster, who had come from Galway, Ireland, owned the shop and dwelling in Johnston Street, Collingwood, and the two cottages directly behind in Sackville Street, where Wren's Tote operated. She also owned forty acres in Olinda, on the outskirts of Melbourne:

> [She was] a hard-headed, strong willed woman, who by her litigious propensities, had achieved some notoriety as an upholder of the rights of property against various municipalities, which had the

> somewhat oppressive honour of numbering this obstinate person amongst their ratepayers.

She claimed to have pursued over a hundred civil cases and lost none. She had once wrangled with the Blackburn and Mitcham Shire Council—over resumption of some land—right up to the Privy Council, and won. The council had had to strike a special 'Granny Foster's rate' to pay the £5,000 damages. She was, said *Truth*, rather immodestly, 'a sort of John Norton [its proprietor/editor] or Joan of Arc'.

Granny Foster seems to have 'adopted' Wren as a lad. She called him Stephen (or Stephen John in her will). Her great-grandson, A. A. Kay, who became a noted tennis player, says Wren used to drive to Olinda 'on weekends' (but surely Sundays rather than sportsdays) 'to discuss tactics for the following week'. Kay maintains Granny Foster was 'closely associated with Wren in business ventures'. Her first husband (Foster) had died in 1888; for a few months in 1902 she was married to William James, a man 'practically without means' from whom she soon separated. She appointed Wren sole executor of her will in 1908. She had 'often remarked that she would "remember him in her will" [but] ... Mr Wren treated the promise as a joke and advised her to buy a motor car and enjoy her health'.

On her death, Wren found he was sole heir. He refused the legacy and divided the estate between 'those whom he considers to be the rightful owners'—Foster's three sons (the oldest was fifty-six) and three daughters. *Truth* exulted:

> John Wren, the professional gambler ... John Wren, the boomer of horse-racing—yes, John Wren who in every respect is regarded as the antithesis of holy Joeism and puritanical pietism, has refused to accept Mrs Foster's fortune 'on moral grounds' ... How now all ye dames and puritans who have fought sons and daughters and other relatives of deceased persons in the law courts on questions of 'undue influence'. Take Jack Wren as the example! Canonise him as a saint! Make the tote promoter and professional gambler a patron saint of self-denial and the upholder of moral principle. For it is written, 'By their fruits ye shall know them'.[50]

Frank Hardy never mentioned Granny Foster. It would have marred his crude characterisation.

Salvation

In an age of sectarianism, Wren did not discriminate against non-Catholics socially or in business. Dick Lean told his son that soon after he began working for Wren he was asked whether he was a Mason. He admitted he was. Wren replied, 'I'm glad of that. You've got to be on one side or the other'. This is not so much taking the competitive spirit too far as being a placatory way of expressing tolerance. While Wren would never have put anything other than 'Catholic' on a census form, he was not given to bigotry. For much of his life he apparently had difficulty with the practice of the religion with which, familially, tribally and philosophically, he was on so many occasions conspicuously identified. John Francis says his father did not attend Sunday Mass until the last years of his life, while one young Xaverian of the early 1940s—John Francis was not at home then—remembers Wren going to the Burke Hall Preparatory School services but not to communion. John Francis said his father used to argue with clerical guests about dogma, questioning in particular how a merciful God could condemn sinners to eternal hellfire. Superficially at least, he was uneasy about his own scepticism. Apparently he continued the practice inculcated in childhood of saying his night prayers on his knees. Once he shared a sleeping compartment with his Sydney rival, HD ('Huge Deal') McIntosh, who recalled:

> Beyond the gruff word or two we didn't speak. To my astonishment, after the berths had been made up and Wren prepared for bed, he knelt down on the floor of the carriage and said his prayers. Say what you will, there cannot be much wrong with the character of a man who has the pluck to do that in front of a tough and hard-bitten rival as I was then.[51]

Towards the end of his life Wren experienced a 'reconversion'. Especially under Nellie's influence, he became a daily communicant.

Four months before his friend and business partner E. G. Theodore died, Wren wrote him a letter firstly about their mining interests in Western Australia and then, somewhat incongruously on the same page (which must have been typed for him):

> Since my recent discussion with you on immortality, I have been very worried in case your convictions on the matter should prove to be erroneous.
>
> If your view is correct, it does not matter but, on the other hand, if it is not so, what a great risk you run and what a great prize to lose. I would dearly love to be associated with you in the here-after enjoying eternal happiness and in my morning and evening prayers I earnestly pray that the Almighty may change your views as I believe He so suddenly changed mine. I was pleased to learn from you that you were baptized a Catholic, that your mother was a devout one and your sister a nun. What a great joy to them and yourself to be united with you in heaven.
>
> Indeed one is fortunate in being fortified with the rights [sic] of the Holy Catholic Church, established by Christ on earth for the redemption of mankind. Even in this troublesome world it is something to look forward to and is most comforting and consoling.
>
> I trust that you will not conclude that I have a bee in my bonnet and that I have suddenly become a religious crank.
>
> Sincerely yours,
>
> John Wren[52]

As it happened, Theodore resisted the approaches of a Catholic priest during his last illness until very near the end, when he appears to have assented to the last rites.[53]

At Tom Tunnecliffe's demise, Wren's zeal seems to have overcome his common sense. An ex-Catholic and obdurate apostate, Tunnecliffe had asked for a 'rationalist' funeral. Labor historian Don Rawson recalled in 1992 that, according to a sceptical and independent Catholic, John Holland MLA:

> [Wren was] so strongly opposed to this, and presumably was taken so seriously, that it was in doubt whether John Cain, Labor parliamentary leader, would feel it prudent to take part.
>
> The matter was of serious concern to the party's leaders, though at a later stage Holland was informed by Pat Kennelly, the party's state secretary, that the matter had been resolved and Cain would indeed speak. It is a fact that the service itself was held at

> Tunnecliffe's house, prior to the more formal state occasion at the crematorium ...[54]

However simplistic or superstitious this seems to Wren's critics and even admirers, there is little doubt that he approached death in a 'fortified' state rather than beset by the mortuary guilt-ridden terrors projected on him in *Power Without Glory*.

CHAPTER TWO

The Melbourne Milieu

JOHN WREN'S PARENTS witnessed 'Marvellous Melbourne' grow to a metropolis of almost half a million by 1900. The need for skilled labour stimulated the development of trade unions. Building workers set the pace by gaining an eight-hour day in 1856 without loss of wages. The Early Closing Movement gained reduced working hours for shop assistants and, in the longer term, more recreational time for workers, although 'sweating' in non-unionised trades was prevalent, especially for women, and lingered into the twentieth century. But the progress of unionism consolidated a sense of workers' rights even among the unmobilised. Charles Don, an English stonemason and a vice-president of the Victorian Eight Hours League, claimed to be 'the first of his class' to be represented in 'any legislature within the British Empire' when he won the Collingwood seat in the House of Assembly in 1859. At one stage he worked as a mason on Parliament House by day and sat in it as a member by night.[1]

Victoria's governments took measures such as land selection laws and protective tariffs to try to retain the vigorous immigrants who had followed the lure of gold and whose average educational level, by world standards, was remarkably high. Morale-building was self-consciously pursued. On one day in 1854, foundation stones were laid for a university and a public library. Mechanics institutes throve in the suburbs and country towns. Melbourne was going to be no mean city. Optimism that a civil society could develop without castes lay behind the compulsory, free and secular Education Act of 1872, and there was the further hope that it would ultimately eradicate sectarianism.

Sectarianism

'The hatred of Rome here is incredible', said the liberal Anglican, Bishop James Moorhouse of Melbourne. 'Nothing will induce me to join in the bigoted howl' against Rome, he protested.[2] But for Evangelicals and Nonconformists not even the democratic ideal behind providing education for all could be disentangled from the desire to erase Catholicism. The cry of 'No Popery' had been carried from the Old Country. British prosperity was attributed to British constitutionalism, and the bible allegedly provided its justification. On the other hand, at Catholic functions the Pope was toasted before the Sovereign; Catholics were alleged to have political as well as spiritual loyalty above Crown and Empire. Even a Catholic humanitarian like Caroline Chisholm could be deemed by a bigot, albeit a democratic one like John Dunmore Lang, to have a subversive agenda in helping the immigration and settlement of Irish girls.[3] The press was no better. The Melbourne *Age*, run by the Scottish Syme family, had suspected Catholic premiers like (Sir) John O'Shanassy and (Sir) Charles Gavan Duffy of plotting a Roman ascendancy. The *Argus* and the *Herald* were only a little less sectarian.

For its part, Catholic clerical leadership abroad and at home did little to temper traditional prejudice. In 1864, the year of the birth of Wren's archbishop and friend, Daniel Mannix, the Vatican, with the Papal States under siege, anathematised liberalism and democracy in its *Syllabus of Errors* (1864). With such an obscurantist document, Catholic apologetics could hardly expunge from the Protestant mind spectres of the Inquisition and the suppression of dissent. The *Syllabus* was followed in 1870 by the declaration of papal infallibility, which was necessarily construed by non-Catholics as intellectual aggression, although understood by Catholics as having no political application. Whatever popes may have thought, Catholics in Australia realised their welfare was better served by an unfettered church in a democratic state.

Proponents of the Victorian Education Act saw it as a death-blow to obscurantism. The Catholic response to such secularism was to fulminate against state schools as, in the words of a Sydney archbishop, 'seed-plots of future immorality, infidelity, and lawlessness'.[4] However, (inadequate) statistics suggested there were more Catholics than others in gaols, and for some time a large percentage of Catholic children attended state schools and, indefinitely, a fair proportion of state teachers were Catholic. The pastoral letter of the Catholic Plenary Council of 1885 obliged the faithful to send their children to Catholic schools, if at all possible. It also warned against 'mixed marriages' (that is, with non-Catholics) until ultimately a papal decree, *Ne Temere,* of 1907 tried to prevent them altogether. Catholic education survived and flourished, as did mixed marriages. The financial penalty in education entrenched a sense of persecution, even created solidarity. When that most charismatic of prelates, Daniel Mannix, arrived in Melbourne in 1913, he could quite anachronistically, but plausibly, link the education Acts to the penal laws of Ireland.[5] The increasing immigration of Irish priests and religious teachers from 1880 saw that this memory was well absorbed by local Catholics.

That Australian Catholics were predominantly Irish by extraction—or 'race', in popular usage—compounded the sectarian problem. The squalor, both physical and mental, which over centuries British imperialism had created in Ireland, had not been improved by its fraudulent co-option into the United Kingdom in 1801. Naturally the British had to hold those whom they oppressed in contempt. The (Catholic) Irish were stereotyped as ignorant, superstitious, inebriate, incontinent and violent, a menace to civil society. In the United States they had even been deemed 'white niggers'. In contemporary cartoons Paddy and Mick usually had a simian upper lip and often a mouthful of stagey contradictions. The atrocious British inaction during Ireland's Great Famine of 1846–9 was matched by expressions of relief that the population of Ireland had been purged by over a million deaths and two million emigrations. Uniquely among European countries, Ireland's population declined markedly during the nineteenth century.

The Australian colonies received perhaps 5 per cent of the seven million emigrants who left Ireland in the nineteenth century. Leaving convicts aside, the most destitute fugitives generally ran the relatively quick course to America; the Australian colonies gained those who could afford the much higher passage or presented well enough for state assistance. In effect they were more likely to be upper working class, those with greater initiative, as Wren's illiterate parents seem to have been. The worst scars of the 1840s famine were not common here. On arrival the roughly 25 per cent of immigrants who were Irish dispersed fairly evenly throughout colonial society, becoming within all sizeable areas an ethnicity to be reckoned with but far from dominant. This both incited and tempered political clout. Moreover, the distance from the United Kingdom, the white outpost's need for a sense of security which only the Empire could provide, and the fact of Home Rule in all colonies (even Western Australia after 1890) in general dampened republicanism. Wren was prepared to serve the Empire; even Mannix in the 1920s thought dominion status adequate for Australia, though by then not for Ireland.

Nothing, however, seemed to cool the rancour between Orange and Green. Melbourne had its first St Patrick's Day procession in 1843, less than ten years from its foundation. On 12 July 1846 a riposte from Orange men with Battle of the Boyne banners elicited a 'pat-riot' protest, which in turn evoked a volley of shots from the 'King Billies' or 'William-Worshippers'.[6] The attempted assassination in Sydney in 1868 of Queen Victoria's second son, the Duke of Edinburgh, by an alleged Fenian, Henry O'Farrell, confirmed the sense of desperate Irish Catholic disloyalty—and was not appeased when in 1883 Henry's crazed brother, Patrick, even-handedly shot at Catholic Archbishop James Goold.[7] In the later 1870s respectable Victoria had felt itself terrorised by that rampaging off-shoot of Erin, Ned Kelly, hanged in Melbourne in November 1880. It is not fanciful to imagine the Wren family were stirred by Ned's self-justifying Jerilderie letter, like those who protested against his execution, and were riled by the manifest bias at his trial by the Anglo-Irish 'hanging judge', Sir Redmond Barry. The loyalist-Protestant mind was outraged by the fund-raising visits of such Irish notables as the Redmond brothers in 1883 seeking Home Rule, to which the veteran Liberal prime minister of the UK, W. E. Gladstone, had finally been converted in the 1880s. John Wren remembered going to such rallies with his father.[8]

The climax of charges of disloyalty against Irish-Australians came during the First World War, although the percentage of Catholic volunteers was only slightly less than the national average. Rev. F. A. Hagenaeur was far from unique in arguing in 1917 in *The Papal–Kaiser Intrigue* that the Pope had begun the war to regain temporal power; his pamphlet was commended to 'the careful attention of every loyal citizen' by the *Presbyterian Messenger* (20 July 1917).[9] This abusiveness was fanned by Mannix's unsparing retorts. However, no rationality would have curbed the well-educated, prosperous, vocal Orange minority, empire-conscious to the point of supporting even the unconstitutional defiance and mutiny of the Carsonites against Home Rule for Ireland in 1913–14. The outlook of Dr Alex Leeper, for over forty years warden of Trinity College, Melbourne, was so imperialist that he was repelled by 'Australian nationalism, even in forms as trivial as a kangaroo stamp'.[10] After the defeat in December 1917 of the second conscription referendum, the headmaster of Presbyterian Ladies College, J. P. Wilson, who during 1910–32 was a member of the university and Scotch College councils, wrote (18 January 1918) to the commander of the Australian forces, John Monash, in the following vein:

> All the powers of hell were banded together to defeat conscription and led by that archdevil of hypocrisy, lying and treachery—Herr Mannix—who has just bought Wrixon's mansion in Kew and has spent thousands lavishly in bringing it up to his ideas of luxury. Now where did he get the money for it all? He gathered under his wing all the Irish whose highest ideal is to shoot a man from behind a hedge, the cold footers, the shirkers, sentimental old women and factory girls who in every recruit see a possible husband vanish. The feeling was bitter beyond belief. On the prior Saturday I saw vanloads of gibbering apes howling up and down Swanston and Collins Streets—creatures with no teeth, google eyes, dishevelled and frenzied men.[11]

With such rabid sentiments among members of the 'establishment', it is not surprising that Protestant entrepreneurs, when advertising jobs and lodgings in the 1920s and 1930s, could specify 'No Catholics need apply'.

Marvellous Smellbourne

The achievement of Melbourne in the late-nineteenth century was put into contemporary world perspective by Asa Briggs, in *Victorian Cities*. Dubbed 'Marvellous Melbourne' in 1885 by an overseas journalist, G. A. Sala, it was, says Briggs, also 'the Paris of the Antipodes' or 'the Chicago of the South'. Its rateable value in 1891 was surpassed only by London and (barely) by Glasgow.[12] From the beginning, speculation in land was the basis of quick riches and recurrent slumps and, with the development of public transport, provided opportunities for political graft. The general prosperity ostensibly based on popular self-government was reflected in municipal development and its status symbol, the imposing town hall with massive portico and clock tower. Not only was there the Metropolitan Town Hall in the centre of Melbourne, its foundation stone laid by the Duke of Edinburgh in 1867 but, within relatively short distances, comparable structures were erected in inner suburbs such as Collingwood, Fitzroy, Richmond, South Melbourne, Hawthorn, Prahran, North Melbourne, Malvern and St Kilda. Government House dared to have a ballroom larger than the one in Buckingham Palace.

For its International Exhibition of 1880, Melbourne erected within twenty months a grandiose edifice, its Florentine dome higher than St Paul's. The success of the Australian Centennial Exhibition in 1888 seemed to justify the civic expense. Over two million visited the exhibition, in which 93 countries participated. Some 5,000 singers chorused and half a million citizens attended symphony concerts. Yet while such events brought out the 'quality' of society, they did not necessarily engender greater respect among 'the lower orders', cramped as they were by sabbatarian restraints. 'Wowsers', as puritanical city fathers came to be known, even succeeded in having a clause inserted in the Railways Construction Act preventing the commissioners authorising Sunday trains on new lines. Illogically, they could run in some places for church attendance but not for family visits or pleasure, until the rules were gradually breached from 1884. London had twenty Sunday newspapers, Sydney a few but, in 1889, the Sunday Newspapers Act stifled any in Melbourne for eighty years. In 1904 Melbourne became the last city in the British Empire to open its Public Library, National Gallery and Museum on Sundays.[13]

But Melbourne was also deservedly known as 'Marvellous Smellbourne'. Open drains carried sewage through the centre of the city. Government House, set in spacious parkland, was not free of noisome vapours. Even when the young aspiring diva, Nellie (Melba) Armstrong, sang there, parlous air could mingle with parlour song. Lord Normanby complained of 'the extreme inconvenience experienced at Government House from the stench which arises from the Yarra'. In 1890 the *Argus* marvelled about the 'indifference' of inhabitants; their city was 'in some respects ... even in advance of the times, [but] in others is some three or four hundred years behind them'. Only in 1892 did Normanby's successor, Earl Hopetoun, no doubt with haughty relief, turn the first sod of the main outfall sewer that would, before the century ended, flow to beyond-the-suburbs Werribee. So in Melbourne there were notable epidemics of typhoid and diptheria (in Sydney there were alarms of bubonic plague).[14] Antiseptic medicine was in its infancy, and asepsis barely conceived. The anxieties of city life differed from those of today. If they affected the 'quality' of society, how much more did they depress those in the poorer suburbs.

Smellboom

Metaphorically there was another malodour over Melbourne in the 1880s which in the 1890s precipitated for many a fatal financial stench. It was one cause of the worst depression in its history. The radical Sydney *Bulletin* called it the 'Smellboom'. When considering John Wren's attitude to money-making and the law, it would be hypocritical to ignore the mores of his social *betters* or those of the lowly *bettors* who were to make his fortune. If Wren is to be labelled a racketeer, extortionist or, as Manning Clark would have it, a 'preyer on humanity',[15] then we might well ask what pejorative terms can be justly applied to the political and moral leaders and speculators so graphically discussed in Michael Cannon's *The Land Boomers*. A couple of examples will suffice.

Sir Matthew Davies, Victoria's first native-born Speaker, was knighted for his donations to public bodies. They came from investments in thirty-four major companies, some of them so hopelessly insolvent that the creditors simply let them wither without the formality of liquidation. Losses to the public amounted to over £4,000,000. Davies had been a founder and honorary secretary of the Young Men's Christian Association (YMCA) in Melbourne and a conspicuous opener of church bazaars. The *Bulletin* dubbed him 'a miserable, lucre-loving trafficker in the temple'. He too absconded on one occasion and was arrested in Colombo. His brother, Sir John Mark Davies, 'made the first and only known application of Marxist principles' to the liquidation of the General Land Co Ltd, of which he was chairman. With debts of £450,000 and not more than £16,000 forthcoming, it was decided not to force insolvency on shareholders. Those who could should pay; those who could not should try to borrow from their friends or mortgage their futures. But Davies was then faced with a Supreme Court action over an allegation of a fraudulent balance sheet. It was strangely dropped. Yet Davies went on to become variously attorney-general and solicitor-general in the McLean, Irvine and Bent ministries, was unanimously elected president of the Legislative Council, and was knighted in 1918.[16] In the 1990s the brothers Davies would have been in gaol with Alan Bond or on Majorca with Christopher Skase.

Equally impressive as Davies 'in the solemn red plush surroundings of the Victorian Upper House', and an interesting yardstick by which to judge Wren's business practices, was William Lawrence Baillieu, head of the famous family that had intermarried with the Myer, Hordern and Latham fortunes. His eldest son, Clive Latham Baillieu, became Australia's second baron in 1953. Baillieu in 1885 went into partnership with a son of the crooked future premier, James Munro, in an estate agency. In 1887 Baillieu became a foundation director of the Real Estate Bank, 'founded largely to buy at inflated prices the unsold properties owned by Munro'. With a paid-up capital of £58,000, the directors approved 'within twelve months the purchase of land to the value of £922,000'. Eventually Baillieu became insolvent. Cannon estimates his debts at £225,598 in 1892; the composition accepted by creditors was sixpence in the pound. In the Insolvency Court he was said to have concealed the extent of his overdraft at the Federal Bank each balancing day. His indebtedness then was 'kindly written off the books of that wayward institution', and so on. Baillieu proceeded as though nothing had happened. The full story of Munro's Federal Bank did not come out until exposed by *Table Talk* in June 1893. Munro had lent himself, family and friends nearly three-quarters of a million of the public's money. Baillieu and his Munro-Baillieu partnership took £230,000 of it. Australia's future governor-general, (Sir) Isaac Isaacs, described 'the farce of advancing to A on B's guarantee and to B on A's guarantee. For instance, W. L. Baillieu obtained an advance and got Munro's guarantee and then Munro got an advance, and Baillieu went security'.[17]

Let us see how Baillieu is treated in the *Australian Dictionary of Biography*:

> More remarkable than W. L.'s involvement in the land boom was his exceptionally expert recovery from the depression, though the later success of the Baillieus made it inevitable that this early

> discomfiture would echo in public memory ... If there remained an enigmatic quality in his personality, it lay less in any ethical ambiguity—despite the murmuring of rivals less clever than he—than in his reticence concerning his deepest motives ... he twice rebuffed offers of a knighthood.[18]

But this rebuff is easily understood; being proposed for a knighthood would have meant scrutiny of his past. For his 'deepest motive' there is no need to look further than greed. But what a masterly blanding of a gentleman crook who became 'The Money King of Australia'! Imagine what would have been written if Baillieu's scam had been pulled by John Wren.

Public memory of these scandals was roused in 1929 when George Dick Meudell published *The Pleasant Career of a Spendthrift.* An idiosyncratic stockbroker, Meudell had kept records of the boom and bust years. Attempts, mainly successful, were made to keep the book from circulating by people who wished to blot out their former dubious activities. Among them was Theodore Fink, chairman of the *Herald*, who had been perhaps the most slippery lawyer of the bust years. He probably made legal history by making two secret compositions of his lawful debts in one year, and advised the Davies, the Baillieus and his notorious elder brother, Benjamin Fink, how to offload theirs. Theodore Fink had become one of Melbourne's outstanding citizens, chairing some of Victoria's most important educational commissions and patronising the arts. He persuaded Meudell to prepare a sanitised edition, *The Pleasant Career of a Spendthrift and his Later Reflections* (1935), misleadingly labelled a 'second impression'. As Michael Cannon observed:

> all mention of Theodore's brother, B. J. Fink was omitted from pages 20, 23, 27, 32, 60, 66 and 82. A long list of insolvent land boomers was omitted and Meudell's few flattering remarks were retained, to give a completely opposite version to his original intention ...
>
> Another new section claimed that B. J. [Benjamin] Fink 'retained throughout the confidence of all the important people with whom he dealt'. Other sections gave quite tendentious accounts of the law cases ... both defended by the young solicitor, Theodore Fink. Thus was history rewritten.[19]

And it was thought that money had changed hands. Baillieu in the intervening years had had a mental collapse. He had to be restrained after assaulting his chauffeur, and was shipped unobtrusively to London. Meudell's conscience-pricking 1929 volume was blamed by some, but Baillieu was probably too shameless for that. Interestingly Theodore Fink and John Wren were later on friendly terms.[20] They had at least one interest in common: making money.

Fink was also a friend of Alfred Deakin, the self-conscious model of political rectitude. They had been to Melbourne Grammar School together. Again, Michael Cannon:

> Deakin's part in the land boom remains an enigma … Deakin was a Cabinet Minister during almost the entire period of the 1880s … he was not the man to prosecute the authors of financial disaster with any vigour … was too closely involved with several of the biggest land boomers … became chairman of the City of Melbourne Building Society when Sir Matthew Davies retired … was also a director of James Munro's Australian Property and Investment Co. Ltd. when it crashed. Ambition, if not desire for a quick fortune, makes strange bedfellows … The Gillies-Deakin government, engorged, bloated and rotten fell in October 1890.[21]

With the financial crash of the 1890s 'Marvellous Melbourne' had become 'Smellbourne' in another sense. Nothing, however, would dampen the self-righteousness or the sectarianism of the wowser parsons, even in adversity. True, the Free Presbyterians in 1892 would undertake a solemn fast and the Wesleyans a Week of Self-Denial to 'humble themselves before God on account of His hand on the community … and also to confess the sins that were the procuring causes of God's wrath'. However, not only were covetousness, immorality and irreligion to be deplored but also 'the insidious advances of Romanism', although Catholics were not prominent among the boomers. In May 1893 the Anglican bishop, Dr Field Flower Goe, had proclaimed a Special Day of Humiliation and Prayer. At a special combined service in the Melbourne Town Hall there were lofty groans of corporate self-deprecation but no specifics about who were to blame: there were too many boomers in the congregation. The Rev. Alex Marshall of Scots Church in Collins Street 'actually denied the existence of some notorious, individual cases'. The men who directed the great financial institutions were 'upright honourable men' with whom 'we could sympathise in their misfortunes, whatever blame we might be disposed to attach to the general policy'. Someone found time to remember God's 'providence towards the English people in the face of the Spanish Armada [1588] and after the Great Fire [of London, 1666]', meaning the benign 'Protestant wind' that preserved them from Rome.[22]

It was fortunate for the vituperative energies of the parsons that in proletarian Collingwood, Catholic John Wren was beginning (as they thought) 'to prey' on his impoverished kind by providing the fantasy and entertainment of a scrupulously conducted shilling tote. He also provided an excellent diversion for bigots to ignore the causes of social distress. The young Wren, out of work, could hardly be expected to debate the fine line between investment and speculation when it was ignored by society's moral guardians. Nor would he concede that only the 'toffs' in their snug clubs had an exclusive right to off-course gambling. Wren said that the five-day closure of the banks in 1893 had filled him with 'a burning hatred'.[23]

Collingwood

Australia in the late-nineteenth century had the most urbanised population in the English-speaking world and can claim to have been the first nation of suburbanites. Of Melbourne's suburbs, Collingwood, named after a famous English admiral, was the most conscious of being a distinct community, and to other areas was the most problematic. It was born, says Robin Boyd,

> with a wooden spoon in its mouth, but not because it was underprivileged by nature. It occupied the morning side of a pleasant hill with a river at its foot. It just happened to be a convenient backyard where a busy adolescent town could sweep its junk more or less out of sight if not always out of smell.[24]

The Yarra River divided the gregarious and grey proletarian habitat from the genteel and green municipalities of Hawthorn and Kew, part of what Manning Clark called 'Yarraside', the haven of 'respectability-mongers'. The bible belt also started at the river: in 1891 only 9.4 per cent of 'professing adherents' were Church of England and 17.4 per cent

Presbyterian, compared with 27 and 27.8 per cent respectively in Kew, 22.9 and 59.9 per cent in St Kilda.[25] In 1901, 39.3 per cent were nominally Church of England, 21.8 Roman Catholic, 9.6 Methodist, 8.8 Presbyterian, 6.3 Baptist. The population lived 28.8 per acre.[26]

With flat ground between Melbourne's residential Eastern Hill/ Fitzroy area and the river, Collingwood inevitably became a conduit for insanitary muck and the river a sewer as well as a reservoir. But it had to endure more than this: it was the only inner suburb to have begun as an industrial area. Proximity to the Yarra attracted industries derived from animal products. With West Richmond it became the metropolitan centre not only for bootmaking, breweries and brickworks but also for noxious slaughterhouses, tanneries and soap and candle making. While it was a suburb of low-paid workers (population about 36,000 in 1890) and, in Australian terms, was regarded as a slum, it was never comparable to London's East End, or a place apart like New York's Harlem or Manila's Tondo. It was drab, without buildings of distinction, rather than being just squalid. Zymotic diseases (diptheria, typhoid, dysentry, fevers) were common, but Collingwood was 'not remarkably unhealthy'. The death rate was about the same for the whole metropolitan area, although the proportion of doctors to population was 1:7,000, compared to 1:1,391 in Hawthorn and 1:661 in St Kilda[27]—perhaps a reflection on contemporary medical practice.

Streets were narrow with back lanes providing access for night-soil carts. Except for the more middle-class section of Clifton Hill, houses were typically low cost, and were one-storey dwellings occupied by one family. Collingwood had one of the lowest ratios of owner- or purchaser-occupiers in Melbourne: 36 per cent in 1888–9 compared to 61 per cent in Hawthorn and 62 per cent in Footscray.[28] Even in comparison with neighbouring Fitzroy, it was a weatherboard rather than a brick area; it did not regulate the size of rooms. A typical frontage was 16 to 20 feet, the smallest in Melbourne. Low rents and piecework industries attracted hardship families, widows and deserted wives. Sweating was prevalent. By 1890 one-third of factory workers were female. Artisans made up 30 per cent of householders, another 18 per cent were unskilled labourers, while 15 per cent were in unskilled city service jobs. In such an industrial area protectionism was 'a faith and a dogma'.[29] As early as the 1860s Collingwood had a state-wide reputation for radicalism (and recalcitrance) as represented in the career of Charles Don. By the time Wren was born it had developed a defiant ethos in which the proprieties of Collins Street and Government House were not accepted at face value. The brashness of Collingwood was notorious.

An editorial borrowed from the *Empire* appeared in the rural *Ovens and Murray Advertiser* in 1866, entitled 'COLLINGWOOD ROUGHS'. It reviled the suburb as 'the hotbed of democracy ... the training school of stump orators'. A Collingwood MLA during the current constitutional struggle over the tariff had had 'the impudence' to say of an official in England that 'they [the Victorian people] had not come 10,000 miles to be dictated to by a pup from Downing Street'. Such language, said the editorial, 'was worthy of the great [Charles] DON himself ... of the veriest mongrel that was ever kicked out of a decent man's presence ... of a drunken virago in a taproom'. It urged parliament to take steps 'to terminate these discreditable proceedings'.[30] The pomposity with which Wren's popular initiatives were to be spurned by 'establishment' figures is anticipated here.

Collingwood was not a dormitory suburb. As a larger proportion of the locally employed lived in the suburb, solidarity was enhanced. It was exemplified by rabid support for the local football club which cut across sectarianism and even class distinctions. At a seminar on *Power Without Glory* in 1976 Dr June Hearn, whose family had resided in Collingwood for a long period, pointed out that during hard times

> working class solidarity ... compensated for a lot of the impoverishment. When people were evicted others took them in ... you lived in appalling conditions but you did live. People sent round food, or offered loans of money if they had it ... There was no such thing as loneliness in C'wood; your house was always open and people always felt it their right to come and go as if they lived there ... I think that, more than anything else, enabled working class people, particularly women, to survive.

Hearn was speaking of the 1930s depression but Collingwood had also been badly affected in the 1890s depression. Factory workers like Wren were laid off. Between 1892 and 1895 Melbourne lost 56,000 in population, some 5,085 from Collingwood. It seems ironic that Wren's Tote should rise and prosper exactly at this time. Disagreeing with Niall

Brennan, who saw the characters in *Power Without Glory* as a 'caricature' of the people of Collingwood, Hearn commented:

> Economic impoverishment and despair do, very often, encourage people to gamble … they use, out of desperation, what they should be using for survival … Gambling was looked upon as the panacea for all ills by all the people I ever knew and by all the friends of my family. People bet on anything. And because there was so much wastage of talent … in Collingwood, the most sharp-witted people … usually set themselves up as gambling operators … There were dozens of little John Wrens … my father was one of them. He operated in exactly the same way, albeit on a much less grand scale.
>
> Like John Wren, he gathered around himself the same coterie of thieves, pickpockets, forgers, all sorts of petty criminals … Anyone with any 'go' found themselves living on the shadier side of the law … what seemed to be a novelty for upper or middle class people was, in fact, the norm for the working class of Collingwood.[31]

Although the reality may lie somewhere in between the views of Brennan and Hearn, what is clear is that people were not ostracised permanently because of problems with the law. Few in Collingwood would have thought Wren odious because he employed former criminals at his Tote. They were disowned only for atrocious crimes. Monty Grover's title, 'Wren and His Ruffians', in his famous exposé in the *Lone Hand*,[32] disconcerted mostly Yarrasiders.

Visitors commented on the prevalence of gangs and the culture of larrikinism in Australian cities. R. E. N. Twopenny in *Town Life in Australia* (1883) was particularly appalled by the 'practical demonstration of latent sympathy with crime' shown during the Ned Kelly trial and execution. He complained that even the chairman of committees in the Legislative Assembly gave leadership to thousands agitating for reprieve. A Trades Hall Council sub-committee at a royal commission on employees in 1884 attributed larrikinism to abuses in factories and the lack of recreational facilities for youth, who in any case were put to work much too early.[33] The liberal *Bulletin* thought the cause was lower-class affluence:

> The youth who chooses to indulge in riotous living does not come to absolute want in the inevitable fashion which obtains in the old

> country. An occasional spell of work puts him in funds ... the idle and lazy do not here necessarily disappear, ground under the wheels of the social machine.[34]

Collingwood naturally contributed to this reputation. Dr Hearn remembers the gangs of her youth taking their names from streets and warring with intruders from neighbouring Fitzroy. Most young males took up boxing for self-defence; too many thought of bouts at the Stadium. Collingwood had its own argot. But it was not a notorious centre of vice or crime in spite of its 87 hotels in 1885 (compared to 64 in Richmond, 9 in Hawthorn, 7 in Kew). 'Dozens of little John Wrens' had sprouted before and would do so long after the Tote closed in 1907. They felt they attracted unnecessary discrimination by the police.[35]

Police

Social dissidence derived also from the convict legacy and the libertinism of a fluid society. This showed itself especially in attitudes towards the police. Many of those who did not punt on Wren's Tote still enjoyed his triumphant evasions of the law. Even chief commissioners were not held in high regard. Frederick Standish, chief from 1855 to 1880, was a notorious gambler and boozer who was alleged to have suspended one hunt for the Kelly gang pending declaration of weights for the Melbourne Cup.[36] The Longmore Royal Commission into the Police in 1882 deemed a certain Thomas O'Callaghan 'most untrustworthy'. He had a bleak record, on five occasions being charged formally for breaches of discipline, even once being reduced in rank. He rose to become inspecting superintendent and chief commissioner during the Tote's heyday. The Cameron Royal Commission of 1905–6 considered his administration had 'many blemishes'.[37]

The *Lone Hand*'s blistering attack on Wren in May 1907 presented a retrospect of the career of one Paddy Boardman, who became an associate of Wren at his City Tattersalls Club. It was impossible, it said, 'to deny Boardman's claim to sympathy in the long ago. Certain detectives did deliberately plan a disreputable career for the young man and Thomas O'Callaghan ... must be held responsible for the Boardman of then and now.' Boardman gave evidence to the Longmore Commission of police chicanery, as a result of which they tried to frame him. The *Lone Hand*, however, had no doubt of Boardman's subsequent 'cronk' practices, such as jury-squaring, providing false evidence and running 'hazard schools'. But he was still being fairly candid before the Cameron Commission twenty-four years later.[38]

Detective Patrick Macmanamny was described by his superintendent in 1899 as 'without exception the smartest thief taker and the best commercial detective I ever met'; his service sheet was studded with commendations.[39] He successfully raided Wren's Tote in 1896 but was passed over in 1900 when new top-level plans to bust Wren were to be put in motion. Perhaps this was because even at that time he had begun to appear sympathetic. By 1907 the *Bulletin* could record:

> at any time last Friday afternoon in Melbourne, anyone with a camera might have secured an interesting snapshot photo of Jack Wren in earnest confab with Macmanamny. At 1.40 pm they were standing together at the Town Hall corner ... previously and subsequently they were seen elsewhere.[40]

At the Cameron Commission, several hearsay allegations of corruption were made, and it was suggested that Macmanamny 'lived in more affluence than a member of the police force in his condition should'.[41] Wren's nemesis, Detective-Sergeant David O'Donnell, indubitably honest, rejected the charges against Patrick MacManamny, who continued his distinguished career; but O'Donnell observed how they were 'surrounded ... by crooked, unscrupulous and untrustworthy people' who were 'in deep sympathy' with lawbreakers like Wren.[42] So there is a problem here. If O'Donnell's estimate of Macmanamny was correct, could it be that the latter saw something more in Wren than just a lawbreaker? Might he have seen a man who would have been a pillar of law and order, if those whom Manning Clark called the 'straiteners' and 'frowners', the sabbatarian repressors, had had more respect for the impulses of those they deemed the 'lower orders'? These were the moralists who restricted trains and trams on Sundays, even closed the Public Library and removed the swings from children's playgrounds, because the Lord had ordained a day of rest rather than recreation.

Naturally the general public of Collingwood thought little of 'fixing' the law enforcers. All this will surprise no one who remembers the collusion between starting price (SP) bookmakers and police in Melbourne before the TAB era, or between publicans and police in the days of 6 o'clock closing, or between police and abortionists. The butt of Collingwood's scorn was the informer and the 'nark'. O'Donnell despised them too. 'Informers were a class I never had any regard for', he wrote, 'Very unreliable ... such dirty tools ... many of them were rascals, who would rig up evidence, swear anything that suited them ... wherever they are used, perjury and rascality may be looked for'. He should have added condign retribution too, from such as Wren and his so-called ruffians. To O'Donnell 'it was ever a puzzle' as to whether gamblers or informers 'caused the greatest mischief'.[43] Equally, the denizens of Collingwood perceived a contradiction between class-based regulations and a genuinely democratic morality.

Sport

Young Melbourne was well equipped for the development of competitive spectator sport. Ample land, a temperate climate (but without more individualistic counter-attractions of much-of-the-year swimming, surfing and sailing), a favourable percentage of single young men, a high standard of living which guaranteed substantial prizes, and recreational time for the general citizen—all made commercial sport viable and innovative. Anthony Trollope, the English novelist, who visited Australia in the year of Wren's birth, remarked how sport 'is not a national necessity with the Americans, whereas with the Australians it is almost as much so as at home. Cricket, athletics, rowing matches, shooting, hunting, flat-racing and steeple chasing are dear to them.'[44]

From the 1870s Saturday afternoons became free for most clerical, building and factory workers; in this regard Australia was probably leading the world. Sports mania developed. A unique football game, Australian Rules, emerged in the 1850s; the Melbourne and Geelong clubs were formed before any existed in the English Football League. The game became so popular that when two undefeated teams, South Melbourne and Geelong, played in 1887 for an unofficial 'premiership', 34,121 people paid to see it, probably a world record at that time.[45]

Australian sportsmen began to shine internationally. After Edmund Trickett from Sydney won the world's sculling title in England in 1876, 25,000 'fans' welcomed him home and a purse of £850 was subscribed. He defended his title twice in his hometown. Between 1876 and 1907 seven New South Welshmen held the world sculling championship for twenty-two years. Australians were 'no puny, degenerate race that are reared under the Southern Cross', as might have been expected of those with a convict tradition. 'Banjo' Patterson wrote of 'Gladiators stalking through the degenerate Romans'. In 1888 'the Clarence Comet', Henry Searle, became world sculling champion, and he defended his title in London the following year. He died of typhoid on the way home, and 120,000 people attended his funeral.[46] Intercolonial cricket began in 1856, an English team visited in 1862, an Aboriginal team went to England in 1868, and the first Test match took place in 1877 at the Melbourne Cricket Ground, an oval as grand as Kennington in London. Australia won, and went on holding its own against the Mother Country.

Horse-racing, however, was the premier sport. Ownership of horses was general; grass plentiful and free. Trollope observed that 'There is hardly a town to be called a town which has not its racecourse and there are many racecourses where there are no towns'.[47] Melbourne's first race meeting took place in 1838, within three years of its foundation, and the soon-to-be-famous Flemington racecourse was established in 1840. In 1857 a match race between a Victorian and Sydney champion drew 40,000 spectators, inspiring an Australian Champion Sweepstakes. The Melbourne Cup over two miles was inaugurated in 1861. It caught the public imagination so quickly that as early as 1865 many employees were given a half-holiday to see it. In time, wowser employers were obliged to concur in the holiday; they sponsored picnics at the beach or in the hills away from the gambling demon:

> the Methodist grocery firm of Moran and Cato closed all their shops on Cup day 1884 'not … in honour of Cup day', one of the principals explained, 'but simply because men get a holiday then, and we do not like our men to be working while others are enjoying themselves'. But all their staff got a circular saying 'if we discover any of them dealing in sweeps or betting on the racing, the connection between us must end'. Moran and Cato's would never employ a Catholic.[48]

But equine 'demons' emerged to draw crowds. In 1866 a three-year-old colt, The Barb, the 'Black Demon', the turf's first out-and-out champion, won the cup with only 6 stone 8 pounds (41.4 kilograms) in front of 25,000 spectators. He would later win two Sydney cups as well, in

1868–9, the second with 10 stone 8 pounds (66.6 kilograms). The cups were democratic handicaps; well-performed horses had to lug weights to bring them back to the field. By 1880, 100,000 people (one third of Melbourne's population) watched the never-to-be-beaten three-year-old, Grand Flaneur, notch the fifth of his nine wins. During Cup week the Governor of Victoria was expected to entertain colleagues and their entourages from other colonies. The Marquess of Normanby advised his successor, Sir Henry Loch:

> It would be a kind of High Treason for a Governor not to attend the Flemington Races. I know nothing about Races, but I have always done so and it is no great hardship as it is the finest course in the world and they make you very comfortable. I do not know whether you drive four in hand. I always drove my team to the races and it is a popular thing to do.[49]

In 1890 Carbine broke all records, 100,000 turned up, and the Cup was worth £10,000 plus sweepstakes, a prize which fell markedly with the 1890s depression and was never equalled until Bitalli won in 1923. Walter Hickenbotham, Carbine's trainer, handed out hairs from the horse's tail to ladies; legends persisted that there was efficacy in them. In 1895 a crowd wept on the wharf to see 'Old Jack' (Carbine) exported to England as a sire. His skeleton was returned years later and used to stand near Phar Lap's fully stuffed hide in the Melbourne Museum. When the intrepid Tommy Corrigan—winning jockey in seven Grand Nationals, and celebrated in verse by 'Banjo' Patterson—was killed in 1894, all Melbourne mourned, shops were closed, flags flew at half mast, the Governor and Lady Hopetoun sent a wreath. The funeral procession took two hours to pass, as though 'the remains of a great warrior or statesman were being carried to a grave'.[50]

Mark Twain, creator of Huckleberry Finn, was in Australia and New Zealand in 1895. Although it was a year of depression, he described Melbourne as 'the mitred Metropolitan of the Horse-Racing Cult':

> Its raceground is the Mecca of Australasia, They come 100,000 strong … and they pack the spacious grounds …
>
> … the grandstands make a brilliant … spectacle, a delirium of color, a vision of [female] beauty. The champagne flows, everybody

> is vivacious, excited, happy; everybody bets, and gloves [exchanged among ladies for betting] and fortunes change hands … and when each day is done the people dance all night so as to be fresh for the race in the morning …
>
> … the Melbourne Cup is the Australasian National Day … unique, solitary, unfellowed; and likely to last a long time.[51]

Gambling

Without gambling there would have been little horse-racing. Not that Australians gambled only on horses, but the turf was the hub of an important industry. Anyone familiar with eighteenth-century and Regency literature knows of the British propensity to gamble. It travelled with emigrants, perhaps more so with bored and desperate convicts. Factors such as a climate of extremes, 'a sunburnt country', 'of droughts and flooding rains', and a land which provoked gold rushes (a mineral lottery with instant wealth for a few) are alleged by some commentators to have stimulated risk-taking and fatalism. Also Irish-Catholic culture had been hospitable to horse-racing and at least moderate gambling in contrast to evangelical Protestantism which regarded it as sinful. Worry about the effect of such pleasures on its languishing church attendances could obscure genuine concern that money needed for personal and family support was being squandered. In an era before the welfare state, even the trade unions discouraged gambling because they had to act as a resource for needy members. However, wowser authority was often exercised in such a hectoring way as to incite rather than to eradicate the evil. Prosecuting adolescents for playing pitch and toss was unlikely to be salutary. Colonel Hoskin of the Salvation Army told a 'HORRIBLE GAMBLING STORY' to a crowded Collingwood Town Hall, according to an *Argus* headline (19 August 1905). Two boys had bet a shilling that one would go further than the other in amputating his fingers. Three digits were removed, he said, before they were stopped. Several sceptics in the audience cried 'Over!' amidst laughter.

Both proponents and antagonists have been responsible for romanticising the idea that Australians are the greatest gamblers in the world (and boozers too). While this is exaggerated there can be no doubt that gambling was ineradicable and, as with Prohibition in the United States, attempts to suppress it, particularly among the poorer classes, made 'criminals' out of otherwise law-abiding citizens. On the causes of gambling Geoffrey Caldwell concludes that:

> Gambling in Western society is an interesting complement to the meritocratic system where the rich, the competent, the educated score the bulk of society's rewards. At least gambling is more democratic; at least all who enter have a real chance, long though the odds may at times be; and it is an alternative reward and distributive system.[52]

An inspiration to young John Wren was George Adams of Tattersall's fame. Adams had arrived in Sydney in 1855, worked as a stock dealer and butcher and from 1875 as a hotelier. Tattersall's Club members met in his hotel, subscribing to sweepstakes on race meetings. They became public in 1881. When in 1892 legislation driven by religious bodies prohibited letters containing sweep investments, Adams moved to Brisbane and, after being curtailed there, to Tasmania in 1895, where the government found it beneficial to legalise and tax his lotteries. From there he solicited patronage nation-wide and flourished.[53]

The question arose as to what was the fairest mode of gambling on the turf from the point of view of both punter and stakeholder. The totalisator had originated in France in the 1860s with the *Pari-mutuel* system. It was preferable to sweepstakes, where even drawing a horse was a matter of chance. On the tote a person made his own selection, and it seemed to offer a means of expunging some of the worst features of betting. By aggregating the wagers and dispensing them to the winners, minus a service percentage to the operator, and by insisting on cash transactions, the redistribution that gambling entailed seemed fairer than with the improvised prices of bookmakers. It reduced rash credit betting with its risks of bankruptcies and suicides. Both the racing club and the state would find opportunity for facile taxation, even if this created an approving, lucratively symbiotic relationship with gambling. Moreover it was expected that the totalisator would curb the temptation to try to manipulate results, as it would be no concern to the tote operator who won. It was hoped it would push less reliable bookmakers out and eliminate conflict of interest. With additional funds the racing club could offer better prizes and facilities. But this is what wowsers did not want. Many opposed the tote because it *was* the fairest.

Clandestine totes operated in Victoria, but at Melbourne Cup time in 1879 the aptly named Mr H. Gamble, chemist of 150 Bourke Street East, Melbourne, the proprietor of Gamble's Celebrated Cough Lozenges and Safe Hair Vigor, openly advertised shares at £1 each in his Totalizer (sic) Company. Prizes were to be distributed, with the winner getting 50 per cent, second 30 per cent, third 10 per cent (naturally Mr Gamble got the other 10 per cent). Subscribers were to select the horse of their fancy, forward their remittance 'with exchange added' and state how many shares they wanted. Business would be by letter only and the share list would close on 1 November. On Cup Eve Gamble and two other men with their clerks were arrested and charged with keeping 'a common gaming house'. Gamble's house was searched and nearly £400 in cash seized, as were his ledger, circulars and sweepstake butts. He was eventually fined £10 with five guineas costs. But when he was bailed his premises were besieged with people anxious to invest on the Cup. The press as well as the public praised the tote system and many racing men thought it ought to be run officially on the courses. R. C. Bagot, Victoria Racing Club (VRC) secretary and the imaginative engineer who designed both Flemington and the Melbourne Cricket Ground, pleaded for totalisator betting: it would end 'the mushroom bookmakers on the Hill (the moderately priced area for spectators) who, last Cup Day, numbered some 700'.[54]

The totalisator was tried in Adelaide from 1879 to 1884, successfully as far as its two racing clubs were concerned. Its opponents, however, were able to point out that a major objective, to reduce the volume of gambling, had not been achieved, and even that bookmakers had been helped by the expansion of racing consequent on more revenue for the clubs. Partly due to the influence of Congregationalists in parliament, both the tote and bookmaking became illegal in 1884. Racing declined and there was an exodus of horse-breeders and others interested in the sport, a decline in adjunct industries and a rise in unemployment. It was estimated that GDP (gross domestic product) dropped by over a percentage point. After the 1887 election cleared out some of its opponents, the tote was reinstated.[55]

Melbourne, however, resisted. Bills put up by notables such as David Gaunson and Dr L. L. Smith in 1881 passed the lower house only to fail in the Legislative Council.[56] The VRC was divided. In 1892 a future premier, John Murray, submitted a private Bill stipulating only a limited number of machines to be used at any race course and a responsible division of the 10 per cent levy. Bookmakers were not excluded. Again the press was in favour. The Bill passed in the Legislative Assembly. The historian of the VRC explains why it failed ignominiously, 29 to 6, in the conservative upper house:

> Ministers of religion and their blindly faithful, but shortsighted congregations held special 'prayer' meetings all over Melbourne exhorting the public to rise up against the terrible Totalizator machine which was the work of the Devil himself. They flooded the private letter boxes of every Legislative Council member ... The Temperance Society and Women's League demonstrated outside Parliament ... assuring any Council members who voted for it they would never enter heaven [that is, parliament again?].[57]

And there were also influential VRC members who preferred bookmakers and exclusiveness to the democratic tote.

That it was expensive to operate in its earlier days and could not carry out the complete process automatically probably retarded acceptance of the tote to some degree, but there was no impediment once the distinguished engineer (Sir) George Julius had operated the first completely mechanical machine in Auckland in 1913.[58] When it was installed in Sydney in 1917–18 only Victoria did not have it. The financial exigencies of the next depression settled the issue in Victoria in 1931,[59] almost forty years after Wren had been reviled for popularising it in Collingwood. Today the TAB is everywhere, enticingly appointed, and the state takes 18 per cent. Wren took 10 per cent plus the loose change.

Wannabet?

In 2000, C. J. Wren (a grandson) launched a book *Wannabet?*, one of the authors of which was the Rev. Tim Costello, brother of the federal Treasurer and the incumbent of the Collins Street Baptist Church, where the Rev. T. E. Ruth used to fulminate against Collingwood's notorious gambler. 'In the act of gambling', Ruth seriously maintained, 'God is dethroned and chance is substituted. All that Christ taught of the fatherhood of God is repudiated. Men are marionettes made to move by chance.'[60]

The locale for the launch was the woodyard behind Wren's original Tote at 136 Johnston Street, Collingwood—the venue for efficient, small-scale gambling at the turn of the twentieth century. The concern of Costello and his co-author, Royce Millar, was that 'a crucial turning-point' had been reached in contemporary gambling regulations 'when government turned its attention from people to money and embraced an industry it once outlawed'. No less than the premier of Victoria had declared that the magniloquent Crown Casino represented 'the new spirit of Victoria' and had in effect condemned critical church leaders as 'wowsers'. What Costello and his supporters (Catholics now as well as Protestants) were concerned about was the romanticisation of gambling as a quintessential Australian trait, and such statistics as these: the loss by the unlucky in 1999 of $12.4 billion from an outlay of approximately $100 billion; 21 per cent of the world's 'most sophisticated' poker machines being in Australia and causing more than half of all losses; 42 per cent of poker machine revenue coming from problem gamblers, and so on.[61]

On any view, Wren's illegal shilling tote can hardly be morally condemned in view of today's all-pervasive, state-sanctioned, Australia-wide gambling industry.

CHAPTER THREE

The Mammoth and Marvellous Machine

Beginner's luck

HUGH BUGGY, 'one of the most colourful journalists of his time', ace crime reporter and sports journalist, a man with an extravagant memory for detail who covered over 200 murder investigations in 83 murder trials and attended nine hangings,[1] was at the age of eighteen hired by Wren as a shorthand writer for his racing and trotting clubs. His instructions were:

> They tell me you can write 150 words a minute. I want verbatim reports of stewards' enquiries into crook running and appeals against disqualifications. And I want the transcript on my desk at half past eight on the morning after an enquiry. So the job's yours, although you're younger than I thought.[2]

That is an apt illustration of the way Wren worked. At the time there was no such facility as a typewriter in his office and Buggy had to produce at night in longhand. Buggy became an occasional associate, and intimate enough for the usually taciturn tycoon to reminisce in his company. After Wren's death in 1953 Buggy wrote daily articles for the Melbourne *Argus* through December 1956 and January 1957 to try to repair Wren's reputation. The paper expired after publishing only 24 of the 38 articles in the series. They subsequently became the property of the Wren family, who in 1977 published them *in toto* as a book, *The Real John Wren*, in response to the ABC's serialising of *Power Without Glory* without regard to its objectives or defamatory character.

Wren told Buggy that a wager on the great Carbine in the 1890 Melbourne Cup, a month before weights were declared in June, laid the foundation of his fortune. In this mythopoeic story the timing is important. Carbine's price had depended on the weight he would receive. He had already won two Sydney cups, at well over weight-for-age, and came second as a four-year-old carrying 10 stone (63 kilograms) in the 1889 Melbourne Cup. When in August 'Old Jack', as Carbine was known, was given 10 stone 5 pounds (66 kilograms), only Nat Gould of the racing writers supported him. That prolific novelist's maxim, however, was 'Back a good horse and a good jockey and damn the weight'.[3] So Wren liked to believe that even at nineteen he had been shrewd. Carbine's subsequent form was such that his price firmed and he started favourite in the Cup at four to one against.

Buggy makes a neat story of that crucial day in the career of the apprentice boot clicker, short, sturdy, sandy-haired, with 'a firm dogged jaw and steel-grey eyes … natty and clean-shaven—an oddity in the age of the walrus moustache and the luxuriant handlebar'. He was (probably) wearing his 'harsh blue serge "Sunday best", the applied livery of Democracy', while on his head was 'a sporty grey hat, forerunner to the pork pie as he hated the sombre bowler'. Buggy believes the 'patrician hacks' of 'quality' and 'the haughty beauties in the landaus left him unmoved' as he trudged through their dust. 'Defiantly unimpressed' may have better described a non-smoking, teetotalling youth whose brother was in gaol and had been flogged for abetting a rape, something never mentioned by Buggy. Carbine won by two-and-a-half lengths, in fact heroically, with a split hoof in record time against a record field of 39 starters.[4] This was the stuff of legend, and it happened.

Wren told Buggy this win was the beginning of 'an extraordinary run' in which he 'couldn't lose for six months and picked up quite a few hundreds'—'a sweeping understatement' according to 'some of his old friends' who believed that 'in the six months after Carbine's historic victory, "J W" won almost enough to buy out Whybrow's boot factory where he worked'.[5] This is quite unlikely, but Wren seems to have been supplementing his income running a 'doubles' book or 'a few somewhat furtive transactions in threepenny place cards'. After he lost his job in the slump of 1891–2 he is believed to have worked for a tote or bookie for a time, learning the trade. Richard Stremski in his scholarly history of the Collingwood Football Club, *Kill For Collingwood*, gives a more sophisticated explanation of the origin of Wren's foundation capital. Stremski, on the basis of reputable interviews, concludes:

> Wren had developed a low-key, loan sharking operation ... at Whybrow's. Frugal to a fault he lent money to his workmates between pay packets and collected interest at threepence a month on ten shillings (that is, 2.5 per cent a month). One large loan on a prospecting adventure may have netted a particularly lucrative return. Thus, Wren was able to shift to the slightly more respectable enterprise of 'making book' [sic] in the boot factory. In 1893 he transferred the bookmaking activities to the back of a tea shop on Johnston Street and quickly expanded into the woodyard behind it which fronted Sackville Street.[6]

What has been unknown to commentators is that the owner of that tea shop and dwelling in Johnston Street was Eliza 'Granny' Foster, who may well have helped to stake Wren. At first patrons passed behind the counter of the shop into the betting room but in time, probably no later than 1896,[7] owing to the need for greater security from police raids, they entered the yard through Sackville Street and 'reached it through devious ways ... between the shop and Gold Street'. This was not a slum area; Johnston Street was a main thoroughfare to 'Yarraside'. At that point it used to 'drop rather steeply onto the river plain of the Collingwood flats'. Almost opposite was the Galloway Arms Hotel, which had a special parlour for the playing of bagatelle'. Police raids were not facile affairs in the 1890s. They were made in whatever lumbering, hired four-horse cabs the city police could get. On one occasion police had to hide on a cart under a load of hay—in order to surprise their lawbreakers. An extensive off-course network existed before Wren's Tote and continued during his paramountcy. Buggy's research revealed that none of the illegal operators won anything like Wren's notoriety. The wowsers whose 'oratorical fire was never diverted from Wren' regarded them as nonentities.[8]

The Tote opens

Wren opened his tote business in 1893. At first wagers could be as small as threepence or sixpence; by 1895 they were in shillings. Wren is alleged at the early stage to have appropriated a third of the takings, but from this time on the takings were aggregated and Wren took 10 per cent plus the extra 'pence' (that is, winnings were paid only to the base sixpence).[9] Order and fair dealing were mandatory. A special notice in Wren's yard read:

> A man is especially engaged and kept in the back yard to do all the shouting and swearing that is required in this establishment. A dog is also kept to do all the barking. A fighting man—or chucker-out … has won 75 class fights and is a splendid shot with a revolver. An undertaker calls every day for orders.[10]

There can be little doubt that many of Wren's 'minders' and 'bouncers' were what Yarrasiders (and Manning Clark) would have regarded as 'unsavoury types': pugnacious men with criminal records, often recidivists. To signal the imminence of police raids there had to be 'nitkeepers', 'cockatoos' and a 'mulga wireless'—characters with names like Copper O'Rourke and Sauce McQuirk. As McConville writes:

> Wren, with stouter defences and a string of informers extending into the Russell Street Detective Office, survived longer than less methodical competitors … The Tote survived because of support from inner city residents with established careers in crime. The stand-over men and grafters on the Tote payroll looked to Robert Roberts or Paddy Boardman for direction rather than to Wren himself.[11]

What seems clear, from lack of evidence to the contrary, is that they were loyal to Wren—or too respectful to complain. There are no recorded shoot-outs, brawls or mutinies among the henchmen. And there was no unsavoury accretive commerce: no prostitution, bootlegging or drug-selling. Women and minors were kept away. Their bets would have been mediated through agents (for example, tobacconists, barbers). In time Wren had feeder branches, allegedly five in Lygon Street, Carlton, and others scattered elsewhere.[12]

Inevitably the police turned their attention to what from its beginning was a popular venue, all the more so for its reputation of prompt payment and honesty. Even the vinegary *Argus* would report in 1895:

> Everything is done fairly and above board. The tote sheets hang before you and every number registered is seen. There can be no deception. If the institution has a virtue it is its openness. That no one may dispute its honesty the tote sheets are kept on exhibition days after a race meeting. They can be critically examined by anyone to whom a ticket may have been sold. The very strength of the tote lies in its honesty.[13]

A reporter stated that 15,000 shillings had been known to follow a single race. On one occasion £19 was paid for a one shilling investment, odds of 380 to 1. This did not impress the *Bulletin*, which complained that 'the splendid odds' had been augmented by Wren's 'all-in' principle whereby the tote even swallowed up monies invested on non-starters. Thus when 'congratulating himself on the splendid odds of 50 bob to five, the average ass punter forgets that he has sacrificed many previous shillings in a vain attempt to spot a runner'[14]—let alone a winner. In fairness to Wren the *Bulletin* might have added that the winners profited more than Wren did from the extra inputs into the consolidated wagers. Also, in an enterprise organised for emergency closures, the extra administration involved in repayments would have complicated procedures. It is notable that the Collingwood *Observer* defended Wren's 'enterprise' on at least nine occasions during 1903–6.[15]

The police nabbed Wren three times in 1893. John Wren, 'tobacconist of 136 Johnston Street', was arrested on 18 March and fined £5 with five shilling costs.[16] In May he was fined £10. In November, on the eve of Tarcoola's Cup, police changed tactics and swooped by forced march from north and west. Wren's spotting service had broken down. Inspector Connolly summarily breached the defences and rounded up fifty-five punters. While there was only a threepenny bit in the cash box, he collected lists of horses with other documents.[17]

This time Wren was not on the premises—or got away—but he was arrested and fined £50 or three months gaol. It cost Joe, his brother and a first offender, £25 or two months. Each punter caught paid five shillings with one shilling costs, except for William Thomas, who resisted arrest and paid forty shillings. As it happened, the horse laid by Inspector Connolly's informant won and, according to Brennan, Wren had his winnings delivered to the police station next day.[18] Wren had a sardonic sense of humour, as well as being a 'sport'. The *Lone Hand* made the point that, even at this early stage, Wren suborned a witness who refused to repeat in court what, allegedly, she had told the police previously, that sometimes John and sometimes Joe paid her mother the rent.[19] Obviously the girl was of Foster origin and just as obviously the police may have been telling lies. In any case, she was being loyal. In Collingwood there would have been little need for a bribe. The *Lone Hand* thought that already Wren's 'money had begun to talk, but he was not yet a privileged flouter of the law'. What is more interesting is that he was thought to have made so much so soon—at twenty-two. Wren did not appeal against his 1893 convictions, perhaps because the amount did not warrant it.

From the beginning Wren was defended by David Gaunson MLA, a cogent and blustering barrister, demagogic politician and inveterate toper, who had defended Ned Kelly in 1880 at his last trial and been prominent in mass protests against his execution. His brother-in-law, even further back in 1854, had acted without fee for some of the Eureka stockaders accused of treason. Gaunson was also solicitor to Madame Brussells, the most notorious of Melbourne's brothel-keepers, who figures later in this story. He 'once boasted that he had cheated Pentridge [prison] of more deserving tenants than any other practitioner in Victoria'. Perhaps Wren did not appeal at this stage because it was not clear even to Gaunson, though this is unlikely, how loopholes in the anti-gambling laws would enable him to evade further convictions and prison. What Gaunson would certainly have impressed on Wren were 'his rights' as a householder. As McConville relates:

> In 1894 when [Wren] threw Senior Constable Daly out of the Tote he defended himself in most respectable terms. Shouting through the barred gate of the woodyard, Wren reminded the policeman that it was his house, 'and every man's house is his castle'.

Ultimately, Wren and premier Bent were to be among Gaunson's pall-bearers.[20]

In 1894 the Collingwood *Mercury* recorded another raid on 'Wren's shop' and on Levy's, a tobacconist of varying addresses. Wren's shop was 'packed'. There was panic as 'All tried to get over the back fence which was covered with barbed wire' which retained scraps of clothing. Hats, walking sticks and umbrellas littered the yard. Wren was not there. Thomas Oldroyd was said to be conducting the business. The police found £150 in the front shop beneath a heap of rubbish under the counter. Gaunson pleaded that his client should not be sent to gaol. The prosecutor said he did not desire that, and Oldroyd was fined £10 with £7 7s costs.[21] In July 1895 it was Edward Mills who took the rap. Constable Watson had succeeded in 'effecting an entrance' in spite of 'elaborate security arrangements'. He found a crowd of two hundred, with Mills 'distributing tickets'. Mills pleaded he could not find work in the country, had to feed a wife and three children and so, as a 'last resort', was thankful to accept a billet at the tote shop. Sub-Inspector Gray said it did not matter what the fine would be, someone would be willing to pay it, and as soon as one man was caught another would take his place. So it was difficult to get a second conviction. Mills was fined £10 with 25s costs. He was allowed only half an hour to pay, but no doubt there was an agent on the spot. Mills was to appear in court again for gambling.[22] The *Mercury* expostulated in late 1895:

> When will this tote sham cease? The totes (not just Wren's) do a roaring business, and bare-footed children, out-of-elbows men, and slip-shod, scantily attired women are to be seen daily spending shillings which have a right to go for food and clothing. There are some people who have to be protected against themselves and we greatly fear that many of those who patronise the tote are amongst the number.[23]

The *Mercury* maintained that the government was virtually 'supporting' the totes through the inaction of police who could see 'as plain as a pike staff' what was going on.[24] Why, the authorities directed police to keep the traffic clear near the tote shops in Johnston Street! 'Isn't it a case of straining at the gnat and swallowing the horse?' So the question was: 'To be or not to be: tolerate totes or put them out of business. Let us have no more farce.'[25]

Wren's wonderful Tote

Victoria's Street Betting Suppression Act did not include betting within a building while the Police Offences Act of 1890, on which prosecution relied was inadequate, although in the past it had won convictions. Among the problems faced were how to prove either that 'a common gaming house existed', or the identity of 'owner or occupier', and whether that person knew how the building was being used, and how to show that a building was actually being used for 'betting with persons resorting thereto'. Doubt as to ownership or occupancy, and lack of documentation relating to betting, made convictions of those with shrewd legal representation difficult. Strangely, says Buggy, until the end of the century 'nobody appeared to be very clear as to who controlled' the Collingwood tote although, according to Stremski, the local 'moralistic *Mercury* in this period cited Wren as proprietor on no less than ten occasions'.[26] Wren was being referred to in parliament as 'a man we all know' or 'a prominent sportsman who is known to us' and 'a certain man you know who I mean'.[27] Wren by temperament probably enjoyed this hugger-mugger, and the mystification helped to keep him out of court. The local populace may also have been stirred by the gradual bracing of the Johnston Street fortress and its baffling organisation. In 1903 *Truth* would describe the tote at its most formidable:

WREN'S WONDERFUL TOTE

HOW CONCEALED, CONSTRUCTED AND CONDUCTED

POLICE HYPOCRISY AND POLICE HYSTERIA

MAMMOTH AND MARVELLOUS MACHINE

Wren's Tote is now an Australian institution on par with Tatt's Sweep. It has also been the subject of similar popular patronage, accompanied all the time by abortive attempts to suppress it ... consequently spread over ten years or so, the public have been diverted from time to time by more or less fatuous and foolish forays by the men in blue against the redoubtable Tote. On one of these occasions the officers of the Law hid themselves in a cart under some bags of chaff and suddenly descended upon the premises.

ATTACKING IT WITH AXES

But in vain. At the first stroke the place was as empty as a rabbit burrow taken possession of by a ferret. Nothing came of this effort but a laugh against the police. Nothing remains of it except a few axe marks visible to this day as historical records. From start to finish the police have been outgeneralled, and the present farcical proceedings of the force [i.e. at Cup time 1903] adds rather to the gaiety of nations than detracts from the prevalence of gambling. But one of the chief commissioners [O'Callaghan's] first official act was to increase the ranks by fifty constables and this is apparently just a desperate device to keep the men employed. Well, they are having a time of it, playing cards, draughts and dominoes all day long, varied with an occasional investment on the Tote energetically run all the time just around the corner. You have only to examine the premises to at once understand how the law has been so successfully defied and ludicrously derided. It is a marvel of construction, exhibiting a crude skill in engineering which would do credit to an expert.

THE ENTRANCE

is from Sackville Street through a door in a wall built across a twelve foot right of way … This admits you to a small, square yard, where there is another door. In this enclosure visitors are scrutinised, and there are ready and willing chuckers-out at hand to eject any 'crook' character. The door in the second wall which is protected at the top by plenty of barbed wire, leads into the main yard. This is paved with pitchers, as gutter running down the centre, and presents the appearance of a milking-shed more than anything else. In one corner is a water-closet, humourously labelled 'Vockler Villa' and in another a urinal. All along one side is a Tote. It is a very long structure, looking from outside like a cage at the Zoo built to retain ferocious animals. The lower part is battened stoutly and the upper portion is defended by thick iron water piping … immediately behind this rampart is a raised platform about a foot high and three feet behind this again are the lists of the horses entered in the current races of the day. At night a bright light is thrown on these from big tin lamps fixed in every post. When the Tote is in full swing, the attendants, cowled and gowned from head to foot like medieval torturers, pass up and down the platform, rapidly adding the new investments against the horses' names.

THE TOTE FROM OUTSIDE

It should be said that running right behind its innermost wall is a secret passage 40 feet long and about 16 inches wide. The existence of this cleverly devised get-away was only discovered during the last raid, and it has explained to the police much which hitherto baffled the mighty intellects of the force. But it is the Tote-room, where the chief conductors operate, that main interest centres … What cannot be shown in the drawing is the peculiar constitution of the … [shute] through which the money is passed in by the punters, and the winnings are passed out by the operators. It twists in the shape of a square Z, necessitating a snaky curving of the arm to get the hand to the end of it. This device prevents outsiders from obtaining any view of whoever are within or whatever is going on. [There are] means of sudden exit and escape … The first is a sliding panel leading to the secret passage above described, and the second is a direct cut to a yard next door. The strong box … is where the money is placed as it is received. It is constructed of heavy wood, and is of triangular shape, two of its sides being the walls of the room …

… The Tote is connected by telephone. Of course, the authorities did not do this knowingly. What was done, however, was to get the connections put in down the street. Then it was cunningly switched on to the main Tote office. Altogether Wren's Tote is a mammoth and marvellous machine for meeting the needs of a large portion of the community, and at the same time evading the law. Its administration is as wonderful as its construction. Wren has a mastermind and is said to pay his legal advisers a retaining fee of £300 a year.

Truth, always on the lookout for impostors—and 'establishment' hypocrites—was unequivocal about Wren's dealings with his clients:

> He owes his success to his absolute integrity and all-round straightness, and certainly is tolerated in the community with far more sympathy than censure in his constant war against the forces of humbug and stupidly exercised authority.[28]

Suborning witnesses

Wren's success led to other illegal bookmakers adopting his prices—eventually advertised as 'Wren's prices'—and to the establishment of profitable sub-agencies about which little information is available. But he did not, as an Al Capone might have, seek any monopoly. The notoriety of the Tote attracted rivals to Collingwood and inspired an outcry in which the renowned Dr L. D. Bevan of Collins Street Independent Church[29] played a lead. Chief commissioner Chomley was moved by accusations of laxity to put Detective Macmanamny to raiding the Tote. With an array of high and special commendations, Macmanamny rose from constable in 1887 to sub-inspector in 1910, 'capable of any class of criminal investigation work'.[30] Showing what the *Lone Hand* called 'strategical skill', Macmanamny in November 1896 arrested Wren and had him convicted in the lower court. Wren appealed to the Supreme Court and won. The *Lone Hand* marvelled retrospectively at how he came to escape conviction; the newspapers were almost silent:

> Never was so little said in the public journals about so readable a subject as the allegations that resulted from the raiding of Wren's Tote in October 1896. The direct charge of Tote keeping paled into insignificance beside the incidental accusation which Detective Macmanamny fired at Jack Wren. Two witnesses were employed to put money on the Tote, and testify to the character of the business. These two men—Beesby and Conn—were the formal informants … During one of the weekly adjournments of the case, according to the detective's charge, Wren tracked them down to Bendigo and offered them each £58 to go away and lose themselves. On the word of Detective Macmanamny the influential Tote proprietor had been guilty of an attempt to corrupt the course of justice. But what of that? Nothing came of it. He was not even convicted on the charge of Tote-keeping, nor did anybody seem very shocked at the failure of the case. He went on rejoicing.[31]

It would appear that the Supreme Court was not impressed by police conduct. McConville provides a 'typical' case of Wren suborning a police informer in 1899:

> Police claimed that Wren had 'got at' several witnesses in a Tote prosecution. One, James Allison, proved stubborn and wrote to police in December recording that he 'was personally approached by an agent of Wren with an offer of £50 or more to turn against the police failing—doing so, a threat of prosecution for perjury was held out'. Allison's wife was met by Wren and other Tote men four times, 'twice with an offer of a permanent billet for myself and subsequently to tell me to clear out as Wren was determined to charge me with perjury if his offer was not accepted'.[32]

Isaac Isaacs, Victorian attorney-general, attempted to amend the Police Offences Act in November 1898, closing the gaps in the law by proposing that owners and not just occupiers of premises be made responsible for their use. This would be applied also to adjoining premises used for access to illegal ones. Police, however, could not enter without a warrant, for which it was necessary to show some evidence of illegal activities. When introducing the Bill in the Legislative Council, Sir Henry Cuthbert was quite explicit, referring to unsuccessful raids in Collingwood. The Bill was directed particularly at Wren. At this stage Wren (aged twenty-seven) was rumoured to be making £20,000 a year and to have a ring of betting shops or at least imitators who quoted Collingwood prices. The council passed the Bill down to the Legislative Assembly but not without noting its inconsistencies which were then taken up. Isaacs described the tea shop at 136 Johnston Street and the problems of access. Necessarily, the Bill was opposed by Labor and anti-wowser MPs who detected the double standard whereby 'gentlemen could bet in clubs but workers not'. However, the Bill foundered more on the fears of landlords that their rights were infringed and that surveillance of the uses of their property could prove vexatious. The Bill was beaten by a majority of one, 23 to 22.[33]

On Caulfield Guineas Day (October) 1899 Macmanamny led another raid, battered in the door with axes, and found the place empty; all inmates escaped into Johnston Street. Raids seemed futile.

The 'Stacey'/Smythe affair

The most heinous offence with which Hardy charges 'John West' (Wren) during his Tote days is the murder of a police informer, Arthur 'Stacey' (Smythe). It was repeated in the television serial. 'Stacey' is ultimately shanghai'ed onto a boat travelling to the Orient, and disposed of at sea.

The build-up to this incident in *Power Without Glory* begins with a successful raid on the Tote in 1899 led by two young detectives, 'Armfield' (Armstrong) and 'Williams' (Wilson). Three of 'West's operatives are arrested. David 'Garside' (Gaunson) discovers that the chief witness against them is a police pimp, Arthur 'Stacey', whom the police are hiding in a back street in Carlton. 'West' and 'Garside's' clerk, 'Daniel Cummin' (J. B. Cullen) contact 'Stacey' and offer a bribe if he will say he has never been near the Tote in his life and has not made any statement to the police. They even suggest that he disappear from Melbourne. 'Armfield' and 'Williams' then set a trap for 'West': when he and 'Cummin' return to 'Stacey's' house to concoct this perjury, the detectives will be eavesdropping outside the window. When the sovereigns are being handed over, they will pounce. Things go according to plan; 'West' and 'Cummin' are arrested for attempting to bribe a witness. 'Stacey' is then put out of 'West's' reach.

The detectives, however, have overlooked the tentacles of the Catholic Church. 'West's' fiancée's mother, Mrs 'Moran' (Mahon), is 'president of the Women's Sodality at St Joseph's' and 'a friend of the Archbishop [sic] of Ballarat himself, who used to be a priest in Carringbush'. She prevails on the current parish priest to persuade Fr 'Carroll' of Carlton ('a hard case 'tis true—he likes his little drink and his little bet on the horses—but he's a fine and pious priest') to go and see 'Stacey', who turns out to be a Catholic too. Does 'Stacey' know, asks 'Fr Carroll', that 'West' and 'Cummin' are also Catholics and that the detectives are Orangemen, Freemasons—the 'poltroons'! No, it will not be perjury to change evidence and allege 'that the whole thing is a conspiracy against West and Cummin'! 'Stacey' is spiritually cowed and does as he is told. The judge has also been bribed by 'Garside' with 400 sovereigns. Unfortunately, the detectives are inexperienced and contradict each other. 'Garside' dominates the court. The judge sums up in 'West's' and 'Cummin's' favour. The jury finds them not guilty.

Then comes the trial of 'West's' three Tote operatives. This time 'Stacey' tries to satisfy the detectives and says he has placed bets on the Tote and can identify the men who accepted them, although they wore masks. Puffed up now with self-importance, he plays to the gallery revealing, writes Hardy, 'his ignorance and utter stupidity'. He has difficulty remembering which of the two cases he is involved in and at one stage even says: 'I am a truthful man and a Catholic. I have been telling the truth since Fr Carroll came to see me on behalf of Mr West'. Before the trial can recommence on the second morning, 'Stacey', although under police guard, is smashed on the skull with an iron bar by Arthur 'West' outside the 'Carringbush' (Collingwood) court and abducted by him, 'One-eyed Tommy', 'Cauliflower Dick' and 'Piggy'. Three months later, 'One-eyed Tommy' delivers 'Stacey' to 'a cut-throat captain' trafficking in drugs and prostitutes. 'Stacey' is never to return to Australia, 'even if you have to murder the bloody pimp'. The day that 'Stacey' is 'thrown overboard to the sharks', 'John and Nellie West' board a ship 'bound for an idyllic honeymoon in New Zealand during which John West forgot that Stacey had ever existed'.[34]

In fact, there was a raid on Wren's Tote led by a Detective Wilson on 4 March 1899. Arrests were made and there was litigation of intense public interest in the subsequent months. This was reported in the newspapers. The *Leader*, in particular, covered Tote cases between March and July 1899 and it has been scanned from mid-1899 to January 1902. Five men, not three, were charged following Wilson's raid. They were remanded for eight days to prepare their case. Gaunson was their counsel. On 14–15 March four of them were fined for breaches of the Gaming Act; charges against the fifth were dismissed. The four appealed, but only one appeal was reported on 13 April when it was adjourned, because the trial of Wren and Cullen supervened and because of pressure on the bench. No further reportage of these appeals has been sighted, although the *Lone Hand* said they were upheld. But the *Lone Hand* inaccurately referred to only two arrests being made in March 1899.[35]

On 12 March Wren and his cousin, J. B. Cullen, who had been 'the managing common law clerk' with Gaunson & Wallace, Solicitors, were charged at Carlton Watchhouse at 11.30 pm. It was alleged that:

> On 9 March, at 61 Kay Street, Carlton, they intended to pervert the due course of law and justice, did unlawfully corrupt, wilfully and maliciously solicit and attempt to suborn, instigate and persuade one, Arthur Smythe, who, as they knew, had been summoned to appear and give evidence in certain cases, to commit wilful and corrupt perjury by falsely swearing that he, Arthur Smythe, had never been in the Tote yard, or made any statement to anyone that he had been in or on such yard or premises.

They were also to be charged with inducing Smythe 'to suppress evidence … by withdrawing into the country and remaining there during the hearing of the informations'. Wren described himself as '27, financier' where previously, the *Leader* noted, he had been 'styled a gentleman'. Bail was fixed at £200 and 'each accused in his own bond for a similar amount'. The necessary surety was at once forthcoming from Wren's father. On 13 March both accused were remanded for eight days.

On 21 March the hearing began at Carlton Court, and Wilson's testimony was very much as that attributed to 'Williams' in *Power Without Glory*.

In what the *Leader* captioned 'a sensational development', Smythe, described as a 'blacksmith', 'appeared to be ill and looked anxious and care-worn'. He denied handing over any notes of conversations to Wren or Cullen and then caused considerable excitement by ejaculating: 'This thing is a conspiracy against these two men. There are not four words of truth in it all. I was dragged into it against my will, and I'm losing weight ever since. I have lost over a stone in weight already.' Smythe went on to say that he had 'signed a paper at Wilson's house without knowing what it contained'. Wren had visited him on Sunday (5 March) and asked him to produce certain information as to who the witnesses against him in the Tote cases were, giving him £2 for doing so. Smythe said that when he had told Wilson and Armstrong that Wren and Cullen had been to see him, Wilson said, 'That's right. Lay a trap.' Smythe accused Wilson of 'twisting things about' and obliging him 'to sign things … without knowing what they were, including, under threat of gaol, a blank sheet of paper.' He denied that Wren and Cullen had told him what to say in court, or advised him 'to go away on any occasion'. He did get the names of the witnesses against Wren's men, but it was from Wilson, whom he had told that the information was for Wren. He had received £8 altogether from Wren even though he was a Crown witness, but the money was supposed to be handed to the detectives as part of the 'trap'. Wren and Cullen were committed for trial. Smythe was later (13 April) to complain to the bench of being constantly stalked by police.

The case opened on 25 April with a charge of conspiracy unexpectedly added to that of subornation of perjury against Wren and Cullen. There was 'a large attendance of spectators' who laughed inordinately when Wilson could not attend because of what defending counsel called 'a stomach ache'. The trial reopened on 27 April. Purves QC mocked Wilson to the amusement of the crowd. When Wilson gave the impression he must have seen through a wall, he was asked: 'What are you, a Röntgen ray [X-ray]? (laughter)'. Later Purves sarcastically described Wilson as 'a human phonograph'. Purves made the police seem incompetent and manipulative. Smythe admitted that a trap had been set for Wren and Cullen to be caught paying for information on witnesses. The police promised him in return a position in Customs and half the fines in the totalisator case or £50 cash. He said the police told him that the alternative for him was gaol. In concluding, Purves QC alleged the detectives were guilty of conspiracy to obtain commission of a crime, and that this reflected the greatest discredit on the police force.

Mr Justice Hood summed up, saying that there were 'a number of peculiar facts about the defence among which were the giving of £6 and £2 to almost a stranger to accomplish an indefinite object'. And there were also peculiar features in the evidence for the prosecution. 'Wilson and Armstrong had at least acted very foolishly', he said, 'dictating to one another and reading and rehearsing the evidence for the prosecution. Either the explanation was coloured, or the whole story was a deliberate concoction of lies.' Wilson 'certainly made statements which were hard to understand and, taken literally, his statement that he had not given Smythe a copy of the statement he was to make was not true'. Finally Hood said:

> If the detectives had concocted their evidence for the purpose of convicting Wren particularly who was a reputed owner of the Totalizator, which the police had failed to crush, and whose conviction, therefore, would lead to promotion for them, the police force was rotten from top to bottom. The idea … was appalling, and, on the evidence before him, he hesitated to accept it.[36]

The jury retired at five minutes past five, and at six o'clock returned with a verdict of not guilty. The Catholic *Advocate* called for a royal commission into police methods.[37]

On 6 May, at the incidence of John Francis Byrne of Carlton, warrants were issued against Wilson and Armstrong for perjury. On 17 May the City Court decided a *prima facie* case had been made out against Wilson and he was committed to trial before the Supreme Court. On 27 June in the Supreme Court Wren (and Cullen) declined to give evidence on the grounds that 'I have been subject to a criminal prosecution, and a further charge might arise out of what I might say'. Cross-examining, Mr Duffy asked Wren:

> You are a speculator? – Yes.
> What sort of speculator? – Mines, horses, racing.

> Totes? – Yes, totes (laughter).
>
> Where is your tote? – I decline to answer.

At this stage His Honour intervened to disallow further questioning. Eventually the detectives were given the benefit of the doubt but came in for some severe criticism from the bench.[38]

The events on which the *Power Without Glory* 'Stacey' affair is based are garbled. There is no mention of a Fr Carroll in the court proceedings; the involvement of the clergy is mere scurrility (and there has never been an 'archbishop' of Ballarat). 'Stacey's' farcical performance in court is just invention. He is supposed to have been violently abducted while guarded by police, and then kept in captivity by 'One-eyed Tommy' for three months before being disposed of. Surely Smythe's kidnapping would have been a sensational event for the newspapers, but it was not reported and no mystery surrounds his exit from public view. Quite simply, Smythe, afraid of the police, absconded. On 13 April he complained to the judge that the police were following him.[39] He gave evidence that Armstrong had 'told me that if I didn't swear up to the mark he would tear my inside out and hang it on a fence'.[40]

In Grover's *Lone Hand* article of 1907, the 1899 raid and subsequent actions of Wilson, Armstrong and Smythe (described as 'this unstable blacksmith') are described. Had there been any credible suggestions that events occurred as described by Hardy, Grover would have known about them and publicised them. Instead Grover was obliged to say that the public were left without definite jury guidance to decide whether the two detectives entered into a conspiracy to defame Wren by charging him with suborning a witness, or whether Wren, 'faced with an ugly accusation, used his money resources to smother up the evidence against him'.[41] The jury could have thought it was both. It is noteworthy that the police records of both detectives are marked on 31 March 1900 '*Not reliable*', although both subsequently earned approbation. It is pertinent that the records of both men are tarnished by episodes involving evidence in the form of documents.[42] However, Grover was not prepared to exonerate Wren until he was proven not guilty. A gambler, he did not seem to deserve the benefit of any doubt.

This affair has been carefully investigated. Clearly, there are better possibilities than fantasising that Smythe was thrown off a drug-runner's boat in the tropics. According to newspaper reports he was about thirty in 1899. One only Arthur Smythe is registered as dying in Victoria between 1900 and 1985. He died mundanely from diabetes and cardio-renal failure at '71 years (about)' in the Alfred Hospital, Prahran, on 12 February 1939.[43] There is other evidence to suggest that the two persons are the same, but none for Hardy's appalling accusation.

Not satisfied with accusing Wren of a hanging offence, Hardy alleges that Mr Justice Hood accepted '400 sovereigns' to influence the jury.[44] As Hood had died in 1922, Hardy was safe. Not only is there no evidence against Hood but he is held in the highest regard by legal historians as a fearless and independent judge who, among other verdicts, sent numerous corrupt land boomers to gaol in the 1890s.[45] For this cowardly slander there can be no excuse

CHAPTER FOUR

The Gambling Mania

The incorruptible cop

WREN SEEMS TO HAVE HAD little harassment between 1900 and late 1903; he continued to flourish and the parsons' outrage grew with Wren's prosperity. Anti-Catholicism was also more vocal. The Prohibition and Public Morals League of Collingwood agitated for action against gambling, and was obsessed about Wren and his church. The parsons habitually referred to having the support of all churches but one. Rev. Pearce Carey was to tell an Orange meeting in the Masonic Hall how one Saturday afternoon between 3.10 and 5.10 he and 'five brave men' (all parsons) had hidden near the Collingwood Tote (later revealed to be the vestry of the Baptist Tabernacle in Sackville Street) and counted the number of bettors going in. There were 1,571. The audience would be horrified if they knew what was going on at Wren's Tote, he said. And at the same time Wren had made a £100 donation to St Vincent's Hospital. Shame on the Roman Catholic Church for encouraging gambling! Incidentally, the watchers admitted to seeing an actual Orangeman entering the Tote. They were able to agree, however, that he must have been an Orangeman in name only.[1]

With Sergeant Gleeson promoted to headquarters, cabinet instructed chief commissioner Chomley in 1900 to put a reliable man in charge of the Gaming Squad, one 'who did not bet or associate with betting men, who could not be seen hob-nobbing with them before the whole public of Melbourne'. Just promoted from Senior Constable to Sergeant, David O'Donnell was such a man. Said to be superlatively fit through regular running and swimming, he stood well over 6 feet and (allegedly) weighed 22 stone (140 kilograms). He had twenty-two years of service behind him, including 'extra special duty' against Ned Kelly's gang. He had been awarded the Royal Humane Society's Bronze Medal for rescuing a drowning woman and her baby in Port Phillip Bay. An expert in fraud investigation, he had on one occasion chased three suspects en route to England, catching one in Colombo, one in Egypt and one in England.[2] He came from an exemplary family; his brother, Dr Nicholas O'Donnell, was the leader of the Irish Home Rule Movement in Australia and a Gaelic scholar. Resourceful, studious and honest, David O'Donnell may have found promotion slow because he was alert to corruption in the force. In his memoirs he said that he objected to this new 'class of duty' being forced on him. Chomley, however, insisted that he 'must' accept the role: 'You are the only man fit to wear Mr Gleeson's mantle. I cannot appoint anyone else.' O'Donnell tried several times 'to get rid of it' but was told 'no one else could be trusted'.

O'Donnell thought gambling was 'a sort of monomania'. Trying to cure it by acts of parliament was 'just as difficult as trying to drain Port Phillip Bay with a tea cup', particularly as he had to do the best he could 'with statutes that lawyers could drive a coach and horses through'. 'Valuable time' wasted on gambling would have been better spent attacking 'serious crime'. He 'detested ... the enforcement of such repressive laws' and having to use 'such dirty tools' as informers. Many were 'unreliable ... rascals, who would rig up evidence, swear anything that suited them ... wherever they are used, perjury and rascality may be looked for ... it was ever a puzzle' as to whether gambling or informants 'caused the greatest mischief'.[3] The gamblers found O'Donnell baffling. He maintained that he had 'no grudge against totemen or gamblers of any sort, though many people thought I had on account of my continually prosecuting them'. However, he asserted that as a matter of principle:

> I had no truck with any of them, and kept them as far from me as possible. Some of them wanted to be very friendly to me ... I sternly refused their attentions ... they were lawbreakers, and it was my duty to stop them, therefore I could not see the logic, if they could,

> of associating with or making friends with people of their class, and I told some of them so too. The consequence was, I became, in their eyes, a most unreasoning and dangerous man. I checked every move they made, and, very quietly, engineered every act done to rid society of such people. That was the whole front of my offence. I knew that they were afraid of me ... and made up their minds that, as I could not be bought over, I must be removed by violence.[4]

Eventually he was forced to carry a revolver. His prowess made him a household name in Melbourne. Nevertheless the *Age* described him as:

> The soul of good humour and geniality and by his tact and well known fairness has right throughout his career obviated, when dealing with criminals, the necessity to resort to the extraordinary muscular force which he possesses. When occasionally his duty calls him to the Pentridge Stockade [gaol] he is welcomed on all sides as a friend who, if he cannot help a man in misfortune, never necessarily oppresses him.[5]

However, O'Donnell in his turn was undermined by fellow detectives, some of whom were 'hand in glove with the gamblers and betting shop owners'. On one occasion O'Donnell gave 'a certain contemptible police officer—a perfect bounder too' some manufactured information which was duly passed on to 'his friends, the gamblers. Next morning it was all back [to him]'. He cites others who were 'more loyal to the gamblers than the Crown'. So, no one but his superintendent was allowed to know what he was doing. But not only 'crooked, unscrupulous and untrustworthy people' put him in danger:

> One elderly detective in his office who was somewhat puritanically inclined ... knew all the Collingwood gamblers and their histories, and simply detested drink and gambling, and all who indulged in either. He was continually assisting a certain religious party to get rid of both evils, and supplied the press and clergy with all the information he could get regarding the gamblers.

The gamblers 'had no idea' that this man was the source and blamed O'Donnell:

> I told him at the time that if he did not desist from stirring the gamblers up, he would be the means of bringing about my assassination, but it was no use. His religious principles were so strong against the vice that, if he had had his way, he would have caused every gambler in existence to be imprisoned for life … a daily paper gave a fabricated history of certain supposed frequenters of a tote and the gamblers said it was the work of O'Donnell, but it was not; it was pure fake on the part of the reporters. Gamblers are a most unreasoning class, and they are just as murderously inclined as they are unreasoning.[6]

The Melbourne Cup raid

On Melbourne Cup eve 1903 Sir William Irvine's cabinet ordered O'Donnell to seize and occupy Wren's Tote 'right or wrong'. He knew that 'unless the police could drop down upon it from the clouds, they could not enter it … legally … or prosecute anyone … under the law as it existed'. In fact the crown prosecutor had advised O'Donnell 'to have nothing to do' with Wren's Tote 'till the law was amended and made sufficiently strong to warrant any action' he might take. Still, although the crown prosecutor 'knew that the police occupation was illegal, he said I … had no alternative but to obey'. A short act of parliament would have solved the problem, but for years 'the government fooled with the matter and placed the police in a false and uncalled for position'.[7]

O'Donnell therefore obtained a special warrant ordering him to enter 'any house, premises or place' which enabled him to reach the Tote, by force if needed. At 3 am seventy-five police with siege tools in horse cabs moved on the Sackville Street woodyard. As the raiders stood with axes poised to smash their way in, it was discovered that the gate was ajar. The same in the interior. They rushed into the 'birdcage' (where bets were made) without a squeak or a splinter. Not a fugitive ran to the trapdoors. Wren had heard the well-kept secret and had moved his activities elsewhere, and no doubt did a satisfactory if less comfortable trade nearby as the lightly weighted (6 stone 8 pounds, or 40.2 kilograms) colt, Lord Cardigan, ran down the overloaded (10 stone, or 63.5 kilograms), greatest of mares, Wakeful, to take the Cup by half a head. As the *Bulletin* reported:

> During the whole of Cup Day casual gamblers who came to back Sweet Nell or Abundance, or some other beast, were buttonholed by certain unostentatious individuals, who were strolling about outside, and advised to go and get their hair cut at an adjacent shop. They went. Wren was running his tote of yore, under some slight inconvenience certainly, but he ran it and paid his dividends on [Lord] Cardigan with his usual promptitude. These bettors, having backed their particular prads, came back and gave three cheers for the stolid [police] ... Meanwhile the Government was admiring its withered laurels and declared its resolve to hold the place until Wren came back and claimed it, and thereby prove his criminality. But Wren reckoned that the Government was losing more money than he was and would cave in first, so he naturally made no sign. Besides he was too busy making money at his new address to argue small matters like that.[8]

The *Advocate* reported that tens of thousands had been gambling in Bourke Street.[9]

At first, twenty-five police were left at the Tote as a garrison, then sixty with cut lunches were deployed to take three eight-hour shifts in the cheerless precincts near what one reporter described as 'the baser adjuncts of the adjoining cottages' (that is, the dunnies). The police chief commissioner and the chief secretary did an inspection. Melbourne became increasingly amused as, without detection, someone on 9 November posted on the Sackville Street fence, 'The Collingwood Tote has moved to more commodious premises'.[10] Dummy betting sheets were stuck to the back of the Rev. Carey's house and at the Salvation Army citadel, and the odds were called outside.[11] As no owner of the premises came forward and none could be found, the newspapers became restive about sixty police doing nothing when there were thieves to be caught. To placate them O'Donnell was directed to make a highly critical report to the Collingwood Council of the sanitary conditions in the Tote yard and its surroundings. The Tote might then be physically demolished. The Collingwood Council called it 'monstrous and reckless' to assert that the cottages that sheltered the tote should be condemned as unfit to live in. The *Argus* called the whole exercise 'a humiliating exhibition of impotence'.

A wood and coal dealer served a summons on O'Donnell on

9 December, claiming £500 for trespass. It did not get to court.[12] Gradually the garrison was whittled down until one policeman on shift was left dozing in the heat. On 7 January Constable Armstrong was manhandled out into Sackville Street by masked men, and his helmet, coat and revolver hurled after him.[13] Four men—the nominal owner of the woodyard and two henchmen with criminal records, and Wren himself—were arrested for that and were defended by Gaunson. His submission was that the police warrant did not cover the woodyard through which they passed but only the Tote yard. Gaunson had fun. The Act covering the alleged offence went back to Richard II in the late fourteenth century. He interrogated police witnesses: Did the 'strong invading force … have Gatlings, ammunition, wagons, battering rams and all the paraphenalia of warfare in the time of Richard II?' And weren't the police playing cards, and even gambling to pass the days?'[14] The coverage in the papers made the police a laughing stock. So ended sixty-five days of farce which must have glamorised Wren among the less affluent classes, and not just those of Irish origin or in the environs of Collingwood. However, the wowsers became more vociferous and more determined than ever to expunge 'the pestilential citizen'.

The clubs

Still, within a year of the Melbourne Cup farce, the *Age* was able to commend the police on suppressing many (but not Wren's) suburban betting shops. Inspector Milne had found Section 51 of the Police Offences Act sufficiently elastic and comprehensive to call on landlords or their agents to stop their tenants from using their premises for gambling. Yet eight months later, captioned 'The Gambling Evil', the *Age* lamented:

> It is an extraordinary thing that while the police authorities are acting with quite extraordinary energy in putting down suburban tote shops, they show no eagerness in dealing with the spurious betting clubs which abound throughout the city. These betting clubs are not genuine associations of persons gathered for any common purpose. They exist in each instance for the profit of one individual who in some cases is actually the proprietor of more than one club. The reluctance of the police to take action in these cases is due to the fact that the astute owners of the more nefarious

> gambling dens have fortified themselves behind an imposing array of legal formulas in the shape of so-called 'articles of association' which appeared to have paralysed any efforts that would have been otherwise put forward for their immediate extinction. It has been shown that the pseudo companies, with directors, officers and secretary, into which most of the clubs have formed themselves, are the most transparent subterfuge.[15]

At the same time the *Argus* ran a series of articles captioned 'The Gambling Mania'.

An indication that gambling had increased was the emergence of four new betting clubs within the Melbourne city area. They followed the style of Solomon (Sol) Green's Tattersalls Club, which seems to have been established at 224 Bourke Street in 1891–2 and was licensed to sell liquor. In early April 1903 it moved to allegedly 'more commodious' premises in Royal Lane off Little Collins Street. Green, who advertised himself as 'the Leviathan of the Turf', was to become a famous racing personality not only as bookmaker but also as horse-owner (he won the 1910 Melbourne Cup with Comedy King, the 1928 Victoria Derby with Strephon, two Newmarkets and a Futurity with Gothic in 1927–8). He was also to become a reputable philanthropist. In contrast to Wren, Green, a cockney Jew from London, was a notable dandy, a big man with Havana cigar who used to dress in 'a long morning coat with black silk lapels, striped pants, topper and a gold cable watch carrying costly bric-a-brac'. He later attended the races in a gold-plated Rolls Royce.

Buggy says that when the Licensing Court refused to renew Green's licence, Wren 'moved in and set up City Tattersalls Club'.[16] Monty Grover, in anti-semitic mode, maintained that two of Wren's sleazy mates, Paddy Boardman and 'Squash' Lenny, 'went to the landlord and offered him double the rent he was getting from his co-religionist, Sol, whereupon, for the sake of their ancient faith, the landlord gave his tenant the option of doubling his rent, but Sol scornfully declined the honour. Exit Sol Green from the premises, his head full of wrath.'[17]

Green called his new club Melbourne Tattersalls. He had for years advertised his long prices with no limit on starting price. Wren took up the challenge, with prices received from the course and doubles. At the same time he offered tote facilities, consolidating outlays with those at Collingwood where there was some falling off in patronage. Green boasted that clients addressed their correspondence, '**Sol Green, Australia**'; Wren countered with '**J. Wren, Melbourne**'.[18] All that was required to enter Wren's club, according to the *Argus*, was an introduction from a member and the payment of five shillings.[19] The *Lone Hand*, however, says members of City Tatts 'paid a shilling [only] subscription or were passed in gratis, and were certain to be thrown out with great violence if Wren doubted their disrespectability'. There was no hint in the first balance sheet of 1904 that Wren was the boss.[20] City Tatts was not incorporated until August 1905.

Three other city clubs registered as companies were formed in 1893: the Metropolitan Club Ltd, the National Sporting Club Ltd and Fitzroy Tattersalls Ltd. Joining fees for them were two shillings, in return for which a piece of scrip was issued and two shillings returned for wagering. The *Argus* declared:

> Not one of these places is a 'club' in the general acceptation of the word. They have practically only one room [but also a billiard table] in which the betting is conducted. Neither food nor liquor can be obtained at them, nor sleeping accommodation. If bars were opened the 'clubs' would come under the Licensing Acts and their proceedings would be brought under supervision. The three which have been registered under the Companies Act cannot be seriously regarded as genuine companies. They issue shares but the scrip is not negotiable. The shares cannot be transferred because the scrip is simply a ticket of admission. Nor have they any capital, since the money paid for shares is immediately returned to those who deposit it. Again, it is practically impossible to obtain more than one share.

Wren's City and Green's Melbourne Tattersalls issued metal passes.[21]

The *Argus* estimated that altogether the five clubs had 20,000 members, but every member in turn would act as an agent for friends and acquaintances. Wren's club, it said, probably had 7,000 members with Green's not far behind.[22] These estimates could have been exaggerated for purposes of sensationalism. From the rate books we know that the dimensions of the Melbourne Tatts and National Sporting clubs were 36 by 50 feet (about 11 by 15 metres) and 34 by 60 feet (about 10 by 18 metres) respectively.[23] Five hundred people could not have assembled in these buildings, although the *Argus* may have meant that their patronage was spread out over a race-day afternoon. Also, the *Argus* has equated share capital with actual members, but where company records survive it is clear that not all share capital was issued and of that substantial parcels were held by a few directors or initial subscribers. From figures published in allotments, the estimate of 20,000 overall members may have been exaggerated by as much as five times.

While the *Argus* refers to the clubrooms as 'black miserable places', barely furnished, 'where a few dirty, crushed sporting papers are thrown on a deal table' in the 'reading room', it is not as scathing as the *Lone Hand*, which two years later alleged of Wren's premises in particular that 'the degraded character of the boss's constant adherence was symbolised by vermin crawling on the seats and walls'. The *Argus*, cited by Buggy, said, however, that City Tatts 'safeguarded itself by giving greater attention to the social side of its function' than Melbourne Tatts. It is difficult to envisage Senator Dawson, very briefly Labor premier of Queensland (1899)[24] and recently the federal minister for Defence, giving his lecture there on social democracy in late 1904, even if not quite sober, in a 'verminous room'. At least when Dawson toasted and Senator Findley seconded before 500 persons Murmur's victory in the 1904 Caulfield Cup, the anti-Wren *Australasian Typographical Journal* described the 'large clubroom decorated with flags and potplants'.[25]

Green's club, said the *Argus*, was better furnished than the others. Its members belonged to 'a higher grade of society'—and for this, they were obviously not harassed by the police to the same degree. Respectable citizens did belong to the other clubs but inevitably, what the *Argus* called 'the riff-raff of the city', men who lived by their wits, youths who band together and call themselves 'pushers' ... gathered at these clubs.[26]

Monty Grover of *Lone Hand* had probably never been in City Tatts. He is patently a hostile commentator relying on hearsay and seemingly disturbed by the existence of knockabout Collingwood blokes, though not by the raffish chaps around the *Bulletin*. The rate books describe the City Tatts building as 'a brick hall'. Among the various Objects of its Memorandum and Articles of Association are the maintenance of 'a reading room'. Its Statutory Report of 1905 cited billiard room receipts of £46. Its 1906 Annual Report mentions a 'levy on members participating in the many pastimes available'; that is, 'Billiard Tables, Card and

Reading Rooms' being 'extensively patronised' and 'Current literature of all descriptions being supplied to members'. The financial data shows receipts of £115 under 'Billiard Room', indicating significant activity, but the amount spent on books shows a meagre £12 12s—obviously window dressing. The capital of the club was specified as £2,500 divided into 50,000 shares of one shilling each. Surviving records show no evidence of Wren's involvement in any official capacity, neither as director, company employee, initial subscriber or anything other than 'John Wren, Financier', a single shareholder (like Gaunson and the police spy, Goodson) among the several hundred others. Frank Lawrence is listed as 'manager' by 18 September 1905, while Sugar Roberts is then one of three directors.[27]

The following years brought Wren widespread notoriety. The rumours that implicated him in fixing the Austral Wheel Race of 1901 will be discussed in a later chapter, along with other ventures in racing, boxing and even theatre. Around 1904 Wren began to develop a stable of thoroughbreds, only one of which achieved fame: Murmur. Even this was accompanied by allegations of fixing—Hardy and Manning Clark, but not Monty Grover,[28] were sure of it—and when in the spring of 1905 the Victoria Racing Club and Victorian Amateur Turf Club refused to accept Wren nominations, it was assumed that corruption was the reason rather than the rejection and punishment of a gambling competitor. With his enterprises expanding, Wren became even more the focus of wowser protests against 'the gambling mania'. Wren seems to have developed a stake in the short-lived betting club in Sydney set up by the notable public relations 'fixer' Dan Green on three floors of a building in Pitt Street, in 1904–5. It had over 6,000 members and was backed ostensibly by Joseph Wren, but almost certainly that means John. Dan Green's reputable biographers do not suggest criminality, although he had links with all levels of politics and society. A New South Wales Gaming and Betting Act in 1906 led to police raids.[29] The *Bulletin* reported that 'Nothing seemed to come of this and Green had to seek refuge in bankruptcy'. But it also gloated:

> John Wren has met his first rebuff in Sydney, where the police raided the Sydney Club, and made a record haul of civil servants, including, so rumor sayeth, one Under-Secretary. Meanwhile John Wren is understood to be in treaty for the purchase of the

> Cyclorama building, opposite the railway station, which he will, it is said, turn into a hippodrome, boxing hall and place of general entertainment.[30]

But nothing seems to have come of this either.

From mid-1905 the police were pressured into staging a more vigorous campaign against betting. It was led by O'Donnell. On 27 October the *Argus* reported that O'Donnell and his men, in response to their blitz, were being 'shadowed by gambling personnel who resorted to violence and intimidation'. One article in its series on 'The Gambling Mania' was subtitled 'A Reign of Terror'. It listed the prior convictions of twenty people 'employed in the gambling trade' for criminal assault, larceny, house breaking and unlawful wounding. Using *Argus* reports between June and December 1905, it has been possible to build a database of at least 156 persons charged during the police blitz. Wren is not among them. The database is not exhaustive, but it is evident that Wren's was far from being the only gambling interest with a motive to try to intimidate O'Donnell. Nevertheless, commentators have always thought of Wren as the number one suspect; they have not taken the trouble to identify any other. The names and addresses of potential suspects are known and were available to Hardy and his researchers, who were so assiduous in scrutinising the *Argus*. Of 156 persons charged, at least 96 were convicted, but that number is likely to be much higher because not all trials were reported. O'Donnell is known to have been involved in the cases of 56 offenders, but the number is also likely to be higher because he may have been giving instructions behind the scenes and the *Argus* did not necessarily report his involvement in every case.[31]

Large numbers of people were caught, ranging from the 'directors' of the Metropolitan Club (Louis Solomon, Wolf and Michael Cohen, Louis and Henry Meyers, who might have provoked another anti-semitic Grover jibe) down to small bookmakers in tobacconist stores and lolly shops; from small-time street bettors and children playing pitch and toss to the biggest two-up school in Melbourne; from dozens of Chinese lottery promoters to poker-machine owners, card-playing groups and Calcutta sweepstake organisers. Some two-up players had prior convictions for assault. One arrested Chinese lottery promoter was abusive and threatening to police, saying 'no savee' until O'Donnell, whom he knew by sight, showed his face. And there were 34 other convicted Chinese lottery promoters discomfited by O'Donnell.

It was assumed that Wren wanted to make some pre-emptive strike against O'Donnell although, in view of the poor police record in prosecuting him, it is difficult to fathom why this should be so. On 12 October (reported in the *Argus* for Wren to read) Inspector Lawrence Gleeson told the Royal Commission on the Victorian Police Force that Wren's Tote was 'almost impervious to attack' because it was 'almost impossible to secure the evidence necessary to secure a conviction'. Gleeson said he had been in charge of gambling prosecutions when the Collingwood Tote was in 'full swing'. He had been given instructions to attack it but admitted candidly, 'Wren's Tote had got too strong (laughter). I had been pretty successful up to that, and I didn't want to spoil my record (laughter)'.[32]

Commissioner A. A. Billson was presumably referring to Wren's Tote when he told Gleeson, 'The whole force of the law seems to be directed against one tote. The people imagine there are no others. Now we find that there are many though no action is taken against them.' Gleeson replied that there were 'a number of totes in North Melbourne and other suburbs' that had been suppressed. He also denied having any special consideration for Wren. At first Gleeson said that he knew of 'no reputable club which conducts a tote … Victorian Club members deal only with each other'. However, when asked specifically by Billson about totes in 'toffy' clubs such as the Melbourne Club and the Commercial Travellers Club, he replied that they were 'run not for profit but really for the delight and edification of members'. Gleeson made it clear that, while no instructions had been given to avoid raids, he saw 'no use in attacking respectable clubs for carrying on a paltry tote while the city is full of totes and bogus clubs'.[33] So much for class distinction.

A half-daft sort of fellow

The Royal Commission into the Victorian Police Force, presided over by seven parliamentarians, was initiated on 15 August 1905 and continued into 1906. Among the more sensational witnesses was Cornelius Crowe who, over a number of years, had conducted a relentless campaign against Wren. Born in Tipperary, Ireland in 1853, Crowe was a prolific pamphleteer. His titles include his *Australian Slang Dictionary: Containing the Words and Phrases of the Thieving Fraternity* (1895);

Duties of a Police Constable (1896); *Crowe Versus Police Department* (1902); *Bribery in the Federal and State Parliaments, Unjust Judges, Perjured Police, Innocent People Imprisoned* (1903); *Bribery Commission: How Montague Usurped the Factions of the Peacock Government* (1904); *Serious Tampering with the Course of Justice* (1907); *The Inquiry Agent: A Drama of Real Life, Played on the Stage of the World* (1909); and *One Big Crime: Startling Stories of Australian Crimes and Corruption—Reminiscences and Reflections* (1920). Others are lost (for example, *MacManamny and his Co-Conspirators*) or exist only on library catalogue cards (for example, *Policemen and Politicians* and *Police in League with Thieving Nightwatchmen*).

Crowe's special target at the commission was Wren, although he also made allegations of corruption against premier Bent, chief commissioner O'Callaghan and Detective-Sergeant Macmanamny. A large humourless man, Crowe had joined the New Zealand police force in 1876 but was dismissed for drunkenness the following year. He did not mention this when joining the Victorian police force in 1880. His service record between 1882 and 1896 cites six breaches of regulations involving 'being under the influence' and an unproven allegation that he had tipped off a publican about an impending licensing raid. In early 1896 his superintendent wrote on his record: 'No further opportunity will be given to this constable should he offend again'. Crowe resigned in May 1897 and set up a night patrol firm. He claimed to have had an early encounter with Wren when trying to have some police investigated for aiding burglars who were robbing stores he was supposed to protect. Wren, he said, ordered me 'to leave it alone, as the police were friends of his, and he did not want new men in their places to annoy the working of the Tote'[34]—a not implausible story.

Crowe would not desist. He attacked Wren for corrupting the police. 'On 10 December 1904 at 10 pm', he wrote later, 'two ruffians attacked me with iron bars while attending to my duties … and though knocked down suddenly, I saw sufficient to know they were strangers who could have nothing personal against me, and could be no other than hired assassins'. Three days later two men came to him, he said, and told him that Wren had the day before offered them money to make false affidavits against him. They said they were told that there was no danger, as chief commissioner O'Callaghan wanted Crowe in prison and the chief secretary, Sir Samuel Gillott, was legal adviser to the proceedings. Crowe said he wrote to the detective and to premier Bent pointing out his attempted murder and the conspiracy to imprison him. He suggested they both 'emanated from the same source'—Wren. Bent denied the allegations against his colleagues.[35]

O'Donnell recalled to the royal commission on 24 November 1905 that he had investigated the assault on Crowe, who had told him of the 'conspiracy' about 'four or five weeks' after he became aware of it. O'Donnell had followed it up; two men had admitted to speaking to Crowe in the terms described but said that they were 'pulling his leg'. According to O'Donnell, Crowe 'gave theories of a bomb explosion, but they blew out (laughter). I think Crowe has a bee in his bonnet (laughter)'. Crowe had already said that he had heard that both Wren and Macmanamny had gone to Wilkins MLA to try to have the enquiry stopped. His source was Gaunson's clerk, J. B. Cullen, who could not be found at first and, when he was, refused to take the oath. When Wilkins appeared he strongly denied that Wren and Macmanamny had seen him on the issue, or that Wren had threatened to have him defeated at the next election. Crowe had also sent the commission a letter saying that an accountant who audited Wren's books could give them particulars of money paid by Wren to the police. On examination, Crowe admitted that he had not personally seen the books and had been given the information by sources he refused to identify. The commissioner understandably regarded his evidence as hearsay.[36]

Worse was to follow for Crowe when ex-Sergeant O'Hara, who had been at Fitzroy police station with Crowe in 1886–7, stated that there had always been 'trouble' while he was there. Former Inspecting Superintendent Sadler remembered Crowe's being transferred from office work to the beat because 'he was not to be trusted'. Then 'Paddy' Boardman appeared with five statutory declarations which seemed to implicate Crowe in several illegal actions. One declaration from a C. S. Levy of Fitzroy alleged that when in the police force, Crowe had demanded a bribe from Levy, who ran a betting shop, in return for secret information about prospective police raids. 'I paid him hundreds of pounds', said Levy. Cross-examined by Crowe, Boardman admitted that he had sought the declarations

> On account of the remarks that you [Crowe] published about me … to show you that you are not the clean potato yourself. You are

> trying to show everyone else corrupt ... I may tell you there is a man who informed me in the first place, and I'd rather you had that statement from him—John Wren ... He will come and show how I came to make these enquiries.

Boardman admitted that he was a member of a 'club', not Wren's club ... he has not got one'[37]—which could not have impressed the commission.

Not surprisingly, Crowe wrote withdrawing from the commission on 29 November. The chairman, J. Cameron MLA, said:

> This letter was from a man who had flooded the country with pamphlets bringing charges against the police and against other people. The Commissioner has tested every case to be a mare's nest. His (the Chairman's) candid opinion was that the writer of the letter was a most unreliable man. He had been discredited by every witness who had come before the Commission.

Actually, Crowe's letter of withdrawal stated that he wished to withdraw 'at present'. Cameron omitted these last words perhaps out of exasperation, choosing not to have Crowe confuse issues again. Crowe chose to see it as part of a deliberate suppression of 'everything likely to expose the existing deplorable state of affairs'. To him, the royal commission was a 'sham'. [38]

Crowe soon had further reason to feel he was being harassed. On 23 March 1906 he received a summons signed 'George Walker' for blackmailing by letter G. H. Bennett MLA (Richmond). Bennett had handed the letter to Macmanamny. Crowe denied signing or sending such a letter. No one seemed to know who this private informant, 'George Walker', was and, in the course of three trials of Crowe, he did not put in an appearance. During at least the first trial, while Macmanamny prosecuted, Wren 'sat in the press box opposite the jury', some of whom Crowe alleged had been 'squared'. Crowe also alleged he was denied adequate time to prove that there was a conspiracy against him. At the first two trials, experts swore the signature on the letter to Bennett was Crowe's, but at the third trial they were dispensed with, 'Macmanamny having discovered a witness who swore that he signed the letter' at Crowe's request. However, the witness was so completely contradicted that the judge directed the jury to return a verdict of not guilty. Crowe understandably complained that he 'had been put to the cost and ignominy' of defending himself against 'a malicious prosecution'. However, he was unbalanced and should never be quoted against Wren without reservation. Wren, he believed, had succeeded in getting O'Callaghan made chief commissioner so that he could 'start a gambling shop on a colossal scale in Bourke Street'. He even went so far as to insinuate that the clean O'Donnell had 'smoodged' to Wren and that he had received £200 'from Wren's delegate before the Commission to compound a felony'. A few years later Crowe was even more extravagant:

> the Commission, composed as it was of seven members of Parliament … dispensed with all honour and honesty, and arranged with the lowest dregs of humanity to put forward perjured affidavits vilifying my character … The world's history in despotism can show no parrellel [sic] … The demons in hell would blush at the fiendish perfidy …[39]

Crowe re-emerged into the public eye in December 1915 for libelling the then Superintendent Macmanamny, whom he was to admit he had never met. The matter was raised in the Victorian parliament and Detective Dungey was quoted as calling Crowe, among other things, a sacked New Zealand police constable, a blackmailer, a cheat, a pimp, a drunkard, a standover man and trouble maker. Chief secretary D. McLeod referred to Crowe's 'mania'. A four-page leaflet had been circulated, making 'astounding accusations' of corruption by none other than a person named 'George Walker'! Crowe was charged with criminal libel. He disavowed authorship but a jury found him guilty. Before being sentenced to three years imprisonment, he pleaded for the benefit of the First Offenders Act.[40] He continued to write. *One Big Crime* (1920) ranges from the Eureka Stockade and the Kelly Gang to his own grievances against police and government. In spite of his unreliability, Crowe's commentaries and compilations of scurrilous articles, innuendos and sensational snippets have influenced opinions on Wren.

O'Donnell deserves the last word on Crowe:

> A half-daft sort of fellow, who nursed a grievance against members of parliament and all from the Chief Commissioner downwards … pamphleteering and preaching all sorts of wild, imaginary and

> unsupportable statements about all and sundry … He was continually making false and libellous statements which emanated from his crazy cranium … I have no doubt, from reiteration, he eventually managed to believe his own fabrications were nearly true.
>
> Some police officers and a few members of parliament … who are either too ready to grab hold of any garbage or were extremely gullible, swallowed all the vile, unsubstantiated fiction brought them … [and which were] in such widespread circulation … [The Royal Commission] fairly knocked the bottom out of the whole wild and woolly statements, hints and innuendoes [in circulation over the previous four years].

O'Donnell thought the government was justified in winding up the royal commission when 'not one of the mendacious assertions were shown to have any truth'.[41]

Bombing O'Donnell's house

O'Donnell's jibe at Crowe having 'a bee in his bonnet' about explosions may have haunted him some two months later. At 2.25 am on 6 January 1906 a 'young, active' man broke a window of O'Donnell's terrace in Nicholson Street opposite the Exhibition Building, and threw in a Stone's ginger beer bottle stuffed with gunpowder and bound with coiled wire. It struck the venetian blind and fell to the floor, limiting the damage to one side of the sitting-room. The studious O'Donnell had left the sofa, which was damaged, at 2 am and was with his wife and two children asleep upstairs. No one was hurt. O'Donnell recovered from the shock in time to see a short, thick-set man running away in the distance. He was unable to use his revolver as his wife had put it out of reach of the children, and himself.[42]

O'Donnell's house was not destroyed. The fire brigade arrived to find the window sash and curtain burning and only one side of the sitting-room damaged. The *Argus* deduced that

> All the facts indicated intimidation only. The man who threw the bomb did so in full belief he was throwing into an empty room. This home-made bomb was not sufficiently formidable for anyone to expect it would cause injury, except that such a bomb would

> burst through the ceiling of the drawing room and blow up O'Donnell in the room above.[43]

However, O'Donnell was naturally enough enraged, especially as he and his wife had contemplated on that humid night putting their sickly young daughter to bed near the sitting-room window. In his first press interview he said:

> I've got no doubt whatever where the guilt lies. I don't know the man who actually threw the bomb but I know the brain which was directly behind him. There is no doubt in my mind that the gambling gang now controlling a portion of Melbourne organised this outrage … I can't make out why they should try to kill me particularly. I'm only one of a number of persons who do their duty … and my part is not one which brings me into direct touch with them … it is not going to intimidate me. It will only add fuel to the fire.

O'Donnell went on to detail a number of intimidating acts of recent years, in particular mentioning gamblers in Prahran, several suburbs away from Collingwood. He knew 'nothing to prove that all the gambling shops of the metropolis were controlled by one head' but—and this was ominous—boulders used to smash windows in Prahran had come 'not from Prahran but from the banks of the Yarra'.[44]

Wren was quick to take umbrage. He wrote to the *Herald:*

> Sir—I trust that you will see fit to pardon any warmth that may inadvertently find its way into this communication, for it touches upon a matter that affects me … much more … than any person … [Detective O'Donnell] imputed … [this bombing] to certain evilly-disposed betting and gambling men. He mentions a 'Tammany ring' and its 'boss' and to this combination, or supposed combination, he attributes the perpetration of one of the most dastardly deeds conceivable …
>
> He is manifestly attempting to direct suspicion against me: this fact is so plainly discernible that my family and friends have called on me to speak out, if not for my own sake, then for theirs …
>
> Detective O'Donnell has achieved by the occurrence certain

> benefits and probably very justly so; for instance, there is the admiration of his officers, the sympathy of the public and kudos so warmly bestowed by the press. But for me, if I do not clearly and fully exonerate myself … I will be looked upon as a cold-blooded assassin of innocent little children. Am I not the most deeply concerned person mentioned? Of course, only by inference.
>
> Now I distinctly characterise the insinuations … as an open insult to my humanity. What act in the whole of my life would justify or give colour to such an accusation? It is also an insult to my common sense. My intelligence revolts at such silly means of injuring a person even had I a bitter enemy whom I wished to injure.
>
> Why should I injure O'Donnell? He has never, either directly or indirectly given me any cause for offence. On the contrary, though our relations have been that of the slightest, they have been cordial.
>
> As no direct charge has been made that I can lay hold of and refute, I am compelled to adopt a course calculated by Detective O'Donnell to be the best one for adoption under the circumstances.
>
> Detective O'Donnell may have suspicions based on what appear to him fairly sound reasons, and one could not find fault with him on that account; but when the seeds of suspicion are so sown that they grow through or provide a harvest of evil, that is what I take exception to.

Wren then augmented the government reward of £500 with a further £500 from himself. He also offered £1,000 to O'Donnell if it was proven that he 'was implicated in the outrage even in the most indirect way possible'.[45]

If Wren had been involved, this letter, even if not composed by him, would be consummately cynical. It was supported by his friend Senator Dawson. He deprecated the sensationalism of the press reports and thought it only natural that in the first shock Detective O'Donnell should become hysterical and lose his head. He pointed to some anomalies in the accounts of what really happened; for example, how the desperado allegedly allowed only a few seconds for his escape, how he ran away not into shadows but into an arc of light, how the deed was scarcely planned by 'a master brain', etc. 'The bomb outrage is abominable', he said, but so is 'the outrage on a respectable citizen wantonly charged with a foul crime'[46]—an accolade which must have drawn snorts from the parsons. The following day both premier Bent and chief secretary Gillott acknowledged Wren's offer of a reward and expressed confidence that he would not have been involved in a bombing.[47]

Meanwhile O'Donnell stated that Wren was

> quite wrong when he says I attempted to direct suspicion against him. I did no such thing. I never imagined for one moment that John Wren had anything to do with this outrage, or that he was even cognisant of it. I hold a different opinion of him altogether. Indeed I feel that had he known such a cowardly act was contemplated, he would have used all the power he has at his disposal, and that is by no means small, to prevent it.

O'Donnell added that, if Wren's personal influence had failed, he was confident that Wren would have informed him and put him on guard (implying that he was, however, a 'boss'):

> He is quite safe in offering me £1,000 if I could prove that he was implicated in the outrage or even if he knew of it. He might as well offer me a thousand pounds if I could prove he was a Chinese. It would be just as reasonable [meaning that Wren perpetrated foolproof wrongs?]. What I intended to convey was that there are fellows connected with gambling who would be quite capable of such a crime. It is towards those that my suspicions were directed. No man who knows anything about the betting crowd, and the way they work, would think that John Wren instigated or took part in the outrage.[48]

This is still a somewhat ambiguous rejoinder, a barbed exoneration even, and Wren was quick to reply to the editor of the *Herald*:

> Sir—Detective O'Donnell, in his latest interview with the press, disavows all intentions of saddling me with any responsibility of complicity in the recent outrage at his house …
>
> I never said or wrote that the detective ever imagined or believed that I had anything to do with the outrage. I said, and I say

now, that his melodramatic utterances when he was under the 'limelight' were calculated to direct suspicion towards me.

... There is a leading daily in the city that writes of all betting operations that are not conducted under the control or the interests of the VRC as 'gambling'. In my turf transactions—the most extensive in Australia, I believe—I do not recognise any such authority; hence according to the VRC's champion, I am a gambler. The same journal, when championing the cause of the VRC in the discussion that arose, owing to the rejection of my nominations by that body, characterise those who consider me unjustly treated, and voice that opinion, as 'member of a Tammany ring' and in the columns of that same journal I am repeatedly referred to as a 'Boss'. According to this journal, I am a 'gambler' and a 'Boss' and those who view the actions of the VRC as arbitrary and unjust were Tammany men ...

I quote the remarks of the journal referred to for the sole purpose of proving that Detective O'Donnell had me in his mind during his sensational outpouring to the press. All through his communications the words 'Tammany' and the 'Boss' are given utmost prominence. There is no other betting man of my acquaintance that has, to my knowledge, ever had such epithets applied to him. Then, is this not reasonable to assume that I was the 'person' he so constantly alluded to? That fact cannot be disguised, and any attempt to shirk the issue by either Mr O'Donnell or myself will be but a silly subterfuge that would deceive no one but ourselves.

Referring to the boulders from the banks of the Yarra River, Wren continued:

Now, I reside upon the banks of our much-abused river at Kew. Here, apparently, we are asked to presume that I am so extremely thorough in my methods of destruction that I actually supply my 'Tammany' creatures with rocks from my own back yard, wherewith to break the windows of an inoffensive law-abiding citizen who never harmed me, by word or deed.

Despite all these innuendos, and many more, Mr O'Donnell now claims that he never for a moment suspected me of any

> complicity in the Nicholson Street explosion. If I could accept his disavowal, it would be necessary to convince myself that Detective O'Donnell had been attempting to induce the press and public to accept as a truth something he has no belief in. I confess my understanding is unequal to the task Detective O'Donnell wishes to impose on it.
>
> ... Mr O'Donnell, in his denial that his suspicions were not aimed in my direction, does not express one single word of regret for the irreparable wrong he has done me and mine by the utterances which would be highly amusing were it not for their far-reaching and harmful effects.
>
> ... Detective O'Donnell, as to all men, must be granted the right of forming and holding any opinion he chooses. He says, 'I have no doubt whatever as to where the guilt lies. I do not know the bomb thrower, but I do know the brain that planned the act'. That is a very decent opinion. I have formed one too, on the same subject, for I am willing to enlighten Detective O'Donnell by imparting them [sic] to him, if he elects to call upon me for the purpose of receiving them.
>
> JOHN WREN[49]

Of course, O'Donnell did not. But a puzzling aspect is that he said 'he had a clear view of the offender and would know him again'.[50]

O'Donnell seems to have withdrawn from the argument at that stage, but in his 1926 memoirs he returned to the bombing. He referred to himself as 'the marked man of all' because 'all the burden of the gambling suppression fell on him'. The bombing at his home 'was hatched and carried out 'by the 'gamblers':

> There was no doubt in my mind over that matter ... all through they tried to terrify and corrupt everyone who was opposed to their nefarious, law-breaking tactics. However, the lunacy only recoiled upon themselves ... one of the most childish explanations circulated was ... that I bombed my own house in order to gain notoriety. One fellow, who has written to the papers attempting to veneer certain totes as legitimate clubs and was continually in company with the man suspected of being the offender who put the bomb in my house, used to hold forth near St John's Church, Clifton Hill, on Sunday, to that effect. Before I could get sufficient

evidence to put him on trial for criminal libel, however, he seems to have got the hint to cease his puerility.

> … grave suspicions, according to Dame Rumour, were attached by members of the criminal class to a man, who by his burglaries, ware-house breaking and serious crime, had made himself notorious. The man was to be seen continually close to a certain bookie on racecourses, who was deeply interested in trying to get his fellows to believe that I bombed my own house. The unfortunate suspect has since paid the extreme penalty for another capital offence.[51]

Two individuals who could conceivably have fitted the descriptions given by O'Donnell were John Jackson, who was hanged for shooting Constable McGrath at the Trades Hall break-in (see pp. 222–3) in November 1916, and garrulous, feckless Sugar Roberts. However, there is no evidence of their having had such an association. Hugh Anderson describes Jackson as 'one of Melbourne's master cracksmen who combined singular daring with infinite care'. If it was he who was involved, he probably did not wish to kill O'Donnell or any member of his family.[52] This seems more likely than Brennans's surmise that it could have been, on Jackson's part, 'a crude and vengeful piece of retaliation against a policeman on his trail for many things'.[53] Jackson was very 'professional'. But if O'Donnell really did believe that he could recognise the bomber if he saw him again, why did he not name Jackson, at least after his execution and the publicity he had received with his trial?

The cynical Sydneyside *Bulletin* could not take the events and the flourish of Smellbourne cheques following the bombing seriously. Perhaps it was 'a put up job'—even by O'Donnell?—which could 'be explained by advertisement':

> The detective was getting such gorgeous notices because the nitroglycerine or the ginger pop, or whatever it was, exploded and wrecked the sofa on which his daughter wasn't sleeping, that perhaps Wren rushes to share the boom, and now testimonials may begin to pour on to him from old gamblers testifying they have lost money to him frequently but he has never used dynamite on them. What with Bent and bombs and Wren, and the crying smell of the Yarra, Melbourne is getting to be a noisy place.[54]

CHAPTER FIVE

Judkins Closes the Tote

The sizzling Savonarola[1]

THE BOMBING of O'Donnell's room was a boon to the parsons and wowsers,[2] especially to their most vociferous preacher of 1905–6, William Judkins. Although he should have known the facts (or lack of them) of that outrage only months before, he chose to write in W. T. Stead's *Review of Reviews of Australasia*, of which he was editor:

> The death of Detective-Sergeant O'Donnell and some members of his family was almost accomplished by some ruffians who threw through the window into O'Donnell's room about midnight, a bomb which, exploding, wrecked the furniture of the room. How the occupants of the room escaped with their lives is a marvel.[3]

Nothing that had been said or implied to the contrary at the royal commission or elsewhere could deflect Judkins's purpose: to establish in the public mind that an Australian 'Tammany' led by the Catholic Wren was conducting a 'reign of terror':

> [It was] as perfectly organised as in New York when some of the members of our parliaments are the openly avowed friends of some of the chief members of these gangs … It is easy to see how far the ramifications of the Tote extend. But *cui bono,* is not Sir Philip

> Fysh,[4] a beneficiary of Tattersalls ... and are not Senator Dawson and Mr Solly MLA professed friends of Mr Wren?
>
> ... it would be difficult to find an organisation capable of working more political and social evil than this. The very foundations of law and order are shaken if it works unmolested and, while instances I have given are surface indications, patent to everybody, one trembles to think what may be even now the real condition of affairs.[5]

Judkins had been born in Maryborough, Victoria, and became a school teacher at Creswick, but resigned to study for the Methodist ministry. He failed to achieve ordination apparently because, as a probationer in New Zealand, his zeal in teaching temperance debilitated his health. He was short, wiry, with sharp features and the wags said that he and Wren could have been mistaken for each other. In Melbourne from 1902 he first became secretary of a patent medicine company which, his deriders were delighted to reveal, advised 'a specific decoction called *UNEEDSOME*', allegedly a 'bronchial balm', but one 'which was supplied for other purposes of which some men and women did not approve'—apparently because of some erotic intent. On the prospectus was 'a young woman showing a large amount of her legs'.[6] However, Judkins had more than enough gall to absorb this sort of hooting from *Truth* and the *Bulletin*. It did nothing to abate his vituperation, both oratorical and literary, against the 'social evils' of the day: gambling, racing, drinking, boxing, dancing and even the employment of barmaids. While he believed the Roman Catholic Church was a protagonist of these evils, 'the one thing in Mr Judkins's favour', said the Catholic *Tribune*,

> is that so far [6 May 1906] he has not publicly insinuated that 'Rome's feet of wool' are visible in Wren's gambling shop. But he has the practice of unreasoning abuse and the same sort of unhealthy suspicious mind which is forever suggesting to him bad motives and crooked theories'.

Judkins's ego expanded with his rhetoric about social evils which he thought should be stamped out by legislation. He was to declare that only committed Christians (presumably not including Catholics) rather than merely respectable members of society 'should be entrusted with the moral oversight of the community'. Remove the occasions of sin and people would reform.[7]

He was particularly outraged by Wren's moves into boxing and pony racing. He seemed irrepressible. The ban on his horses by the Victoria Racing Club (VRC) in October 1905 had provoked Wren to offer to buy Flemington racecourse for £25,000 from the government, which had leased it to that controlling body virtually for nothing. Premier Bent toyed only mischievously with the proposal, but the possibility that this could happen shocked the staid VRC and the wowsers.[8] Then in late April 1906 Wren promoted a Bill Squires–Tim Murphy stoush at the Exhibition Building (site of the opening of the hallowed first federal parliament by royalty in 1901). It was for the 'Championship of Australia'. An estimated crowd of 10,000 attended including, *horribile dictu,* one woman, who procured a seat in the organ gallery. Judkins felt a call to raise his evangelical status a notch or two—publicly he was often to be referred to as the 'Rev. Judkins'. He sought and gained permission from the Methodist Committee on the Amendment of Betting Laws to campaign specifically against gambling and to target Wren.[9]

His attack was launched at Melbourne Central Wesley Church in Lonsdale Street where, following British Methodist practice, a 'Pleasant Sunday Afternoon' was held each week. The highlight on 13 March 1906, between items of sacred music, was advertised as 'A Demonstration Against John Wren'. Judkins seemed to have excelled himself. Not only was the Collingwood Tote operated 'by the filth and off-scourings of the jails', it was 'a hideous underworld of vice' corrupting sport:

> a Vesuvius of carnality and greed ... a seething mass of flaming animalism ... tainting the community, corrupting the youth, luring to destruction the weak and foolish, and scattering among the hard-working clean living people the seeds of crime, debauchery and miserable poverty.

Wren, said Judkins, clouded his criminality by large cynical benefactions to his victims in the Catholic Church. Worse and—Judkins said this sorrowfully and 'only at the Lord's bidding'—Wren was bribing the police, and this was done with the connivance of the Victorian chief secretary, Sir Samuel Gillott. Gillott, a wealthy former leading barrister, thrice mayor and first lord mayor of Melbourne, may have been 'respectable' and democratically elected but he was not one of those committed Christians who had the right to prescribe the moral code of society. It was idle for him to claim that the existing law was defective and that he 'refused to allow a man to be arrested who would hold the law to ridicule at his trial'. There was an obvious reply to this but, before the parsons uttered it, premier Bent, sniffing the political wind, promised to strengthen the laws. Sensing victory, Judkins became indefatigable, using church resources, ranting at rallies several nights of the week, and drawing large audiences, especially females, until eventually he lost his voice for a month. His interjectors were likely to be 'interrupted with the clamour of dainty parasols and shoes striking the floor'. His effrontery stirred both enthusiasts and scoffers. In June he breasted Collingwood, where four women scuffled with some youths over a banner which declared, 'Dolly Judkins, the good young man who never went wrong'. The women won.

On 20 June 1906 Judkins rallied a deputation of some 5,000 to wait on the premier to demand stricter controls of gambling. They represented churches, the teaching profession, the Chamber of Commerce, the Employers' Federation and even the Trades Hall. Bent could not fit them into his office. With Judkins at their head they then paraded to the Exhibition Building with Bent in pursuit. He listened to 'a petition with over 60 detailed suggestions which virtually amounted to a bill'. Four days later Bent announced that 'the betting that was going on in many places was to be stopped'. His government would foster only 'clean sport'. Yet, however much Bent thought about the wowser vote for the 1907 election, he would also have known of the concurrent pastoral letter of the normally irenic Catholic archbishop, Thomas Carr, who saw little chance of self-respecting members of his flock co-operating with their Protestant traducers. Catholics had votes too; Bent needed to proceed cautiously.

It is impossible to know if Judkins was being canny in appealing for a united Christian approach to his 'social evils', knowing that if the Catholic Church refused to join it could be stigmatised through its association with Wren. Weren't many of the leading gamblers and publicans Catholics? Didn't it depend on raffles and bazaars through schools and charities? Archbishop Carr might point out that Catholic children were encouraged to take the pledge against alcohol until at least the age of twenty-one, and that in morality Catholics needed no lessons from bigots whom the diocesan *Advocate* came to describe as 'foul-mouthed ranters'. Judkins's close associate, the Orangeman Rev. George Tregear, in an illuminating phrase, said that 'if his little girl wrote such twaddle [as Carr's] he would horsewhip her'. Sectarian tempers rose as the Methodist *Spectator* wrote that the Catholic Church had justified 'the Reformation by pandering to the vices of society while today it enjoys the shameful distinction of being the one religious organisation which fattens by means of gambling and whisky'. Inevitably Catholics were taught that it was Protestant-sponsored 'godless' state education that led to immorality. This in turn raised the issue of Catholic opposition to Bible lessons in state-funded schools favouring, it believed, Protestant exegesis. Tregear in particular added insult by denouncing the Abbotsford (a ward of Collingwood) Good Shepherd Reformatory Convent for Wayward Girls as a slave sweatshop. Sectarian bitterness may have been as intense as at any time in Australian history—and John Wren, gambler, was a focus of it.[10]

Battery at Flemington

Then in mid-July 1906 another spectacular outrage occurred to boost the parsons' purpose. An overweight (95 kilograms), unregistered 23-year-old bookmaker, operating on the unregulated Flat at Flemington Racecourse on Grand National Day, was bashed and kicked to death. With £20 to pay out and only £2 7s in his bag, Donald 'Big Mick' McLeod was set upon by hundreds of punters for 'scaling'—that is, returning the wagers while unable to pay the winnings. McLeod offered to settle outside City Tatts on the Monday but, finding that unacceptable to his punters, ran for it. He was easily overtaken and mercilessly battered. A post-mortem, days later, found that his death was due not to the beating but to a lacerated spinal cord and suffocation when he fell, but that naturally made little difference to the public horror. Judkins and Co had a victim (hardly a martyr) to illustrate the great evil of gambling. Wren attempted a creative response. A young boxer, Ted Nelson, had tried valiantly to defend McLeod. A collection was taken up for him at the Cyclorama, not then under Wren control. Wren not only supplemented this gratuity but stepped into the ring to commend Nelson and the noble art of boxing, and to condemn those who 'used their boots in a cowardly un-Australian fashion'. Nelson had 'shown everyone the class of men that professional boxing produces'.[11] Wren could hardly have made converts in the current hysteria and may only have shown the wowsers what a vulgar fellow he could be.

The McLeod tragedy was a golden opportunity for the Rev. Henry Worrall, pastor of the Golden Square Methodist Church, Bendigo, and dubbed by *Truth* 'Wowser Worrall' and 'Worry-all'. Born in Lancashire he came to Australia in 1898 via missionary work in Fiji, where he 'became renowned for his stamina, preaching, evangelism and opposition to Catholicism'. Described as 'thick-necked, deep-chested, fitted with a heavy jaw, a large moustache, and an expression of bank-like security and stolidity',[12] when assigned to a small circuit in Tasmania he, not quite modestly, described it as 'putting a Dreadnought in a duck-pond'. He became a stern critic of Tattersall's and Sir Philip Fysh. The week after McLeod's death, Worrall preached a sermon depicting him as a simple country lad contaminated by the city and asked, 'Who slaughtered the body and murdered the soul of Donald McLeod?' Worrall's answer was sensational:

> There is a man standing in your parliament on whose hands rests his blood ... Sir Samuel Gillott stands in high authority and I impeach that man tonight in God's name with the blood that has been flowing from the wounds of the gamblers. I impeach him with the responsibility for the evils that are around about us. It is nonsense for him to plead that he is powerless to stop the scourge which is creating around us a very Gethsemane of woe and trouble.

This was too strong for the people's representatives. They impeached Worrall instead. Bent, affecting horror, proclaimed Worrall's sermon 'an awful thing': if the members of parliament were 'guilty of what this gentleman says', he would 'not want to remain in the House a day longer'.

Publicity was just what Worrall wanted. He was defiant, unrepentant. Whatever penalty was imposed on him, said Worrall, he would 'look up and exclaim, "Oh God, I thank thee for having allowed me to come into Thy fellowship of sufferers." (applause).' However, Worrall still asked for a police escort, but Bent disregarded his request and told the press that Worrall could have a brass band, if he liked, provided there was a man with a tin whistle at the head of it. Worrall hired a special train for his journey to Melbourne on 31 July together with 250 supporters. Bent, who was also minister for railways, said he welcomed the increase in revenue. Some 2,000 well-wishers sang 'Onward Christian Soldiers' as the train departed from Bendigo. At each stop hundreds more wished him 'God speed'. Some 5,000 met him in Melbourne and proceeded to Parliament House. *Truth* observed that while the Son of Man had entered Jerusalem on an ass, Worrall had chartered a special train.

The impeachment turned into farce in spite of the solemnity with which it was treated by the Queen's Hall officials. *Table Talk* published an apt parable about David (Worrall) about to slay the fat giant, Tummibent (premier Bent, whose paunch was a caricaturist's delight). The galleries overflowed; the prayerful knelt on the lawns outside singing hymns. Worrall probably hoped for martyrdom in the form of a gaol sentence. Judkins became envious: he said he would give £50 to stand before the bar of parliament. However, he arrived late for the session, was at first mistaken for John Wren, but eventually managed to squeeze into standing room. But parliament had no clear procedures for dealing with this alleged breach of its privileges and libel of its members. The honourable gentlemen lapsed into their customary chiacking and raillery. Even before Worrall was admitted, verbal insults flying around the chamber included 'alcoholic epileptic', 'cackling jackdaw', 'guttersnipe' and 'goat'. At the bar of the House Worrall withdrew nothing, expressed no regret and demanded anti-gambling legislation. Then Bent bumbled one of the worst speeches ever heard in parliament. In putting the censure motion he played the buffoon. Worrall's speech, he said, reminded him of a hymn he used to know:

> The Lord delights in those who speak
> The words of truth; but every liar
> Must have his portion in the Lake
> That burns with brimstone and with fire.

Bent then said reflectively that 'If I were a girl I would not run one hundred miles after him'.[13]

Worrall was found guilty and was severely censured by the Speaker, but Bent was surprised that his motion was lost by as much as 26 to 36 votes. Although the Trades Hall had joined Judkins's deputation in June,

Laborites now realised that the wowser reformers were upholding class discrimination. Radical Frank Anstey, as he was to do so often in his long career, castigated the reformers for promoting 'a form of society in which the spirit of gambling and of speculation is deeply rooted'. Labor voted against the censure. A short time previously, in what Bongiorno calls 'perhaps the most extraordinary resolution ever carried at a public meeting in Australia', a Labor group calling themselves Christian Socialists declared:

> That in the opinion in this great gathering of free and God-fearing citizens the howling 'push' of sanctimonious snufflebusters who denounced the poor man for gambling a shilling as a child of wrath, and cringe and crawl to the gilded 'crooks' of the Stock Exchange and the VRC [Victoria Racing Club], are a standing menace to the peace, progress, and prosperity of Australia; favourable to a piebald population, under Chow-Japanese rule; free trade, a 10-bob-a-week wage, 14 hours work for one hour's pay, sweating, prison labour, and to every other political and economic abomination that may tend to an additional greasing of 'the fat sow', and should therefore, be immediately banished from the Commonwealth ....[14]

Judkins would not debate Anstey's or any other Labor point. He believed Labor was being manipulated by Wren and Rome.

Over the top

City Tatts was raided in May, and Wren, Frank Lawrence, Sugar Roberts and other 'directors' were charged with betting. Key evidence came from two young constables operating in plain clothes. One claimed he had bet with Wren himself, but the defence could prove that Wren was in Sydney on that day. The other constable, Goodson, maintained that, after becoming a member of the club, Wren and a companion had called at his home to see if he were one of O'Donnell's squad. He had allowed Wren to search him, to no avail. Wren then offered him a job at one of his racecourses, but he had said that his mother would never agree to that. Goodson's testimony was accepted in court. Wren and six others were fined £100 each; Lawrence and Roberts were exonerated. *Punch* cartooned a profile of Wren and exulted:

> The Czar of Gambling humbled. That great man, Mr John Wren, has been fined … the maximum penalty … Shame! Surely, Wren is above the law … Wren was not like other men … in fact, he was aces. Nobody had a chance with John … He could do anything he liked, law or no law, and make money doing it … for he was the Bismarck of Betting, the Roosevelt of the Ring, the Talleyrand of the Tote, the Napoleon of Pony Racing. How are the mighty fallen!

However, resurrection soon followed. With Gaunson representing him, Wren appealed. Acting Judge George Neighbour agonised for ten hours before he found the police evidence unsatisfactory. The fines were quashed.

Wren then charged Goodson with perjury, as he had done to detectives in 1899. The case was dismissed in the police court. Grover called this 'a policy of intimidation' and made much of Goodson's allegation that Wren had said to him that O'Donnell deserved 'to be kicked to pieces for ruining young fellows like you'; that is, turning them into (hated) informers. While Grover chose to equate this common expression of exasperation with advocacy of 'murder', he immediately went on to say that this should not 'be accepted as evidence' that Wren had ordered the bombing of O'Donnell's house or that he was

> personally directing the maltreatment of suspected 'narks' which happened about that time. The Tote and the Club provided food and drink and occasional luxuries for a whole mob of bad characters. They would think little of gratuitously obliterating a dozen 'narks' if twelve murders were deemed to be essential in the preservation of Jack Wren's business.

This is an observation that needs, however, to be related to the hypocrisy of the laws on gambling, the corruption they provoked and what seemed to lawbreakers their legitimate need to protect themselves.

Judkins was appalled by Judge Neighbour's decision. In September he went too far with his reckless (even mendacious) accusations. At the Pleasant Sunday Afternoon following the appeal, he virtually alleged that Wren had bribed Judge Neighbour:

> If I were to tell you all I could, you would hold your breath ... some of you have been pretty well scared over the revelations of what it has been possible for money to do in connection with some of our great institutions over the last few months.
>
> Matters are so serious in some departments of our public life that you would shiver if you knew of what has been going on ... We know some things but there is a time and place to save them. I'm holding up the red flag of danger. We are attacking things of which some of you have not the remotest idea. I am not talking platitudes now. We are going on until this kind of thing is impossible in Australia.

The innuendos were clear: parliament, the law, the police and Judge Neighbour were corrupt. An inference was patent: John Wren and the Catholic Church were behind this corruption. Neighbour, after consulting the attorney–general, did an unprecedented thing: he remonstrated publicly. Again unprecedentedly, he claimed a judge's integrity had been impugned. He was 'willing to meet the accusing man anywhere at any time'. Premier Bent was no help, and tried to buffoon away his responsibility: 'How do I know whom John Wren influences', he said. 'There are all kinds of rumours about ... He won't influence me. Of that you may be sure.'

The *Argus* demanded an immediate enquiry. Still Bent said: 'What do I care about Mr Judkins'. The *Argus* insisted that 'either Mr Judkins must be discredited or the administration of justice must be proven to be corrupt'. Then Bent offered Judkins a royal commission: it was his duty, in today's parlance, to put up or shut up. Nothing daunted, Judkins promised further revelations at Wesley Church on Sunday 23 September. Some 2,000 crowded inside, another 1,000 outside in the precincts. But they heard nothing specific against any individual, only that Judkins had been following certain gamblers 'as closely as if he lived by their sides' and that he could, if he wanted to (but obviously did not), disclose names of prominent city men who frequented the 'gambling hells'. He wrote to the premier refusing the royal commission, repeating the vague accusations, justifying his stance as that of a military scout flagging advance information to his commander and reiterating criticism of the O'Callaghan regime under which gambling, illicit drinking and prostitution had flourished.

Wren had intended at this time to travel to the United States for reasons of health, he said, but also to survey opportunities for his boxing promotion. Naturally there were rumours that he was actually removing himself from embarrassing exposures. A farewell was organised for 'the king of sport' at the (Catholic) Cathedral Hall on 21 September. To the surprise of his fans he began: 'I'm not going to America'. He refuted Judkins's infamous lies. He held his reputation dearer than his health, he said. He would stay and face every enquiry as long as he lived. He was no coward, he said. He had never claimed he was able to influence thirty members of parliament, in fact was independent of all of them and had never given any of them a shilling. Judkins was trying to intimidate the MPs, many of whom were weak-kneed. He wrote to the *Argus* challenging 'the mountebanking humbug' to charge him openly with corruption. He would then sue him for libel and, whoever won the case, he would pay the costs. But Judkins cannily replied that he would choose his own weapon.[15]

By then not only the press but officials of the Methodist Church were becoming wary of their champion. (Anglican Archbishop Lowther Clarke had months before deplored his extremism.) Rev. W. H. Fitchett, principal of Methodist Ladies' College and prestigious author of the 100,000 copies best seller, *Deeds that Won the Empire*, publicly deplored Judkins's unsubstantiated allegations. The *Age* thought that he had incurred 'universal odium as a scandal monger', but the press had relished his publicity-seeking. The *Argus* entertained its readers with an ode:

Hail, Mr Judkins (abridged) Hail Jud!
Sapient sutler of the Lud,
Peace on your hud,
And strength for the just and gud.
Joust, O Jud, for purity
Smite the LBA and the VRC
Restore genuine neck-to-knee
And fill the tavern with lukewarm tea
Smite pot, trots,
And petting parties on vacant lots
Purge the land 'neath the Southern Cross
From ponies, punters, pitch and toss

Help Madame Grundy
Stop hiking on Sunday
And cram the churches from crypt to steeple
With jerked-by-Judkins-from-Hell young people

Oh, Jud, Jud (added to Kins)
Cleanse us please of our manifold sins
Purge us, scourge us, ring us dry—
And let us crawl back to the Mallee to die.[16]

Judkins' most boisterous rally occurred on 30 September at the Gaiety Theatre, where he was billed to speak on 'Melbourne's Sins and Follies' to men only, plus one female vocalist, who were to be admitted by ticket. What was alleged to be a 'Wren mob' was there to hear that 'hell is right here in Melbourne'. A salvo of eggs hit the stage; one spluttered on Judkins's forehead, another on the vocalist's arm. But Judkins was far from mortified; *Punch* said he bore his yolk bravely. 'Friends', he shouted, 'it is a small thing to suffer in the cause of righteousness. Ten thousand blows like that will not stop me.' There was capital to be made out of this affray. Next day in the city court two youths, acknowledged Wren supporters, were arraigned. It was argued that a sacrilege had been committed. A more severe penalty than £5 for offensive behaviour would have been exacted if the Bench could have been persuaded that the old Gaiety theatre had hosted a quasi-divine service.

The Tote closes

However ridiculous Judkins eventually appeared, he was able at least to claim a partial victory over Wren and the gamblers. On 14 August 1906 Gillott introduced a Lotteries Gaming and Betting (or Gambling Suppression) Bill into parliament. Premier Bent, still smarting under the Worrall humiliation and mindful of other vested interests such as those of the Victoria Racing Club (VRC), the Victorian Amateur Turf Club (VATC) and elite clubs, was not going to capitulate to extreme demands such as the suppression of proprietary racecourses like Wren's as Judkins wanted. But Gillott at first defined the 'places used for betting so vaguely that the term could have included the Flemington (VRC) and Caulfield (VATC) courses. All courses, according to the Bill, had to be at least 6 furlongs in circumference, which would have closed Wren's pony courses. His three tracks were to be limited to 16 meetings each per year, where previously he had had 156 days. The police were given powers to enter gaming houses and dwellings nearby, and owners and occupiers were to be responsible for any illegal activities therein. Sweepstakes were severely restricted while public raffles, guessing competitions, art unions such as were run at Catholic functions and by the Trades Hall, and lotteries such as Tattersall's were to be prohibited. The pre-publication of race betting details was to be forbidden. Bookmakers had to be licensed by the VRC but, mindful of Donald McLeod, only on the people's Flat at Flemington and Caulfield if an entrance fee was paid.

That last provision outraged MPs already complaining of discrimination against the lower classes. Frank Anstey fulminated that the legislation was a 'hypocritical subterfuge', with no intent to tackle the gambling evil at its source. When Gillott cited Seebohm Rowntree's famous definition in *Betting and Gambling*, 'the craze of endeavouring to obtain wealth without labour', Bob Solly (Labor) interjected: 'On the Stock Exchange, did you say?' He was later to upbraid the Rev. Dr Fitchett as 'a very large gambler' in mining stocks at Broken Hill. When Gillott claimed that the Bill made no distinction between rich and poor, Edgar Wilkins pointed out that to be a VRC member one needed a £25 premium and a £5 annual subscription. The future Labor premier, G. M. Prendergast, complained that the Bill was 'too drastic' and 'interfered with … freedom'. There was no doubt, he said, that 'Mr Wren had done a great deal to purify pony racing about Melbourne, by excluding men who have been guilty of disreputable practices and ponies that have been run improperly'. He had 'elevated the sport'. The premier interjected: 'To do him justice, he has done that'. Gaunson denounced the Wesleyan 'slang-whanging' and advocated legitimising the totalisator as in New Zealand, where it had 'the most beneficial results'.

William Watt, a future Liberal premier and acting prime minister, observed that 'many provisions were chiefly aimed at Wren'. In an adjournment motion to discuss the status of the VRC, Watt said, 'I like John Wren. I have met him frequently. He is as straight as a rush. I also admire the man who trains John Wren's horses as a straight and able fellow.' E. C. Warde (Flemington) instanced the wealthy man who goes to Collingwood to bet because it is 'the squarest institution … with the fairest odds … fairly conducted'. Bob Solly topped these comments by comparing Wren to Napoleon, 'though he has done wrong things'. It would appear that these legislators did not think that Wren had caused the bombing of O'Donnell's house.

Gaunson, who thought the whole proceedings 'perfect humbug', provided the light relief. During the debate on the contemporaneous Licensing Bill he referred to 'one club that had at least four thousand members, and there was not a more sober club in the whole world … because there was not one solitary drop of drink supplied or sold'. 'Where is that?' quizzed Sir Alexander Peacock (thrice premier of Victoria). City Tattersalls or what is popularly known as Wren's Tote, Gaunson replied. 'Do they meet there for social or literary purposes?' asked Peacock owlishly. Yes, there was a copy of the *Encyclopaedia Britannica* there, said Gaunson. 'It has never been opened, I should say', opined Peacock. Gaunson insisted it had. 'Why, when giving evidence in court recently, Constable De Lany [sic] affirmed that he had gone to the club one day, and who did he see perusing it but John Wren'. When Gaunson agreed that City Tatts, and 'Sol Green's Club' (Melbourne Tatts) too, had 'tried very hard' for a liquor licence, Prendergast (Labor) queried: 'The proprietor of the club you referred to is a life-long teetotaller, is he not?' 'Yes', said Gaunson gravely, 'that is right enough. I [myself] am a teetotaller as long as I do not get a drop of drink on board. I am quite satisfied teetotallers have the best of the fun.'

After prolonged and acrimonious debates lasting twenty-two days and nights between the beginning of the second reading on 13 September and 18 December, with time off naturally for the Spring Carnival Cup meetings, VRC members were aghast at prohibition of the publication of pre-post betting in newspapers and elsewhere. Without betting, the racecourses—and the industries they supported—would die, it was claimed. Then one evening with members soporific Anstey, at the instigation of J. A. Boyd, moved that certain words after 'place' in the Bill should be omitted. A drowsy premier, unaware of the consequence, accepted the amendment only to find, after the amendment had passed, that betting even at Flemington was to be banned. It was the carnival season: the great three-year-old, Poseidon, had just won the Caulfield Cup and was dead set for the Melbourne Cup, the first horse to achieve that double. Race clubs throughout Victoria protested against the ban.

Bent quickly put through a corrective amendment. Others followed. Betting details could be published *after* a race. It was no longer necessary to charge for entry to the Flat. Wren's pony tracks were given 24 days each and the two trotting associations, hitherto ignored, were given 20 days. Four furlong courses were permitted. Restrictions on lotteries, raffles and guessing games were relaxed particularly at charity bazaars. However, Bent would not budge on suggestions, especially from Labor members, that an official totalisator would cure many ills associated with gambling. Wren had demonstrated that a tote would be popular; it would not discourage betting. Bookmakers and elite clients were against it because of competition for gamblers' shillings and distaste for Wren's origin, associations and success. Labor MPs continued their opposition to the Bill on grounds that either all gambling should be forbidden or none, and that it was discreditable to the poorer classes that the wealthy should be privileged in law to gamble. Others frequently alleged that Labor was protecting Wren's interests and even that some MPs were in his pay. Prendergast defended his colleagues against the accusation and insisted that he had only slight contact with Wren, and had refused to negotiate with him over the possibility of founding a Labor newspaper. There was no need for Wren to suborn Labor MPs when they were ideologically committed to oppose inequality and wanted reform, the reform of capitalist society. As Anstey said of the churches:

> They want sobriety; they want honesty and they want cleanliness of character; they want a lack of the gambling spirit, and yet they uphold a form of society in which the spirit of gambling and speculation is deeply rooted—man struggling with man and woman with woman.

And Wren, not just because of his largesse, but because he was a lower-class person who had resourcefully opposed the establishment, had become a working-class hero.

The Bill passed the Legislative Assembly on 18 December, and went briskly through the upper house. In the New Year of 1907 the Act came into operation. According to Buggy the four police who surveyed the tote yard on 3 January 'found one group of young men throwing balls at an Aunt Sally' while another was playing nine-pins. To the sergeant who asked 'How much a shy?', the reply was 'Nothing'. We're playing for love' On the more or less unbreachable rampart was a notice: 'BETTING STRICTLY PROHIBITED'. Wren would have authorised this. City

Tattersalls also capitulated, although Wren was considering testing the legislation. However, when Inspector Gleeson applied under the new legislation for a declaration of quarantine against both the Tote and Club premises, Wren had second thoughts because quarantine 'would adversely affect the interest of innocent people'. In late March 1907 he sent an emissary to the chief of the CIB with an assurance that the Tote and Tattersalls Club would be closed and the keys handed in to the commissioner of police. He would not start up elsewhere. However, O'Callaghan refused any bargaining with a law-breaker and the application for the quarantine continued. There appears to be no truth whatever in stories that Wren threatened the commissioner that he would re-open the Tote and that Detective-Sergeant O'Donnell, also present, then fulminated that in that case he would call out the military and 'blow the Tote off the map'.[17] Wren may well have felt, now that he was married and having a family, that to continue illicit activities was not in his long-term interests. One assumes his eminently respectable wife felt this even more so.

Blackmail

Meanwhile, there were desperate attempts to stop the Bill. On Friday 30 November 1906 another scandal had burst. Chief secretary Gillott had long survived allegations of administrative paralysis and even of deliberate inaction with regard to Wren's Tote, but he could not weather John Norton's open letter to him entitled 'LECHERY AND LUCRE'. 'This morally putrescent prostitute's pimp', crowed *Truth,* had since 1877 been holding mortgages for properties occupied by 'a feculent fiend in female form', Melbourne's most fashionable brothel keeper, Madame Brussells. Within the inner city she ran an opulent bagnio to which favoured clients, even from nearby parliament, had private keys. Gillott had been lending her money at 10 per cent. Judkins also trumpeted the scandal at his next Pleasant Sunday Afternoon (2 December). It was futile for Gillott to protest that he was engaged only in an ordinary business transaction somewhat negligently supervised. He felt obliged to resign, and sailed for London forthwith.

Norton was furious with Judkins for claiming credit for his scoop, and the following week, in a leader entitled 'JUDKINS THE JACKAL' accused the preacher of being 'a prevaricating perfidious plagiarist'. The Christian name, 'Jakes', would be appropriate for this 'gospel-grinding, gammoning ghoul', he wrote. Referring to a Total Abstainers' Picnic where Judkins had been crowned with a ti-tree coronet, Norton suggested that 'a nightpan would better become your brazen brow'. A rumour around Melbourne attributed the exposure to a Wren spy who was supposed to have given the information to Norton and Judkins independently. On this basis, Wren has been accused of blackmail, presumably to halt the anti-gambling Bill, by Grover and Manning Clark. Confirmation seemed to come in the New Year of 1907 when the Labor leader, G. M. Prendergast, revealed that Wren had proffered similar information to him but he had refused to use it. However, Norton said in his 'JUDKINS THE JACKAL' leader:

> The pecuniary partnership between marvellously moral Melbourne's ex-Lord Mayor and Madame Brussells … was known to the Law Court officials, to nearly every lawyer and lawyer's clerk in Melbourne [and] many Members of Parliament, to the editors and proprietors of the newspapers … as well as to a great and greedy galaxy of Bible-banging, pulpit-punching, penny-pinching, pelf-pursuing, 'tray-bit trapping', pharisaical parasites like [Judkins] … for many months and years past.

Gillott's dealings were not publicised before because too many people from Toorak and Parliament House might have been embarrassed. If Norton had suspected that Judkins had received a briefing from Wren identical with the one he allegedly had, he would hardly have continued his charge of plagiarism (*Truth*, 15 December). It is noteworthy that the *Lone Hand* states that *Truth* published *after* Judkins's oration at Wesley Church. It was in fact two days *before*.[18]

Moreover, unfortunately for this allegation of blackmail, Judkins wrote to the *Lone Hand* (1 June 1907) a month *after* its denunciation of Wren, claiming that he had done his own research:

> … my information [about Gillott] was given to me by a police officer long before I announced it, and a Melbourne firm of lawyers, on my instruction, searched the titles and produced for me the particulars, for which I paid. Moreover, it was common property among members of Parliament, the police and prominent men.

To discredit Gillott, Wren's 'underground' had not been needed. Even in New Zealand Judkins was remembered for his vindictiveness. *Labor Call* (13 December) quoted the New Zealand *Times* which, it implied, 'knows Judkins': 'In the case of Samuel Gillott, Mr Judkins, always zealous, and long ago spoiled by the limelight of his own lurid atmosphere, would be incapable of charity'.

In the light of this it is instructive to read a much-quoted passage from Grover's *Lone Hand* diatribe, which became the seminal document used authoritatively by Hardy, Manning Clark and others against Wren:

> The intimidation practised by Boss Wren has been largely in the nature of blackmail. He has demanded freedom from prosecution as the price of preservation from exposure. Anything discoverable to the discredit of men in high or low places, if it seemed advisable to bribe or frighten them, has been discovered by the frowsy 'shadowers' or expert spies attached to the service of the gambling hells. A legislator who does not hold out his hand for a *douceur* will shrink at the threat of the whip. Whilst the Anti-Gambling Bill was being blocked in the Victorian Assembly by members of the Labor Party, the crack of Wren's intimidating whip echoed along the corridors of the House. Craven Samuel Gillott, the old thieves' lawyer and partner of bookmaker Joe Thompson, cowered at the thought of revelations, whilst stout-hearted Premier Bent [NB. in power at that time] put a bolder face on his own personal perturbation. At last the screaming Mr Judkins uttered a first consignment of unpleasant reflections on the character of Chief Secretary Gillott and the Judkins oration was followed [but it was *not*] by an article in TRUTH newspaper, the same material, in duplicate, having been supplied to both parties by—*Wren*! The whipstroke that drove Gillott to Europe was a threat to Premier Bent who sailed away for the benefit of his health ere the anti-Wren legislation had been seriously enforced. Happily it was the pestilent Boss's turn to be exposed when Mr Prendergast … had to defend himself against a charge of being visited by Wren at Parliament House … Wren offered the whip to the Labor Party, whose leader declined to use it. It was then passed along to other hands.

Manning Clark put an idiosyncratic, lurid gloss on this:

> Those whose private lives were inconsistent with their public posture as pillars of respectability trembled in their shoes at … [Wren's] threat to reveal all. Sir Samuel Gillott, the one-time barrister for the thieves of Melbourne, was terrified of revelations. Some members of the Labor Party, outwardly the purest of the pure, but inwardly ravening wolves in the presence of alcohol or women, cowered in the corridors of Parliament House when a hireling of John Wren whispered what might happen to them if they did not toe the line. Tommy Bent, the Premier of the state which had turned respectability into a gold mine, trembled when John Wren hired a scribe to write up Bent's sport in the brothels of Melbourne. The police did not take action because, as the *Bulletin* pointed out, any day of the week the detectives in charge of investigating vice and corruption could be seen swilling the champagne bought for them by John Wren.[19]

A simple analysis of these two statements by Grover and Clark respectively will expose their dubiety. Grover's reference to Wren's premises as 'gambling hells' is at odds with their reputation for fair dealing and orderliness. What contrasting words would he have used for the Victoria Racing Club's race track or Sol Green's Melbourne Tattersalls or the Victorian Club? References in both statements to Gillott's being a 'thieves' lawyer' is a crude *ad hominem*, as though practising in a criminal jurisdiction was in itself corrupt. The repetition of this jibe by Clark is improvident; he gives no indication, for example, of having consulted any other source on Gillott. Clark's hyperbolic reference to 'some Labor politicians' as 'ravening wolves' is pharisaical bombast (and why just *Labor* politicians?). Note that Grover did not say Labor MPs 'cowered'; he said that Gillott did. Clark's charge that Wren was continually ('any day of the week'?) corrupting vice squad detectives with champagne is based on a *Bulletin* paragraph of 4 October 1906, which in effect said: 'Long time before … [in 1902] this journal referred to the commonplace spectacle of Jack Wren shouting champagne for a couple of detectives'.

Furthermore, both paragraphs refer to premier Bent. Unlike Clark, I know of no place where Wren is accused of hiring a scribe to write up

Bent's sexual capers. And neither does Clark tell us where this information comes from. More to the point, Grover would have known why Bent was suddenly, as the *Age* put it, 'persuaded by his colleagues to take a trip to England' on 19 March 1907, four days after the state election. The answer was in the *Bulletin* of 30 May. Bent's trip was not simply for the benefit of his health, as Grover put it. It is curious that Grover should call Gillott 'craven' while Bent is 'stout-hearted' when they both fled from disgrace:

> The sweetest story ever told about any notable Australian politician is the yarn that has a pretty little stage lady for its heroine. She was boarding at a hotel in the city, where she was then performing. The politician was a frequent and privileged visitor at the pub, and one night when whisky had got into his elderly head, and the common sense was out of it, he found his way to the room of the stage lady, and aroused her from her slumbers. Whereupon she screamed … Next day the lady put the scandal in a lawyer's hands … The alarmed politician went and confessed … to the principal legal member of the Cabinet; the legal man consulted his colleagues and it was unanimously decided that the culprit had better quit the scene … until this particular scandal had blown over … Her lawyer, after demanding £300 mercifully reduced the amount to £250 … In this incident, and others almost as glaringly scandalous—the dullest-eyed cynic may see the fallacy of the argument that a politician's usefulness to the State is in no way affected by his character.[20]

The principal legal member in cabinet referred to in the *Bulletin* story was John Mark Davies, a former leading 'land boomer' and ingeniously dishonest liquidator of lawful debts. Like W. M. Baillieu, J. M. Davies 'fought his way back into parliament and respectability', became attorney-general from 1903 to 1910, and then with Baillieu sat in the red plush of the Legislative Council as president until 1919.[21] Could it be said that cabinet connived at Bent's offence? Cornelius Crowe, of course, barked vindictively that cabinet 'had compounded a felony'.[22] Yet Grover could call Bent simply 'stout-hearted' while Wren was 'pestilential'. Double standards were a part of the political culture.

Finally, we may ask two questions. If the accusation that Wren was behind Gillott's disgrace had reputable sources—and it did not—one may well ask what is the difference between the enquiries and the alleged exposure imputed to Wren (which was in the public interest?) and today's 'investigative journalism' and its usage in politics. I have yet to find a case of Wren's having extorted money or compliance from a parliamentarian with threats; withdrawal of patronage must always have been a possibility and therefore a pressure point, but there is no evidence that it happened either. On the other hand, one does not need to be versed in Collingwood lore to understand why Paddy Boardman, for instance, would feel justified in throwing back to Cornelius Crowe: 'You are not the clean potato yourself'. There should be a difference between recriminations, the exposure of hypocrisy and blackmail.

Monty Grover concluded his *Lone Hand* indictment with the acknowledgment that Wren had made peace with the police following the Anti-Gambling Act but, portentously, he warned that 'The ruffians of Wrenism thus thrown out of employment started to talk as they had never talked before. They are still talking. And the public awaits with curiosity the next step.'

There was no 'next step'. None of Wren's employees, no *ruffian* or otherwise, that I know of, 'tipped a bucket' on him. What does this tell us about him? Experience tells that it is not possible to intimidate everyone. Grover melodramatically claimed that he had to carry a revolver for his safety. There is no evidence that anyone was ever in any mortal danger from Wren. It is notable that the *Lone Hand* did not make any further scurrilous attacks on Wren. Obviously it had no cause. No other article between 1907 and 1921 dealt with Wren as subject, although there are six references to him: three of them in 1907, two in 1909. After that there is only a report on 1 October 1917 of Wren, 'so well-known in sporting and military circles, as a fund-raiser for and governor of St Vincent's Hospital'. So, were his Tote and its related activities his only 'crimes' in the eyes of the *Bulletin*'s social reformers? Certainly its closure did not end illegal gambling in Melbourne.

The Swinburne ruckus

George Swinburne, businessman, engineer, educationist, philanthropist and politician, was a powerful figure behind the anti-gambling legislation A fervent Methodist, he represented the middle-class electorate of Hawthorn, of which he had been mayor and which included Kew where he and Wren both lived. Swinburne was 'grieved to find a definite alliance between the Political Labor Council, the party interested in gambling and the liquor interests and said so vehemently'. His distinguished hagiographers, E. H. Sugden, Master of Queen's College at the University of Melbourne, and (Sir) Frederick Eggleston, politician, author and diplomat, thought Wren 'a menace to the moral health of society', but saw nothing anomalous about Bent's being Swinburne's 'friend and leader'. They must have been aware of Bent's past swindles and his sexual caper of March 1907, but wrote blandly that the premier left for England 'the day after the election ... [where he] combined a search for health and a purpose to do business'. That rationale creaks. They were scornful of Frank Anstey's plea that there should not be different gambling laws for rich and poor. To them that was 'hypocritical subterfuge' couched in 'cynical verbiage'.

Swinburne and Wren were headed for conflict when the latter signed the nomination paper of Dr James Marmaduke Rose as Swinburne's opponent in the general state election. Rose was the previously defeated candidate. Sugden and Eggleston thought that 'Wren [in 1907] had not the political ability that he subsequently acquired or he would never have backed a steed of the calibre of Rose'. On 8 March, Swinburne pointed out that Rose was a nominee of the foremost lobbyist against anti-gambling and anti-licensing legislation (supported by 'the worst elements in gambling and drink'). Both Wren and Labor leaders inferred that he was being accused of bribing them. He declared he would attend Swinburne's next political rally on 14 March at the Hawthorn Town Hall, as he was entitled to do, and issue a challenge. Swinburne took the precaution of having a number of athletic 'well-dressed young gentlemen' behind him on the stage.

The *Age*, *Argus* and *Australasian* have left reports of what they thought actually happened and the accounts, when analysed, caution against simple arrogation of blame. If there had been some preconceived plan to disrupt the meeting by violence rather than by rowdyism, it was hardly in Wren's interest to attend and insist on speaking. That would not have enhanced his credibility. On his feet Swinburne accused Rose of having raised only one issue of public policy: the question of whether there should be a referendum on having scripture lessons in state schools. The Labor Party, said Swinburne, 'had been guilty of a most impudent action in sending out a circular to state school teachers on the matter'. A little later, to mingle the sectarian issue with gambling, Swinburne instanced corruption in 'Art Unions' in 1902, another glancing shot at Catholics. Rose, he said, was simply put up 'to damn the Gambling and Licensing Act'. Although Rose was an ex-MLA, he represented 'the worst elements of gambling and drinking'. In a voice which the *Age* (15 March) said 'rose to a shriek', Swinburne declared that 'when gambling and drinking become public vices and nuisances ... the Government has to interfere with them'. (But one might exclude the VRC and the well-behaved upper-class clubs?) Why, said Swinburne, Wren tries to influence electorates other than Hawthorn! He 'had the audacity to distribute throughout the [federal] electorate [of Maribyrnong last December] a long letter against Mr Mauger [MHR, 1901–10] in favour of the Labor candidate'.

Wren attempted from the platform to make a speech but was confined to questions. He did slap his £500 cheque down, offering to forfeit it to local charity if Swinburne could prove that he had 'suggested to any member of Parliament to use his vote in my direction'. Swinburne protested that he had 'only said [that] ... the men whom Wren interviewed were the men that battled against the gaming Bill in Parliament'. When Wren asked if Swinburne had ever seen him in Parliament House before the gaming Bill became law, Swinburne admitted he had never personally done so. Wren also asked Swinburne why he had sent him, 'the biggest gambler in the community, a letter asking me to provide a vehicle for him on polling day'. At this the embarrassed chairman (R. J. Alcock) admitted that 'it was done by some blundering ass on ... [their] committee' (whom, one hopes, was present). Apparently, however, Swinburne had no qualms about soliciting logistics from wealthy electors. Amid laughter and cheers Wren followed this by accusing Swinburne of having voted in 1902 to reduce the wages of the impoverished workers on the Waranga Basin. Swinburne could not remember doing so, but Wren flourished a document. Swinburne then protested, however, that he 'had raised their wages a shilling a day not so long ago'. As Wren demanded 'a straight-out answer' his supporters, according to the *Argus*, began to move towards the stage shouting 'Give him an answer, you coward'. No speaker could be heard over the clamour. Then:

> The chairman walked to where Mr Wren was standing and taking him by the arm, apparently remonstrated with him ... Mr Wren

> faced the audience with his right hand raised in the air and clenched fist. The chairman continued to hurriedly address him, and the two men swayed for a moment in wrist grips.

From that point, a melee began. The *Age* report is the most detailed. When Wren persisted with his question,

> The chairman rushed towards him, and in an attempt to induce him to sit down, took hold of him by the wrists. Mr Wren's face grew hot with protest. He tore his hands away and said something that was inaudible. At the same time the chairman still keeping hold on Mr Wren's straining wrist was understood to make a signal for a policeman.
>
> Two of the policemen rushed forward and the torrent of sturdy shouting men whom they had kept in check burst its bounds. Instantaneously these men made a wild charge over the reporters' table for the platform. At the same time the crowd of Mr Swinburne's supporters on the platform were seen to be in the throes of a violent commotion also. Someone was making awkward left arm strokes at Mr Wren who hit out with both hands at a surging group jostling and shouting around him. Mr Thompson Moore stood amidst the crashing chairs and the surging mass valiantly protecting his tall hat …
>
> The mob which conducted the assault from the body of the hall who were acting for the safety of Mr Wren found the charge a very trying one … [they were] repulsed at every point.
>
> During a cessation of hostilities … Mr Wren's followers surged around in front of the platform shouting, 'Where's Jack Wren?' 'Where's his 500 quid?'
>
> Mr Wren forced his way from the back of the stage to the front … his supporters yelled with glee at his appearance. Some said 'Jack, did you get your 500 jim?' Mr Wren showed a cut near the eye and blood was smeared upon his face but it was proudly said by his supporters that he had 'given far more than he got'. His burly supporters lifted him shoulder high, and amidst a perfect pandemonium bore him out of the hall.
>
> Mr Swinburne stood amongst his followers discussing the stirring events of the previous few minutes. Shortly afterwards the

> meeting dispersed. Mr Wren's supporters gathered in Burwood Road, and cheered him. Hundreds still loitered at the scene of the turmoil until late in the night, but there was no further disturbance. The supporters of Mr Wren, who took part in the charge on the platform, were not prepared to give their names. Asked why they adopted such tactics they coolly observed that they were merely rushing forward 'to ask the candidate a question' …
>
> Some time after the meeting … the chairman told … the *Age* that the calling up of the policemen was the signal for the disorder. He said he thought he had given Mr Wren a good deal of latitude but when Mr Wren threatened to throw him off the stage he thought matters had gone far enough … All he sought the assistance of the police for, was to see that order was preserved and that the meeting was not taken out of his hands. He had no intention at any time of giving Mr Wren into custody.

Not even *Truth* saw any excuse for Wren's conduct. 'WREN IN THE WRONG' was its caption for an article extolling freedom from ruffianism at public meetings: 'otherwise the knell of democracy will be sounded', it said grandly. It could, however, be pointed out that the flash point for the melee came when chairman Alcock grabbed Wren's wrist, alarming his supporters and probably Swinburne too. (NB: the brief account in Sugden and Eggleston's biography of Swinburne is glib and without detail.) Technically, it could be said that it is not a chairman's role to restrain physically even someone not entitled to speak, let alone someone like Wren who in this case was entitled to ask questions. This was a task for the police who were present. However, it was not technical points that Collingwood men crossed the Yarra to observe when they rallied to their leader. In view of these accounts having been written by witnesses hostile to Wren, the affray seems by today's standards relatively mild. Wren and Collingwood hardly presented a grave challenge, even when provoked, to the gentility of Yarraside.

Physically, Wren came out of this incident badly, as the *Argus* reported:

> Mr John Wren, who was considerably jostled … on Thursday night, was just yesterday forced to summon medical advice. A blow he had received over the heart had left a bruise, and so indisposed did he become that he was confined to his bed.

A week later, the Catholic *Advocate* reported that 'He is still suffering from the effects of the rough handling he received ... last week. Dr Barrett, Mr Wren's medical adviser, announced a slight improvement in his condition on Wednesday.' Swinburne won Hawthorn decisively, but by only the same margin over Rose as in 1904.

One consolation in the elections for Wren would have been the defeat of Judkins in working-class Brunswick by Frank Anstey, who increased his majority from 55 to 59 per cent with a 30 per cent increased turnout. Although Judkins 'carefully selected his constituency', said the *Argus*, 'he found that a large majority were not favourable to the extreme views which he expounded'. Not unexpectedly Judkins had a different (and extreme) explanation:

> The victory was won by the other side by pandering to the social evils, to the drink trade and to gambling. Some of our people were not able to vote because when they went to the polling booth they found that others had voted for them, and in their names.

However, no one seems to have complained officially and no hue and cry went up. That was just Judkins, never punctilious with the truth. The Rechabite Samuel Mauger had revenge on Wren. After being made postmaster general in the Deakin federal ministry later in the year, he closed mail and telephone services to Wren, putting him on a level with purveyors of indecent literature, quack medicines and lottery tickets although he was no longer running the Tote. Mauger was soon obliged to relent.

The death of Judkins

In August 1911 it was announced that Judkins was suffering from an incurable cancer. A public appeal was opened to raise at least a thousand pounds 'with a view of bringing immediate relief to Mr Judkins' mind and making subsequent provision for his wife and child'. Eventually over £1,800 was raised. Among those contributing were Andrew Fisher, Labor prime minister, and 'two non-teetotallers', while the secretary of the Licensed Victuallers' Association paid a sympathetic visit. A certain 'R. Roberts', contributed £1. *Labor Call* (24 August) could not resist jibing: 'Poor little Juddy's sufferings may perchance be alleviated by the knowledge that sympathy and charity are a bigger and wider thing than he imagined'. Some doggerel entitled 'Sympathy' followed:

The party veil is torn aside
Surrounding the bed of pain;
And sympathy vast as the ocean wide
Breaks the sectarian chain.
From far and near, both sinner and saint,
Are joined in kindly feeling;
To the sufferer dire whose heart beats feint,
To his fellow men are appealing.

The Catholic *Tribune* concurred, praising 'his honesty of purpose' in trying 'to clean up some of the plague spots of the community'. Even if he had identified himself with 'the many bitter enemies of Catholicity' who supported him, the paper 'would not, of course, withhold our sympathy'.[23] On his death at forty-three in September 1912 the obituarists were generous, the Catholic *Advocate* calling Judkins a 'hard but fair fighter' and repeating that 'unlike others on the same platform he did not stoop to the abuse of the Catholic church'.[24] This can be profitably compared with the remarks of Rev. Irving Benson, minister of the Wesley Church, Melbourne, on the demise of Wren. A memorial window there 'commends the courageous devotion of [Judkins], this modern Sir Galahad in the cause of reform'. Curiously, Manning Clark called Wren the 'most generous donor' to Judkins' testimonial.[25] There is no mention of Wren in any place that I know of or in any published list of subscribers. If Wren had been a subscriber—and it would not have been uncharacteristic—it surely would have been newsworthy. Although it may appear to be the usual Clark muddle when dealing with Wren, it would be ironic if he also got this apparent furphy from Hardy, who claimed to be Clark's adviser on Wren. Judkins and Wren both lie in Booroondara Cemetery, Kew.

One notable person who mimicked the absurdities of Judkins was the young R. G. Menzies, as his biographer relates:

> Judkins' florid style of fiery, righteous oratory invited lampooning, and Menzies [then at school] proved himself to be the uncannily accurate lad for that. Once his talent had been discovered, he was repeatedly put up to 'do' Judkins for the boys. That gave him a … nickname, 'Judkins'—'Juddy' for short.[26]

A fatuous legend

That fatuous legends from the period still cling to Wren can be seen in Lorna Osborn's life of her grandfather, Rev. T. S. B. Woodfull, published in 1995. She accuses Wren of having put his Tote profits into real estate of degenerate quality, becoming in effect a rack-renter. Her crusading ancestor was thus brought into conflict with Collingwood councillors 'influenced by Wren'. I have not heard, not even from Hardy, that Wren was involved in rack-renting. Osborn is convinced that Wren inspired the bombing of O'Donnell's house. Moreover, she thinks, it took some seventy police with battering rams and guns to close down Wren's Tote in 1907 when it was wide open to receive the four police who came for the capitulation. The earliest memory of Osborn's uncle, Colin Woodfull, aged three, was 'the sound of parsonage windows being shattered by John Wren's henchmen' (or so the family believed). But Colin was not born until 1908. The parsonage was not in Collingwood but in genteel Albert Street, East Melbourne, two suburbs away. The Tote had been closed for more than four years. Another Woodfull family recollection is of their girls being stoned by Wren's roughs on their way along the riverside to Methodist Ladies' College in Hawthorn. That must have been an even more perverse pastime for Wren, then a millionaire entrepreneur. The key to the family's fantasies could lie in what Osborn calls 'the feared links of the Labor movement with Roman Catholicism and the activities of John Wren'.[27]

Rev. Woodfull was a worthy committed social reformer, but indications of his impressionable mentality lie not just in his rapid shift from pacifism to jingoism during the First World War but also in his attitude to those who dissented. During the 1919 federal election, when some Nationalist Party returned soldiers near Ararat tarred and feathered the poet and politician J. K. McDougall for writing anti-war verses, Woodfull told a Protestant Federation meeting that McDougall 'would bear the marks of his attack to his dying day, and he deserved to do so'. In fact the Nationalists used reworded verses from McDougall's poem, 'The White Man's Burden', written in 1900, as 'evidence' that Labor was contemptuous of the diggers. Rev. Henry ('Worry') Worrall provided an even sterner verdict at a temperance meeting in Wesley Church: 'God damn the man who wrote words like that (loud applause). He withdrew that prayer. It was unnecessary. The writer was damned already.' A certain B. Cohen replied in the *Age*: 'If this is supposed to be Christianity, then thank God I am only a Jew'.[28]

To balance the bullying parsons one should cite a contemporary example of Catholic clericalism. At the *Te Deum* at Melbourne's St Patrick's Cathedral in November 1918 to thank God for the end of the Great War, John Wren's friend, Bishop Patrick Phelan, reassured Catholic mothers that their fallen sons had automatically gained salvation, whereas 'even this comfort was denied the Protestant mother who was taught … [her] prayers were useless'. Outside his church there might be no salvation—or so the bishop seemed to think at the time.[29]

CHAPTER SIX

A Tammany Boss?

THE TERM 'TAMMANY' (derived from the notoriously corrupt urban organisation which influenced the United States Democrat Party and gained control of New York) has been prodigally applied by Wren's critics to his so-called political 'machine'. An authoritative article in *Labour History* by Chris McConville, entitled 'John Wren: Machine Boss, Irish Chieftain or Meddling Millionaire?', clarifies the issue. To account adequately for inner-Melbourne politics, writes McConville:

> [we should] treat machine models with suspicion. Collingwood, like inner areas of American cities, may have made work and housing available to poor immigrants. But political practice in American ethnic ghettos rarely presents us with a model applicable to the working class suburbs of either Melbourne or Sydney.

The lack of ethnic segregation was a feature of Australian urban society. The channels for upward mobility were not controlled by local 'godfathers'. Wealthy though they might be, their patronage was limited in scope. Irish-Australian Catholics—through their own education system, which operated under a public examination process within what was largely a meritocracy—did not have to accept dependency to get on in life. Not only were the inner-suburban municipalities each a small part of the whole city, they were relatively powerless:

> Education (and so, school buildings), railways and tramways, the police, the courts, water supply, street lighting, and sanitation all lay beyond the control of a Collingwood-based machine. It only dealt in honest graft of a limited nature. For lucrative contracts, the machine needed to control the Colonial and Federal legislatures and, more hopefully the Melbourne City Council [and the Melbourne and Metropolitan Board of Works and other statutory bodies]. So, any boss in the municipalities of inner Melbourne dealt with little rather than big business, with small operators who looked on the Collingwood street cleaning contract or a post as a Richmond City Baths attendant as worthwhile perks.[1]

And Wren was not involved in protection, prostitution or bootlegging rackets. He was involved in gambling, certainly, but as an illegal service until 1907 rather than as a 'racket', and no doubt in association with 'types' whom genteel Yarrasiders, who inspired the repressive laws, found unsavoury.

Of the three titles in McConville's querying headline, only 'meddling millionaire' (as he is aware) is not wide of the mark. 'Machine boss' is inapplicable, in spite of the ludicrous assertion in the *Review of Reviews* that the Tote 'is as perfectly organised as the New York Tammany'.[2] Wren's role in supporting self-determination for Ireland was a natural one for someone of his ethnic background, resources and contentiousness, but in this he was more a senior liegeman of Archbishop Daniel Mannix than a 'Chief'. As for 'meddling' in politics, that capacity existed for any wealthy man through donations to electoral and surplus expenses. It is easily forgotten how poor Labor politicians could be until the post-war period, how they generally lacked inherited wealth (sometimes even home ownership), needed transport for themselves and their supporters, venues for meetings, and cash for publicity, entertainment, how-to-vote cards and telephone bills, and even for charitable handouts. And parliamentary tenure was itself so uncertain, not just because of unsafe seats but through challenge from within. Parker Moloney was minister for markets and transport under Scullin, and lost his seat in December 1931. 'In an era before parliamentary pensions', says his biographer, 'he was left virtually destitute [the Depression was on] ... sold his house ... and moved his family into an aunt's home'.[3] A letter from the then organising secretary of the Victorian party, the legendary stammering 'numbers man', Pat Kennelly, to Wren on Legislative Council notepaper, having to ask for a small loan on the security of his mortgaged home in 1940, also makes the point:

> Dear Mr Wren,
>
> Further to our conversation today, relative to my election account and your donation thereto of £200. I now submit the following proposal, that you advance me the remainder of the account namely £337 as a loan. I will submit to you the deeds of my home and am agreeable to pay you £4.0.0 per week until such account is liquidated. Naturally the necessary papers will be signed by me should you desire same.
>
> Trusting to receive a favourable reply to the above request,
>
> Yours faithfully
>
> P. J. KENNELLY[4]

This need for patrons led facilely enough to payment of branch fees for participatory, nominal and even non-existent members, and stacking branches at crucial times using bogus union tickets—as was done in later times by unions themselves, communists and Santamaria Movement men. As for actually dominating the Labor Party, any aspiring boss had to contend with its structure, its supervising central executive and the predominance of the affiliated unions which no single person could control.

The Labor Party was an impoverished organisation; finance for elections was a mere fraction of that available to more conservative parties, backed as they were by commercial interests. Writing in 1955, L. F. Crisp could say:

> Never, in all probability, has a major party been so unwilling as the Labor Party to tax its members sufficiently to provide an adequate national treasury …
>
> As Forgan Smith [Queensland Premier] said to the 1939 Federal Conference, 'we have the cheapest Labor Party in the world as far as cost of organization goes'.
>
> … For the first thirty years of its existence the Federal Executive lived on budgets which would have shamed an outer-suburban football team.[5]

Labor had to rely on their branches' meagre membership fees, chook raffles, fetes and socials, or slush funds from breweries, hoteliers and bookmakers, or loans and gifts from their cobbers.

Only in 1950 did the federal party meet the salary of a full-time federal secretary (or, for that matter, stenographer), but relied on state services. Even then, the salary paid to Kennelly took into account that he was drawing salary and allowances as Leader of the Opposition in the Victorian Legislative Council. When the Santamaria Movement gained control of the Victorian branch and deprived him of his seat in 1951, Kennelly was in a desperate personal situation. The Movement realised that, with only his secretarial salary, Kennelly would be unable to effectively oppose their faction. Kennelly was saved by a federal double dissolution which saw him gain endorsement for and victory in the Senate. This was not without impact on the development of the 1954–5 Split.[6] At the fatal election of 1949, after eight years in office, the total expenditure of Labor was £100,000, a large part of it voluntary levies on unionists and members. The Menzies coalition parties, financed by the banks (terrified of nationalisation), doctors (ditto), major commercial interests and anti-socialist zealots, spent ten times that amount.[7]

Wren was not unique. There were other benefactors, less publicised: J. P. Jones, who began work in stables aged eight, renounced Catholicism, became Melbourne's first pay-as-you-wear tailor in the 1890s, subsidised the Labor paper *Tocsin*, of which he became founding secretary, became secretary of the North Melbourne branch of the Labor Party, became a most successful businessman and MLC, held portfolios under Labor premiers Prendergast and Hogan, and, like Hogan, was eventually expelled from the party.[8]

Then there was J. J. Liston, the noted spokesman for the liquor trades who has been neglected by historians. Born in Ireland in 1872, a Catholic, he began life as a hairdresser, became a publican and by 1906 was secretary of the Liquor Trades Defence Union, naturally detested by the suppressionists like Judkins, Worrall and Woodfull. Liston was seven times mayor of Williamstown, and in the 1920s was said to 'run the town'. In 1930 he resigned from the council after being cleared of 'grave irregularities'. After vigorous service on the Melbourne City Council from 1923, he was defeated by one vote in 1931 for the lord mayoralty. He led the 'wets' in the anti-prohibition victories in the 1930 and 1938 referenda. Mannix attended his funeral; Scullin was a pallbearer. He is commemorated by the trophy for the best and fairest player in the Victorian Football Association and by the noted weight-for-age horse race, the J. J. Liston Stakes. David Dunstan rightly notes:

> In his rise from humble origins and in the scope of his influence Liston may be compared with his co-religionist John Wren … bestowing patronage on sporting and charitable associations and performing unpublicized acts of kindness during the Depression.[9]

Later we will see Wren take his place as an organiser, publicist and even orator among some of the foremost Labor politicians of his time, but it is unlikely to erase the sleazy image so cultivated by uninformed Yarrasiders, ethnosectarians and academics who have experienced only the post-1960s gentrification of Melbourne's inner suburbs. However, Sir John Jungwirth, for example, who worked for thirteen Victorian premiers either as a private secretary or secretary of the premier's department, has recorded how he first met Wren when travelling with premier E. J. Hogan to Sydney, to a premiers' conference. Wren and Hogan 'were acquainted', he wrote succinctly and, although himself a self-confessed wowser, he sensed nothing sinister:

> Wren and Hogan close associates? I never really knew. Certainly confidants of Wren saw Hogan at Parliament House from time to time. These interviews were always private. I had no knowledge of the matters discussed. Of course, in my young days I had been warned about Wren's Collingwood 'Tote'. To me gambling was a social evil which never helped needy people. Wren's great crime was that the Tote made him wealthy.

Obviously there is naivety here, but it shows what a lack of reliance on hearsay and scurrility can do for first impressions:

> Soon after we left Spencer Street station … [Harold] Glowrey MLA [who managed Moroco East property in the Riverina for Wren] … a member of the Country Progressives [and so a link with a later premier, Albert Dunstan] brought Wren to our reserved compartment. We had a general discussion just as any group of men would do. Wren invited us along to the Sydney Stadium the

> following night to see the boxing. It was an interesting experience. The more blood the fighters shed, the more the women in the audience cheered. Fifty years have gone by and I have never seen a second fight. On that and other occasions Wren appeared to be a mild-mannered, so softly spoken man with a wide knowledge of public affairs. He was reputedly influential in some of our leading financial and publishing institutions.[10]

Wren was singled out for particular denunciation among potential 'godfathers', not just because he was so spectacularly successful in business and seemed insidiously influential in politics but also because he was Catholic, 'Irish' and 'Labor'—hence, the 'Tammany' label. At the beginning of the twentieth century Catholic clergy were increasingly supporting the Labor Party, once it was clear that pragmatic rather than 'continental', doctrinaire (that is, anti-religious) socialism was its objective. While efforts to discredit Labor ('riding the socialistic tiger') by the Conservative former prime minister George Reid were supported by the Protestant Defence Association, they were opposed by Cardinal Moran, who went so far as to say that 'if some insisted on calling Australian Socialism what he called Australian democracy, then he was prepared to identify his name with Australian Socialism'. [11]

From 1901 to 1906 Labor representation in the federal parliament rose from 14 to 26; in New South Wales from 1898 to 1907 it rose from 19 to 32, among whom Catholics increased from 1 to 12; in Victoria from 1897 to 1907 the increase was from 8 to 21.[12] Catholics found Labor congenial for reasons of class but also because of its lack of sectarianism; while it did not support State Aid it did oppose teaching the bible in state schools, which Catholics saw as, effectively, Protestant proselytism. Moreover, Irish-Australians (and Laborites) had not shown loyalty to the Empire during the Boer War—Moran saying that 'He understood that one of the special purposes for which their volunteers had gone to South Africa was to assist in annexing certain goldfields that had become very attractive to their British friends'.[13]

To cap this there was the question of Home Rule for Ireland, anathema to Orangemen. The Commonwealth parliament resolved in favour of it in 1905, prompting 'a political mobilisation of Protestant loyalists'. To one prominent 'temperance movement enthusiast' and member of the Protestant Electors' Committee, the main issue at the

1906 federal election was 'whether Australia was to be ruled from the Thames or from the Tiber'. To be able to smear Labor and the Catholic Church with tales of corruption through association with Wren was too good an opportunity to miss. Even the radical *Bulletin* (and its offshoot, the *Lone Hand*), which had its own agenda for a non-socialist Labor Party—the party was allegedly 'full of cranks and extremists'—fostered the idea that its opposition to the 1906 Anti-Gambling Bill was due to corruption rather than to principle and preference.[14]

Early interventions?

The 1898 Police Offences Act, drawn up by (Sir) Isaac Isaacs, is a credible point from which to try to trace Wren's interventions in politics. The *Australasian Typographical Journal* suggested that John Hancock (Labor) had caused its defeat. But any single contrary vote could be regarded as decisive. A future premier, John Murray, was one who later regretted his negative vote. Hancock did speak passionately against privileged clubs such as Tattersalls and the Victorian Club, but Bongiorno properly says there is no evidence of any association between Hancock and Wren. Nevertheless, given Wren's personality and his identification with Labor in his youth, he may well have participated in Hancock's campaign in the by-election in 1891 in Collingwood. With vigorous support from unionists, Hancock won easily against the opposition of the *Age* and the local *Observer*. 'Every boot-factory in Collingwood was turned into a Hancock Committee Room'.[15] Although Hancock had transferred to Footscray by 1894, it would be surprising if he did not know the Tote owner whom Isaacs suggested was earning £20,000 a year in 1898 and against whom particularly his Bill was aimed. That does not mean Hancock was being bribed. In any case, anti-Labor MLAs were just as decisive. Frank Madden, no admirer of Wren, spoke derisively against the Bill. It reminded him of the Irish St Stephen's (Boxing) Day sport of 'hunting the wren':

> all the farm hands, stalwart fellows with sticks in their hands, hunting the wren from furze bush to furze bush. When one man, perhaps a bigger fellow than myself, struck a wren to the ground, he would glory in it and say: 'I killed a wren with one stroke of my two-handled wattle.' This Bill is the two-handed wattle of the Attorney-General to kill the Collingwood Wren.

At the very least it is impossible to say that Wren money defeated the Isaacs Bill; at the most it is improbable.

The *Lone Hand* said that it was not until 1901 that Wren was 'openly spoken of as an influential wire-puller by members of the local Labor Party'. The 'Bootmakers of Collingwood', it said, claimed that by backing P. J. O'Connor in a state by-election in Fitzroy, Wren had caused the defeat of P. W. McGrath, the Trades Hall candidate. But here, already, there is a problem. The *Lone Hand* went on to say that O'Connor was 'soon to lose his seat through supporting Premier Irvine [no admirer of Wren], so he is not to be accused of having truckled to the Tote Boss'. Then what was the point the *Lone Hand* was trying to make? Only that any support by Wren for particular politicians was, because it was *Wren*, reprehensible? The *Tocsin* suggested that the rowdyism and brawls at McGrath's meetings were connected with Wren and 'Tammany tactics', but the melees in Fitzroy (and Collingwood and Richmond) could be quite independent.

Sectarianism was a lively issue in this election. The Catholic *Tribune* saw the Trades Hall politicians who supported McGrath as having 'a dead set on Catholic candidates'. O'Connor was not only a prominent Catholic but a former mayor of Richmond, a current member of its City Council and a member of the Board of Works. Moreover, many Fitzroy residents 'resented what they considered to be Trades Hall dictation'. The *Tocsin* (2 May 1901) also noted that the Victorian Political Labor Council turned down a deputation of the Fitzroy branch in favour of O'Connor because it wanted a 'Labor candidate'. McGrath finished at the bottom of the poll with 478 votes; O'Connor won with 1,187. This was hardly a vote of confidence in the Trades Hall and scarcely the sort of result where money was decisive.

Janet McCalman calls O'Connor the first 'Wren man' in the Victorian parliament. If so, O'Connor was no use to Wren after the general election of 1902, when he was defeated. No mention is made of O'Connor's third out of four candidates in the federal election of 1901 in Yarra (including Richmond), where he polled 27 per cent of the votes and the Congregationalist teetotaller, Frank Tudor, won 33 per cent. Again, in 1904, after intrigues and compositions in the Labor branches within the Legislative Council's Melbourne East electorate, O'Connor failed to win Labor preselection and finished at the bottom of the poll behind both Labor and non-Labor candidates. As Bongiorno says, 'If

Wren was already a puppeteer in 1904, he certainly had not perfected the art'.

The *Bulletin* alleged in 1904 that Wren was branch-stacking in Abbotsford in favour of Labor candidate W. D. Beazley. As Beazley was opposed to legalising the totalisator, the *Bulletin* thought that he was necessarily trying to protect Wren's patch! In fact, Beazley's eminence in Collingwood far preceded Wren's. He was founding president of the Collingwood Football Club and thereafter president for twenty years, MLA for Collingwood from 1889 until his death in 1912, three times mayor, and founding president of the Collingwood Cricket Club. Beazley did not need Wren; in 1904 he was elected unopposed.[16]

Federal influence

Quite ridiculous was the claim in *Liberty and Progress* (25 May 1907), the journal of the Victorian Employers' Federation, that in the federal government of 1904 'John Wren was of much more importance to Cabinet councils than the Prime Minister, J. C. Watson'. Federation in 1901 had added a tier to government in Australia, so that a 'meddling millionaire' with a club in the middle of Melbourne, from then to 1927 the acting capital city, could be expected to know some politicians. However, notwithstanding what comes later in regard to H. V. Evatt and others, only an obsessional mind could conceive (without any evidence) of Wren nobbling J. C. Watson, W. M. Hughes, Andrew Fisher and H. B. Higgins in 1904, when federal politics did not in any case impinge directly on his interests. The *Liberty and Progress* article was reprinted in Cornelius Crowe's *The Inquiry Agent* (1909) and dredged up for the Victorian Protestant Federation's (or Herbert Brookes's) *Vigilant* in 1920—both fitting contexts.

A little weight was given to this allegation by the flaunted friendship between Wren and Labor senators Anderson (né Andrew) Dawson and Ted Findley. They had proposed and seconded respectively Wren's health at the City Tattersalls celebration of Murmur's Caulfield Cup victory in 1904. Dawson also defended Wren rather impetuously in 1906 against suspicion that he had engineered the O'Donnell bombing. He had gained immortality for one reason only: he had been premier of 'the first Labor government in the world' (from 1 to 7 December 1899 in Queensland). He gave a public lecture on 'socialism' at City Tattersalls in 1904 with Wren in the chair. Whatever it was he said would have been very pragmatic as he was 'a reformer rather than an ideologue', who favoured 'judicious alliances with Liberals'. This later estranged him from Labor but would not have worried Wren, no ideologue himself. Dawson may have found congenial company at City Tatts, although he would not have been able to slake his 'thirst for strong liquor' on its unlicensed premises.[17] But he was an impecunious and lonely figure. However, as minister for defence, during Watson's brief four months of office, his usefulness to Wren must have been for window-dressing only, unless the allegedly villainous gambler was simply capable of friendship. Obviously it was Dawson whom the *Bulletin* meant to be Wren's 'own tame senator', a characteristically fleering quip.

Nor was Findley a likely Wren acolyte, although some eyebrows would have been raised because he was a fellow-Catholic. Findley had been president of the Trades Hall Council in 1896–7, and a founder with G. M. Prendergast of the Labour papers *Boomerang* (1894) and *Tocsin* (1896). He had been expelled from the Legislative Assembly in 1901 for printing and publishing a 'seditious libel' of King Edward VII in *Tocsin*. He served in the Senate for many years and was an honorary minister in the Fisher cabinet in 1910–13. Having opposed compulsory military service as early as 1908, he remained with Labor in 1916. Ross McMullin refers to the 'conspicuous' presence of the two senators at Murmur's victory celebrations, and implies that this was reprehensible, if not sinister. 'The race was rumoured to be rigged by the winning owner,' McMullin writes.[18] There were indeed rumours. But the race was certainly not rigged.

Influential?

Edgar Wilkins, in spite of twenty years' public service was, according to the wowsers and the Orange Lodge, contaminated. Although he was an Anglican and a Freemason, and sent his sons to Scotch College and his daughters to Presbyterian Ladies' College, he admitted to friendship with Wren. Wilkins had been a butcher in Collingwood, entered the Council in 1889 and been three times elected mayor. He defeated Hancock, Beazley and others for the Legislative Assembly in 1892, by a very large majority. According to the *Cyclopaedia of Victoria* (1903) he was 'successful in obtaining the insertion of a clause in the Shops and Factories Act, giving employees a half-holiday every week, and shortening the hours of labour'. He had also participated on the 1897 Royal

Commission into Law Reform and became a Labor member.

In June 1908, however, Wilkins had the temerity to challenge the Rev. T. S. B. Woodfull to a debate on whether the worthy parson had exaggerated the state of poverty and insanitary conditions in Collingwood. The mayor, Councillor Rain, presided. Rev. Woodfull was supported by Rev. George Tregear, Grand Chaplain of the Orange Lodge. Doors were shut at 6.50 pm, and the debate scheduled for 8 pm. There was 'great cheering from both sides'. The ladies, who had taken up positions early, waved their handkerchiefs at Woodfull. Aside from the subject at issue, Woodfull alleged Wilkins had shirked crucial votes in the House of Assembly and 'had been a champion of the Tote which was a disgrace to Collingwood'. Wilkins protested:

> [Woodfull must have known that he] had gone all the way in the reform of the gaming laws and the Licensing Act. He was never associated with the Tote in his life and had never put a shilling on it, but he was not afraid to say that John Wren was a friend of his (laughter, oh-oh, and cheers).

Woodfull accused Wilkins of 'defending the worst form of sweating … landlordism … vice … breakdown of family life'. In the parliament Wilkins had never denounced the Tote (it was then eighteen months since it closed) and had received Wren 'at his banquet', alleged Rev. Woodfull (which, according to Scripture, may have been what Jesus would have done).

Rev. Tregear triumphantly took this up in his column in the Orange Lodge's *Australian Sentinel*: Wilkins, he said, had suffered 'an unmerciful castigation' from Woodfull and had shown his 'mental incapacity'; he was a 'Wren supporter, beer sellers' friend and general "smoodger" … Rome's champion'. He did not know 'how little Rome cares for him'. Wilkins had been too ecumenical. Tregear continued:

> The Sunday band concerts, the frequent guzzles, the fawning speeches at the notorious Abbotsford Convent (of the Good Shepherd) are bearing fruit … For twenty years, by truckling to Romanism … he has been a little king in Collingwood.

Tregear aimed to bring 'the Roman Catholic sweating den at Abbotsford

… under proper government control', which would be 'a victory for British justice'. Probably because Wilkins had progressed by this time from being a retail butcher to a wholesale business at the Metropolitan Meat Market, it was useless to suggest he needed Wren's lucre. But being a 'friend' was enough to incur Tregear's Christian contumely.[19]

Apart from Frank Anstey, the other notable Labor MP of this period whose name is associated with Wren's is Robert Solly. As a bootmaker Solly had worked in Collingwood in 1886, and become prominent in the Victorian Operative Bootmakers' Union and its secretary during 1901–4. He was a founding member of the Richmond branch of what became the Labor Party; in 1901 he was president of the Trades Hall Council, and in 1903–9 the first Labor member of the Richmond City Council. A short period as MLA representing the Railway Officers during 1904–6 was interspersed with five unsuccessful attempts to win federal and state seats. The *Lone Hand* asserted that Solly's meetings were attended by intimidating Wren ruffians, not a foolproof way of influencing secret ballots. Was Wren so crass or was rowdyism simply a feature of inner-suburban politics? In 1907 Solly won only a quarter of the votes in Richmond against a Catholic cordial manufacturer, a philanthropist and 'fair employer', G. H. Bennett, who had held his seat through seven elections since 1889. So much for Wren's alleged power—if, indeed, he had seriously applied it then in favour of Solly, whose biographer sums him up as 'a man of sincerity, loyalty and fairness and admired as a self-educated man … Consistent in his principles, he remained on the left of the labour movement.'[20]

When Solly was preselected by Labor for a Carlton by-election in 1908, the *Bulletin* alleged that Wren's lieutenant, Frank Lawrence, had finagled the 300-strong ballot by introducing members of a two-up school. Gaunson was also in the contest, allegedly at Wren's behest, to draw off the 'liberal' vote for Solly. Whatever influence Wren may have applied in the ballot, Solly, as Bongiorno says, 'must have had [with his record as above] strong claims on the seat' of Carlton, which he was to hold until his death in 1932. The *Bulletin*'s allegations 'may have been partly sour grapes at the defeat of the type of middle-class radical intellectual [a former editor of *Labor Call*], with whom the journal had long identified'. Interestingly, a few weeks prior to his election Solly, even with Wren's help, had been unable to defeat E. J. 'Ted' Cotter for preselection in Richmond, allegedly Wren's territory. Cotter went on to hold the Richmond seat until 1946. Of him, McCalman writes: 'There are suspicions that he had connections in the 1930s with John Wren, but his early and best years in politics reveal him as no captive of the millionaire sportsman'.[21] Both Solly and Cotter appear to fit the pattern outlined by F. B. Smith: 'Once a working man ensconced himself there [in Parliament], he [often] lost his lower class allegiance in the douce world of clubs, patronage and patriotic functions'.[22] Although hostile to Wren, the historian of the Tobacco Workers' Union does not see Solly as some capitalistic stooge:

> it is clear that whatever his dealings might have been with Wren those dealings were considered minor compared to his overall influence and achievements in the labour movement spanning more than fifty years.[23]

Contrary to legend, not many Labor MPs seem to have known Wren well at this time. Martin Hannah MLA, who with Solly represented the Railway Workers' Union in 1904, said in 1905 that 'he did not know Wren and never had met him in his life'. Hannah led the Building Workers' strike in 1906–7 and should have met Wren then. But he 'opposed Wren's gambling interests in the Assembly'. When a Liberal MLA, R. F. Toutcher, claimed there was a corrupt association between G. M. Prendergast (later Labor premier in 1924) and Wren, the Tote boss wrote to the *Argus* saying he had spoken to Prendergast twice but not on any legislative or business matter. This was confirmed by Prendergast, who said the occasions related to unsuccessful attempts by Wren to get him to expose Sir Samuel Gillott's relationship with Madame . Prendergast must have forgotten having been approached by Wren with a scheme for a Labor daily in Melbourne, or perhaps it was just rumoured. This is not to say that Wren did not attempt to meddle in Labor politics at this time. According to minutes of the Political Labor Council of 1906, Frank Lawrence, secretary of Wren's City Tattersalls, offered it a donation of £80 to canvass the Essendon electorate—which was turned down. Frank Bongiorno is clear that there is no evidence of a close relationship between Wren and Labor politicians until 1907.[24]

However, Wren was obviously developing ideas of becoming influential in politics. The *Advocate* reported on 9 June 1906:

MR JOHN WREN CONTEMPLATES
STARTING A DAILY PAPER
IN MELBOURNE.

In reply to a testimonial which he had recently received at the Cathedral Hotel, Mr Wren, according to the *Sporting Dramatic Views*, said:

> He appreciated the address as coming from his friends, many of whom he had known as a boy, worked with them on the bench, battled with them on the cricket and football fields, and, later on, met them in the business walks of life. He had been subjected to much misrepresentation of late. That from the platform was not of very great account, but he had also to suffer from the statements of a section of the press, which had displayed the greatest amount of personal bias against him. He thought the time was opportune when a serious setback should be made against a paper of this class. It was his intention at no distant date to run a morning newspaper in Melbourne, which would be second to none in the world.

On 29 August the *Town and Country Journal* reported that Wren was about to spend £120,000 establishing 'a Labour daily', and that he intended to stand for state parliament. This was fantasy. Wren was too engrossed in his promotions and, even years later when he did become a proprietor, he showed little aptitude for newspaper management.

Trying to divine what association there was between Wren and a politician like Prendergast exposes the thinness of our evidence. Arthur Calwell (prominent in the Victorian ALP from the 1920s and in a good position to know) maintained that Prendergast was as much 'a Wren man' (that is, in receipt of financial assistance and under some obligation) as were other identities of that period such as Ned Hogan, Tom Tunnecliffe and Albert Dunstan. Ross McMullin agrees with Calwell that Wren 'knew Prendergast well'. His biographer in the *Australian Dictionary of Biography*, Geoffrey Serle, disliked this idea because of Prendergast's 'almost religious' faith in the labour movement and his reputation for integrity: 'as honest as the day's light … entirely trusted by his caucus as dependable, unselfish and always a cheery optimist'. Serle, a distinguished scholar, always found it difficult to accept that

Wren might not have been a malignant force in Labor politics.[25] The two positions can be reconciled only by scrutinising how Wren's reputation has been constructed and by whom.

The strikers' friend

'Historians have not been kind to … Wren … that most mysterious of Australian rogue-heroes', says Bongiorno who, though not over-judgmental himself, nevertheless seems reluctant to see Wren acting to help Labor or unionists without self-interest. Wren's intervention in the ten week Building Workers' strike between early November 1906 and January 1907 is revealing. This time he did more than meddle. The strike affected some 5,000 workers, who therefore received no wages over the Christmas period. The issue was the reduction of the working week from 48 to 44 hours. From the outset Wren supported the strikers, twice donating £200 to a public strike fund. He claimed that he also contributed a £5,000 lump sum. No firm evidence has been found for this; but, in view of the large private donations he made during his life, it cannot be ruled out. Bongiorno puts one such donation at £830.

Wren's most dramatic intervention came in January, when he offered to start his own brick works as a countermeasure against the 'combine' which had locked out workers and refused to supply contractors prepared to concede to the strikers. Wren offered to buy land at Thornbury, a northern suburb, but premier Bent declined the offer because—Wren was prepared to believe—the government wished to remain neutral in the dispute. Wren's bitter critics, Revs Woodfull and Carey, had made an attempt to mediate in late November, to no avail; it is not reported that their sympathies were with the strikers. The timing of Wren's offer (6 January 1907) appears to have been most opportune, as a mediating conference of employers and strikers and the highly respected Mr Justice Leo Cussen was to meet soon after. Wren supported the Cussen conference and did not attempt to upstage it. Rather, his offer would have acted as a goad to the brick suppliers to make concessions, although strike fatigue had set in and union funds were low.

Wren's letter of 5 January to the secretary, Builders' Strike Committee, Trades Hall, published in both the *Herald* and the *Argus*, is worth reprinting for its mixture of candour, rationality and artful partisanship:

Dear Sir,

Kindly notify your comrades that my offer to the premier for the purchase of State brickworks has been rejected. The refusal will, no doubt, temporarily retard me in my efforts to force a settlement, but I do not think that the premier is in any way blameable for his attitude of neutrality, which he is evidently desirous of maintaining. Rather let us refrain from any act or word that could be construed into an indication of partisanship. Most of his predecessors, as you know from past experience, would long ere this, have declared for the 'big battalions'.

In striking out in some new direction—now that we have failed in our initial attempt—I must almost unreservedly place myself in your hands, for I have no practical knowledge of this brickmaking business whatever, so put your experts on the scent of anything purchasable and probably profitable. I do not emphasize the word 'profitable', as I am willing to take chances—big chances—in an enterprise of this kind, as it is one that promises a beneficial result to those deserving it and a corresponding setback to the 'gold bag combination' who have adopted the 'thumbscrew' and the 'rack' of the boycott in preference to the legal reasoning and judicial calm of an equitable conference.

I have made your people a promise that I stand prepared to take a big financial risk in fulfilling, but I want to take every businesslike precaution in endeavouring to minimise that risk and, with that end in view, I ask you to provide me with some form of fair guarantee, which I would like to see endorsed by your unions, as to the measure of support to be accorded in the proposed venture.

At the conclusion of the strike, contractors requiring bricks will naturally look askance at the products of one who has been largely instrumental in opposing them in the hour of strife, and though in quality and price my bricks will be equal to those of competitors, still in the open market I must inevitably suffer as a penalty for having so openly identified with your cause. Now what protective measure can you suggest in such a case as I have outlined and what steps can you take to enforce such protective measures assuming that you succeed in devising one? Satisfactory answers to these questions and I am into business as far as my available capital will take me.

> I have not hitherto presumed to bother you with suggestions but I feel you should give the *Herald* proposition [for a settlement of the strike] the fullest consideration, for with a righteous cause and a just judge it is long odds on you passing the post with your head in front.
>
> Yours to the end in any case,
>
> JOHN WREN

Wren's subsequent interview with the *Herald* suggests he was quite capable of having composed the letter without assistance:

> 'Have you been offered any other land by private owners?' he was asked.
>
> 'Yes', replied Mr Wren, laughingly, 'I have been inundated with letters from people wishing to sell. I have not had time to inspect the properties but, unfortunately, some of them are too far out of Melbourne to be of any use'.
>
> 'Are you determined to start manufacturing bricks?'
>
> 'Yes, if the strikers give me certain guarantees. I do not intend to go into business for the purpose of flinging my money away'.
>
> 'Where are the properties you speak of situated?'
>
> 'It would not do for me to indicate them definitely until things are settled. I want to get good land so that I can turn out a better brick than the combine. In my opinion the action of the combine in refusing to supply bricks to contractors who concede the forty-four hours is intolerable'.
>
> 'When do you expect the workers to inform you of their attitude in regard to the guarantee you mentioned?'
>
> 'I understand there has been a meeting held already but that the committee considered points in my letter rather vague. I have explained those matters, and probably a decision will be arrived at today'.

The Master Builders' response was predictably sophistic: Wren's proposal would put workers in a contradictory position, it said. If unionists were to lay bricks only for contractors who bought from Wren then, horrible to relate, he would become a 'great monopolist', the very thing unions were supposed to abhor! As things turned out, Mr Justice

Cussen recommended a rise in wages though not the 44-hour week. The Master Builders accepted that; the strikers went back to work. The *Bulletin* could only see Wren as 'setting himself to bag the Melbourne Trades Hall bodily'. Bongiorno thinks Wren 'had his eye on the State Labor Party, as he made his donations to the striking building workers during the debate on the Gaming Bill'. This coincidence of the early part of the strike and the debates on the Gaming Suppression Bill was hardly Wren's doing. We can surely assume that his donations would have been made in any case, as they were on other occasions to strikers' funds. Moreover, Wren's letter of 6 January was written weeks after the anti-gambling Bill was passed and three days after the Tote was closed. Martin Hannah, who had led the strike, had voted for the Bill. As Bongiorno says, modifying somewhat his earlier attitude:

> Wren's relationship with Labor was evidently rather more complicated than most historians have allowed … it is possible that the motives for Wren's generosity were more directly commercial than most of his critics recognized. For a man who provided popular entertainment to Melbourne's working class, notoriety was valuable publicity. In 1906 there were even rumours that Wren would stand as a Labor candidate for parliament. 'Next to Mr Frank Tudor, MHR,' declared *Liberty and Progress* 'Wren is the popular hero.' At a rowdy election meeting in 1906 the crowd gave three cheers for Maloney (the Labor candidate, and a Protestant) and Jack Wren.

However, Wren's generosity can also be construed as going beyond cynical self-interest—more than enough to enrage the sanctimonious Woodfulls, Tregears and Careys. What an upstart he must have seemed to them and the employers. Why, he did not have the decency to be mealy-mouthed and at least pretend to be altruistic about his brick-works proposition. He made it look as though the business of business was gambling.[26]

Thirty-five years later Wren recalled to Jim Scullin, a former prime minister and his friend:

> As a mark of appreciation of my efforts on behalf of the various Trades Unions engaged in the great building strike … I was privileged

> to be presented with five beautiful illuminated addresses, which I have at my home. During the course of this strike, to which I contributed £5,000 ... At a public meeting, in a speech which was reported in the press of the day, I stated that I would try to prevent the men being starved into submission ... My support of the men in this strike created bitter hostility towards myself from the opponents of Labor. In nearly every strike, before and after Arbitration, I have never refused a genuine appeal for financial assistance.
>
> At all elections, both Federal and State, I have never hesitated to support, in a practical way, the Party and individual candidates, very often to my material disadvantage. My predominant desire is to help the class from which I sprang.[27]

Patronage

While the Tote operated, Wren's influence even in municipal politics seems negligible. In 1905 only one endorsed Labor man sat on the Collingwood Council, while one of Wren's associates, G. Pinkerton, finished last in the poll. Also in 1905 the next year's mayor presided at an anti-gambling crusade, and 9 of his 15 councillors in 1907 were teetotallers—unlikely pro-gamblers. Electors only slowly turned to Labor, and early politicians owed their success to pro-protectionism. This applies even to Wilkins and Beazley, who represented Labor before Wren entered the Tote and then outlived it. But Wren would not have discouraged his confidants from pursuing office within Labor branches. It is difficult to believe Frank Lawrence when, as vice-president in the Fitzroy branch, he denied that 'he had joined the branch as a nominee or at the instigation of Mr John Wren' and declared that he had 'nothing whatsoever to do with that gentleman'. His role at City Tattersalls had been more as 'public accountant' than secretary, he said. P. Kierce, active in the Collingwood branch, was Wren's official measurer at 'his pony meetings'. Still, as Bongiorno says, 'this is hardly compelling evidence of branch-stacking or Wren domination'.

There is no doubt that Wren paid at least the cab fares, and that Lawrence and Roberts manipulated ballots to insure Frank Brennan's Labor preselection for the federal Batman (Fitzroy–Collingwood area) by-election in 1911—although it has been suggested that there were candidates with better Labor credentials. Brennan was a lawyer specialising in union business who had nearly defeated no less than Sir John Quick in Bendigo in 1910. A state executive enquiry found no evidence in Batman of ballot-rigging or improper conduct by Brennan himself. His parliamentary career was to extend to 1949 (except 1931–34), including a term as attorney-general in the Scullin government. He was a pacifist opposed to involvement in the First World War, while in the Second he opposed at first even Curtin's introduction of limited conscription for overseas service. A staunch Catholic, he nevertheless in the 1930s was prepared to be accused of being a dupe or fellow-traveller for his support of communist-front peace organisations. His biographer writes: 'He always opposed any form of bloc activity within the Labor Party, Catholic or otherwise. He was a Labor politician who was Catholic, not a Catholic acting as a Labor politician'.

Wren had nothing personal to gain by being Brennan's patron unless it was respectability, in spite of opinions that he did nothing for nothing. Niall Brennan, Frank's son—in the 1940s a writer of satirical verses against Wren which his family found distasteful—gives a memorable description of going to Wren's office, aged eighteen, in the late 1930s to collect 'something which was waiting for' his father there:

> When I was finally admitted to the presence, I was conscious of a huge desk with a small head peering over the far side of it, as if the desk was too big for the man … He spoke a few words, slightly interested that I was 'Frank's boy', but no more than that, and handed me a wad of notes. It was about £80, and never in my life had I ever handled so much cash. The manner of his handing it over seemed furtive, and I felt like a person being slipped a bribe.

However, no one who knows anything of Frank Brennan (or, better, Brennan and his politically involved siblings) would accept that there were strings attached to what were legitimate contributions to a cash-strapped political party. An obvious enough example of Brennan's independence of Wren was his support of Maurice Blackburn, contrary to Roberts's machinations, in the notorious Fitzroy by-election of 1925.[28]

CHAPTER SEVEN

Wheels, Hooves and Sulkies

Plugging the Austral

IT HAS BEEN IMPORTANT for Wren's detractors to brand him not only as an extortionist tote owner but also as a cheat, a 'fixer' of sporting contests. The first serious allegation that Wren rigged a sports event concerned the victory of the famous Irish-American, 'Plugger' Bill Martin, in the Austral Wheel Race of 1901 held at the Melbourne Cricket Ground. Cycling was then a most popular sport. High cash prizes made competition torrid and rough. Team riding was rampant. Cycle agents sometimes acted as officials, so that disqualifications were not always fair. Cycling firms gave additional prizes to those who rode their machines. Although betting was illegal, successful wagers could be more lucrative than the prizes.[1] The Austral was the Melbourne Cup of cycling. In that year there were 152 starters. To reach the final a rider had to win several heats.

Martin was thought by some pundits to be past his prime for a hard two-mile ride on grass in which he was the scratch marker, conceding handicaps of up to 300 yards. Monty Grover in the *Lone Hand* was 'quite certain' that:

> Martin did not win [in the final] from nineteen [in fact, fifteen] striving opponents ... Several days before the final heat was decided the 'books' complained bitterly and figuratively that they were in

> the soup … Wren had taken all the money available about Martin's chance … consequently the 'books' found themselves unable to lay any odds whatever against the majority of starters. With the exception of Mick Lewis and one or two others … Martin's opponents were 'dead' and the whole community of racing cyclists knew of their decease. The doughty Plugger, acting by arrangement with Wren, made terms with the corrupted ones.[2]

But what did the reputable contemporary papers say? On 7 December, the day of the Austral heats, the *Age* reported 'some very high wagering'. Among others named, Mick Lewis was said to be 'much fancied'. So was F. Beauchamp, because of 'his brilliant finishes'. Martin was mentioned as having 'disappointed … last Saturday' [30 November], but it was chilly and 'it is well known that Martin always performs better in hot than in cold weather'. On the day of the preliminaries, however, Martin won not only his heat but also the Ten Miles International Scratch Race—which, one imagines, was not calculated to improve his price for the Austral. He was in good form, and the weather had been warm. Beauchamp was second. On the final day (14 December), the *Age* editorialised:

> With 'Bill' Martin who has, so far, never won an Austral, an unprecedented warm favourite for this year's big cycling event, together with the fact that several of the champions … will be competitors, more than usual interest centres in the great final struggle … The remarkable developments that have occurred in the betting have given rise to many extraordinary rumours as to intrigue, in which several of those remaining in the contest are alleged to have been concerned. It is quite possible … that there may be no truth whatever in any of these extremely discreditable rumours, but there is good reason for believing that the committee of the Melbourne Bicycle Club will be found quite prepared to take drastic action in the event of any reasonable ground for such action being shown by the running. The competitors will be very vigilantly watched. For this purpose two additional timekeepers and four additional umpires have been appointed … In the event of any coup being effected by 'crooked practices', the club is endowed with full power … to declare a 'no-race' … and to order the race to be

> run again at such a time as they think fit. We understand the stewards … will not hesitate … to bring the rule into force … In the event of a 'no race' all bets will lapse as a matter of course.

Dodgy punters could have been unnerved by this.

The *Herald* (14 December) reported the result. The chief steward had read the 'riot act' to the competitors about the possibility of 'no race'. The afternoon had turned warm. Martin, in his white guernsey with a black ball back and front, 'looked fit to ride for a kingdom let alone the seven thousand pounds or so that his supporters had wagered' on him. Mick Lewis on 250 yards went to the front of his bunch in the third of the eight laps 'and there was an easy swing to his riding which must have made a few of the men who had backed Martin and others very heavily feel nervous'. At the mile Lewis went to the front on his own. With the end in view he was still riding 'as easily as a lawn mower'. However, in the back division:

> [Beauchamp] gave him his quietus with a stinging bit of pace to which Martin hung like a leech … Round the far corner Bill Martin humped his back, and moving all over the track, but with the speed of a deer, he passed the whole lot, and to the delight of the crowd … shoved his wheel home three lengths ahead. There was great applause, and it was renewed when Plugger, pale of face and sinking at the knees, was led up to the Lieutenant-Governor [Sir John Madden] and the Prime Minister [Edmund Barton] …

Barton's congratulations were 'enthusiastic'; he had 'apparently selected Martin' to win, said the *Age* on the following Monday. But it also reported that Beauchamp (10 yards) had been disqualified for a year (subsequently reduced to three months) for allegedly pacing 'in Martin's interest' instead of his own. However, 'most people who saw the race concede that the best man won'. 'His victory was clearly anticipated by many of the strident voiced callers of the odds'. The *Argus* agreed with both the popularity of the win and the fact that the best man won (16 December). Later (20 December) the *Argus* remarked on the 'many unpleasant rumours abroad during the three or four days prior to the contest'. Several starters were 'nominal contestants only', it said:

> But it would require a lot of money to buy out the Austral, and it would appear that the arranging had been overdone in certain directions with the result that some differences arose, and things resolved themselves almost into their original state: hence, on the morning of the race it was hoped, and some appeared reasonably certain, that the big race would be run on its merits.

The *Argus*, like the *Age*, deplored the betting that attended cycling and remarked that not only Martin was 'backed heavily'; so also were Beauchamp, Lewis and several others. When Beauchamp broke from his bunch he 'was seen to look back, ease up, look back again, and then bend down to work in earnest, and apparently for these antics was severely dealt with'. Lewis was too tired to gain a place. So apparently was Beauchamp. 'Plugger' Bill had to be helped to the victory stand, although the time for the race was relatively slow. He swore off competition events for the future:

> If anybody comes along with a match, pursuit, straightaway, or anything other like, I'll take them on, league patronage or not. But I'm sick of being pulled up in front of the crowd like a small boy, every time any fellow that's lost a few shillings opens his mouth. I can't ride on cold days that's the truth of it. When the sun's shining I can go, but directly the cold wind comes up, I'm all out, and then the crowd start hootin' because I don't win everything. I didn't win anything but the stake on Saturday but I've saved a little an' I'm goin' to settle down in Melbourne.[3]

An enquiry was held on 19–20 December at which a large number of persons connected with cycling were present, including several credited with having won large sums of money over the race. The winner, W. Martin, was also in attendance and, each time any of the officials appeared, he asked, 'When am I going to get my money?'

Seven riders (including Mick Lewis) were charged with not doing their best. One was absent from the enquiry and of the other six five refused to take an oath, although all denied the charges. A sworn statement by another rider, submitted on the second night of the enquiry, was not admitted. The officials submitted a report to the League of Victorian Wheelmen disclosing 'a most undesirable state of affairs which, if allowed to continue, must eventually destroy the sport of cycling'.[4] Plugger did get his money and no one suggested involvement by Wren.

Illegal betting at the Austral Wheel Race remained a problem. In 1905 the Melbourne Bicycle Club (MBC) collected fees from 'a strong force of bookmakers' operating at the race (that is, practically licensed them) in spite of the posting of notices stressing their illegality under the Sports Betting Suppression Act 1901. The Victorian chief secretary, Sir Samuel Gillott, responsible for the administration of the anti-gaming laws, was also president of the MBC! When complaints were made he denied personal knowledge of this bookmaking as he was barely involved with the club, he said—in spite of being president. He called an enquiry, which confirmed that, yes, betting had taken place.[5]

Oppy's disgust

More convincingly, because there is some corroboration, Grover went on to allege that Wren—through his 'commissioner', Sugar Roberts—rigged the 1903 Westral Wheel Race at Kalgoorlie, then rich in gold mining. A Yankee, Floyd McFarland was, he says, 'the fastest rider [Wren] ... ever had in his stable'. His victory could not 'be briefly brought to their financial bearings', says Grover in his article.[6] The corroboration comes seventy years later in the autobiography of the great cyclist and Liberal federal minister, (Sir) Hubert Opperman. He saw Wren as

> the current millionaire mastermind behind sporting promotions to which he had graduated from ownership of illegal suburban two-up schools [untrue] and dubious [also untrue] pony courses. He used the money for power, *entrée* into political corridors, gambling rings and sporting 'ramps'.

He alleged that Wren, quite unblushingly, confided in him and a group of bike-riders:

> MacFarland who had been backed heavily by the Wren syndicate, fell while training some three weeks before the big race. Immediately ... he began claiming a broken collarbone. His odds ... lengthened considerably. Only the select few knew he was training vigorously ... 'On the day of the race I asked him how he was

> feeling', Wren said, 'I'll win', he said, 'on a flat tyre' but, added this arch intriguer, 'To make sure, we paid a few to slow the front bunches'. MacFarland, a champion in his own right, won splendidly.

Wren allegedly went on to say that 'we had won 8000 pounds' and then, 'with breath-taking effrontery' complained that 'a couple of thieving bookmakers welshed on us for 2,000 pounds'[7]. However, there is an immediate problem with Opperman's story. Wren did not go to Kalgoorlie but sent Sugar Roberts as his 'commissioner' (necessarily by sea, via Perth), and there was no telephone contact across the Nullarbor until 1930.[8]

Still, my preference is to give some credit to Opperman's story rather than believe that Grover had reliable evidence which he was unable to disclose—and apparently never did—even though Opperman dispels the accepted image of Wren as taciturn and not given to expansive self-incrimination. However, the story needs to be put in context. Opperman's companions, battling cyclists, had been anticipating—'promised', they believed—that Wren's Motordome would stage a £500 Austral Wheel Race. However, its manager, Jack Campbell, under pressure, told them that Wren had decided not to do so. The National Cycling Union asked (Sir) Bruce Small to lead a deputation to Wren. Small was then the manufacturer of Malvern Star bicycles, made famous by 'Oppy'. He was evangelical in religion, director of the Melbourne YMCA for twenty-five years and, post-war, the most prominent tourism booster-developer of the Gold Coast, of which he became mayor and 'chairman of over 100 organisations' and for which he developed a vision of an Australian Las Vegas. He listed himself as a member of the Rotary and Masonic clubs.[9] His deputation to Wren in the 1920s was pessimistic because Campbell had said Wren never changed his mind. Opperman recalled:

> Five of us entered the room. Wren looked up with cold appraising eyes, opened his mouth and began what was obviously to be a sentence ending with a negative. 'If you've come about the Austral Wheel ...', when Bruce quickly interposed, 'Mr Wren, yes, we have come about the Austral—merely as a matter of form and to fix a date. We have heard rumours it is not to be held, but we gave no attention to that just saying, as I am saying to you now, John Wren

> promised a 500 pound Austral, and John Wren has never been known to break his word'.
>
> Wren pondered and then said: 'Quite correct, Mr Small, quite correct. Now what date would be the best for such a big event?'
>
> We settled that quite amicably and then Wren, still glowing from the rare and erroneous eulogy, became expansive and revealed a depth of chicanery in cycling affairs with which he has often been credited, but never personally revealed. He proceeded in detail as a mentor advising inexperienced worshipping youth, without a twinge of self-consciousness or indication in his thinking that there had been the slightest malpractice [in the 1903 Westral Wheel Race].[10]

It is interesting to note Opperman's disapproval of a man who was helping to keep professional cycling viable. Even though Small implies that Wren normally kept his word, and Wren accepts that he should live up to the cyclists' *expectations*—not necessarily his *promise*—he gets no credit for it, only contempt. Furthermore, as said before, gamesmanship and team riding were, and are, commonplace in cycling. As McFarland seems to have been the best rider in the Westral, at least some justice was done to the competitors if not the bettors. The problem with these denunciations of Wren is that they do not bear close scrutiny, rather than there being no grounds for suspicion. With motorpacing—as with wrestling—a serious problem was that it had to provide close contests that were entertaining. As Opperman said, 'demands from the box office for … fortuitous results became pressing … water interfered with carburration, leads were found to be dislodged from spark plugs'.[11] The impresario had to provide excitement or lose his patrons. Cyclists had to co-operate or lose patronage. This was not pure sport.

Some years later Small and Wren became involved in litigation over the contract of an Italian rider, Giuseppe Pancera, whom Small had signed up overseas on behalf of Wren's Melbourne Carnivals Ltd (the Motordrome). However, soon after Pancera arrived he hurt his ankle and 'performed indifferently in his first trials behind motorpace'. He was 'immediately disowned', says Opperman. Small paid him off and then sued. Opperman was in court when:

> Johnny Wren appeared from the shadows for the verdict; I sat alongside him … His dismay at the unpalatable judgement, with

> costs against [his] Melbourne Carnivals, was more that of a back-lane starting price bookmaker than the public image of an urbane millionaire gambler. He turned to a subdued [Richard] Lean [manager of Melbourne Carnivals] with the wildest and most irrelevant requests. 'Put in an appeal, send cables to Europe, find out all about him'. His bluster must have evaporated under more dispassionate advice for legally the incident disappeared from our [that is, Opperman's as well as Small's] lives. But the rancour lingered on and a break with the Motordrome became inevitable.[12]

For nearly a quarter of a century after Wren's death, this incident (as well as his general 'style') somehow lingered to irk the great wheelman. Oppy went up in the world, became a Liberal MHR and a federal minister and completed his career as high commissioner to Malta. When he returned to Australia in 1972, he expressed shock at what he saw as ugly changes in society: brawling at football, road rage, criminal behaviour in the streets, pollution. Prime minister John Gorton had had 'fatal flaws'; his successor, William McMahon, 'proved more durable'; and, sad to relate:

> The general citizenry, it seemed by choice, dressed like a depression-forced dole line and, *as with John Wren's old felt hat, symbolised a casual approach to wealth* [emphasis added]. The atrocious nasality of short-cut Australian speech and accent, even more intensified and ocker-educated by radio and television, smote harder on our ears ...[13]

Oppy's distaste for the *mores* of Collingwood and his native land mark him as overly class-conscious and unlikely to be an unprejudiced rapporteur where Wren is concerned. Like Opperman, Wren should obviously have become *nouveau riche.*

Murmur at the races

If the allegation that Wren rigged the Austral Wheel Race is at least possible, that he 'squared' enough of the thirty jockeys in the 1904 Caulfield Cup so that his 5-year-old gelding, Murmur, could win is fanciful in the extreme and shows ignorance of the Melbourne turf. Of all important handicaps—taking into account the special features of Caulfield over

$1^1/_2$ miles and with invariably class horses as starters—this race, as the accompanying note shows, would be almost impossible to rig.[14] Even Grover maintained that the allegation against Wren 'was probably an erroneous rather than a groundless suspicion'. 'The horse', he wrote, 'achieved an honourable success by three lengths'.[15] In spite of this, Manning Clark says Wren 'fixed *all* starters [emphasis added]'.[16]

The credible facts about Murmur's Caulfield Cup are related in Maurice Cavanough's *The Caulfield Cup* and by Hugh Buggy.[17] In 1903 for £200 Wren bought Murmur, 'a better than average sprinter', in Tasmania; but it was incapable of getting a distance, it was thought, although sired by the 1886 Melbourne Cup winner, Arsenal. Murmur won an undistinguished handicap at the Caulfield spring meeting that year, after which Wren put it in the charge of Frank Musgrave, one day to be trainer of the renowned Ajax. The handicappers dismissed Murmur with a mere 6 stone 12 pounds (43.6 kilograms) when weights were declared for the 1904 Caulfield Cup. To this point Murmur had contested only sprints. But the gelding showed promise under a stayer's preparation, and Wren began backing it at odds of 100 to 1 down to 20 to 1, even before weights were declared. He made no secret of his optimism and even seemed to revel in giving this tip to police and anyone in Collingwood. Murmur's form on the training track became well-known,[18] and in August and September it won two handicaps at 8 to 1 and 2 to 1.

However, there were better horses: Emir and Demas and, particularly, the mare Gladsome, belonging to that 'sartorial poem', Sol Green, the 'Leviathan of the turf' and proprietor of the Melbourne Tattersalls Club. The plainly suited Wren actually tried to do a deal with Green: let Gladsome and Murmur have a secret trial race, he proposed, so that the two of them would know what their respective chances were.[19] Green declined, although Gladsome would carry more than 2 stone more than Murmur. Gladsome went out a 7-to-2 favourite, with Demas at 6 to 1, Murmur and Wingaroon at 10 to 1 and Emir, brilliant but 'a cranky brute', at 100 to 7.[20]

Hardy, not surprisingly, gives a false but plausible account of the running of the Cup. But the facts are: Demas did go to the front too soon but then, at the barrier, he had drawn the rails; then in the scramble for a good position, he found himself in the lead but no pace-maker took over. Emir had the too-formidable weight of 9 stone 4 pounds (59 kilograms). Gladsome proved not to be adept in a handicap; it showed its class by winning the 10 furlong weight-for-age Mackinnon Stakes a fortnight later and the 1905–6 Futurity Stakes of 7 furlongs—twenty-four wins in all during its career.[21] However, the mare that finished second, Acrasia, won the Melbourne Cup a fortnight later and equalled Carbine's race record time. As Cavanough says:

> Murmur won because he was superbly trained, extremely well ridden, and most of all, because he got under the handicapper's guard. There was no inquiry into the race, by either the VATC or the VRC or any reason for an inquiry.[22]

And, as the *Australasian* said, 'No Caulfield Cup favourite had ever had a better run than Gladsome … she was not good enough'.[23] Murmur was given a 10 pounds (4 kilograms) penalty for the Melbourne Cup; that additional impost and a leg injury in a training gallop saw his price lapse to 33 to 1. He finished in the ruck. Wren had backed him to win £35,000. Acrasia's owner, the leading Sydney bookmaker Humphrey Oxenham, owner and founder of Oxenham's Consultations, rival to George Adams's Tattersall's Consultations, won over £40,000 in bets, but confided to Sol Green that he would not have backed his mare at all had he not known that Murmur was a doubtful starter. It had to be passed by three vets 'as likely to get through the race without undue pain'.[24]

However, Wren had already won £51,000 on the Caulfield Cup, a record win for any Victorian punter to that time, although quickly eclipsed by Sir Hugh Denison's double cups coup with Poseidon in 1906.[25] Wren gave Musgrave two-thirds of the £2,500 prize money, with one-third to the jockey, and £500 to the mayor of Collingwood for distribution to the needy—and he told two publicans in Collingwood to hold open night for all. Such largesse enraged Wren's enemies. He had special satisfaction in defeating Sol Green. But Green, by way of compensation, had purchased for £250 the ticket of the drawer of Murmur in George Adams's Tattersall's sweep, and won £6,000.[26]

Challenging the VRC

Wren seems to have first become an owner during the 1900–1 season when he paid 500 guineas for a mare, Melodius, with a colt at foot.[27]

Some unsuccessful purchases followed, until success with Murmur encouraged him to expand his stable. Nominations for the 1905 cups and Derby closed in August; for the Cups he entered Grand Rapids and, for all three, the winless Pius (most fallibly named after Pope Pius X, then reigning). But when he entered them for lead-up races and four of his colts, Tom Moore, Bob Roberts, Gapon and Winchester, for the 2-year-olds' Maribyrnong Trial Stakes, the nominations were rejected in early October by the VRC (Flemington). The Victorian Amateur Turf Club (Caulfield) followed suit. No reason was given. The *Argus* reported (5 October) that 'Both clubs, in other cases, have taken advantage of a rule which gives them the right to refuse entries without saying why'. However, on further thought they did allow the entries for the cups and the Derby to stand, and races where bets would already have been laid. Wren then tried to lease his horses to Frank Musgrave. The Victoria Racing Club (VRC) insisted on seeing the contract. On Saturday morning, 7 October 1905, both men met with the VRC Committee, which later let it be known that they had discussed whether betting shops were detrimental to racing. Wren had said they were not. A committee man told him that there was no imputation that he had run his horses improperly, although the committee declined to say then that the Tote was the basic reason for rejecting Wren's entries. Simply, there were other grounds.

Wren detractors have chosen to believe that the Murmur victory led to Wren's being virtually run off the major courses. Needless to say, if not 'squaring' the jockeys in the Caulfield Cup, then other forms of malpractice were now imputed to Wren as being those 'other grounds' for his unacceptability. And the VRC let it be so. It could hardly announce that the Collingwood Tote and the City Tatts Club were keeping crowds from Flemington and Caulfield, or that punters were getting a better deal from off-course-betting, or that the plebeian Wren would lower the social tone of the thoroughbred turf if he continued to be successful. How could he be allowed to receive the illustrious Melbourne Cup from the governor, or his wife the sash for the Oaks (the classic for fillies) from the governor's lady? There was much criticism of the injustice done to Wren and of its class bias. The future Liberal premier, John Murray, declared that the VRC's action 'could not be justified',[28] although he regretted that he had voted against the Isaacs Bill of 1898.

The VRC was unmoved, until in late September 1906 its chairman, toadying to premier Bent so that he would exempt the club from certain clauses of the anti-gaming Bill which were contrary to VRC interests, felt that he should stress the prudence with which the club conducted its affairs. Committee man R. G. Casey, father of the future Lord Casey, then explained:

> The decision of the VRC was not a personal one against Mr Wren. His entries were refused because Mr Wren was alleged to be the owner of a tote in Collingwood and it was looked upon as an evil influence in racing.[29]

In other words, the VRC derived nothing from backyard betting. It was no coincidence that Wren was at the time planning to open a racecourse on the fringe of the metropolitan area at Eltham, and proposing an annual £10,000 race—nearly twice the current Melbourne Cup prize.[30] Even the *Argus* thought the timing of the VRC ban on Wren 'rather remarkable'.[31]

Spiritedly, Wren turned to the ponies. Until late 1905 he had only wagered on them, but from that time he invested substantially in courses at Richmond, Fitzroy and Ascot in partnership with Ben Nathan, who had owned them but lacked the flair to make them a success. They were the 'the poor man's courses': six shillings for the Grandstand (a half crown for ladies) and 'two bob' for the Leger (or cheaper section, usually away from the winning post). Nathan, the son of a part-Jewish gold-rush immigrant, was also born in Collingwood.[32] He allegedly played in the original Fitzroy football team (before the Victorian Football League was founded in 1897).[33] A keen racegoer, he ran several horses and in 1896 'made racing history' by being the first punter (as distinct from owner, trainer and jockey) to be disqualified from attending the races for 'offering a £50 bribe to a jockey to pull a horse at Aspendale track'. Andrew Lemon remarks that he gained his revenge by patronising unregistered racecourses with Wren.[34] In 1910 he bought Rippon Lea mansion in south-east Melbourne (once owned by Bent), which became renowned for its garden, especially its orchids. He developed an extensive interstate financial business and an Australia-wide furniture chain-store, Maples ('There's a Maples store right near your door').[35] He died one of the richest men in Australia with an estate valued for probate in 1935 at £945,722, the largest in Victoria during 1935–9.[36] Wren was a pallbearer at his funeral.

The Victorian Pony and Galloway[37] Racing Club was formed with Wren as manager; with three meetings a week, they kept punters from Flemington and Caulfield and reduced the pool of betting money for those courses. But even premier Bent came to acknowledge that Wren had 'done much to purify pony races'.[38] So did moralists like (Sir) Frederick Eggleston.[39] Such a claim in relation to trotting made Monty Grover dyspeptic, but he could not deny it.[40] Most audaciously in 1906 Wren proposed to the Bent government that it lease Flemington to him for £25,000 per year. The VRC paid virtually nothing in rent for it. The premier declined the offer but not without teasing the VRC and causing apprehension.[41] A decade later, when flooding of the Maribyrnong River onto the Flemington course postponed the traditional Tuesday Melbourne Cup meeting, Wren advanced his Ascot Wednesday meeting by a day. As this was a holiday, he made a killing. No doubt it gave him satisfaction, and the VRC chagrin.

Buggy described the pony scene before Wren as 'being gradually throttled by a layer of welshers, scalers, race-riggers and ferret-faced crooks eager to turn a dishonest quid'.[42] Jocularly referring to him as 'St Wren', *Truth* enthused about his ruthless methods with the 'hooks and crooks' on the one hand and his disciplined procedures on the other.[43] Having regard to his treatment by the VRC, Wren decreed that a nomination would be withdrawn only if the owner was guilty of malpractice, and all inquiries were open to the press. He was well ahead of the VRC in his use of stewards, whom at first he chaired himself. They could prevent a jockey from riding in a race if his mount's price fell without an adequate reason or if prices did not match performance. The stewards were empowered to replace a jockey, and gained a reputation for independence of owners, trainers, riders and bookmakers.

Among those eventually warned off the pony courses was Squizzy Taylor, who was alleged to have threatened to kill Wren as he had threatened other identities such as police commissioners and the committee of the Victorian Amateur Turf Club.[44] Wren was concerned enough about people like Taylor to keep a gun. One trainer who was disqualified for pulling up a hot favourite stormed into Wren's office, threatening to shoot him. According to Buggy:

> Wren quickly drew a pistol from a drawer and slapped it on the desk. 'Well, here's my gun. Now where is yours?' he asked. 'You say I

> ruined you. I would say you sent hundreds home broke yesterday. Now what about that?' The bluff was called and the purple-faced trainer left.'[45]

When the racing dates were savagely cut in 1907, Wren raised his prize money and increased his program from six to seven races. An Ascot Five Hundred Pounds was instituted for ponies and then, audaciously, a stake of £3,000 was offered for a mile race, the second largest in Australia after the Melbourne Cup. In the short term he failed to break the VRC's ban on horses running on unregistered courses. But pony racing at least became more lucrative to participants and attractive to the public.[46] By early 1908 Wren's reforms and financial backing were such that the VRC had to recognise pony racing officially.[47] On 16 January 1919 the *Hawklet*, a popular sportspaper, commented:

> Pony racing is no longer the Cinderella of horse racing. In fact, Wren's meetings are now established on a sounder basis than many of our other meetings. It is not so long ago that it was not considered fashionable and proper to patronise these meetings, but that time has passed, and the many pony racing reforms, the close control and excellent management have won for these meetings a recognition that no racegoer can challenge.

In harness

Hardy is at odds with Max Agnew, the leading authority on Australian Harness Racing, over Wren's involvement in the sport. *Power Without Glory* has it that 'John West' became interested while in New Zealand on his honeymoon in 1901. On his return he bought three horses. One of them he named Nellie W., after his wife. It won several races but, because it was too much of a back marker, 'West' arranged with a certain 'W. J. Bennett' (W. J. Beckett, a Wren associate in real life), who is referred to as 'The Gentleman Thief', to get his brother, 'H. Bennett', to change the mare's name to Phoebe and take her to New Zealand. This was easily arranged, according to *Power Without Glory*, because 'W. J. Bennett' was the president of the Australian Trotting Association and secretary of the Melbourne Trotting Club (MTC). He issued 'a licence and certificate' to his brother 'in the name of Smith'. 'John West' and

'Bennett' were then said to make big money from Phoebe's wins but, when she returned to Australia, she was recognised as the former Nellie W. and 'Bennett' lost his presidency. 'West' was supposed not to be too concerned because he was already intriguing to get control of the MTC.[48]

Although a search for the alleged 'ring-in' scandal has not been exhaustive, there was no horse (standardbred or thoroughbred) running in New Zealand in the 1903–4 season by the name of Phoebe (or similar) or Nellie W. No placegetter in a horse race was owned by J. Wren or a Beckett or a 'Bennett' or even 'H. Bennett's alleged alias 'Smith'. (It was a forlorn period for Smiths in New Zealand harness racing.) Trotting was corrupt at the turn of the century and there was a New South Wales/New Zealand ring-in case in November 1903, an account of which was published in the Sydney *Sportsman* and reprinted in Melbourne *Truth* (28 November). A certain Charles White and his mare Edna (alias Chieftess, alias Tulip) were disqualified for life and, as this story appeared in *Truth* within a fortnight of one on the Collingwood Tote, this may have given Hardy the idea to fit Wren and Beckett with something similar. Greg Brown in his *One Hundred Years of Trotting* cites a November 1902 report in the *Sydney Mail* announcing a 'new non-proprietary club, the New South Wales Trotting Club' the committee of which came to include an H. Beckett. Brown also discusses the controversial figure of a Robert Beckett who in 1903 was disqualified for life for insulting stewards but only served a few months. It is not known whether they were related to Wren's friend W. J. 'Bill' Beckett, who was an owner-breeder, held office in the Victorian Trotting Association (founded in 1908), was for thirty years chairman of Wren's Victorian Trotting and Racing Association, and a trustee of the Victorian Amateur Turf Club (Caulfield). He was also twice mayor of Fitzroy and three times a Labor minister under Prendergast and Hogan. No evidence has been found that any Beckett was involved in the Edna ring-in, nor was any Victorian-based ring-in reported in 1903 in the *Australasian*, which was published in Melbourne and gave a comprehensive weekly coverage of all sports.[49]

Melbourne's first trotting track, according to Agnew, was at Elsternwick Park, but 'because of … wowsers was forced to close … as it was catering too much for the "working class" unlike thoroughbred racing which they never opposed'. Meetings were also held at

Maribyrnong, with occasional races at Sandown, Moonee Valley, Epsom and elsewhere, each club having its own rules. There was no permanent 'home' for patrons, and tracks varied in shape and size. A Melbourne Trotting Club was formed, but was 'on its way down the well-worn pathway to financial ruin and extinction' when in early 1907 it called a meeting at the Orient Hotel and in desperation invited John Wren. He became 'the salvation of the sport… and made the greatest single impact that trotting in this century has known'. Wren was attracted by the fact that the government allowed the club 20 dates a year. A Victorian Trotting Association (VTA) was formed, with Wren taking full control—promoting and staging meetings at Richmond which could offer proximity to the city (a threepenny horsecab fare) and cheap entrance prices. No doubt Wren saw this gesture of trust as one in the eye for the VRC and, if Wren deserved the ill-repute laid on him, it requires further explanation—never, of course, offered by Hardy and other detractors.[50]

Once appointed, Wren wasted no time. Years before the VRC would do so, he appointed supervisory stewards, of whom he would be chairman. He laid down these rules:

> Any bookmaker found guilty of offering a driver or trainer a bribe would be disqualified for life. Any bookmaker caught taking a bet from a woman or one [person] under age would have his permit revoked. Any trainer or driver found guilty of not allowing a horse to race on its merits, to be given the harshest possible penalty for the offence.[51]

While he accepted all entries unless there was specific evidence of malpractice, 'more than a dozen trainers and drivers were disqualified for life'. The first meeting was held on 11 May 1907. The first event, worth a mere £25, was won by Vermont Patch driven by Lou Robertson who, as a trainer, was to go to greater heights at the gallops, winning a Melbourne Cup with Marabou in 1935 and two Caulfield cups. The main event carried a purse of £100. Another was won by St Elmo driven by an outstanding horseman, Gus Milson, and owned by Bill Beckett. Milson then went to Sydney where he became its 'finest trainer'.[52]

Within weeks the crowds at Richmond were bigger and better than at any trotting venue in Australia. Other tracks were phased out. Some dissenters had formed the Epsom Trotting Club, but it lasted only three meetings. As Agnew put it, 'Wren had the happy knack of being able to provide the public with what it wanted'. He understood publicity and co-operated with C. J. Meehan, who founded the *Australasian Trotting Record* in 1906, a time when the dailies took little notice of such a struggling sport. Meehan was rewarded in 1914 when he became secretary of the Victorian Trotting Association. Trotting was included in what became J. J. Miller's famous *Guide*; Beckett compiled that section.[53]

The Richmond course in Melbourne and the Epping track in Sydney competed in raising stakes. There was a difference between the New South Wales Trotting Club and the proprietary Melbourne club, however, that was necessarily remarked on in New South Wales; for there the profits were ploughed back, while at Richmond they went to Wren. He had to keep Melbourne clients happy by offering higher stakes. Within two years a handicap was introduced worth £500. Wren foresaw that, having made trotting profitable, he would face objections to proprietary control. So the glamorous Melbourne Thousand event was born in 1911. A Sydney Thousand had to follow, and did in 1914. They were the counterparts in trotting to the Melbourne and Sydney cups.[54]

When the First World War necessarily reduced participation in sport, trotting was particularly hard hit. Furthermore, although all the investigations of the stewards had been open to the press in the interest of fair hearings, Wren, says Agnew, was to develop an 'arrogant and dictatorial attitude', acting with 'ruthlessness that almost bordered on cruelty towards any man who dared stand up against him'. Agnew insists that he used his power of disqualification 'as a means of getting rid of anyone who dared oppose him'. He does not, however, insinuate venality.

Hugh Coulter was a case in point—an outstanding horseman who was, it seems, vindictively put under life disqualification by Wren, but later returned to the sport to play 'an important role'. Prejudiced against Wren by a prominent owner, Coulter gratuitously upbraided him for his injustices while he was showing visitors around the Richmond course. Wren retorted with a threat of excluding Coulter, which he eventually carried out on what appears to have been a technicality. However, during the war, three years after Coulter's disqualification for life, Wren declared, 'in a display of vanity', an amnesty for those who would attend the course 'on a special day'. Agnew continues:

> Typical of Wren's manner in doing things, he had invited members of the press and other distinguished guests to be present to see him personally hand back the licences of those who came forward to accept this patriotic gesture from the all-powerful ruler of Melbourne trotting. John Wren seemed surprised to find among them the name of Hugh Coulter, who had traveled all the way from Adelaide to attend.
>
> When handing back his licence, Wren was heard to say, 'It hurts me to have to give you yours back, but it will only be temporary, I'm sure.' It was accepted without comment. The Adelaide horseman left the room, never again to return to Victorian trotting. Hugh Coulter went back into trotting in South Australia.

This is Max Agnew's unsourced story which, in view of his ungrudging attitude to Wren's early achievement in the sport, is acceptable.[55]

Among real Australians

One evening in 1909 after working back in the office, a lunchless Wren was dining at the sedate (St Paul's) Cathedral Hotel in Swanston Street, possibly contemplating through the window the promising cafeteria site opposite which he would eventually own as the Criterion. Pat Reynolds, the licensee, was a friend. Famous Young and Jackson's, owned by the Cody family, was further down on Flinders Street corner, but too boisterous even for a Collingwood alumnus now engaged in diverse respectable business speculation. As Buggy tells it, the waitress's greeting, 'Good night, Mr Wren', alerted 'a dapper, well-tailored man' at the nearby table. While Buggy prefers to believe in the mystique of pure chance, it is probable that Wesley Castles from Brisbane had been told where to find the risk-taking entrepreneur, because he introduced himself and came to the point immediately: 'So you're John Wren; I believe you're interested in racecourses'. Apparently Wren sized Castles up as 'an honest, straightforward citizen'. Castles does not seem to have told Wren why he had bought Albion Park in Brisbane from the Royal Bank for £30,000; now because it was losing money, he offered to sell it to Wren for £31,000. Looking at those bare facts Wren might have driven Castles to sell at a loss, but he jumped at the expedience that Albion Park—unknown to him as he had never been to Queensland—had 45 racing dates. Next morning Wren went to his solicitor, the federation father Sir

George Turner, and arranged a deposit of £1,000. Wren saw his backstop, Ben Nathan, and they sent the latter's brother and Barney Reynolds, his publicity officer, to Brisbane to clinch the deal. Wren could not make the 23-hour journey for another six weeks.

Wren told Buggy that he felt more at home in Brisbane: 'I felt I was among real Australians. I didn't want to be thought English like so many people in Melbourne. I liked the happy-go-lucky atmosphere of the city—even its soggy humidity.'[56] However, when he visited Albion Park the following day, he was 'staggered' to see an uncomfortably sandy, six furlong course with a notorious 'ti-tree turn'. He attended a race meeting which altogether attracted only about eighty-five patrons to pay the five shillings or half a crown admittance. Only twenty-one horses competed at the whole meeting, and the appointments were 'primitive' and the administration 'hopeless'. He immediately instructed Barney Reynolds to take out in his flowery prose full-page advertisements in the dailies for a £2,000 stakes program to be held in six weeks time. The Queensland Cup, run by the Queensland Turf Club (QTC) at its Eagle Farm course, was worth only £500. Wren went on to develop Albion Park, adorning it with tropical vegetation, grading the track, and planning 'classic' events such as a Sires Produce Stakes (£1,000), a Derby (£1,000) and a Futurity Stakes (£2,000). The Futurity attracted thirty-two acceptances, more than had run at the whole meeting that Wren had first attended there. By 1914 the renamed Albion Park Jockey Club was returning a profit of £30,000 a year. The QTC was obliged to raise its stakes. By 1923 they were greater than Albion Park's, QTC having the advantage of valuable cost-free land.

Meanwhile, and also with Nathan, Wren bought another unprofitable course at Sandgate (also known as Deagon). They made it pay, although transferring racing dates to Albion Park. It operated intermittently until 1941. In 1912 Wren and Nathan bought Kedron Park racetrack for £18,000 from J. B. Sharpe, and took a lease of night racing at Wooloongabba in the name of Frederick Thomas of Melbourne. Making no secret of their drive towards a monopoly of proprietary racing in the Brisbane environs, they leased Bundamba (Ipswich) in 1915. In 1919–20 a Wren-Nathan company, Doomben Park Recreation Grounds Ltd, bought out a Doomben Park Syndicate of some forty members who had each contributed £500 to buy a potential race course near the present aerodrome. D. J. 'Dan' O'Mara of the legal firm O'Mara and Robinson was its secretary. It began constructing a grass track and grandstands, but racing did not begin there until 1933.[57]

According to Buggy, the Sydney magnate (Sir) J. Joynton Smith unsuccessfully offered £350,000 for Albion Park and Kedron Park in 1918. However, realising that a Wren/Nathan 'monopoly' with its exodus of money southwards was being keenly resented, Wren proposed to a consortium led by George Dash, a Nationalist Party organiser and managing director of the *Sun*, that it lease Albion Park, although it was earning from £1,200 to £2,000 a meeting. This was refused, as it would have maintained the proprietary system Dash opposed. After some hard bargaining by Dash in Melbourne, a straightout purchase was offered and accepted. An option was also given on Doomben. The price has been variously assessed. Dash said the cost of the two courses was 'slightly more than' £275,000 with £58,000 paid in the first year and £4,000 a month after. Buggy and the Queensland Royal Commission into racing of 1929 said £450,000. The first year's repayments caused outcry as such profits were 'unheard of in racing'.

In 1923 the consortium was registered as the Brisbane Amateur Turf Club (BATC), with Cr Allen Oxlade as its first chairman. He was followed by T. M. 'Terry' Ahern, licensee of the popular Gresham Hotel where Wren stayed when in Brisbane, and then by Dan O'Mara. In 1954 the Irish hotelier John Delany was briefly chairman. In 1924 he had owned the Bohemia Theatre, which became a stadium, but negotiations for the sale of the building to Wren fell through. Personal links between Wren and BATC officials are obvious.[58]

As Andrew Lemon observes, the scheme Wren arranged for Kedron Park was remarkably similar to that of the BATC. After failing to attract a buyer, in March 1923 a Kedron Park Amateur Racing Club was formed with E. J. Lawrence (not Frank Lawrence) as secretary. The purchase price paid by the club in August was £21,000 with £229,000 goodwill. The management then paid £20,000 instalments each year to Wren, nearly double its presumed profits. After expressing concern, the purchasers were indemnified from liability. The terms were renegotiated in about 1929. The hostile commission reported that the bona fides of the club were 'generally doubted by the racing community'.

The Ipswich Amateur Turf Club was granted registration by the QTC after 1931. Lemon notes that the 1929 commission found that this club, though bona fide, was influenced by proprietary interests. Wren allowed the club to use his Bundamba course for racing, provided its meetings were not held within a week of his own. Then there was Goodna. According to the commission, the lease over Goodna was secured by two men in 1920, one of whom was E. J. Lawrence. There was also Strathpine, which in 1922 was bought by T. G. Jones of Melbourne, a son-in-law of Nathan. Finally, Coorparoo was acquired by Wren/Nathan interests in 1922. No attempt to trace the later history of these arrangements has been made. It appears that by 1922 Wren and Nathan had owned or leased all Brisbane and Ipswich racecourses with the exception of QTC's Eagle Farm.

Out west

Wren turned in 1912 to Western Australia, where some eighty-seven race clubs were conducted under Western Australian Turf Club (WATC) rules. According to Lemon, the West had for Wren similar attractions to Queensland, 'combining a growing economy with lax government controls on racing'.[59] A. E. Cockram, who claimed to be 'the largest owner in Australia of [120] horses and courses' with 'more capital invested in ... [them] than any man out here', leased Belmont Park to a Wren company, Belmont Racing Club Ltd, for £2,000 per annum. He had cut the course from the bush and spent £30,000 in improvements over the past fifteen years. It was run on a proprietary basis but under WATC rules. It had only six dates a year, while trotting 'was racing about 60', and Canning Park [also proprietary] had 'about 20 or 30.' He had 'originally paid £28,000 for the land, making his total investment £58,000'. He had, he said, 'refused £70,000 for the course', which was 'returning dividends of about £3,000 a year'.[60]

Of Belmont Park's first meeting under Wren management in May 1912, the *Australasian* correspondent said:

> [It] was boomed as no other meeting of a similar kind has been boomed in this State, and the result was an attendance of 3,000 people, which is easily a record for a proprietary course. Personally I thought more people were present. The prize money amounted to 890 sovs [sovereigns], 500 sovs being devoted to the principal event of the day. The other clubs give 375 sovs and on rare occasions 400 sovs.[61]

By August the correspondent was writing:

> Proprietary racing clubs are of late receiving exceptionally big entries for their meetings. For the Belmont Park meeting to be held this month, 173 entries were received for half a dozen races, and no fewer than 38 came to hand for the Belmont Handicap of a mile and a quarter. Proprietary clubs were not in the past favourably disposed towards the policy of the WATC of encouraging long distance racing, but if they continue to receive such big nominations they should have little to complain of. The total received for the Belmont Park meeting is said to be a record. The total for the long race certainly is.

The same month Wren announced that he would stage in December a race worth £2,000, the same value as the WATC's Perth Cup (except for its £100 trophy), which would be held as usual a fortnight later. It was hoped that this would attract 'a good class of horse' from the eastern states.[62] The meeting was so successful, with 6,000 present,[63] that in 1913 the WATC asked Belmont 'not to give a good stake' at that time because 'it interfered with their meeting'. Apparently that meeting was then cut out. On 20 June 1914 the *Australasian* described the Belmont Racing Club as follows:

> after a spell of four months, [it] held a meeting on June 6. The fixture was well attended, and it was noticed that since the last meeting a substantial amount of money has been spent on the course. Mr Wren evidently intends to make the property in every way attractive, and the racing track is a first-class one. Drastic measures have been taken to put the running track in order.

Lemon suggests that WATC restrictions may have prompted Cockram to build the seven furlong (1,400 metres) course adjacent to Belmont. He put it into the ownership of his brother, Horace, who in turn leased it to Ben Nathan, Wren's Melbourne partner. Goodwood opened in July 1912 as an unregistered course under the ponderously named Andrew Clydesdale (later to become an MLA). Although, when Wren had acquired Belmont, the *Australasian* said it was 'understood' that he had no intention of 'purchasing the unregistered course that had been laid down opposite', Lemon sees Goodwood as having had all Wren's 'trademarks', with £1,000 as initial prize money to induce owners and trainers into unregistered racing.[64] It was generally agreed that larger stakes resulted in 'straight racing'. As Detective-Sergeant Henry Mann told the 1915 Parliamentary Select Committee on Racing, 'If a race is worth only £30 or £40, a bookmaker can probably give more than that for a man to pull his horse up'.[65] Interestingly, the *Australasian* reported that on Saturday 31 December 1912:

> There was no registered racing ... and the Goodwood club held their 'Thousand' meeting. The stake money for the day amounted to £1,400. There was a large attendance, some 4,000 ... including the [Labor] premier [John Scaddan] and several members of the Parliamentary Labour Party.[66]

That Wren had himself been in the West and discussed his interests with Labor MPs is a reasonable surmise.

Clydesdale took control of racing on the Kalgoorlie–Coolgardie goldfields in 1914. In 1915, together with some founders of the Fremantle Race Club, he formed a Western Australian Racing Association (WARA) to control unregistered racing and extend the use of the totalisator at its meetings. Wren was involved in these developments. He had amended his Belmont Park fixture in favour of the Goldfields Racing Club in 1912.[67] As Clydesdale and WARA were also involved at Bicton and Kensington Park courses, a Wren link there is also possible. To the 1915 Select Committee of Parliament, the future Liberal/National premier (Sir) Hal Colebatch said he had no doubt that Wren had improved unregistered racing.[68]

However, the 1915 select committee found there was too much racing in the state—particularly during wartime—and that business and profit came before sport or breeding. The committee also found that the WATC had lost effective control of racing to the unregistered sector. As Lemon says:

> Its solutions were for a government board to be created to license courses, grant dates and issue totalizator permits, and so gradually reduce the number of meetings. It suggested the abolition of bookmakers, the suppression of street betting, and the banning of

> night racing. It indicated that the tote should not be permitted at privately owned courses and that members of racing club committees should not be allowed to own or lease horses which run at their courses. In short, the committee managed to offend almost every vested interest in the industry.

The government tried to legislate 'along these lines' in late 1916, but the attempt was abandoned. In March 1917 a Racing Restriction Act was passed which 'abolished unregistered racing but allowed Goodwood to be converted into a registered course'. The WATC was given power to allocate 76 days racing per year maximum within thirty miles of Perth (including the fortnightly and mid-week meetings at Goodwood). The number of race days was cut back from 102, in response also to the fact that it was wartime.

Racing historian Jenny Tomlinson suggests that the Act did not fully achieve its objectives: 'in fact, there were many other unregistered courses which continued to be governed by the WA Racing Association'. And, in her view, the proprietary and unregistered courses were not necessarily harmful:

> [They] did an enormous amount to promote racing, and they played a large part in establishing a strong basis on which racing in WA could grow and develop.
>
> However, Parliament was anxious that racing be more controlled and, although it was reluctant, the WATC decided it would be more beneficial to the racing industry as a whole in Western Australia if all racing was carried out under the WATC Rules.[69]

Wren and/or his agents appear to have tried to frustrate competition from the West Australian Trotting Association (WATA), which from 1914 was to be the first Australian club to run night (electric light) meetings. The WATA had been affiliated with Wren's Victorian Trotting Association, but in early 1917, as the *Australasian* stated:

> [The Victorian Trotting Association] cancelled the affiliation, and recognise[d] only the Westral Trotting Association—a body that has sprung into existence with surprising suddenness. The first club

> to ask the new association's permission to hold a race was the Goodwood Race Club (unregistered with the West Australian Turf Club).[70]

Resisting competition, the WATA's foundation president, James Brennan, at a dinner in April 1913, with a sympathetic Labor minister for works (W. D. Johnston) in attendance, attacked unregistered and proprietary racing for depriving the WATA of dates—and Wren, the interloper from 't'other side', personally:

> With the man who was endeavouring to secure the control of racing in Western Australia, money and the craving for money have ever been his whole desire. Was he the man they wanted to take charge of trotting here? (No). Was he the man they wanted to take charge of proprietary … and possibly also of unregistered racing? … Surely it was impossible for a man to come here and regulate the racing dates for the state![71]

To the 1915 select committee Brennan complained of dirty tricks (for example, bribes to cause dissension in WATA, and attempts to stack its membership, but also bigger stakes to lure patrons away). However, it is difficult to see how Wren could have spent much time (or any?) in the West to supervise such tactics personally. A reputation had preceded him … 'never been anything but a parasite',[72] said Brennan. This was far from being a universal opinion. Whatever his impact on trotting in the West—and no further information has become available—Wren had certainly given a boost to racing there.

CHAPTER EIGHT

Showmanship

WITH HIS FLAIR for showmanship it was hardly surprising that, free of the Tote by 1907, Wren's first major venture outside the sporting world was in live theatre—which had its heyday in Melbourne prior to the First World War, before its conquest by the cinema. The historic playhouse Theatre Royal was almost next door to the City Tattersalls Club. In 1908 its flamboyant manager Bland Holt retired after having made his fortune, especially with Drury Lane melodramas. One can imagine the disgust of the wowsers, not themselves ardent theatre-goers, when the billboards announced that Wren was partnering no less than Sir Rupert Clarke MLC of Kismet Park, governor of the Colonial Bank of Australia, in backing entrepreneurs Clyde Meynell and John Gunn to lease the Royal in Melbourne and the Criterion in Sydney.

The new management of the Royal showed initiative and vigour. The appointments and fittings were refurbished and its programs revised to challenge J. C. Williamson's Productions, which was just staging its *tour de force*, Lehar's *The Merry Widow*. The Royal repatriated from London the celebrated Oscar Asche, an old Melbourne Grammarian of 'matchless elocution', together with his wife Lily Brayton, to perform Shakespeare's *The Taming of the Shrew* and *Othello* to packed houses. Williamson's responded with renowned artists such as Sir Henry Irving and Dame Nellie Melba. Both companies cut entrance prices until both decided they were 'enriching their patrons at the price of impoverishing themselves'.[1]

In 1911 they combined. Meynell became a Williamson's board member. Wren withdrew, not having made much money but no doubt richer in experience. Since 1908 he had removed his name from the billboards, according to Buggy because he 'felt he had received enough publicity—much of it misleading and mischievous—to suffice for a lifetime ... he receded into the background ... and did not grant press interviews'.[2]

However, on his own accord Wren had announced in July 1908 the formation of a grandly named 'The National Opera Company under the Direction of Mr John Wren'. He was acting, he said, 'in compliance with a frequently expressed public demand' to revive 'a number of the world's standard musical works'. He was 'taking immediate steps to establish The National Opera Company in congenial surroundings as a firmly-based permanent Australian institution'. He had commissioned the noted impresario, George Musgrove, to recruit a conductor and principals in London. The season opened in August with Planquette's *Les Cloches de Corneville*, followed by 'the sweetly familiar' Anglo-Irish melodies of Balfe's *The Bohemian Girl*, Benedict's *The Lily of Killarney*, and Wallace's *Maritana*. Before moving to Sydney at the end of October, he announced with panache that his company would be recruiting the conductor Gustave Slapoffsky from Musgrove's 1907 German Opera Company. Grand opera—Gounod's *Faust* and Verdi's *Il Trovatore*—would be added to the repertoire before the season ended at Christmas. But then The National Opera Company ended too.[3]

Characteristically, Wren loaned his soloists for church services. When in September 1908 the United States Great White Fleet on its Pacific tour visited Melbourne, 100,000 people were said to have 'greeted 1,200 officers and men on their way to Pontifical High Mass' at St Patrick's Cathedral:

> Gounod's *Messe Sollenelle* (St Cecilia) was rendered, under the direction of Professor Fredrick Beard by an augmented choir. Miss Aileen Hodgson (prima donna) and Mr J. Ryan (baritone) of the new National Opera Company, by permission of Messrs John Wren and Geo Musgrove, took part in the solo portions.

On the next three Sundays Wren provided singers for other major churches.[4] The following year there was a report of a farewell to Mr Allen Doone, 'the Irish-American singing comedian', who attributed his success to John Wren's management of his Melbourne season. Doone brought the house down by galloping onto the stage on Murmur, Wren's famous Caulfield Cup winner of 1904.[5] In Melbourne in 1922 Wren backed the theatre and film entrepreneur E. J. Carroll, a devout Catholic, in bringing out the Sistine Chapel Choir, and in 1925 the famous violinist Fritz Kreisler. Ray Betts, a principal with Wren's accountants, Buckley & Hughes, says Wren anonymously sponsored musicians from Europe and New Zealand, not for money nor for his own entertainment, but just because it 'pleased him'.[6] In the Wren papers (19 April 1934) there is a cable from Longdon Care Musgroves Perth reporting on bookings in Perth and Kalgoorlie for concerts obviously promoted by Wren, to whom 'all good wishes' are sent by the diva Florence Austral and her husband, the flautist John Amadio.[7]

In 1915 Wren contracted with John Cranstead, a film exhibitor, to present vaudeville in conjunction with boxing at the West Melbourne Stadium. A notice in the *Melbourne Herald* in April 1915 details 'a strong program' in which Lilian Thomas's 'charming voice' will render 'Your King and Country Need You', together with

> Will Rollo a Comedian, Carno and Mack Gymnasts, Will Carroll Rag-Time Singer, Merlo Brothers Wire Walkers, Miss Elsie Norris Male Impersonator, Jessie Lee Sketch Artist, Jim Harris and Le Nords Expert Acrobats and Balancers. There will be several boxing contests and [champions] Hughie Meaghan [Mehegan] and Frank Thorn will be seen in action with their respective sparring partners.

Wren later acquired the freehold in Park Street, Sydney, of the Criterion Theatre and, in the same building, the Criterion Hotel (where he used to stay). He leased the theatre to Williamson's. Eventually he 'came to own the greater part of the block facing Park Street and bounded by Pitt and Castlereagh Streets'. In 1927, when the Labor-controlled City Council opened up the Bathurst to Park Street block to provide for the flow of traffic, the Criterion Theatre was demolished, although the hotel was rebuilt on a narrower site. A plaque there tells the story. Wren was paid £267,000 compensation which, inevitably, some critics felt was £80,000 too much and was due to his influence with councillors.[8]

In 1923 Wren became the financier behind Frank Talbot Pty Ltd, which succeeded Carroll in leasing the Athenaeum Hall, 188 Collins Street.[9] Talbot, 'genial and diplomatic ... last of the showmen of the old school', had managed tours by celebrities such as Emma Calvé, Sir Harry Lauder and Dame Clara Butt and travelled with the film of C. J. Dennis's *The Sentimental Bloke*. At the Athenaeum:

> it was largely Wren's finances which gave Melbourne its first 'intimate theatre'. This small and cosy playhouse was ideal for the presentation of drawing room comedies and dramas. Elaborate spectacles were not attempted and one of the earliest offerings was Barrie's *Dear Brutus* ... The Athenaeum attracted a distinctive audience. Its patrons became 'regulars' ... an intelligent, discriminating and critical patronage of a type which Gregan McMahon attracted to the Comedy Theatre in the 30s.

Between 1923 and 1929 a bracket of plays of high quality charmed Athenaeum audiences. They included *The Ghost Train*, *Outward Bound*, *The Sport of Kings*, *Give and Take*, *The Alarm Clock*, *Eliza Comes to Stay* and the Barrie plays, *Mary Rose* and *Quality Street*.[10]

When talking pictures depressed the appeal of live drama, Wren had the Athenaeum wired for sound and changed into a cinema. He was the first to show the initial talkie hit, Al Jolson in *The Jazz Singer*. In 1933 Wren and Talbot were persuaded by British Dominion Films Ltd (registered in Victoria in 1927–8) that the Athenaeum was 'ideally suited' for the launching of 'the first all British Theatre in the empire'. They were to break open 'the thraldom of Hollywood'. Although Buggy says that 'Wren and Talbot took a heavy hammering in the early years' before 'the vindication of their faith in the British industry', the imperialist *National Products Handbook of Australian Industries* (1934) was triumphant:

> Never in the history of the moving picture industry has a policy received such enthusiastic public endorsement as the all-British theatre policy introduced by British Dominion Films Ltd. It is interesting to note that both in Canada and India, all-British theatres have lately been established. Thus Australia has once again pointed the way.[11]

In the 1940s British films such as Laurence Olivier's *Hamlet, The Young Mr Pitt* and *Spring in Park Lane* became box office successes.

Wren also promoted some local film-making, putting up large sums of money, according to Dick Lean Jnr:

> He would have a crack at anything. Some thought him a 'soft touch' ... Failure often ensued. He sent a fellow named E. J. Stewart out the back of Broome ... [who] chartered a pearling lugger, took photos and made a movie, right round the outback, from Broome to Wyndham, of the ... [tribal] Aborigines. Then later—I can't recall the guy's name—they sent this guy over to America to sell the film, and that was the last they saw of the film or the guy.[12]

Wren's Criterion Theatres Ltd was incorporated in Sydney in June 1919 to facilitate transfers and to be used as a 'cash box' for family purposes. It obtained the major shareholding in Frank Talbot Pty Ltd soon after registration (2,990 out of 3,997 fully paid £1 shares, Talbot holding 997). Dick Lean was company secretary, and with Talbot and Wren constituted the board until Talbot died in July 1949. He was not replaced. When Frank Talbot Pty Ltd was liquidated in April 1968, Criterion Theatres remained the major shareholder and, out of total payments of £24,163, received a distribution of £4,861 and a dividend of £16,350.

Wren also appears to have had a substantial interest in three Melbourne cinemas: the Glen cinema and the Glen Palais ballroom in Hawthorn,[13] the Rialto in Kew and the Cinema in Richmond. Only the Cinema has been researched. Registered under Richard Lean Pty Ltd in September 1927, it was built on a prime piece of land in Bridge Road, Richmond, which had been leased by Lean. Among the initial shareholders and directors was Bernard Nolan, Wren's solicitor, with one share of the 25,000 at £1. Lean sub-let the Cinema to Hoyts Theatres. The Cinema venture was a typically complex scheme in which Wren's control was kept at a respectable distance. Wren did not deal directly with the owners of the site—the Church of England. Not that there was a great risk of scandal, the cinema being a legitimate recreational activity (cf. the Tote or Sir Samuel Gillott and Mme Brussells). The Church of England was not so vehement against Wren, but there could have been complaints that it was paid £850 a year (over thirty years that amounts to £25,500). Would the deal have gone through if signed by

Wren? But the church would have known who Lean was. A long-term lease required high-level approval, including the signature of the archbishop. Keeping Wren at arm's length was satisfactory to both sides, and the church protected its interests by the insertion of special moral and political clauses. In June 1934 Wren replaced Nolan as director, and in July bonus shares to the value of £1,400 were issued. Wren received the bulk of the bonus shares, suggesting he had taken over the major shareholding.[14]

The House of Stoush

While he was still running the Tote, Wren saw that there was a large potential audience for boxing in Melbourne but insufficient promotion—in spite of the enthusiasm at the turn of the century for tidings of Sullivan, Corbett, Fitzsimons and Jeffries, and pride in the past triumphs of Australians Peter Jackson and Young Griffo.[15] Only the Exhibition Building seemed to provide a suitable venue, and that had been sanctified by a royal visit, the opening of federal parliament in 1901 and other parliamentary and grand commercial occasions. Nevertheless, Wren managed to procure it for several of his earliest ventures in spite of howls of near sacrilege from the Judkinses. At a fight in Sydney in early 1905 Wren believed he had discerned a future world champion in the Newcastle miner Bill Squires, who packed a hefty punch in each hand but little else. He matched him in August 1905 against a Melbourne pug, Dick Kernick, who was one of Wren's Tote janissaries. Wren spent £1,600 in all, of which the stake, purse and belt at £650 was less than half. His advertising henchman, Barney Reynolds, filled over four columns in the *Argus* with ballyhoo, when displays of this kind were unusual. Reynolds extolled 'this greatest Fistic Festival ever presented to the Australian people' and a brass band heralded fans into the Stadium, where seats were priced from twenty shillings to half a crown. Kernick was felled in the first round but survived till the seventh. *Power Without Glory* portrays this combat not just as an opportunistic mismatch but as a farce. If so, the 7,000 crowd seem to have had their moneys worth.[16]

Ten thousand people packed the Exhibition in late April 1906 to see Squires defeat the well-performed American, Tim Murphy, in three rounds. Although Murphy conceded 8 kilograms, the puff was such that the *Argus* thought Squires was 'without doubt the finest fighter

Australia had produced in the last ten years if not in all time'. Judkins, at the Pleasant Sunday Afternoon on 13 May, denounced the fight as 'a menace to the morality of the community'. Hideously, one woman had gained admittance too.[17] Typically, without any apparent evidence, Manning Clark is in no doubt that 'Professional boxers received [Wren's] ... bounty in return for agreeing to rig a fight'.[18] However, Wren's promotions were so popular that the next Squires fight, with Peter Kling, had to be staged at his Ascot racecourse. In a fourth major contest, Wren had to fit out his Richmond racecourse, where 13,500 fans, the largest crowd ever seen at a Melbourne bout, saw Squires drop South African champion Mike Williams in the first round under a scorching midsummer sun.[19] Squires then by-passed a chance to fight the not yet so famous but much feared future world champion, the Afro-American Jack Johnson, in order to notch a win in America.

Wren sent Squires to the United States with Barney Reynolds as chaperon and publicity agent. On 4 July Squires fought Tommy Burns[20] for the world heavyweight championship; having won nineteen fights and lost only one, and that one on a foul, the Australian was favourite at 6 to 4 on. Wren had Reynolds wager £3,000 for him. But Squires had no finesse. His alleged 'cyclonic velocity' lasted 2 minutes 8 seconds. Wren was stoical as always when he gambled and lost. Squires had never been flattened before. Australians, he had to realise, were not in world class after all. One American commentator said Squires 'proved the biggest failure, who ever entered the championship ring in America. He showed no defensive tactics whatever.' Another said that Squires 'has a glass jaw'. 'Take your time, Tommy', said a Burns second; 'It's too easy'. Squires fought Burns twice later, in Paris lasting eight rounds, and in Sydney thirteen. At least his ringcraft had improved[21]—or Tommy's patience. Meanwhile, Wren seized the chance to pit Jack Johnson against the local lad, Bill Lang, at Richmond. After lavish advertising, but in slithering rain, 15,000 turned up to see Johnson toy with the local champion for nine rounds before knocking him out.[22]

Unable to hire the Exhibition Building after mid-1907, and having been prevented by anti-gambling legislation from staging fights at his racecourses, Wren had been using the restricted spaces of the Cyclorama and his Athletic Pavilion as best he could. During the state elections of March 1907 a pamphlet and leaflet campaign took place, advertising a League of Sportsmen with, imaginatively, 10,000 members. It aimed to return MPs who would modify or repeal the anti-gambling laws. It was attributed to Wren. It was unsuccessful. Bent and his supporters (but not Judkins) were returned convincingly. Conservatives were outraged that Wren was instigating what would today be called a 'pressure group', but in those days, says Buggy, considered almost seditious.[23]

It is ludicrous to sneer at 'citizen Wren', as Manning Clark does,[24] for promoting (and personally enjoying) a sport which was accepted ninety years ago and still is today—described by some as 'the noble art of self-defence'. Among Australia's champions were the lieutenant-governor of Papua, Sir Hubert Murray, a future governor-general, Sir William McKell and the celebrated doctor and war hero Sir Edward 'Weary' Dunlop. *Snowy Baker's Magazine* emphasised the patriotic need for pugilistic skill. An advertisement for one of its correspondence courses read:

> SOME DAY YOU'LL BE SORRY that you cannot box. When you find yourself facing the bully your size and strength will not help you—but SCIENCE will. Think how humiliating it would be to be beaten by a man smaller than yourself, think of the fuss of the onlookers and the taunts of your pals.[25]

The best-selling novelist Jack London was in Sydney on Boxing Day 1908 to describe the Johnson–Burns world championship bout. It was the most historic fight ever in Australia, attended by 20,000 with, he said, a throng of thousands outside the Rushcutter's Bay Stadium. Ringside seats cost £10. The gate drew £26,000. London wrote:

> The fight. The word is a misnomer. There was no fight. No massacre would compare with the hopeless slaughter that took place ... It had all the seeming of a playful Ethiopian at loggerheads with a small and futile White man, of a grown man suffering a naughty child ... of a funeral, with Burns as the late deceased, and Johnson as the undertaker, grave-digger and sexton ... It was hopeless, preposterous, heroic.[26]

Johnson notoriously taunted Burns, protracting the demolition to avenge the racist slurs he had endured. The police stopped the slaughter at the start of the fourteenth round. Unfortunately perhaps, people still like to read about it. Clark's squeamishness was anachronistic.

The Johnson–Burns fight, promoted by H. D. 'Huge Deal' McIntosh, made Sydney the mainstay of a high-level boxing industry. In December 1912 his interests were bought out for £30,000 by R. L. 'Snowy' Baker, an Olympic silver medallist in boxing and Australia's most famous all-round athlete. In 1913 Baker built an open-air stadium at West Melbourne and in 1914 founded Stadiums Ltd. It co-ordinated his own promotions in Brisbane and Sydney, and those in Melbourne with Wren's. In the following October he convened a conference which Wren attended to establish championship conditions and rules, bringing Australia into line with England with standard weights for all divisions. Early in 1915 Wren gained full control of Stadiums Ltd and domination of Australian boxing. He finally roofed and refurbished the West Melbourne Stadium, which became his boxing headquarters under Richard Lean. Similarly, he roofed what became the Brisbane Stadium.[27]

The capacities of the stadia were 11,000 in Sydney, 7,000 in Melbourne and 5,000 in Brisbane. Registers of Stadiums Ltd in 1914–15 show Wren to be personally in possession of nearly two-thirds of the 93,007 shares, with Baker holding just over one-tenth. Subsequently a number of transfers occurred, very few listed under Wren's name.[28] The 'well-written, comprehensive and professionally prepared' minute-books of Stadiums Ltd compare favourably with those of other companies and belie the perception that Stadiums Ltd was a 'brutal, primitive' organisation. At the inaugural meeting of 28 May 1914 it was reported that time-keeper McCarthy had been dismissed for betting on contests, and it was decided that no official in Stadiums' employ should be allowed to bet on any contest or have any interest in any match. In the following month it is reported that chairman Wren had suggested to Baker to get rid of the Rolls Royce. Eventually only a hire car was deemed necessary. In June 1917 Jimmy Hill was disqualified and forfeited all moneys for not being a bona fide contestant. In December, Lean of his own accord reduced his salary by half because of slack business. In July 1918 Baker retired because there was not enough work to do. The future of the company looked uncertain. However, it survived, and it is evident that the management was not simply self-serving.[29]

Peter Corris, a reputable historian as well as a notable novelist, has weighed the merits and shortcomings of Stadiums Ltd without accusing it of rigging fights; but the boxing historian Richard Broome has referred to John Wren's 'monopoly' being to the eventual detriment of the sport, without being specific.[30] What was a near monopoly swallowed smaller companies and insisted on exclusive contracts with its prize fighters. Its style was autocratic, even 'harsh and unimaginative', says Corris. It probably used political influence to foil any statutory control through a National Boxing Commission, and discouraged unionism. As a result it could dictate terms to fighters' managers and discriminate against those who dissented from them. (It could, if it wished, also protect fighters against managers who might take not only one-third of a purse but charge expenses as well.) Only the 1952–4 world bantamweight champion, Jimmy Carruthers, ever got more than 25 per cent of the gate, says Corris. The firm closed down several times rather than pay higher purses. Statistics reveal that a relatively high proportion of gross takings was allocated to servicing all boxer and wrestler participants, ranging from about 36–7 per cent to 50 per cent.[31]

Corris believes that by keeping its drawcards at home, the firm discouraged Australian champions from going overseas, although currency regulations did nothing to advance travel abroad. Still, it may have been fortunate that local stars were generally not set against obviously superior overseas fighters, if the performances of the Afro-American Freddy Dawson against the Australian lightweight champion Vic Patrick and others in the immediate post-war are any guide. Enough fighters were scarred or dulled for life. However, Lean's fear that Australian world champions would demand more than 25 per cent of the gates also kept them at home.

Lean made visits to Europe and the United States, carefully matching prospects with local stars to provide optimal entertainment. Ideally, it was said, the local champion should be able to just defeat the import. That certainly did not happen with Freddy Dawson, but did so often enough with others. There was no colour bar, white and coloured fighters were treated equally, but the company was slow in encouraging women to attend. The dressing rooms were austere—'what was good enough for Les Darcy ought to be good enough for anyone'—and amenities for patrons rudimentary. Dick Lean, to whom Wren delegated full authority in the 'house of stoush', prided himself on being 'tough but fair', on keeping his word in a hard game in hard times. Lean was extraordinarily competent if rigid in his dealings, and employed talented staff and judicious referees. It is impossible to know what the sport would have been like without the control of Stadiums Ltd, but firm control there was. It was able to thwart competition from the likes of Frank Packer and McIntosh. What is important here is that the gangsterism which fouled the sport in America did not exist in Australia.[32]

Wren has been unjustly blamed for the tragic fate of the great Maitland boxer Les Darcy, after Darcy absconded to the United States in breach of the War Precautions Act on the very day of the first conscription plebiscite in Australia (28 October 1916). US fight promoters were induced not to give Darcy fights. He was branded a coward. Falling ill with 'blood poisoning' in Memphis, he died aged twenty-one. His body was returned to Australia; his funeral processions were crowded; he became an instant folk hero. D'Arcy Niland, an accomplished novelist and major biographer of Les Darcy (after whom he is named), interviewed many people who had known Darcy well. He completely exonerated Wren, but not H. D. McIntosh and 'Snowy' Baker, from having persecuted the young champion:

> For a long time some people, particularly in Victoria, went around saying that it was John Wren … who brought Darcy down … But he had many diverse interests … Darcy was small stuff to him. I can state categorically that in all the hundreds of interviews I've done, Wren has never been mentioned. That story was cooked up later, when certain people were set on blackguarding Wren's name.[33]

The minutes of the board of directors of Stadiums Ltd in 1916–17 support this to a degree. Baker, who was managing director until July 1918, visited Darcy to discuss his 'reported enlistment' in late August or early September. 'The position was fully explained to the satisfaction to the Board.' On 1 November Baker 'was instructed to take every possible means to ascertain the accuracy or otherwise of the rumour of Darcy's departure and to afford all information to the civil or military authorities'—as the board was obliged to do. Wren was absent from those meetings. There is no further mention of Darcy. Baker and McIntosh, not Wren, were Darcy's nemesis.[34]

Stadiums Ltd expected crowd-pleasing aggression from its fighters, and that inevitably meant some blood would often flow. Although attempts were made to ensure that boxers were physically durable, the supervision was inefficient. Corris thinks Stadiums Ltd made 'comebacks' too easy:

> A review of the careers of professional fighters is not cheering—it has been estimated that more than half of the men who have pursued boxing seriously have emerged from it with some permanent injury, often incurred in a gymnasium.[35]

The most publicised case was that of the Aboriginal Ron Richards, triple champion (middle, light and heavyweight) of Australia. Corris relates that Stadiums Ltd was more concerned about Richards than has often been suggested, and there is evidence that some other successful fighters (for example, Fred Kay and Tommy Burns) were grateful to Wren for his personal interest in their welfare.[36] Nevertheless, it has been suggested that in order to please the crowds, Joe Wallis, Stadium Ltd's Sydney referee from 1914 to 1950, 'prolonged some unequal fights', notably the 'hard-hitting' 1949 Australian lightweight title bout between Jack Hassan and Archie Kemp, after which the latter died. On the other hand, no less than the great American fighter Archie Moore, after seven bouts in Australia, called Wallis 'one of the greatest referees in the world'. Merv Williams in Melbourne was sacked after an unpopular decision against Micky Miller, the Australian featherweight champion in 1938. Subsequently hired by the *Sporting Globe* as a commentator, he 'fearlessly suggested foul play' in a subsequent bout. No other such incidents have been noted. Williams eventually became editor, whose reminiscences of Wren over four issues at Wren's death were eulogistic.

A report to the National Health and Medical Research Council in 1974 revealed that 61 deaths had occurred in boxing during 1910–39 and 24 in 1939–74, with only 10 per cent occurring in amateur boxing. A high percentage must have happened under Stadiums Ltd's auspices. (But an item in the *Hawklet* on 1 January 1920 has Wren contributing to the funeral expenses of Mons Victor, a noted wrestler of the 1890s—before Wren's time—who had committed suicide.) In the Archie Kemp disaster, Corris says that the promoters paid £1,000 compensation, Wren contributed £100 personally, Kemp's opponent £100, a public appeal £357, while Kemp's share of the gate was £842.[37] There is no need to discuss here the inadequacy of this or to discuss the desirability of boxing. Wren was simply a man of his time and place. To quote Dr June Hearn again in her reminiscence of Collingwood: most male youths wanted to learn to box, and go on to fight at the Stadium.[38] It nurtured novices, and in Melbourne, put on three one-minute round bouts for kids. If sufficiently aggressive, they were rewarded with showers of coins.

Part of the success of Stadiums Ltd between the wars was the diversity of its programs: boxing on Friday nights, wrestling on Saturdays, a mixture of vaudeville and the lesser lights of boxing on Wednesdays. Wrestling matches were part of public entertainment throughout the nineteenth century, in both Greco-Roman and catch-as-catch-can style. There was a revival of interest in 1904–7. Wren was involved by 1907 and was showing, in successfully defending himself against a charge of breach of contract by the noted grapplers Bhutan Singh and Gus Rennert, that he was not to be trifled with.[39] A major problem was that the matches were usually non-stop and governed by falls, not rounds. This made for periods of inactivity and boredom, and had to be changed. However, interest 'decreased sharply after 1907' until the 1920s when, with lively media coverage, particularly radio—it was broadcast on 3LO, 3DB and 3AW—public enthusiasm revived again, but because it was now an entertainment as much as, if not more than, a display of skill. Richard Lean Jnr points out that while superior skills were not ignored, victory was decided in the 'bull-ring' at the back of the office, not in front of the audiences:

> because if you put two wrestlers in front of the public and they got into a hold and sat there all night nobody was going to pay to see the contest. So your world champions are genuine, but the wrestle they put on is a public performance.[40]

Showmanship was everything. A wild ethnic image could be a crowd-puller for the crushing King Kong or Big Chief Little Wolf with his 'Indian deathlock'. Other fearful 'holds'—hammerlocks, headlocks and the 'Boston crab'—became the signatures of other grapplers, while 'Strangler' Lewis and 'Jumpin' Joe Savoldi with his 'lethal' flying drop kick inspired awe. Little Wolf was allegedly a Navaho, Cherokee or whatever, but his real surname was latinate.

No allowance for simulation seems to have been made by a young sports broadcaster and journalist, Clyde Palmer, for what only a semi-otician like Roland Barthes could call 'a great Spectacle of Suffering, Defeat and Justice'.[41] Palmer was outraged by what he discerned as mockery, not by the ancient noble Greco-Roman art. He relentlessly lampooned Tom Thye, the entrepreneur of a group of eight wrestlers visiting Australia in 1928–9. Someone tried to bribe Palmer to stop satirising, but he handed the cheque over to his editor and it ended up with Keith Murdoch, chairman of the *Herald and Weekly Times.* Murdoch kept it for years, it was said, in his office drawer, presumably against a day when he himself might be in conflict with Wren, its alleged source. It was never cashed. However, we should note Wren's reluctance to write cheques. As pressure to have Palmer sacked failed, Thye during a bout 'contrived to fall on to the press table [at the ringside] at which Palmer was writing'. Palmer was kicked across the bridge of the nose,[42] and for the rest of his life had difficulty breathing through his nose. Wren and Lean have been seen as sanctioning this assault, but Tom Thye and his group hardly needed their permission to fall on top of a journalist with inflammatory opinions and the nerve to ridicule their livelihood. Wren himself apparently enjoyed wrestling, and barracked from the ringside even when he probably knew the result in advance.

In the mid-1950s the 'house of stoush' began to change its character as showbiz personalities like the 'groaner', Frank Sinatra, and lachrymose crooners like Johnny Ray, packed the stalls with a less macho audience than Wren had enticed in his heyday. In January 1955 the Stadium burned down; it was rebuilt as Festival Hall which, while maintaining some old sporting traditions, became the venue for the Beatles, the Seekers, and nearly all major entertainers. It reached its peak of popularity in the 1960s and thereafter declined.

CHAPTER NINE

Floreat Pica: Magpies Forever

MELBOURNE IS PASSIONATE about Australian Rules football, and Collingwood has been its most famous and ardently supported club; conversely it has been the most reviled. Between the wars, a premiership in 1919, four successive ones in 1927–30, two more in 1935–6 and seven times runners-up cemented the popular notion that money provided this success and that it came from John Wren, the only non-player or non-official privileged to enter the dressing rooms during 'closed doors sessions'. Fans of other clubs wanted to believe it. Absurd stories have been accepted. People have believed that Wren gave or sold the Victoria Park ground to the city of Collingwood for the purposes of football. In fact, the municipal council acquired Victoria Park when Wren was seven years old.[1]

In Wren's time some of Collingwood's success must have been due to the baseborn suburb's fierce pride and the enthusiastic promotion of the club by the council. Many of its players, 'born into a Magpie family and reared in the Magpie nest', were recruited from youths who wanted nothing more than to wear the famous black and white [magpie] jumper. Harry Collier (captain 1935–9; best and fairest 1928, 1930; equal Brownlow medallist 1930), who went to school opposite Victoria Park, was 'so honoured to play for the club he was shocked to learn he would be paid'.[2] Lou Richards, captain of the 1953 premier side and later media star comedian-commentator, was one of a third generation of his family to play for the club. His grandfather had also captained the Magpies in a grand final in 1905; each of two uncles played in five grand finals and two premiership teams between 1917–22 and 1935–9, one of them becoming captain. To be selected to play in 1941, said Richards, 'was bliss'. Champions stared down from photos on the walls, while in the flesh there was the most domineering and durable of coaches (1913–49), Jock McHale.[3] Collingwood believed it had an inimitable, unimpeachable tradition. Wren shared this fervour.

Fortunately there is a professionally researched history of the Collingwood Football Club with a devout title, *Kill for Collingwood*, by Richard Stremski. He points out that, although Wren had played in local teams when an adolescent and had been an official patron of the club in 1897–1901, he had then, with the exception of 1911, allowed his membership to lapse until 1914. Although previously a member of the Fitzroy Cricket Club, he became a member of the Collingwood Cricket Club from its inception in 1906. Stremski thinks Wren kept aloof from the football club because of rivalry with the Maddens. Sir John (fhief justice and lieutenant-governor) 'was appointed number one patron in 1896', while Frank (secretary of the Victoria Racing Club) was 'reputed ... an implacable foe of Wren'. Their mansions in Studley Park were near Wren's; probably they made it clear to the club that they would not associate with the Tote man whose horses had been barred from the VRC-registered courses. Also, Wren may not have had the self-confidence at that stage to outface this upper crust, socially that is. According to Stremski, Wren's patronage resumed during the First World War, as the Maddens retreated.[4]

Leonie Sandercock and Ian Turner are incorrect in calling Wren a committee man in 1903, as well as in blaming him for initiating illegal player payments and thus the professionalisation of football:

> [Wren] was known to be a generous supporter of the Collingwood club. So, when—in the aftermath of Collingwood's premiership of 1903 (the second in a row)—there was talk of professionalism among the players, it was Wren's name that came to mind.[5]

But, unusually for academics, they do not say whose 'mind' was involved. Was it their own? Most of their sources are not given in *Up Where, Cazaly*? (which Manning Clark cites more decorously as *Up*

There, Cazaly?). As they used the *Australasian* extensively, their source may be an article by 'Markwell' (19 September 1903) but, if so, they did not follow that journalist's 'mind' because he says specifically: 'there is no scintilla of reason for believing that anything underhand was being done at Collingwood'. Intensive research into football scandals of the early years of the Victorian Football League does not record Wren giving handouts to Collingwood players 'until well into the Jock McHale era'.[6] There were calls in the press to investigate payment of players as early as 1896, Essendon and Melbourne being prime suspects.[7]

The *Bulletin* (3 August 1982) has also asserted that Collingwood was 'one of the first clubs to pay its players adequately because Wren feathered the Magpie nest'. Not so, says Stremski, who points out that 'Wren's contributions never formed part of the players' wage structure'. When he became a regular patron he offered glad-handers, especially to goal-kickers like Gordon Coventry rather than defenders, who were less exhilarating. He personally paid players under suspension when club rules forbade them to be paid officially. Only in 1936 did he give for the first time a substantial sum (£100) to a premiership side, probably to match another patron's gesture of the previous year. It was only in the late 1940s that Wren began to offer incentives against less than full-bodied performances.[8] Bob Rose, deemed to have been the greatest Magpie, winner of four Copeland trophies for best-and-fairest player between 1949 and 1953, used to find Wren occasionally popping into his sports store on Monday mornings to reward him with perhaps £10 or £20 for an outstanding game. He found Wren informal and genial with no hint of underhand patronage. Collingwood, says Rose, kept strictly to uniform payments for players irrespective of ability or performance. This was to cost the club dearly as it otherwise could have recruited greater talent. Rose himself left the club prematurely at the age of twenty-seven to coach a country club for better pay.[9] As Lou Richards confirms:

> football wasn't our [the players'] major source ... of income ... Bonuses were frowned upon during the season but were allowed to an extent at finals time, when all the payments were increased ... [However] Many a player in financial difficulties would hit John Wren for 100 or even 200 quid to get them over bad times. The money was never repaid; it was rarely expected.[10]

Wren acted as the club's main employment officer during the Depression, but could not in 1932 persuade the Collingwood Council to put the great Brownlow medallist Albert Collier on wages, even when Sugar Roberts and four other councillors endorsed the club's request. Collier had had to leave Victoria to work in Tasmania in 1931–2. In the latter year the club had to impose a pay cut on players who responded by being 'late onto the field on one occasion, while debating possible strike action'. When the team made the finals the lost wages were made up.[11] Wren proved more influential for three other players in the late 1930s when the Depression had eased. Only Wren's 'all-time favourite player', Gordon Coventry, gained a job in a Wren firm, Effront Yeast. Most needy players ended up in Carlton and United Brewery, where coach Jock McHale worked and Wren had influence—as did, to a less extent, some other clubs.[12]

Wren was ever a 'fixer'. He made a dramatic intervention in the wrangle between the football and cricket clubs over tenancy rights at Victoria Park in 1933–4. It was said that when the cricket club delegates saw Wren turn up as one of the football club's representatives, they knew 'it had to be fixed'. The resolution, however, was a most tactful compromise: 'everybody won', but mostly the football club.[13] To pay for new clubrooms, costed in 1935 at £8,100, the local MLA, Labor Party leader and Wren protégé Tom Tunnecliffe, wangled a £5,000 subsidy from the state government's unemployment relief fund. Collingwood might have seen this as a Keynesian boost to joblessness—but other clubs would hardly have thought so.[14] (Note that Wren's friend, Albert Dunstan, had become premier in April 1935.)

With war looming in 1939, Collingwood club officials coveted the lucrative liquor licence of the Tivoli (German) Club, which would surely have had to be forfeited once hostilities began. Wren was instrumental in getting the licence transferred to the football club. A back-dated supposititious social club was rigged up, with a concocted membership and 'an unlabelled Visitors Book, which showed the Prince of Wales and the Earl of Hopeton [sic; Australia's first governor general], to be among the alleged … guests'. (Sir) Eugene Gorman, 'Victoria's greatest trial lawyer' and a long-time friend of John Wren, was employed as advocate, but withdrew when he believed it to be a hopeless case:

> It was obvious that the club had no real case for registration, but it did have 'a man who could get to someone else'. Some might call it political corruption; Collingwood members preferred to regard it as political influence. The man with the clout was John Wren ... Tom Tunnecliffe 'got to' the Chief Secretary–Attorney General ... H. S. Bailey. Bailey in turn 'got to' at least one of the licensing court magistrates, J. L. Harty. There was no bribe; no money changed hands. It was just a favour for a friend of a friend, who it was well known always returned favours.[15]

Tunnecliffe or Bailey may also have spoken to a second magistrate, H. J. Compton. So the chairman of the Licensing Court, D. Heardey, who strongly opposed the move, lost. The Collingwood Football Social Club then opened officially on 23 April 1941. The strain of this epic struggle caused the club secretary to suffer 'a burst blood vessel in his brain, but [he] declared that the battle was worth the cost' because money rolled into the club. Most other clubs had to wait at least twenty years for another Liquor Control Act to enable them to acquire a similar licence.[16] An interesting sidelight on Wren is that he never forgave Gorman. Encountering him in a lift soon after his withdrawal, Wren responded to his greeting with a Collingwood growl, 'You mongrel!'[17]

There was an occasion when a Wren political alliance superseded his devotion to Collingwood. The attempt by a young champion, Len Fitzgerald, to gain a clearance to Sturt in Adelaide became a *cause célèbre.* He was offered better employment and emoluments and the prospect of being captain-coach. Collingwood was adamant in its refusal, but Fitzgerald moved to Adelaide, even forfeiting £181 in provident funds. There was a media furore about a player's rights versus his loyalties. Less abstractly, there was a local politician in Sturt whose backers thought his election prospects could depend on the Fitzgerald clearance. They were in some way associated with Wren, who tried to influence the Collingwood Club committee in Fitzgerald's favour. This cause a rift between Wren and a new club secretary, Gordon Carlyon, who said that 'the club was not there to do the old man's bidding'. Eventually a compromise had to be reached, as Fitzgerald was also adamant. In the event, he played the last four home-and-away games with Collingwood, after which he was cleared. He won the Margarey medal for the best and fairest in South Australia three times in the 1950s.[18]

Stremski believes that 'Wren's influence at the Club was at its zenith in the later 40s. Not only his incentives increased but he had close relationships with Club leaders.' However, in the 'revolution of 1950' over the aborted appointment as coach of Bervyn Woods instead of former champion player Phonse Kyne, Wren found himself caught between the old and new guards in the administrative shake-up. His advice to his son, John F. Wren, 'not to get involved in club politics' was disregarded. In a 'packed meeting' at the Collingwood Town Hall the younger Wrens and Frank Galbally, a former player and prominent Melbourne barrister, led the rebels to a victory which, however, accommodated the 'old guard'. Wren mostly 'kept out of the donnybrook until it was virtually over'. Old friends were spilled from executive positions. His impact had been neither dictatorial nor decisive. As with many other of his activities, he had influence but not control.[19] As a consolation, Woods managed Wren's Rose Hotel in Fitzroy for the next twenty-three years.[20]

Commentators occasionally show their prejudice against Wren by what one can only hope are slips of the pen and tongue. It was, for example, quite surprising to find a professor of history refer to Wren, rather than John Norton, as the proprietor of *Truth*[21]—in spite of admiration for Manning Clark, who actually got that much right. Bob Pratt, South Melbourne's great full-forward of the 1930s, said in an interview that he had received a direct phone call from Squizzy Taylor 'before the 1935 grand final offering him £100 to play dead'.[22] This was retold to me personally as being a phone call from John Wren, and the sum offered was £80. I was expected to believe that, if Wren wanted to bribe Pratt, he would not hire a go-between but would incriminate himself. Moreover, it seemed to be thought impossible that someone would impersonate Wren. Unfortunately for the Pratt story, Squizzy Taylor had been killed in 1927! Furthermore, Stremski had revealed that Pratt could not play in the 1935 grand final because on the previous evening he had been 'knocked by a lorry laden with five tons of bricks as he alighted from a tram' in a suburb distant from Collingwood. Of course it was conceivable that Wren had sent the lorry (with bricks) around Melbourne prowling for Pratt, and may even have been himself in the shotgun seat. However, the South Melbourne triple Brownlow medal winner and captain, Bob Skilton, has the last word. In Pratt's obituary he is quoted as saying: 'Everyone at South Melbourne reckoned that Collingwood had paid the truck driver, but it turned out that the truck driver was a South supporter'. Actually, he had turned up the next evening at Pratt's house with some compensatory cigarettes.[23] Legend making history? Or perhaps Wren *ought to have* been prowling in Prahran for Pratt!

Another particularly silly fable concerning Wren, still current among Essendon (and other) football fans, blames its loss of the 1951 premiership on a Wren bribe. Essendon had been premiers in 1949–50 and were favoured for a triple premiership. However, in the last home-and-away game of the season between Essendon and Carlton, the latter's defender, Harry Casper, had so provoked the great and normally unaggressive full-forward John Coleman that blows were struck and Coleman was suspended from playing during the final series. Deprived of Coleman, Essendon lost the premiership. Only John Wren could have been responsible for the catastrophe. He was said to have bribed Casper to goad Coleman to an uncharacteristic offence! I personally worked over a Christmas vacation with Casper while his memory was still relatively green (1954–5). He was still incredulous. His remarks to Stremski, 'I hate Collingwood. I'd never do anything to help them in any bloody way',[24] were consistent with what he expressed to his friends at the Portsea pub.

In the 1930s the most robust contests were probably between Collingwood and Richmond, and the most feared player in the league was the Richmond ruckman Jack Dyer, whose name was execrated at Victoria Park. The feeling was mutual. Even in later years, when Dyer was a leading television commentator, he refused to dine at the Collingwood clubrooms. He had once been disqualified for deliberate violence against Jock McHale's son. McHale had called him 'a bloody mongrel'. However, on retiring as a policeman, Dyer asked a former football identity and cobber to help him set up in a pub. He tells the story in his autobiography:

> [Ted] Rippon found a few pubs he thought would suit me and finally the one we settled on was in the toughest area of Port Melbourne—its clientele was largely waterside workers, painters and dockers and quite a few crims—not the best place for a retiring copper to set up shop. There were more guys with records than you would find in a year at Brash's [a well-known music store]. Still, they loved their football and 90 per cent of them were straight as gun barrels.

We figured it was worth a shot but when I tried to get the lease on the pub I ran into a brick wall. Pubs were hard to get because they were a licence to print money and the hotel broker handling it told me not to waste my time. He already had somebody in mind.

It happened it was owned by John Wren, the Collingwood tycoon and infamous manipulator of politics, business and sport. Ray Dunn [Richmond president and noted barrister] told me to ring Wren and ask him for the lease.

I laughed with scorn. 'He's Collingwood mad. He knows how I hate the bastards—he'd spit in my eye'.

Ray was insistent. 'You never know until you try. He likes doing favours for people'. Well, I didn't want to be under any obligation to Wren. You never know what he would want when he called in the debt. Again Ray said there would be no obligation for me to do anything that I wasn't prepared to do.

I'd heard the stories about Wren and how he controlled the underworld. But I phoned him anyway.

'Come around and see me, Mr Dyer', said John Wren.

So I went to his office, told him I wanted his pub but the broker had slammed the door in my face. He picked up the phone, dialled a number and got the broker on his hot line. 'Give Jack Dyer that Port Melbourne pub—and give it to him on his terms.'

There was a protest at the other end and Wren snarled: 'I don't care who you've promised it to—it's Dyer's. Get it all straightened out now! He'll be in to do the paperwork tomorrow'.

He slammed down the phone.

Wren turned back to me. 'Right Jack. It's yours. See that fellow in the morning and it will be all fixed. Do you need any money?'

'No Mr Wren, that's all I wanted.'

His broker had the red carpet and silver service waiting for me the next morning and by that afternoon the pub was mine.

John Wren never called in that favor. In fact, we never spoke to each other again. I have always been told to take a fellow as you find him. I found John Wren a man's man and a man of his word.[25]

This was a sporting gesture towards an old rival. But, if Dyer has related it accurately, the way it was made betrays a peremptory side to Wren which must have affronted dependents in other circumstances.

CHAPTER TEN

Not a Media Mogul

AS EARLY AS 1906 Wren declared he would start a daily newspaper in Melbourne, pro-Labor of course, but no evidence has come to light of negotiations to do so. His own treatment by the press had made him keen to influence public opinion, although it is doubtful that he entertained fantasies of being an Australian Northcliffe.[1] Wren lacked the know-how and would soon have realised it. However, association with the flourishing Labor Party in Queensland revived this aspiration and, in 1915 with his friend Ben Nathan, he purchased the languishing *Daily Mail* (established 1903) using Norman White of Sydney as his nominee. At least early on he employed capable editors such as A. J. Buchanan, also a novelist and literary critic, and W. Farmer Whyte,[2] later a biographer of Billy Hughes. By 1921 the *Daily Mail* carried twenty reporters; the *Sunday Mail* ran to thirty-two pages.

Ross Fitzgerald believes that Wren already had a close association with 'Red Ted' Theodore when he bought into the *Daily Mail.* As his source is Niall Brennan,[3] who is himself surmising, we cannot be sure but, in view of Wren's expanding activities and his Labor predilection, it is not an unreasonable inference that he became friendly with Theodore, T. J. Ryan (premier, 1915–19) and other Labor MLAs not long after he purchased Albion Park Racecourse in 1909 and became enthusiastic about its climate and people. Although Wren and Theodore were a contrast in personal style, there was obvious compatibility in background, temperament and acquisitive interest. Theodore had come from Liverpool Irish Catholic/Rumanian Orthodox parentage, left school at twelve, worked as an underground miner, become a vigorous organiser for the Australian Workers' Union, entered Queensland parliament at twenty-five in 1909, had been elected deputy leader of the state Labor Party and treasurer in 1915 and would be premier by 1919.[4]

If Wren had delusions of great power as a media mogul, he had his wings clipped by several defamation actions soon after his proprietorship of the *Daily Mail* began. In June the *Mail* accused its rival, the *Brisbane Courier*, of 'GULLING THE PUBLIC—THE COURIER'S SPURIOUS PATRIOTISM—PUBLIC FUNDS SCANDALOUSLY MISAPPLIED'. It was alleging that the *Courier*'s patriotic funds for the relief of victims of war were being misused. 'The whole business smells abominably' said its editorial. The *Courier* took out a writ for £25,000 damages, but reported it only in a tiny article on 1 July. The *Mail* was obviously delighted to be able to display a new image as a 'fighting paper', as it liked to call itself. It was openly defiant: 'the suit will be defended' it declared, but the suit did not get to trial. Realising the issue was mismanaged, Wren went to Brisbane on 13 August to sort things out—the very day he enlisted in the army. On 24 and 25 August the *Mail* admitted that the accusations were unfounded, apologised, donated £500 to the patriotic funds as evidence of faith in their honest administration, and undertook to pay all expenses. The *Courier* responded through Ernest J. Stevens, one of its proprietors, in a personal note to Wren dated 30 August 1915 under the letterhead of The Brisbane Newspaper Company Ltd:

> Dear Sir,
>
> I am very pleased to receive yours of 25th inst. As it confirms my belief that although you are a hard fighter you are a manly man, & not easily hoodwinked by any member of the legal fraternity. I can assure you there is no feeling of hostility to you in my mind.
>
> Yours sincerely ,
>
> ERNEST J STEVENS[5]

Wren's letter must have been conciliatory. We may ask whether Wren the showman had pushed his editor into pugnacity or whether the editor had acted on his own judgment. The *Courier*'s letter suggests the latter.

However, a further defamation suit was laid in July by H. B. Ellerton, Inspector of Asylums in Queensland, as a result of accusations such as these:

ASYLUM HORRORS. SHOCKING CONDITIONS AT GOODNA.
RATS AND VERMIN INFESTED WARDS. INADEQUATE
MEDICAL STAFF. A SEARCHING INQUIRY IS NEEDED.

The government was advised to look at the 'revolutionary' reforms in medical supervision being carried out in Victoria. This too sounds like Wren showmanship: giving the paper a kick-start. He had to pay £3,325 plus costs, but his paper had shaken off its dreary image and within twelve months showed a profit again.[6]

The bitterly divisive issue of conscription in 1916–17 shows Wren riding two horses simultaneously. While he supported Archbishop Mannix and Sinn Fein in Melbourne, he personally supported conscription. The *Daily Mail* on 3 August 1916 praised Theodore as 'a Treasurer who takes infinite pains, who possesses prudence and who has not hesitated to exercise proper economy'. However, on 5 August, while Theodore is praised for 'no half-heartedness' towards the war in line with Wren's overt patriotism, on 28 September the Queensland deputy premier declared that conscription 'was one of the greatest frauds that was ever attempted to be put before a free democracy'.[7] This could hardly have pleased Wren but, on 26 October, two days before the first conscription plebiscite, Wren was with Mr and Mrs Theodore at South Brisbane wharf applauding 4,000 volunteers going overseas, among them Theodore's brother. The troops offered three cheers for Theodore. Next day Buchanan (as he had to) signed the editorial declaring that 'the path of duty is the path chosen by every man and woman who greets the ballot box to vote "yes"'.[8] The *Bulletin* called the *Mail* 'a sort of pseudo-Labor journal'.[9]

The previous Saturday (21 October 1916), the *Mail* editorial entitled 'Roman Catholic Church's Attitude', signed by Buchanan, had favourably quoted Archbishop James Duhig of Brisbane who, while stressing that the Catholic Church itself had no policy on conscription, had urged Catholic men to 'do their duty'. This, said the editorial, lay along 'the road to which the Prime Minister is pointing'. This was a palpable hit at Mannix in Melbourne, who was declaring conscription to be inherently 'evil'. (Did Wren deliberately go to Brisbane for plebiscite day—to feel more comfortable there?) On the following Monday an editorial numbered Wren's friend, Frank Anstey, among Australia's 'unscrupulous enemies', calling him sarcastically 'Our brilliant anti-conscription tactician', and on Wednesday wrote 'You will be helping shirkers by voting "no" and you will be injuring all the rest'. With Queensland being the only state government to oppose conscription, 52 per cent voted NO. On 10 November an unsigned editorial said, 'Germany is glad and has reason to be glad'.[10] What influence did Wren have on this? The issue is inscrutable.

At the start of the second plebiscite campaign in November 1917, Buchanan again sarcastically attacked Theodore's loyalty and his chairmanship of the Anti-Conscription Literature Committee, whose headquarters was at the *Worker* building in Brisbane. He rushed to the defence of prime minister Hughes, of whom Theodore had said that 'once he is given the power to seize and deport men, that power will become unlimited and unrestricted'. This was, according to Buchanan, disloyal and dishonest: the prime minister would never break a solemn promise![11] In view of Hughes's apostasy in 1916 how could even 'a sort of pseudo-Labor journal' believe that?

Its editorial of 17 December, three days before the second plebiscite, could hardly have been more partisan in its focus on the Irish-Australian vote—contrary to premier Tom Ryan and his fiery Irish-born minister, J. A. Fihelly, whose rhetoric inspired 'the pejorative term 'Fihellyism', signifying disloyalty and support for Germany and the Sinn Fein rebels'.[12]

> There is an impression abroad which may or may not be well founded, that the majority of people of Irish descent are likely to vote 'No' at the referendum on Thursday. It is certain that the attitude of one of the newspapers [the Brisbane Catholic diocesan *Advocate*] has done something to foster that impression … in doing so it has not followed the advice or the precept of its own Archbishop, Dr Duhig, who has declared … that the Church … leaves the question an open one. …

Then come three sentences: the first does not accord with Sinn Fein, but the others would have expressed Wren's attitude:

> Is any Englishman outside of a madhouse anxious to injure Ireland … has not Australia been as good to Irishmen as it has been to Englishmen … If Australia is worth living in, it is worth defending.

While it is difficult to reconcile the attacks on Theodore with the idea that Wren was supervising the editorials, it is possible both saw such rhetoric cynically, just part of the political game. It would be inconsistent of Wren to believe Englishmen were considerate to the Irish, but he did on other occasions praise British values and their transfer to Australia.

Sharpe versus Wren

Wren's original partner in the *Daily Mail* was soon bought out by J. B. Sharpe, then MHR for Oxley. In the early 1900s Sharpe had become involved in horse-racing and trotting and, according to the *Labor Daily*'s obituary, established night footrunning in Brisbane, which boomed during the careers of world champions Arthur Postle and Jack Donaldson. Andrew Lemon described him as a bookmaker.[13] He owned Kedron Park Racecourse in 1912 before it was bought by Wren and Nathan. Sharpe was active in the Labor movement and a leading figure in launching its evening paper, the *Daily Standard*, in December 1912. He purchased a building for the paper as well as 'all the necessary equipment and material' but, when he was unable to provide all the capital he had promised, the directors were forced to call on the unions to take up extra shares.[14] Sharpe was a curiosity in the Labor movement. He had favoured conscription; but when prime minister Hughes had dramatically walked out of caucus forever on 14 November 1916, the minutes show that Sharpe had aligned himself with both sides.[15] Subsequently he contested Oxley for Labor on three occasions, unsuccessfully. He died in Sydney in 1935, having finally been a life-insurance salesman.

In view of their mutual interests it is possible that Sharpe was more involved in Wren's acquisition than is apparent. In November 1915 he offered to become a partner and did so. As part of the deal he became manager in December, but fell out with Wren at least in part because he failed to supply his share of the capital. In March 1916 an understanding was reached whereby Wren agreed to lend Sharpe £5,000 at 5 per cent, on the security of a Brisbane property. Sharpe then became managing director, but his tenure was short as in August he issued a writ to restrain

Wren from controlling management, and claimed damages for breach of contract. When the case was heard in March 1917 Sharpe tried to withdraw. Wren also wanted the case dismissed, but with costs paid by Sharpe and finality assured. Sharpe was allowed to discontinue but had to pay £200 against future action.[16] Despite this bitter antagonism, Sharpe was managing director again from April to December 1917.

Sharpe wrote a letter[17] to the Queensland premier, Tom Ryan, on 20 November 1918, complaining that he had been 'ejected from office by a majority of shareholders (being the nominees of Wren)'. The 40,007 shares in the company had been divided between Wren's nominees: Norman White (20,000), three members of his family (three shares in all), three other nominees (one each) and Sharpe (20,001), putting the latter in a minority position and, if Wren so chose, a powerless one. Since his ejection, Sharpe said, the company had been run down by Wren so that 'the value of my interest … is being whittled away deliberately'. The only offer Wren was prepared to make for Sharpe's shares was £4,000, although he (Sharpe) had offered the shareholders £8,000 for their shares alone but 'had been met with a curt refusal'. Wren, he said, was 'willing and financially able to have the business conducted at a loss with the desire of ousting me on his own terms'. He also claimed victimisation because of his 'political views' and asked for some action by the government to prevent being 'robbed of my rights and property'. Sharpe sold his shares to White in January 1919 at Wren's price.

Wren's agreement with Norman White, acting as nominal owner of the *Daily Mail* from 16 January 1919, is instructive. Obviously Wren, in view of his extensive racing interests, did not want to be perceived as owning a substantial interest in the newspaper. As White was not 'in a position' to purchase Sharpe's shares 'without financial assistance', Wren was to advance the necessary £4,000 only if 'the said John Wren shall simultaneously be granted the right to ultimately acquire the said shares'. Wren was to lend the £4,000 without interest to White if he 'agrees not to sell or dispose of the shares for 20 years, without the prior written consent of John Wren in any way', and Wren also agreed to purchase the 20,001 from White on or before 16 January 1939 for the sum of £5,000. White was to repay simultaneously the £4,000 borrowed. If Wren failed 'to effect purchase' on or before that date, White could sell or dispose of the shares in any way he liked, provided he had repaid the £4,000 within seven days of 16 January 1939.[18] So White was to get

£1,000 simply by holding shares on Wren's behalf. His 'loyalty' was thereby guaranteed. The public and perhaps the government was none the wiser, and Wren was using, not breaking the law in a legally executed agreement. Both parties emerged winners. But some may see this as a 'shady', because convoluted, manoeuvre.

Amalgamation

Even if Wren had had the literary talent and the appropriate grasp of public affairs required, he would have been far too busy and residentially too remote at that time to exert constant influence on the *Daily Mail.* In any case, pressure from conservative advertisers would have forestalled a militant Labor posture. Labor papers elsewhere, as Buggy maintained, were beset by 'meddlesome union presidents and secretaries who intruded with disastrous results'.[19] By 1929 there was no sign of deterioration; the *Mail* seems to have been a healthy, readable publication. The masthead boasted: 'Net circulation has been proved by unanswered challenge to be greater than any other newspaper in Queensland'. This was contested by the *Courier* with 28 pages in 1929, more classified advertisements but less columns: 'First in circulation, coverage, advertising and influence'. Rivalry had been keen and apparently beneficial. However, by 1931 both papers had lost size, probably due to costs in the Depression. The *Daily Mail* was down to 18 pages, the *Sunday Mail* to 22. The *Courier* ranged from 20 to 24. Predatory southern eyes were focusing on both of them.

As research constraints limited scrutiny of the *Daily Mail*, the issues for October 1929 and October 1931 were looked at—the former date to ascertain its approach to the Royal Commission on Racing, which was unfavourable to Wren, and both dates because they coincide with events in Canberra relating to the whisky tariff allegedly influenced by Wren. If anything, the *Mail* gave more coverage to the royal commission than did the *Courier.* On 25 October it had no qualms about reporting over three columns the evidence of James Jack, the insurance manager of the Brisbane Amateur Turf Club, who argued that the £450,000 paid to Wren for Albion Park was 'an iniquitous price'. There is no evidence of attempts to correct reports with favourable editorials or diminished reportage. Clearly the proprietor was not 'leaning on' the editor.

The same can be said about the controversial whisky tariff of 1929–31. As the debates in federal parliament in 1929 do not seem to be covered in the *Mail* at key dates, this may be an indication of bias, but it must also be recognised that there was not much to report with the Scullin government stifling debate on the whole tariff, not just whisky. On 13 December 1929 the *Mail* reported Treasurer Theodore's denial of Senator M. Reid's allegation that the Queensland Licensed Victuallers' Association had paid him £10,000 'not to interfere' with their licences for three years. But there is no editorial expressing a line on the issue, and an equivalent amount of space is given to Reid's reply on 14 December. In 1931 the *Mail* does not withhold criticism of Scullin. For example, an editorial of 23 October on the Seamens' Strike calls on him to take a much tougher line with militants. The *Mail* kept to an unexciting centrist position, but gradually the circulation of both papers failed to keep up with increased costs.

Keith Murdoch (jocularly known in the media as 'Lord Southcliffe') had in the early 1920s successfully remodelled the Melbourne *Herald* for the old 'boomer' directors, Theodore Fink, W. L. Baillieu and his son, (Lord) Clive. In 1926 a syndicate including Baillieu, Broken Hill's W. S. Robinson and the *Herald* board acquired the *West Australian*, but resentment at Melbourne ownership led to Murdoch's abandoning direct control in the 1930s and disposing of the syndicate's interest. In 1929 he had begun acquiring a monopoly of Adelaide's major newspapers.[20] From there he trawled to Brisbane, aware that the *Daily Mail* was 'feeling the pinch of the Depression'. Wren agreed that the paper needed invigoration and sold Murdoch a share. In 1933, together, they bought the *Courier*. With both papers finding competition unprofitable, a merger into the *Courier-Mail* was agreed in July 1933, under the aegis of Queensland Newspapers Ltd. Wren acquired 29.3 per cent; the Herald and Weekly Times Ltd, 33.7 per cent. The *Courier-Mail's* manifesto (2 September) proclaimed:

> It will be thoroughly Queensland in outlook ... will not be attached to any political party. It will be thoroughly independent, praising that which it believes to be in the interests of Queensland and of Australia, and condemning that which it believes to be opposed to the best interests of State and Commonwealth.

These were unexceptionable ideals, but Wren could hardly have had any illusions that the drift of Murdoch's policy would not be pro-Labor now that he had, says Desmond Zwar, for the first time 'a controlling personal interest in a newspaper'.[21]

However, Zwar is incorrect in asserting that Murdoch 'had the right to nominate the entire board of directors during his lifetime'. Peter Norris, who acted for (Sir) John Williams, editor of the *Courier-Mail* and later chairman of the Herald and Weekly Times Ltd, recorded this:

> Williams described a battle for the right to nominate directors to the company taking over the newspaper and said there was a toe-to-toe slog between Mr Wren and Murdoch with Mr Wren finally winning the battle and getting the right to appoint two directors to the Board. [He threatened to call the deal off.] This having been agreed, Wren did not appoint any directors. Sir John Williams said that he queried Mr Wren about this at a later stage and asked why, having put up such a battle for the right to appoint directors, he had failed to appoint anyone.
>
> Wren's reply was, 'Murdoch knows all about the newspaper industry. I know nothing ... Murdoch can run it any way he likes. If he gets a quid for himself, he must get one for me too'.
>
> Sir John said that in all the subsequent years Wren made no attempt whatever to influence editorial policy [which was generally anti-Labor] on any occasion. His only visits were once annually when he called at the office in Brisbane and asked two questions: one, 'What is the circulation?'; two, 'What is the bank balance?'[22]

Zwar states that Murdoch 'never became close' to Wren and 'dealt with the business of control by letter', as though the media baron was too fastidious to meet personally the former tote-owner.[23] However, either money waives such distinctions or Murdoch came to see Wren as quite respectable, because a handwritten letter from Murdoch to Wren concludes, 'I am coming to Melbourne next Monday and hope to see you later'. Norris also recalled an incident 'shortly after the war in the mid-forties during Wren's wind-up with Murdoch of Qld Newspapers:

> JW and Murdoch had an argument over £1,200 in land tax. Each one refused to pay. Finally, proceedings were issued which went to a single judge of the Qld Supreme Court and then to the High Court. I heard the judgement. JW won it, but the costs involved,

even in those days, would have far outweighed the amount involved. But JW fought it as a matter of principle; he wasn't going to let Murdoch get away with something.[24]

Bednall's boss

A pertinent reminiscence of Wren comes from Colin Bednall, a highly respected journalist and pioneer television manager, who from 1946 to 1954 was managing director of Queensland Newspapers Pty Ltd.[25] After Murdoch's sudden death on 4 October 1952, Bednall learned that:

> in one of Murdoch's various financial deals, he had surrendered to Wren and heirs the right to take the newspaper [*Courier-Mail*] and associate enterprises over in the event of his own death. Wren's name did not appear on any of the Company records because he operated through nominees …

Bednall was not disposed to think well of Wren:

> [I had heard] vague stories about John Wren and his underworld associations, but I was engrossed in my job too much to worry much about them. Then Frank Hardy's *Power Without Glory* hit the bookshops and I was stunned. I even stayed away from the office for a week and I might never have returned had there not been a need to sign the pay cheques.

Then in late 1952, to Bednall's surprise:

> [I] suddenly found … [myself] to be, as the local boxing promoter explained to me, one of the team—John Wren's team, along with a cabinet minister, a police commissioner, a turf club chairman, sundry lawyers and the boxing promoter … [who], hungry for free plugs for the stadium he managed, had [previously] lost no time in explaining that his boss may one day also be my boss.

The new 'boss' immediately re-appointed Bednall to the board. But how 'sinister' did Bednall's new master actually turn out to be when, in 1952, they met for the first time?

> Walking through the general office I saw sitting on a hard bench reserved for petty debtors, a short bandy-legged old man. Passing the bench again thirty minutes later, I saw he was still there. His legs did not reach the floor so he could swing them, and this way he made it appear that he was happy. However, I walked over to him and asked if he was attended to.
>
> 'I am hoping to see Mr Bednall', said John Wren, 'but they tell me he is a very busy man'.
>
> Wren continued to treat me with consideration. He had the right to appoint three new directors to take over control of the board of the company, but as a gesture to me he forfeited his right to do so.

Although Wren had been involved in the *Daily Mail* from 1915, Bednall found that he 'was fascinated by the workings of a newspaper office':

> He asked me at once to publish some pictures of the pugilists booked to fight in his local stadium, and I did so. The next request was for free editorial space to sing the praises of a beauty aid that was being promoted by his son. Explaining that to disguise advertising matter as news would be out of character with the type of newspaper I was trying to develop, I refused that one. Thereafter, the only favour he asked of me was that I take one of his daughters on a guided tour of the *Courier-Mail* building.[26]

Obviously Wren was sizing up his new situation with Queensland Newspapers. However, the courtesy he showed Bednall when he could have simply pulled rank is not inconsistent with reports of his consideration for others and respect, in particular, for 'men of principle'. 'The only embarrassment he caused me', wrote Bednall, 'was to press constantly that he be allowed to do me or the *Courier-Mail* some favour'. Again, this was typical of Wren in his dealings with trusted staff and others, although it could reasonably be thought that he was trying to put Bednall under some obligation. I would think rather that he also wanted to demonstrate something of his wide influence—vanity was a factor in his 'meddling'—especially when he had revealed (and had realised?) that he was no master of the media. In any case the opportunity to show his mettle soon came when Bednall went to Melbourne:

> [Williams] soon got wind of Wren's attitude to me and when I went to Melbourne on a visit, he asked me to get Wren to use his political friends to block a piece of legislation that was unwelcome to the Melbourne *Herald*. I was so astonished to be asked a favour by Jack [Williams] that I steeled myself and walked down Flinders Lane and put the request to Mr Wren. He unhesitatingly agreed to have his creatures block the Bill before it left the party room. To do so, he simply picked up a telephone, called Parliament House, and asked that a prominent member of the party be brought to the phone.
>
> 'Is it true you're thinking of setting up a Government board to run the newsagents?' he asked as I sat on the other side of his desk in the office of Stadiums Ltd. 'It is?' … 'Well, I don't care for that … please have it stopped'.[27]

Stopped it must have been, for a check of parliamentary records for 1944–53 has not revealed such a Bill or papers related to it. Maybe, because of Wren, the issue was never canvassed in caucus. So it is unclear what the Bill proposed to do and how Wren could have been concerned about it—other than doing a favour for a business associate, something he liked to do, showing off his putative influence.

Bednall did not seem to realise how damaged Wren's reputation had been in spite of his own reaction to *Power Without Glory*. On his return to Brisbane, he recalled:

> I was foolish enough to send Jack [Williams] a telegram saying Wren had taken action as requested. Back came an urgent telegram from Jack stating for the record that he was at a loss to know what my telegram was about as he would never dream of asking any favour of the likes of John Wren.[28]

Twenty-seven years later, in 1979, Peter Norris raised the question of Wren's reputation with Williams, now knighted and retired. They were on cordial terms. Apart from the Tote, said Williams, himself noted for 'integrity', he knew nothing to Wren's discredit. However, he said that Wren 'unquestionably wielded a good deal of influence politically and he was powerful financially'. He admired Wren's contributions to charity 'without seeking any publicity'.[29] Naturally, he said nothing of his fear of having been thought an associate of Wren; it would have been barefaced for a protégé of Murdoch to demur at political wirepulling.

But in Sydney ...

Wren seems to have also been involved in a Sydney *Daily Mail*, which had been set up in the early 1920s by members of the Protestant Federation—'sectarians' who, said Jack Lang, made headlines out of the Sister Ligouri scandal of 1921.[30] Sir George Fuller, the Nationalist premier, recommended purchase to his followers, but an option on all unissued shares was acquired by the impresario Sir Ben Fuller (no relation) on behalf of the Irish-born P. J. Minahan MLA (Labor), a wealthy retailer known as the 'Boot King', foundation chairman of the Catholic Club and of the Knights of the Southern Cross. Lang alleged that Wren was Minahan's partner in the *Daily Mail*; 'the Irish have captured the Protestant paper', he scoffed. However, the Sydney venture was unsuccessful and was taken over by the New South Wales Labor Party in 1923 and then by the *Labor Daily*, established by Lang on 23 January 1924.[31]

CHAPTER ELEVEN

The Patriot

PREJUDICE AGAINST WREN has been such that allegedly authoritative commentators disparage his patriotic gestures during the First World War even to the point of denial. On news of the Gallipoli landing on 25 April 1915, Wren offered £500 and a gold watch to Australia's first Victoria Cross winner. It looked to be a flamboyant, rather vulgar gesture, but Wren was supporting the war as enthusiastically as (and more materially than?) his antagonists. That he was sincere is clear enough from his gift to the Belgian Relief Fund a few weeks before the Anzac landing. When his crack miler, Garlin, won the Doncaster Handicap at Randwick on Easter Saturday, Wren wrote to the secretary of the Australian Jockey Club asking that his prize money of £2,125 be given to 'these brave allies ... [to whom] we owe a debt of gratitude for which Australia should show its fullest appreciation in a generous and practical manner'.[1]

Wren thought the rich should lead by example. However, Albert Jacka's biographer, Ian Grant, says that Jacka, according to 'family sources' (which turns out to be a 'great nephew', and which he uncritically accepts), declined Wren's gift.[2] There does not appear to be any suggestion of this refusal before the publication of *Power Without Glory*. On the contrary, the *Advocate* of 31 July 1915 reports that Wren did give Jacka's parents the sum of £500 and a gold medal, while the *Argus* of 14 August reports that 'Wren expressed his pleasure recently when he was able to pay that sum [£500] over to Private Jacka's relatives'. Lloyd Robson in *The First AIF* confirms this, as does the entry on Jacka in the *Australian Dictionary of Biography*.[3]

Nor did Jacka spurn what Grant calls the 'cunning and ruthless' Wren's 'business expertise'. Grant concedes that it was Wren's 'drive' that in 1920 set up an electrical goods importing and exporting house, Roxburgh, Jacka & Co Pty Ltd (from 1923, Jacka, Edmunds & Co Pty Ltd), in central Melbourne. John and Arthur Wren, Richard Lean and Jacka became directors. Jacka contributed £700 of the paid-up capital. By the time the company was floated on the stock market, Arthur Wren nominally had 420 of 800 shares, Roxburgh 170 and Jacka 140. When Roxburgh withdrew, Arthur Wren's shares increased to 525 (66 per cent) and Jacka's to 170.[4] The company prospered, and moved its show-rooms to larger premises in 1925. Jacka in 1926 bought a fashionable home in St Kilda and became a councillor there in September 1929.[5] Up to this point it is impossible to know what Grant means by saying Jacka was 'easy prey' for Wren, especially as the latter had alternative and, little doubt, more productive uses for his lucre. Then in 1930 in the trough of the Great Depression, the Scullin government totally banned the import of some items of hardware and most electrical goods, and put a 50 per cent or more tariff on others. At this point Grant's chronology is confusing:

> Wren was impressed with the popular public support Jacka had won as a councillor and later [in September 1930] as mayor and he offered to secure him a safe seat in Federal Parliament as part of his own manipulative powers within the Labor Party. The task was within Wren's capabilities …

Jacka (apparently because he was a man of integrity) refused: 'they [whoever, unspecified; was it Labor politicians?] are not my style', he is supposed to have said, while people would say, 'Look at Jacka—a failure in business climbing into a safe job as an MP'. So in August 1930 Wren allegedly persuaded his brother Arthur to sell his own share at a loss because, spitefully, Wren 'did not like taking "no" for an answer'.[6] In fact, in September the company did go into 'voluntary liquidation', not bank-ruptcy as has been alleged. The company owed £21,289; its deficiency of assets to meet liabilities was £19,942. The National Bank (£11,544) and

Wren (£6,051) were the two major unsecured creditors. The reasons for liquidation were overwhelmingly economic, with the National Bank having more reason than Wren to 'pull the plug'. At the winding-up the creditors, all unsecured, received 8.73 pence in the pound.[7] Yet Grant seriously states that 'in these early months of 1930 Jacka had accepted the political onslaught [of protectionism?] and was successfully fighting his way clear until the intervention of John Wren'.[8] In fact, as though to safeguard his wife's interest in the event of a depression, Wren had taken out a life insurance policy in July 1929 in her favour. The following year Wren, who had agreed to act as guarantor for the new Xavier College memorial chapel, was forced to withdraw his patronage. Millionaires can also lose liquidity.[9] There are several other incidents in 1929–30, which strongly suggest that even Wren was feeling the pinch—at least on income.

Jacka is supposed to have sold his house 'to pay accumulated debts', while the family 'moved into rental accommodation'. A more reliable account based on the St Kilda rate books has Jacka renting his house in late 1929 and moving back into it in late 1930.[10] Jacka's mayoral allowance of £500 per annum (several times the basic wage) was at least enough to keep the family (a wife and one adopted daughter) together. Jacka is described as 'probably the only mayor in Australia unemployed throughout most of his time in office'. However, on leaving office he did get a job as a salaried employee with a car, 'not working on a commission basis' with 'Anglo-Dominion Soap Co, a subsidiary of W. Angliss & Co', where 'his acquired salesmanship skills would have suited the employment'. His brother said he 'did well at this till his health failed suddenly'.[11] However, Manning Clark, fudging his sources, has Jacka 'knocking at suburban doors, and pleading with housewives to buy his soap'. This sob story is repeated without acknowledgment by Stuart Macintyre.[12] At least Grant does not blame the break-up of Jacka's marriage—only 'good in parts', said his wife—on Wren. But, summing up, Grant says that 'in private life ... Jacka was incapable of recognising that if he crossed a man like Wren then Wren would somehow seek retaliation to save face'.[13]

How to make sense of this? Wren is accused of ruining a hero for whom he had virtually underwritten a decade of prosperity because that beneficiary would not accept a glittering prize as compensation for a failing venture (assuming that Wren did actually make such an offer).

That is really what Grant is saying. He is unaware that Arthur Wren may have had problems with his own liquidity in the Depression. Astonishingly, near the beginning of his biography Grant claims that 'Wren would even more drastically affect … [Jacka's] life after the war' than he did by offering him a reward for valour—which Grant says Jacka did not accept![14]

The source for the story of Wren's alleged ultimatum that Jacka enter politics or forfeit his financial support is E. J. Rule, the author of *Jacka's Mob* (1933): he was reminiscing in *Reveille*, the journal of the RSL, although Wren is not explicitly mentioned.[15] There is another version in Anne Longmire's *History of St Kilda*, where Jacka is reported as having told a friend: 'I am being closed down. Wren, thinking that he bought me, wants to take a course of action politically but I refuse to do so. He said, 'Alright, if you don't I'll close you down.' I prefer to be closed down.'

This is described as an 'unsourced quote in a folio of materials prepared by City Librarians, St Kilda Public Library'. Longmire in her text is careful to state that this 'was rumoured'. There is also a problem with dates. Wren is alleged to have withdrawn 'his support in 1929', which is said to be 'the same year … [that] Jacka's firm went into liquidation'.[16] It was not. It must also be asked whether the Labor Party itself, with or without Wren's 'fixing', could have found a seat for Jacka in its unhappy years 1930–2. In the 1931 federal election, Labor in Victoria won only four seats. Who was to give one up at Wren's behest for Jacka? It is at least credible that Wren could have contrived a Labor or Country Party backbench seat for Jacka in the state parliament, but a federal seat at that time is fantasy. It is impossible to believe that Grant knows much about Wren's capabilities or Jacka's relations with him. Sad to relate, Grant's book was published in association with the Australian War Memorial.

Enlistment

Grant's gratuitous condemnation does not end there. One of Wren's more publicised actions was his short-lived enlistment in the AIF in August 1915. It has been customary among Wren's denigrators to regard it as a stunt. Grant even describes Wren's eventual discharge as cowardice: 'Wren had … declared he was ready to serve anywhere. When the realities and dangers of army life became apparent to him he was able to successfully seek demobilisation on the basis of an ear infection.'[17]

There was no 'stunt'. Wren did not approach the recruiting office in what Don Garden in his *History of Victoria* calls 'a convenient well-publicised enlistment'.[18] The greying Wren simply 'presented himself' at the Melbourne Town Hall 'shortly after 1 pm' on 13 August to be greeted by MacDonald, the officer in charge, 'with a cheery "Want to enlist, lad"'. There were no reporters even fortuitously standing by. Taking down his particulars, MacDonald asked: "By the way, are you John Wren senior or John Wren junior?" Wren—his father was long dead and young John was at home with five siblings—answered, 'John Wren junior'. Then MacDonald, 'looking up from his papers for the first time with curiosity', added, 'Are you John Wren, the owner of racehorses?' The evening *Herald* of 13 August was then tipped off and reported as above. It said Wren was reputed to have been 'in his young days a keen athlete … a prominent cricketer and footballer … also did a great deal of boxing … is a crack revolver shot'.

Wren left that afternoon by train for Brisbane to finalise business, no doubt to deal with the defence of his newspaper, the *Daily Mail*, in a £25,000 defamation suit. The *Argus* caught up with him at Seymour railway station. The news was acknowledged rather than hailed in the major Victorian papers next day, but it was not news in the *Sydney Morning Herald* or the Brisbane *Courier*, and rated only a paragraph in the Adelaide *Register*. It was left to the weeklies, *Labor Call* (successor to the *Tocsin*) and *Truth* to do the hailing, while the *Bulletin* was not yet antagonistic. There was a pleasant enough sketch of 'John Wren—Recruit' by Boz and a quite uncritical reference to Wren's spartan habits at home, suggesting he would not 'find it cold camping out'.[19] *Labor Call* was effusive, suggesting that Wren enjoyed the goodwill of many in the Labor Party:

> If Jack entrenches himself in Gallipoli as he did in Collingwood, when he defied the whole Police Force of Victoria to enter his Tote establishment, then the Blanky Turk will have Buckley's chance of shifting Wren, even with the assistance of the German Jack Johnsons.[20]

The muse of *Table Talk*[21] was stirred by Wren's enrolment 'as a private':

When young and old and rich and poor
Have crowded through the depot door
Enlisting,
We've seen a figure, here and there,
Of squatter or of millionaire,
A dot, within the barrack square
Enlisting.

No doubt there are some thousands more
Of millionaires who've longed for war
But hid it;
Yes, heaps of brave and wealthy men
To beard the German in his den
But here's the point about Jack Wren
He did it.

Though Wren to-day is just one man
Of thousands doing what he can;
Example.
Has got a value in this game
That hangs upon a well-known name
A sample.

Jack Wren to-day is just Jack Wren,
The same as any other men
Who hear him
Say quietly, "yes, I'll enlist,
Give me a rifle in my fist";
There comes a call we can't resist
To cheer him

We've given, judging by our talk,
Old Kaiser Bill a miss in baulk,
But, knowing
How hard a job we have to do
And what 'twill cost to see us through,
Wren had the bulge on me and you—
He's going.

John Wren after the closure of the Tote

John Wren in old age at the Stadium

ABOVE: John Wren, googly bowler (standing, third from left), with Collingwood Trades Cricket Club, 1902–3

OPPOSITE LEFT: Arthur Wren, John's younger brother, at the time of his conviction, 1889

OPPOSITE RIGHT: Arthur Wren as a philanthropic bootmaker

OPPOSITE: Studley House, John Wren's home, now part of Xavier Preparatory School

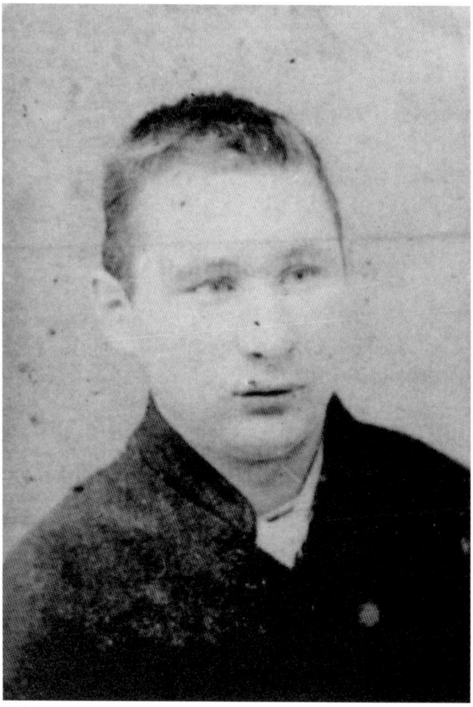

John Wren with Collingwood worthies

Ellen (Nellie) Wren with (left to right) Margaret and John (standing), Mary, baby Joseph and Anthony, and Elinor reading

ABOVE: Elinor Wren

OPPOSITE TOP: John Wren and daughter Margaret, c. 1907

OPPOSITE LEFT: John (left), Mary and Anthony Wren

OPPOSITE RIGHT: Margaret Wren

Jack Wren at the races [caricature by David Low]

OPPOSITE TOP: Mary Wren

OPPOSITE: Holidaying in Dublin (from left), Margaret and daughter Erika, Mary, a German friend and Ellen

SUPPRESSING HIM
(Mr. Bent is determined on taking action that will stop the Collingwood Tote.)
Mr. Bent (when he gets him). — 'Now I've got him there, I wonder if I can keep him?'
J. Wren. — 'Ten to one you don't.'

[Melbourne *Punch*, 16 August 1906]

AN APPALLING FUTURE

Young Australia (facing 1907 with its new lot of legislative 'Don'ts'). — 'Gosh!'

[*Bulletin*, 10 January 1907]

Frank Anstey MHR, socialist orator and Wren's cobber

[Melbourne *Punch*, 26 March 1925]

W. H. Judkins, the platform fighter against the evils of gambling

[Melbourne *Punch*, 28 June 1906]

'May I not enter,' said The Bird
'My steed as swift as a bee.'
'Not much!' said Fatso, 'the request's absurd
While I'm running the VRC.'

[*Truth*, 21 October 1905]

'He who shall hurt the little Wren
shall never be beloved by men' —
Auguries of Innocence,
Wm. Blake, 1789.

[Melbourne *Punch*, 19 October 1905]

LEFT: Albert Dunstan—torpid premier, 1935–45

[*Table Talk*, 13 September 1928]

RIGHT: Tom Tunnecliffe, as new minister for railways, forfeits his idealism

[*Table Talk*, 18 August 1927]

LEFT: Ted Theodore sings, 'Yes, we have no Munganas'

[*Bulletin*, 9 July 1930]

RIGHT: James Scullin, leader of the federal Labor Party, on high moral ground

[*Table Talk*, 17 May 1927]

Archbishop Daniel Mannix, 'a divil of a holy man'

[Melbourne *Punch*, 22 December 1920]

JOHN WREN, RECRUIT.

John Wren, enthusiastic recruit, does his duty

[*Bulletin*, 26 August 1915]

But *Truth*, as usual, provided the bite:

> the announcement that John Wren had enlisted … came with no hints or symptoms of martial fever … he did not preface the step … by issuing challenges to do likewise. …No doubt John Wren likes a little bit of advertisement as well as the next man, but when it came to doing his bit for his country, he made no fuss about it. … How different from the 'hold-me-back let-me-at-him' attitude of 'the blather-skite from Balaclava' … Willie Watt [former Victorian premier, future Australian acting prime minister, a non-volunteer but a notorious taunter of non-enlisters] … what a great thing … for the country if [Wren's] … example were followed by the horde of tommies, touts, tick-tackers, and take-downs that seek plunder on the various racing Wrendevous around Melbourne … It would then be up to the cold water crowd to get busy with Worry Worrall at their head, while Larry Rentoul [both leading parsons] would probably … raise a battalion of real merino wowsers.[22]

Wren joined the 22nd Battalion on 1 September; he remained until 4 November, when he was transferred to the 24th. On 6 September the *Herald* had Wren on the front page with a report of his first weeks in camp and pictures of him swinging a pick and standing with four comrades, but no reports in this or other papers have been found about Wren speaking out at recruiting rallies as Garden alleges. *Table Talk* on 9 September has a full-page group of seven photos of Wren at Royal Park. On the same day *Punch* published an excellent shot. *The Age* on 7 September reports 'ideal conditions' in the camp, although on the 6th it had reported that four soldiers had died from cerebro-spinal meningitis, which was present in the camps. The *Age* found that Wren had already been elected honorary secretary of the recreation committee, had donated £50 to the entertainment fund and arranged with 'the theatrical management for regular entertainment'. He was reported as saying that 'he was never more contented or happier in his life'.

All this, and probably something else, led *Truth* on 11 September to change its tune and attack the *Herald* and *Table Talk* for their 'sickening slobber' about Wren. This developed into a tirade, captioned 'playing at soldiers' on 25 September, because Wren was by then a corporal and had gained leave to see Garlin win the Chelmsford Stakes in Sydney while other recruits had difficulty getting permission to see their families. He had also 'advanced' £300 for musical instruments, to be paid for eventually by public subscription. Later he lectured the troops on fitness and the evils of booze and womanising. *Truth* expected Wren would soon be a colonel! But was it just publicity, for which it blamed Wren, that roused *Truth's* spleen?

> replicas of the photographs of him have also found place in … the Brisbane *Daily Mail*, the paper that Wren recently bought … and in connection with which he started off by having a writ of £25,000 banged into him … the *Mail* … had to print in the leading papers of Australia one of the MOST ABJECT APOLOGIES that has ever been seen in print … to get out of the action brought by the Brisbane *Courier* … though his money may bring the dilly dailies of Melbourne… there are some things he cannot boss.

Showing its malice, *Truth* went on to suggest Wren's enlistment might be a tax dodge. Politicians were discussing a Commonwealth income tax, never levied before, and soldiers would not pay tax. It seems far-fetched that Wren would risk his life to avoid a relatively small tax. But then *Truth* was also sure by this stage that Wren would never see a troopship.

No more was heard from *Truth* until its prophecy came true. Wren was hospitalised on 20 November, approved for discharge as medically unfit on the 24th and demobbed on 8 December. On 27 November, under the heading 'THE CORPORAL'S CHALLENGE', *Truth* wrote that 'Kaiser Bill and the successor of Abdul the Damned must have heaved tremendous sighs of relief … for has not the pony autocrat been photographed times without number?' Two days earlier the *Bulletin* had also been cynical:

> Please don't—this is no laughing matter. J. Wren went on a 26-mile route march the other day and now he has varicose veins or something, and won't be able to go to Gallipoli, so they say. Still Wren provided an excellent example—while it lasted.

In spite of such scepticism there is no reason to doubt Wren's medical condition. It was officially diagnosed as 'chronic suppurative otitis media'. Wren had been sent to hospital by Major Percy Webster, and declared unfit by him and the president of the Medical Board and three members.

Wren's 'Detailed Medical History of an Invalid', signed by Webster, says:

> Has had R. Chronic Otitis Medea for years. On 18/9/15 got cold and again got very bad 19/11/15. Is again very bad. Has now laryngitis and C. 20/11/15. Chronic Superlative Catarrh of R Middle Ear originating in childhood.

He became 'very deaf in the left ear' and was 'liable to recurrence of acute attacks'. This was not a problem that could be faked. Before antibiotics were devised, it provided very persuasive grounds for rejection, particularly in view of Wren's age. Older recruits did tend to become a burden unless completely fit, even though they were not incapacitated from 'earning a full livelihood in the general labour market'. His condition was 'not due to service'; he had had it chronically 'for years'.[23]

An article in the 1910 *Encyclopaedia Britannica* by E. C. Baver, a London ear, nose and throat specialist, clarifies Wren's condition as seen at the time. Professor Adam Polytzer's *A Textbook of the Diseases of the Ear* (1902) finds cold and moist air 'decidedly injurious'. While ear infection did not rival trench feet or scabies as a chronic soldiers' disease, it still warrants references in official medical records. A. G. Butler's *Official History of the Australian Army Medical Services* records that 'middle ear disease as a sequel to pharyngeal infections was a feature of the sick parade' and was reported as 'very prevalent' at No. 3 Australian General Hospital (Lemnos) in the Gallipoli area between September and October 1915. Wren would surely have been susceptible in that environment. A study of the last 2,000 cases of Australians 'boarded' for invalidity in England showed 'ear diseases' comprised 6.13 per cent (cf. shellshock, 9.38 per cent). Butler points out that disabilities which may on active service be a bar to soldiering do not prevent a man from being a productive wage earner. He also cites the 'Consulting Physician and the Consulting Surgeon AIF' reporting on 'the unfitness for front-line service of men over 44 years of age'. Such men became a burden on the war effort and, they say, should not have been recruited.[24]

And Wren was forty-four, although he had given his age as '43 years blank months', perhaps to seem further below the ceiling of forty-five. He was supposed to have been adequately checked on enlistment, but recruiting officers were not averse to ignoring uncertain conditions. One wonders in fact how his 'bandy leg' was ignored, in view of the route marching involved, but he had played sport competently and he did perform the drills and rifle exercises satisfactorily. However, Don Garden, who was so sure that Wren's was a studiously well-publicised enlistment, is also knowledgeable about his service experience: 'Wren did not find army life very hard as his main duties involved addressing recruiting rallies accompanied by a band for which he paid'.[25] Garden provides no source for this sneer.

The *Herald* on 6 September has Wren sleeping on straw palliasses, with stew for breakfast, a mug of water for lunch and bread and jam in the evening. A photo of Wren swinging a pick was obviously posed, but it is clear that he was engaged in routine duties. The evidence does not show Wren involved in a grandstanding stunt or taking a coward's exit. Rather, as a middle-aged married man with six children, his gesture appears quixotically patriotic—again, even flamboyant. He laid himself open to ridicule as well as disease. But the dailies did not knock him. The *Herald* on 23 November simply reported the situation; in the acting state commandant's words, 'He did his duty … his example, however, must have been an inspiration to the younger men of the community, especially to sportsmen'.

Wren also contributed to the welfare of the troops, providing some recreational amenities and giving £500 to a board of trustees to grant for interest-free loans to men who had suffered loss through enlistment. What no commentator seems to mention is the pecuniary loss to the hands-on entrepreneur himself as a result of three months in an environment not without serious medical risk.[26]

During the Second World War Wren apparently gave Sir Gilbert Dyett, president of the RSL, a cheque for £47,500 as a contribution to the public appeal to replace *HMAS Sydney*, sunk by a German war boat off the Western Australian coast. Dyett took the cheque to Canberra, but the appeal flopped. Wren's cheque ended up in consolidated revenue, a gift to the government. Labor leaders Curtin and Chifley, who disliked Wren's influence on Labor, would have enjoyed that. However, Wren does not seem to have complained about income tax. Paddy Kelly remembered that during the war, Wren 'must have been forking out about 18s 6d in the £', and that he rebuked a whinger by saying: ' "What are you moaning about. If the Japs take the country they will take everything you've got". Whatever we pay in tax is worth it for the protection we receive.'[27]

CHAPTER TWELVE

Murder Most Foul

The Grey Ghost

APART FROM ALLEGATIONS that he instigated the murder of 'Stacey' (Arthur Smythe; see Chapter 3), Hardy implicates 'John West' in four other capital crimes in *Power Without Glory*. Three of them are based on actual events, but the narrative is falsified. There is no reason to believe that John Wren was involved in any of them. On the contrary, evidence points the other way, even if one agrees with Hugh Buggy that:

> In the days of the Collingwood tote [Wren] would not have hesitated to take a swing at the jaw of a police informer. Nor would he have rebuked one of his employees if they had knocked over such a snooper who, in his day, had less status than a private eye who seeks divorce evidence. But it is a far cry from thumping a paid informer to hiring a killer and ordering murder.[1]

Hardy wove the notorious gunman Richard 'Dick' Buckley into his saga as 'Dick Bradley' knowing, as he surely must have, that Buckley was then still alive. In 1946, at the age of eighty-three, Buckley had been released from gaol on compassionate grounds. Known in the underworld as the 'Grey Ghost', he was shuffling around Port Melbourne and would have been a rich subject for the pub scuttlebutt of informants like Cornelius 'Con' Loughnan on whom Hardy relied. Hardy makes no suggestion that he sought even to speak to Buckley. It may have taken more nerve than he could boast of. According to Buggy, Wren in his youth had some slight acquaintance with Buckley in Collingwood. In 1883, at the age of twenty, Buckley had been sentenced to four years gaol and three twelve-stroke whippings for a near-fatal bashing of which he was innocent. The mistake was officially acknowledged and he was released, but he became a 'soured and sullen misanthrope'.[2] He was to spend some fifty years in Pentridge.

'Dick Bradley' befriends 'Arthur West' in gaol, comforts the younger man when he has in his turn to bear the pain and ignominy of two floggings. 'Arthur's gratitude is almost canine and, on his own release, he tries to get 'John West' to spring 'Bradley' from prison. Subsequently 'Arthur' remains a staunch mate and expects 'John' to help 'Bradley' too.[3] It is quite possible that Buckley and Arthur Wren were on friendly terms in gaol. The indications in real life, however, are that after his release Arthur was well cured of crime—always excepting work on the Tote—and that he led a law-abiding life until his death in 1935.

Hardy also links Wren with Melbourne's squalid petty gangster Squizzy Taylor ('Snoopy Tanner'), although Wren on several occasions had him barred from his racecourses and from his stadium when Squizzy tried to rig fights. Hardy, however, has to be melodramatic, exaggerating Squizzy's scope:

> Tanner's word was law in the Melbourne underworld and no wonder. He had risen to a position of great power with John West's secret protection. He ... by dint of cunning, daring and treachery ... controlled Melbourne's biggest two-up schools [an honour belonging to Henry Stokes], [and] had under his sway a large gang of shop-breakers, pickpockets and murderers.[4]

In his biography of Squizzy Taylor, Hugh Anderson spikes this notoriety and finds no association with Wren whatever. The only mention of Wren in his book is an episode when Taylor brags that he could get a corrupted gaol warder a job on a Wren racecourse.[5] Quite fantastic is the claim that, with Taylor, Wren contemplated running bootleg liquor to the United States during Prohibition in the 1920s, in spite of the risks involved through distance and, at landfall, from the surveillance of American coastguards.[6] In relation to ballot rigging, Buggy, a basically truthful man if biassed toward Wren, consulted some reformed associates of Squizzy, who denied involvement:

> They declared that neither Taylor nor those who tagged along with him possessed the political 'know how' or the finesse to involve themselves in subterranean election manipulation. To visit the home of a crown witness at night and advise him to break down his testimony was one thing. To overawe a juryman was a less complex transaction [than manipulating elections].[7]

Trades Hall break-in

Hardy alleges that 'West', in his quest for control of the Labor Party, organised the notorious attempted robbery of the Trades Hall on the fringe of Melbourne's city centre on 1 October 1915. He was supposed to want the account books and the ballot box from a recent election in a (significantly) unnamed union. In *Power Without Glory* the executants are 'Dick Bradley' (Buckley), 'Sam Ward' (Alexander Ward) and 'Piggy Wood' (John Jackson). In one getaway car outside are 'Snoopy Tanner' and 'Arthur West'; in another, 'John West' and 'Ron Lassiter' (Richard Loughnan) of the Builders' Labourers' Union. The crime goes awry, police intervene from their nearby headquarters, a constable is shot dead, and 'Bradley' and 'Piggy' are wounded. Although the conspirators believe 'Bradley' fired the fatal shot, they determine that 'Piggy' should take the rap. Assured that the jury will be 'squared', 'Piggy' admits shooting the constable in self-defence, but he is 'betrayed' and hanged. 'Bradley' and 'Ward' are tried twice for murder before being convicted on a lesser charge, and are given six and five years gaol respectively, because three jurymen 'had received substantial payments'. The 'West' brothers, 'Lassiter' and 'Tanner' escape altogether.

Hardy's version is 'farcical', says Buggy, and this is confirmed by Hugh Anderson. Wren on 1 October 1915 was in Royal Park military barracks. Hardy is careful to avoid giving a date for Wren's military service. Quotations from contemporary newspapers, with dates suppressed, show that he knew that Wren was in camp from August to November. Slyly, he changes the period of enlistment from 'August' to 'Autumn',[8] a neat deceptive assonance. As for Jackson, he had no choice but to admit killing Constable McGrath because the bullets in the policeman's body came from his automatic pistol. McGrath was not shot by Buckley, as Hardy asserts; he had 'fired six shots from a heavy Webley revolver', a different gun.[9] No record of appeal against Jackson's sentence seems to exist. It is absurd to say under those circumstances that he allowed himself to be 'betrayed' in a diabolical conspiracy. Jackson had been a master cracksman who had never before been convicted, although he had almost certainly broken into the Trades Hall the previous year. He had nothing to do, porcinely or otherwise, with the 'Piggy Wood' caricature in the early section of *Power Without Glory*, and had never been a henchman at the Tote.

'Apart from the novel', says Anderson, 'nothing is known that connects the Wrens, Loughnan or Taylor' with the crime.[10] Buggy says Taylor 'was never questioned by detectives ... because they knew where [he] spent that night and it was remote from ... the Trades Hall'.[11] Buggy later saw the police list of the contents of the Trades Hall safe; it had contained no ballot box or ballot papers—and only £21 in cash.[12] It is noteworthy that Frank Hardy's daughter, Shirley Hardy-Rix, married to a police officer, has published an historical account of the Trades Hall raid. There is no suggestion of any involvement by John or Arthur Wren. Presumably she accepted that the *Power Without Glory* account was untrue.[13] So, belatedly, did Hardy.

The assassination of Barney Reynolds

Barney Reynolds ('Barney Robinson' in *Power Without Glory*), 'one of the best known sports in Australia', had been one of Wren's right-hand men, publicity officer and manager of the Melbourne Athletic Pavilion (formerly the Cyclorama). He wrote florid advertising copy for Wren's boxing matches. At Wren's behest he had taken Newcastle heavyweight Bill Squires to the United States in 1907 to contest the world championship. However, 'Barney Robinson' in *Power Without Glory* has a good heart and eventually falls out with 'John West', whom he accuses of being 'an accessory before the fact' in the tragic death in the United States of the great boxer and folk hero, 'Lou Darby' (Les Darcy). 'Barney' leaves 'West's employment and has to eke out a bare livelihood writing for a Melbourne sports journal, the *Hawklet*, which actually existed at that time. However, in 1919 'Barney' receives a summons from 'West'. There is a task for him in Perth, involving an all-expenses trip (with wife) and the promise of his old job back. 'West' has had 'a trunk line telephone call from his manager in Perth' (although there was no such linkage until 1930): the Western Australian government is going to wipe out proprietary racing. 'West' owns two racecourses there and he believes the projected Bill to be 'an attempt by his rivals ... to drive him out. They were a well-organized gang and worked on similar lines to himself. The trip ... was a dangerous, delicate job.' 'Barney' is given £5,000 for 'influence and money' and told to carry a gun, because 'we are up against a tough mob'.

Even at this point Hardy is unconvincing, because the 'tough mob' seems to be only the Western Australian government. However, no sooner have 'Barney' and his wife landed at Perth wharf and are looking for a taxi than 'Barney' is gunned down by an unknown assassin. His dying words to 'Florrie', his wife, are to take the £5,000, go into hiding and do not go near 'West' again. Hardy relates that the Melbourne newspapers reported the murder of someone called Jackson on the wharf. Police are stymied because they believe that the victim travelled under an assumed name and the female companion had disappeared. So the murderers are not caught. As for 'West', he decides to leave the 'tough mob' alone and, in any case, he 'sold one of his racecourses and leased the other on most favourable terms'. 'Florrie' can keep the £5,000 because this way she will be quiet. 'West' cooks up a story that 'Barney' had a bad heart and died suddenly in South Australia. With consummate hypocrisy he laments Barney's death: 'Fine fella, Barney, a real wit and a great personality'.[14]

All this is a Hardy concoction, or perhaps based on a yarn told to him by his pub informants. In fact, Barney Reynolds died on 17 March 1916—that is, seven months *before* Les Darcy fled to the United States. Reynolds had been working for Wren in Brisbane supervising his racing interests. According to the *Referee*, the popular boxing journal, he had been 'in indifferent health for some years but his end came suddenly, being due to a paralytic stroke'. He was on 'one of his periodical visits to Melbourne' at the time. A caption called him 'the Keenest of Keen Judges and the Prince of Good Fellows'. He was 'generous to a fault ... Peace be to his ashes', said the *Referee*. Reynolds died at Mt St Evins, the private wing of St Vincent's hospital, of which Wren was a patron.[15]

The Glenferrie murder

Another 'diabolical plan' conceived by 'Arthur West', alone this time, leads to the hanging of another accomplice rather than the culprit,

'Bradley'. This story is based on the much-publicised robbery and murder of a Glenferrie bank manager in 1923. Hardy dates the event to the Victorian police strike of 8 November—'The time was ripe to take risks!'—instead of its actual occurrence on 2 October. On that day, according to Hardy, the bank manager, following his normal weekly routine, approaches the railway station carrying about $2,000 worth of surplus and grimy notes en route to the city. He is shot by 'Bradley', whose accomplice 'Martin' [Angas Murray], allegedly 'a young newcomer to Snoopy's gang', grabs the money bag. The getaway car is driven by 'Snoopy', with 'Arthur West' in the other front seat. Implausibly, 'Arthur' is dropped in the city (which was not on the direct route home), after which 'Snoopy' takes the two criminals to hide in his house in St Kilda. The bank manager dies not immediately but after contracting blood poisoning and identifying 'Bradley' as the killer.

But 'Arthur' deliberates that if 'Martin' is caught first and hanged, 'the public conscience will be placated' and then, even if eventually arrested, 'Bradley' will escape the death penalty. 'Snoopy' is only too willing to save himself. So he separates 'Bradley' and 'Martin' and rings a friendly detective to pick up both himself and 'Martin' and then release only himself, 'to allay suspicion'. This goes according to plan, except that the leader of a rival gang visits 'Martin' in the death cell and wises him up to the betrayal. This can be fatal to 'Snoopy's gang and his protector, 'West'. So 'Snoopy' conceives another plan: he will pretend to spring 'Martin' from gaol but arrange to have him shot while trying to escape. 'Martin' discovers this and asks to be locked up for his own protection. How to unravel all this outstrips Hardy's imagination. He contrives a *deus ex machina* in the form of the inevitable smoodging Catholic priest who sets 'Martin's mind and soul at rest'. Martin then 'calmly' waits for the hangman's noose and refrains from grassing his former comrades.[16]

In fact, bank manager Thomas Berriman had kept to his 11 am schedule on 8 October 1923, with £1,851 in notes in his leather case. He was shot by Richard Buckley while Angas Murray ('Martin'), a Geelong gaol escapee, ran off with the money. Berriman died on 21 October. Murray was arrested at Squizzy's house and charged with murder. Squizzy was at first charged with being an accessory, but won a *nolle prosequi* (not to proceed) because of insufficient evidence and an official desire, in the event of his acquittal, not to prejudice the case against

Murray. No proceedings were taken against Arthur Wren because he was never in the getaway car; Buggy claims 'irrefutable proof' of that.[17] Arthur had nothing whatever to do with Squizzy's crimes but, as he was dead when *Power Without Glory* was published, Hardy was able to defame him at will. Nor is there anything to suggest that John Wren was asked by Arthur to finance the defence of Murray and Buckley. Nor did Squizzy 'shelf' Murray, who was convicted of acting 'in concert' with the acknowledged killer, Buckley, and sentenced to be hanged as equally culpable. Squizzy did make two attempts to enforce Murray's escape from gaol, because he feared the prisoner would break down and implicate him. He also wanted to make it clear to the underworld that it was not he who had informed on Murray. His attempts ended in debacle.[18]

As Murray had never been involved in violence before, his plight excited the sympathy of many members of the public as well as those who were in principle against capital punishment. This was heightened when two jurors broke silence to declare that they had assumed, because Murray had not fired the fatal gun, that the death sentence would be commuted. Otherwise, they said, they would have insisted on a recommendation to mercy. Protest meetings were held, including one of 12,000 people at the Exhibition Building; a petition with 70,000 signatories was presented to the governor of Victoria. The future prime minister, Jim Scullin, moved at a Melbourne Town Hall meeting that 'Cabinet's determination [to hang] … Angus Murray … outrages the public sense of justice and seriously weakens that respect for law on which society is founded'. Anderson says, that during a protest march in Melbourne, 'Squizzy appeared on the outskirts of the crowd in his motor car, and like a potentate, returned the salute of numerous hands raised to caps as the protestors walked past'.[19]

The conservative Lawson government was unmoved. As for Murray's being silenced and reconciled to his fate by Hardy's fictionally ubiquitous Catholic priest, Buggy was told by the governor of the gaol that Murray spent his last hours with Rev. E. H. Davis, the official Anglican chaplain. Squizzy was the only person to visit Murray in his last weeks. Buggy was among the reporters gathered below the gallows:

> We were all prepared to take a note of the condemned man's statement naming Taylor as the planner of the Glenferrie hold-up. But Murray made no dying revelations. He merely said that never

> in his life had he done anything to justify the extreme penalty being passed upon him. He left it at that and Squizzy Taylor breathed again.[20]

From outside the gaol the strains of 'Nearer My God to Thee' drifted into the death chamber.[21] Meanwhile, Dick Buckley had evaded capture and, until 1930, hid successfully in suburbs mainly around Moonee Ponds.

Squizzy's shootout

Squizzy Taylor's life ended on 27 October 1927 in a shootout with another criminal, John Daniel 'Snowy' Cutmore, in the latter's bedroom in Carlton. The immediate enmity between them arose from Cutmore's violence against a woman running sly-grog, who was under Squizzy's protection. Squizzy, accompanied by another man, burst in on Cutmore while he was laid up with a heavy cold—possibly only to remonstrate with him, but Cutmore had a gun under his pillow and a crossfire began. Cutmore died immediately; his mother, who was in the house, was clipped in the shoulder; and Squizzy was fatally wounded. The third man disappeared and was never identified. Melbourne *Truth* maintained that eighteen bullets were fired, but only fifteen could have been discharged by the revolvers of Cutmore and Squizzy. There were various theories as to what happened, even old Mrs Cutmore being thought by a few to have shot Squizzy in defence of her son. Buggy could 'recall at least six versions of this bedroom fusillade'.[22] It was an opportunity for Hardy to provide another.

According to *Power Without Glory*, 'Snoopy Tanner' (Squizzy Taylor) becomes murderous when he is warned off 'West's racecourses. In a drunken fury he bursts into 'West's office and threatens to kill him if the ban is not lifted. 'West' gets very edgy; comically so. At home he shifts his chair away from windows; in bed he worries that 'Snoopy' might be up a pine tree, 'peering ... in the darkness'. He decides to take 'Arthur's advice: 'Tanner must be killed and buried with all proof that he had ever worked for John West'. So he hires a gun from Sydney, the mysterious third man, who accompanies 'Snoopy' to 'Slasher Cutting's (Cutmore's) house but, under orders, shoots Snoopy instead and absconds.[23] Hardy, however, fails even to make it fictionally credible that a tycoon with the material power and political clout he attributes to 'West' would need to stoop to such risky measures to immobilise a petty gangster. Anderson concludes:

> Only one thing has remained constant over the years: that more people than the official version allows were involved in the killing, and that these shadowy central characters and the police were both content to let the shooting of Cutmore and Taylor stand as a simple gun duel between opposing criminals. It was, in effect, a declared 'open season' and no questions asked.[24]

Before he died, and no doubt sucking sagaciously on his pipe, Hardy could say that perhaps Wren was not involved in 'Squizzy's demise. No new evidence would have provoked this belated rumination. It was just a feckless Hardy afterthought without regard for contradictions. A legend, however, had been created.

Buckley's last hope

Hardy could not resist linking concealment of Dick Buckley during the 1920s to the Wrens. In *Power Without Glory* 'Arthur West' keeps in constant contact with him ('nearly every night') and badgers 'John' for money for Buckley's upkeep. 'Arthur' also has over-curious and potentially treacherous old lags bashed and silenced. In view of the relentless pursuit of Buckley by the police, this is quite improbable. If what Hardy said of the 'Bradley–West' relationship was true, Arthur Wren would have been under close surveillance. Moreover, if the police had known of any improper Wren involvement, it would have been an easy matter to drop Wren's name to some part of what was a diverse press. Whatever corruption can be imputed to the police, a number of them would not have had fond memories of Wren, and there were sectarian and political reasons for discrediting him.

Buckley was eventually captured in a raid by detectives which was carefully planned by the future field marshal Thomas Blamey, then commissioner of police (although in *Power Without Glory* he is supposed to have been appointed with West's approval). A squad with sledgehammers simultaneously broke down the front door and side gate of a house in Moonee Ponds where a semi-recluse named 'Mr Konsul' lived. According to Anderson, they acted on a tip from the baccarat and two-up 'king' Henry Stokes, who had become 'tired of financing the fugitive'.[25] The *Argus* reported that Buckley was 'tended only by his granddaughter'.[26] *Truth* said he had been 'guarded by loyal friends'. Buckley was alleged to have enjoyed parties that lasted till dawn. Memoranda were found in the house with names of jockeys and bookmakers opposite financial contributions. The Wrens were not mentioned. However, *Truth* did say:

> For some time one of Buckley's benefactors was a citizen of Melbourne whose philanthropic turn of mind led him to befriend criminals in the belief that by kindness he might lead them back to the straight and narrow path. He had the reputation of being absolutely staunch to those he took under his wing, and was known to be averse to giving assistance to the police …

Truth also claimed that early in Buckley's time on the run he had formed a relationship with the daughter of a respectable businessman; but, it would seem, not the same person as the above benefactor:

> This woman was young and beautiful and, remarkable to relate, was not of the underworld herself. Rather, she came of a very good family, her father being … quite well known in commercial circles in Melbourne, and she lived at home.[27]

Had Wren been mooted here, the clues would surely have been clearer.

Hardy may have picked up some inkling of all this; but, if he did, he used only the part concerning Buckley's granddaughter. It must be remembered that *Truth* retailed sensational stories, and this one is romantic and vague. There may have been nothing to it. If Wren was in mind, some hint of his gambling, sporting and political interests would surely have been made. This would have been particularly noted when the Hogan Labor government commuted Buckley's death sentence to life imprisonment—although Angas Murray, who had not himself fired a shot, had been hanged seven years earlier for the killing of Berriman. However, capital punishment was against Labor ideology and, at sixty-seven, a man who qualified for the pension was thought a little old for it.[28] There was no need for any Wren influence.

Buckley was finally released by the Cain Labor government on 20 December 1946, the last day of the parliamentary session for that year, no doubt so that any awkward question would be deferred until at least 22 April 1947 when parliament would meet again. There had been many requests for Buckley to be freed, and the Dunstan governments, allegedly under Wren's control, had reviewed the case 'at times' but were said to be determined that Buckley would die in gaol.[29] And premier Cain was hostile to Wren's influence with some members of parliament. This places a query over Buggy's claim that Buckley's release followed an approach from a 'woman relative' who asked Wren to use his influence on humanitarian grounds.[30] Normally, Buggy would have had some warrant for his statement, but press reports at the time give no suggestion of any influence by Wren. The *Age* reported:

> In the last stages of the disease of dropsy, Buckley's health has failed so markedly during the last few weeks that his release was sanctioned on the grounds of mercy, following repeated requests by his relatives that he be allowed to die 'out of gaol and with his family'.[31]

The inspector-general of prisons, Joseph Akenroyd, notable for his reforms in Victoria's penal system,[32] stressed that action was taken 'less out of consideration for Buckley than for his close relatives, who throughout the years of his sentence had displayed extraordinary solicitude'.[33]

Oddly, a search of the Victorian Executive Council minutes for July–December 1946 has yielded nothing relating to Buckley's release,[34] nor do the indexes to the Victorian premier's departmental register of inward and outward correspondence for the years 1940–6[35] have any specific references to either Buckley or Wren. (It is possible they have been made elsewhere—for example, the chief secretary's or other departmental correspondence—but limited resources have made an exhaustive search impractical.) However, if Wren did make some approach for Buckley's release, it might have been informally through his Labor Party network, rather than through the bureaucracy. Hardy simply has 'Frank Lammence' (Lawrence) threaten a reluctant 'Carr' (Cain) that 'if you don't release 'Bradley' (Buckley) and leave 'West's galloping meetings alone he ['West'] will bring your Government down if it costs a million'. The late Arthur 'West' (Wren) had made 'a death bed request for Bradley's release' and, scoundrel though he might be, 'West' obviously retained loyal family feelings, though Hardy does not make a fine point of it. Premier 'Carr' is supposed to have found this irresistible.

Dropsy did not claim Buckley as expected. He saw seven Christmases after his release, dying at ninety of tuberculosis in September 1953, a few weeks before Wren himself. But Buckley was no longer a headline item, rating only page seven in the *Sun*.[36] *Truth* was more respectful, featuring him on page three, and it revived its cryptic reference to Buckley's benefactor: 'Some said a wealthy businessman who had underworld connections had ordered that he should want for nothing. It was believed that this was payment for a past service of Buckley's.'[37]

By that time *Power Without Glory*, with its clear references to 'Bradley'/Buckley, had been published, but *Truth* did not point the finger at Wren, then or later. Nor had the intrepid Hardy tried to interview Buckley, who was very visible in Port Melbourne while he was writing the book—or with callow relish he would have bragged, as he liked to do, about putting his own life in danger, and about his connections in the criminal world.

Thirty-two years after the *Power Without Glory* trial, Hardy allegedly 'broke … silence to tell of a plot to kill him'. The contract had been let out to Freddie Harrison, a notorious Melbourne gunman. But whoever the instigator was—and who could it have been other than the man on Studley Hill?—he had reckoned without the virile seamen and dockers who had been 'running guard' on Frank Hardy's young family. Two of their 'chiefs' called in 'Hughie' (no surname supplied), who 'had been King of Pentridge … while serving twenty years and a flogging for shooting a policeman in the Coles Book Arcade robbery'. Romantically, he'd been in the Irish Republican Army and was called 'the best shot in the world'; Hardy deserving no less a protector. So Hughie told Freddie: 'If anything happens to Frank … if he suffers a heart attack or falls off a Bourke Street bus, you'll be dead in 24 hours'. Seven years later, 'Harrison's face was blown off' (*Sunday Press*, 11 December 1983). This was a typically puerile Hardy fantasy.

CHAPTER THIRTEEN

The Good Friend of Democracy

Higher status

WREN SUPPORTED AUSTRALIAN participation in the First World War enthusiastically. There is no need to see his joining the army in mid-1915 as just a stunt, nor to see only insincerity and self-promotion when, for example, he chaired the organising committee for a gymkhana 'to raise funds for a seaside home for slum children', even if the main event was the John Wren Cup for draught horses. Similarly, there is no need to see Wren's involvement in the Irish cause between 1916 and 1923 as the cynical pose of 'a church benefactor' angling to 'exact some indebtedness from Catholic Labour men'. Chris McConville may see too much craftiness in Wren's more frequent appearances at Catholic functions at this time, whereas 'Before 1917 … [he] rarely appeared … alongside wealthy Catholic barristers, surgeons and real estate agents as a patron to parochial societies'. [1]

By 1917 Wren, an extraordinarily busy man, had acquired greater standing and respectability. He was becoming principal patron of the Collingwood Football Club and had been appointed a governor of St Vincent's Hospital. Perhaps the professional men and reputable dealers were more willing to be seen with Wren by then. But was his patronage at Catholic functions so rare before 1917? Like most Irish-Australians he was genuinely stirred by the woes and justifiable expectations of Ireland at that time. The failure of the British government to implement

Home Rule in 1914 because of Ulster intransigence, even though due constitutional process had been observed, had added a fresh layer of indignation to the cause. Wren told Buggy quite credibly that when the Irish MPs Joe Devlin and John Donovan visited Melbourne in 1906, he had attended all their meetings. In 1911 he donated £50 to the Irish Envoys' Fund. Similarly, when William Redmond, brother of John, the leader of the Irish parliamentary party, visited in 1913, Wren contributed generously to their fund-raising.[2]

And from 1913 there was the phenomenon of Archbishop Daniel Mannix. Manifestly a scholarly and saintly leader, allegedly a world eminence,[3] Mannix infatuated Wren as he did even many Catholic sophisticates. Wren—and hangers-on like Sugar Roberts, men without education—were flattered to be of service. We would need to know much more about Wren's benefactions to the church, and how unpublicised they were, to be sure that they were somehow dramatically increased because he perceived political opportunity in the furore over the Easter Rising in 1916 and its aftermath. Bishop Patrick Phelan's public acknowledgment of Wren in September 1916 as 'a personal friend' and prime donor suggests a sequence of past benefactions, not just a splurge of untoward generosity.[4]

Wren would have been exhilarated by the triumphalism of Mannix's rise to fame, not just national but international, once prime minister Hughes chose—as he did after his narrow conscription defeat in October 1916—to exploit sectarian antipathies and elevate Mannix to the status of his major public enemy. Somehow Wren succeeded in reconciling his support for conscription with his allegiance to Mannix on issues Irish. Editorials in his *Daily Mail*, unequivocally pro-conscription, do not appear to have affected his relationships with Queensland's Labor (and Irish) premier Tom Ryan, or treasurer E. G. Theodore, whose state government was the only one in Australia to be anti. Wren was hardly going to join those middle-class 'loyal' Catholics like Benjamin Hoare and T. C. Brennan in Melbourne, or Judge C. A. Heydon and Sir Thomas Hughes in Sydney, or former Catholics like the Maddens,[5] whom Mannix flailed so contemptuously and among many of whom Wren was socially unacceptable. Nor was he going to shrink from the limelight or pass over the opportunity to justify himself, perhaps wipe away some of the past sleaze. It was understandable that he would want to enhance his own status and influence by putting resources at the service of his tribe and its imperious prelate. But he did it without compromising his own belief about the war.

Sinn Fein

The Young Ireland Society applied in October 1917 for the use of the Exhibition Building for a rally. Predictably the Loyal Orange Institution and the Protestant Alliance Friendly Society opposed it. Their representatives, led by some of the usual bigots, Drs Rentoul and Leeper and Oswald Snowball MHA,[6] waited on the premier, Sir Alexander Peacock, to express their alleged 'fears that the peace would be disturbed'. Peacock asked them for a list of the resolutions that would be moved at the rally. They could not produce any. However, Mannix would be present and that was a sufficient reason for the rally to be forbidden. They then confronted the Exhibition trustees (who included Bob Solly). The trustees capitulated, so that Mannix the following Sunday said they were either pro-Orange or had 'just as much backbone as a stick of boiled asparagus'. It was 'very peculiar', he said, that from the time the meeting was talked of, the *Argus* had received every morning a cablegram about 'those awful Sinn Feiners'. In fact, special cables always seemed to arrive when they were wanted. For example, when conscription was being promoted, 'the paper was told of smashing defeats at the front', but a week later 'perhaps they forgot all they had said, the great offensive was pushing on to Berlin, and there were scarcely any casualties unless among the enemy, who had suffered frightful slaughter'.[7] With such populist sarcasm, it was no wonder that there was a throng (Catholic estimate over 100,000; Protestant over 30,000) at Wren's Richmond racecourse next evening (Cup Eve) to hear the archbishop.

Wren had been reluctant at first to lend his arena without being assured that speeches would be confined to the Irish question. A deputation representing the Young Ireland Society, the Catholic Federation, St Patrick's Society, the Hibernian-Australian Catholic Benefit Society, the Irish National Foresters, Catholic Young Men's Society, Catholic Workers' Association, Shamrock Club and the Gaelic League waited on Wren. With an eye no doubt on the War Precautions Act and the security police, but in terms quite consistent with his own known beliefs and in a tone utterly different from that of Mannix, Wren admonished the deputation for putting him in 'an unenviable position'. He would not, he said, allow a meeting which would 'create dissension'. This was a time 'when every sensible person in the community must realise the desperate position in which Great Britain and her Allies are placed'. Then, in what could almost be a tilt at Mannix, he went on:

> Unfortunately, in Australia a great bulk of the people have, ever since the War started, taken it for granted that the Allies must win. ... We in Australia are up to our necks in the fight, and I ask you to picture the position Australia will be in if Great Britain and her allies go down ... This is no time for quarrelling amongst ourselves ... all differences, political and religious, should be dropped. I cannot understand the bitterness that apparently exists between his Grace, Archbishop Mannix, and our Prime Minister. They are both staunch Home Rulers. [Mannix's conversion to republicanism for Ireland was not clear at this stage.] I remember a few years ago Mr Hughes, in the Exhibition Building, being cheered to the echo by the largest Irish meeting ever held in this State for his great speech on behalf of Ireland. It is a great pity Dr Mannix, Mr Hughes and Mr Tudor [Labor leader of the Opposition] cannot get together ... our men at the front need every possible assistance we can give them.

One member of the deputation then pointed out that the settlement of the question would be beneficial 'to the Empire and to the Dominions ... Their aims were neither revolutionary nor republican'. Another said recruiting would increase if the issue were settled and Sinn Fein was not 'in any way connected with our utterances'. He then asked, 'Why should they fight for liberty abroad when they could not get liberty here', to which the former notorious law-breaker replied: 'Liberty can be misused just now. The liberty of our country is at stake, and we must all conform to the regulations.'

D. G. Carter, president of Young Ireland Society, stressed that he was a Protestant, with his only son and eighteen blood relations at the front. Of course he would not want to act against his country. A certain Mr Ryan said they were resolved that Ireland should, like Australia and Canada, have a voice at the peace conference; half a million Irish had fought for the empire. Wren concluded:

> After considering your request, and noting the modified tone of your resolutions, I have decided to grant you permission to hold the

> meeting on the Richmond racecourse. … Whatever differences existed before the war have been wiped out by the blood of gallant Irishmen … Mr Lloyd George and all the members of the British Government are anxious for a happy solution … and no one … would welcome it more heartily than our own Prime Minister. Mr Hughes is a lifelong Home Ruler. … I think that in the interest of recruiting … it would be unwise of me to refuse permission to use the racecourse … You have assured me no sectarian issue will be raised … this is no time for dissension … I feel certain that nothing will be said at the meeting that will affect the feeling of any section of the community and I also feel that no disloyal sentiment will be uttered … The merits of Home Rule, surely, can be discussed with calmness … Your assurance that nothing will be said to offend anybody, though unnecessary, is, however, gratifying to me.[8]

Nothing, however, was going to stop the implacable Mannix from giving offence, and Wren may well have realised it. Still, at least he could claim to have uttered the appropriate cautions. As it turned out, Mannix did not fail his more ardent supporters, revelling in provocative semantics:

> You here in Australia are Sinn Feiners, though you do not call yourselves by that name (Applause). With you here in Australia, with all good Australians I mean, it is Australia first and Empire second, if there is a conflict of interests (Applause). I know right well that a great many people will say this is sedition, and that in making this assertion I am absolutely disloyal. I am very glad indeed that my type of loyalty is different from theirs (Applause). I am very glad that my loyalty to the Empire, *such as it is,* does not prevent me from being loyal in the first place to Australia, my adopted country, and to Ireland, the land of my birth (Prolonged applause) [emphasis added]. [9]

Wren's position on the war and the gravity of its outcome for Australia—something Mannix seemed unaware of—was quite different from his intemperate archbishop's. The latter's concern was not just his standing in Australia but the need to repair his reputation in his native land, which had rejected him in 1912–13. Mannix had relished the sectarianism so rife pre-war; he had aggravated it and 'together with the Orange bigots, bellicose parsons and conspicuous loyalists, had polarised much of the Australian community. Wren would never have supported the sort of statements Mannix made in America in 1920—for example, that the Irish flag was the only one he recognised, or that Britain had been, was and would always be America's enemy. Wren would eventually share the exasperation that Bishop Phelan and most other Australian Catholic clergy felt when Mannix supported the Irish Republican leader, Eamonn de Valera, against those who accepted the Anglo-Irish settlement of 1921. Mannix was the only bishop in Ireland or Australia to do so at that time. 'Reasoned argument is lost on Mannix on the Irish question', said Phelan.[10]

However, to a feisty Irish-Australian Catholic and Laborite in such a political climate, Mannix was irresistible. In 1917 Mannix was a hero of the working classes; no one had more influence with them, claimed the governor-general. It was equally important for his critics to diabolise him. Linking him in disloyalty with a former notorious law-breaker and reputed Tammany boss was effective propaganda. Herbert Brookes was not alone in thinking that Mannix and his henchmen (including, of course, the Jesuits) wanted the elite of younger Protestants to be slaughtered on the Somme, leaving their women to be proselytised and impregnated by stay-at-home anti-imperial Catholics. That Catholics volunteered in almost equal proportions for overseas service mattered little to Brookes and others (or that Sydney's Archbishop Michael Kelly and Wren had favoured conscription). So Brookes plotted his own kind of reactionary perfidy—secret armies—concealed beneath muck-raking anti-Catholic publicity in journals such as the *Vigilant*.[11]

Wren's prestige both locally and with the Labor movement grew after the war, independently of his association with Mannix. So did his patronage. On 24 July 1919 he staged a peace banquet in the Collingwood Town Hall. The *Labor Call* reported it:

> With characteristic thoughtfulness and undoubted hospitality, the one and only John Wren last Thursday entertained the citizens of Collingwood ... It was none of your Gaud Night Mayor or Government 'Ouse shivoos—all swank, swagger, swollen chests and snobbishness. It was a real people's festival of 2000 odd men, women and children. The sight was splendid. Nothing was spared;

> everybody was satisfied. It was necessary to relay the tables and extend the accommodation in order to provide for the guests, who were present by open invitation. Greville Ltd. catered with proficiency and General John Wren supervised the arrangements which, with the aid of an enthusiastic staff, consisting of Fr McGinnis, Frank Lawrence and Co, had been well thought out, and were smoothly carried out.
>
> Appropriate speeches were delivered by Cr Kiernan MLC, Frank Tudor MP,[12] and Martin Hannah MLA, while the host himself addressed all present in the different parts of the building. Following the dinner a grand musical programme was performed by leading artists ... while Mrs E. L. Kiernan capably presided at the piano. John Wren is to be cordially congratulated upon his happy thought, and he and his fellow helpers-citizens and citizenesses—upon its thoroughly successful realisation.[13]

The *Advocate* said 4,000 were 'entertained'. The 'guests were the people of Collingwood, whose breadwinners were out of work owing to the present industrial crisis'. A fund organised by Wren raised £3,000.[14]

In September, Wren announced that 'he was disposing of his business interests and going to settle in Argentina'. Whether he was serious or whether it was some quixotic way of testing his status is unknown. According to the *Advocate*, an overflowing gathering of Collingwood citizens entertained him in the Town Hall and presented him 'with an enlarged flashlight picture of a notable assembly in which he was the moving spirit—the Peace display and entertainment to the residents of the municipality with which his name has been so much associated'.[15] Several MPs paid tribute to him, notably W. J. Beckett MLC[16] (Hardy's 'Bennett'), who described Wren as 'a white man and a true man in every sense of the word' and a generous benefactor. It was here, Wren said, that 'a person of means had a duty to spend his money for the benefit of his fellow-men'.[17]

No more seems to have been heard of the proposed exodus to Argentina, for Wren was soon caught up in preparations for the Australasian Irish Race Convention, which Mannix proposed should be held in Melbourne Cup week, on 3 November. The aim was to press Ireland's claim to self-determination and to support the leadership of de Valera who, with other Sinn Fein candidates, had recently been elected to Westminster but had formed their own parliament (Dail Eireann). The Melbourne convention of 2000 delegates was chaired by the Queensland premier Tom Ryan, who at the invitation of the federal Labor conference in October was to transfer to the safe federal seat of West Sydney—ironically Billy Hughes's seat until 1917, when he had deserted the Labor Party. Although Dennis Murphy, Ryan's biographer, writes that 'despite frequent visits to Melbourne, Ryan does not seem to have evinced any great desire for a close friendship with the Archbishop', Mannix cast himself as king-maker, calling Ryan 'the prospective prime minister of the Commonwealth'.[18] The *Argus* reported Mannix calling Ryan 'the one honest man in the whole political field ... An honourable and honest man ... who may help to save Australia from the economic domination [Great Britain's?] that embitters life and stays her true progress'.[19]

Before Ryan could contest the seat, arrangements had to be made for Cornelius Wallace, the sitting Labor member, to resign. He had doubled his opponent's vote in 1917.[20] Murphy asks:

> What quaint persuasion was used on Wallace remains a mystery—the good of the party, a name in history or an alternative winnable seat? Wallace subsequently accepted nomination for the seat of Nepean, held by Labor during the 1910–13 Government [but not subsequently in 1914 and 1917]. He was to lose Nepean and was then given a position in the Harbours and Marine Department in Queensland.[21]

It is not implausible that an extra sweetener was offered to Wallace to move aside for Ryan, and that Wren paid it. The problem is that there is no evidence. It should also then be easy to believe that some consideration was offered to local aspirants in, say, Bendigo in 1917 to create a haven for 'Billy' Hughes when working-class West Sydney became untenable.[22] But again, no evidence. Still, in such matters Hughes would hardly be more moral than Ryan. And how often has some similar political trade-off or reward been fixed? The important issue seems to be the way such things are done; best not to frighten parsons (and priests) and pharisaical commentators.

Homage to St Patrick

The St Patrick's Day procession in 1918 saw Mannix at his most provocative. Amid Sinn Fein banners and slogans, a float celebrating the 'martyrs' of the Easter Rising passed the official car containing Mannix, Bishop Daniel Foley of Ballarat (his cousin) and the Apostolic Delegate. Mannix reverently doffed his purple biretta. However, when a band stopped in front of the car to play the National Anthem, only two prelates 'took the salute'. His biretta sat fast on Mannix's head. Mannix was virtually censured in camera by his fellow bishops the following May for actions like this, but he was spared public humiliation. In any case his defiant actions were too demagogically productive, too cheering to his Catholic supporters and too inflammatory to his church's enemies, like Hughes and Brookes, to have him lose face among his flock or other working-class admirers.[23]

The Melbourne City Council refused permission for the 1919 procession. The organisers declined a confrontation and used the excuse of the then-current influenza pandemic to save face.[24] Presumably sometime towards New Year 1920, with the war over, Wren conceived, or was given the idea, of a surpassing procession demonstrating the authentic loyalty of Catholics to their archbishop and to Australia, rather than to an empire which was denying self-determination to Ireland. Wren was to show, on this above all other occasions, his flair for organisation, show-business even, while pandering to Mannix's love of participatory pageantry.

Wren was probably aware that Mannix, like the other Australian bishops, was planning his regulation *ad liminem* visit to make his official report to the Pope later in 1920. There was doubt as to how Mannix would be received in Rome. His blatant politicking had certainly displeased a previous Apostolic Delegate, Archbishop (later Cardinal) Cerretti, who had virtually ruled that the clergy should be neutral in the conscription controversy.[25] The British government was making adverse representations. On the other hand, Cerretti would have reported Mannix's popularity with the faithful. There were also rumours that Mannix could be translated to the see of Dublin where the incumbent, William Walsh, was then in his eightieth year. On 10 March at an 'Irish National Concert', Mannix said he knew nothing of this. Where once 'a section of the community sought to bring about his degradation … now apparently they were working for his promotion. He would come back when his business was done in the old world.'[26]

Finally, there was clear agitation in Australia by Brookes and his like that Mannix should not be allowed to return to Australia—not without taking some oath of loyalty at least—and prime minister Hughes was sympathetic to that idea. Mannix also intended to visit Ireland, to perform an act of filial piety: his nonogenarian mother was alive. If he did, with the dastardly Black and Tans loose on the Irish population, Mannix might even be assassinated. Wren wrote, or got someone to write under Mannix's name, some verses, 'Come Back to Australia', to the tune of the popular Irish song 'Come Back to Erin':

> Come back to Australia, our prince and great leader,
> Come back to Australia, the land you have blessed;
> Bring back the news that old Ireland has her freedom,
> Australia will clasp you with love to her breast.

An executive of former soldiers, the St Patrick's Day Celebration Committee, was formed. It exacted permission from the state commandant, brigadier-general C. H. Brand, for the participation of ex-servicemen. Permission was granted for a 3 inch piece of green ribbon to be attached to military tunics, but nothing else extraneous.[27] In accordance with RSL policy, the proceedings had to be non-sectarian. Mobilising names of soldiers eligible to march was most easily done after mass on two Sundays at parish churches. Including nurses, they tallied some 10,000. Wren's most dramatic idea was to invite some Victoria Cross winners (mostly non-Catholics) to participate, pay their expenses, and put them on white chargers as a guard of honour for Mannix. Naturally they would be sympathetic to self-determination for Ireland. Fourteen VCs signed up. No doubt Gilbert Dyett, president of the RSL and chairman of Wren's Victorian Trotting and Racing Association, assisted. In 1927 Wren boasted to Hugh Buggy;

> It seemed to me that most people who owned a really good and smart white horse in Victoria were opposed to Irish independence and also to the views of Dr Mannix. It was very hard to secure the loan of a white horse or even buy one. So I advised my agents in New South Wales and Queensland ... to buy the finest white horses they could lay their hands on. I reminded them also that they must not quibble about the price asked for the horses. Their main job was to

> get them to Melbourne quick and lively. But I beat all the doubters and scoffers. I got those fourteen white horses—fine horses too.[28]

Not all the VCs could ride comfortably—one had not ridden before—but they all stayed in the saddle or rather, in a few cases, the horses stayed under them.

Various (Protestant) loyalist bodies privately approached the Victorian premier, (Sir) Harry Lawson, to have the procession baulked on the specious ground that it could lead to public disorder. This could only have meant that it might provoke a riot, led by loyalists, for which there was an obvious precaution—to be taken by themselves. Mannix admonished his flock not to give deliberate offence, but refused 'to make an Irish procession look like an English procession ... It would not be British at all'. Lawson directed the loyalists to the lord mayor, Councillor Aikman, who said he deplored sectarianism, especially at a time when the Prince of Wales (the future Edward VIII) was due to visit. Aikman was satisfied that the procession would be loyal, without disloyal emblems, and that the Union Jack would be emblazoned on the leading banner and the Australian coat of arms on another. He had listened attentively to soldiers who wanted to know why they could not march post-war as they had done pre-war. Aikman had to withstand further loyalist deputations, including one from the Women's Nationalist League. The *Argus* complained that it was not enough to abstain from disloyalty; it wanted a display of loyalty.[29]

The days that followed must have been the most exhilarating of Wren's life, better even than Collingwood's fourth successive premiership in 1930. Wren involved himself in preparations for Mannix's departure. At the Cathedral Hall on 12 March he launched a £50,000 presentation fund, initiating it with a gift of £5,000. That first night, £23,000 was pledged, but Mannix declined to accept any such personal gift on principle.[30] The offer lapsed. Wren personally met the train with the Western Australian VCs on it. They came, he said, 'in the name of Ireland for whom they would lay down their lives. They would restore Ireland to the free nations of the world.' He met the New South Wales contingent, 'defenders of liberty and champions of Ireland's sacred cause'. He hired the Exhibition Building for a Welcome Home to Catholic service personnel. Gatecrashers, non-Catholic ones at least, were supposed to be excluded: guests who had lost their cards had to make the Sign of the Cross.[31]

The St Patrick's Night concert was held on Wednesday 17 March in the Town Hall, which had seldom witnessed 'such an amiable spectacle'. Mannix arrived to waving flags and cheers, flanked by Bishops Foley and Phelan and the advance guard of six VCs. Ambrose McMahon 'with power and expression' sang 'For the Green', 'Who Fears to Speak of '98', and 'O'Donnell Aboo'. Melbourne's most lyrical tenor, Walter Kirby, chirruped 'Macushla' and 'Mother Machree'. After Alice Lynch had 'aroused the enthusiasm of the audience to fever heat by her spirited rendering' of 'Ireland a Nation—Sinn Fein, Sinn Fein', Corporal T. L. Axford VC 'elicited tremendous applause' by rising and kissing her hand, causing Mannix to call him:

> one among them, more daring than the rest … [who] managed to capture another distinction … for himself which all of them coveted (laughter and applause) … We should all like to award him another decoration for the gallantry and good taste he displayed in paying a signal compliment to the lady who so well interpreted the feelings of the audience by her singing of that fine song, *Ireland a Nation, Sinn Fein, Sinn Fein.*

Mannix said he was delighted that the Christian Brothers boys had begun the evening not with 'God Save the King', 'or even '"God Save Ireland"' but with 'My Australia'. The Australian flag should also have 'its proper place'. In Australia, from Australians, 'Australia … should have first place'. But there was no room for neutrality on the Irish question:

> The Irishmen or the Irish-Australians who love Ireland most, love Australia best—and that man who is a traitor and renegade to Ireland is a very poor Australian (Cheers). He has ceased to be an Irishman without becoming an Australian. He is just a Britisher in a bad exclusive sense (Loud applause).[32]

The St Patrick's procession, or rather, military parade, took place on 20 March. It can be regarded as a prototype for the first full-scale Anzac Day march of 1925. Wren had it filmed. The film was released as *Ireland Will Be Free.* Incorporated with it was part of an overseas-made *Martyrs of the Easter Weekend 1916.* At least part of the film has survived in the

National Film and Sound Archive in Canberra. It has been expertly analysed by Dr Elizabeth Kwan. No Union Jack other than the one in the upper canton of the Australian flag was shown. According to the *Argus* reporter, the Union Jack was 12 x 15 inches within a 2½ feet square Australian flag within a 10 x 12 feet banner featuring St Patrick. So the procession was, as Mannix said, 'not to be British at all'. But it was spectacular. Mannix in his car was led to Parliament House by mounted police and his fourteen VCs on white steeds. Then came 6,000 ex-servicemen, almost all in uniform, with the wounded and maimed in cars. Then came the banners, the men of Catholic and Irish societies, and schoolboys—all in all 30,000, according to the film, but probably 20,000.[33] While ostentatiously it was a legitimation of Irish resistance to imperial rule, Kwan points out that 'the film also implied a threat that these *Australian* soldiers were prepared to defend that view against *England*'s government'. Instead of being, as Niall Brennan believes, 'a testimony for all to see that Dr Mannix was as loyal as the best of them',[34] Kwan believes that the procession and the film did quite the opposite. It was put together carefully. Being a silent film the accompanying statements had to be carefully worded, the symbols highlighted and carefully chosen: 'The film effectively turned English rhetoric of Empire and its role in the Great War on its head so that England represented oppression, not liberty … [but] there was no specific reference to the British Empire'.[35]

Mannix would make that reference himself at the first showing of the film. 'These pictures', he said, 'would go all round the world to shame … those who stood behind the outrages that are done under the shadow of the Union Jack'.[36] However, the film did not mention the word 'republic' or show the green, white and orange tricolour or the words of the republican anthem ('Soldiers' Song'). It used rather the largely discredited and more conciliatory green harp flag and 'God Save Ireland'. It encouraged viewers, whoever they were, to see Ireland's cause as a reasonable one for 'self-government'. In this it is not unreasonable to see Wren's own restraining hand, as in his admonition to the Young Ireland Society in November 1917. The day after the procession, at the final rally of the VCs with the archbishop—the opening of a school church in Caulfield—Wren, 'whom the diggers call their old general', was given 'a flattering reception' and invited to speak. A severe cold prevented him from saying more than a few sentences, but the last one was: 'Ireland would yet come into her own, aided thereto by the democracy of England',[37] a concept not invoked by Mannix but reiterated by Wren elsewhere.

Attempts by loyalists in 1921 to prevent the St Patrick's Day march failed, but conditions were imposed: the Australian flag and Union Jack, each measuring 6 x 3 feet, had to be carried in front of the procession. The organisers responded by having a derelict carry the Union Jack, to the derision of the crowd. Police had to surround him to prevent physical attack. Bishop Phelan—Mannix was overseas—exulted afterwards that Irish Australians had that day 'danced on the Union Jack' which stood for 'unparalleled crimes in Ireland'. Wren was not involved and may well have disapproved of such gestures. For as he told Buggy:

> He considered that there was no further call to demonstrate the essential loyalty of Irish Australians of Melbourne. He was satisfied that he had proved his point beyond all doubt in 1920 in a way that would have convinced all reasonable minded citizens. But as he told me himself had the St Patrick's Day marches in the turbulent twenties moved through Bourke Street under a canopy of Union Jacks the scene would not have mollified the anti-Irish bias of certain relentless critics of the procession.[38]

The Jerger deportation

Wren was involved in organising the near-ecstatic public scenes in May 1920 which caused Mannix to miss his train to Sydney, where he was to board the SS *Ventura* en route to the United States. When Mannix had gone, there was the urgent business of the deportation of Fr Charles Jerger. Jerger had been born in Germany but had moved to England as a small child. His mother's second husband was a naturalised British subject and a member of the Prince of Wales Rifles. Apparently Jerger was acculturated and did not speak German particularly well. In 1893 he joined the Passionist Order. Stationed at Marrickville in Western Sydney, just prior to the first conscription referendum, he made remarks on the issue which were interpreted by one parishoner as traitorous. They were related to the police. During the second referendum campaign a fellow Catholic priest and two lay persons complained about his attitude. The issue was taken up by, among others, Alderman John Ness, chairman of the Marrickville Recruiting Committee and a former president of the Protestant Federation, who thought 'it was necessary to take off the gloves and fight the Catholic Church itself'. By 1920 this meant dealing with 'Archbishops Mannix, Kelly, Duhig and a few others'. Jerger had not been naturalised in spite of over forty years under the British flag.

The government decided around August 1919 to deport Jerger under war-time powers which were still operative. Following various petitions and a High Court injunction, an inquiry was set up in June 1920 under the solicitor-general, Sir Robert Garran. He refused the claim of Jerger's counsel, Tom Ryan KC, for a jury trial. Garran's report, says Gerard Henderson, 'gives weight to the view that the hearing was something of a show trial'.[39] A second injunction was then taken out to restrain Senator G. Pearce, minister of defence, from deporting Jerger. Defence counsel, the future Nationalist Party leader and later chief justice. J. G. Latham, was asked by Mr Justice H. E. Starke (father of Hardy's counsel at his trial in 1951) whether any grave danger would be caused to the Commonwealth if the deportation was delayed for a fortnight while the matter was referred to the Full Court. Latham said the government thought so, and Starke's adverse ruling was acted on immediately, in spite of widespread political protest.

Wren's involvement in all this was extensive and vigorous. He had given an undertaking to Mannix that he would use his resources to help Jerger. Both the Labor Party and some unions protested against the deportation, Frank Anstey claiming that the War Precautions Act was anti-working-class. The government had to change its deportation plans, moving Jerger from Sydney to Melbourne and ultimately to Adelaide on the SS *Nestor,* on which the crew had refused to work unless Jerger was given a fair trial. He was then moved to the P & O liner *Khyber,* 'manned by a coolie crew', which set sail for Fremantle. Wren pursued it by train, rallied a demonstration in Perth and tried to issue a writ of *habeas corpus.* Having taken on extra coal, the *Khyber* did not have to berth and sailed to Europe with its prisoner. Wren returned to Melbourne on the Transcontinental to 'an enthusiastic demonstration at the Spencer Street station':

> Several hundreds assembled, and as Mr Wren stepped off the express he was surrounded by friends and warmly cheered. Hearty congratulations were showered upon him for the great fight he had

> made … and Mr Wren unhesitatingly stated that Fr Jerger would never have got out of Australia but for trickery and deception. Various Catholic bodies were represented in the gathering, which also included many of Mr Wren's personal friends and members of various trades organisations. Mr Wren was made to feel that his efforts to secure a fair trial for Fr Jerger had given satisfaction to all fair-minded people. In the afternoon at Richmond, and in the evening at the Bijou Theatre, Mr Wren addressed largely attended gatherings.

Wren's speech at the Bijou ranged from an appeal to Magna Carta and the right to trial by jury to a review of the Jerger saga. A deputation representing 2,000 soldiers had waited on him in Perth where, he said:

> I told them drastic action such as they suggested was not the thing, and that we did not want this country running in blood … I impressed on them that we could remedy these matters by constitutional means. If all workers join their organisations, and become active propagandists we can achieve a great deal. We will then be in a position to prevent deportation without trial.[40]

Wren was obviously a commonsensical and cogent speaker—certainly no rabble-rouser, although a supporter of trade unions. It is difficult to discern anything sinister or crafty in his speeches. The *Advocate* also reported resolutions by the 'Sailors and Soldiers Democratic Association' endorsing the actions of the Seamen's and Waterside Workers' Unions of South Australia. Those resolutions had been forwarded to the *Age*, *Argus* and *Herald*, but not printed. The Sydney *Daily Telegraph* leader was quoted:

> The deplorable thing is that this question is being fought on the most fanatical sectarian grounds … [one] sees in the government's 'excessive zeal' over Fr Jerger a desire for vengeance against those Catholics who had spoken out against it during and after the war.[41]

That vengeance was to culminate in November 1920 in the opportunistic expulsion of Wren's friend Hugh Mahon from parliament, for denouncing British rule in Ireland as 'this bloody and accursed despotism' at an open-air meeting organised by the Irish Ireland League. When moving the expulsion, Hughes, handkerchief in hand to staunch the crocodile tears of outraged loyalism, put on such cynical histrionics that even (Sir) Earle Page, leader of the newly formed Country Party, almost voted against him.[42] Another coup, however, was being anticipated: the chance of blocking Mannix's re-entry to Australia if he refused a loyalty oath. Cabinet seriously deliberated on this in July 1921, the government relenting on the pretext of deference to the Anglo-Irish peace talks then in progress. Still, expelling a priest with a German name was one thing; an archbishop with Mannix's following was another. There would have been high drama for Wren if that had happened. The possible consequences for democratic governance of such vindictive sectarianism was well put by the liberal ideologue, (Sir) Frederick Eggleston, in a letter to the *Age*. While finding it imperative to declare himself anti-Catholic, he wrote:

> If Father Jerger is a danger to the community why cannot it be proved in open court in the ordinary way? Surely, in the 20th century, it is hardly necessary to recall the evolution of British ideas of justice and to point out that if the court abdicates its functions as a protector of liberty and Parliament refuses to stand up against the arbitrary exercise of executive authority the liberties of each one of us are in jeopardy.[43]

The greatest democrat in Australia

The Amalgamated Catholic Clubs entertained Wren at a complimentary concert at Cathedral Hall on 16 November. In view of Roberts's presidency, this gesture may seem manipulative, but on the platform with the administrator of St Patrick's Cathedral, Fr Barry, were Tom Ryan, Hugh Mahon, L. L. Cunningham MHR, E. J. Hogan MLA, R. Solly MLA and Roberts. Ryan made the presentation of 'an easy chair, bearing the crest of an open arm with raised scimitar and a lion rampant on a ground of ermine'. It was 'the original coat of arms of Wren's ancestors' with, in Irish, 'Ruhan Abu' (Wren to Victory). It was 'flanked by beautifully designed horseshoes', embroidered by the Sisters of the Good Shepherd, Abbotsford. A Limerick lace scarf was presented to Mrs Wren, also 'in his own name and the name of the Catholic people generally'. Ryan spoke about Wren:

> [He] had taken a fearless stand on many occasions and ... was an all-round sport and a bountiful giver to charity and good work (Applause). Some ... would have them believe that such clubs were for narrow and sectarian purposes but that was not the case. They were first of all, for the general improvement and uplifting of the members ... [which] could be done without hostility to anyone ... It was not because Fr Jerger was a priest that Mr Wren interested himself, but because he was demanding a fair trial from a British jury.
>
> ... To Australian democracy as a whole Mr Wren was a good friend (Applause). Why should not Ireland have the same right of self-determination as any other small nation? ...Why should not Mr Mahon have the right to criticise trenchantly the doings of the British Government ... the same right as [former British prime minister] Mr Asquith who before an audience of Scotsmen at Ayr ... said the doings in Ireland were comparable to those of the Germans in Belgium ... He would rather cut off his right hand than do an injustice to a man because he differed from him in religion (Applause).

Ryan concluded by tracing 'the history of the progenitors of Mr Wren who ... was descended from a race of kings'. Hugh Mahon went one better in stating that Mrs Wren, being by birth a Mahon, was a descendant of King Brian Boru. Wren was 'the most strenuous and stalwart friend of democracy and liberty in Australia today'. He was not sure about Wren's pedigree but 'of him he would say that he was a king in himself'. Of his own expulsion from parliament, he said he had at least been expelled by his enemies whereas Hughes was 'booted out' of the Labor Party 'not by his enemies, but by his lifelong personal political friends'.

Wren's reply was not lacking in humour:

> Mr Ryan was an eminent barrister, and had the reputation of being able to prove that black was white (Laughter). That evening he had gone close to proving the impossible in his case (laughter and applause). However, with all his eloquence Mr Ryan would find it

> hard to convince some people that he (Mr Wren) was not really a half-brother to Satan (Laughter).

Wren was not loath to stress his links with Mannix, both through patronising the Amalgamated Catholic Clubs and being his agent (as in the Jerger case) during the archbishop's absence:

> He [Wren] had watched the rapid progress of the Catholic clubs since His Grace had given the movement his support and blessing (Applause). The clubs were a great need in the community and were destined to be a great power for good (Applause). In His Grace the Archbishop the clubs had a great spiritual guide and in Mr Roberts they had an enthusiastic president who worked untiringly and gave generously … His Grace … was never in better health in his life. He had been in constant touch with the Archbishop since he left Sydney … they would be pleased to know that he would come back to Australia for a certainty.

But Wren was, as usual, careful not to denounce British values:

> He was delighted to see … many of his English friends. In his opinion, the democracy of England would eventually insist on Ireland securing its just rights (Applause). It was a sign of the times when a British Labour Party decided that it was within the rights of the Irish people to have a Republic if they so desired. This party represented the great masses of England and very soon the English people would not tolerate the present ruling class … a drastic change would occur at the next British elections.[44]

The formal proceedings ended with a chorus of 'God Save Ireland'; then, 'at the invitation of Mr Roberts, a number of guests assembled in the supper room' for refreshments. There the twice future premier of Victoria, E. J. 'Ned' Hogan, proposed the health of Mr Roberts. J. F. Hannan,[45] variously MHR, MLA and senator, and C. Bennett 'spoke appreciatively of Mr Wren's kindly interest and sympathy in industrial matters' and described him 'as the greatest democrat in Australia'.

A month later, at the close of the *Ireland Will Be Free* film season, the Princess Theatre was 'packed to the doors'. Among the audience with

Ellen Wren were the famous soprano Amy Castles and the aviator Raymond Parer.[46] National songs were sung by local artists and there was a 'powerful rendering' of 'Emmet's Speech from the Dock' ('Let no man write my epitaph': the rebel Robert Emmet's speech before execution in 1803). It was announced that a cable message would be sent to Mannix stating that '30,000 joined in fervently singing "Come Back to Australia" during the season'. Wren was unable to be there to receive a presentation because he 'had to leave in the afternoon for Sydney on urgent business'. A letter from him was read by Ambrose McMahon and is worth quoting for what it says about Wren. At least it should be conceded that it is not the epistolary style of an Al Capone:

> Studley Park,
> December 18th, 1920
>
> My Dear Mr McMahon,
>
> I regret exceedingly that I will not be able to attend at the Princess' Theatre this evening. Extremely urgent business, which has cropped up suddenly, has called me away to Sydney. If any of my Irish friends are disappointed—and I am vain enough to hope that some will be—place all the blame on my shoulders. I trust that none of my friends will think that I have had an attack of 'cold feet'. They will, I feel sure, give me credit for having sufficient courage to take a gift that I have neither earned or deserved.
>
> As you know, Mr McMahon, I was strongly opposed to the suggestion of a presentation to me. I have done nothing meriting the thanks of the Irish citizens of Victoria. Anything that I have done, or attempted to do, pales into insignificance when compared with the deeds of those brave men who appeared on the screen of the Princess nightly. The country that has produced men like Padraic Pearse, Terence McSwiney, and thousands of other heroes, is one to which anybody should be proud to belong, and I deem it a privilege and honour to be able to render even remote service to gallant little Ireland. I have done very little for the land of my father and mother. I only wish that I could have done or been able to do a thousand times more. My great regret is that we here, in far away Australia, cannot do anything practical to help to bring peace to poor, long-suffering Erin. We can, however, at least express our sympathy, with Ireland, and our admiration for her wonderfully courageous people.

We can do that without being any the less true Australians.

I am unaware of the nature of the presentation you intend to make, but highly as I would prize any gift that was made to me in the name of Ireland, I will value even more the good opinion of the Irish people of Australia should I ever be able to gain it. As an Irish-Australian, though not of the material of which brave men are made, I would feel proud to earn the esteem of my Irish friends, I can assure them all that it will be the happiest period of my life when I am able, God willing, to pay a visit to peaceful, happy, free Ireland. My prayer and your prayer will be 'God Save Ireland'.

JOHN WREN[47]

Wren was too absorbed in Australia ever to visit Ireland, although his wife and daughters did so.

Responsible citizen

Something of Wren's standing in 'industrial matters', and the hatred of him by the *Argus*, emerged in February 1921 when he was invited by Tom Walsh and the executive of the Seamen's Federation to act as mediator in a shipping dispute. On 26 February the *Argus* wrote 'a spiteful letter', says the *Advocate*, to which Wren replied. The *Argus* cut his letter by close to half; but the *Advocate* (on 3 March) published it in full. The parts reproduced in italics were not published in the *Argus*.

Sir,—Your leading article of today begins as follows: 'Notwithstanding the intervention of Mr John Wren, the shipping dispute has been settled. *The community breathes more fully because of this fact. Evil counsellors, unscrupulous plotters were at work making ready for a formidable attack upon public liberties had the negotiations for settlement broken down'. What justification have you for such statements?*

My position in relation to the negotiations that immediately preceded the settlement arrived at is simple. On Wednesday I was asked to represent the seamen in a conference with a representation of the shipowners. My personal inclination was to refuse, but it was urged upon me by Mr Walsh, president of the Seamen's Federation, and members of his executive council, that I might be able to do something to end the unhappy state of affairs that existed. I consented to act, and met Mr Elliot, representative of the shipowners, who, I understood, was given by his side the same full powers as were given to me by the seamen. We met under the chairmanship of Admiral Sir William Clarkson, and discussed certain proposals. On one point, considered most vital by both sides, we could not agree, and the conference ended. Subsequently, I reported the result of the conference to the seamen's executive and, in doing so, offered some suggestions.

I do not claim any credit for being in any way responsible for the settlement of the dispute. Your implied insinuation that I was endeavouring to block a settlement is, of course, too absurd as to be seriously considered. I would like to point out one or two facts. My direct connection with the dispute began at about midday on Thursday. At 5 p.m. on Friday, or less than 30 hours after I was asked to act as mediator, the trouble was settled. *Prior to my being approached by the seamen with a view to acting on their behalf, the dispute had existed for about five weeks, which period does not include the period the stewards' strike lasted. I will leave the public to judge whether or not the dispute was settled 'notwithstanding the intervention of Mr John Wren'.*

Yours, etc

JOHN WREN

The *Tribune* on the same day said that 'Mr Wren settled the strike; of that there is no doubt. He did not ask to be allowed to intervene; yet he did so when asked with consummate success.' On 24 March it published a letter from Walsh and his executive recording their thanks to Wren for having 'very materially aided the process of negotiations'.

Wren had a last opportunity, in July, to pay tribute to Tom Ryan before his premature death on 1 August at age forty-five. Ryan had lost a libel case against the Hobart *Mercury* by a three-quarter jury majority in dubious circumstances. An editorial in 1919 had stated that Ryan has 'been as open in ... sedition' as the 'anarchists' who had recently marched through the streets of Brisbane. The jury was unable to agree on what constituted 'fair comment' in an editorial, and asked Mr Justice Starke whether it needed to base a judgment wholly on the evidence or whether their 'private views [could] be brought to bear'. Starke naturally ruled out anything other than what was in the evidence. However, hearsay and prejudice were not excluded, and Ryan faced £5,000 costs. Wren organised an appeal fund in Sydney, Melbourne and Brisbane to raise it. Speaking at 'a preliminary meeting' of Ryan's supporters in Melbourne on 21 July, Wren cited jury prejudice:

> On the morning after the verdict had been given the foreman of the jury visited Parliament House and in his (Mr Wren's) presence said that he was so disturbed in mind over what had taken place in the jury room that he had come to unburden himself, and let the public know how the verdict had been arrived at … one of them [the jurors] said, 'I don't care what the judge said. My brother-in-law has told me all about Mr Ryan and his former government in Queensland. I know that his administration ruined the State of Queensland, and I don't care a rap what I heard in court'. That was how the verdict was arrived at. Mr Ryan was found guilty by the jury of a serious offence of sedition.

Ironically, in view of what happened at the criminal-libel trial in 1951, Wren then deplored the class basis of jury decisions:

> It was regrettable [he said] that there were so many class-conscious people in this community. When these people denied fair play in a court of law … because of his [a person's] political views and sympathies with the workers, it was high time the special jury system should be altered. Special juries were selected on property qualifications. If trial by jury in civil cases were to continue he thought that jurors should be selected from the jury apart from any property qualifications. Frequently there was more capacity in a man not possessed of property than in one having vested rights. Yet the former were ineligible to sit on a special jury! Mr Ryan's case had been decided … on the conscription issue. Whatever views they held on conscription they were aware that the majority of the Australian people voted with Mr Ryan on two occasions …

The case was to go to the Privy Council if necessary. Wren interpolated later at the meeting that he 'cast no aspersions on the learned judge'. Mr Justice Starke was 'as fair as a judge could be'. Wren was 'appointed president of the fund-raising committee'.[48]

No doubt Wren had a hand in organising Mannix's triumphant return via Thursday Island (30 July) and Brisbane (1 August), where he was on the official welcoming platform. In Melbourne Wren showed his film again, this time at the Palace Cinema. It was so packed that those with reserved seats could not get admission. A special supplement to the *Tribune* on 18 July reported 'great disappointment' when he announced that the archbishop was too fatigued to attend, but 'The audience expressed sympathy ... and gave Wren a rousing reception'. On 29 September the *Sydney Morning Herald* reported how the Labor lord mayor of Sydney, W. H. Lambert, had returned 'greatly pleased' with the reception accorded to him in the past week in Melbourne:

> He said he had been invited specially for the purpose of presenting to Archbishop Mannix a painting in oils of Mr John Wren which had been subscribed for by the citizens of Melbourne who were both admirers of Mannix and Mr Wren.

As the return of Mannix roughly coincided with the truce in Ireland, tensions were reduced in Australia. On 6 December 1921 a treaty was signed partitioning Ireland into the twenty-six counties of the Irish Free State and the six of 'Northern Ireland', but retaining the monarchy over both. By June 1922 civil war had broken out, with Mannix obdurately supporting his machiavellian hero, de Valera, and the republicans. He was unique among bishops of Australia and Ireland in doing so. All others in Australia supported their Irish colleagues, while Catholics in general were bewildered by the viciousness with which former Sinn Feiners attacked each other. Passionate commitments in Australia cooled; even interest waned. As said before, Wren probably agreed with his old friend Phelan that reasoned argument was lost on Mannix on the Irish question, although his awe of and desire for friendship with the archbishop remained. The curtain had been rung, however, on the heady drama of Irish nationalism and imputed disloyalty in Australia.[49] Peace came to Ireland on 24 May 1923—but not to Mannix, at least until de Valera became prime minister in 1932 and moved the Irish Free State towards republicanism. Even then, St Patrick's Night concerts in Melbourne mourned the partition of the Emerald Isle, while during the 1939–45 war Mannix intransigently defended its neutrality, a position rejected by Wren.

CHAPTER FOURTEEN

A Champion Wire-puller?: federal politics

WE HAVE SEEN the absurd allegation made in 1904 by a conservative journal that prime minister Watson consulted Wren on the formation of his cabinet. We also saw that Wren socialised with federal politicians like Senators Dawson and Findley while they sat in Melbourne. With the shift of federal parliament from Melbourne to Canberra in 1927 such intimacy must have become more difficult. And even Wren's detractors seemed unable to find anything suspiciously nefarious in the national arena to attribute to Wren, until the Dalley election beat-up of 1928.

Perhaps they could have made something of a letter from Wren to prime minister Hughes, dated 18 September 1917, but one can only guess what it might have been. Australia was in the slough of the First World War. The federal government wanted greater social austerity, Hughes had abandoned the Labor Party the year before, and Wren was the good friend of Hughes's arch-enemy, Daniel Mannix:

> Dear Mr Hughes,
>
> I regret having to write again re restriction of racing, more especially as you must be very worried over your son's illness, but if you could arrange that the number of days allowed by the Government under the War Precautions Act would commence from the 1st October, you would do me a great favour, for which I

> would feel ever grateful. As I will lose quite £10,000 per year by the restrictions, I am sure you will do all you can to obtain the above request.
>
> I trust your son will make a happy recovery very soon. I leave for Brisbane this evening & will be away for a week or 10 days.
>
> Yours faithfully,
>
> JOHN WREN[1]

The letter suggests ongoing familiarity between Hughes and Wren. Hughes's son Charles had had a serious motor-bike accident,[2] about which Wren felt it appropriate to express sympathy, just as he thought it necessary to refer to his own imminent absence from Melbourne. He seemed to imply that he might expect a ready personal response, although a previous letter from him to Hughes had not been acknowledged. Hughes had not yet announced (8 November) his second conscription plebiscite but, in any case, in spite of any Wren–Mannix nexus, the *Daily Mail* had supported conscription in 1916. Hughes knew that, and expected that it would do so again.

Apparently Wren did get three additional dates for his registered courses in Brisbane. An irate John MacGregor, editor of the *Brisbane Courier*, which was a rival to Wren's *Daily Mail*, wrote to Hughes on 12 January 1918:

> You may or may not be aware that the Minister for Defence telegraphed this week to the Queensland Turf Club that he had agreed to give 'John Wren' three more racing date[s] in respect of his registered courses in Brisbane. The thing is a very grave scandal, so grave that even the QTC, usually most solicitous to forward and protect the interests of Wren, cannot acquiesce in the granting of those dates to him. What is the influence in your [non-Labor] Cabinet, or in the Defence Dept., which secures for him the official consideration that is shown him? He races for private profit—is said to have made £36,000 out of his Brisbane courses last year, and £1,200 out of a one-day race meeting a week ago—and yet can get concessions, over and above those originally agreed upon, of more racing dates when the Queensland Turf Club, which now gives all its profits to patriotic funds, is denied them. I think you can scarcely be personally aware of what is going on, and of what people are

> saying, or these things would not happen. I am not mincing matters, first for the reason that *I think the Wren influence in this country is about the worst* [emphasis added], and second, because I take a personal pride in saying while I have little faith in the honesty of many of our parliamentarians, I believe that W. M. Hughes, whatever his faults, is incapable of either doing or sanctioning a dishonest act ...[3]

Unfortunately, MacGregor was not more explicit about the Wren influence, but a comparison of the courtesies in these two letters to Hughes suggests more toadying or naivety in the *Courier*'s editor than in the racing baron. Was Hughes rewarding Wren for the *Daily Mail*'s support on conscription? Like the editor of the *Daily Mail*, MacGregor deluded himself that Hughes was incapable of dishonesty, despite his running a flagrantly devious campaign.

The Dalley affair

Just as Tom Ryan moved into federal politics through a New South Wales seat, so Theodore, after unsuccessfully contesting and unexpectedly not winning the Herbert (Townsville area) seat in 1925, moved to Sydney and won the Dalley electorate in January 1927. However, for Theodore there was no facile route into national politics. His analytical abilities and easy dominance on the floor of the house alarmed his political opponents in the shaky Bruce–Page government. On the other hand his aloofness and indulgent life-style aroused resentment in the Lang and Australian Workers' Union factions of Labor, while his antagonism to communists, whose exclusion from the party he supported, alienated the extreme radical wing.

In May 1928 the *Daily Telegraph Pictorial* published a statement by William Lambert, the Labor MHR for West Sydney from 1921 to 1926, who had recently lost pre-selection in his electorate. He said that in 1925 he had been offered £8,000 to resign his seat in favour of Theodore, an allegation he had subsequently denied in the *Evening News*. He further alleged that P. E. Coleman, Labor MHR for Reid, had disclosed a similar offer from an agent of Theodore. Coleman had previously been prominent in denouncing a notorious Labor ballot-rigging scam, and was also a marked man. He denied the allegation. Now over a year after Theodore was elected, Lambert alleged that the previous incumbent for Dalley, William Mahoney, had received £5,000 to traffic his seat. Mahoney maintained that a win on Spearfelt in the 1926 Melbourne Cup had enabled him to purchase the Commercial Hotel in Brisbane. Before he entered the Senate in 1928, J. J. Daly had provided an affidavit supporting Mahoney. It was disregarded.

Here was an opportunity to destroy Theodore that was too good to miss. The Bruce government set up a royal commission which examined Theodore's bank account but could find no fault. However, it did not believe that Mahoney, not a known punter, had won the money at the races. Two nationalist senators gave evidence that Coleman had named Wren as the source of the bribe:

> The commissioner found that Mahoney had been given about 5,000 reasons for resigning by an unspecified donor while acting in Theodore's interests ... As well as discrediting Mahoney ... [he] disbelieved Coleman's denial that he had been offered £8,000 to vacate his seat for Theodore.[4]

Wren was summoned but said it was of no interest to him who won Dalley. The commissioner apologised for taking up his time. Nevertheless, it was generally believed the money had come from him. Stuart Macintyre insists that there is 'strong evidence' for Wren's bribe in spite of the commissioner, but what it is he does not or cannot say; nor are his footnotes helpful. He also thinks Theodore was not himself 'short of money', because of the Mungana scam,[5] but there is extant a letter from Theodore to Wren during this period asking for a loan of £1,000. Written on Commonwealth parliament paper on 2 July 1928 but marked 'Personal', it is noteworthy that it begins most familiarly but is formally signed off:

> Dear Jack,
>
> When I purchased my Sydney house I expected to sell the Brisbane house within reasonable time but I have not succeeded so far. So I am carrying a big overdraft at the bank, and the cost of the Roy. Com. (nearly a thousand pounds) has left me embarrassed. I expect the *Comth Govt* to meet my costs but I am not confident they will, [Prime Minister] Bruce is very petty and mean. If you can lend me £1,000 I will be eternally grateful. If this request is not

> inconvenient to you, will you let me know when you are likely to be in Sydney on your next visit.
>
> Yours Truly
>
> EDWARD G. THEODORE

Wren annotated the margin: 'Granted—£1,000 in bank paid to him, JW'.[6]

Years later, Theodore told one of his secretaries that the Labor Party had raised the money to compensate Mahoney. He 'wasn't bloody well silly enough to pay it'.[7] The foremost authority on Labor in the period, Bede Nairn, believes Theodore raised the money from his own resources and donations. This would have included help from Wren.[8] Labor was unable to provide it. There were also businessmen who, although generally anti-Labor, supported Theodore's cogent protectionist views and did not want him out of politics. But the conservative newspapers were jubilant, affecting deep indignation as they publicised the seemingly sordid transactions that had allegedly taken place. Frank Anstey was equal to their humbug, as Ross McMullin relates:

> [He outlined to his constituents] in his inimitable style the Ready-Earle scandal of 1917, the donation of £25,000 to Hughes in 1920 by grateful admirers of the Prime Minister, the payment of £3,000 to a Nationalist Party official in 1922 for standing aside in North Sydney when Hughes wanted to switch to a safer seat, the attempts to bring down the Theodore government by blatant bribery, and the more sophisticated corruption which succeeded in maiming the Gunn Government [South Australia] by seducing its leader.[9]

In his unpublished papers, Anstey wrote how the then-current prime minister, S. M. Bruce, was organised into a seat in 1917:

> To save civilisation from the Germans he joined [in 1914] a crack British regiment, was wounded, and retired. As he was chief director of an English corporation with branches in Australia he went there to recuperate. The holder of a Nationalist stronghold conveniently resigned for a better-paid position and the visitor took his place as a Federal member.[10]

Theodore went on to become deputy leader in the parliamentary party in February 1929 and, after Labor's landslide victory in October, deputy prime minister and treasurer. Theodore is believed to have been influenced by Wren and his interests, especially in the matter of tariffs. Theodore had always been an ardent protectionist, but for cronies may have been especially solicitous over some products more than others.

Local representatives

The character of the MPs who represented Wren's urban patch and contiguous electorates in Melbourne may help to tell us why there is so little evidence of his influence at the federal level. Moreover, between 1916 and 1941 Labor was in office only between October 1929 and January 1932. With Scullin then in office Wren's influence was not implausible but, from 1941 to 1949, under prime ministers Curtin and Chifley, only a future Maoist like Ted Hill, or a political naif like Frank Hardy, could suggest that John Wren was dictating or could dictate federal policy. Between 1901 and 1922 Labor's safest Victorian seat of Yarra, which included Richmond, was represented by Frank Tudor, who had succeeded to the Labor leadership after the expulsion of W. M. Hughes in late 1916. He is characterised by Janet McCalman:

> Tudor was the archetypal artisan radical. A lifelong teetotaller and deacon of the Congregational church, he had a moral breadth that embraced Home Rule for Ireland, to the horror of many Richmond Protestants. At the time of his election he was President of the Melbourne Trades Hall Council … Tudor served in three Labor ministries as Minister for Customs.[11]

To my knowledge, no taint of shady practice or even a close association with Wren has been suggested about Tudor. It was his campaign secretary, Richard Loughnan, founder of the Builders' Labourers' Federation, who helped Tudor build up 'a solid Labor following in Richmond'.[12] He was also well known as having been Squizzy Taylor's bondsman, not that that necessarily makes him a consort. But it is difficult to envisage Tudor being enmeshed in some semi-criminal web involving, ultimately, even John Wren—especially because, for sectarians, Tudor had the advantage of *not* being a Catholic. It was not the custom in Richmond and Collingwood to shun those of dubious repute, just as in 'Yarraside' there was tolerance of white-collar graft.

According to his biographer, Tudor's successor in Yarra from 1922 to 1949, James Scullin, disdained to have anything to do with Wren at all, even though there is epistolary and reliable anecdotal evidence to the contrary. After describing Scullin's 'somewhat puritanical character', John Robertson writes:

> It is hard to imagine him finding congenial companionship in John Wren, a shady Roman Catholic entrepreneur, who made money through catering for some of mankind's less exalted pastimes, by arranging boxing matches and running an illegal totalizator. Wren was known to Labor politicians in Scullin's area … however, suggestions that he exercised political influence are not supported by evidence and do not square with the latter's nature.[13]

This is most prissily put: 'shady Roman Catholic' almost implies an expectation of dishonesty, while 'arranging' rather than 'promoting' or 'staging' boxing bouts seems gratuitous on Robertson's part. And the idea that a politician can invariably guard his 'nature' from unwanted influence is just too naive. An interesting point, however, is that in a thorough-going biography, Robertson found nothing to suggest a close association between Scullin and Wren, let alone corrupt dealings. Although he must surely have read Jack Lang's books, he says nothing to discount Lang's assertion that Wren through Senator Daly, acting as attorney-general, was behind the appointment of E. McTiernan and H. V. Evatt to the High Court bench in 1930. Scullin had forbidden filling the vacancies and was at the time on the high seas returning from England. Wren's motive, said Lang, was to provide judicial sympathy for Theodore in the event that there would be High Court litigation arising from the Queensland royal commission on the Mungana issue.[14] Lang also asserted 'the champion wire-puller of the period' influenced Scullin to take Theodore back into cabinet in January 1931 'for his own purposes', but does not state what these purposes were[15]—the tariff, or just power?

McMullin seems to have no doubt that Wren hovered around the Scullin government. 'There was also dark speculation in some quarters', he says, 'about Wren's role in [Scullin's] ministerial selection'. Although

Victoria (with 48.9 per cent of the vote) had returned only 13 MHRs, five of the thirteen cabinet positions went to Victorians, while only four went to New South Wales—one to Wren's friend Parker Moloney, whose electorate was in the Riverina. Lang saw the Australian Workers' Union and Wren colluding in the arrangement.[16] John Curtin, it was said, found his exclusion from cabinet 'heart-breaking', especially as Western Australia's allotted place went to the outback MHR, 'Texas' Green. Any suggestion that it was Wren who had Curtin sidelined is refuted by Arthur Calwell:

> [Curtin's] rejection was a great humiliation. He blamed the Treasurer, Ted Theodore, for it. Curtin told me that Theodore walked down the Caucus room when voting was about to take place and said, 'One Anstey in the Cabinet is enough'. Theodore believed in orthodox finance but Anstey and Curtin did not. Curtin later modified his view but, at that time, he and Anstey were playing around with social credit theories.[17]

Quite possibly Theodore discussed the formation of cabinet with Wren, but it is difficult to believe that he would defer to Wren in such a matter. These decisions were not for Wren to make, irrespective of reciprocal favours in other matters. What is perplexing here is that Lang cannot be dismissed out of hand, and that Labor historians can have such opposing views about Wren's relationship with Scullin. (By contrast, Gavin Souter is of the opinion that there was no evidence that Scullin was influenced by Mannix, '[n]or was there any evidence that Labor's new leader was helped or influenced by John Wren'.)[18]

Scullin was succeeded in Yarra in 1949 by S. M. Keon, whose denunciation of Wren in the Victorian parliament in 1948 is described later. Keon won federal pre-selection over John Cremean. However, the electorate was then divided and Cremean won the new seat of Hoddle. In spite of the long-standing friendship between the Wren and Cremean families and rivalry with Keon, John Cremean sided with the anti-Evatt faction in the Labor Party split of 1954–5 when other old 'Wrenites' like Jack Galbally held firm. Both Keon and Cremean lost their seats. It is clear from the character and performance of the MPs in Labor's safest federal seat in Victoria that Wren was hardly a corrupting influence on its representation or representatives.

As we have seen, Frank Brennan won the Batman seat, which enveloped Collingwood, in a by-election in 1911 and retained it, except for 1932–4, until 1949. We know he had assistance from Wren but he was certainly no 'creature'. Idealistic, largely ineffectual, he had opposed participation in the First World War, supported the suspension of military service in 1930 and at first opposed limited conscription for overseas in 1942[19]—which were not Wren policies any more than was his support for Maurice Blackburn in 1924. The electorate of Melbourne was represented between 1904 and 1940 by Dr William Maloney. Maloney, eccentric and wealthy, more of a social worker in politics than a crusading Laborite, had no need of Wren.[20] Nor would Wren have been so naive as to try to 'purchase' his support.

Arthur Calwell, who succeeded Maloney in Melbourne in 1940, acknowledged that he was 'well acquainted' with Wren, and his final favourable judgment of the 'wire puller' will be reserved until later. Calwell, as will be seen, was prepared to use Wren's influence in forming a Country Party–Labor alliance in Victoria in 1935. But again, there has not been any suggestion of Calwell being a Wren puppet. The same is the case with both James Matthews and E. J. Holloway, who represented Labor in Melbourne Ports during 1906–32 and 1932–51 respectively. Similarly with James Fenton and Arthur Drakeford in Maribyrnong during 1910–34 and 1934–55. Fenton had been a Methodist lay preacher and a wowser when he first entered the Victorian parliament in 1908. He was unlikely to have become a client of Wren. A long-standing friend of Scullin, he was acting prime minister during Scullin's absence in London in 1930 and defected with Lyons to the United Australia Party in 1931, becoming a minister and remaining in parliament until his defeat in 1934.[21] Drakeford, who was minister for air during 1941–9, at least did a favour for John Wren when he secured an early demobilisation from the air force for John F. Wren in 1945.[22] Other than that, this former national president of the Australian Federated Union of Locomotive Engineers, Ben Chifley's union, is not known to be linked with Wren.[23] Joseph Hannan was the only Labor representative of Fawkner in this period. He was at least well-disposed towards Wren but was unable to regain a federal seat in the lower house. His biographer does not appear to suspect him of 'Wrenism'. Hannan's 'parliamentary speeches', he says, 'reflected deep knowledge of union affairs and scrupulous regard for party principles and policy'.[24]

In the Melbourne environs of Collingwood, this leaves us to account for only Frank Anstey, MLA for Brunswick area 1902–10 and then MHR for Bourke (Brunswick-Coburg) 1910–34, where he was succeeded by Maurice Blackburn until 1943. This would have given Wren no pleasure. Nor the future prime minister, John Curtin, who wrote to Anstey:

> I do not regard Blackburn as a Messiah of the Latter Day. He is a blanc mange—clever perhaps; a man without sin, he is really destitute of virtue. He is really too good to be personally worth a damn[25][meaning that Blackburn lacked the stomach for hard politics but was apt at posturing].

Blackburn was excluded from the Labor Party in 1941, and was defeated in 1943 by the official Labor candidate, W. G. Bryson, a Catholic who lost the seat between 1946 and 1949 through a sympathy vote for Blackburn's widow, Doris (Independent Labor). He then defeated her for the new seat of Wills and held it until the Labor Split, when he followed the anti-communist group out of the party.[26]

Revolutionary *manqué*

Communist and radical commentators have particularly lamented the influence Wren allegedly had over the socialist orator Frank Anstey. Anstey was a founder and president of the Tramways Employees' Association, wrote for *Labor Call* and *Tocsin*, and became MLA for East Bourke (later Brunswick) in 1902. His interest in boxing may have drawn him to Wren. In March 1918 Anstey went to Europe, where he became enthusiastic about the Russian revolution, but money from Wren for an improvident lifestyle is alleged to have kept him off the revolutionary path and out of the Communist Party in the 1920s and 1930s. There is no question that Anstey accepted Wren's patronage, but he was far from being a puppet. Wren failed to get him to resign his seat in favour of Tom Ryan in 1920. There was no penalty. Similarly, Wren would hardly have approved of Anstey's fulminations in 1929–30 against Scullin's insistence on governing in the face of a hostile Senate.

Wren sent Anstey for his health to Salamaua in New Guinea in 1926 at the time of the Edie Creek gold discoveries—also, it seems, to look at investment opportunities. The *Herald* reported that he had brought back nuggets from Bulolo, 3,000 feet up in the mountains. He thought

New Guinea 'a Utopia', said the headline. After Wren had registered in July 1927 the Upper Watut Goldmining Company Pty Ltd, with mining and dredging leases totalling 480 acres, Anstey declared: 'I thank God the day is passed when it is necessary for me to work hard'.[27] Of 104,000 shares of £1 each, 75,000 went to Wren, 25,000 to Anstey and four lots of 1,000 to four New Guinea miners, of whom three were Germans, former enemies. In September 1929 Wren shed half his shares, most going to Theodore and some to Ben Nathan. Theodore withdrew the following year.[28] With Labor in power, the iconoclastic *Smith's Weekly* had a cracking opportunity to expose hypocrisy:

LABOR'S UNHOLY ALLIANCE WITH JOHN WREN
SCULLIN—THEODORE—ANSTEY POLICY EXPOSED
Kicks White Miners Out
New Guinea Gold Fields Closed to Small Men
How 'Vultures' Met on Watut Gold Lease

Smith's declared that 'white labour' had been abandoned in favour of 'niggers' ('a black labour Eldorado') and deplored the presence of German shareholders. It was unimpressed by Anstey's declaration that the country was 'too unhealthy for white miners', who in any case needed a stake of £5,000. 'No', railed *Smith's*, 'it is Anstey–Wren–Kanaka country'.[29]

Fortunes were made at Bulolo, but not by Wren and Anstey. However, Upper Watut was not a costly failure, as there is no evidence of expenses incurred between 1927 and 1930 and none of the capital was subscribed in cash. Nonetheless, it must have hurt Anstey's reputation. Even an obituary of 1940 would say that 'Gold mining interests in New Guinea engaged his attention in later years'.[30] According to David Day, John Curtin tried ardently to dissuade his old comrade from leaving politics in 1934 but:

> He had … been quietly amassing a nest egg: partly courtesy of his association with John Wren, which he had invested in a block of beachside flats in Sydney where he was content to spend his time soaking up the winter sun and lazily watching the passing parade of bathers.[31]

Some Anstey admirers choose to believe that in retirement he wrote an exposé of Wren's corruption of the Labor Party which he was induced to incinerate in some final act of immolation. In *The Hard Way* Hardy says that Anstey's mistress, Harriet Middlecoat, gave him what she had of his papers but, to 'his utter disappointment ... he found nothing directly relating ... to the Wren political octopus'.[32] A not unbiassed A. W. Sheppard told his biographers that Anstey had 'confided' in him that 'he had started to write a book about John Wren's manipulation of the Labor Party'.[33] A journalist, Hector Tonkin, gave a small collection of papers to the biographer of S. M. Bruce, Cecil Edwards, who included some passages and deposited all of them in the National Library, Canberra. Tonkin is said to have 'taken typed copies of the memoirs shortly before they, and other papers, were burnt after Anstey's death',[34] but obviously he did not say by whom they were burnt. But were these papers incriminating? Or has it been wishful thinking?

A notable Melbourne journalist, Herbert Mishael, who like Anstey lived in Brunswick, told Tonkin:

> Anstey would not have a bar of Wren once he realised what a harmful influence he was in Labor Party affairs! Wren had tried and failed to persuade Anstey to give up his Parliamentary seat to make way for T. J. Ryan because Wren regarded Ryan as a future Prime Minister of Australia.[35]

This is another garbled recollection. Did Anstey come to realise that Wren was a 'harmful influence' in 1920? Or was it only in his old age when, according to David Day, he was hatching Wren's 'nest egg'? While it is useful to compare Anstey's alleged disillusionment to that reported about Tom Tunnecliffe, *Labor Call* in its obituary did not see Anstey as having been corrupted by anyone, and claimed that Anstey had 'carried the banner of Labor as high as any man carried it'. A biographer, the radical historian (and former communist) Ian Turner, judged him 'A free-thinker and a Freemason ... [who] enjoyed the friendship and favour of John Wren; but he never betrayed his deeply held beliefs'.[36] But did Wren ever ask him to?

Interstate politics: Sydney

Before turning to the broader Victorian scene, where one would expect Wren's political interventions to be most evident, the little that is readily known about his activities in other mainland states should be recorded. Earlier chapters on his sporting and business interests indicate the political lobbying that Wren probably undertook. However, nothing has been uncovered to indicate anything resembling Wren's alleged 'control' outside Victoria.

Ross McMullin asserts that 'Racing, newspapers and Labor politics dominated Wren's interests in Sydney'.[37] Wren's abortive interest in 1922–3 with the 'Boot King' and Labor MLA P. J. Minahan in an unremunerative Sydney *Daily Mail* has already been mentioned. I know of no other investment in newspapers in New South Wales by Wren. As to racing, Wren owned no courses for Sydney gallopers, and only slight oral evidence and a photograph of both of them in a sulky inspecting a track[38] suggest that he could have been in partnership with J. J. Joynton Smith, 'hotelier and racecourse and newspaper owner'. He obviously knew this proprietor of the fleering, independent *Smith's Weekly*, who was chairman of the Australian Trotting and Victoria Park Racing Clubs—but his biographer found no evidence of any partnership with Wren. Wren's obituary in the *Sydney Morning Herald*[39] asserts that he owned a pony course until the inauguration of the Sydney Turf Club in 1943, but this has not been investigated. Wren had a close association with the Donohoe racing family, who were also close to Joynton Smith. Frank Donohoe was a director of both Stadiums Ltd and Smith's Newspapers Ltd, while Bill Donohoe was a trustee of Joynton Smith's will.[40] Where necessary, Wren would have lobbied on behalf of Stadiums Ltd and his business interests in New South Wales.

There are suggestions that Wren dabbled in Sydney politics. Aside from the favourable sale of his Criterion Hotel, little is known, but McMullin asserts that Wren 'carefully observed the [notorious] Willis versus Bailey contest [in 1922–3] over the sliding panel ballot boxes and allegedly sought to influence it'. Although he sees Wren as 'a seasoned practitioner' in voter impersonation and multiple voting on union tickets, 'the systematic use of ballot boxes [in NSW] was another dimension altogether'.[41] Bede Nairn quotes a *Sydney Morning Herald*-based allegation (14 April 1923) that Wren tried 'through an agent to influence proceedings' in an ALP inquiry in Sydney in 1923, but for what purposes is unclear.

If Jack Lang can be believed, Wren probed the possibilities of an association with him. The future High Court judge, Edward McTiernan, then a young Labor barrister (of whom Bede Nairn says: 'his integrity was invulnerable, his ability exceptional, his opinions much respected'),[42] thought well enough of Wren to suggest to Lang in 1922 that he should 'meet a man who could do him and Labor a lot of good'. Lang went along to the Criterion Hotel, which Wren owned and where he stayed when in Sydney. But Lang could not work out what this 'small, shrewd … taciturn' man wanted. They 'sparred' but got nowhere: 'He must have decided there and then he couldn't get anywhere with me … Had I been prepared to make the opening, then the history of this State may have been different. But I just didn't believe the Labor Party was for sale.'

'A champion wire-puller' was Lang's summation of Wren, but he did not specify gross corruption. Whether Wren was subsequently involved in any anti-Lang faction is unknown but far from inconceivable, in view of Theodore's move from Queensland to New South Wales in 1926 (following Ryan's precedent) and Lang's hatred of him.[43] When considering Lang's opinion of Wren, Evatt's judgment in 1927 that Lang himself was 'the biggest crook in the labour movement' must be remembered.[44] The lack of respect was mutual.

Interstate politics: Adelaide

McMullin states that Wren had associates in South Australia who included 'Labor's extraordinary firebrand' Bert Edwards, 'King of the West End', MHA for Adelaide (1919) and city councillor: 'flashy friend of the destitute [to whom he left his estate of £45,492], and reputedly the homosexual, illegitimate son of former premier [and Federation Father] C. C. Kingston'. A hotelier, politician and philanthropist, he was a Catholic and, when campaigning with Wren for Father Jerger, had allegedly (according to the Commonwealth police) bribed the Australian Workers' Union seamen to strike in 1920. He was described by an opponent as 'a Tammany Hall boss', 'using aggressive tactics … to win pre-selection for a crony … "A man is justified in doing anything to win it", was his pragmatic approach to ballots [an attitude not unknown in modern politics!].'

However, Edwards was a slum clearer, an opponent of land sharks and rack renters, and a prison reformer who had himself been incarcerated for sodomy (but quite possibly was framed). His flamboyance ('White suits with Homburg hat, bow tie and suede shoes, favouring silk pyjamas and gold-tipped cigarettes') made him an odd associate for the dour Collingwood tycoon. They have, however, been described, oddly it must be said, as 'similar types'. Edwards favoured licensing offcourse bookmakers and opposed prohibition, and Wren is supposed to have helped him on his release from prison to resume hotel keeping. Their friendship did not stop Edwards campaigning for Lang in 1930, nor did it win him a seat in either federal (1940) or state (1950) elections.[45]

That South Australia's Senator J. J. Daly could have been Wren's 'pea' (as Lang said) gets endorsement from ex-communist memoirist Tony McGillick, who had been to the same Catholic school and resisted Daly's encouragement to seek pre-selection as a Labor politician. McGillick called him 'a protégé of Wren' and writes of 'a powerful Wren force' in his state. Confidence in McGillick's opinion is not helped by his having been an organiser for the Friends of the Soviet Union in 1938 and having visited the USSR. At one stage McGillick wrote that 'the Soviet people, clear-eyed, strong in body and mind, proudly march on from victory to victory' (in, presumably, socio-economic reform).

Daly came from a devout, poor Catholic family, left school at thirteen, became secretary of the Self-Determination League of Australia in 1916 and led the state delegation to the Sydney Eucharistic Congress in 1928. He became a lawyer and a prominent member of the Australian Workers' Union; a state president of the Labor Party in 1927 and a member of its federal executive in 1928–34; a senator in 1928–34, Senate leader, acting attorney-general in 1930–1 and then minister for defence. A partner of Anstey and Beasley in opposing the Niemeyer deflationary advice,[46] he was in March 1931 spilt from cabinet and expelled from the South Australian branch of the party. The loss of his ministry was thought to be retribution by Scullin over the Evatt–McTiernan appointments and by Theodore for lack of support in restoring him to cabinet. Daly soon recanted and was made minister without portfolio. In 1934 he failed to gain pre-selection and eventually became 'an avowed pacifist'. Daly's biographer says nothing about a Wren connection.[47] Some association does seem quite credible but, with a highly regarded legal practice and a robust personality, his being a Victorian tycoon's 'creature' is unlikely.[48] I know of no visit of Wren to Adelaide other than that during 1920 in pursuit of Fr Jerger.

Tariff tout?

Jack Lang saw Wren as being at the zenith of his power after the landslide victory of Scullin as Labor leader in October 1929. Labor had won 47 of 75 lower house seats but held only 7 of 36 in the Senate. Protection had, however, been Labor's settled policy since Federation and Scullin had, since 1925, been scornful of the Tariff Board's low-excise policy. Jack Lang recalled:

> Scullin's favourite theme was the protection of Australian industries. The quickest way to provide employment was in Australian factories. The trade balance was drifting, so imports should be reduced.
>
> For the first time Labor was making a direct appeal to the Chamber of Manufacturers. They suspected [PM] Bruce. He was an importers' man. Theodore gave pledges for increased protection if Labor won the elections. So the Party had more money than it normally had ...
>
> [It] must have satisfied some of the big financial interests of the city who normally detested Labor ...[49]

Within a month of Labor coming to power, a tariff schedule was tabled in parliament on 21 November 1929 raising import duties on 240 items by an average of more than 30 per cent on previous rates. Among them was a heavy tariff on liquor, which was seen by critics as being too favourable to the Wren/Cody interests. This was 'the most scientific protective tariff we have had', claimed Scullin. With the economy collapsing, Scullin had neither the time nor inclination for public hearings or the niceties of debate that summoning the Tariff Board would involve. Labor riled the opposition by stifling discussion, and enraged Latham, leader of the opposition, by denying him the right to discuss customs duties at all.[50] Other means of raising revenue would have met with obstruction from the opposition-dominated Senate or the conservative Commonwealth Bank. Further schedules followed from 1929 to 1931, with radical laborites like J. B. Chifley advocating high tariffs whatever their impact on exports.[51] Simple cronyism does not explain the rise in duties on imported spirits, although it is understandable that discriminating topers should not have wanted to consume Wren/Cody Corio or Old Court whiskies or Vickers gin rather than imports. An 'industrial patriot', however, Theodore 'was fanatical about Australia's manufacturing potential. In private life he looked for the "Made in

Australia" label, even specifying that only Australian whisky should be served when he entertained at the Hotel Australia.'[52]

However, McMullin sees the 'whisky tariff' as 'one of the more notorious ... [unspecified] shady rackets' that were 'implemented'—'very lucrative for Wren and his company, Federal Distilleries Pty Ltd'.[53] Not all Labor MPs were supportive. The opposition seized on this opportunity immediately. On 27 November, Senator James Ogden asked:

> Can it be argued that this was done in the interest of the Australian whisky man or to provide employment? May we not assume that the intention was to increase the profits of the Federal Distilleries in which Mr John Wren has a controlling interest? Unquestionably this is another instance of a surrender of the Labor Party to the money power.[54]

National MHR, Henry Gullett, remarked a few days later: 'A request for these duties did not come before me while I was in charge of the Department of Trade and Customs.'[55]

Six Labor backbenchers voted on 12 May 1931 against their own party's further proposal to lower the duty placed 'on certain spirits'. A special meeting of caucus was called to consider this defeat. Scullin was conciliatory, and expressed the opinion that nothing should be moved that 'would bind members on items affecting them in their electorates'.[56] There was, however, an angry debate in 1931, after which the tariff Bill was carried by one vote. Even 'enthusiastic protectionists' made 'frequent and furious condemnations' against tariff proposals which were 'often ill-considered in detail'. John Curtin (as a Western Australian, in an unsafe seat, perhaps wary of tariffs) and six other Labor MPs voted with the opposition, while Joseph Lyons (who had by this time defected from Labor) and two other opposition members went with the government. This was consistent with an increasing fear, even among a few Labor men, that over-protection would lead to retaliation overseas.

C. B. Schedvin provides a persuasive context within which to explicate the tariff problem:

> The instincts of many Labor men were isolationist: the Depression had been caused by forces beyond Australia's control and the country must, it was argued, isolate itself from the international

> economy as far as possible. Moreover, the tariff was the most convenient instrument available to the Government. A new schedule simply had to be tabled in Parliament to become effective immediately. To a Government which was constantly hamstrung by a hostile Senate, the simplicity of this procedure was a haven. It is not difficult to understand, therefore, the Government's constant resort to the tariff when it was being urged to reduce costs and wages—a course which it found intolerable.[57]

The tariff on liquor was not exacted just for Wren's benefit, but it could be asked whether some aspects of it were not too indulgent. Suspicion remained and, in any case, the opposition had to make a point. As the patrician MP Charles Hawker put it in 1931:

> This discriminatory duty … was 'wangled', originally to the benefit of Federal Distilleries Limited, whose product was the only Australian whisky that was manufactured in large quantities at that time, and was mature enough to market in bulk … Mr John Wren was a large share holder. The fact … led to some resentment on the part of a local distillery that was being established by the Scottish combine … Within a few weeks … a second schedule was brought down giving the Scottish combine the same advantage over its small competitors in regard to imported whisky as was enjoyed by Federal Distilleries Limited, and what the former gained over its small competitors made up for any disadvantage suffered with regard to locally distilled whisky. Failing that, it enabled Federal Distilleries … to make an advantageous amalgamation with the big combine which now has the smaller importers as well as the smaller Australian distilleries in a position of great disadvantage. A large quantity of Australian-made whisky is being consumed today …[58]

A further tariff schedule placed a duty of 28 shillings per proof gallon on whisky bottled under customs supervision, but 33 shillings on whisky bottled out of bond. This favoured big producers and distributors, and threatened the old hoteliers' practice of free bottling from hogsheads of bulk spirits.[59] A few weeks later a second schedule gave the 'Scottish combine' the same advantage over its small competitors in regard to imported whisky as was enjoyed by Federal Distilleries. Parker

Moloney, Labor minister for markets and transport, and a friend of Wren, defended the revised tariff by claiming that the executive of the Victorian Licensed Victuallers' Association (VLVA) was in favour of the new arrangements. To which Hawker retorted that the chairman of the VLVA was a licensee of a hotel owned by Federal Distilleries. Its executive had since been dumped.[60]

Contemporary newspapers confirm that there was turmoil within VLVA—but it appeared to be more concerned about excise on beer than on whisky, such that one of its first decisions was not to pass on the duty to the public. However, the redoubtable Labor MP, Don Cameron, pointed out that no other country had whisky bottled out of bond. He thought the tax unjust.[61] Whatever the degree of connivance in levying this excise, the government still had good reasons for placing an extra five shillings duty on whisky bottled out of bond. It encouraged all whisky to be bottled under supervision, ensuring that it would be true to its label, and increasing revenue and creating employment through the manufacture of bottles and cases and in the bottling and packing of spirits in the bond stores.[62] These were credible reasons—in the five years to 1930 there had been twenty-five convictions for illicit stills in Australia—but they were unlikely to convince those who like John Curtin thought that Wren had too 'big a hold' on the Labor Party.[63]

Rebuffed

A decade later, on 22 November 1941 (that is, less than two months after Curtin became prime minister), Scullin, then only a senior backbench statesman, was lobbied by Wren over double taxation of Fijian gold:

> Dear Jim,
>
> I desire to convey to you my sincere thanks and appreciation of your just efforts on my behalf, in connection with my Fijian gold mining interests …
>
> It makes me very sad to now find that the Party which I have supported so fully in the past should now select me and my friends for the harsh and unjust treatment of what amounts to confiscation of our Fijian gold mining interests, for this is what the Government proposals really mean …
>
> Why the Government should differentiate against these Fijian

> mines as compared with gold mines in Australia, New Guinea and Papua, all being component parts of our British Empire, is a mystery to me. I spoke to Mr Curtin … and the only reason he gave me was that the Australian and New Guinea gold mines paid an Australian gold tax of apparently 20/- per oz. Well, why not impose a similar levy on the Fijian mines than practically confiscate them. At the present time, these mines are subject to a royalty charge of 5 per cent and an export tax of 1 per cent and, in addition, they are subject to Fijian income tax.
>
> Under the Government's proposals, I would be subjected to very heavy taxation on my Australian income but I do not object to this because it is income and the asset is preserved whereas in Fiji it is a wasting asset.
>
> Again thanking you for your assistance,
> I remain,
> Yours sincerely,
> JOHN WREN [64]

Wren also telephoned Curtin personally and complained:

> 'This Bill hits Mr Theodore and myself very severely, and I want you to do something about it'. Curtin replied: 'It's a taxation measure about which I know very little but I'll speak to the Treasurer about it'. Wren retorted: 'Well, you'll have to do something about it as I propose to talk to Mr Theodore'. The following night Wren rang up again and Curtin gave him the uncomforting reply: 'I have spoken to Mr Chifley about your taxation difficulty. He said to inform you that the Bill is going on and to let Mr Theodore know that the Senate rejected a similar provision introduced by him in the days of the Scullin Government'.[65]

To administer this rebuff must have given Curtin not a little satisfaction. Wren's curtness, which comes through, even in this précis, suggests that he was accustomed to talk bluntly to politicians: but this was not 1930, nor was Curtin an old mate. There is no doubt that he had in the past regularly lobbied Scullin's ministers. Stan Keon said he had evidence of this from Scullin's secretary, and Richmond's ex-mayor, James Loughnan, one of Scullin's aides and no enemy of Wren, agreed.[66]

After a long interview in 1947 with prime minister Chifley on the Fiji question, Theodore wrote to Wren on 24 January 1947:

> I gave Mr Chifley a list of the taxes and imposts that apply in Fiji to gold mining companies. I quoted from a memorandum I had put before a Taxation Committee in Fiji. At Mr Chifley's request I left a copy of this memorandum with him …
>
> I explained to Mr Chifley that we had been unable to distribute dividends to shareholders since 1941 (with the exception of one 1/- dividend for Loloma in 1944). Because what remained for distribution after heavy taxes in Fiji would have been subject again to most severe taxation here.
>
> After discussing the matter a little he said he realised it was pretty tough treatment especially as there was no allowance for depletion of ore reserves or for the wasting assets.
>
> Mr Chifley told me he would ask Mr Scullin to go into the question and make a recommendation. He, Mr Chifley, expressed the view that it might be practicable to enter into a reciprocal arrangement with Fiji whereunder company income that was taxable there should be exempt here and vice versa. I said such an arrangement would be quite satisfactory and the Fiji government would agree on those lines.[67]

Theodore would appear to have received a more amicable response than Wren. In April a disgruntled Wren concluded a letter to Scullin:

> Common honesty demands just treatment and equitable legislation on a par with shareholders in Australian Mining Companies, otherwise discrimination against Fiji Mining Company shareholders is obvious and distinctly unjust.

A more formal note on the same day to 'Mr Scullin' (rather than 'Dear Jim') expresses great disappointment with amendments made to the relevant Act:

> My opinion is that the only sensible course for the Directors to pursue is to invest the whole of the profits in sound Australian securities and pay dividends from the earned income in Australia

> and thereby preserve the whole of the accumulated assets instead of paying most of it away in taxes. Any shareholder who is in need of money can sell these shares as there is a good market for same.[68]

Chifley in 1947–8 again rebuffed Wren when the Brisbane Amateur Turf Club sought approval from the Commonwealth Bank—with adequate security for a loan of £300,000 from the National Bank—for the purchase of Doomben racecourse from a Wren/Nathan company, Doomben Recreation Grounds Pty Ltd. Wren got both Scullin and E. J. Holloway (then minister for labour and national service) to use their good offices with Chifley. He, however, was not impressed even with the proposal to invest the greater part of the purchase money in Commonwealth loans. This would still be inflationary and contrary to government policy, Chifley said.[69] Whatever may have happened in Scullin's day or was going on in Victoria, it is ludicrous that anyone should think that the Curtin–Chifley governments were influenced by John Wren. Yet this was when those behind *Power Without Glory* were telling the Australian people that Wren controlled the Labor government.

Jobbery in context

Just as it should be instructive to provide a context of boodlers, Baillieus and Bents to understand why spirited members of 'the lower orders' in Collingwood may have been contemptuous of the law in the 1890s, so it is useful to be reminded how conservative statesmen and even members of the judiciary could deal in the 1920s and 1930s in offices of state. It should help with any moral assessment of Wren's political interventions—at least comparatively. One chain of events at the highest level can suffice.

Joseph Lyons was relieved of the Treasury portfolio in the Scullin government in January 1931 when E. G. Theodore returned to cabinet, although still under a cloud of suspicion in relation to alleged corruption while premier of Queensland. Not just piqued, Lyons thought this improper. He was already lunching at the Herald and Weekly Times, of which Keith Murdoch was managing director. On 4 February he was asked to abandon the Labor Party by conservative commercial and political identities (for example, Staniforth Ricketson of J. B. Were and Co), with R. G. Menzies as spokesman, and support from Keith Murdoch. The reward would be leadership of a new political force, a

United Australia Party (UAP), to replace the abject Nationalist Party. It was too glittering a prize for a parochial Tasmanian to resist, and Lyons accepted in May. The leader of the opposition and alternative prime minister, (Sir) John Latham, moved aside.

Latham's friend W. Kent Hughes trusted that his 'sacrifice' would 'not be in vain' and that the 'service' he was rendering would 'not be unrewarded in the future'.[70] In due course, in 1935, Lyons not only put Latham on the High Court bench but, as he had requested, made him chief justice of Australia—although, as Menzies in particular knew, Mr Justice (Sir) Owen Dixon was the most eminent jurist in the country. To conservatives who harped on 'the sanctity of contracts', albeit in a great depression when equality of sacrifice should have been in order, even a backroom deal was a deal. Quoting one of his colleagues, Dixon wrote in his diary that Latham's appointment was 'a job'.[71]

The jobbery was suave. When Latham resigned his Kooyong seat in parliament in 1934, UAP pre-selection for this most blue ribbon of conservative electorates went to the then Victorian attorney-general, R. G. Menzies, obviously a UAP federal leader of the future. The octogenarian High Court chief justice Sir Frank Gavan Duffy was prepared to take a timely retirement and make way for Latham once his [Gavan Duffy's] son, Charles, was appointed to the Victorian Supreme Court bench.[72] Menzies had been able to fix that in June 1933. As the distinguished biographer of Jack Lang says, 'Ricketson and Menzies and their fellow plotters would have earned the qualified admiration of Jack Bailey, Jock Garden and Albert Willis [notorious trade union fixers], past masters at this kind of Tammany game'.[73]

This is the same Latham who, as attorney-general, dropped the prosecution of the 'coal baron', John Brown, for his illegal lockout of workers in 1929.[74] That same Brown was the 'old and intimate friend' of the then High Court chief justice Sir Adrian Knox, who became 'the residual legatee' of Brown's will, such that he felt he had to resign as chief justice.[75]

Some historians finesse Latham's appointment to the bench. Sir Zelman Cowen[76] is one example but, more blandly, Stuart Macintyre in the *Australian Dictionary of Biography* says simply that by 1933 Latham 'had set his sights on the post of chief justice', and mention of the earlier 1931 'understanding' is avoided. Similarly with Latham's conflicts of interest, when he was a reactionary federal attorney-general under S. M.

Bruce and held 'general retainers from a wide range of shipping, mining and other clients'. For example, Latham was being paid a retainer by the Commonwealth Steamship Owners Association early in 1929—although he was that year principal author of the Maritime Industries Bill which sought to transfer industrial regulation back to the states, except for the maritime and stevedoring industries. This was clearly a legislative measure of enormous importance to shipowners. Such conflicts of interest are passed over by Macintyre as yielding 'no evidence to impugn his integrity'.[77]

In 1933 attorney-general Latham urged Victoria and New South Wales (both with conservative governments) to act against communism. As the Commonwealth could legislate only if there were an actual or threatened revolution in this case, Latham cited, oddly enough, the Victorian government's suppression of Wren's Tote in 1906 as an example of what might be done. In 1951 he was the only one of seven federal justices who refused to accept that the Menzies Communist Party Dissolution Act was *ultra vires.* Quite plausibly, he is suspected of having helped to draw up the legislation in secret conclave with Menzies and his then attorney-general, John Spicer, at the Australian Club in Melbourne. After the Act was declared invalid, Latham admitted that he had seen Menzies and had made some suggestions on amendments.[78] Latham seemed unaware that the judiciary's role was to appraise legislation, not help draft it. As Gough Whitlam has pointed out, 'It should not be thought that the judges of that era did not show a reciprocal solicitude for Menzies'.[79] Bourgeois historians rarely treat the motives of Collingwood (and Balmain) boys with such generosity. John Wren was sufficiently aware how rubbery the political ethics of the moralising conservative politicians could be, and must have had little compunction about emulating them, albeit in a far less sophisticated manner.

CHAPTER FIFTEEN

A Friend Like You: Evatt to Wren

THE FRIENDSHIP OF John Wren and Dr H. V. 'Bert' Evatt warrants lengthier analysis if only, but not only, because it is documented through ten letters written to Wren by Evatt between 1938 and 1946, a period when the latter moved from the High Court of Australia to federal politics and to being, ultimately, deputy prime minister. There is also a somewhat corroborative letter by Wren to Sir Gilbert Dyett. These letters were not discovered until after the death of Wren's last surviving and eldest son, John Francis, in 1992. One wonders what Manning Clark (d. 1991) would have made of the friendship and whether, in the light of it, he would have modified his esteem of Evatt, 'the man who had the image of Christ in his heart and the teaching of the Enlightenment in his mind'.[1] Or would he have revised his opinion of Wren's life as 'a vaudeville of devils'.[2]

There is no record of Evatt's first acquaintance with Wren. It could have been as early as 1919 when Evatt was junior counsel for Tom Ryan in a libel suit against the *Argus*.[3] More likely it would have been in 1923–5. Wren would have taken an interest, at least at Archbishop Mannix's behest, in the 1923 federal deportation order against the Irish envoys Michael O'Flanagan and J. J. O'Kelly, who had come to Australia to raise funds and support for Irish republicanism. Evatt had been hired as their junior counsel.[4] Wren was friendly with (Mr Justice) E. T. McTiernan, who tried to form an association between Wren and New

South Wales Labor leader J. T. Lang. As state MLA for Balmain, Evatt campaigned in the corresponding federal electorate of Dalley in 1927 for Theodore, who had moved from Queensland to Sydney.[5] Evatt may have represented Wren in commercial litigation. All three men were antagonistic to Lang. Lang would go on to allege that Wren was responsible for the elevation of Evatt and McTiernan to the High Court in 1930.[6] Arthur Calwell was to recall that he was introduced to the then Mr Justice Evatt for the first time by John Wren at a Collingwood–Melbourne football match in 1932. Evatt was Wren's guest.[7]

John Francis Wren was insistent that Evatt and his father were friends and that the Evatts visited the Wren home. He recalled being at the High Court with his father in the 1930s during a case at which Evatt was on the Bench. He said that after the verdict was delivered, 'Evatt, still robed, ran down the corridor after my father to say, "I daresay you were satisfied with that result, Mr Wren"—or words to that effect'. Some research has uncovered only one High Court case involving Wren. It was 1935. Evatt did preside, but with his fellow judges. Wren lost and had to pay £12,505 plus costs, a considerable sum in those days.[8] This hardly seems to be the case to which Wren's son was referring. But the reminiscence raises issues of propriety, as does what follows.

Evatt's letters to Wren begin with two cryptic ones on High Court notepaper, and can be dated 29 and 30 March 1938. The men have already been in contact, as Evatt thanks Wren for a prior 'note' which is 'a result of your own and partly my interventions'. These would appear to have been to prevent a non-Labor senator being appointed to replace Victorian Labor senator-elect John Barnes, who had died on 31 January. The letter suggests that 'RGM' (R. G. Menzies), then federal attorney-general, was attempting to defy the convention that, when a senator died before his term expired, the relevant state government chose a replacement on the advice of the dead senator's party. However, this 1938 case is not strictly a foreshadowing of the infamous Bjelke-Petersen/Bert Field manipulation of 1974, as Barnes had died before taking his seat. Evatt opines that 'RGM' should not have practically invited litigation as he did. It is the responsibility of the Victorian premier, Albert Dunstan, 'to see to it that the Labor nominee gets the vacancy'. If not, he 'will get the blame', whether the new appointee be 'Red or Black or Tan or Brindle'. Obviously, it is up to Wren to see that his friend Dunstan gets the benefit of this [Evatt's] expert legal advice.

A Labor man, J. M. Sheehan, did replace Barnes on 12 July.

However, the bulk of the letter is mysteriously concerned with 'the other matter we discussed', which it would not be discreet for Evatt to mention explicitly in writing. So it is later referred to as 'the thing'. Evatt was to leave Sydney on the *Franconia* on 17 April for sabbatical leave in England via New York. Before that, his and Wren's 'mutual friend' will be 'out of Australia'—and so unable to fix this 'thing'? It must be done immediately and, as he will be, while in London, an official delegate to the Imperial Cricket Conference, 'this will make it easier to act'. His claim to whatever it is that he wants is 'broader than mere judicial office for over seven years'. He cites his scholarly publications: his seventh book—*The Rum Rebellion*, on Governor Bligh—is about to be published, while *Australian Labor Leader*, on William Holman, will probably be published while he is abroad. He is president of the Mitchell Library, Sydney, 'the most scholarly institution of its kind in the world'. And, apart from his career in law, he himself is 'one of the greatest scholars in the history of NSW'.

Evatt acknowledges that all this sounds 'd—d boastful', but he must have 'immediate action'. 'It will be harder later', he says. He points out that in his book he has praised prime minister Lyons for his part in the anti-conscription campaign of 1916–17 (although Lyons had 'ratted' on Labor in 1931). He has also praised Tom Ryan and Archbishop Mannix. He believes that Frank Brennan (who became Scullin's attorney-general in 1929–31) and John Curtin (now leader of the opposition) 'would work to oppose me'; he 'greatly fears to breathe a word to them'. So this 'thing' has to be done by Wren 'on your own responsibility'.

A sweetener follows. Wren must give his daughter Mary 'fondest regards from my wife and myself'. They hope to see Mary Wren in London. They think the trip will do her good and, if they can, they will be 'always at her service'. He concludes:

> Pardon my frankness but the matter is too delicate for you to handle except successfully: or, in other words, *you* [emphasis Evatt's] should be successful.
>
> With very best wishes,
> H. V. Evatt

But there is an exasperated postscript: 'Please advise me what to do about Curtin and Brennan. (I hope it will not be necessary for me to see or write to them).'

Evatt wrote again two days later. Wren in the meantime had phoned, but Evatt 'could not grasp everything you said'. However, Evatt would 'try and see Joe [Lyons]' before he leaves. He is 'puzzled':

> Joe has it in his power to do the thing from here and it would be easier to do it from here. The other persons would probably prefer something that would give their wives a *handle* [that is, a knighthood?]. You know what I mean. After all, I am the one who is going abroad—I will not be doing so for another 7 years: the only time that the thing would be really interesting and valuable is *now* [emphases Evatt's].

There are '50 ways of doing a thing', continues Evatt, 'and a hundred of refusing':

> Like you, I prefer straight out refusal. It would be a shocking thing if your kindly thought and action only resulted in other people getting everything. I do not know J's [Lyons's] movements: I would much prefer him to send for me ... to deal with the matter here and now—before I leave: of course I could do anything abroad which was wanted but others will be there for that purpose. The delay and uncertainty are provoking.
>
> Yours sincerely,
>
> B.E.

What was Wren's 'kindly thought and action' that only resulted—so 'shockingly'—in 'other people getting everything'? The most obvious explanation of 'the thing' is that Evatt wanted to become a privy councillor and believed Wren had enough clout to procure it for him, even from a non-Labor prime minister whose most formidable cabinet colleague (and rival) was Evatt's *bête noire*, 'RGM'—who had been made a privy councillor in 1937, as was Evatt's 'indolent' colleague Mr Justice Rich.[9] But then Lyons had been a Labor premier and federal minister, and was an exemplary Catholic. Evatt would have known that Joe and Enid Lyons were on friendly, even visiting, terms with the Wrens, as John Francis Wren said they were. The same was true of the Evatts, as the remarks about Mary imply. As things turned out, Evatt did not become privy councillor until he became attorney-general in 1942. Evatt seems naive in this matter; Wren pretentious—if, as seems likely, he was encouraging Evatt to think he was a masterful puppeteer. (Evatt has addressed Wren as 'Dear Mr Wren' in these first two letters; henceforth it will be 'Dear J.W.', except for the one dated 29 September 1943 which is typed and therefore dictated, and the 1946 cable from the United Nations.)

Evatt resigned from the High Court on 30 August 1940, and on 21 September contested and won comfortably the previously conservative seat of Barton (NSW) in the federal election. In her authorised biography of Evatt, Kylie Tennant attributes the highest motives to Evatt's decision, as did many of those who voted for him. In a time of national peril—the European war was a year old and the Battle for Britain in progress—Evatt could be seen as providing possible alternative leadership to the weak, disunited government of Menzies, who had become prime minister on the death of Lyons on 7 April 1939. 'Certainly', wrote Tennant, 'Evatt had ideas of being prime minister—why should he not? If Menzies could be prime minister, then the position should be well within his grasp'.[10]

Wren thought so too. Two days after the 1940 election (6 October), he wrote to Sir Gilbert Dyett, who had been president since 1919 of the influential organisation that became known as the Returned Services League (RSL). Dyett had also been secretary of the Wren-controlled Victorian Trotting and Racing Association since 1919, but Wren addresses him formally:

> Dear Sir Gilbert
>
> The various happenings such as industrial disputes, strikes etc. together with the sinking of our ships in the Pacific by raiders must be retarding Australia's war effort and certainly is causing myself and many others in the community grave concern.
>
> It appears to me that unless steps are taken to remedy this deplorable position, very serious developments and possible disaster to this country will occur.
>
> I am wondering whether you could in your capacity as Chief President of the Australian Soldiers Association [that is, RSL] do something practical to improve the present state of affairs.

For instance the value of the services to the Commonwealth of such a learned and distinguished person as Dr Evatt M P could not be estimated.

He is undoubtedly the ablest and most outstanding man in the Federal House of Parliament, not only has he the ability to think, combined with industry and extraordinary energy with the added essential assett [sic], plenty of guts.

The position this country is in at present appears alarming and is fast drifting towards a state of anarchy. Some of your own soldier representatives at your last Canberra Conference thought the matter so serious that they actually talked of a Dictitatorship [sic].

The Government passes legislation and misguided persons declare not to work unless the legislation effecting them is withdrawn, action, which if carried out and developed, may mean Civil War.

This government is apparently too weak to give effect to its own laws.

I think very seriously it is time some highly capable man in the community such as Dr Evatt should arise and set about putting Australia on a sound basis.

I know you were desirous of bringing about the formation of a national government and that is my primary reason of writing to you.

However I should be glad to hear your views on the matter and whether you think any good purpose might be served if negotiations were undertaken by you.

Yours faithfully
JOHN WREN

Two days later, when the election results were declared, the combined Labor representation (that is, official ALP and Lang Labor) was thirty-six seats, equalling the conservative (United Australia Party and Country Party) number. There were two conservative independents whose votes would prove crucial. Menzies wanted to form an all-party national government, as Churchill had done in England. Evatt was in favour; he was desperate to be in office, but preferably as leader of such a government. Alternatively, he wanted to overthrow the Menzies conservative government and was exasperated by what he believed to be

Labor leader Curtin's timidity in not trying to do so. Labor agreed only to an Advisory War Council (AWC) of eight, later ten, with equal representation from both sides of parliament.[11]

Evatt was not elected to the AWC until 18 March 1941. Earlier than that, it would seem, there are two undated letters from Evatt mentioning only the day of the week and 'Sydney'. On the first of them, on paper bearing the letterhead of the Advisory War Council, the word 'War' has a cancelling stroke through it. Evatt writes that Menzies may attempt 'closer political unity' through a more powerful War Council or a new executive war committee, but it is by no means certain. He will do so if Curtin agrees, but Curtin leans too much on Wren's 'great friend Scullin', says Evatt. He reminds Wren that 'Scullin failed as PM, admittedly in difficult circumstances. But now he is against almost every change, either a national government or a minority Labor government.' Scullin, says Evatt, may favour a new executive committee, but he himself 'can do nothing with him'. Perhaps Wren can. Where previously he signed off as 'H. V. Evatt' and 'B E.', he is now 'Bert Evatt'.

The second letter is on the letterhead of the Federal Members' Room, Sydney but is from Chambers, 182 Phillip St, Sydney (handwritten). Evatt and Wren, it appears, have been discussing 'ideas' with 'Gilbert'; the 'key' to carrying them out is in the AWC 'which can be, later on, very useful as an instrument'. (For what? Making Evatt prime minister?) As the official Labor Party and Lang Labor (four MPs) had by then united, there was to be reconsideration of representation on the AWC. Last time Evatt tied with Norman Makin but was defeated when one of his supporters changed sides, but he believes his 'strength has increased'. Curtin has told Evatt (so he says) that Forde and Makin are 'of little or no use and that he would like me to become a member. But he may not fight very hard to produce a change.' The matter 'could be clinched' by Forgan Smith, Queensland premier, who can persuade the Queensland MPs to support him. 'You and only you', writes Evatt, 'could persuade Forgan' (implying that Wren has him in his pocket?). Scullin and Calwell are also important, while 'Gilbert might help with Curtin'. There are intimations of the later tragic Evatt as he accuses Forde of having 'promised me support and betrayed me' at the last ballot. Meanwhile he does 'not want to get another kick—if I can avoid it'. He believes he 'can do a job for this country. They asked me to resign to help Labor to win this terrible war—yet after I did so and we won so easily in NSW—they keep me powerless to do anything.' The rest of the letter is somewhat peremptory about 'Gilbert': 'I've already told Gilbert to tell Forgan that, in the event of future adjustment, he can stand in [for?—illegible] me ... Perhaps Gilbert might report to me—Curtin will be in Melbourne this week.' The letter was signed 'B. Evatt'.

A further three letters are dated 14, 17 and 26 May 1941. Among other things, they deal with a by-election in Boothby, South Australia, on 24 May, where the Coalition's 'effective majority' was reduced from 20,000 to 8,000. Evatt had thrown himself zealously into this campaign, as he had in the Swan electorate (Western Australia) the previous December.[12] (He had been the only prominent federal MP to do so and had to pay his own expenses, possibly with some help from Wren.) The first of the three letters is on AWC paper and encloses a copy of 'the circular ... which did an enormous amount of good' in Boothby. It was meant to have the same impact as one delivered in Barton in the previous October, signed by himself and delivered to electors by post 'on the Friday before the vote'. As there were 70,000 on the Boothby roll, he will not tell the party about it 'so that it will come as a bombshell'. The cost will be somewhere near £150. It seems likely that Wren is to pay this sum. (Did he also pay some or all of the £1,500 that Kylie Tennant said it cost Evatt to win Barton? That seems likely too.)[13] The letter of 17 May, written from the Hotel Windsor, Melbourne, suggests Wren did pay in Boothby, because Evatt raises the 'imposition' to £200 but says 'it was Ted Theodore's idea in Queensland [although Theodore was out of politics?] and it may be very important'. The third letter, of 24 May, after the Boothby election, encloses a copy of Evatt's circular which he says did 'an enormous amount of good':

> We could toss this govt out and I think [Alexander] Wilson [Independent Country Party] would support us. But the trouble is Curtin's complete lack of will power. He'll not form a Labor Govt nor will he allow us to join 50–50 with Menzies. That is why I am keeping closely in touch with Gilbert [Dyett]—we must be ready for every event. Menzies seemed somewhat truculent and overbearing towards his colleagues on Saturday when he arrived [back from England] but there may be a change after Boothby.
>
> Yours Ever,
>
> Bert E.

There are two personal issues in that triad of letters. Once again, reference is made to Mary Wren, to whom Evatt's wife, he says, 'sends her special love'. Second, two of them have references to Evatt's brother Clive who, in 1936, was elected MLA in New South Wales. Evatt says, mysteriously, that 'he got the message from our [unnamed, unknown] friend that Clive will get into cabinet I think but [William] McKell [premier] wants him to take Education not the Law job.' He thinks 'this is a good idea personally'. Later he tells Wren that 'Clive got into the team and is very pleased to take Education'. (Did Wren really have some influence in that too or, rather, did Evatt just think so?)

By 1941 Wren's opinion of Menzies's leadership was shared by much of the Australian press, which was also critical of his extended absence overseas. While Menzies was prepared to resign and serve in a national government under a Labor prime minister, Curtin realised that this would provoke dissension in his own party and declined to take office except with a total Labor cabinet.[14] Jack Lang observed:

> Evatt realised that the key to the situation was the votes of [Alexander] Wilson and [A. W.] Coles [Independent] … so he set out to capture them. Wilson was a member of the State-controlled Victorian Country Party, which was a breakaway from the Federal organization … Evatt then enlisted the support of … John Wren, who had some influence with … Dyett, and directly or indirectly used these as his intermediaries.[15]

Wren would have known Alexander Wilson through his alleged puppet, Victorian Country Party premier Dunstan, to whose faction Wilson in effect belonged. In the 1920s and 1930s Wilson was prominent in the Victorian Wheatgrowers' Association, its president in 1937, and vice-president of the federal branch in the same year under Sir Earle Page.

Another connection between Wren and Wilson was Harold Glowrey, MLA for Ouyen, within Wilson's federal electorate of Wimmera. Glowrey, who when young had been assistant secretary of the Victorian Farmers' Union and editor of the *Farmer's Advocate*, became a member of Dunstan's Country Progressive Party group. He was an associate of Wren and had managed the Wren property Moroco East in the Riverina in the 1930s. (Glowrey is nominally its owner in the *Australian Pastoral Directories* from the 1930s to the 1950s.) Dunstan controversially appointed Glowrey chairman and general manager of the Grain Elevators Board in 1940 at £500 per annum. Allan Dalziel asserts that:

> Evatt was able to influence … Alex Wilson … who was a great admirer of Evatt and felt that Australia was in grave danger if the war effort was left to Menzies. He so cultivated Wilson that on an occasion when Evatt was at his Sydney home recovering from an attack of 'flu which had prevented his attendance at the Advisory War Council in Canberra … he caught the train to Melbourne, and to the astonishment and annoyance of Curtin, turned up in Wilson's electorate of Wimmera. He toured the electorate with Wilson, making speeches and receiving deputations.[16]

Influencing the less impressionable and wealthy A. W. Coles was left to the soldier Gilbert Dyett.

Menzies was to resign on 28 August in favour of Country Party leader Arthur Fadden, who as prime minister lasted less than six weeks. Dalziel recalled 'many others whom Evatt cultivated in this intense period of his planning to bring down the Menzies–Fadden government':

> one afternoon in 1941 … He called me to his first-floor window which looked down on Phillip Street and said, 'do you see that tall man on the other side of the street?' I looked across the street and saw a tall, thin man walking up and down. The distinguishing feature of his dress was that he wore a bowler hat. Evatt told me the man was Sir Gilbert Dyett … I was told to go down into the street, introduce myself to Sir Gilbert, bring him up to the first floor of Denham Chambers and wait in another room until Evatt gave me a signal to bring Sir Gilbert into his chambers …
>
> It did not surprise me that a public man like Sir Gilbert, with his leadership of the RSL and his strong links with powerful personages in Melbourne, was another with whom Evatt had made contact to promote his plans for dislodging the tottery anti-Labor wartime Coalition Government.
>
> So, on a historic day in October 1941 Wilson, with Arthur Coles … crossed the floor of the House and Fadden was out and Curtin was in.

> When people talk about the Curtin wartime government saving Australia, it is well to remember that, if it had not been for Evatt, a Curtin Administration might never have taken office.[17]

Clearly, the meddlesome millionaire may have had some catalytic though not indispensable role here. It would be confronting for some if it had to be said that the sinister Wren was an instrument in bringing about the accession of John Curtin to the prime ministership in the days of national peril.

The Labor Party repaid Wilson in 1945 by appointing him administrator of Norfolk Island for seven years at £1,000 per annum with 'free furnished quarters and an entertainment allowance of £150 pa'. The position had not been advertised. Not surprisingly, this was criticised by the opposition, which would never do such a thing. But was Wilson a so-called 'Wren man' or just an 'independent'? On 19 June 1941, before his apostasy, he had asked prime minister Menzies if the government contemplated 'taking any action to curtail organised and commercialised sport so that people's minds might be more properly directed to the winning of the war'[18]—not a Wren-inspired question one would think. But Wilson did not pursue the issue. Did he need to? At the risk of feeding Wren's obsessive critics I should also mention that Curtin was only a few weeks in power when Wilson asked for the examination of the possibility of mining Victoria's brown coal deposits to produce motor spirits and other oils.[19] Wren held coal deposits (including Altona)—but the link is too tenuous and, again, Wilson does not pursue the issue. If Curtin had thought Wren interests were involved, he would not have entertained it unless necessary. When Wilson was appointed to Norfolk Island, no one seems to have breathed Wren's name or any Wren connection in the affairs of 1941.

Evatt became attorney-general and minister for external affairs in the Curtin and Chifley governments. There is one letter from Evatt to Wren in the war years, dated 29 September 1943. It is from the attorney-general's office, has 'Confidential' written on it by Evatt, and encloses a 'full Cabinet document' which 'conveniently sets out the story' he wishes to tell and which he asks to be 'returned'. The letter begins by thanking Wren for his 'very generous donation' to the M. A. Noble Testimonial Fund ('Monty' Noble having been a notable Australian Test captain), but moves quickly to criticism of Dyett. He, it seems, had supported the minister for repatriation, C. W. Frost, in his opposition to Evatt's setting up a legal bureau for soldiers through the Crown solicitor's office. Dyett had intervened while Evatt was abroad, presumably because he thought it not in the best interests of his RSL. Evatt deeply resented Dyett's action and wanted Wren to 'look into this matter' and persuade Dyett 'to cooperate … in the work I am doing to help the soldiers instead of stabbing me in the back and helping the people whose object occasionally seems to me to be to put every obstacle in the way of the returned soldier'.

So here we have Evatt drawing Australia's influential ex-servicemen's organisation into line on an inter-departmental policy issue, the presumption being that, as a virtual employee of Wren's, Dyett was also his 'creature'. And the demand is accompanied by the impropriety of enclosing with it a confidential cabinet document.

Perhaps the most remarkable piece of correspondence from Evatt to Wren was a deciphered cablegram on 10 June 1946 from 'New York', where the minister for foreign affairs was engaged in frenetic diplomacy at the infant United Nations. The question of the status of Franco's Spain was one about which Evatt was not prepared to be opportunistic, although the Spanish question had divided factions of the Labor Party in the 1930s and support for Franco had been of passionate concern to the Catholic Church. As Alan Renouf says:

> For him [Evatt], the survival of the Franco regime in Spain was abhorrent, because this was inconsistent with his two guiding precepts, security and justice; a Dictatorship, instituted by force, including foreign force, and which had aided the enemy in the Second World War was both dangerous to the peace and unjust.[20]

The issue became inflamed when in April 1946 Poland proposed that the Security Council break diplomatic relations with Spain. Evatt disagreed on the matter of procedure, and proposed a committee of investigation to ascertain the facts.

The Australian Catholic hierarchy, led by Mannix and Duhig, evidently protested against Evatt's 'pro-communist' position and enlisted Wren to contact Evatt. Wren did, by 'telephone message', of which there would be no record. Evatt replied at length. He protested that his stance in the Security Council was 'in no sense pro-communist' and 'is actually opposed to the extreme [and 'undemocratic'] course recommended by the Soviets'. Evatt says his proposed course of action was 'moderate' and 'the only possible course in the circumstances':

> By referring the matter to the General Assembly time is given to the Spanish people themselves to set their house in order and they are encouraged to do so. ... [There were] no grounds for thinking that the removal of the Franco regime 'would throw the Spanish people into the arms of the communists'.

On the contrary, Evatt continued, lack of interest in the welfare of the Spanish people would turn them towards communism. This had not resulted in Germany and Italy when free elections followed the removal of Nazism and Fascism. Moreover, only harmful results for the Catholic faith, he maintained, could come from association with Franco, the basic principles of whose regime 'are fundamentally opposed to the tenets of Catholicism'. This notion may have surprised Mannix and Duhig, as would Evatt's solicitude for the integrity of their faith. As the last remnant of Fascism, said Evatt, Franco's regime is 'an avowed enemy of the labour movement'.

Evatt says that he 'strongly resents statements like that attributed to the state member of the Victorian Legislative Assembly for Richmond', Stan Keon, who was notorious for intemperate criticism of anyone suspected of temporising with communism:

> No one has been more consistently critical of the Soviet wherever their [sic] view has been undemocratic ... it is utter madness to overlook the menace presented by Franco to international good will and especially to the Catholic Church. I look to you to explain this to the two Archbishops ... remembering always that the New South Wales Labor policy has always been opposed to International Fascism which nearly brought about our overthrow by Hitler, Mussolini and Hirohito. I must adhere to the principles consistently advocated by me on behalf of Australia and I trust you will give a fair and just interpretation of all my actions.

This cablegram concludes with 'best wishes to you all. Mary is much improved in health and my wife saw a great deal of her in London. Mary is anxious to return to Australia for a visit and if I can assist, I shall gladly do so.'

Four days later (14 June 1946), Wren would have received from 'The Australian Delegation, United Nations Delegation, New York', a cablegram which began: 'Following extracts from press in New York regarding Spanish question may be of interest'. It was suggested Wren 'may have been able to make use' of them. Firstly, there were 'Extracts from Catholic Weeklies'—the (American) *Commonweal* and the (British) *Tablet*. The former advocated Franco's 'disappearance' and 'fair elections in Spain'; the latter warned that 'the fate of the Church must not anywhere be identified with the fortunes of any specific political regime' and that Evatt 'deserved the applause of every lover of freedom and true democracy'. The 'liberal weekly', the *Nation*, said that Evatt 'sounded a note long awaited on the Security Council, the note of moral realism', in relation to Franco's Spain.

Wren would have shown these cables to Mannix and Duhig as soon as possible. There exists a covering note to Duhig dated 25 June with the second cablegram, now in the archdiocesan archives in Brisbane, which states baldly: 'Enclosing further cables from Dr Evatt. I am pleased my telephone conversation was the means of separating him from the Russian representative Gromyko'.

It can be deduced that Wren had actually talked directly to Evatt by telephone between 10 and 14 June, his first communication on this matter having been a 'telephone message', although this is not altogether clear. The first cablegram is not in the Brisbane Catholic archives, but Duhig did receive it. Wren's claim that he was responsible for some 'separation' of Evatt and Russian ambassador Gromyko is surely vainglorious, but Duhig did not think so. He wrote to Wren on 17 July:

> With regard to Dr Evatt, I have been greatly interested not only in the cablegrams … but in his change of front on hearing from you as evidenced in his utterances ever since. I think you may congratulate yourself that you did an excellent service to Australia and to the Government of which Evatt is a minister.

Duhig's distrust of Evatt emerges in later letters to Wren. On 22 December 1948 he believes the federal Labor government has lost support. He likes Calwell, a very honest, straightforward man, although Chifley needs to be 'more moderate and conciliatory'. But 'Evatt has not done them any good'. On 20 December 1950 he thinks 'our friend Evatt is now coming out in his true colours'. This would be because he has led the High Court challenge against the Communist Party Dissolution Bill. What Wren thought about that is not known. Mannix was ambivalent about the Bill, if not about Evatt's appearance in court defending the communists.

The final letter in the Evatt–Wren series is dated only '4 October' on 'Minister for Foreign Affairs' paper, but the year is certainly 1946, and it is six days after the federal election which Labor won with a reduced majority. The letter is marked 'Personal'. Evatt says he is 'enclosing a cutting from today's *Telegraph*[21] in which you will be specially interested'. This must be an item tipping that J. J. Dedman, the minister for postwar reconstruction, would become deputy prime minister if Frank Forde lost his seat, as seemed likely. Forde did. The cutting says that not only has Dedman done sterling work as a minister but, unlike his prime minister, he is not from New South Wales. As a Victorian, Dedman will provide more federal balance. Evatt, on the other hand, is also from New South Wales and, in spite of his prestige, his duties take him away from Australia and therefore the immediate political scene. What Evatt does not seem to know is that Dedman has been 'encouraged by promises of support volunteered by Chifley, Scullin and others'.[22] He mentions to Wren that there are reports that Calwell will stand. He thinks Calwell has no chance and 'it all is rather strange'. Evatt tells Wren:

> I would hope you might do something through people like Scullin, Senator Sheehan, Hendrickson *but only* [double underlining] if you can move with absolute certainty: in such a situation I really need a friend like you because I am 2nd to Chifley (if Forde is beaten). I have worked flat out to help the party as they all know.
>
> Yours Sincerely
> Bert Evatt

As it turned out, there were five candidates, who on the first ballot scored as follows: Evatt (NSW) 27, Ward (NSW) 22, Dedman (Vic) 12, Calwell (Vic) 11, Drakeford (SA) 4. Evatt won Dedman's and Drakeford's preferences; Ward won all of Calwell's. Evatt defeated his fellow New South Welshman 43–33. At the time, the result was seen as a right-versus-left victory, Calwell like Ward having been dissident on occasion during the war. But he too was a friend of Wren and a fellow Melbourne Catholic. It is difficult to think that, with his intellectual prestige, Evatt needed Wren at all in this matter.

After his death in 1965, Evatt's family commissioned Kylie Tennant to write his biography. His widow, said Tennant, 'showed exemplary patience in answering questions, checking facts, recalling details known to no one else'. She must have forgotten the visits to Studley House and her solicitude for Mary Wren. This is the only reference to Wren in the biography:

> [One of Archbishop Mannix's] early mistakes ... [was] a friendship with a generous member of his church, the wealthy John Wren, who had a finger in the underworld and more than a finger in Labor politics. It was to such men as John Wren that the IWW [International Workers of the World] pointed when they cried out that the Labor Party was bought by the Roman Catholic Church and the liquor interests.[23]

The sectarianism of these remarks hardly needs explication. *Power Without Glory* had done its work well.

Soon after the cache of Evatt–Wren letters was discovered, I wrote a three-part analysis of them, which was published in *Eureka Street* from August to October 1992. Naively, I imagined that even if political historians were not interested in what the letters said about Wren, they would be enthusiastically read by students of the controversial career of Evatt.

Evatt's centennial biography, sponsored by the Evatt Foundation, was then being written under the leadership of Ken Buckley, who took steps to authenticate the letters and who wrote the chapter in which there is some discussion of them. I was surprised that he referred to only two of the letters: the one asking for Wren's assistance to gain the deputy leadership, and the cables from the United Nations referring to Franco,[24] He later claimed that he did not have access to the other eight letters,[25] although all the letters are housed together.

Buckley speculates as to how 'a highly respectable Labor leader was covertly soliciting a favour [only one?] from a man with a sleazy reputation' who 'no doubt worked on the basis of a return of favours'. His explanation is simple: Evatt lacked a trade union base and 'had to cast around for support as occasion arose'. Wren was just any port in a storm. There is no suggestion either that 'the highly respectable' Evatt's regard for Wren might modify the latter's ill repute or, alternatively, that it reflected badly on Evatt himself. There is, however, room for a sneer at Wren's religion: Wren 'anticipated benefits in return for his money—in the case of the Church, a cynic would say that Wren aimed to buy his way into heaven'.[26] Buckley, like others, has no hesitation in attributing motives to someone whose career he had not studied, and has no concrete suggestions as to what Wren could have hoped to gain from his friendship with Evatt.

There seems to be a reluctance among some historians to see Wren as a person of at least normal vanity and gregariousness who enjoyed association with notables and felt a sense of achievement as an uneducated native of Collingwood. This should not be too difficult to understand for any reasonable person who can empathise with Wren's working-class origins.

Finally, a decade after the discovery of this significant collection of Evatt letters there has been, to my knowledge, no request by the Evatt Foundation for copies for their archive.

CHAPTER SIXTEEN

Control or Connivance?

Inner suburbs

WREN'S CRITICS HAVE HAD no doubts that he controlled, at least from the First World War to the later 1940s, the inner suburb municipal politics of Richmond, Collingwood and Fitzroy. He is said not only to have dominated the local branches of the Labor Party, in which resident unionists had an automatic right to vote, but also to have created bogus trade unions. His capacity to do so was enhanced by 'the increased working class character of the core of the city [where] most of the old ring of the suburbs became more Catholic'. While in 1891 in Richmond, Collingwood and Fitzroy, Catholics accounted respectively for 23, 19 and 19 per cent of the population, in 1921 it was 30, 26 and 28 per cent.[1] My query is whether 'control' is the appropriate word. Did Wren play an ongoing and decisive role in the dynamics of local politics, or was he mostly just a financial resource for old cronies, their descendants and favoured 'godsons' and causes? Without doubt he provided money to influence and enforce Labor Party branch pre-selections for the three tiers of government. But Wren would come to see that his wealth could be more productively employed smoodging individual parliamentarians (not just of the Labor Party) than oiling local so-called 'machines'—which, in any case, could split into factions. Together with protecting his own interests, there was also a sentimental desire to be a man of mark and to exercise patronage in his home base, just as many ordinary denizens want to enjoy prestige from association with a ruling clique.

A second question arises. Would the manipulation and farce of Collingwood politics or the sleaze and intimidation of Richmond's, and the incompetence and mismanagement in both places, have been much different without the putative godfather on Studley Hill? Conceivably worse, perhaps? Melbourne's violent crime wave between 1919 and 1923 had nothing to do with Wren. Chris McConville points to 'disintegration of authority within the underworld and competition for liquor and vice rackets', which were not Wren's concern.[2] Wren did not, as Hardy portrayed, preside over some 'reign of terror'. Richmond had some respite from corruption during the ascendancy of Stan Keon and his (particularly Catholic Social Movement) supporters from the mid-1940s until the 1955 Labor Split. But afterwards it re-emerged, until eventually the Victorian government had to move in to quash it. By then Wren was long dead.

McConville has pointed out how limited was the capacity for graft in inner municipalities. Jim Cairns has contrasted them with other more affluent suburbs, such as Kew, Hawthorn and Camberwell:

> [There] corruption is different … councillors don't accept £10 or £50 like they do in Richmond but they benefit … through their business activities and thereby get far more money, many many more times money as a result. But they don't even see it as corruption.[3]

Commentators have often assumed that the dominance of the Labor Party in the councils between the wars created greater morality in public affairs. Janet McCalman, in her perceptive and humane *Struggletown* (that is, Richmond) observes:

> The story of Labor's blemished record in Richmond [and also Collingwood] tells more of the special problems of working class communities than it does of proletarian moral viciousness. Society tends to expect greater virtue in Labor politicians and remains blind to the pressures that afflict and tempt them … Labor-controlled municipal government in Australia [has] … often been regarded as … a legitimate source of jobs, political patronage and financial

> kickbacks ... Poor people would insist that such lurks were essential to survival; equally [unpaid] working class councillors would assert that municipal office imposed financial burdens of entertainment, transport and the maintenance of the telephone in their homes that a working man's wage could not remotely pay for.[4]

Wren's money enabled him to indulge such clients and, without any purposive ideology or policies, he contributed to the contemporary political torpor. The following anecdote from Granny Foster's descendant, the believable Abel Kay, suggests both an abiding Wren surveillance of the Richmond Council and an almost benign complacency:

> A friend of mine told me that at one stage he had to make improvements to his factory in Richmond and he had to put in more amenities for his staff. He put up a plan to the Council and it was knocked back. He went to John Wren and said: 'Can you help me in any way?'
>
> 'All right', Wren said. 'I'll do what I can'. 'Put your plan up in time for the next Council meeting.' At the next Council meeting it was passed without any problem. My friend went back to Wren and said, 'Is there anything I should do, Mr Wren?'
>
> 'The usual thing is ten pounds for each councillor', Wren said.[5]

Stan Keon maintained that:

> The ALP recognised certain areas as Wren's. He dominated the Party machine and the preselection process in Richmond. He would pay the membership fees to the Central Executive and nominate the candidates he wanted there, and you did not get anywhere in politics unless you met with Wren's favour.[6]

However, as we shall see, with determination Keon did break the boss's hold, and said he 'never received any threats of violence from Wren'.

A factor complicating judgment of what is said of Richmond/Collingwood is that not all Wren favourites were corrupt. Not only were the devout Catholics and old family friends, H. M. 'Bert' and J. L. 'Jack' Cremean untainted, but they were related to the raffish O'Connell clan and worked amiably with it. Bert's wife, an O'Connell, was her brother's mayoress in 1926–7, while Bert was Australia's youngest mayor of his time in 1928–9. Bert had won the state seat of Dandenong in 1929, but lost it in the reaction against Labor in 1932 during the Depression.

Back on home turf Bert Cremean gained the vigorously contested pre-selection for the Clifton Hill (part of Collingwood) by-election in 1934 and necessarily won the seat. Pre-selections were decided in a Labor Party caucus. It was decided that another ballot should be held for an endorsed candidate in the regular election of 1935. Cremean's previous runner-up, Laurie Marshall, contested again. He was a colourful local butcher who had been a Boer War volunteer at fifteen, a top-level athlete, once victorious over the legendary sprinter Jack Donaldson, and a champion weight-lifter. A staunch Labor supporter and a pacifist, in May 1934 he had been mysteriously 'knocked out' within 50 yards of a police station and the Collingwood Town Hall. He was on his way to a council meeting, where he would have made up a quorum to support Mayor Roberts on the vexed question of control of the Victoria Park sports ground. (That issue is dealt with in Stremski's *Kill for Collingwood.*) This assault was clearly not done by so-called 'Wren ruffians', but indicates the endemic violence of the inner suburbs and its effect on local politics.

Against three other candidates Cremean gained an absolute majority of 709 to 602, with Marshall gaining 354 votes. Marshall protested against irregularities and breaches of party rules but, as such a protest was also against the rules, he withdrew. The *Herald* reported that, at the official poll, Marshall wrote on the margin of his ballot paper, after loyally supporting his fellow Laborite, 'the hardest vote I have ever recorded'. But, said the *Herald*:

> Before he could release the pencil a flood of emotion surged through him. He turned the paper over and thus poured forth his soul: 'Hail, despot Preselection! A blight upon the eyes of Democracy, as fleas upon the People's back.' Having signed his name he felt better.

The *Herald* wondered whether 'poetry on the back of a ballot paper is not as informal as fleas on the back of the people'.[7] Still, Marshall had his turn as mayor in 1936–7. Harry Dummett, however, a declared independent elected to council in 1930, was excluded from all committees, although after twenty-six years he was allowed to become mayor in 1956.[8]

A returning officer at the 1935 pre-selection was the 21-year-old A. W. 'Alex' Sheppard, a future notable intelligence colonel and Sydney bookseller who, as a branch member, had advertised his integrity by protesting against corruption. He told his biographers that at 9 am on the Saturday of the ballot, Sugar Roberts, 'then mayor of Collingwood', entered the polling booth but, after voting, overstayed his time chatting up the scrutineers. Conscientiously, Sheppard demanded that he leave. When Roberts tried to pull rank, Sheppard threatened him with the police. Roberts left protesting, 'Don't be so bloody difficult! I'm going.' Sometime later 'a man came in and said to him, "Sugar and an important member of the Party are outside. They want to make it up to you. Go out and speak to them, there's a pal"'.

Outside, there were no introductions. The important man put out his hand and said, 'You're the sort of chap we want in the [Labor] Movement. Glad to meet you'. As their hands released Sheppard felt a cylinder in his palm which he let drop on the footpath. He thought it was a bundle of bank notes held by a rubber band. Sheppard left it on the ground. Roberts called after him, 'Hey you've dropped something'. Alex replied over his shoulder, 'No, you have ... A big brick'.

Sheppard returned to his invigilation, to find that whereas at the North Fitzroy polling booth he had left 200 ballot papers, of which the scrutineers returned 50 unused, there were 280 in the ballot box. Nor could one tell the difference between the fraudulent and the validly completed. When Sheppard reported this to the central executive of the party, a 'no ballot' was declared, but no new pre-selection was held and Cremean remained the official Labor candidate (as would almost certainly have happened anyway). Sheppard was disgusted. The man who had greased his palm 'he later discovered was John Wren'—one is tempted to say, the ubiquitous John Wren, who has figured in so many dubious recollections.[9]

So, how to interpret this anecdote? The characterisation of Roberts is persuasive, although the story is a little spoiled by the fact that he was not at the time the mayor. I would hesitate to say either that Sheppard was mistaken or that Wren was incapable of such a crude gesture. However, at that stage of Wren's career an intervention on behalf of an already victorious and suitable candidate seems unnecessary and demeaning. Sheppard was notably hostile to Catholics[10] and also sympathetic to communism. (Post-war he was attacked by the Stalinists for 'Titoist deviationism'). It does not help Sheppard's story that it was only later that Wren's identity 'was discovered'. Knowledge of how this happened would be interesting. It must be remembered that Cremean's predecessor was the leftist Maurice Blackburn, Roberts's *bête rouge* and Curtin's *blancmange*, whose tenure in Fitzroy and Clifton Hill showed that Wren was certainly not in absolute control of his precincts. It is possible that he was making a supervisory effort to ensure that no one like Blackburn was elected again. Following ructions over the choice of mayor in 1934, Roberts was again disendorsed as Labor councillor, together with three others. He came only fourth in the 1935 elections. He resurfaced on council in 1936, but the 'boss' seems not to have been directing affairs effectually to the benefit of his old mate.[11]

The most lurid character in Richmond's local politics was Cornelius 'Con' Loughnan, important here not just because of the notoriety with which he tainted Richmond Council but also because Hardy portrayed him as a key informant for *Power Without Glory*.[12] McCalman describes the eloquent ex-seminarian vividly:

> Chronically disputatious, impulsive and capable of sudden sadistic violence, he was clearly afflicted with a severe personality disorder that by middle age sank him into alcoholism. His crude voice belied his taste for stylish dress; in later life he would sport an elegant cane that concealed a rapier. In his final years of decline he was to be disfigured by a grotesque wen on his neck that completed the bizarre menace of his physiognomy.

Cornelius carried a revolver and 'had obliged the police in May 1925 by firing four shots at a man suspected of breaking into a factory at 2.00 am'. Among his other occasional armaments were a sword-stick and a hypodermic needle. He drank with Squizzy Taylor. He was elected to council unopposed in 1924 and was soon implicated in 'preselection ballots … [abounding] in smears, intimidation and accusations of branch stacking'. In 1926 Richmond Labor 'was in chaos' and Cornelius was accused of working against Bert Cremean, although he was an endorsed candidate. This caused Cornelius to lose his own pre-selection the following year. A trade union appointment in 1928 as general secretary of the Hospital Employees' Association of Australia revived his career. He 'slipped back' into the council in a by-election in 1928, and in 1932 he was elected mayor. (Cremean, his critic, was then MLA for Dandenong.) He avenged himself years later on a colleague who did not support him for a second term by striking him on the ear with an axe. (After conciliation he sent the victim a 'Happy New 'Ear' postcard.) In order to gain a kickback from the purchase of a new steamroller for the council he was alleged, in the dead of night, to have driven its still operable machine into the Yarra. The 1930s was a dark age of negligence and chicanery; council accounts were in the red. In 1937 Con's young brother, Jimmy Loughnan, was elected for the first time in what was to become a record five terms as mayor. 'Richmond', says McCalman 'had developed a Labor ruling class, bonded by dynastic and factional loyalties'. Five councillors lived in the prestigious West Ward, three of them in the one 'charming street'.[13] Must we believe that Wren was waving a conductor's wand over these affairs, especially once his Richmond racecourse was resumed in 1931?

One of Hardy's more swaggering vignettes in *The Hard Way* is his description of meeting Cornelius, whom he saw 'often in the weeks that followed'. Cornelius delighted him with a story of having, when he was mayor, brought along a prostitute as his mayoress to a reception for the duke of Gloucester. 'A red hot dill he was', said Cornelius. His consort 'done a good job but ... she had a snake's hiss in the wash-basin at one stage'.[14] Hardy did not remember that the duke was in Melbourne in late 1934 when Cornelius was *not* mayor. This unreliability is characteristic of Hardy's 'research'. As they might have asked in Richmond, 'Who saw who coming?'

A more serious question is what control could Wren have had over Cornelius or any other of the second-generation Loughnans. How to reconcile this with his friendship with the very proper Cremeans? Or his alleged role as 'a machine boss'? Further, what was the performance of the representatives sent to the state and federal parliaments as a result of pre-selection processes allegedly controlled by Wren? Were the representatives more suitable elsewhere? There were dynamics in inner-suburban politics not steered by Wren.

Just after Wren's death in October 1953, there occurred an ironic postlude to all this. In March 1953 a former Collingwood mayor,

William Johnstone, had as a councillor resigned so that he could apply for a salaried council position (in effect, deputy town clerk). His appointment was opposed by a current councillor and opponent, W. A. Livy, who said Johnstone had solicited John Wren for the job. He protested vigorously to his Clifton Hill branch, to council and to the ALP central executive that Johnstone was unqualified for the position and that the appointment was unnecessary and unethical. The Labor Party executive had then directed that no appointment be made and that there should be no further publicity. But Johnstone sued Livy for libel and slander. Under cross-examination in March 1954 he denied that he had ever spoken to John Wren or gained his approval for his application. In court, the following exchange took place:

> *Mr Adams* (for defendant): Did you believe that the late Mr John Wren had influence in municipal matters in Collingwood?
> *Johnstone*: I would not believe that.
> *Mr Adams*: Did you believe he had any influence in Collingwood municipal affairs?
> *Johnstone*: I don't think he had any influence whatever.[15]

Johnstone received £150 damages. The presiding judge was Mr Justice (Sir) J. V. Barry, who had once, through hearsay, entertained a contrary view (see below). Perhaps Johnstone was referring only to the most recent past. Perhaps Wren had since the later 1940s ceased to interest himself in local affairs. Perhaps Johnstone was being evasive. Perhaps we should simply accept what the general historians have been telling us about Wren and the inner suburbs. Or, as Socrates might have asked, is the unexamined history not worth reading?

State politics

(Sir) Frederic Eggleston, liberal politician, distinguished diplomat and widely published author, with ministerial experience in Victoria during the 1920s, was dismissive of the abilities of Labor representatives in state politics:

> [They were] nearly all small, limited men—nearly all very small men—most of them opportunists, some worse than that. It is necessary to appreciate the natural history of a party of this kind. It

> is entirely false to treat such a party as the standard-bearer of a great crusade of the people. They were ordinary men, representing constituents or pursuing their interests and chosen by these men because they were men most like themselves. They were good husbands and fathers, but they had forgotten that they were part of a great movement and would have regarded ideas as an embarrassment.

Eggleston was in no doubt that Wren had 'complete control' of the Victorian Labor Party.[16] If so, he had not enhanced its electoral prospects at least until the 1920s, nor could Labor have been of much use to him. The only Labor government before then lasted fourteen days in December 1913 under George Elmslie.

Although Wren was supposed to have the inner-suburban branches 'sewn up', pre-selections did not always go to Wren's preferred candidates. He failed in 1908 to have Richard Loughnan contest the Richmond Legislative Assembly seat as the official Labor representative. This prize went for thirty-seven years to the benevolent but ineffectual E. J. 'Ted' Cotter, also nominally Catholic, of whom McCalman writes:

> parliamentary conviviality rather than social ambition was to be his undoing. There are suspicions that he had connections in the 1930s with John Wren, but his earliest and best years in politics reveal him as no captive of the millionaire sportsman and his shady political machine. Something quenched the fire in Cotter's belly, however, and in the twilight of his career he did little other than inspire some of Richmond's dirtiest tricks as rivals conspired to defeat him for the pre-selection.[17]

As if to warn against slick generalisations, McCalman also notes 'one of Richmond's political ironies'. Referring to the vote in the state parliament in 1916 on six o'clock closing of hotels, she quotes the local *Guardian*:

> Richmond's parliamentary representatives are an enigma if not a conundrum. Tudor is a teetotaller who was present at the Liquor Trades' picnic. 'Gor Save' Webber, now the MLA for Abbotsford, is also a teetotaller, but voted against six o'clock closing and Ted

> Cotter who will enjoy a drink with either a lord or a labourer voted *for* the Bill.[18]

Conspicuously, Wren failed to prevent the noted agnostic, teetotaller and anti-Catholic socialist, Maurice Blackburn, from winning pre-selection for Fitzroy in a 1925 state by-election against thirty-one candidates. Blackburn had opposed Australian participation in the First World War and Theodore's proposal at the 1924 Labor conference to exclude communists from the party; but he had also, in the 1921 federal Labor conference, moved the Blackburn Declaration, qualifying the aim of the socialisation of industry. Blackburn won the Fitzroy pre-selection on preferences but with just 190 of the 600 primary votes. Wren's candidate, E. A. Painter, 'a trenchant anti-Communist', came only third. (The future federal Labor leader, Arthur Calwell, came fourth.) Outside Fitzroy, Blackburn's pre-selection was not popular; he was thought to be too radical. A local councillor, J. A. Boell, came forward, standing as Independent (Labor). As Blackburn favoured local option,[19] Boell ran a policy of longer hours for pubs, with the support of hotel-keepers. More important was 'Keep Communism out of Fitzroy', for which Sugar Roberts provided leaflets to be distributed outside Catholic churches among other places. Blackburn, it was alleged, was not only a crypto-party member, 'a trustee of Soviet Russia', but also opposed self-determination for Ireland. Communist Party members came forward to testify that they had been approached to tell this lie. Blackburn beat Boell easily, 4,317 to 2,800. Roberts was exposed, and made himself more ridiculous when a Labor enquiry into malpractices and member opposition to an endorsed candidate was set up. He resigned from Labor, 'ostensibly refusing to be in the same party as Blackburn, but his resignation was refused on the ground that his own conduct was being investigated'.[20]

'One of the worst elections I have ever conducted', complained the returning officer, referring to intimidation and impersonation. Frank Brennan, however, thanked the electors for Blackburn's 'magnificent victory', although 'many old supporters of the Labor Party have found that someone else had voted in their name'. Brennan had backed Blackburn as had other alleged puppets of Wren like Scullin, Anstey, Prendergast, E. J. Holloway and Esmond Kiernan. Roberts was expelled from Labor. Submissions to have him reinstated were abject and did not suggest that domineering patronage was exercised on his behalf. The boot trade unionist, Tom Richards, 'who had given vital support to Blackburn', testified to a special party meeting in 1927 that Roberts's 'heart and soul' was for Labor, 'notwithstanding the one unfortunate occasion of nearly three years ago':

> He had worked hard to turn Clunes [where he and Wren had a substantial interest in a knitting mill] to Labor from solid anti-Labor ... None had a better record in the Party extending back to his early days when he was a blacksmith's striker.[21]

Blackburn was elected to the new seat of Clifton Hill, well within Collingwood, in 1927. (What was Wren doing to allow this?) He entered federal parliament in 1934, but later was twice expelled from the Labor Party: temporarily in 1935 for belonging to the Movement Against War and Fascism, and in 1941 for participating in the Australia–Soviet Friendship League. He thought the Soviet Union was 'a great experiment in government'.[22] In the light of his own ideology, Wren was not astray in his judgment of Blackburn in 1925—and one assumes some Catholic clergy encouraged Roberts—but it is noteworthy that differing factions of Labor, including so-called 'Wren-men', would not countenance Roberts's malpractice.

A brief look at several other 'Wren-men' also suggests much less than 'complete control'. W. P. 'Bill' Barry, former secretary of the Tobacco Workers' Union, was not Wren's choice to succeed Bob Solly in 1932 in the by-election for the blue-ribbon Labor seat of Carlton. Wren would have preferred left-leaning William Slater of the Clerks' Union, for whose legal education he was said to have paid. Slater had been attorney-general under Prendergast and Hogan, but lost his seat in the debacle of 1932. He was to win another seat in a by-election soon after. He was backed by John Cain and became attorney-general again in all three Cain ministries. (During the war John Curtin was to accredit Slater to the Soviet Union as Australian representative for a few months in 1942–3.) Barry faced sixteen other candidates for pre-selection, including J. V. Stout, later secretary of the Trades Hall Council. He defeated Slater by 9 votes and won the seat by a mere 183, compared to Solly's previous majority of 4,362. (The communist candidate polled 2,253). However, Barry became a Wren 'favourite',[23] secretary of the state parliamentary Labor Party from 1938 to 1955 and 'leader of the right-wing faction'. Barry held portfolios in all three Cain ministries.

McMullin refers to 'persistent rumours of corruption involving his Wren-linked ministers Bill Barry and Archie Fraser'. They 'overshadowed the Cain government's achievements'. Fraser, a lawyer, succeeded Kiernan as MLC for Melbourne North, held ministries under Cain, then became a County Court judge and chairman of the Victorian Licensing Court. He belonged to Melbourne's three leading racing clubs and the Lawn Tennis Association of Victoria, and was the father of Wimbledon tennis champion and Davis Cup captain, Neale Fraser. Kate White provides some details of the rumoured corruption of Barry and Fraser, without involving Wren. Other members of the Wren faction were alleged to be 'wealthy publican, Les Coleman [susceptible to Wren's money?], and ex-railwayman, Tom Hayes'.[24] On the other hand, John Holland MLA occupied Footscray and Flemington seats from 1924 to 1955. Labor historian Don Rawson described him as a 'sceptical and independent Catholic of the "I take my religion from Rome but not my politics" school'. He was not a Wren-man.[25]

Among Labor leaders of the 1920s and 1930s Wren's name is consistently linked with those of Tom Tunnecliffe and Edmund John Hogan. Tunnecliffe opened a bootmaker's shop in North Melbourne in 1886, which 'became a centre for earnest discussion of contemporary social issues'. A delegate to the International Socialist Congress in Sydney in 1888 he was, with Prendergast, Findley, Jones and Bernard O'Dowd, a co-founder of *Tocsin* and, with Frank Anstey, co-founder of the Victorian Labour Federation in 1898. Later he was president of the Trades Hall Council. In spite of his limited education, he became a cultivated pamphleteer, author of *The Problem of Poverty* (1904) and *Successful Socialism* (1906), and wrote poetry. He won the West Melbourne seat in a by-election in 1903, but the seat was abolished. He represented Eaglehawk near Bendigo from 1907 to 1920, when he was defeated by nine votes on Nationalist preferences by wheat farmer and future premier, Albert Dunstan. This can be explained by the decline of mining in the electorate. Tunnecliffe then became secretary of the Public Service Association. In 1921, no doubt with patronage from Wren, he re-entered parliament as MLA for Collingwood, until 1947. (At the time Wren could hardly have patronised a worthier and more experienced Labor candidate.) He became chief secretary in

Prendergast's short-lived Labor government in 1924 and, when Hogan became premier in 1927, minister for railways and electrical undertakings. In Hogan's second ministry, Tunnecliffe was again chief secretary.[26]

'Ned' Hogan, a devout Catholic had, after an early career as a union organiser, become a farmer and won the rural seat of Warrenheip in 1913. He held it for thirty years. Forthright, self-educated, rugged, athletic, he was a champion caber-tosser, weight-putter and hammer-thrower. In 1927, with 28 Labor out of 65 lower house seats plus the support of Dunstan's breakaway Country Progressive Party (CPP), Hogan became premier. How well Wren knew Dunstan at this stage is uncertain. Kate White says Wren had backed the CPP in the 1920s and given financial support to several of its members;[27] Arthur Calwell refers to him as 'a close friend' of Dunstan, at least by 1935, and recalled:

> The Country Party was really a breakaway party of the section of the farming community that usually voted Labor before World War One. But … under the influence of men like Sir Earle Page, it became the party of the squatters, the party of country townspeople … [a] most reactionary force …[28]

It was believed Hogan consulted Wren before settling his ministry. Sir John Jungwirth, who for twenty-seven years was permanent head of the Premier's Department and 'worked closely with thirteen successive Victorian premiers', recalled:

> confidants of Wren such as Gilbert Dyett, Frank Lawrence, Cr Roberts (Collingwood) and Dick Lean saw Hogan at Parliament House from time to time. These interviews were always private. I had no knowledge of the matters discussed.[29]

Wren naturally expected his enterprises to be protected, but did he try to influence policies in which he had no financial or personal interest? It seems unlikely, and we lack evidence of it. With his bias towards Labor, one assumes Wren favoured its attempt at the mild redistribution of seats, which ostensibly caused the CPP to withdraw support in late 1928. Dunstan wanted to keep the Victorian gerrymander which, at that time, had a ratio of 39 country votes to every 100 metropolitan. Hogan was defeated by one vote on 22 November. He was also under criticism for his handling of a waterside workers' strike during which police 'ran out of blanks and fired bullets, wounding several men'.[30] However, the Catholic *Tribune* on 15 November had reported:

> The benefactions of Mr John Wren are numerous and largely unknown, but many have been assisted by his kindly generosity and dozens of deserving institutions aided by him. The latest exhibition of Mr Wren's charity was the donating of £1,000 to relieve 'the distress caused by the present trouble in the waterfront'.

In a letter to the acting secretary of the union, Wren wrote:

> Whatever the merits or demerits of the dispute, there is no doubt that a large number of women and children are undergoing extreme hardship … innocent victims who should not be allowed to continue to suffer. I am enclosing a cheque of £1,000 …[31]

Hogan returned to power in October 1929 with the support firstly of Dunstan's CPP and later of a reunited Country Party, only to find himself governing in the trough of the Great Depression. Hogan became offside with the industrial wing of Labor when he accepted, as did Dunstan, the conservative deflationary Premiers' Plan of 1931.[32] When Hogan was obliged to travel overseas to recuperate his health in March 1932, Tunnecliffe became acting premier.

Political historians give varying accounts of where Tunnecliffe (and so, presumably, Wren) stood. Ross McMullin sees Tunnecliffe as 'noncommittal' about the Premiers' Plan, whereas Kate White says he led the faction that 'rejected' it as being contrary to Labor policy, while Don Garden says that Tunnecliffe advocated 'a policy in Hogan's name which was far softer on continuing the Premiers' Plan than Hogan would have approved'. Peter Love says Tunnecliffe 'refused' to implement the plan. McMullin further complicates the issue by asserting that Hogan's endorsement of the plan was supported by various rural branches of the Labor Party and by 'Wren-controlled urban areas in Collingwood [which Tunnecliffe represented!] and Clifton Hill [represented by the noble Blackburn, who was outspoken against both Wren and the plan!][33] This is confusing. On such an important issue I would expect the puppeteer to have had firm hands on the strings. There is little evidence that he did—but, in spite of contradictions, his critics are confident that they know.

The government fell in April 1932, and the number of Labor MLAs was greatly reduced in the election that ensued. Premier Hogan and four colleagues were excluded from Labor but in the election retained their seats in a landslide win by a United Australia–Country Party coalition under Sir Stanley Argyle. Tunnecliffe, who had been acting premier, became Labor leader. In 1935 Hogan joined Dunstan's group, eventually becoming a minister in the government that was supported by Labor until 1942. Where did the allegedly king-making Wren stand in all this?

As the economy picked up, contention over the Premiers' Plan receded, and disappeared once the Country Party–Labor alliance was forged in 1935. There is no doubting Wren's role here. Arthur Calwell tells the story. Then a public servant, Calwell had been transferred in 1934 out of Treasury to the Housing Commission—quite unfairly, he thought—for criticising the Argyle government. He 'later had the satisfaction' of initiating the move that destroyed it:

> It was my idea, and mine alone, that with the help of the Labor Party, the Country Party could form a government. Nobody else had thought of it ... I went to John Wren, who was a close friend of Albert Dunstan. In fact, Dunstan was as much a Wren man as were ... Prendergast, Ned Hogan and Tom Tunnecliffe, all of whom were greatly helped [not controlled?] from time to time by Wren ... Wren was enthusiastic about the idea ... it was not until Dunstan became leader [of the Country Party] soon afterwards that the want of confidence motion was moved and carried. Some Labor men were reluctant to vote for it. One of these was E. J. (Ted) Cotter of Richmond. I would not like to say money was offered but I had a suspicion that votes were being bought by promises of rewards of some sort to those in the Labor Party who would oppose [that is, would have opposed] the motion. When the vote was taken, all Labor and Country Party members voted for it and carried it.

Oddly, in his entry on Calwell in the *Australian Dictionary of Biography*, Graham Freudenberg makes no mention of Wren's role in this. Whatever money was circulated would appear to have been his. Under Dunstan, Labor held no ministries, but in 1937 Tunnecliffe cemented Labor support by accepting the speakership. Calwell justified support for Dunstan on the grounds that 'it enacted a lot of legislation that the Labor Party wanted', such as increased democratisation through the reduction of property qualifications for the Legislative Council, and the abolition of the position of alderman in the Melbourne City Council. Other concessions to Labor policy were a Farmers' Debt Adjustment Act, some amendment to the workers' Compensation, Factories and Shop legislation, establishment of a housing commission and hire purchase relief, but such Labor demands as a more equitable electoral distribution and the abolition of dole payments in favour of award wages were not met.[34]

Against this, because Labor did not stand candidates in electorates held by the Country Party, its branches, already weak, lost support. Government was inert as Dunstan's frugality and lower taxes starved education, social welfare and public utilities. In this way, he deprived the bureaucracy of initiative and favoured rural interests. While the Depression and then the onset of war reduced state capacity, the blame for Dunstan's shiftless regime has to be shared by anyone who facilitated and helped to maintain it. That must include the meddlesome millionaire whose dull adhocery and self-interest must have obscured vision. It is noteworthy, however, that the alliance was supported by John Lemmon, who was MLA for Williamstown (in J. J. Liston's precinct) for a Commonwealth record-breaking fifty years, had been four times minister for public instruction, and had opposed the Premiers' Plan. In 1937 he boasted of the 'most satisfactory results' for the people of Victoria, achieved by allying 'the common interest of the man on the land and the worker in industry'.[35] It is idle to blame the Dunstan stagnancy simply on Wren.

The pragmatic John Cain was Tunnecliffe's deputy leader until 1937. Cain, ex-Catholic and agnostic, became parliamentary leader of a small party riven by ideological and sectarian animosities and endemic conflict between its industrial and political wings. Cain disliked Wren's influence and the Catholic pressure which so vehemently opposed, in particular, a united front with the Communist Party. His deputy was Bert Cremean, who is credited with having put forward the original proposal in 1941 for the anti-communist Movement subsequently directed by B. A. Santamaria. But it is doubtful that he would have had any part in the latter's fantasy of Catholic control of the Labor Party.[36] Frank McManus, assistant secretary of the Victorian Labor Party and later a Democratic Labor Party senator, was to say that had Cremean not died prematurely, the Labor Split would not have occurred.[37] To apply the term 'Wrenite' to Cremean should modify its connotations.

There were other paradoxes. Led by Cremean and Calwell, who were members of the state Labor executive, the 1935 annual conference ruled the Victorian Council Against War and Fascism to be pro-communist and out of bounds to Labor Party members. However, Wren had allowed the use of his stadium for the rumbustious Egon Kisch rally of 1934. International events such as the Italian invasion of Abyssinia in 1936 and the Spanish civil war passionately divided Catholic isolationists from Laborites sympathetic to communist pressure for a 'popular front'. Cain's lack of partisanship made him an acceptable compromise leader—and in this he and Wren, although mutually hostile, were more alike than they knew. It was something that founders of the Santamaria Movement were to discover. Moreover, anyone asserting that Wren controlled the Labor Party has to explain how Cain became and remained leader for so long. It has not been done.

The Milk Board scandal

Truth addressed a lengthy column to The Members of the State Parliament, Melbourne, C.1. on 2 September 1939, entitled '*Truth* Will Talk if Money Talks'. It had been 'gravely disturbed for some time at the growth of the practice known in the Australian vernacular as "rattling the can"'. It alleged that there were 'certain members' who were all too ready to accept bribes or contributions to party funds from interest groups wanting legislation defeated, deferred indefinitely, or amended to the point of innocuousness. *Truth* believed that such an attempt had been made the previous year in relation to the Money Lenders' Bill, through the creation and disbursement of a 'defence fund' used to buy amendments. Something similar was currently being attempted in order to defeat a Bill amending the Milk Board Act. Pressure to control milk retailing and profiteering went back at least to 1927. Among the aims of the new Bill were the prevention of excessive margins between wholesale and retail prices, the provision of a fair share of the retail price to farmers, and the protection of the consumer in relation to the price and quality of the product. The Bill was finally passed on 20 November.

Pushed by the Legislative Council's decision to appoint a select committee to look at the issue, Dunstan announced on 23 November a royal commission to investigate 'certain allegations against members of Parliament'. According to Dunstan's biographer, J. B. Paul, Dunstan had vacillated for so long in initiating an investigation that one could infer only that he had something to hide or that some crony would be embarrassed in the event of public scrutiny.[38] The prime mover in the Legislative Council was E. L. Kiernan, a former Collingwood councillor and associate of Wren, and MLC for Melbourne North. Kiernan fell out with Wren, probably when he deplored the tactics against Blackburn in the Fitzroy by-election of 1924–5. Subsequently, like Hogan, he supported the Premiers' Plan and was expelled from the Labor Party in 1932. He became minister for sustenance in the 1929–32 Hogan ministry. He was an active Catholic of independent mind, was strangely unopposed in the 1934 Legislative Council election (that is, Wren fielded no candidate against him!), but would have realised that he could not hold his seat without Labor endorsement in the 1940 elections, and did not stand.[39]

In fact, *Truth* did not 'talk', as it had threatened, and its editor refused to divulge his sources, perhaps because he had none except Hogan's speech on 10 August in parliament when he mentioned the dairymen's defence fund. Summing up, Mr Justice (Sir) Charles Gavan Duffy found no impropriety in relation to the Money Lenders Bill, but in reference to the Milk Board Act inferred that Welsh and two others, Frank Gillies (president of the Milk Distributors) and Robert Morris (committee), had agreed 'to bribe some members of Parliament'. However, the commission found that there was no evidence that any MP 'with the exception of Tunnecliffe' had 'acted improperly'. There was 'no evidence against Messrs Kennelly, Barry or Hayes [another alleged Wren-man said to be involved]'. All three had been called as witnesses; each denied on oath having any improper relations with the Milk Retailers. 'Nothing', said the judge 'came to light that would in any way justify a finding against any of them'. In relation to Tunnecliffe, however, the judge said that, if he could believe the key informant (Frank Gillies), he 'should conclude that … [Tunnecliffe] was soliciting bribes'; but he found Gillies 'an untruthful and evasive witness throughout', who could not be relied on to make 'a definite finding against anyone else'. Tunnecliffe was off the hook. Therefore, although Duffy reported that Welsh, Gillies and Morris 'entered into an agreement to be accepted by any Members of Parliament', no bribe 'was accepted or agreed to be accepted by any Member of Parliament' and neither was 'any bribe ... offered to any Member of Parliament'. Nor was any charge laid against the three Milk Distributor officials. When the new executive of that organisation was elected in September 1940, all three were returned to their former positions.

No mention of Wren has been found in the hundreds of pages of transcribed evidence in the report. He is not mentioned in the *Parliamentary Debates* in which prominent figures in the milk industry are singled out for criticism. Surviving defunct company records do not include Wren's name among lists of directors and shareholders (of those companies identified as controversial). Minutes of meetings of the Milk Distributors' Association show no evidence of Wren's involvement in the milk industry in the 1930s. No metropolitan dairy is listed as either licensed or owned by Wren at 24 August 1939, nor is it apparent that any of his better-known associates held such a licence—although his friend, Harold Glowrey, had between 1919 and 1925 been secretary of the Metropolitan Co-operative Milk Co. In spite of enemies and critics, involvement of Wren in the scandal is not even alleged, as far as can be ascertained, in publications such as the *Vigilant*, *Bulletin*, *Labor Call*, *Argus* (throughout the 1930s), *Australasian*, *Weekly Times* or Communist *Guardian* (which took a highly critical interest in the affair).[40] One object among many of Wren's Australian Food Exporters company (AFEX) was the merchandising of milk products. But AFEX was formed a decade after the milk scandal. Wren may possibly have had more interest in the outcome of the investigation of the Money Lenders Bill as, according to his son, he did have some involvement in hire-purchase finance (through Benjamin Nathan?), but no record of this has been seen.

John Cain's biographer, Kate White, believes that 'Dunstan's reluctance to call a royal commission was at least influenced by his association with Wren and, in turn, Wren's links with Labor'.[41] To defend Tunnecliffe before the commission Wren had briefed the future distinguished Mr Justice (Sir) John Barry, then a leading barrister, who became an endorsed candidate in the federal elections of 1943 and a member of the state central executive of the Labor Party in 1945–7. Wren wrote to Barry in terms which suggest that his concern was to salvage his all too compliable friends:

> I was very worried … over the matter as I feared that if it was found there was a miscreant or two, it would have perhaps reflected itself on the great Labor Party, *which I have helped to create and establish in this Country, and has achieved so much on behalf of the working class of Australia* [emphasis added].
>
> The party would indeed have been in grave danger of a serious setback, from which it might not recover for many years.

Barry wrote at the bottom of Wren's letter: 'From John Wren, multi-millionaire and controller of the Victorian Labor Party'.[42] Is this just a loose, casual comment, or did Barry really believe in Wren's 'control'? My impression of Barry is that he was aloof from the day-to-day workings of the Labor Party. (He was a reluctant Labor candidate in 1943 for a blue-ribbon United Australia Party seat and, as the Curtin landslide became apparent, he was aghast that he might win, his eyes being on a future in the judiciary.)[43] Wren's letter is also interesting for its sanctimony and self-promotion—providing a clue to Wren's motivation, which was far from just making money. If he was involved in the scandal, Wren's hypocrisy was consummate. (For biographer he would need a Molière, particularly as the fallout from the accusations of the 'Wrenite' Hogan was to be the destruction of 'Wrenite' Tunnecliffe.) Wren's other remarks to Barry suggest that he wished to enjoy the jurist's esteem, as he did that of other distinguished citizens, but on his own terms.

Behind the scenes

On 14 March 1940 the *Vigilant* was again in pursuit of Wren. Many appointments made by Dunstan, it said, 'have occasioned grave concern among not only members of the Country Party but the Protestant community at large'. There was the recent appointment of Wren's agent, Harold Glowrey, a Catholic, to the chair of the Grain Elevators Board. Previously, in 1936, Hector Hercules Bell had succeeded to the chair of the Melbourne and Metropolitan Tramways Board. Bell, a 'tough operator' who had been for twenty-six years a leader of the Labor group in

Richmond Council politics and not aloof from 'some electoral irregularities', was to be involved with Wren in land speculation at Altona in outer suburban Melbourne, on a one-third basis.[44] If anything, Bell was a lapsed Anglican. To show that political alignments were not simply patterned, it was once again the 'active Catholic' and former associate of Wren, E. L. Kiernan, who criticised the Bell appointment:

> There is a saying … that the Government runs the Tramways but that a certain influence outside the Government—in Swanston Street—runs the Government. That makes me feel that any expenditure in tramway extension should be carefully watched by honourable members … The suggestion is that Mr Wren controls … most of the appointments made by the Government.

If Wren did, Bell seems at least to have been a competent choice. The *Vigilant* went much further. Wren influence was to be found anywhere 'in Melbourne where in a Department controlled by the State Government twenty-nine temporary girls were appointed and twenty-six … are Catholic'.

This was vigilance indeed. The editorial admitted that Dunstan was not a Catholic, but said the number of Catholics being elected to parliament in recent years was alarming. How far, it asked, can 'the Country Party and other electors … allow the Bailey, Hogan, Roman Catholic influences … to control the affairs of the State?' It was never difficult to concoct a sectarian issue. It was not in the *Vigilant*'s interest to ask if the policies of Scullin, Lyons, Hogan, Ryan and other Catholic leaders of that period had a more specifically religious bias than those of non-Catholics.

In the Barry papers is an item, 'Rome's Domination of the Parliamentary Labor Party', authorised for electoral purposes in 1943 by Rev. Walter Albiston, chief secretary of the Victorian Protestant Federation. It traced 'a carefully prepared plan' back to a Mannix address reported in the *Age* of 4 July 1913, a few months after he arrived in Australia. Albiston listed the names of those in current politics he thought were Catholics, irrespective of whether they were supine, impervious to prelatical dicta, lapsed or apostate. Among sinister Romanists cited from the federal cabinet were Curtin and Chifley; on the Victorian state parliament list were Cotter, Field and Charles

Mutton; Arthur Calwell MHR was an ominous member of the Melbourne City Council; while among prominent 'RC candidates in the forthcoming elections' was John V. Barry KC! Apparently the hex of Catholic baptism determined inexorably future political alignments. Such was the lunacy of bigots—by no means all on one side.

CHAPTER SEVENTEEN

Carnivals and the Demise of Proprietary Racing

WREN SHOWED his promotional skills in occasional 'carnivals'. Over 60,000 spectators supported the Returned Soldiers' Amelioration Funds on 23 March 1918 at Collingwood's Deep Rock and Live (sic) Saving Swimming Club, of which Wren was patron and president. In 1916, at the deepest spot upstream from Dight's Falls on the Yarra, where he swam and dived himself, he had provided concrete terracing, a separate pool for children and a diving tower. There was to be a star attraction:

> Prince Wickyama [will] undertake the most PERILOUS Dive that has ever been attempted in any part of the WORLD, leaping off the Dangerous Cliffs on the Yarra at Dight's Falls, Studley Park, from a height of 250 FEET 250.
>
> It is estimated that PRINCE WICKYAMA, in his hazardous descent, will be going at the rate of 100 MILES PER MINUTE by the time he strikes the water.

Wren was to give upwards of £100 in prizes to attract 'the best swimmers of Australia to compete'. Unfortunately the Victorian Amateur Swimming Association barred its members from competing. Not so the Ladies' Amateur Swimming Association, which conducted a series of races of which Miss Lily Beaurepaire, sister of the great Olympian, Frank, won the hundred yards from scratch.

'Prince Wickyama' was Alick Wickham, whose father had been one of the earliest white traders to settle in the Solomon Islands. He disliked his stage name. Although the *Encyclopaedia Britannica* credits 'Henry' Wickham with introducing Europeans to the 'crawl' freestyle stroke copied from Pacific Islanders, commentators usually attribute the innovation to Alick. In the 1920s it was popularised by Olympic champion, Johnny Weissmuller, later the fabulous filmic Tarzan. Alick is also credited with starting the surfboard craze in Sydney in 1908, and in 1910 setting a world record there for the fifty yard sprint.

The great event was staged 'in ideal weather' with dramatic effect. At 5 pm, after previously having been beaten by a 'touch' in a handicap race, Prince Wickyama appeared. There was a burst of cheering, followed by a bugle call which hushed the crowd as he mounted the platform. Another bugle call signalled his dive was about to begin. It was a masterful performance. As he came to the surface, cheering could be heard 'for miles away'. Some sceptics estimated the dive to be between 100 and 150 feet, while a seasoned travel writer on the Solomons, who in 1972 described Wickyama as 'the half-breed son of a European planter', depressed this to 'actually … about 96 feet'.[1] In the *Oxford Companion to Australian Sport* the dive is said to have been of 205 feet (62.7 metres), which 'still stands as a world record'. Until Dick Eve, Australia's only medal winner at the Paris Olympics in 1924, won first place in (plain high) diving, Australia had not distinguished itself in this event. Wren may well have given a fillip to the sport.[2]

The Motordrome

In what from 1933 became well known as Olympic Park, Wren opened the Motordrome in 1924. It is a choice site near the north bank of the Yarra, close to the Melbourne Cricket Ground and within the city municipality. In view of the political controversy surrounding its inception, the attempt in the mid-1930s to pressure the Richmond Football Club to use it rather than its traditional ground, and Hardy's allegation in *Power Without Glory* that Wren tried to suppress an alternative venue at the Exhibition Gardens, here is an opportunity to see the so-called 'Wren machine' at work. The story has been followed mainly through the pages of the *Argus*—no admirer of Wren—and, to a lesser extent, through other papers and the *Parliamentary Debates.*

This was not Wren's first venture into motor sport. In 1913 he was associated with 'Jeffkins, the speed king' in promoting it at Richmond racecourse—something, said *Table Talk*, 'Australia has been long waiting to see'. Jeffkins had been racing in America and was 'the only Australian racing pilot recognised by the American Automobile Association'. He had won 'the most Homeric contest of the motoring world' in a Pacific coast race in 1912, attaining speeds of 110–122 miles per hour on the straightway. Seventeen miles in the lead, with one and a half laps to go for a prize of US$75,000, he and his co-driver ran out of oil and had to push the car over 1,000 yards to the winning post. However, in spite of the enthusiasm generated by Wren and Jeffkins in Melbourne, plans that were allegedly in readiness for a big speedway had to wait another decade.[3]

The Olympic Park ground had in the later nineteenth century been known as the Friendly Societies' Reserve, and was used for amateur public events such as the Eight Hour Day or St Patrick's Day picnics. Inability to maintain it led in 1909 to the formation of the Amateur Sports Ground under a board of management nominated by the Victorian Lands Department. However, the various users still failed to contribute to maintenance and, without intentions being made clear or tenders being called, a lease of five years with another five-year option was granted in 1923 on moderate terms to a Wren company, Melbourne Carnivals Pty Ltd. It was registered in April 1923 with an initial capital of £300 divided into shares of £1 each. Wren's solicitor, Bernard Nolan, handled the company formation. Its stated objects were comprehensive including the ownership, rental or lease of sports grounds for the 'holding of cycle racing, sports, carnivals, displays, and contests of every description, including cycle, motor cycle and motor car racing, and also racing of any other nature, sports, games, athletics, boxing, concerts and/or any other kind of sport or recreation'. At 30 November 1924, the day after the Motordrome opened, the shareholders included Wren, Richard Lean and Jacob 'Jack' Campbell, cycle manufacturer of Prahran. The same three individuals were appointed as directors.[4]

The Motordrome, designed to accommodate 70,000 spectators, was so quickly remodelled with a grandstand and 'saucer' track (an innovation, even by world standards) that it seems to have taken many citizens by surprise. Following a protest letter to the *Argus* and just before the first motor races were held, the city council 'vigorously protested to the Lands Department (which had endorsed the action of the committee of management in granting the lease)'. A further three-quarters of an acre plus a smaller portion of the 'Yarra Park' had also been enclosed for parking facilities. The Lands Department asserted that this was crown land reclaimed when the Yarra was straightened thirty years before, and therefore not under the control of the city council.[5]

The *Argus* and correspondents thought it unfair, even if legal, that the public had had no say in the conversion of public land for a commercial activity. No reference was made in the *Argus* to Wren although his long-time critic, the redoubtable Orangeman Oswald Snowball MLA, champion of Tommy Bent, insisted that all relevant papers be tabled in the House. The chairman of the Amateur Sports Ground trustees gave an assurance that continued public access was guaranteed and that the deal was financially worthwhile. Not everyone agreed. Sir James Barrett, the notable conservative 'fixer', president of the Town Planning Association and future university vice-chancellor and chancellor, asked for a royal commission 'to inquire minutely into the transaction'. The honorary secretary of the Grounds Management Committee said he had no objection. Snowball thought a royal commission 'inadvisable' and a ministerial enquiry preferable, while Barrett suggested that a complaint about noise would be fruitful. However, the (future Country Party) premier, John Allan, did not think there was 'very much wrong with the lease'.[6]

Meanwhile, 15,000 people turned up in 'ideal' weather on 10 January 1925 to 'several thrilling contests', the most popular victory being by Miss Marie Jenkins, whose nine horse-power DFP sports model passed J. Flanagan's Gwynne in the ninth lap to win by a quarter of the course. With even Motor Push-ball proving popular, nothing more seemed to come of the move for an inquiry and, at least in the *Argus*, the 'sinister' Wren was not mentioned. In time, the search for novelty reached farcical lengths, with children driving two-wheeled carts pulled by billy-goats. Ostriches imported from South Africa were set up with cardboard cut-outs of jockeys and names of well-known horses to race around the track. The ostriches, however, refused to perform past their bedtime. Money had to be refunded.[7] However, the ground trustees seemed satisfied with the site's productivity, £40,000 having been spent on the ground. Top European cyclists arrived, and Opperman broke the record in the dangerous five-mile motor-paced event. For motorcycles the first dirt-track race was held in October 1928. Aside from two fatalities which led to professional cyclists having to wear skull caps, not much of moment was reported for the next four years.[8] However, when the Motordrome's second five-year lease was coming to an end, a deputation of amateur bodies called on Dunstan, then minister for lands, to prevent any renewal. He retorted:

> Had it not been for Melbourne Carnivals … the ground would still be as it was—a quagmire … There is a bird which comes along and takes over a nest which some other bird has prepared … If I had been Minister for Lands when the lease was drawn up, I would not have agreed to it, because I am not in favour of such things, but at the time the Amateur Association … said it was agreeable … it would not be fair to turn Melbourne Carnivals out …[9]

Football

One fear of the amateur organisations may well have been that the Motordrome would become devoted, at least in the colder months, to professional football. Although staging such matches was not explicitly one of Melbourne Carnival's stated objects, its manager, Dick Lean, had proposed that it become a Victorian Football League (VFL) venue now that a new tenth club was to be invited into its competition to replace University, which had dropped out during the war.[10] Lean proposed that either the new club could have its home at Olympic Park, or all teams could play one match there, or the VFL could use it as its own ground (as Waverley became in the 1970s). There would be no clash of interests with a cricket club, as at the Melbourne Cricket Ground (MCG) and elsewhere. As it happened, in 1925 three new clubs (Hawthorn, North Melbourne and Footscray) were admitted to the VFL. They were chosen over other Victorian Football Association (VFA, rival to VFL) clubs because of the absence of cricket club controls. Now cricket dominated only six of twelve rather than six of nine VFL clubs. But none of Lean's proposals was taken up.[11]

An extraordinary situation had developed in 1927 when the first and second semi-finals of the VFA had been tied, and the final day postponed because of wet weather. The games had been transferred to the Motordrome. In subsequent years it became one of a half-dozen alternative venues for football. In April 1932 the need to top-dress the

MCG led to a proposal for the Melbourne Football Club (part of the VFL) to play there for the time being. By December, arrangements were being made to use the Motordrome as a central weekly venue for the VFA. Alterations, said the VFA, would make it an ideal ground. Lean announced that the 'saucer' track would be broken up and a 45 feet wide dirt track used in summer. In April, Sid Gower's outfit wound up nine years of high speed motor-cycling on the saucer, with Sid himself breaking the record and winning a championship. Promotion obviously continued to be vigorous. However, the agreement with the VFA fell through owing to the effect it would have had on some clubs which would have been deprived of home games. Olympic Park was to remain the venue for VFA finals only; Hakoah Soccer was to take up the weekly option.[12]

In November 1934 a new situation arose when that year's premiers, the Richmond Football Club (VFL), announced it was considering a move to Olympic Park. Its dissatisfaction with ground control by the local cricket club was shared with a number of other VFL clubs. Among special concessions to cricket club members in the grounds they controlled were reduced admittance prices to football matches.[13]

Olympic Park must have seemed an even more eligible replacement when in April 1935 a practice game, 'the first match ever played between League teams in electric light', was held. It attracted 25,000 spectators and the clubs were delighted with their share of the takings. Richmond's contract with its cricket club ended in September, but Dunstan's minister for lands (A. Lind) opposed a transfer to Olympic Park. A deputation from the cricket club was introduced by Labor MLA for Richmond, Ted Cotter, but was followed by one from the VFL sub-committee declaring the Richmond ground 'not suitable', although official VFL approval for a transfer had not yet been given. Dunstan said it was no concern of his. Meanwhile, the Richmond Cricket Club planned to increase capacity to 60,000, and a new agreement for fifteen years was signed with the football club.[14] It is difficult to discern at that stage any conspiracy between Wren's interests and his political friends.

Once the 1936 football season began, Lean (and no doubt Wren) decided to test whether admission charges violated the charter under which the land had been granted, or the terms of permissive occupancy. If so, they would try to force the Richmond Football Club to play at Olympic Park. One Saturday a certain William Kreutzer, a private enquiry agent, demanded the right of free access to the Richmond ground, a public space. He brought a charge of technical assault against the constable who ejected him. His barrister was the eminent Eugene Gorman KC, who warned on 22 May that 'Unless this matter is decided before the next football match at Richmond on May 30, there is danger that a disturbance may arise'. Accordingly, a group of men and women organised by another private detective, Percy Jones, instructed by Bernard Nolan, entered the Richmond ground without paying and then returned to block the turnstiles. Jones said they were protesting against 'the filching of park lands'. He denied it had anything to do with Olympic Park. Kreutzer was there. He admitted he wanted the gatemen to assault him. However, the gate had been instructed to give free access, if necessary.

There was a legal problem: the cricket club had had permissive occupancy since 1855; the land was reserved as a park in 1873; in 1889 a law had prevented trustees collecting admission fees. To Labor Party leader Tunnecliffe the solution was for cricket and football clubs to control the ground for six months each. He called for the abolition of the Grounds Management Committee and the surrender of the cricket club's permissive occupancy. For some weeks the campaign against payment continued, but without violence and with patrons generally affirming that they wanted to pay for admittance. It was not until 31 July that Wren and Lean were named by the *Argus* as the masterminds, and in court it was alleged that they were trying to entice Richmond Football Club to Olympic Park.[15] One affidavit deposed that Lean was seen with Kreutzer and Jones advising about fifty men in Yarra Park:

> Tickets were handed to each man, with name and number and Jones instructed them as follows. Go and block the turnstiles but do not use violence. Come back here and you will each earn ten shillings. One of the persons issued with a ticket said, 'This is the easiest ten shillings I have earned in my life. John Wren does not make mistakes. He must be right'. Since the issue of the [current] writ, the affidavit continued, the group of persons referred to have ceased to be in attendance at matches.[16]

The court decision upheld admission payments. The Lands Department amended the legislation.

Stan Keon was one of no doubt many observers not impressed by

Wren's tactics in this episode. In 1948 he told the Victorian parliament with some hyperbole:

> One of the reasons I have always viewed the activities [of Wren] with a great deal of suspicion is that I can well remember going to the Richmond Cricket Ground and seeing a gang of thugs handing out one pound notes to force the Richmond Club to Olympic Park.

This was a role reversal for 'thugs'. But Wren's plans did not eventuate. He had dismantled his world class motor-racing track for his beloved football. Compared to Sydney's concrete oval track at Maroubra, the Motordrome's high-banked steep gradient was said to be like a soup bowl to a plate, and had been the venue for intrepid motor and side-car racing. This was replaced in December 1934 by midget car (or speedcar) racing.[17]

At the exhibition

In *Power Without Glory*, Hardy takes up a not dissimilar issue in relation to the Oval at the Exhibition Building,[18] where for years there had been a 'great towering wooden building ... [with a] five lap asphalt track'. The trustees relied on the Oval for revenue. However, when their entrepreneurial secretary tried to promote greyhound racing, George Prendergast, chief secretary in the 1927–8 Labor government, refused consent. His Crown Solicitor advised that without the permission of the governor-in-council, such a contract or admission charges were illegal. Prendergast must have objected to the particular sport, because at the same time he endorsed cycle, motorcycle and athletic events. In 1936 Jack Campbell, who had been a promoter of cycling at the Oval before he became in 1923 an initial director of Melbourne Carnivals, returned to promote boxing as well in opposition to Stadiums Ltd. Some residents of Carlton with their MLA, Bill Barry, protested in February 1938 against the use of such public land for commercial purposes. Barry personally turned up in March at the Palmer–Kelly fight and 'noisily demanded free admittance'. The Exhibition secretary offered to buy him a £1 ringside seat, to no avail. So he was refused admittance to a public space, and the Dunstan government took out an injunction to terminate Campbell's lease. Mr Justice Martin, in February 1939, found in favour of Barry and the government.[19]

Naturally enough it was inferred by many that it was the advent of boxing, a rival to Stadiums Ltd, and not the 'nuisance' of a board track, that caused the complaint. Barry was seen as a protégé of Wren. However, Barry did have a history of opposing the alienation of public parkland. He had pulled a stunt in 1933 when he pegged the old Carlton Cricket Ground for gold, and even for an oil bore, to prevent the land being acquired for the University Women's College.[20] He also seemed to oppose the alienation of Fawkner Park for a military camp in 1939–40. As David Dunstan points out, Barry wished to prove himself a tribune of the people. He 'claimed to have found out about Campbell's five-year lease on the Oval only when he had himself sought to obtain its use for charitable purposes'. Whatever his motives, the trustees no longer had an Oval and the cyclists' interests were ignored. The trustees gained £1,000 per year compensation, but this was lost when, at the beginning of the war, the site was resumed by the air force and never revived for sport.[21] Campbell revived his fortunes with cycling promotion at Essendon, but there were no further challenges to Wren's boxing at West Melbourne. In the course of the law case Campbell had been asked about his connection with Melbourne Carnivals. He said he still had £2,500 invested there but had not been invited to a directors' meeting for seven years.[22]

Barry was feted at a dinner given by the Carlton Citizens' League. On behalf of 'all true democrats' the president of the Victorian branch of the ALP and former MHR Parker Moloney, proposed the toast in front of Dr Maloney MHR and notables friendly to Wren: H. Cremean, R. Solly and T. Hayes. Barry replied:

> If the public were to lose its right of free access to the Exhibition Oval it were better that the land should be used for homes for the people than for a business for private profit ... If an appeal is made to the High Court and I lose it, I shall still have won, for the board track will no longer be on the Oval.[23]

The appeal was withdrawn. No doubt the most ostensible beneficiary of the judicial decision approved of Barry's sentiments, but we have to ask whether in this case we need to be cynical.

Several conclusions emerge from these episodes. Although the Victorian governments were not unsympathetic to Wren's interests, there is no evidence of naked partisanship; Wren did not get what presumably he wanted for Olympic Park, in spite of his alleged dominance. The tactics used by Lean were harsh and manipulative but not illegal, and their ineffectuality was accepted without duress. Wren was less powerful or less inclined to use his power than thought, while Bill Barry seems more public-spirited and less under Wren's instruction than Hardy could imagine. Wren's so-called 'clients' were not mere ciphers.

Athletics

If only because of legends associated with it, professional footrunning at Wren's Motordrome deserves a brief mention. As a sport it is notoriously easy to abuse, as an athlete can feign indisposition or falter or, when handicapping is involved, 'run dead' until a satisfactory mark is achieved. So dubious stories abound and memories can be astray. An informant of Pauline Armstrong, Ted Seedsman, who was 'prominent in the Victorian Athletic League' (VAL), related how Wren had summoned him to his Swanston Street café to 'discuss some matters'. He wanted the VAL 'to waive/bend the rules to enable footrunning to be held at the Motordrome'.[24] Apparently the VAL consented, because in 1928 Wren organised The Melbourne Thousand with £500 to the winner, the rest to placegetters and heat winners. This was the world's richest professional foot race. A prize of £500 was also attached to a separate non-handicap championship race.[25] According to Seedsman, 'Wren had set Jack Donaldson up to win, but a drunken footballer/athlete from Brunswick called Henry Chase took off the prize, much to Wren's chagrin'.[26] This is, however, another preposterous story. Donaldson, known as The Blue Streak, had been the world's greatest professional sprinter and record holder between 1908 and 1912, with a time for the 100 yards of 9³/₈ seconds, which was unexcelled even by amateur Olympic champions for decades. He was forty-two in 1928 and had been living since the end of the First World War in the United States. (He gassed himself to death in 1933.)[27]

The Melbourne Thousand of 1928 was won by Austin Robertson from 8³/₄ yards in his first professional race. In a race of 130 yards the famous Tim Banner was on scratch; the limit man on 12 yards. Inevitably, there had to be a story. Robertson had been a sensational schoolboy sprinter at Xavier College, where he had also been a capable fast bowler in the Cricket XI, captained by his friend John Francis Wren.

He had won the Victorian Associated Public Schools 100 yards championship three years in a row. (He was eventually to be a star South Melbourne footballer.) So had the handicapper given him an unfair mark? Robertson called that 'pure baloney'; the handicapper was 'an honest man' who had simply made a 'miscalculation in assessing ... a first up-runner'. There was not, he said, much betting on the race, but his father had won £500 from Sugar Roberts. If there had been shenanigans, one imagines Roberts would not have been a casualty.

The professional world championship and the Thousand continued to be held at the Motordrome until 1932, but prizemoney had been reduced from 1930 owing to 'heavy losses due to wet weather and other causes'. Melbourne Carnivals had spent some £4,000 popularising the sport, and was surprised when the VAL in November 1932 diverted its patronage to the Maribyrnong Athletic Club. Dick Lean refused to accept any compromise over the arrangements. So Melbourne Carnivals moved out of athletics.[28] But a legend still attaches to the World Professional Championship of 1935 when Eddie Tolan, the Olympic winner of 1932, visited Melbourne and won three (over 75 yards, 100 yards and 220 yards) of the four contests. The unfamiliar 'Australian sprint distance' of 130 yards was won by Robertson, allegedly because Tolan allowed him to and Wren money was available. There is no authoritative ground for this story. The *Argus* reported that 'At no stage of his career has Robertson run so brilliantly. He created a record for the track. Tolan said that Austin Robertson was the only man in the world who had finished faster than he had'.[29] No doubt a cynic will shrug: 'Well, he would say that, wouldn't he?'

Royal treatment?

With his activities diversifying, Wren formed a Victorian Trotting and Racing Association (VTRA) in June 1919, to replace the Victorian Trotting Association (VTA) and modify criticism of proprietary racing. He sold the freehold of Fitzroy, 75 per cent of Ascot and the leasehold of Richmond to the VTRA. Bill Beckett became president while the part-time secretary was a Gallipoli hero, (Sir) Gilbert Dyett. According to his biographer:

> Wren is said to have chosen him as a respectable frontman. Dyett did not smoke, drink or gamble, and knew little about the racing side of trotting, but he performed his duties with military precision,

> honesty and enthusiasm. He was on the Racecourse Licences Board of Victoria in 1930–51 and was central registrar of trotting names for Australia for many years.[30]

No doubt Dyett's 'respectability' was a factor in his appointment, but it is difficult to believe that he would have tolerated sharp practice by Wren or not known about it if it existed. Stern measures, however, were not foolproof. Max Agnew records how on one occasion Dyett locked up overnight a horse he believed to be a 'ring-in', only to find next morning that another official with a key had allowed it to escape. In any case, Wren's personal involvement diminished during the 1920s until he had little to do with trotting in the 1930s. However, after a period of prosperity in the early 1920s, the VTRA came increasingly under challenge from owners and trainers. As the economy weakened, attendances dropped off; in 1929 trotting was compulsorily transferred to Ascot, but stakes continued to decline and facilities to deteriorate. Attempts to have night trotting approved were narrowly defeated.[31] Already some trotting match-races (not race meetings) had been held at night at Wren's Olympic Park. They did not escape the notice of the Rev. Walter Albiston, who told the Victorian Protestant Federation that this was 'the thin end of the wedge' and that if night trotting were approved 'it would be a menace to Victoria':

> Vested interests ought not to be allowed to dominate the cabinet without a vigorous protest from Christian organisations.
>
> One would like some assurance from the chief secretary that if night trotting is introduced these … events will be held in different parts of the State and not in the metropolitan area, which is controlled by John Wren's interests.[32]

A Select Committee of the Victorian Legislative Council on Race Courses and Race Meetings recommended in 1928 that horse and pony racing be controlled by one authority, the Victoria Racing Club (VRC), and that pony racing be curtailed.[33] The following year the chief secretary in the MacPherson Nationalist government, Stanley Argyle, introduced a Police Offences (Race Meetings) Bill reminiscent of the original Police Offences Act 1906 of the Tote days.[34] In the background, Wren seemed to be the potential target. There was to be a slight reduction in the number of race meetings, but the real issue was one of control. Instead of the chief secretary allotting them to the various clubs, Victoria would be divided into districts, to each of which he would grant 'a certain maximum' of racing, pony and trotting meetings. These would in turn be allotted under licence to the various clubs by a representative board.[35]

Wren's Fitzroy and Richmond courses were now doomed, but when Ned Hogan (Labor) led the opposition to the Bill his main protest was that the Epsom and Mentone courses were being retained while Sandown and Aspendale were to be closed. They were the best and next-best courses of those involved, he argued. One MLA asserted that Sandown was the best in the state.[36] Hogan's amendment to leave Sandown off the condemned list was narrowly defeated. Of other alleged Wren 'clients', Tunnecliffe thought the legislation 'ridiculous'; Dunstan called for it to be scrapped and then changed his mind; and Prendergast thought licences should remain with the chief secretary but in the end supported the Bill. On the other hand, Maurice Blackburn warned against putting 'a very important piece of patronage' in the hands of a chief secretary who might turn out to be 'unscrupulous'. A compromise was reached whereby board members would be nominated 'after consultation with the chairman of the VRC'.[37] Pony meetings, particularly those held on Mondays, outraged conservative MPs because they took people away from their workplaces.[38]

The formidable (Sir) R. G. Menzies MLC entered the debate on 15–16 October, although he said he had 'not the most rudimentary knowledge of racing'. Menzies's point was that course owners were being offered compensation only for tangible items of property and not for loss of business. This was not important in the case of Richmond and Fitzroy, both close to the city, because they were potentially rich subdivisions; while extra dates had been given to Ascot. The owners of Aspendale and Sandown were not so fortunate, being much further away from the metropolitan area. Menzies alleged that 'the powerful influence which owns Richmond, Fitzroy and Ascot has been royally treated'. The MacPherson government strongly disputed this, while Bill Beckett MLC, the VTRA president, alleged that Menzies was holding 'a brief' for Aspendale and Sandown interests. 'Sneering and dishonest', retorted Menzies about that inference. It was a 'lie', he said, and was asked to withdraw the remark.[39]

On 31 October, the day after the MacPherson government collapsed, the Bill received the royal assent. Four weeks later, after a general election, Ned Hogan became premier again. However, Wren was not complaining about the Bill which had been supported by VTRA's Bill Beckett. It seems reasonable to conclude that Wren accepted the changes because of the possibilities of profits from subdivision, increased meetings at Ascot, stronger control, a reduction in competition; and perhaps in his long-headed way he saw the possibility of acquiring Sandown on the cheap and reopening it some time in the future. But it is doubtful that this can be said to amount to 'royal treatment' from a government which no one has alleged was in Wren's pocket. Menzies was the main person making this claim, and even his speeches were vague. As he complained, he had trouble himself in working out what the government was really offering as compensation.

The rearrangements made, which were due to become effective on 1 August 1931, left Wren's Ascot with fifteen race and twenty trotting meetings. Out of a Racing Clubs Compensation Fund to be levied on those remaining open, compensation would be paid to owners of the closed courses of Fitzroy, Richmond, Aspendale and Sandown. The major impact was on pony meetings, which were reduced from a maximum of 45 to 15. Both these and trotting were to be held at Ascot.

Metropolitan trotting ceased during the Second World War, and in the aftermath the growth of opposition to the VTRA saw a new body emerge, the Metropolitan and Country Trotting Association, which 'paved the way for the setting up of the first Trotting Control Board' by the Cain government. Ascot had been resumed for public housing. The Royal Agricultural Showgrounds, having the best course and amenities, became enthusiastic about the profits available from night trotting. Even some of Wren's political 'clients' could see that proprietary trotting must come to an end.

War and a gracious exit

The old feud between Wren and the Victoria Racing Club seems to have re-emerged during the Second World War when prime minister Curtin called for national austerity but allowed the states to run their own racing. South Australia stopped meetings altogether; in Victoria racing dates were restricted; the Melbourne Cup in 1942–3 had to be run on a Saturday! The VRC cooperated with the federal government; but premier Dunstan did not. While the VRC did not compensate for its loss of dates by cramming more races into its programs, at one stage Wren's Ascot ran fifteen races on a Saturday, at twenty-minute intervals. Dunstan treated the VRC at Flemington and Wren's Victorian Racing and Trotting Association (VTRA) at Ascot on equal terms. The VRC historian says coyly that Dunstan had 'insufficient understanding' of the VRC's role as the principal club, so that Flemington and Ascot were given the same number of meetings although their allocated stakes were £118,000 and £25,000 respectively. Very decently he makes no mention of the possible influence of Dunstan's friend and occasional consultant.[40]

Curtin, who disliked Wren's influence, would have surmised why Dunstan accepted VTRA proposals. He bitterly attacked the cost of non-cooperation:

> Victoria is so short of firewood, due supposedly to lack of manpower ... [it] expects me to release troops for the work while civilians are devoting their full time to training horses and dogs ... the pageantry of racing continues in full stride. How much feed is consumed by horses and how much meat by dogs?[41]

Curtin must have relished the resumption of Ascot on 1 September 1942 for defence purposes. The VTRA turned to the VRC. Although previously knocked back when its inferior facilities could not cope, it again asked if it could use Flemington for the duration of the war. The VRC had pleasure in seeing VTRA sent to outer suburban Mentone. After the war Ascot was resumed, this time by the state government for housing. In 1948 the Hollway (non-Labor) government legislated for the final destruction of proprietary clubs and the reduction of racing to four metropolitan courses. In early March the VTRA purchased the unused Sandown Park track for £44,000[42] and negotiations began to merge the VTRA with the non-proprietary Williamstown Racing Club (WRC), which had (it thought temporarily) lost its course during the war. WRC members voted against merging with the less reputable VTRA. On 11 June the government announced it would license the four existing non-proprietary clubs—the Victoria Racing Club (Flemington), Victorian Amateur Turf Club (Caulfield), Moonee Valley Racing Club and Williamstown Racing Club.

Two days later the government and the VRC were surprised to learn that the Victorian Trotting and Racing Association had decided to go out of existence on 31 July and that it was presenting the VRC with the Sandown Park racecourse 'with no strings attached'. This, said Wren's old general, Bill Beckett, was VTRA's farewell thank-you gift to the racing public. It constituted the VTRA's profit from racing in Victoria, which it wanted to give back to the people.[43] With no course of its own the WRC, somewhat chagrined, was obliged to accept the merger, which occurred after further wrangling. The new entity became the Melbourne Racing Club (MRC), and Sandown was to become its racecourse. Stan Keon's fulminations later in July were astray. Proprietary clubs were abolished; government inspections became mandatory; and the VRC retained control of the state's racing. Wren became simply an owner, gambler and spectator—and an unacknowledged benefactor. No plaque acknowledges the donor at Sandown Park, which opened officially in 1965, the MRC having merged with the VATC two years before. In 1929 Wren had told the Queensland royal commission that he did not initiate proprietary racing: he had made it profitable. Less affluent patrons turned up and enjoyed it, and in the process Wren challenged privileged clubs to raise their performance. Ironically, he had made a gracious if unapplauded exit.

Jeers and cheers in Queensland

The antagonistic anti-Labor A. E. Moore government set up a royal commission into racing in 1929. Wren's association with Theodore and other Labor identities would have been in mind. It was determined to destroy proprietary racing, which a secretary for railways was subsequently to declare was sending £70,000 per year out of Queensland. During the proceedings the Albion Park deal was severely criticised by the liquor merchant, W. H. Buchanan, who proposed that sufficient payments had been made. Wren told the 'unbelievable' story of his acquisition of Albion Park and expostulated:

> Everywhere I have gone I have been a success and I have kept on increasing my profits. That has been my misfortune. It has been the subject of attack in every State I have gone to.
>
> Any man who confiscates another's property is guilty of wrongdoing. I would like to know what Mr Buchanan would say about his liquor interests if prohibition came about …

> When I came to Queensland, the Queensland Turf Club knew no more about running a meeting than Billy the Blackfellow.[44]

A Racing Regulation Amendment Act put an end to proprietary and unregistered racing in 1931, but it did not mean the end of Wren's involvement in Queensland. He appears to have found a way around it by distancing himself from the ownership of courses, or by long-term sale arrangements. This does not necessarily mean the arrangements were corrupt or illegal, or that Wren was still controlling the day-to-day management of racing on some courses (although he may have been involved in some way). The Queensland Turf Club now had ultimate control of racing in Queensland.

In 1930 the Brisbane Amateur Turf Club had leased Doomben course; it began racing there in May 1933. Wren's involvement continued. He developed the course through the Doomben Park Racecourse Company. One innovation was a Newmarket Handicap along a straight six-furlong course (as at Flemington). With stakes of £3,000, greater than its Melbourne prototype, it attracted patrons. The race developed into the Doomben Ten Thousand sprint (later the T. M. Ahern Memorial Handicap and then the Rothman's Hundred Thousand)—which was made nationally famous in 1946 through the victories of the great Queensland stallion Bernborough, under monstrous weights in both the sprint (10 stone, 3 pounds) and the Doomben Cup (10 stone, 8 pounds) (later the Fourex Cup). Both races, worth £10,000, and a Brisbane Cup of £12,000 were, immediately postwar, the richest in Australia after the Melbourne Cup. Queensland racing rose to a new level.

Negotiations for the sale of the Doomben Company to the BATC were initiated post-war, but were negated by an inability to get Commonwealth government approval for a loan. Revived in the early 1950s, they were in progress as Wren lay dying. The correspondence which follows illustrates the rancour that Wren's success could elicit as well as the loyalty of his associates.

(Sir) Clive Uhr (BATC chairman), radiologist, sportsman, and ex-prisoner of war, was eventually chief negotiator. Exasperated at delays due to a compensation hearing involving Wren's company, Uhr moved that negotiations start at £300,000. When O'Mara informed him that Wren was very sick, Uhr replied:

> I have no time for him whatsoever. He has taken something like £800,000 out of the Club's profits and it is up to ourselves to protect ourselves ... we are leaving ourselves in the lurch ... Wren is a hard-bitten gentleman ... if Wren has taken a coronary he can easily take another ...

O'Mara said that he told Uhr he 'probably did not know that when we were purchasing the BATC, Mr Wren actually agreed to an amount of £60,000 which would put us in a position of purchasing the Club's interest at Albion Park'. Uhr's response typified the accusation Wren could never shake off: 'He only gave you any money of that kind as he knew that he was getting more out of the Club than he was entitled to'.[45] Doomben was sold in 1954 for £444,000, less £46,000 compensation for losing the 'straight six' and £16,000 for cash assets of the defunct Doomben Park Recreation Company. This was shared equally between the Wren and Nathan families.[46]

There was an ironic postlude in 1982 when racing terminated at Albion Park in favour of trotting promoted by Russ Hinze, Queensland minister for both racing and police, and himself an unfazed owner. A piper played 'Auld Lang Syne' at the winning post, and at the celebrations the owners gave three cheers for John Wren.[47]

Wren's luck

It is impossible to know whether Wren made a profit from his own race-horses as his friend, the famous punter and student of 'form' Eric Connolly, had done.[48] Wren was not always lucky. I have found no evidence from 1906–7 until 1913–14 of Wren horses racing, although one nomination was accepted by the VRC in 1912–13. In the spring of 1915 he bought Garlin for £812 after it had won a race at Randwick on Metropolitan Handicap Day. It then started in the Caulfield Cup, in which it finished seventh of nineteen runners at 9 to 1, and so was reasonably well supported. In the autumn of 1915 Garlin triumphed in the Doncaster Handicap at 8 to 1 in an open betting race. Wren gave the stakes of £2,200 to the Belgian Relief Fund; his wagering earned him between £27,000 and £28,000 when he backed Garlin from 25 to 10 to 1. In the following spring Garlin won the weight-for-age Chelmsford Stakes at 10 to 1, came fourth in both Caulfield and Melbourne cups and had several notable placings, including second in the Mackinnon

Stakes and Williamstown Cup. 'Bobby' Lewis, riding the second of his four Melbourne Cup winners, Patrobas, recalled that, rounding the home turn, 'Garlin seemed to me a sure winner'. But its jockey, Albert Wood, had never ridden Garlin before and was unaware of his 'short blistering finish' and made his run too soon.[49]

The coveted Cup would continue to elude Wren. His best chance came in 1920–1 with The Rover. According to Buggy, Wren in 1920 had directed agents in New South Wales, Queensland and South Australia to back it at a certain time on a certain day. He stood to collect £100,000 if the horse won. However, on Cup Eve, The Rover bolted for some eight miles. The betting coup was cancelled. The following autumn, The Rover was saddled up for the Australian Cup of 2¼ miles, which it won with ease under a featherweight of 7 stone 2 pounds. According to its strapper, Alf Sleigh, brother of its jockey, Vic Sleigh, The Rover's stable was ostensibly also running the favourite Nautilus. To forestall any suspicion that Nautilus might not run, both horses were conveyed to Flemington. Then, an hour before starting time, Nautilus was scratched and The Rover heavily backed from 14 to 1 to 5 to 2 favouritism. Such a coup was tolerated in 1921. Wren must have done well. However, in the spring in the Melbourne Cup, The Rover carried 8 stone 4 pounds and started at 10 to 1. It was beaten into second place by three-quarters of a length by a lightly weighted (6 stone, 8 pounds) 3-year-old filly, Sister Olive, which was never to win another race. But the favourite, the great Eurythmic, carrying Carbine's weight of 10 stone 5 pounds (66 kilograms), had the worst luck, limping past the post with a wrenched fetlock after catching a barrier strand in its mouth. Wren is alleged to have had £150,000 riding on a victory for The Rover, but displayed his usual *sangfroid*.[50]

On one occasion Wren's jockey dropped his hands with a race virtually won, and another horse flashed up to win. 'Don't worry, son', Wren is supposed to have said to the crest-fallen hoop, 'It's just one of those things'.[51] The noted earthy *Sporting Globe* journalist Merv Williams, writing soon after Wren's death, stressed his refusal to allow a jockey to 'pull' any of his horses. But he would not 'shelf' a favourite jockey, Paddy Kelly, when he audaciously took an inside rather than his allotted outside barrier position and beat Wren's horse. Trainer Musgrave was upset. 'What's wrong with you, Frank', Wren chipped in. 'Your jockey just wasn't smart enough to do the same as Kelly'.[52] Drawing a long bow, one could perceive here some tolerance of sharp practice as well as being just 'a good sport'—if, that is, one wanted to.

Wren had other hard luck stories, although he did not make a great deal of them. At the Sydney yearling sales in 1916 'a small but powerfully built colt' failed at first to attract the reserve price of 300 guineas set by its owners, probably because of its 'parrot mouth' (an upper jaw protruding beyond the lower, which could impede mastication). However, Wren was attracted by the colt's breeding, the granddam being by Gozo, sire of three Melbourne Cup winners, and the great-granddam by Newminster, sire of Newhaven, which in 1896 had romped in, easing up, by six lengths, in only a quarter of a second outside Carbine's record time. No doubt the then 25-year-old Wren had seen that 3-year-old's triumph—and by 1896, not from the poor man's Flat either. It had taken the lead after the first of the sixteen furlongs. Wren, like all Collingwood and other punters, had a strong opinion about these things and thought Newhaven better than Carbine; and truth to tell, Walter Hickenbotham, who had trained both (and two other Cup winners) said that he did not know how fast the ill-fated Newhaven could run. So Wren offered 300 guineas for its descendant, parrot-mouth notwithstanding, providing it was delivered free of charge in Sydney. The breeders refused, and stood firm on the £6 transport fee. So did Wren. It was the principle of the thing! In another story, Buggy puts the blame on 'the excessive caution of Jim Donohue', Wren's agent. Either way, Wren missed out on owning Poitrel, who lugged 10 stone to win the 1920 Melbourne Cup, an impost exceeded before or since only by Carbine's 10 stone 5 pounds in 1890 and Archer's 10 stone 2 pounds in his and Melbourne's second Cup in 1862.[53]

Wren's only other notable horses in the 1920s seem to have been Beedos and Figure. Beedos won the 1926 Hotham (now Dalgety) Handicap, staged on Derby Day, the Saturday before the Melbourne Cup, and regarded as an excellent guide to a horse's chances. Wren lost heavily on the Cup. Figure, the sprinter, which was second in both the Oakleigh Plate of 5½ furlongs and Newmarket Handicap of 6 furlongs in 1929, won the Oakleigh Plate and William Reid Stakes in 1930 and was third to two notables (Amounis and Greenline) in that year's Futurity Stakes (7 furlongs). Dunwill in 1921–2 showed promise when second in the Epsom to the outstanding Beauford, and won four minor races. Other 'fine' if not well-known horses owned by Wren at the time included Biscay, Galenist, Kildennis, Kilroy, Kingsfield, Liberty Law and Little Flower (St Thérèse of Liseux), the last two apparently named during some patriotic and religious fervour.

However, Wren finally managed a few 'classics': the judicially named Pandect won the AJC (Australian Jockey Club) Derby in 1940, while Pure Fire took out both the AJC and VRC Sires Produce Stakes in 1952. In spite of being the outstanding colt of its year, Pure Fire did not develop as a top-class stayer in the spring, but in Easter 1953, when the champions went to the Sydney carnival, he won the less illustrious Victoria Handicap at Flemington. In May he failed to win the Ten Thousand at Doomben. As Wren lay dying in 1953, Walu won the Ascot Vale Stakes for 3-year-olds; the Saturday after his death, a speedy and handsome colt, Fascinating, won the most prestigious race for 2-year-olds in the Melbourne spring carnival, the Maribyrnong Plate, on Derby Day.[54]

In fifty years of investment in horses, Wren achieved moderate success. With regard to such investment on horses there can be no balance sheet, but it seems as though he may, like nearly all gamblers, have paid for his entertainment.

CHAPTER EIGHTEEN

The Bishops' Adviser

A staunch friend

THE ASSOCIATION of Mannix and Wren has been a problem for Catholic historians. To magisterial Patrick O'Farrell, it did 'grave damage to the image of Australian Catholicism', being 'utterly scandalous' to Protestants and linking 'priestcraft, sedition, moral corruption and underworld power'.[1] Of the eight monographs on Mannix, only Niall Brennan (1964) has not been coy in confronting his association with Wren—one of his 'staunchest friends', as Mannix said publicly in 1921. This did Mannix 'untold damage', says Brennan, and was the result of 'a strange blindness'. He tells of 'a sturdy Irish housewife' looking at a photograph of Mannix between Wren and his stalwart, Sugar Roberts. 'My God!' she cried; 'Christ between two thieves!' Monsignor Lonergan, Mannix's cathedral administrator, is said to have declined to ride with the archbishop in a car provided by Wren. 'And if I might say so, Your Grace', he reproved, 'neither should you'.[2]

But how to describe the exuberant Richmond racecourse rally of 1917, or the triumphal St Patrick's Day march of 1920, without mentioning Wren's role, or at least his gift for organisation? In the first edition (1948) of his quasi-official biography of Mannix, Frank Murphy would have achieved this feat, except that he felt obliged to reproduce the montage of photographs of the 1920 march which hung in Mannix's study at Raheen. Mannix is imperiously centred at eye level, Wren below and smaller, both surrounded by individual snaps of the VCs. A caption identifies each of them. Murphy's 1972 updated edition excludes even that plate, and so Wren's name, from the book. Hardy's *Power Without Glory,* published in 1950, must have created a greater cringe. Mannix was dead by the time Murphy's update appeared, and Wren was apparently an embarrassment.[3] Gilchrist (1982) and Santamaria (1984) in their worshipful biographies evade any controversy over Wren. Fr Ebsworth (1977), of older vintage, is less wary, although about Mannix almost idolatrous, comparing him to Aquinas and Athanasius. It is 'ridiculous', he says, to assume that Mannix 'was ignorant of ... [Wren's] unusual history.[4]

The historiography of Raheen indicates how the archdiocese handled awkward questions and responded to *Power Without Glory.* In 1948 Murphy noted that 'shortly after his succession to the see in Melbourne [1917], a group of Catholic laity provided him with a residence more suitable for his requirements as the archbishop of a great city'. (The previous incumbents had found the cathedral presbytery adequate to their needs.) Raheen, says Murphy, 'was henceforth to be his', suggesting that he rented it before purchase. In the 1972 edition there is an inconspicuous emendation: 'Shortly after his succession ... a favourable acquisition provided him with a residence'[5]—which is even less informative. As noted above, by that time Murphy would have read *Power Without Glory,* while Brennan in his life of Wren (1971) had said that 'Wren bought the property and presented it to the church for the use of the archbishop'.[6] This belief persists, as in Don Garden's *Victoria* (1984), where Wren allegedly 'presented the Church with a new archbishop's residence' in 1913, when Mannix was not even the titular hierarch. (Ominously Garden notes that it was opposite Wren's mansion but, mercifully, there is no mention of a secret tunnel.)[7] Brennan asserts that Wren was 'revenged on the archbishop for the refusal of the £50,000 testimonial' that he tried to organise prior to Mannix's departure for Europe in 1920:

> Word got around that Protestant interests were going to build a fellmongery on the river bank below Raheen. They were going to smoke him out and stink him out, declared the loyal Irish. So Wren got to work, and took out options on enough river bank to keep the archiepiscopal air unpolluted. He gave the deeds to the Archbishop. Which cost him only £38,000.[8]

Garden has also accepted this unsourced 'story'. John F. Wren, in the best position to know and with no reason to deny it, was adamant that this did not happen.[9] It was left to Ebsworth finally to phrase an official Raheen story:

> When the sale was pending, Mr John Wren forwarded a substantial donation towards its purchase, a cheque that was promptly returned by the Archbishop with a letter of thanks, and the property was bought with diocesan money ... The suggestion to purchase Raheen came from a group of Kew Catholics headed by Mr Pierce Cody [no Wren involvement?], but he [Mannix] always insisted that he bought it himself.[10]

In a note in his autobiography, Santamaria took this further: he asserted that a Roman Catholic Trusts Corporation purchased Raheen for £9,800 on 14 September 1917 (six months after Mannix became titular archbishop).[11] However, until it is clear how that fund was raised, it will continue to be believed that Wren was the major contributor, in view of the millions he is said to have given the church in other ways. Other donors would almost certainly have been Count Thomas O'Loughlin, the real estate investor T. M. Burke and Wren's good friend and partner Patrick Cody. If the purchase of Raheen is seen as occurring simply through a diocesan fund, some iconoclast will inevitably ask why such moneys, which could have built a state unaided school, were used in that way.

Wren's most public association with Mannix was during the latter's Sinn Fein campaign of 1917 to 1922. Reports show how little the image of a dour, vicious, barely literate, ruthlessly acquisitive, larrikin megalomaniac (Hardy's 'Al Capone') seemed to fit Wren. When Mannix settled in Melbourne in March 1913 he must have discussed prominent personalities and prospective patrons with leading clergy and laity: for example, Archbishop Thomas Carr, Bishop Patrick Phelan, Dr A. L. Kenny, Dr Nicholas O'Donnell and T. C. Brennan—men of irreproachable integrity, careful of the dignity of their church and its custodians. Carr must have followed the scurrilous accusations made against Wren in, for example, the *Lone Hand*. He seems to have been studiously aloof from any discussion of Wren, although prepared to defend publicly the right to gamble moderately. Phelan has been mentioned as parish priest in Collingwood when Wren's Tote was in its heyday but was (later) prepared to acknowledge him publicly as a friend—and Phelan was acknowledged even by Protestant clergy as a man of learning and integrity. Kenny was an outstanding ophthalmologist, honoured in medical circles and twice decorated by the papacy, and reputed to be a close associate of Mannix. O'Donnell was a noted Gaelic scholar and Home Ruler on excellent social terms with his archbishop. He was the brother of Detective Sergeant O'Donnell, whose home and family Wren was supposed to have bombed in 1906. T. C. Brennan was the first president of the Australian Catholic Federation, editor of the diocesan *Advocate*, and a federal senator.[12] Could Wren have been such a scoundrel and Mannix not warned?

It is difficult to believe that such men tolerated Wren solely for his money. No doubt Mannix, soon after his arrival, noted how Wren returned 'Granny' Foster's money to its rightful heirs in 1913 and donated his winnings on Garlin to the Belgian Relief Fund in 1915, and his generosity to the church, as noted in the diocesan *Advocate*. In the sectarian atmosphere of the time and without a clear demonstration, Mannix would have dismissed any but reputable allegations against Wren. Even Hardy lamented that his 'researchers' could find no dirt on Wren during 1907–16,[13] and there was little backroom activity that would not appear to an aloof bishop to be normative politics and commercial sport at that time. And for every sectarian action there was bound to be an obdurate Mannix reaction.

It is a pity that Hardy, and the *Vigilant*, could not have read the following vignette by Fred Archer, for years the chief desk clerk at Menzies Hotel in Melbourne:

> during the depressed thirties John Wren was the whispered name. Apparently he was that rare thing a cash millionaire. Menzies wasn't his stamping ground but he called one night about 9 o'clock. I was always interested in people who came in at odd hours, so I noted this small man with thin lips wearing an Australian-made hat. 'I wish to see Cardinal Cerretti'. 'Your name, sir?' 'Wren, John Wren'. He gave me an assessing look and waited. 'I'll bet this is no believer, I thought'. 'Will you please go right up, sir, the liftman will direct you'. I never saw him again but it made Frank Hardy's book ... all the more interesting.[14]

Archer admits to communist (Maoist) sympathies and may also have had his perception sharpened by hindsight, but it is interesting to see how unsympathetically Wren could strike people. More important though is why he should be calling on Cerretti (not in the 1930s but in 1928 when the cardinal returned to Australia as Papal Legate for the Sydney Eucharistic Congress). Scarcely for a popish plot if Wren gave his name. Hardly without Mannix's consent. Certainly not without invitation. Cerretti would have known him personally, or at least about him, when he was resident Apostolic Delegate in Australia during 1914–17. Possibly Wren was summoned for a personal commendation instead of that papal knighthood. In May 1929, arising out of the Eucharistic Congress, five Melbourne priests were created *monsignori*, while Dr A. L. Kenny's and Count O'Loughlin's papal honours were upgraded. Ceretti was in Melbourne, where he blessed 'the large new wing of Corpus Christi College', the seminary founded by Mannix in Werribee, outside the metropolis. He also blessed the foundation stone of extensions to St Vincent's Hospital.[15] Wren would no doubt have been a generous donor on this as on other occasions, and he appears on 24 January 1929 in the *Advocate* having given £100 to a 'Rome appeal' for the Irish College there.

Fund-raising and its acknowledgement would be a simple explanation for Wren's visit to Cerretti. In view of Cerretti's going to Brisbane to bless the extensions to St Stephen's Cathedral, and in view of Archbishop Duhig's unreliable financial schemes, it is not impossible that Wren was being consulted on this as well. Cerretti may also have been intimating to Wren that he was not eligible for a papal honour, not only because of his former illegal conduct but also because he was not at the time a fully practising Catholic. However, no doubt someone more percipient in vaticanology—perhaps someone like Hardy or his mentors Ted Hill and Ralph Gibson, or parsons like T. B. Ruth or W. Albiston, or Herbert Brookes himself—would have been able to conjure a more appropriate and sinister explanation.

None of this is meant to deny that Mannix could have influenced Wren to use whatever power he had on issues of concern to the Catholic Church. Not implausibly, Hardy refers in *Power Without Glory* to the 'Davison' (Dunstan) government being manoeuvred by 'West' (Wren) and 'Malone' (Mannix) into passing a Church Rates Bill 'exempting local Catholic Church properties from paying rates to Municipal

Councils'. A search of parliamentary *Votes and Proceedings* for the period has not revealed any Bill of that name or similar. Exemption of church properties, by no means just Catholic, from payment of local rates went back to 1863 in Victoria, but exemption for ministers' residences and other church-owned properties not used exclusively for public worship had been removed in 1874.[16] However, in 1941 and 1944 Dunstan's government amended the Local Government Act to restore the exemption for ministers' residences and for land used for 'the education and training of persons to be ministers of religion'. Typical of the premier, this was a significant cost to municipal rate payers, not to the state government. Dunstan employed 'some splendidly muddled metaphors':

> In these days of peril ... we should offer assistance to the churches. I am not the best church man in the world, but I believe Christianity is the rock upon which civilisation rests. If that rock is allowed to crumble, or if the churches lose their grip on the people, our boasted civilisation will prove nothing more than sinking sands and we shall find ourselves in a state of degeneracy.[17]

The Labor Party agreed, with the devout H. M. Cremean and another Catholic—this time ranting J. M. Mullins—prominent in the debate. Criticism came mainly from the United Australia Party. One could expect that Mannix and Wren fostered these amendments through Catholic politicians and in whatever interpersonal dealings Wren had with Dunstan. This would have been an opportunity to show his worth to Mannix, the man he admired most, as happened also in his negotiations with Dr Evatt in 1946. However, Hardy affects to believe that Wren and Mannix had wanted the amendments to apply exclusively to Catholic properties, which would have been a folly neither would have contemplated, and would have been out of character. Cremean extolled the principle that 'this state, as a Christian nation, shall give the maximum support by concessions of this character to the Christian churches generally'.[18]

In the immediate aftermath of the publication of *Power Without Glory*, Mannix spoke to his clergy, expressing shock and dismay at its allegations. Various priests reported informally how shaken he was. Niall Brennan, who would have had some access to these reports, has Mannix expostulating:

> this terrible book … this dreadful book, but it seems, that many of the things alleged against Mr Wren … are based … are based … upon some degree of fact. I want you to know … that I have had no knowledge of this at all. I want to make it quite clear to my priests that I have never had any idea or suspicion that Mr Wren was engaged in any of these activities.

Later, according to Brennan, Mannix was to say that he had 'never visited Mr Wren's house. I called once when he was ill but I did not go in'.[19] According to Ebsworth, who should be more reliable because he was at the meeting, Mannix said, 'I have never been inside the front gate'. However, the diocesan *Tribune* has Mannix among the guests at a reception for and concert by the Sistine Chapel Choir at Studley House in 1921. (And Wren's son Joseph remembered sitting on the archiepiscopal knee at the Wren home and counting the buttons on his cassock.) There is no question that Wren used to meet Mannix—many times, suggests Ebsworth—on the Studley Park road at the beginning or end of Mannix's long daily walks between Raheen and the Cathedral.[20]

While Ebsworth claims that 'no one would have thought of doubting … [His Grace's] truthfulness', a person familiar with the sequence of Mannix's political utterances would hardly credit him with an infallible or inconvenient memory. To take one issue, not long before *Power Without Glory* was published, Mannix had to know of the Keon–Wren clash of 1948. Surely he was not incurious about Keon's allegations; the latter had visited Raheen often enough. Even if Mannix thought Keon's strictures were just politically motivated at the time, he should have been aware of their origin in the tough realities of Richmond politics and commercial sport.

On the other hand, his closest courtier, Fr William Hackett SJ, allegedly his 'eyes and ears' and a familiar of the Wren household, wrote to his sister in Ireland just after the 'monstrous' verdict in Hardy's trial:

> People have been speaking against Mr Wren for years. Is there any truth in the rumours? Some of his activities were illegal, such as a tote but beyond that I have no facts to go on. I always find him a man of high principle, of deep religious feeling. He is not an educated man but he has a sure judgement …
>
> His friends say he is maligned because successful. I am sure

> there is a lot of truth in this ... I find Mr Wren most Catholic—somewhat dull because his main interests are money and the power that results ...

The force of Hackett's opinion lies in the fact that he would never have imagined that anyone but his sister would read the chit-chat he wrote so fraternally to her in his dutiful monthly airletters ('flimsies', he called them). He had no reason not to be frank with her. Hackett was undoubtedly naive and rather unworldly. Was Mannix equally remote except where clerical and Irish interests were concerned? There is no evidence of a Wren–Mannix association after the trial, but Mannix would not have cut him. It must be remembered that Wren was unsympathetic, even hostile, to Santamaria's Movement, which absorbed the archbishop at this time. However, when Wren died Mannix was 'much moved', wrote Hackett. 'I have lost one who has been a loyal supporter for forty years', he said—off the record, naturally.[21]

James the builder

Ted Theodore may have introduced Wren to his 'friend' (Sir) James Duhig, Archbishop of Brisbane, who in 1906 had been the youngest bishop in the universal church and at his death the longest in office. In 1959 he was the first Catholic hierarch in Australia to be knighted for services to society, an honour which would hardly have been offered to, or accepted, by Mannix. The deference paid to Duhig in the *Daily Mail* editorials during the conscription period suggests Wren knew him at that time—but if not, at the very latest when with Mannix and Tom Ryan and Jim Scullin in November 1919 he led 80,000 people at the Irish Race Convention at Wren's Richmond course. Wren would have been more at ease with the affable, ursine Queenslander than with his own awesome, gaunt archbishop, who liked to put people down where Duhig preferred to placate his opponents. Like Wren, Duhig had not opposed conscription or ridiculed the empire. Unlike Mannix, he would go on to support the Irish bishops and the Irish Free State and to oppose de Valera's belligerent republicanism. In August 1921 Wren was on the Brisbane platform with Duhig, Theodore and Fihelly, defying prime minister Hughes to impose an oath of allegiance on Mannix on his return from Europe. Later that day they buried Tom Ryan.

One can also infer from correspondence that Duhig felt free to solicit financial help from Wren for both worthy religious causes and his well-intentioned but often impracticable attempts to finance them. 'James the Builder' was to erect over four hundred edifices during his regime, juggling accounts and always in debt. His investments were wanton and generally futile. Not even the optimism of a geologist like Theodore's nemesis, H. I. Jensen, could strike oil for him or Wren at Roma in the 1920s, while in the early 1950s Duhig was still seeking to cut his friend into dry deals in Longreach, Beaudesert and, once again, Roma. In his lifetime he had interests in twenty-six gold mines in Queensland and three elsewhere, including a failure in Bougainville. Wren was too shrewd to get involved with a certain Morley Cutlack, Duhig's 'prospector and promoter of cloud-capped companies to plumb the Dead Heart' for Lasseter's legendary reef. Duhig even failed to share in Wren's one successful mining venture in Queensland, Golden Plateau. As T. P. Boland says: 'There have been few followers of the Australian Grail so persistent and single-minded as James Duhig. He was a true knight, never soiling his hands with actual lucre, finding in all his journeying nothing so precious as the quest itself.'[22]

Duhig in return tried to be of use to Wren. When the anti-Labor Moore government began to attack Wren's proprietary racing interests, Duhig in January 1930 'hurriedly' wrote him a letter of introduction to the premier. In his letter of thanks, Wren said:

> I had some diffidence about accepting your advice to see him, because of my political leanings in the past having been towards the Labor Party, though I must confess, between ourselves, that this Party has been of no practical use to me, but on the other hand, has been the means of providing me with a plentiful supply of political enemies and taxation imposts, that have been a heavy burden on capital.
>
> I was much impressed with Mr Moore, who strikes me as a sensible man of integrity and fair dealing ... not likely to be stampeded into doing unjust acts.[23]

Wren may well have changed his mind by October, as the Royal Commission on Racing proved adverse. Duhig was naively pleading for Wren, telling the treasurer, W. H. Barnes, that Wren was 'one of the most abstemious men' he had ever met and also 'one of the most charitable'. Barnes was glad to hear it but said that his anti-Wren Bill would proceed just the same. Duhig then assured Wren that 'he had personally arranged for a hot reception for Barnes in the house'.[24]

In the 1930s Wren was amicably sending at least an occasional news-clipping to Duhig on matters concerning the church (for example, an item on the papal encyclical, *Quadragesimo Anno*). We have seen how Mannix and Duhig used Wren as an intermediary to lobby Evatt at the United Nations in New York in 1946. Subsequent correspondence alludes to Duhig's increasing distrust of Evatt's socialism, where Mannix had supported the 1944 'powers' referendum and, with qualification, bank nationalisation. Duhig made his support for Menzies explicit in 1949, even on grounds of Catholic social principles. One can infer from his letters that he had reason to think that this was compatible with Wren's own drift from Labor. A letter to Wren in 1952 reveals that Duhig has written to the then federal treasurer, Arthur Fadden (a fellow Queenslander), requesting some favour for Wren, to which Fadden appears to have replied favourably.[25]

Wren's advice created no bonanzas for Duhig's apostolate, but neither was he 'a soft touch'. In 1929 he refused Duhig a loan of £5,000 because he said his investment in land in Western Australia had left him short.[26] The correspondence available is not particularly informative. In 1946 Wren gives £500 to a Duhig Jubilee testimonial and £500 again to one of his schools in 1948.[27] It is not revealed whether he loaned Duhig the £5,000 to £10,000 he asked for after the court award of £25,720 to the architect of his grandiose phantom cathedral. Duhig offered 'in exchange ... the deed of a valuable property right on the Brisbane River near the Story Bridge ... a wonderful site of one and a half acres'.[28]

Just as Wren was having his fatal heart attack in September 1953, another letter appealing to his kindness of heart arrived. There was 'a real bargain', a 'providential' one, an agricultural property for £24,000 to which Duhig would like to bring the Irish monks of Mount Melleray to teach Queensland youth rural skills.[29] In view of the persistence of such requests, Wren must have been at times quite indulgent. Duhig's letter of condolence to Nellie states, 'I knew Mr Wren for many years. I greatly admired him for his honesty, his uprightness, his kindness and generosity and I have the happiest memories of his friendship.'[30]

In spite of his wobbly speculations, Duhig was an honourable, ecumenical and constructive citizen. He must have known Wren's reputation. It is difficult to believe that he would have turned a blind eye to criminality in order to benefit from Wren's largesse, or that his opinion of Wren was simply venal.

CHAPTER NINETEEN

Disillusion

A maudlin confession

CHARLES MEEKING was a state roundsman for the Melbourne *Age* in the middle 1930s, press secretary for R. G. Menzies in Canberra for three years, and later federal public relations officer for the Liberal Party. He was, he said, 'well acquainted with politicians of both sides' of parliament. In a letter to the *Bulletin* (25 December 1976), he recalled that his 'most extraordinary interview' was with Tom Tunnecliffe, 'long after he'd been [acting] Premier but while he was still in the Legislative Assembly':

> Walking through Queen's Hall in Parliament House one evening I encountered Tunnecliffe. He talked briefly, and then, obviously wanting company, he asked me into his office and began yarning. It seemed he was in a confessional mood, and there was no need to tell me he was not talking for publication.
>
> Wren's name came up. Tunnecliffe recalled a few episodes, and was curiously depressed. 'When I first went into politics for the Collingwood seat', he said, 'I was full of ideals. I believed I was going to reform the world, to put right every wrong. But as time went on, with Wren always around, I lost all my ideals.
>
> 'I can say I became completely corrupted. I was no longer my own man. It's caused me long grief. I believe I've been a complete failure.'

> [During the period 1907–20 Tunnecliffe represented rural Eaglehawk, not the Wrenite suburb of Collingwood.]

Even allowing that Meeking's recollection is sound, one cannot infer much from an informal conversation like this. It is a pity the 'few episodes' were not recalled by Meeking, as I suggest they would more readily have been had they been nefarious. He does not imply that they were particularly odious. He may have been referring to the stagnancy of the Dunstan government. (Tunnecliffe was only *curiously* depressed.) It is reasonable to infer from the letter that Wren had no depressing impact on Tunnecliffe while he was MLA for Eaglehawk (1907–20), in fact not until he won Collingwood in 1921. And it is not unreasonable to suggest that, in view of the Milk Board finding that Tunnecliffe may well have accepted a bribe, he may have felt compelled to curry some self-justification with Meeking. In 1927 *Table Talk* remembered him:

> [Tunnecliffe] stewed over inductive and deductive logic and won a prize for the former at the Working Men's College at a time when most young men were prancing away their leisure at the polka and schottische ... [He] was a tiger for subjects generally considered both dead and dismal—political economy, sociology, philosophy and the like ... Nowadays ... he reads with more catholicity of vision, browsing on Galsworthy, Wells, Bennett, Shaw *et al*, and lending a reflective ear at the Repertory Theatre, of which both he and Mrs Tunnecliffe are members.[1]

With this background, Tunnecliffe may have become maudlin (in his cups?) in old age as he reflected how the dreary grip of parliamentary pragmatism, trade union parochialism and Dunstan parsimony had crushed his youthful Labor idealism. The tantalising thing for a biographer of Wren is that there are intermittent suggestions of some major corruptions having been perpetrated, but they remain phantoms. The unromantic fact is that Tunnecliffe was not '*completely* corrupted' or 'a *complete* failure', even if he had accepted patronage or bribes. But if he had, it was ignominious of someone with such a cultivated sensibility to blame Wren who, after all, had no lien on his life, limb or conscience. It is pathetic to read of seasoned politicians blaming Wren for their acceptance of *his* money and then feeling some obligation. Or, in view of the penury of the Labor Party, was he offering them an essential service?

Catholic Action

Victorian Labor leader John Cain was by 1941 under increasing pressure to withdraw support from Dunstan—but it did not come from Wren. While Cain said the alliance with Dunstan was 'a complete betrayal of all ... principles', and agreed privately with Labor's state conference that a move away should be made, he waited for a sustainable issue that would not disrupt the party. That came in 1942, when Dunstan attacked prime minister Curtin's imposition of uniform taxation, which had become constitutionally possible under emergency defence powers. Cain moved to the opposition benches, the United Australia Party (UAP) taking its place behind Dunstan. However, an alliance in 1943 between Labor and the UAP to enforce a redistribution with Cain as premier lasted only four days, after which Dunstan returned to power. Wren's relations with Dunstan remained as before. With the UAP in disarray, Labor won even press support in the post-war elections of November 1945, and gained eight seats from the Country Party. Cain was again commissioned to form a government, which lasted until November 1947. A basically Catholic fraction deriving from the anti-communist Santamaria 'Movement' and the Industrial Groups was not enthusiastic about Cain, but its leader, Wren's friend but non-client Bert Cremean, had died in May 1945. Frank Field, his successor as deputy, was also a Catholic, but he had no links with Santamaria or Wren;[2] in fact he was regarded by many fellow-Catholics as insufficiently anti-communist, even sympathetic.[3] A successful Cain–Field ticket was a sign that Wren's influence in the Labor Party must have slipped. In Richmond, with the amiable, pliable Ted Cotter finally retiring, a pre-selection contest for the Richmond seat in the Legislative Assembly saw the defeat of the so-called 'Wren machine's' candidate, James 'Jimmy' Loughnan of the notorious and unreliable clan. The victor was Standish Michael Keon.

Born in Richmond of a 'battling' family, Keon had left school at twelve, was largely self-educated and actively participated in the Catholic Young Mens' Society. He became well read, assisted Arthur Calwell and his wife to write and produce *The Irish Review* and, in 1939, after some unemployment during the Depression, became general secretary of the Victorian Public Service Association. Editing the *Public Service Journal* was one of his functions, and Keon brought to it an aggressive zeal that would pressure Dunstan into conceding at least the first stages of an independent Public Service Board, finally achieved under Cain. Through shrewd timing and mobilisation Keon won Labor pre-selection. The contest between Cain and Cremean for leadership had meant that neither's candidate was acceptable to the other's supporters in Richmond. Keon had nominated 'out of the blue and [he said] got the preferences from both sides'. To forestall those who voted early and often, voters had to show their wartime ration books, identity cards and union tickets at the polling booths. 'Fixing' was impossible.[4]

Keon was fiercely anti-communist and dogmatically committed to Catholic social principles as laid down in the papal encyclicals. A moderate socialist, he supported, for example, bank nationalisation and increased welfare services. Skilled in excoriating rhetoric, he attacked wheeler-dealing politics as played by Dunstan and Wren. During 1945–55 he dominated Richmond, setting up *Richmond News* as a vehicle for his crusade, cleansing the council of corruption and promoting local welfare. A bachelor, intolerant of erotic books and films, he denounced a visiting French exhibition in 1953 as 'leprous rubbish' in spite of becoming an art connoisseur himself. When he spoke, several anti-clerical MPs liked to remark, 'You can smell the faggots burning'. To many he seemed to be a priest manqué.

The Cain Labor government lost office in November 1947, mainly over the Chifley federal government's determination to nationalise the banks but also because of poor administration, failure to quell union strikes, and even rumours of corruption involving Bill Barry and Archie Fraser, both allegedly close to Wren. Labor lost fourteen seats, notably those of Frank Field and Bill Slater who, as ministers, had not protected Wren's interests.[5] Rumours flew that the 'old man' had bank-rolled this defeat. Field had to contend with even his local Catholic pro-Movement curate campaigning against him.[6]

Wren was roused from sleep by telephone on the night of 27 July 1948, to be told that Keon had called for a royal commission into his activities. This arose from the proposal to amalgamate Wren's Victorian Trotting and Racing Association (VTRA) with the Williamstown Racing Club—thereby forming a club, ultimately using the Sandown Park racecourse and finally destroying proprietary racing in Victoria. Keon combined a rash prediction with a cogent summation of the traditional charges against Wren which would have pleased Mr Judkins:

> The new [racing] club will be as much a creature of John Wren as was the ... [VTRA]. The same methods and the same technique will be used. Those who can be bought will be bought. Those who can be intimidated will be intimidated. Those who have honour and integrity will be won over by donations to some charitable cause.[7]

Keon alleged that Wren had contributed to the Country Party's electoral campaign funds in 1947 because Cain had replaced Wren's pre-war monopoly over trotting with a non-profit public instrumentality, the Trotting Control Board. Robert Murray remarks:

> Wren swore vengeance as it was rumoured that he contributed heavily to the funds of other parties ... There were signs, impossible to be sure about, that he tried to stir up trouble for Cain and Field ... who introduced the legislation and lost his seat ... and for Slater, the Attorney-General and Chief Secretary, who drew it up.[8]

Keon maintained that Wren 'had corrupted every sport'. Dunstan (then minister for health), he said, was in touch with Wren 'almost every day'. And other Country Party notables—Hyland, Dodgson and Lind—were 'in the bag' (although he was to withdraw his charges at least against the last two named). Acting premier J. G. McDonald called Keon 'a political stink bomb' and a 'skunk' with his 'dirty, filthy, slimy innuendoes'. He denied that Wren had contributed to Country Party campaign funds, as did the party manager. McDonald said that before this incident he had never had any contact with Wren 'either by word of mouth, letter or intermediary'. Dunstan called Keon 'an unmitigated liar' for saying that his past campaigns had been financed by Wren and that the latter's influence had kept Dunstan in power for years. But the cagey countryman would not be interviewed outside the House.

Wren contacted McDonald by letter, enclosing a cheque. He denied next day any supply of funds—presumably in 1947 only, although he left that open. He wrote an open letter to Keon: if he could prove that Wren 'had contributed one shilling to the Country Party or any other member of the Party, he would donate £1,000 to the Melbourne

Hospital'. But, if not, Keon would give £200. There was 'not a grain of truth' in Keon's statement, said Wren:

> I will allow you to select any member of Parliament—even though he would be prejudiced against me personally or politically—to carry out the investigation, my only condition being that such an enquiry be open to the Press and the Public.
>
> If there is a spark of manhood in your composition you will, in order to preserve the honour and dignity of parliament, accept my challenge, thereby enabling me to disprove your flagrantly untrue, irresponsible and despicable statement.

McDonald on 28 July suspended standing orders to announce that not only 'the honour of political parties was at stake, but parliament had been … degraded and lowered to the level of the gutter'. He asked Keon to provide 'sufficient grounds' for a royal commission to be appointed 'so that the matter can be immediately investigated in every detail'.

Keon was undaunted. Naturally, he mocked Wren's challenge with its odds of 'five to one'. Never, he crowed, has the House been so belittled than 'in the reading of a letter of this type from a shady sports promoter [Uproar]'. (Later he would retort that McDonald had read the letter only because Wren had ordered him to do so.) McDonald's concern for 'the reputation of this gentleman' was, he said, 'extraordinary'. He had accused the Liberal Party before of accepting money from 'industrial concerns' but never had there been such an outburst of indignation or had House business been suspended because of 'an allegation that someone had made a donation to a Party's fund'. The Liberal Party appealed even in the press for donations, said Keon, and 'normally' there was 'nothing wrong' in that. Quite obviously, he said, no one can produce receipts and cheque butts of money donated to a political party. What he was asking for was a royal commission 'into all aspects of Wren's activities, not only his relations with the Country Party' but one 'with power to send for documents and subpoena witnesses':

> The challenge and money [was] typical of the man who sent it—a man who fought his way through life with money, and believes that money speaks all languages and can do all things. He throws £1,000 on the table from millions, and issues this challenge. I suggest that

> if a man who has been able to corrupt his way through life can come to the door of this House and have the Acting Premier stand with his £1,000 in his hands, then this Parliament has come to a low level.

McDonald's offer of a royal commission, Keon said, was 'a hollow farce'—but then so was Keon's furore without solid evidence. Wren said he did not know why Keon wanted a royal commission. He was willing to produce any witness or document required. He could remember meeting Keon only once and could not understand why he was being attacked. However, Wren's offer of what looked like a *bet* as a pledge of good faith smacked too much of Collingwood and was unconvincing, not to say vulgar—even more so than when he had challenged Sergeant O'Donnell over the bombing in 1906.[9]

But how justifiable was Keon's attack on Wren? Or was it opportunistic? As it happened, negotiations over Sandown Park led to Wren's Victorian Trotting and Racing Association making a free gift of it to the Victoria Racing Club. Keon was to lose his '£1,000 to a gooseberry bet' that there would never be racing at Sandown Park. If Wren had contributed to McDonald's 1947 campaign—and, as Keon said, there was nothing intrinsically wrong with that—his challenge showed extraordinary gall. Yet no bucket-tippers ever seemed to come forward, and surely not everyone would have been too craven to do so, even if there was some intimidation. (One looks in vain for evidence of Wren-sponsored violence.) At least everyone knew Wren subsidised electoral expenses. But Keon was not a disinterested commentator in 1948. He had reasons to proclaim:

> [I had] no intention of being 'a stooge' for Mr Wren or any other interest in gambling or otherwise. If my seat in Parliament is to be held at that price, I will not pay the price. I have no illusions as to what is likely to take place in relation to my seat in this House in due course ...[10]

With Jim Scullin due to resign, Keon's eyes were already on the redistributed federal seat of Yarra; the new middle-class Hawthorn sector would not be displeased by his outburst. Another candidate for preselection was John Cremean, Bert's brother, formerly Calwell's secretary and from that 'respected and honest family' whose friendship with Wren went back a generation. Obviously Wren did not favour Keon, and neither did Scullin, but Keon prevailed in a bitter contest. As Murray says:

> Keon used the Movement … and church youth groups as the base for building up a rival machine of his own. Both sides included many non-Catholics, but the Irish-Catholic flavour of both was strong. St John's Church, East Melbourne, became the Keon camp's virtual headquarters, while the Cremean supporters organised at St Ignatius', Richmond. Keon's appeal—he was then in his early 30s—was to youth, to opposition to Communism, Wren, the local councils and the 'old gang'.[11]

Keon went on to win the Yarra seat with an increased Labor majority, although in an election where the Chifley government was defeated. However, Cremean won the newly created contiguous seat of Hoddle. Keon's state seat went to a protégé, a Movement man, Frank Scully, who was to be the sole survivor of those who were expelled from the Labor Party in 1955, securing a further term as an anti-Evatt Labor/DLP parliamentarian.

Catholic folklore has it that when the news broke of his attack on Wren, Keon was rung up by several priests on the night of 27 July 1948. (Keon specifically mentioned to me only Mgr O'Collins of South Melbourne, but also referred to 'influential people').[12] He was told that he should leave Parliament House by the back door, and by no means walk home as usual through the Fitzroy Gardens. In 1986 Keon thought this danger had all been greatly exaggerated. As he told me, he had never received threats of violence from Wren; the roughs around the Richmond O'Connells and Loughnans did not need to be told by John Wren to be violent. After the 1954–5 Split, when Wren was well interred and the 'incorruptible' Jim Cairns had narrowly won his seat, Keon remarked: 'I had windows broken, dead cats thrown through the window, obscene phone calls. I couldn't get my rubbish bin emptied for years'.

Loutishness was just part of the Richmond (and Collingwood) scene. In later life Keon's criticism was that, in the period before he was elected, Wren 'dominated the party machine … [and] the pre-selection process':

> He did a lot of charitable things but then he exacted a payment in return. It was a Tammany style of politics.
>
> He would pay the membership fees to the central executive. If you wanted to get anywhere in politics in Richmond, Fitzroy or Collingwood, if you didn't meet with Wren's favour, you didn't bother. [*But see above instances where 'Wren's favour' was not decisive. Also, it is evident that Wren's favour fell on honourable men such as Tudor, Scullin and Frank Brennan and failed to stymie someone he disliked, such as Blackburn.*]
>
> And yet a lot of very honorable people swear by him. I never had a great deal to do with him but I knew that I had no chance of making any progress unless I accepted his support.[13]

Yet 'with luck and hard work' Keon *did* outmanoeuvre the so-called 'machine'. My reading is that Wren exercised broad influence in the inner suburbs—no doubt decisive in some specific instances—but not overall *control.*

In Canberra, from 1949 to 1955, Keon was regarded as prime ministerial timber, always providing he could learn to control his verbal intemperance. However, during the fatal Labor split in 1954–5 he became virtual, though not official, leader of the anti-Evatt group. At forty-two his parliamentary career was over. Unnecessarily, the 'Wrenite' John Cremean, although critical of Keon, also sacrificed his political future, while Jack Galbally, who had represented Wren in the Hardy trial, remained with Labor and became its leader in the Legislative Council.

There were no simple patterns here. Keon went on to be a founder of the Democratic Labour Party, but by 1958 was denouncing Santamaria's attempts to make it a church party—for which, Keon said, there was no place in Australia.[14] Although a fierce supporter of the Industrial Groups, Keon had never been a member of the Movement. He wanted a centrist Australian Christian Democrat equivalent. His unique dissidence had led him to denounce Wren, Evatt and Santamaria within a decade. In reality it was Keon and his like, the apostles of Catholic Action who, rather than Wren, were ultimately the target for *Power Without Glory*, as the Industrial Groups had gradually won over key unions from communist control. Post-war prosperity and greater geopolitical sophistication meant a different Australia in which individuals like Wren could no longer wield their former degree of patronage.

In the final political episode of *Power Without Glory* Hardy, convinced of a simplistic anti-communist conspiracy, tries to deal with the eclipse of 'West's' (Wren's) power among Catholics and to reconcile the antagonism between the old corrupt wheeler-dealer and 'Kiely' (Keon), representing the new fanatical Catholic Action. Archbishop 'Malone' (Mannix) is supposed to extract £50,000 from 'West' for his crusade. This is wishful thinking. Wren's son, John Francis, was sure about that. His father, he said, believed that the Movement would destroy the Labor Party by inflaming the sectarianism which Catholic politicians such as Scullin, Ryan and Chifley had shunned. Wren's attitude was in line with that expressed by his friend Ted Theodore in 1925:

> Sectarianism is an influence difficult to combat, because its propaganda is for the most part insidious and underground. It rarely comes out into the open. It performs its lethal work in the dark, with murderous innuendo and slanderous tongue. Sectarianism thrives on ignorance and prejudice and is responsible for more ill-will, hatred and rancour in the community than any single cause.[15]

Mannix probably did extract from Wren some seed-money in 1941–2 for his anti-communist cause. Niall Brennan would appear to be near the mark when he suggests, on the basis of credible hearsay, that '£5,000 had been donated by Wren to the Santamaria cause and that Wren later confessed his regret at doing so'.[16] His eldest son confirmed this. Apparently, after that, nothing.

Denouement

Wren, as noted earlier, felt that in relation to taxing the profits from the Fiji gold mines, the Labor Party had proved ungrateful. He was moving away from it. In his letter to Scullin in late 1941 he complained:

> Apparently, after more than fifty years of effort and practical support of Trades Unionism and Labor in Australia, the number of true friends on whom I can rely for justice, is limited. This is indeed very painful for me.
>
> At the age of fourteen, when I was employed in a boot factory at

> the wages of 5/- a week, my father asked me to accompany him to a meeting at the Melbourne Town Hall, which was held for the purpose of raising funds to help the London Dockyard Employees' Strike. One of the principal speakers was the late Rev. Prior Butler, whose eloquent appeal on behalf of these downtrodden workers, had such an effect upon me that I induced my father to allow me to donate my weekly wages to the strike fund until its termination. From then on I have been an enthusiastic and practical helper in the cause of Trades Unionism and Labor politics, in which period, I have spent in the vicinity of a quarter of a million pounds helping the cause I believed in.
>
> As a mark of appreciation of my efforts on behalf of the various Trades Unions engaged in the great building strike about thirty five years ago, I was privileged to be presented with five beautiful illuminated addresses which I have in my home. During the course of the strike … I contributed £5,000 … my support of the men in this strike created bitter hostility towards myself from the opponents of Labor.
>
> In nearly every strike, before and after arbitration, I have never refused a genuine appeal for financial assistance.
>
> At all elections, both Federal and State, I have never hesitated to support in a practical way, the Party and individual candidates very often to my material disadvantage, my predominant desire being to help the class from which I sprang.[17]

Post-war prosperity rendered Wren's gifts to individual politicians less expedient. Moreover, like his friend Archbishop Duhig of Brisbane, he disapproved of Curtin-Chifley socialism.

On this point, Charles Meeking's letter, referred to above, is persuasive. He had lived in Studley Park, Kew, and had known Wren's solicitor, Bernard Nolan, though not Wren himself. He probably did not suspect that Wren may have spoken with Menzies, who also lived in Kew, had visited Mannix at Raheen, was acquainted with Mannix's confidant, Fr William Hackett SJ, and may even have used the Raheen library when writing the Liberal Party constitution.[18] Meeking recalled:

> In 1948, flying to Melbourne one day, I found myself sitting next to a man who proved extremely knowledgeable about *political affairs*

> and *people.* He made some outspoken comments, including some as we flew over Canberra, and I felt it fair to warn him of my job.
>
> 'That's interesting', he said. 'My name's Smith, and I'm a travelling representative of the hierarchy. Have you met Wren? How long will you be in Melbourne?'
>
> When I told him I'd be in Melbourne a few days but had no wish whatever to see Wren, he replied that it would be important and helpful for me if I did go to see Wren. He asked the name of my hotel, and I reluctantly agreed to be available the following morning.
>
> When I reached Wren's smallish office in Flinder's Lane next day there was no delay.
>
> Ushered straight in, I found the pink face and pink bald head unexpectedly small and unimpressive. I thought of Tunnecliffe and some of the small-time Wren minions I'd known years earlier, but found Wren well informed on politics …
>
> He talked with some venom of Labor bank nationalisation efforts and other socialist policies. He invited my views, but I continued to wonder what the urgency for the interview had been.
>
> Then as I stood up to leave, Wren said, 'You can go and tell Menzies he's going to win the next election'.[19]

There are several, no doubt obvious, points about Meeking's letter, which to me has a ring of authenticity. However, I have never heard of a layman who calls himself 'a travelling representative of the hierarchy'. No wonder his name was 'Smith'! But which hierarch? Was it Mannix who was not opposed to bank nationalisation, providing there were safeguards against monopoly, and had favoured the 1944 'powers' referendum? Or was it Duhig of Brisbane, who believed that bank nationalisation and such 'socialism' as Chifley and Evatt planned were opposed to Catholic principles, who publicly favoured the Liberal–Country Party coalition, and who made a deal in 1949 with Menzies over an eventual position in federal cabinet for the Queensland Catholic politician, Senator Neil O'Sullivan? Or was 'Smith' in reality someone like the Wren factotum, Frank Lawrence, networking?

In a subsequent similar letter to Niall Brennan, Meeking says he reported the aeroplane conversation to Menzies, who told him to go to see Wren. This adds to my supposition that there may have been at some stage contact (though very informal) between Menzies and Wren—but not such that Wren would ring Menzies himself. Menzies KC did represent Wren in a legal case in 1946 in relation to the resumption of the Ascot racecourse. No doubt Wren wanted to suggest that he was still someone to be reckoned with—perhaps even that he might 'kick in' with a donation like the 1949 bank directors, managers and clerks. Meeking saw Menzies later that day in Melbourne Chambers: 'I mentioned to him that I'd seen Wren, and gave him Wren's prediction. He smiled. "Nice to know", he said.'[20] And win Menzies did, for years to come, without any reliance on Wren.

CHAPTER TWENTY

Making Millions

WREN'S INTERESTS ENCOMPASSED sport—as promoter, innovator and manager—and ventures in newspaper publishing. Yet the range of his other commercial activities was if anything even more diverse. His scrutiny of financial opportunities appears almost panoptic. On the one hand were ventures in high-yield Fiji mines or scrapped war assets in Papua or liquor or French cosmetics; on the other, a Sydney 'frock shop' (which I cannot trace), a Melbourne service station, a pub here and there, and Albert Jacka's electrical goods store. An instinctive operator, he probably would have scoffed at formal business education, feasibility studies, cost benefit analyses and the like. Peter Freeman has called the Wren empire 'a corporate labyrinth built on chance not plan, although in most [many?] cases the dice was rolled not by John Wren but by his old friend Pierce Cody and his son Pat'. J. F. Wren complained that 'It took some years to sort out his full legacy': 'I inherited an unwieldy mass of diverse investments which had to be rationalised to remain profitable. The businesses had been too widespread unless we had competent managers. I was left with a nice old mess to clean these things up.'[1]

Neither time nor resources have allowed exhaustive research into Wren's business activities, but what follows should be sufficient to indicate his scope, astuteness or otherwise, preparedness to take risks, resourcefulness and even eccentricity. The miscellaneous nature of his enterprises and his indefatigable interstate travelling (mostly by train) must have precluded efficient personal co-ordination and supervision. One has the feeling that even filing cabinets were not evident in his office. Wren operated with few office staff and delegated responsibility to managers whom he felt he could trust, such as Dick Lean in sport and real estate and his eldest son, John F. Wren, in Marigny cosmetics. As life-long factotum/secretary he had the inscrutable Frank Lawrence, whom Stan Keon called 'urbane and steely'. Unfortunately I have not had any opening to research the activities or character of this obviously reserved and talented man. While not all Wren's managers were efficient, none seem to have cheated him. He operated his discrete enterprises without a coherent structure, putting trusted lieutenants in charge and expecting them to exert control and be directly accountable to him. After Wren's death his son complained that his father had kept on 'too many drones', as he would stand by them if they were loyal to him.[2]

Dick Lean was the exemplar of Wren's success in delegating authority. He had worked in real estate before becoming R. L. Baker's Melbourne manager at Stadiums Ltd. Wren had retained Lean when he bought it 'lock, stock and barrel' in 1914–15. But not before he had tested Lean's loyalty by sending him on a trip to Sydney and arranging for several associates to attempt to subvert him during a train journey. That failed, and Lean remained in his position until retirement, also managing Melbourne Carnivals Ltd as well as attending to most of Wren's land and estate affairs. After a few months in Wren's employment, Lean's work was deemed 'very satisfactory' and his pay raised from £5 to £6 per week—hardly a grand sum. Wren did not pay his staff munificently, but they had access to perks and investments. When he made them nominees for his investments, for example, presumably they were treated generously like Norman White, his Sydney business associate. 'You couldn't wish to work for a better man', said Lean:

> He gave us managers a free hand to spend his money as we thought fit and never complained if we showed a loss … If we did get into the red he would say: 'Don't worry, Lean; you can't win all the time. You'll make it up later on'.

They had had arguments in the past but, about eighteen months before he died, Wren unprecedentedly began to interfere in arranging fights in Melbourne, exasperating Lean to the point where he left his resignation on his boss's desk. As he read the letter Wren called Lean in and, without looking at him, asked how long he'd been with Stadiums Ltd. About forty years, was the reply. Still not looking up, Wren said: 'That's more than two-thirds of your life'. Then, before Lean could say anything, Wren tore up the resignation and threw it in the waste-paper basket: 'Don't be a damn fool, Lean, go back to your office'. Lean did. Apparently the interference ceased.[3]

Mining and petroleum

While Wren had described himself earlier as a mining investor, his first venture in mining of which I have specific knowledge was in Mt Isa Mines Ltd, although he does not appear in its float in January 1924. In February 1924, however, Randolph 'The Reckless' Bedford, mining journalist, novelist and Labor MLA in Queensland, issued with friends a prospectus for Mount Isa Silver Lead Proprietary NL. It offered 80,000 shares at 5 shillings. The largest batch (amount unspecified) went to Wren, his relatives and associates; 500 went to Theodore (then premier of Queensland) and 250 to McCormack (then a Labor minister and later premier) without any concern for conflict of interest. Bedford said, 'I don't expect mean little suburban pikers to understand either mateship, gratitude or generosity'. In July 1924 Bedford sold out to Mt Isa Mines for £65,000 in fully paid shares. In 1929 he issued the prospectus of Mt Isa Pty Silver Lead Co (almost the same name as in 1924) with the same directors, but including Wren. As Bedford's leases were not worked they were eventually forfeited to Mt Isa Mines. Nothing more is known of Wren's involvement except for the 52 shares found in his safe at his death.[4]

'To help the goat that is born every minute', jeered the *Wild Cat Monthly* in October 1929, 'a New Guinea gold mine is floated every week'. It admitted, however, that some fortunes were being made at the Bulolo gold mines. Still, it insisted, some reports were built on a faith that would literally have to move mountains. Prospects were 'located thousands of feet up in some of the most rugged mountain country in the world'. It was too late to warn Wren who, unperturbed by his initial foray into Mt Isa Silver Lead Proprietary NL, had already registered the Upper Watut Gold Mining Company Pty Ltd in Victoria in July 1927.[5] His partner Frank Anstey thought by March 1930, after visiting New

Guinea again, that it would be impossible to move bulky dredges by air, but it was done in the region in pioneering style. However, the company was a failure, but not necessarily a costly one as none of the capital was subscribed in cash and there is no evidence that expenses were incurred between 1927 and 1931. In fact, extant documents suggest that for whatever reason nothing much happened other than the holding of potentially valuable, or valueless, leases.

Wren's shareholding in Upper Watut Gold Mining Company Pty Ltd proved to be one of a number of investments he held in failed mining ventures, including Interstate Mines and Petroleum NL (registered in Victoria in 1928), Kunanalling Gold NL (1932), White Hope South (*Cracow*) *NL* (1932), Baraduda Bucket Dredging NL (1933), Haven Gold Dredging NL (1934), Borneo Gold Explorations NL (1936) and Upper Watut Developments (New Guinea) NL (1935). Ray Betts, former principal with Wren's chartered accountants Buckley & Hughes, Melbourne, remembers that 'There would be a room full of scrip for defunct mining companies that you could line the walls with—of shares that Wren had—he always reckoned they might come good'.[6]

An interesting failure was Roma Mooga Oil Fields NL, registered in Victoria in 1927.[7] It had an oil permit in the Roma district of Queensland and was listed on the Melbourne Stock Exchange in November 1928. Wren's involvement almost certainly owed much to his friendship with Archbishop Duhig of Brisbane[8] and the noted geologist and socialist H. I. Jensen,[9] who had denounced Theodore's and McCormack's part in the Mungana rort. The existence of oil and gas in the Roma district had been known since 1900. Jensen was confident that a bountiful prospect existed along the Mooga Mooga stream rather than around the Hospital Hill area where there was 'feverish activity' in mid–1927 and where the Roma Oil Corporation struck gas and light condensate. Other companies had eleven sites in progress.[10] Duhig, who had recently seen the gushers of California while attending the 1926 Chicago Eucharistic Congress, had visions of financing a grandiose Holy Name cathedral by oil revenue. A permit was purchased for a site generally known as Stewart's Mooga or sometimes Archbishop Duhig's Bore. Roma Mooga's permit adjoined it. Its initial directors were Wren, who stayed with it throughout, and four Melbourne businessmen. Wren, however, was very much behind the scenes, his name on the board being the only evidence of his participation other than his initial nominal holding of 500 shares.[11]

In February 1929 the Stock Exchange of Melbourne's *Official Record* (SEMOR) published the report by Jensen. He said that the area was all oil bearing; the only question was whether it was payable. Jensen almost seemed to be saying that oil searching required faith; if Duhig had the good oil, his neighbours would share in his earthly reward. Jensen chose the site for drilling, which seems to have begun in March 1929. By the end of May it had reached oily shales at 1,055 feet. By mid-September it had reached 1,700 feet without a report of payable oil. On 5 October the *Wild Cat Monthly* reported a crash in Queensland oil stocks. Roma Mooga's annual general meeting on 24 April 1930 agreed to suspend operations, although Jensen thought this 'regrettable'.[12]

Already Roma Mooga had prepared to move on, acquiring 773 acres in East Gippsland near Metung. Oil had been found at Lakes Entrance in 1920 but commercial quantities would not be found until the 1960s when the Broken Hill Proprietary Co. Ltd went offshore. Failure again encouraged the company to recruit a gold prospector. To finance his work, forfeited shares were offered to the public at sixpence each. In June 1933 Roma Mooga secured an option over Wombat Mine near Mitta Mitta in north-east Victoria, where there was a favourable report of payable gold. At 31 October 1933 the balance sheet showed £28 4s of gold won. More significant was the item of £20,907 representing forfeited shares in trust. From this point the company fades away. Roma Mooga investors over four or five years had subscribed more than £41,000 in capital for a return of £28 4s in gold and not one drop of oil. There were no winners at Roma Mooga.[13]

However, Wren must have done well from gold mining at Cracow, Queensland, through Australian Gold Development NL (AGD), registered in Victoria on 14 April 1932, and its associated company, Golden Plateau NL. Gold prices had risen during the Great Depression. 'Fields that had never succeeded', writes Geoffrey Blainey, 'gave hope to companies that used the flotation process and diesel power stations and electric pumps and large scale mining methods, and the advances of the last few decades'. The lack of alternative investments also attracted capital to gold. Where only 28 new companies were registered in Victoria in 1930, there were 160 in 1934. AGD revolved around the genius of mining engineer T. R. Victor, whose 'ability to select mines was uncanny' says Blainey.[14] The company was formed by stockbrokers L. G. May and Wallace Smith, the latter being described as 'the most mercurial mining man on the exchange'. He had been a member of the Stock Exchange of Melbourne since 1898 and died still a member in 1962. He was prominent in the search for oil in Queensland, underwrote the floats for gold in Fiji and, in the 1950s, 'two of his firm's floats were among the rare dividend payers' in the uranium boom. Graeme Adamson, in his history of the Stock Exchange of Melbourne, estimates that 'with its spinoff and own capital appreciation, each £10 AGD share ultimately returned its holders £20,000.[15]

Initially only 100 shares were allotted in AGD and £5,000 raised. On advice, the company bought a reef being developed at Cracow on the Dawson River in central Queensland and floated the Golden Plateau NL mine. It was registered in Victoria on 14 July 1932, and purchased AGD's right, title and interest in approximately 20 acres of Cracow goldfield. In August the company was listed on the Stock Exchange of Melbourne. Of the 150,000 contributory shares issued to the public, 100,000 were reserved for application by shareholders in AGD and the remainder were heavily oversubscribed by the public.[16] By March 1933 the existence of some 50,000 tons of highly payable ore had been established, and in April the mine expanded to the adjoining Sunrise lease.[17] Company capital was increased; production costs fell. In 1934 the crushing mill was recovering 97 per cent of the gold content in the ore treated. The 10 shilling shares (paid up to 7 shillings and 6 pence) were selling as high as £6 1s 6d. The *Bulletin* (22 November 1939) estimated the distributions to that date amounted to £851,000.[18] It is not known how many shares Wren held, but T. P. Boland in his biography of Duhig has no hesitation in saying that Wren made a fortune at Cracow;[19] the archbishop and his cathedral missed out.

Wren's ventures in Fiji in gold mining were spectacularly successful. They involved four companies: Loloma Gold Mines NL, Koroere Gold NL, Emperor Mines Ltd and Tavua Power Pty Ltd. Gold was discovered on Vita Levu by Bill Borthwick in 1931–2 in the Nasivi River region, contrary to the forecast of 'experts'. He was, however, 'grub-staked' by a well-known Suva merchant and publican, Pat Costello, whose trust was rewarded.[20] In October 1934 the Governor of Fiji had told his Legislative Council that private enterprise would be invited to prove and extract the country's gold deposits and that the government intended 'as far as lay in its power, to prevent any form of speculation which may tend to injure its good name.' This was reported in the Stock Exchange of Melbourne's *Official Record* in March the following year. According to K. H. Kennedy it was E. G. Theodore, an acquaintance of Costello, who in early 1933 commissioned a geological survey undertaken with 'financial backing from John Wren, [Frank] Packer, and the liquor merchant, P. F. Cody'. Although the report was adverse, Theodore acquired a property adjacent to Costello's and 'decided to test it in person'.[21] However, S. Salisbury and K. Sweeney attribute the leadership of the Fijian syndicate to Wren and Cody, who 'were joined by' Packer and Theodore.[22] Ross Fitzgerald says that, according to Cody, he and Wren were in Sydney when quartz and gold samples arrived from Fiji with Theodore, who then formed a syndicate to investigate prospects for the full-scale operation. The members were listed on 9 August 1935 in the *Sydney Morning Herald* as Theodore, Wren, Cody and G. Packer (presumably Gretel, Frank Packer's wife). They sent a noted geologist, Dr Loftus Hills, to Fiji. While pessimistic beforehand, Hills changed his mind after assaying fourteen samples which averaged 6 ounces 8 pennyweight per ton. Another sample contained 58 ounces.[23]

Meanwhile, mining engineer T. R. Victor, who was consulting engineer to Australian Gold Development NL on the Cracow Reef, and who had also once been discouraging about Fiji, advised that company on 31 December 1934 'to acquire the necessary capital to develop' the now proven lodes at Tavua and Yanawai. 'It is without doubt', he said, 'the richest surface proposition I have ever had the privilege of sampling and must produce large quantities of gold if the values persist to any degree of depth'.[24] The Stock Exchange of Melbourne's *Official Record* reported in January 1935 that Australian Gold Development shareholders had arranged with directors of Loloma Gold Mines NL (registered 31 January 1935) to be granted priority applications to its shares. The initial subscribers included Wren with 500 shares. Wren, Wallace Smith, P. F. Cody, T. R. Victor, E. G. Banks and Theodore were foundation directors.[25] They were later joined by Sir Maynard Hedstrom of Fiji. Frank Packer's role in the Theodore syndicate is elusive. He does not appear in defunct company records, and writers who mention his involvement are sketchy in details.[26]

A reorganisation began in July 1935, after negotiations with 'London interests … to take over the whole of the undertaking of the old company'. The reason given was 'to provide funds sufficient to carry out a more extensive development campaign, and for the installation of a suitable treatment plant'.[27] In August shares (10 shillings paid up to 3 shillings) were selling as high as £5 18s. In September the new company changed its name to Loloma (Fiji) Gold Mines NL, and London interests were allotted 150,000 new contributing shares. Theodore told shareholders that fellow director, E. G. Banks, a mining engineer, had been to Fiji and 'had never seen a property that was so promising with such a comparatively small amount of work done'.[28] In its second operating period (52 weeks) Loloma made a profit of £193,813 (up £110,020), which was equal to 4 shillings and 9 pence per share.[29] By 1950 Loloma combined with Emperor and Koroere Mines had yielded over 1,000,000 ounces of fine gold and 300,000 ounces of silver.[30]

Koroere Gold NL, registered in Victoria in February 1935, operated at Tova Tova, six miles from Tavua. Apparently E. Byron Moore (sharebroker of Collins Street, Melbourne) originally held an option over 200 acres on the Tavua gold field, comprising properties called Cardigan and Koroere, which backed onto the Emperor Mines Ltd line of lode. In mid-February the Fijian government approved the Cardigan lease and granted a prospecting licence, with an assurance of a lease for Koroere. Original capital was £150,000, divided into 300,000 shares of 10 shillings each. Australian Gold Development Ltd held 50,000 shares. Wren, Victor, Cody and Byron Moore each held 500, while 247,500 were held in trust for the public. Foundation directors included Cody (chairman), Wren, Victor, Byron Moore, Theodore and Hedstrom. In November 1935 contributing shares (paid up to 3 shillings) were selling for as much as £1 6s but then fell heavily, probably because it became clear that it would be some time before returns could be expected. Fijian infrastructure was poor and development expenses high for a small-scale producer. Two calls were made during the first six months of 1936. In early 1937 Theodore declared that tonnages of proved ore reserves were not large enough to warrant the capital expenditure needed for a modern milling plant. He recommended a merger with, say, Emperor. However, Koroere continued for a further twelve months until in April 1938 it sold all its assets to Emperor in exchange for shares in Emperor. By then Koroere's contributing shares had fallen to rock bottom: 1 shilling and 9 pence. It was then absorbed as a going concern.[31]

Emperor Mines Ltd was registered in Victoria in July 1935, with a mining lease and prospecting licence covering approximately 500 acres, six miles from Tavua. Victor reported that it was 'a splendid mine, one with great possibilities'. The company was listed on the Melbourne Stock Exchange in October; 600,000 10 shilling fully paid shares were issued to the vendors, and options over 350,000 shares were granted to the vendors, exercisable at par for 18 months from September 1936. Victor, Wallace Smith and A. G. Campbell were joined on the board by Wren, Cody, Theodore and Hedstrom. In 1943, 1945, 1948 and 1950 the capital of the company was progressively reduced, with money being returned to shareholders. On his death in 1953 Wren was replaced by his son, John F. Wren. Eventually Emperor became part of Western Mining Corporation Limited. In September 1955 Ellen Wren was holding 17,333 shares and was the eleventh biggest shareholder in Western Mining.[32]

An adjunct company to the Fijian mines, Tavua Power Pty Ltd, registered in Victoria in April 1936, was to generate power for lighting, heating, energy etc. and to transmit and supply it to governments, companies, public bodies and individuals. It also engaged in telegraph and telephone installation and maintenance; rail and road construction, transportation etc.; and financing of public works. The initial subscribers were Emperor and Loloma. The first directors were Cody, Banks, Wallace Smith, Campbell, Victor and Theodore. Wren joined the board in July after the death of Campbell in 1936. Again, he remained there until his death and was replaced by J. F. Wren. In 1967 Tavua became Vatukoula Power Pty Ltd.[33]

At his death, Wren held in his safe share scrip for numerous mining and related companies but it is not possible, for any of them, to determine whether he merely had an interest as a passive or speculative investor or whether he had a more active personal involvement. Among the share scrip found were £4,500 shares in Great Boulder Mines Ltd. This interest was acquired through Loloma investments in Great Boulder NL.[34] A letter from Wren to Theodore (4 October 1949) suggests a substantial involvement:

> Dear Ted,
>
> Last week Pat Cody returned from a short visit to West Aust after spending a little time at the Great Boulder Mines in company with the managing director (Mr Coulson) …

> I understand from Pat that, as a result of the recent currency depreciation, the prospects of Great Boulder are now much more favourable than previously …
>
> Whilst at Kalgoorlie, an estimated budget for the calendar year 1950 was discussed … it is expected that a working surplus of £383,000 should be achieved for the year … according to Pat, there should be something like two shillings per share available for distribution …
>
> [Treating slightly higher grades of ore next year] is considered desirable in order to take advantage of the present gold price before any attempt is likely by the government to filch the profits by way of taxation or possibly by the reimposition of the gold bonus payment …
>
> Sincerely yours,
> J. Wren[35]

As defunct company records in Victoria establish that in 1961 or earlier, both Joseph Wren (his third son) and M. J. Cody were directors of Great Boulder Gold Mines Ltd, incorporated in 1957,[36] we may suspect that Wren had been directly involved with Great Boulder Proprietary Gold Mines Ltd, which was made famous by the controversial Claude de Bernales. This was originally registered in 1894, and yielded £100,000,000 in gold at 1963 prices during the next seventy years. However, research has not uncovered even a hint of a Wren association with the company or with Bernales.[37] Wren's involvement may have been due simply to an occasional investment at a time when the company's shares were undervalued.

War disposals

Wren and Cody discerned in war materials abandoned after 1945 an opportunity to avoid taxation, legally as it turned out. They formed a company, War Assets Pty Ltd, registered in Victoria on 24 June 1947 with a capital of £25,000 in £1 shares. War Assets became a two-thirds partner in Milne Bay Merchants Ltd, which was incorporated in Papua on 26 November 1947 with £7 capital paid up. Wren and P. F. Cody were among four promoters. The company took over an assignment that War Assets had with Vacuum Oil Co. for disposal of war materials. A profit of £137,000 was made in two years. The share of War Assets in the profits over two years came to £89,033.[38] The Australian Tax Commissioner in 1952 ruled a liability to pay £63,000 tax on the grounds that 'War Assets have not transferred its right to the disposal of material to the Papuan company [that is, Milne Bay Merchants] and that Cody had retained exclusive control of the Papuan company'. Wren and Cody appealed, whereupon the High Court in 1954 'overruled both these contentions, saying':

> it was obvious that the Melbourne company had intended to transfer the property to the Papuan company for the purpose of avoiding tax and that the directors of the Papuan company had had control on the spot of their activities.
>
> The Milne Bay company made the profit. That was the essence of the transaction.
>
> No income tax could be incurred by the real beneficiaries from the transaction until the Milne Bay company declared a dividend and that could be delayed indefinitely.[39]

In her biography of Sir Leslie Thiess, Joan Priest says that he bought 55 per cent of Milne Bay Merchants Ltd from 'Sir John Wren'. The date is somewhat vague, but appears to be around 1948.[40]

Land, coal, livestock

Wren purchased three grazing properties: Moroco East[41] near Tocumwal/Deniliquin in the Riverina; Bidgemia near Carnarvon, Western Australia; and Spring Hill, Spencers Brook, eight kilometres south of Northam, Western Australia. Moroco East, with 27,000 acres was bought in the name of Ellen Wren in 1916. According to the history of the Murray Shire:

> W. McKee managed it for the next few years possibly until it was taken over by Pattison [Patterson] and Taylor. They are said to have held the property some time after 1926 [actually from 1 January 1927], branching out into agriculture, growing wheat on some of the plain country. But the run reverted to Ellen Wren again for the amount of the mortgage that she still held. Harold Glowrey [later MLA Ouyen, Country Progressive Party] managed the station for many years.[42]

Patterson and Taylor paid £99,047 3s 6d for 14,672 acres freehold and 6,888 acres leasehold. Ellen Wren loaned them £64,047 3s 6d on first mortgage at 6 1/2 per cent. With the Depression and poor seasons, they fell behind in interest payments. Mrs Wren took over the station on 21 March 1932. The mortgage then stood at £59,887 3s 6d, which was what she had paid for it. The Patterson and Taylor partnership had obviously paid too much for Moroco. In 1937 Moroco East ran 239 cattle and 8,653 sheep, which were reduced to 92 and 4,856 respectively by 1951.[43]

Wren and Henry Crosthwaite bought 85,561 £1 shares for £95,000 in the capital of Clifton Downs Pastoral Co Ltd in 1928. Wren was to pay for two-thirds, Crosthwaite one-third. Clifton Downs' main asset was a million-acre sheep and cattle station near Carnarvon in Western Australia's Gascoyne district. Wren loaned Crosthwaite £16,666 13s 4d, and their shares in Clifton Downs were transferred to a company named Bidgemia Pastoral Company Pty Ltd. Crosthwaite agreed to pay off his loan from profits and also mortgaged a property of 90 acres known as Amstel, at Waverley, then on the outskirts of Melbourne. Wren thus effectively controlled the ownership of the Clifton Downs and Amstel properties. J. F. Wren said of Clifton Downs that it was sold, apparently at a considerable loss, 'in the late 1940s after nine years of drought and it has never stopped raining since'. Both properties were sold by 1953.[44]

The second property in Western Australia, Spring Hill, of 4,425 acres near the Agricultural College, Northam, was still in the family in 1984. It was described as rising from the Avon River and consisted of mainly undulating fertile red-loam soils. Annual rainfall was about 17 inches and the homestead was served by a spring producing more than 2000 gallons per day, while scheme water and 'reliable soaks' served the rest of the farm. Spring Hill was used as a fattening staging point for stock going from Bidgemia to the Perth market. During the war the Commonwealth government acquired 252 acres for defence purposes, while an additional area was occupied by the United States defence forces. In July 1946 the Defence Department required a further 230 acres in spite of protests that it would depreciate seriously the rest of the property.[45] Crosthwaite managed the station 'with the help of a lubra and no other assistant except a well oiled rifle'. Coopers & Lybrand, chartered accountants, 'had the greatest difficulty', according to Peter Norris, 'in getting figures from Crosthwaite in order to prepare… tax returns':

> Year in, year out, Crosthwaite would fail to answer urgent requests for information and as often as not when a letter did arrive it would merely say, 'same as last year'. Crosthwaite owned a property which he mortgaged for a substantial sum to Mr Wren … 90 acres … situate[d] in Ferntree Gully Road, Waverley, Victoria, and occupied when I came to know it as Amstel Golf Club.
>
> An extraordinary thing happened in that Joseph Wren when looking into the documents affecting the property discovered the mortgage while duly signed had never been registered and strangely enough he discovered this on the last day of the registration and, of course, took appropriate action … my recollection is [that] the property was sold … for something like £440,000.
>
> It was with a good deal of understanding that Joseph, realising the feelings of the members of Amstel Golf Club who were dispossessed, negotiated with their representatives … A loan from the Wren interests of a substantial sum of money at a favourable rate of interest enabled the Amstel Club to purchase the site of its excellent course outside Cranbourne near Melbourne. The Club honoured Joseph by naming an annual trophy for him …[46]

Hugh Buggy relates that Dick Lean persuaded Wren to invest in 'imported patrician cattle from New Zealand and selling them in Victoria'. The *Wyora* was chartered from Union Steamship Co. and laden with 650 high quality cattle, but only five men as chamberlains. On the first voyage 112 cattle died. Wren lost £3 on the deal. The next shipment boarded twenty-five caretakers. Seven shiploads sold at good prices; Wren made a substantial profit. Buggy does not give the year for this transaction[47] but it was probably around 1916.

Wren was believed to have had some involvement in two coal mines in the Newcastle area, although little documentary evidence has been found. However, it is clear that he speculated with H. H. Bell, chairman of the Melbourne Tramways Board, in a land acquisition and a brown coal prospect at Altona, on the then outskirts of Melbourne, in 1945. According to journalist Peter Freeman, these 'massive' tracts of land were sold to 'a variety of buyers, including property developers and a local council'. Buckley & Hughes noted that in 1954 taxation had been paid on 'the profit resulting from the realisation of certain land

and houses at Altona' and that the profit was of 'a capital nature'. The partnership was two-thirds Wren, one-third Bell.[48]

Liquor

Wren, in partnership with fellow-Catholics Patrick and Matthew Cody, played a leading role in mergers of distillery interests, which resulted in the formation in 1924 of Federal Distilleries Pty Ltd and in 1930 of The United Distillers Pty Ltd. During the mid-nineteenth century it had been found that the Yan Yean water piped into Melbourne and the stream water at the foot of Mount Warrenheip near Ballarat were exceptionally pure, had little iron and were ideal for distilling. Four early firms to distil whisky were: Joshua Brothers Pty Ltd, which began in the 1880s and in about 1900 operated the Federal Distillery in Port Melbourne; The Australian Distillery Company Pty Ltd in Abbotsford; Henry Brind and Co., named after an English chemist who in 1870 had acquired a controlling interest in Myer's Ballarat Distillery on the shore of Lake Wendouree; and Breheny Bros and Kenna's Brewery Pty Ltd, which had begun distilling whisky at Mount Warrenheip in 1917 and amalgamated with Brind's to form Brinds Pty Ltd in 1920. In March 1920 Joshua Brothers Pty Ltd went into voluntary liquidation.[49] It seems that subsequently a syndicate consisting of Wren, P. F. and M. J. Cody and F. A. Leith, trading as the Federal Distillery Company, acquired the assets of Joshua Brothers Pty Ltd from the liquidator.

A new company, Federal Distilleries Pty Ltd, was registered on 22 January 1924, and an agreement was reached between it and four vendors: the Federal Distillery Company (operated by Wren, Cody and Leith), the Australian Distillery Company Pty Ltd, Brinds Pty Ltd, and Breheny Bros and Kenna's Brewery Pty Ltd. All four transferred their assets (and liabilities) to the new company in exchange for shares in that company. The assets transferred by Wren, the Codys and Leith included freehold premises, distilling plant and machinery in Joshua Bros' former establishment in Port Melbourne. There was a clause in the agreement allowing the Codys, Wren and Leith to transfer their shares to 'a new company to be called CWL Ltd'.[50] The acronym CWL stood for Cody, Wren and Leith. CWL Pty Ltd eventually became a holding company for their stakes in Federal Distilleries and the *Courier-Mail*. In September 1929 Federal Distilleries Pty Ltd was marketing such products as Old Court whisky, Brind's gin and Crystal Court gin.

A new joint venture company, United Distillers Proprietary Ltd, was incorporated in October 1930. The joint venture shareholders were the Distillers Company of Edinburgh and the original shareholders of Federal Distilleries Pty Ltd. To complete the restructure, United Distillers Proprietary Ltd then acquired all the shares of Federal Distilleries Pty Ltd, which then became United Distillers operating company.

Pastoralist Benjamin Chaffey of the famous irrigation family became chairman of the United Distillers Board. P. F. Cody, but not Wren, became a director. Wren also stepped down as director of Federal Distilleries, on the board which the great Australian test cricket captain, Warwick Armstrong, then joined. Federal Distilleries continued to make good profits in the mid-1930s, no doubt assisted by favourable budget decisions such as the remission of customs and excise duty on Australian whisky and spirits in 1933.

According to J. F. Wren a feud developed in the early 1930s between producers of Scotch and Australian whisky, with the former endeavouring to give the Australian product 'a bad name' by 'sending agents into bars to disparage Corio whisky, Old Court etc'. His father, he said, offered £500 on one occasion if it could be proved that these whiskies were not 'of the purest'. Wren was prickly, as this story attests:

> being personally unqualified [as a teetotaller] to sample the product, [Wren] got a number of empty whisky bottles of every known brand and filled them all with Old Court. He then invited several whisky fanciers to try out his various 'samples'. Most forthrightly rejected the Old Court bottle's contents, but approved in varying degrees, the rest. After they left, Wren commented to Dick Lean Snr: 'You know, Mr Lean, they don't know what they are talking about'.[51]

Nonetheless, Old Court did not become a commercial success. In 1929 the Scullin government put tariffs on imported spirits, for which Wren had lobbied intensively.[52]

At his death in 1953, Wren had scrip for 197,309 shares in CWL in his safe, as well as scrip for a number of shares in Brinds Ltd, Northern Australian Breweries Ltd , Great Northern Brewery and Melbourne Co-operative Brewery Ltd.

Food and produce

Wren was a minor initial shareholder in Maize Products Pty Ltd (registered in Victoria on 21 November 1912), which produced glucose and household brands such as Kream Cornflower, Columbia Maizena, Nutro Oil and Dandy Starch. The major allotment went to the illustrious confectioner MacPherson Robertson (who in 1934, Victoria's centenary year, provided an endowment of £100,000 for a girls' high school, a bridge in Toorak, a national herbarium and a fountain near the Shrine of Remembrance). In September 1913 Maize Products had twenty-three shareholders of whom Wren was the equal-fifteenth largest. Other confectioners and biscuit makers involved were A. W. Allen, Frederick Brockhoff and, in 1917, Lesley Arnott. David Robertson, MacPherson's son, was also a substantial shareholder.[53] Maize Products was boosted when the First World War cut off glucose supplies to Australia. Within a short time the company was supplying all the glucose required by Australian confectioners.[54] Wren was on friendly terms with MacPherson Robertson, who enjoyed attending boxing at the Stadium, sometimes in his company. They had certain similarities: both lived unpretentious, rather plain personal lives; both were non-smokers and teetotal; both enjoyed sport and physical fitness; both were philanthropists and supporters of trade unions.[55]

Maize Products went into voluntary liquidation in 1920, to be reconstructed in June 1920 with the same name and all former assets. There are no obvious signs of Wren's active involvement after 1920. However, after his death in 1953, 4,575 Maize Product shares were found in his safe. Of these, 3,000 were in the name of David Robertson. There was a declaration of trust indicating that they were held for John Wren as 'executor of Arthur Wren, who left them to JW'; another 850 were in the names of H. W. Buckley and F. M. Robinson (declaration dated 24 January 1950); and another 725 shares in the name of David Robertson (declaration dated 18 January 1950). More research may ascertain what dealings Wren had with David Robertson.

Wren became involved in the manufacture and sale of compressed yeast n 1928. With P. F. Cody and two other partners he acquired the sole Australasian rights to the processes of Jean Effront and Ivan-Aug Effront of France and Belgium respectively. They transferred their rights to Effront Yeast Company Pty Ltd in exchange for 20,000 £1 shares. The agreement also provided for the company to pay a royalty based on the selling price of the compressed yeast sold. The vendors were entitled to purchase at a nominal charge 'all pure yeast cultures from time to time required'. Secrecy clauses concerning manufacture processes were written into the contract. Major shareholders in late 1928 were Wren and Cody. (One interesting early shareholder was solicitor H. E. Cohen, an 'establishment' figure with a distinguished military and legal background.) Wren and Cody were two of the three initial directors. In 1962 Effront became the Yeast Company of Australasia Pty Ltd, which became by February 1965 a subsidiary of Mauri Brothers and Thompson. It was wound up in November 1965.[56]

Whether Morrison's Outdoor Catering Pty Ltd was started by Wren is unclear. It was incorporated in New South Wales in May 1940 with a share capital of £2,500 divided into 2,400 shares of £1 each. The company's letterhead described it as 'official' caterers to Randwick Racecourse, Warwick Farm Racecourse, Sydney Cricket Ground, Sydney Sports Ground, Harold Park Racecourse and Menangle Park. The major shareholders were Wren's second son, Anthony, and J. Goldstein. Correspondence from their accountant refers to the company being essentially Goldstein's after Anthony's death in 1946. Goldstein sought to buy shares held by Anthony's estate in order to treat the firm 'as a family concern', but the Wren estate initially resisted. Because Morrison's was heavily dependent on gaining contracts each year, there was always a risk of failure if one did not eventuate. Presumably Wren had exerted some influence in gaining the initial contract.

Involvement in Australian Food Exporters Ltd (AFEX) was a 'disaster' according to J. F. Wren,[57] and 'an absolute disaster' according to Ray Betts. Registered in August 1948 the company's initial subscribers were Wren, P. F. Cody, P. A. Trouchet (an importer) and an American exporter, L. B. Harford. A surviving report by Trouchet, who was not actively involved, shows that AFEX was involved in shipping frozen and whole cooked crayfish to the United States. He refers to 'our fleet of catcher boats' and to the company's having premises in South Australia, apparently at Port McDonnell and Robe. Ray Betts speaks of 'a processing boat' in South Australia, and 'a very expensive plant for prawn processing at Tweed Heads in Queensland [NSW]'.[58] The results were disappointing. However, in 1960, after Wren's death, AFEX seems to have become an investment company. It was placed in voluntary liquidation in December 1973. Final accounts in 1974 showed investments in approximately fifty leading public companies. Criterion Theatres Pty Ltd (a Wren family company) took the bulk of the distribution of over £1,000,000, with Wren family members getting the rest.[59]

Miscellaneous

'Of all John Wren's extraordinarily diverse interests', wrote Philip Derriman, 'this one was the most unlikely of all—a women's hair products company called Marigny'. Marigny Services Pty Ltd, registered in July 1928, dealt in hairdressing appliances and accessories, electric torches, gramophone records, camera attachments, silk and woollen goods, furs, wigs etc. It also became known as The Realistic Company of Australasia Pty Ltd, and as Lancome Marigny Pty Ltd. A hairdressing salon run by a director, René Henri (or Henry), was part of the operation; it was situated in the Manchester Unity Building, 220–226 Collins Street. Henri became involved some time in the late 1930s or early 1940s. P. F. Cody became a director on 30 December 1940, while J. F. Wren was made manager of Marigny A'asia Pty Ltd and eventually took Cody's place on the board on 3 December 1953.[60] Derriman continues:

> Wren owned a large part of the company, but after his son assumed the position of manager, he took no further interest in it, beyond attending the monthly directors' meeting.
>
> 'In the early days, I never had much to report,' his son says.
>
> However, the business prospered eventually, and to a large extent this was because of an initiative taken while John F. Wren was away serving in the RAAF during World War Two.
>
> A chemist from another Wren company obtained some of the 'cold wave' hair products which American service women brought to Australia with them, analysed them, discovered their ingredients and developed similar formulas.
>
> It is easy to imagine John Wren himself engineering such a ruse, but there is no evidence he had anything to do with it.
>
> Armed with his American cold-wave formulas, Marigny was a jump ahead of its competitors at the end of the war. It opened factories in Melbourne, Adelaide and Perth to make the new products, and it ran classes for hairdressers all over Australia to show them how they should be used.
>
> Eventually the company employed 350 people and when it was

> taken over by L'Oreal of Paris in the mid-1970s the Wrens and other shareholders received £28 for each £1 share.
>
> John F. Wren remained in control of Marigny ... but after his father's death he had to divide his time between the company and the other Wren interests.[61]

Another unlikely interest was the Clunes Knitting Mill. According to *Truth* (April 1930), seven locals in 1922, including Sir Alexander Peacock of Creswick, twice premier of Victoria, formed the Clunes Knitting and Manufacturing Company Ltd. Clunes was 'a decayed mining town' and 'the knitting mills were planned to give the girls, goats and geese something to do'. Business people, farmers and labourers subscribed. In 1924 Wren and Sugar Roberts became involved. (*Truth* erroneously described Roberts as Wren's brother-in-law.) Gradually the Roberts family gained control, with Sugar becoming 'governing director'. In April 1930 Clunes Underwear Mills Pty Ltd purchased the assets of the older company which went into liquidation. The initial directors were Wren, Roberts, William Angas (bread manufacturer of Clifton Hill and Mayor of Collingwood) and T. J. Smith, 'a master carrier' of Malvern, a suburb of Melbourne. About a dozen people, including Wren, received early share allotments, and of the 5,662 shares issued a large number were held by residents of Clunes and Daylesford.

In May 1931 the company resolved to move to Daylesford, to begin operations before 31 December. It changed to public limited liability status as Clunes Underwear Mills Ltd, and to 30 June 1931 only £63 profit was declared. Roberts lamented the 'keen competition that reduced prices as well as having to contend with increased costs of purchases through heavy duties and exchanges'. They had to 'curtail operations through limited capital'. In December 1932 the share list showed thirty-seven shareholders still employed. Wren still had 250 shares. In 1933 a loss of £2,265 was declared, while subscribed capital was still £5,622. The State Bank of Victoria, on 8 February 1934, recorded the following minute:

> Consideration was given to a request by Clunes Underwear that the [Commissioners of the Bank] release the stock and book debts from their mortgage to engage Mr John Wren, a director of the company, to obtain security for his guarantee of the company's o/d

> [overdraft] of £1,750, the Co pointing out that in December 1931 the [Commissioners] were agreeable to a release of those assets for that purpose. It was decided that the request could not now be granted as the circumstances of the company had so materially changed since the previous request was made, the loss on last year's trading having been £2,265.[62]

In April 1936 a general meeting held in Melbourne wound up the company.[63]

Wren had 750 shares in Geelong Theatres Ltd in his safe when he died. There is no record of this at the Public Record Office of Victoria. Also, he had 1,000 preferential shares in Ice Skating Palais Ltd (NSW). In addition to the Criterion and, at one stage, two nearby hotels in Sydney, Wren with the Cody family controlled Connell's in Elizabeth Street, Melbourne, and the New Treasury Hotel in Spring Street opposite Parliament House—and, of course, Jack Dyer's pub in Port Melbourne and the Rose Hotel in Fitzroy, in which he placed Bervyn Woods. It is probable that Wren had interests in other hotels with the Cody family.

At the time of his death, Wren's safe held—in addition to the shareholdings already mentioned—scrip relating to a large number of share parcels of various quantities in a diverse range of private and public companies. As before, it is not possible to determine whether he had any influence or involvement in these companies other than as a passive investor.

One intriguing question is why Wren put various parcels of his own shares in other people's safes. When asked, his accountant Betts replied: 'It was simply to keep his affairs and how much wealth he had, private—not to dodge tax or any other reason—he trusted people. Had to.'[64]

Wren's probate

Wren's will was lodged for probate in Victoria on 22 October 1954. As reported, his Victorian estate alone comprised £25,168 realty and £978,779 personally, included Studley House, valued at £19,695—that is, £1,003,947 in all. It is not possible to determine whether or not his assets were distributed to family members and associates in the years prior to his death. In those days, estate and gift duty minimisation schemes, utilising lawful albeit artificially elaborate legal devices, were in vogue for wealthy members of the community to protect the assets of their estates from Commonwealth and state estate duties levied on the value of the estate at the time of death. (These duties were finally abolished in the late 1970s.) If this practice had been followed in Wren's case, and taking into account the major donations to various charities, individuals and organisations made by him during his lifetime, it is probable that his total assets would have substantially exceeded the amount held by his estate at the time of his death.

CHAPTER TWENTY-ONE

A Literary Hoodlum

Sensation

JOHN WREN PASSED his seventy-ninth birthday with no reason to fear the assault on his character that would soon occur when *Power Without Glory* began to circulate in April 1950—at least nothing worse that Stan Keon's strictures of 1948. His involvement in proprietary sport had been whittled down; his entrepreneurial and financial affairs continued to prosper but were unexceptionable and less conspicuous. He had cut his patronage of Labor politicians, he was avoided by both John Cain and his supporters and by industrial groupers in Victoria; federally, he had voted for Menzies and his successful coalition in the previous December. Old associates such as Frank Anstey, Sugar Roberts, Frank Lawrence, Tom Tunnecliffe and Albert Dunstan were dead. Keon and his supporters were running Richmond.

Nellie Wren's concern, as always, was her family. There were sorrows that had to be borne. Of her nine children, one had not survived infancy, Xavier had not reached three, and in recent years the boisterous Anthony and sophisticated Elinor had died. Mercifully, Margaret had survived the war in Germany and with her two children was in Dublin, having shed her obnoxious husband. Mary, the former live-wire 'Titian beauty', still in her early forties, was married and seemed settled in England, where she saw no more of the solicitous Evatts. Angela was at home and fragile. John Francis and Joseph were steady citizens immersed in business, the law, golf and the Collingwood Football Club. Nothing in Nellie's pious life suggested the sort of Lady Chatterley adultery that Hardy had been concocting for her. Her husband had not been a philanderer but a staid Edwardian—not negligent so much but, as Hackett SJ had said, dull and preoccupied with his business affairs.[1] Hardy's allegation that Nellie had been kept at Studley House under duress has been refuted not only by family and friends but by newspaper reports of her accompanying her husband to official functions.[2] The indulgence of her voyage overseas in 1931–2 hardly suggests ostracism at home.

Nellie's calm refusal to protest against Hardy's salacious defamation, except in legal terms, and John's downright contempt satisfied their friends but did not abate the sniggering prurience of their accusers.

Genesis

Pauline Armstrong has demonstrated in her study *Frank Hardy and the Making of* Power Without Glory that, after 'A close examination of the facts and chronology … the genesis of the novel … must be attributed to Ted Hill and Ralph Gibson and other members of the CPA [Communist Party of Australia].' According to Cedric Ralph, a credible leading communist lawyer, Victorian secretary Ted Hill, 'a master of the offensive', had in the 1940s become increasingly concerned at attacks by Catholic Action on his party's influence in the trade unions. He believed that the campaign was being financed by Wren, allegedly to the tune of £50,000 in the first instance. Ted Hill was a grim ideologue. His brother, Jim Hill, had jeopardised Australian troops in the Second World War by passing classified information to the USSR (which passed it on to Japan). Later, with Stalinism discredited, Ted Hill founded in 1962 a Maoist [Marxist–Leninist] breakaway party.

Ted Hill apparently conceived the anti-Wren project. He discussed it with fellow party executive member Ralph Gibson, who remained an unregenerate Stalinist even into the 1980s. With a Master of Arts from the University of Manchester, Gibson was regarded as 'a formidable researcher' and so became overseer of the project. He was obsessed with the idea that the Victorian premier, Albert Dunstan, was John Wren's puppet. Wren's name was being mentioned in connection with then-current controversies involving milk distribution and proprietary racing. Wren was topical. Les Barnes, secretary and leader of the Tom

Mann Society, 'a kind of labour historical society', had been Gibson's first choice as writer, but declined. He says:

> Gibson suggested the book should be written on the lines of Upton Sinclair, an American writer; it should tell the truth but use names close to people. The truth should be such that the people would not be game to take court action.

If they did, their allegedly evil deeds would endure a blaze of publicity.[3]

The scope of the research for *Power Without Glory* has been exaggerated. With some people, as Les Barnes seemed prepared to admit, this was due to naivety; with others, such as Hardy, both that and dishonesty are apparent. Hardy gives the impression that it was an enormous task. Barnes says he was invited to undertake research until someone with the necessary ability was found to write the book. When Hardy returned from the war 'we had the bloke ... He had the guts, the resourcefulness, the ruthlessness. He was a real scoundrel.' Barnes says that for two years he worked for three or four hours a day with Hardy's wife at the State Library. Having got as far as 1922, they went no further, but 'various others' helped with 'the rest of the book'. Meanwhile 'Frank was running around doing all the cheeky work. He was capable of anything, Frank. He'd lie, cheat, he'd do anything.'[4]

Apparently, collaborators, among them Ted Hill, contributed much more to *Power Without Glory* than Hardy acknowledged. Paul Gray cites a Melbourne academic, Dr June Hearn, who maintains that 'A lot of people from the Communist Party contributed to it and there was a strong feeling of joint ownership of it ... There was a lot of recrimination when Frank Hardy took all the credit for it.'[5] However, Armstrong is convinced that the novel is basically Hardy's. He certainly showed extraordinary resourcefulness in getting it published by 1950.

Compulsive lying

The Melbourne *Age* of 1 March 2003 informed readers that 'the legacy of ... *Power Without Glory* still lingers' in a forthcoming publication on Frank Hardy which would include 'a key to all the identities of the characters'. Such a glossary was circulating even in 1950 and has been published before, but in an international socialist magazine. The new publisher, Ian Syson, former editor of *Overland*, says that 'he isn't worried about libel. Everyone's been afraid to publish it [in Australia] in the past but I think everyone's dead now.' In other words, *Power Without Glory* should continue to be accepted as basically historical fact. According to Syson, *Power Without Glory* 'tells a *history* that no one else seemed prepared to record, of the betrayal of the labor movement, Labor Party and working-class Australians by a self-regarding gangster [emphasis added].[6]

Without directly rebutting Hardy's every allegation, this book has been mostly concerned to present what even non-exhaustive research can reveal about John Wren. The most serious allegations cannot be by-passed, but something must be said about what can only be called Hardy's compulsive lying.

Throughout his life, Hardy boasted that he drew strength and wisdom from being a proletarian, a 'battler from the bush'. He told his champion, the communist polymath, Jack Lindsay,[7] about his 'family's sufferings' and how his own father, Tom Hardy, had to move 'from place to place, working in milk and butter factories'. This puzzled not only persons who knew the Hardy family[8] but, it would seem, members of his family, as their father had been a 'dairy inspector'. On 7 October 1983 an article appeared in the Melbourne *Herald* entitled 'Hardy declares war on poverty'. He said he had a feeling against injustice that went back to his childhood in the Depression in Melbourne, when his family had been twice evicted before he was eight [that is, in 1925, four years before the Depression began]: 'I had to leave home when I was 13 because my dad couldn't get the dole with me at home'. On 6 November Frank's eldest sibling, Jim, replied:

> We were never evicted from any house we lived in. My brother did not leave home so my father could get the dole. There was no reason. Our father never lost a day's work in his working life. He worked for only two companies, Nestles at Dennington [near Warrnambool] and Federal Milk Co-op, Bacchus Marsh, over a period of 34 years. Father retired in 1942 due to illness. He died of cancer in 1943, in his fifties.

And, as Frank himself remarked: 'Ironically he died … in the Hospice for the Dying [Caritas Christi] which Wren had built for the church and which stood opposite Wren's house'.[9]

Frank tried to represent his father as a paragon of working-class solidarity, whereas his mother Winifred's brothers had opposed her marriage to Tom Hardy because he was 'a hard man on farmers', something of a boss's man in effect. Jim Hardy also denies that his father was merely 'a non-practising convert to Catholicism' as Frank claimed.[10] Clearly, Frank is, unreliable, even when talking of his own family.

In an article published soon after Hardy's death, Paul Gray described his siblings as 'well-educated, cultured people', with all eight children having 'a full Catholic education'.[11] In one official document Frank claimed to have been educated to sub-intermediate standard (Year 9).[12] The Hardys were a vivacious, even theatrical, family. Among them was Mary Hardy, described as 'Melbourne's highest rating radio personality (on 3AW), winner of seven of TV's Logies and award winning theatre performer'.[13] Margaret (Peg) studied piano and 'qualified at the Conservatorium with very good results. Later she had her own band.' Jim Hardy was, after the war, a professional entertainer and wrote his own songs. Not surprisingly, 'Frank claimed he wrote Jim's songs which he later sang in Hollywood. Jim said he wrote his own songs and … never went to Hollywood.'[14] Lying seems to have come easily to Frank. As Paul Gray's caption put it: 'Master illusionist: unable to tell the truth, Hardy's talent lay in creating Hardy myths'.

Hardy told varying stories about the age at which he had to leave school and his hard and bitter adolescence during the Depression. As he is his only witness, his hard luck yarns cannot be relied upon. He claimed to have done casual work 'in and around Bacchus Marsh in the milk factory, digging potatoes, picking tomatoes and fruit; for a short time he managed a store where apples were packed'.[15] It is unlikely that he ever was, as he romanced, too poor to buy a newspaper.[16] After the war his only engagement in full-time proletarian work came in 1953–4 when, almost certainly by arrangement with the communist-led Seamen's Union, he signed on to several ships, presumably for some three months' ennobling experience. Toil, however, was not to his liking. He was unpopular—a 'hygiene hazard', according to the crew, because he stayed in his cabin all day. He was 'a super snip' because 'he'd put the "bite" on anyone and everyone', and wrote 'dud cheques which covered the land' and for a while were honoured by his trusting comrades. When employed as a coal-trimmer, he was known as Norman von Nida, the champion golfer, because he was 'never caught in the bunkers'. He discharged himself within a month.[17]

While trying to avoid stagnation in Bacchus Marsh as the Depression rolled on, Hardy did a correspondence course in commercial art and in 1938 left for Melbourne (80 kilometres away) to work for the *Radio Times* as a cartoonist and advertising salesman. In May 1940, in St Patrick's Cathedral, Melbourne, Hardy married Rosslyn Couper, who converted for the occasion to Catholicism and with whom he had three children.[18] Later that year he joined the Communist Party, and would seem to have ended any affiliation with the Catholic Church. As a result of the pact in August 1939 between Germany and the USSR, Hardy, as a communist, opposed the anti-Nazi war which broke out in September. He viewed it as an 'inter-imperialist' conflict, until Germany invaded the USSR in June 1941. Then it became patriotic to join the armed services. He did not enlist as he pretended, but waited to be called up in March 1942, and joined the AIF in May 1943.[19] Hardy had a comfortable war, never leaving Australia.

His friend and obituarist Clement Semmler, a former general manager of the Australian Broadcasting Commission, edited an anthology entitled *A Frank Hardy Swag*. Semmler believed that Hardy had been an autodidactic prodigy who 'after leaving school at 13 began an amazing feat of self-education ... [so that] by the scope of his later reading he could quote from Joseph Conrad, James Joyce and the great Russian novelists'.[20] However, of the time when *Power Without Glory* was being written, the *Age* book reviewer Ian Mair, himself a communist, recalled that 'Frank was so illiterate; his writing so shallow, bloody awful, and he was an unreliable writer. Frank did not understand the world of literature.'[21] Hardy persuaded Semmler that during the subsequent trial he was kept in Pentridge gaol for a considerable period. In fact, he was remanded once—not at Pentridge, and overnight. *Power Without Glory* preceded his grovelling book, *Journey into the Future*, published after a profitable trip in 1952 to the USSR—which he found to be the most democratic state in the world, where Joseph Stalin was an heroic, benign leader and there were no gulags. Later he said it was the 'only dishonest book' he ever wrote. He must have forgotten *Power Without Glory*.

Criminal libel

The blaze of publicity prescribed by Upton Sinclair came when Hardy was charged with criminal libel, on the information not of John Wren but of his wife Nellie. Credible allegations have been made that Wren could have prevented publication by paying £100,000 to a president of the Communist Party of Australia, Lance Sharkey[22] or, as Hardy 'strongly believed', Ted Hill. When it suited Hardy to ingratiate himself, he praised Hill for 'his air of tremendous strength … that inspires to greater fortitude' but later, when he no longer needed him and had read a little psychology, he referred to Hill as 'a psychotic personality with delusions of grandeur and paranoid tendencies—and a dangerous fanatic and blackmailer … a capricious and disloyal man'.[23] Wren's eldest son, John F. Wren, said that when his father's associate, Sir Gilbert Dyett, president of the Returned Services League, brought the book to him, Wren looked at a few pages, dismissed it as 'a lot of rot' and tossed it in the waste-paper basket. (Perhaps he opened it at the page where he and Archbishop 'Malone' (Mannix) are alleged to be involved in stock rustling from a state-run agency with the cognisance of the Queensland premier and future treasurer, recognisable as E. G. Theodore). Both his then living sons, who seem to have known little of their father's reputation, felt that 'he could stand up for himself and that he was not too concerned about it'.

However, they were particularly outraged by the portrayal of their mother as an adulteress. She was 'Nellie West', who has a liaison with a bricklayer, 'Bill Evans' (Egan). He was a lookalike of William S. Hart, the heart-throb film star of the time. 'Evans' was employed to renovate the 'West' mansion in 1917. By him she conceives a child. who is given the unmistakably Catholic name 'Xavier'. Discovering this, her husband assaults her, ostracises her within the family, ignores 'Xavier' and rejoices in his death as a 'child'. As Nellie Wren did bear a child called Xavier, who died aged three in 1922, there could be no mistaking who 'Nellie West' was meant to be, especially as so much carefully collected detail in the novel pointed to the Wren ménage. Until then, Nellie Wren had enjoyed an unblemished, genial reputation. When sent anonymously a copy of the book, she said she was 'disgusted by the novel, it was too absurd to be taken seriously', and she burned it. However, when it was explained to her that *Power Without Glory* was part of a subversive communist plot, she was persuaded to place her name on an information sheet seeking justice against Hardy. His assault on Archbishop Mannix, whom she knew well, would have been especially offensive to her.[24]

The general import of the charge does not mean that literary critic John McLaren is correct in this analysis:

> Hardy's real offence was that he showed government not as a contest between differing views settled by periodic arbitration of a democratic electorate, but as an interlocking series of conspiracies by powerful men furthering their own interests. The full weight of the law had therefore to be brought to bear lest this distorted view should corrupt the populace and destroy their confidence in democracy and their chosen leaders ... Jack Galbally [Nellie Wren's lawyer] virtually admitted this at the preliminary hearing when he argued that not only was the book 'a wicked libel' but also that it was a 'Communist conspiracy against the government' and that 'it defames the parliament, the Church and the Judiciary'.[25]

Galbally did entail all those things, but they were a secondary concern, obligatory forensic rhetoric irresistible to a blustering prosecution—an extra indictment as far as the Wrens were concerned. Without the ascription of adultery, however, no indictment would have been made. McLaren imputes too much power to Hardy's writing. In conservative circles he was rightly regarded as a hack, useful for trampling Wren, Mannix and Labor, but nothing to fear: Mickey Spillane in politics. Galbally MLC was a family friend of the Wrens, a former player for their cherished Collingwood Football Club; his education was alleged to have been partly paid for by Wren, who was also said to have put him into parliament. He too revered Mrs Wren and was outraged by Hardy's slander. It was Galbally who advised the criminal libel charge. There would have been little satisfaction in a civil suit, as Hardy, a man of straw, had no money. 'It was not a hasty decision to take action against Hardy', said John F. Wren: 'We talked it out thoroughly beforehand. We knew it was going to be very nasty.'[26]

It is leftist melodrama to suggest that something called the 'establishment' was showing 'the lengths to which it would go in using legal processes to prevent any questioning of its authority'.[27] Indeed some parts of the 'establishment' may well have contributed to Hardy's defence. Hardy maintained that a win at the races financed the publication of *Power Without Glory* but, as affirmed by Les Barnes, he was a notorious liar. The secretary of the Victorian branch of the Communist

Party said it had given Hardy a loan of £100, which was never repaid in spite of the book's lucrative royalties.[28] That loan (or gift, as it turned out) is undoubted, and there was more. McLaren says that 'the source of the funds for *Power Without Glory*, remains a mystery to this day'. But perhaps not altogether. George Seelaf, secretary of the Amalgamated Meat Industry Employees' (or Butchers') Union, Hardy's confidant, who facilitated his research and writing by giving him a sinecure on his union's journal, told McLaren that the money for the trial came from 'wealthy supporters'. Seelaf had told Hardy 'not to worry—or ask questions' about the source of the defence counsel fees. They would arrive each day. Seelaf also admitted that 'motivated by their anti-Catholicism, the Masons'—who should be 'establishment' enough—helped to collect evidence against Wren.[29]

Why not money too? The radical columnist Philip Adams, in an article 'Beware the moral crusaders', reported 'a theory' that Hardy 'had been fed material from sources not a hundred miles from the Melbourne Club with the specific intention of wrecking the Labor Party'.[30] One not-unreasonable guess about sources of both evidence and money would be the Loyalist and Protestant bigots funded by magnates like Herbert Brookes. Born of an Ulster mother, this wealthy son-in-law of Alfred Deakin and adviser to conservative governments had been outraged by the Sinn Feinism of Mannix during the First World War. He had demanded the Irish prelate's deportation. He wrote in 1918 that 'the work of my later life' would be the destruction of the influence of Mannix (which then meant Wren too):

> I have arranged to be released from business affairs except for a screen. I can serve best ... by keeping in the background. I will give half my working life to the work. I will contribute in money as much as the three most generous contributions per annum in their cause ... [31]

In collaboration with the general secretary of the Victorian Protestant Federation and the Freemason Grand Chaplain, Rev. Walter Albiston,[32] Brookes produced the *Vigilant*, which was, wrote his nephew by marriage Rohan Rivett, 'to wage an unceasing and unrelenting campaign of denunciation, exposure and hostility against the Archbishop, his principal aides and supporters, and such wealthy and colourful associates as John Wren’. Even in the 1950s the *Vigilant* ‘went into 12,000 Protestant homes, including a high proportion of Australia’s parsonages, every week of the year’.[3]’ had been one headline under which Wren was excoriated for defending a certain harmless German priest, Fr Jerger, from deportation.[34] The *Vigilant* even defended the American Ku Klux Klan (KKK), which was anti-negro, anti-Jewish and anti-Catholic: ‘This organisation is opposing the most cunning, deceitful and persistent enemy that Americanism and Protestant Christianity has ever faced—the Jesuits’. The KKK was not a ‘murderous’ organisation, wrote Albiston. However, he was ‘not directly advocating KKK in Australia—at present’, he said.[35]

Albiston had a fitting ally in T. E. Ruth of the Collins Street Independent Church, who because of his self-styled ‘red hot addresses’ was provided with a bodyguard ‘in case Mannix partisans should assault him’. In the 1930s he called Eric Campbell’s pre-fascist New Guard ‘these young men of the dawn’.[36] Brookes also poured money and time into secret armies to deal, if the need arose, with socialist subversion in the 1920s and no doubt later, but it would hardly surprise if Seelaf and his unscrupulous friends milked this source for their assault on the Labor Party. Seelaf told McLaren that ‘the full story of the publication and trial … will never be told. Part of it … was confidential between himself and others now dead, but he was pledged to take the secret with him to his grave.’[37] Unless there were discreditable reasons, there was no need to be so secretive.

While the Communist Party of Australia (CPA) could hardly have planned the publication of *Power Without Glory* to coincide with the Menzies government’s Communist Party Dissolution Act, it understandably grasped advantage from its timing to link the Hardy prosecution with this unprecedented attack on Australian civil liberties. Liberal Party leader, R. G. Menzies, had defeated Labor in November 1949 after a period of industrial turmoil in which communist-led unions had played a militant role. Even the Labor government had that year gaoled union leaders and sent troops into the coal mines to break strikes. The Cold War was at its peak. Internationally, Mao Zedong had led communists to power in China in late 1949; and the Korean War, in which Australia wholeheartedly supported the United Nations force, was being waged from July 1950 to 1953. The Communist Party Dissolution Bill was brought down by Menzies in 1950 and became law on 20 October

1950, only to be thrown out as *ultra vires* by a 6 to1 majority of the High Court on 9 March 1951, on the grounds of its impact on civil liberties and property rights. Another electoral victory in May 1951 was supposed to give Menzies a mandate for his policy, and a referendum to decide the issue was to be held on 22 September. Although in March, Gallup polls had over 70 per cent supporting Menzies, on voting day the referendum was defeated by less than half a per cent, thanks to a relentless civil liberties campaign by the new Labor leader, Dr H. V. Evatt. It was in this atmosphere that Hardy's trial took place.

Although some copies of *Power Without Glory* had been available as early as April 1950, the official launch occurred on 4 August, and from then it gained the attention of press and public. On 29 September Hardy addressed a meeting organised by the Arts Council in conjunction with the Realist Writers Group. The subject was 'Why I Wrote *Power Without Glory*'. The following day the *Age* reported this extract:

> 'Our man John West was ready made', said Mr Hardy, 'I could not have invented him. I have never invented a character in my life.'
>
> 'A man asked me recently who the characters actually were. He did not believe me when I replied that they all came out of my head, and I don't believe anyone here does either.' (Laughter.)[38]

This was three weeks before the Dissolution Act became law. Two days later Hardy was visited by two detectives, and on 25 October he was arrested. Why had he been so provocative? Armstrong offers this explanation:

> The time was certainly ripe for the CPA to remove itself from the spotlight by pulling a rabbit out of the hat … If the CPA had a martyr it could build an even more effective national campaign against the … Act … Apart from the possibility that Hardy had overplayed his address … due to alcohol or excitement, there were three likely scenarios: the address was a carefully conceived plan by the CPA and Hardy to force the Wren family to take legal action; Hardy had made a private decision to become a working-class writer/martyr; or the CPA had, for its own purposes, encouraged Hardy to be provocative without warning him of the possible consequences.[39]

Hardy spent one night in the City Watchhouse on remand. Next day he was released on £500 bail, which was provided by a wealthy CPA member, Mrs A. M. (Molly) Inge of elite Tintern Avenue, Toorak. They 'left the court arm in arm, and posed for photographers'.[40] The Frank Hardy Defence Committee was formed. It included noted writers and unionists. It raised money by selling *Power Without Glory* at meetings, together with a glossary of identifications. It made good use of the time before the committal (or preliminary hearing), which was adjourned from 5 December to 15 January. Hardy was then committed for trial which, after some appeals, took place from 12 to 16 June 1951.

The trial

The key issue, said the well-mannered prosecutor, (Sir) Henry Winneke, later chief justice and governor of Victoria, in his opening address, was whether any reasonable person who knew Ellen Wren would identify her with 'Nellie West'. The defence agreed, but wanted the Crown to prove that the words were calculated to cause a breach of the peace. The crotchety judge, Mr Justice Martin, who had in 1946 sentenced novelist Robert Close to three months gaol for an 'obscene libel', disallowed this.

Hardy's defence was that he was creating 'composite' characters, part fiction, part drawn from life—'as in all historical novels', he was to say later.[41] Yet it was never asked why, in that case, the identities had to be so unmistakably close or how the glossary of identifications emerged so spontaneously. His argument amounted to this: the composite characterisations are meant to be recognisable as real people when not *legally* defamatory, but should be regarded as *fictional* when they are. The prosecution's argument, which should have been sufficiently cogent in this case, was that if personal and familial circumstances alleged to be fiction point beyond a reasonable doubt (the burden of proof required in criminal cases) to living persons, who are then accused of criminal or disreputable conduct which cannot be proven or is not published in the public interest, a criminal libel has been committed. There could be no 'public interest' in the legal sense in pillorying the septuagenarian Nellie Wren for adultery allegedly committed almost four decades before. But there was public interest of a different, both prurient and prejudicial, sort.

While the case has been described as 'a seemingly watertight prosecution that had no hope of succeeding',[42] this does not allow sufficiently for the skill of defence counsel Donald Campbell KC. Noted for his abrasive, relentless cross-examinations and Scots burr, and a polio victim from childhood, he elicited sympathy for his inability to walk without sticks and his ability to display them on cue. He was a friend of Ted Hill.[43] One of Wren's legal advisers, Peter Norris, said that 'Donnie Campbell didn't mind getting into the gutter and behaved that way'.[44] He relished the attack on Catholicism in *Power Without Glory.* During the trial Justice Martin kept muttering to the shorthand writers beside him, 'I have to watch this Campbell'.[45] His junior was the future 'peerless advocate' and Supreme Court justice (Sir) John Starke, who believed that Campbell had suggested his appointment as junior counsel in breach of bar rules. In 1992 Starke reflected that his elevation to the bench in 1964 was due to premier Bolte's determination to get rid of 'a nuisance at the bloody Bar'. In an interview on ABC radio in 1992, he said that he was a frequenter of illegal SP bookmakers, could not stand a female secretary in court, especially if she 'wasn't very attractive', and thought he 'never was ... much of a bloody lawyer' but had the 'flair' for advocacy, particularly in front of juries. 'You've got to bloody well have an urge to win',[46] he said. The legal profession was not at its choicest either on bench or at bar.

Because of his politics and swagger, the defence barristers had little respect for Hardy, and Starke recalled that Campbell wisely said to him:

> 'Hardy, my fees and Jack Starke's fees [£200 *per diem*] are to be paid to our clerk at 10 o'clock each morning of the trial.' Hardy looked a bit taken aback. He said, 'And what will happen if they're not, Mr Campbell?' 'Oh,' he said, 'don't you worry Hardy, don't worry at all. On that day Starkey and I won't be appearing for you.' The fees were paid at 10 o'clock every morning, I can tell you that. [47]

Campbell and Starke knew their only chance of success was to ensure that the jury would become aware of the substance of Hardy's allegations against Wren, and that meant exposure to *Power Without Glory*, which since Hardy's committal had been removed from bookshop sale. That was the only way Hardy could get bail. Starke later said of the committal proceedings:

> We had a pretty weak magistrate ... and we were front page news all over Australia. Campbell got in, one way or another, every piece of

> roguery we could lay our hands on, and there was plenty of it, against old man Wren and it was all published in the papers.[48]

The defence knew that, although most of this material would not be admitted at the trial, every juryman would have read it at least through the newspapers. At the trial Campbell badgered the judge into allowing pertinent excerpts from the book to be read so that the jury was reminded—'in a big way', said Starke—that Wren was believed to have a serious criminal background. In fact, Campbell wanted *Power Without Glory* read in its entirety.

Summing up at the end of the trial, Winneke appealed to the jury 'to put your mother or your sister in the same position' as Ellen Wren 'and see how you like it ... A scurrilous, scandalous libel of the grossest kind had been committed'. Not so, argued Campbell; the case was 'not an issue of truth or falsity' but whether the author referred to real or fictitious characters. Why were the Wrens not called by the Crown? Why have they remained 'the shadowiest of the shadowiest'? Because, said Campbell, they would have been forced to admit that they did not believe 'Nellie West' and Ellen Wren were identical. But in any event, he argued, changing tack, even if an identification was intended, the book depicted 'a good moral and religious woman driven to adultery by the nefarious conduct of her husband [and therefore] she is not to be looked down upon'. He did not allow that 'respectable people' might see an adulteress as depriving someone else's wife of her rights, and therefore culpable.

And there was more, Campbell said. Ellen Wren could still open civil proceedings in which the whole question of truth would arise. A verdict of not guilty would carry no imputation against any one. Criminal libel was a legal anachronism which should not still exist; he referred emotionally to several old statutes, including one providing for a prisoner to be 'kept in irons for the first three years of his imprisonment'. Irrespective of his politics or religion, whether he is a communist or not, Hardy must be given a fair and impartial trial and judged not guilty. The jury needed a mere hour to come to that verdict. According to Hardy, 'Pandemonium broke out. Pressmen jostled with each other to get to a phone. The gallery clapped, cheered and stamped its feet. Judge Martin went livid and kept shouting, "Silence in the Court! Silence in the Court"'.

'Scarlet' would have better described Martin. Having nothing else to hand, he thumped the bench with a copy of the bulky novel. But before he could order 'Release the prisoner', athletic Hardy had sprung out of the dock to embrace his long-supportive (but later discarded) wife. Martin had been outmanoeuvred by defence counsel throughout the trial, and he knew that the gallery was stacked with intimidatory Hardy Defence Fund supporters ready to protest if the communist tribune were to be convicted and to exult if he were released. It seems clear that, as far as Judge Martin was concerned, the law had been cheated.[49] When told the verdict by a reporter, Wren simply mused: 'Not guilty! … Extraordinary'. Nellie was not, it seemed, upset by the verdict. Resignedly, she said that it was just what she had expected.[50]

Juries and justice

Campbell and Starke had expected Hardy to get five years. Starke recalled:

> The night before the jury had gone out, I said, 'Oh, Hardy, you'd better bring in your tooth brush, your razor and your shaving gear tomorrow'. And he said, 'Why? You don't think I'm going to get convicted do you?' And I said, 'Well, that's one of the three possibilities'. And he said, 'What do you think?' And I said, 'Forced to bet, I'd say that probably a conviction, followed by a disagreement, followed by an acquittal'. And Hardy turned white, turned white. And I thought, Well, if he didn't know he was in danger of getting convicted, there's something wrong with him'.[51]

Hardy gleefully admitted that there was no shadow of a doubt that he should have been found guilty at the trial. It was the skilful use of the vagaries of the jury system by his lawyers that saved him.[52] Hardy had publicly represented his novel as based on fact, but the law deemed it to be fiction.

Juries can waive the rigour of the law. It happened, for example, in a true civil liberties case in 1854–5 in Melbourne, when the leaders of the Eureka Stockade resistance were arraigned for patent treason but the jury refused to convict them. It should, however, be difficult to put a writer, who won his greatest notoriety by besmirching the reputation of an elderly woman, on a level with heroic men revolting against gross administrative abuse. Yet many Australians thought the judgment appropriate, even if not strictly just. The Wren sons had taken myopic legal advice. Winneke said years later that he believed criminal libel proceedings were not intended for cases like Ellen Wren's but should be involved only when a serious public mischief was caused by something published about a public figure.[53] Otherwise the charge may appear contrived—and it did.

A few years later Starke met the jury foreman at the races. He had no inhibitions about asking how the jury had reached the verdict of not guilty. There are two versions of the reply, as allegedly told by Starke: 'Listen, Wren had been a very bad man but as soon as he was affected, he runs to the law to protect him—we weren't going to have it',[54] and 'Old Wren had been a bloody scandal all his life and the first time he's hurt by anything, he rushes to the law for protection and we thought to hell with him'.[55] At a reunion forty years later Starke could say cynically to Hardy:

> I've no doubt your trial started me off [in my legal career]. I didn't do much but Campbell let me do a couple of cross-examinations and my name was in the papers every day—something important for a barrister who cannot advertise. We both did well, Frank. You would never have got so much publicity for *Power Without Glory* without the trial and I would never have got a practice like I got. What have we got to complain about?[56]

In a short time Hardy sold 100,000 copies of *Power Without Glory*, as well as thousands of a sequel about the trial itself, *The Hard Way*—not to mention other mediocre fiction on the basis of putative literary merit. In 1976 *Power Without Glory* was made into a long-running series on national television in spite of protests from the Wren family. It was the ABC's greatest success in that genre to that time. Sales of the book were again boosted by repeat series on commercial television. Some estimates suggest a million copies have been sold altogether; there were substantial sales in Eastern Europe under communist patronage, and elsewhere in translation. The readership and television series would have reached millions.

The irony is that if Wren's sons, like their father, had simply dismissed the book, 'no bookshop would have dared to sell the book; but the trial and the not guilty verdict gave the book complete immunity'.[57] The trial also ensured that John Wren was installed in the public imagination as Australia's most sinister and successful racketeer. Most Australian readers see the novel as substantially an accurate biography.

Phantom adultery

Whether or not he had wronged Ellen Wren was still preoccupying Hardy later in life. One consolation was that keeping the issue alive was not unprofitable. But, even with the royalties rolling in, he was uneasy with the charge that he had built his reputation by salaciously defaming and shaming her. In 1978 he wrote: 'I wanted to be known as a courageous political writer-warrior rather than a cowardly assassin of harmless old women'.[58] In the *Sydney Morning Herald*, not quite two years before he died, Hardy summarised the circumstances in which the alleged romance of Bill Egan and Nellie Wren was related to him and how by chance, during a period of writer's block some time later, it had unloosed a new flow of creativity. Hardy wondered how it was possible 'that writing the chapter troubled me not at all'.[59]

The answer to his question lay in Hardy's moral obtuseness, not in his claim to amoral creativity. Even if Ellen Wren had been caught *in* the act, *flagrante delicto*, it would have been despicable to shame an easily recognisable woman, particularly of her years and socio-religious standing, by publicising what she would have preferred her relatives, friends, descendants and people generally not to know. To pile on injury, Hardy attributes the paternity of Ellen Wren's youngest child, Xavier, to Egan. It was not part of Hardy's purpose even to check if this were credible by procuring a birth and death certificate. As the alleged affair was terminated in December 1917, according to *Power Without Glory*, and Xavier was born on 27 September 1919, only an elephantine gestation could have made Egan his father. Hardy was not sufficiently well informed to know when the child had died (10 September 1922), although there is a paragraph about his death in the *Advocate* (14 September). In the book he is eleven when he dies, although this does nothing for the story; elsewhere Hardy insists that he was eight.[60] To anyone who retorts that this shows only that Hardy did not mean the child's existence to be taken literally, one must ask, then why call him 'Xavier' at all? That his callousness would reactivate maternal sorrow was beyond Hardy's ken; a mendacious reference to the child's death served to make the end of an affair more poignant or, perhaps better, more satisfyingly prurient.

In his *Sydney Morning Herald* summary, Hardy tells how a friend, Norm Jury, who belonged to both the Communist and the Labor parties, brought to Hardy's house Alan Hall, a fellow-member of the Malvern ALP branch, who had occasionally denounced John Wren at meetings. Hall ran a second-hand furniture shop, but at some early stage of the acquaintance Hall's wife had told Hardy that Hall was a security agent, a claim confirmed by her husband. This was a most unlikely disclosure, especially to a known communist. He was in the smuggling and immigration section, said Mrs Hall.[61] Hall turned out to be a fascinating raconteur, and among the stories he told was that as an expert in unarmed combat he had shot a notorious criminal, George 'Ape' Kirkland, with the latter's own gun. Hall also recounted how his brother-in-law, Bill Egan, a handsome stud who reminded people of the American film star William S. Hart, had had an affair with Frank Anstey's mistress, Harriet Middlecoat. Hardy decided that Hall was a dangerous man to know, particularly as 'he clearly knew little about Wren's machine'.

Some months later, Hall rang Hardy. Did he remember what he had been told about the lady-killer, Egan? Well, Egan had had an affair with Mrs Wren in 1917 when he was laying bricks at her house. Nellie had sent love letters to Egan in a matchbox and they subsequently had rendevoused at the cinema and in the hills. But why had Hall not told the full story 'during our several earlier conversations'? And why would he tell a story involving his own sister, Egan's wife? On whose behalf? Hardy did not know the answers to these questions, but expected they would be resolved when his ASIO file was finally opened. (Hardy wanted this to be as soon as possible, to advertise his notoriety and the inevitable gaucheries of the spooks.)[62] Meanwhile, he was having problems learning something about 'Wren's personal life for the 15 years to World War I'. He solved them when he found notes he had made at Hall's. They inspired him to begin writing the alleged 1917 love affair into his book. He did not divulge how he came to believe that Wren had had an (unlikely) affair with an actress, as portrayed in *Power Without Glory*.[63]

Hardy and his backers expected some litigation, but not a criminal suit on behalf of Nellie. After being bailed a second time, Hardy barged in on Hall. 'That bloody story you told me has landed me in jail', he jeered. He demanded to know whether Hall could vouch for it. Hall went one better! He would persuade his sister Lucy to testify in court that the scene in *Power Without Glory* where 'Myrtle Evans' (Lucy Egan) confronts 'Nellie West', 'her husband's mistress', was based on fact. George Seelaf drove Hardy to Eltham to meet Lucy, who allegedly 'repeated the Bill Egan/Ellen Wren story', although at no stage did the voluble Hardy recall what she actually said or describe what must have been for him a memorable meeting. Whether Lucy actually related the ludicrous fracas in the novel, when 'Myrtle' smacks 'Nellie West's face, screams abuse and chases her around the garden throwing bricks at her, was not specifically confirmed—because, one assumes, it did not happen. Allegedly, Lucy reluctantly agreed to give evidence.

Don Campbell KC, however, would not 'have a bar of it'. Why would Hall, allegedly a Commonwealth police officer, want to help him, he asked Hardy. Campbell thought Lucy Egan would 'most likely go into the box and swear that the whole story is a pack of lies' invented by Hardy, who would then spend the rest of his life in Pentridge gaol. In that case, argued Hardy, why hadn't the prosecution called her? They knew she existed. (An obvious reason would be that as the Wrens did not know Lucy Egan personally—had not met her—they could not know that she was not part of Hardy's conspiracy. To have approached her themselves would have exposed them to the accusation of nobbling a potential witness.) Campbell thought that perhaps the prosecution expected the defence to call Lucy Egan, because they must have known about Hardy's visit to Eltham. Campbell's strategy then was to subpoena her and, rather than put her in the witness box, just talk conspicuously to her outside the court and study the prosecution's reactions. Hardy alleged this happened, and 'The prosecution entourage watched with great interest and some dismay'. Lucy Egan, 'a plump woman of some charm … wearing an old fashioned hat and fur … as nervous as if she were to face a firing squad', was then sent home, and Hardy did not see her again.[64]

Hardy called this 'the strangest event in the dramatic trial, of which the public remains unaware to this day [1992]'. In *The Hard Way* he said: 'Galbally was obviously dismayed. Reporters sensed a hot story and hovered around [but did not pursue it?]. Campbell then spoke to her and sent her home.'[65]

In the version Hardy had presented in *The Hard Way*, 'Mrs X' (Lucy Egan) appears at the *committal* on 15 January 1951, where she had 'reluctantly agreed to give evidence'. This was *not* the jury trial. However, in the 1992 version the event occurs on the first morning of the *jury trial*; that is, on 12 June 1951. Hardy clearly consulted the version in *The Hard Way* before writing the new expanded version for the *Sydney Morning Herald* and *Sunday Age* decades later. Yet he altered an important fact. He places the event not at the committal hearing but at the jury trial.[66] What game was he playing this time? *The Hard Way* had been written in the mid-1950s, quite close to the real events. Was his memory, as it often was, just sloppy? In any case, there was no way Campbell would have been allowed to call Lucy Egan at the committal, or indeed at the trial, where the defence could not plead public benefit. In a letter to the *Australian* (28 August 1976), after viewing the television portrayal of the alleged adultery, John F. Wren unwittingly corroborated Lucy Egan's presence at the committal, not the trial:

> At the conclusion of my evidence in the lower court in the criminal libel charge against Hardy a lady—'Mrs Evans', the so-called wronged wife in the above episode—said to me, 'I admire you greatly for the way you have defended your mother. It is completely untrue what Hardy has written about my late husband and your mother. We were very happily married'.[67]

This may have been so in 1917 although, according to Armstrong, it seems certain that the couple had separated by 1924 in spite of having ten children. Bill Egan was living at Abbotsford at his death; Lucy in Greensborough at hers, nine years later. A conventional death notice for Bill in the *Age* (30 September 1944) stated that he was Lucy's 'loved' husband. There may have been some explanation for the different residences, such as Bill's proximity to work—Greensborough being an outer suburb while Abbotsford was a ward of Collingwood.

The adultery yarn may have begun simply as raunchy badinage and chiacking among workmates, and with repetition came to be accepted as fact. Armstrong even suggests that if Bill Egan was the source of the adultery story, he may have had a grudge against John Wren and struck at him in a way calculated to wound. He had been a constable in the Carlton–Collingwood area in the early years of the century, in the Tote's heyday, when he surely knew Wren 'at least by sight and reputation'. He had been dismissed from the service after five years 'following a variety of misdemeanours and offences'. The official indictment was 'Conduct very bad'. This was not revealed by Hardy, although one could expect that Hall would have told him that Egan had been in the police force.

But then Hall was also a strange character, 'a big talker' who 'frequently mixed fact with fiction', a 'great yarn spinner' who was a 'bit odd in his mind', a close relative told Armstrong. He had never heard 'any suggestion that Hall had been a Commonwealth policeman'. Nor is there any known record that Hall served in either the Victorian, Commonwealth or federal police. (His father had been a constable in the Victorian police from 1880 to 1900, when 'resignation pre-empted impending dismissal because of heavy drinking'.) Hall had shot and wounded a man, not Kirkland, at a New Year's party at his mother's home in 1919. For some reason the charge against him was dismissed—perhaps, suggests Armstrong, because he had become a police informer.[68] Whatever his subsequent doings, Hall's veracity was to become a crucial factor in Hardy's justification of his scurrilous treatment of Nellie Wren

Hardy returned to Australia in late 1979 after some years abroad, especially in France where, among other distinctions, he had been a 'groupie' of the Greek cabaret singer Nana Mouskouri.[69] He had a novel for publication, *Who Shot George Kirkland? A Novel about the Nature of Truth*. 'The impulse behind this book', he said, 'was a deep inner need to express regret about the so-called adultery allegations':

> When … [it] was published I felt that at least the ghost of Nellie West would be laid to rest because the facts of the source, and the history of the incidents portrayed … were fully revealed. Few people who read it at the time of publication in 1980 [1981], including the critics, failed to see this.[70]

The book is in two parts. The first is a reflection by Hardy's *alter ego*, Ross Franklyn, a name compounded of the first names of his former wife, Rosslyn, and himself, and used previously in both *Power Without Glory* and *The Hard Way*. Franklyn is in a French village anguishing over his treatment of 'Nellie West'. He has been suppressing this anxiety for decades. Had Alan Hall given him false information? Now that Hardy has a carry-bag of Freudian terms, he asks if Hall suffered from *pseudologia fantastica* (simply, compulsive lying)—a pretentious term he flourishes several times. Franklyn concludes that if he can prove that the story of Hall shooting Kirkland is true, then so will be the putative affair of Nellie Wren and Bill Egan (no longer 'Evans'). But then if not, not. He has checked newspaper files for the 1920s and 'the murder columns of the [*Argus*] index for every quarter of the year' until the end of 1927. He has found nothing on Kirkland. So, Kirkland cannot have existed and Hall has lied on both counts. With 'the feeling of self-disgust arising from the return of guilt',[71] our conscience-stricken Franklyn commits suicide.

The narrator in part two is an adulatory clone of the first, a nameless would-be biographer of Franklyn who has abandoned a half-finished first novel to pursue his research on the great author. He interviews acquaintances of Franklyn in Europe and, on returning to Melbourne, Alan's wife Elizabeth Hall, and Alan junior, a psychiatrist. He also resumes research in the Public Library. He gets corroboration of the Lucy Egan story from the Halls, although Elizabeth says that Bill Egan was lost in the war when in fact he dropped dead in central Melbourne in 1944 at the unmilitary age of sixty-six.[72] In the library our biographer finds that Kirkland at least existed and was involved in shootings (but in these accounts there is no mention of Alan Hall). So has Ross Franklyn killed himself in vain? Still, his novel (*Power Corrupts*) was certainly not in vain and was not to be disparaged by doubts about its factuality, because it is great art. We have to be thankful, says our narrator, even if Hall was lying; without his story of the affair there would be no such masterpiece. The 'greatness' of Ross Franklyn lay, continues our narrator, 'in a [profound] sentence in his last writing': 'Alan Hall had led him into the limbo world between truth and fiction and there he had learnt "the true meaning of the irreconcilable feud between literature and reality"'.[73]

'Limbo', a state of nescience, was more apt than Hardy knew for this bafflegab. *Who Shot George Kirkland?* ends in cliché, with our nameless narrator under a veranda sheltered elegiacally 'by a shower of cooling rain', and then 'impulsively walking in the tender cooling rain' still asking the unanswerable question in the title. However, in an interview conducted in December 1980, Hardy said that 'two years ago' he had gone back to the Melbourne Library and 'through the records again more carefully'. There he found George Kirkland 'murdered', not just 'shot' as he had often written ambiguously before. It was 'with his own gun just as this bloke [Alan Hall] had told me thirty years before'. Once again Hardy linked the questions of the Kirkland shooting and Nellie Wren's alleged adultery. As Hall had told the truth about Kirkland then, asked Hardy, was Nellie Wren an adulteress? Was the infant, Xavier Wren, Egan's child? 'It's still not possible', he concluded, 'for me in a simple statement to give my opinion. It's probably legally dangerous, probably physically dangerous.'[74]

But he did give his opinion on several later occasions. He was to say 'on balance' that he thought Ellen Wren had not had that affair. In April 1992 Hardy wrote in the *Sydney Morning Herald* that the impulse behind the Kirkland novel was 'a deep inner need to express regret because it seemed certain that the story was untrue'. By December he had changed his mind again:

> Now Hardy says that he is 'virtually' certain that the adultery story was true after all. He says the *Herald* article had prompted a woman to offer more evidence on the subject. He is putting together the last pieces in the jigsaw just in time for his memoirs.
>
> He won't say very much more right now, thereby guaranteeing another bite at the controversy when his memoirs are published.[75]

And more revenues, naturally—a matter rarely off Hardy's mind. He lived another twenty months without further revelations.

As Pauline Armstrong has pointed out, it can only be concluded that Hardy 'left false trails ... that were designed to confuse any future researcher'. If he had been honest and thorough he would have found, as she did, that Kirkland (b. 1878) had been a 'voluntary patient' for three days in the alcoholism unit in Royal Park Hospital in 1923, and an 'involuntary patient', again as an alcoholic, in June 1925, and had been branded 'an habitual criminal' and gaoled in November 1930. Far from being murdered, Kirkland died in the Royal Park Psychiatric Unit in 1944.[76]

Hardy's concern that he may have assassinated the reputation of a harmless old woman was sheer humbug. He was a flagrant liar. Who then suffered from *pseudologia fantastica*? Who was, as Franklyn's biographer, with a forced flash of dinkum humour, said of Alan Hall, 'the greatest bullshit artist who ever poked his head through a bridle'?[77] But Hardy was worse than that. For a man who over decades would drag out a reckless, unsubstantiated accusation of what was once regarded as a serious sexual misdemeanour (not to mention the fabricated homicides attributed to Wren), a more appropriate term would be 'literary hoodlum'.

Delusion

Hardy believed, and was encouraged to believe, by notable ideologues like Jack Lindsay,[78] that he had written the great Australian novel. More discriminating communist authors, such as Jack Beasley and Rupert Lockwood, demurred.[79] Yet Hardy's lack of invention and even the simplest of his derivations have been overlooked by many critics, while the improvidence of his prose has too often been ignored. The very title of the novel, while resonant, is patently copied from Graham Greene's *The Power and the Glory*, so controversially discussed in the 1940s. Commentators overlook this. 'John West's' spinning sovereign falling into Constable Brogan's palm at the beginning of the book—the corrupt copper had to have an Irish name—'has come to stand', says Kylie Valentine, 'for the whole book in ways not dissimilar to the madeleine cake near the opening of Proust's *Remembrance of Things Past*'. However, she is careful to say, 'to make a surely winning bid for the most obvious statement of the year [Proust and Hardy] have little in common'.[80]

The opening scene is often praised as 'stunning', or words to that effect. Without denying its effectiveness as cheap melodrama, such a street corner scene was a cliché in American B-grade crime films of the time. As for Hardy's vaunted study of Balzac—who also features in the epigraphs—and his having successfully evoked the distinctive indigence of 'Carringbush' (Collingwood), there is not one aspect of Hardy's setting, not one street or building, which shows close observation—nothing to suggest that he had actually visited Collingwood and was familiar with its Labor and Catholic contexts.

In terms of literary merit there is virtually nothing to be said for *Power Without Glory* except for its narrative verve, which results from a vaguely familiar canvas cut crisply enough into episodes involving recognisable personalities. At such a pace, Hardy's inability to sustain discussion or enlivening characterisation or vivid scenarios is more easily overlooked. The story skelters from one scurrilous indictment to another. With a glossary of personal identifications, some readers have been easily gulled. *Power Without Glory* has, as Chris Wallace Crabbe says, 'that peculiar grip that comes from immediate locality and recent events'.[81] Marvellously, biographer Nadia Wheatley explains that Hardy 'skimp[ed] on characterisation', not because of incapacity but because 'the reader shares the specific history unveiled through the story'. As Hardy 'expected the reader to collaborate in the text ... it seemed unnecessary for characters to be fully realized'.[82] I suggest it is more germane to remember Hardy's early career as a cartoonist. So we find on page one that 'John West' has a 'pear-shaped head and ... large-lobed ears, set too low and too far back ... a high sloping forehead ... [and] a thin, hard line ... etched for a mouth'. Towards the end of the novel, premier 'Davison' (Dunstan) resembles 'a happy-go-lucky pig. His nose was a snout, his cheeks were puffed, his ears were large and pointed at the top like those of a pig, and his head was bald except at the sides.' This is Walt Disney or Looney Tunes, not a serious literary work, although even they would have difficulty depicting how, when 'West' discovers 'Nellie's adultery, 'Words poured from his mouth like molten lava'.[83] Even the characterisation of 'West', as Kylie Valentine points out, is restricted to the transformation of an unpleasant young man to an unpleasant old one'.[84]

Apotheosis

Frank Hardy died in January 1994 at his desk in the bayside suburb of Elwood, with a racing form-guide in his hand. Generally this was thought to be fitting; some found it inspiring. It was a facile death, as was most of his life. His obsequies took place at the Collingwood ('Carringbush') Town Hall as though he had belonged in its precincts. Ironically, in the days when Collingwood was a proletarian suburb, trade unionists during the Eight Hour Day procession had been known to stop and give 'Three cheers for John Wren'. But legend had conquered history. The *Age* reporter saw the two-hour celebration of Hardy's life as being held 'among his own—ordinary people who care and battle ... The people were supporting a working-class hero'.

According to reports, the mourners were by then mostly gentrified, as the inner suburbs had become. Gough Whitlam led them and spoke and wept. No speaker remembered that *Power Without Glory* was meant to be primarily a vicious assault on the Labor Party. There was 'a burst of applause from the remaining comrades' when it was mentioned that Hardy had visited the USSR in 1951. The reporter, obviously not having read Hardy's *Journey into the Future*, said that Hardy had 'disapproved of Stalin'. There were well-worn banalities apropos Hardy's heartfelt beliefs. Neither communism nor Christ had failed, someone said; they had never been tried (*more applause*). And without understanding how patronisingly the editor of imperial *Punch* had meant it, Malcolm Muggeridge was quoted approvingly as saying that Hardy was 'the most Australian of Australians' (*encore*). Certainly he recalled Banjo Paterson's barber in *The Man from Ironbark*; he was 'a humorist of note'. Who else would have flattered the first Australians with a pop song, 'Why Don't You Didgeridoo As You Would Be Didgeridone By'. Which belongs, as Beasley says, 'to the finest traditions of "Abo" humour, such as the Jolliffe cartoons, the "Mine Tinkit Dey Fit" Pelaco ads and the grimly named Abo Fertilizer'.[85]

One would like to believe that Hardy's promotion of the land rights of the Gurindji in the late 1960s, and his association with the compassionate eye surgeon Fred Hollows, made some compensation for his offences. Aboriginal problems needed a publicist, no matter how self-regarding and opportunistic. In view of the humane outcomes, Hardy's motivation, his continual quest for notoriety, might then be overlooked. Unfortunately a former comrade, Rupert Lockwood, records:

> The Hardy publicity machine was well oiled. He was credited with decisive support for the Gurindji's struggle for Vestey land at Wave Hill … People directly involved … had other views … Frank was notorious for his one-way borrowings … [A Northern Territory welfare officer reported that] Frank let it be known he was strapped for cash. A Gurindji spokesman … approached Hardy: 'You bin help us, Frank. We bin help you'. The tall tribesman handed the money to Hardy.
>
> My brother Douglas Lockwood, a well-known author and friend of the Aborigines, the Gurindji[,] (he was banned from Vestey station in the Territory) was horrified. 'That Aboriginal money could have only come from the Gurindji's meagre welfare allowance', he told me. Some Communist Party members were also not pleased.[86]

The Gurindji probably derived pleasure from their act of reciprocity, but Hardy could not imagine that the money given to him could be paid into their strike fund, or that he might have paid them some part of the proceeds from his book, *The Unlucky Australians*, and the various media appearances he made, ostensibly on their behalf.[87] Two Gurindji came to the funeral. Old Mick Rangiari said that Hardy 'sat in the dust with us fellas. He had a yarn and he put our true word in a book about the Vestey mob. He was a really true man.'[88] It was a touching reminder that opportunism and a quest for publicity can be put to beneficial effect.

Hardy's coffin was draped with the Eureka and Aboriginal flags. As it was borne to the hearse, the Trades Hall choir resurrected old fantasies with the Internationale, now just a hollow anthem evoking a ghostly brotherhood of man.

Conclusion

Obsequies

THE COLLINGWOOD FOOTBALL team, in September 1953, confronted Geelong, the 'classiest' side seen post-war, which had won premierships in 1951–2. Collingwood had arrested Geelong's winning streak of twenty-three games in August, but even then was not considered favourite for the two finals matches they played. The grand final was fiercely contested and, although the Magpies were almost five goals in front at three-quarter time, 'a desperate onslaught' by Geelong took it to within a two-goal margin at the final bell. Wren and his old friend, the legendary coach Jock McHale, left the members' enclosure at the final change and bustled with the crowd in the outer ground behind Collingwood's goal. It was the Magpies' first premiership since 1936. Wren gave the team £500. The next day McHale had a heart attack, and died within a week.

Wren was hardier. He had had the additional excitement of his son advising him during the afternoon that his horse, Walu, named after a river near the Fiji mines, had won the Moonee Valley Stakes at set weights for three-year-olds. This augured well for the colt's future. Wren was elated. However, within thirty-six hours of Collingwood's victory, at five o'clock on Monday morning, 28 September, he had a heart attack in his healthful sleepout. At seven o'clock he crawled along the passage upstairs and, not wishing to disturb Nellie, he woke Angela. She rang John

Francis, who took him to Mount St Evin's Hospital, the private wing of St Vincent's. 'You cannot have a pain like that and live', his father said.[1] Wren survived until 26 October, and he died with his two remaining sons, John Francis and Joseph, and his doctor at his bedside. Two death notices appeared in the daily papers, a matter-of-fact statement from the Wren family, and from the officials and players of the Collingwood Football Club 'a tribute to our great friend, generous patron and active supporter ... His loss is mourned by all at Collingwood'.[2]

At St Patrick's Cathedral, Wren's obsequies were not conducted with the customary requiem Mass for the Dead on a bare altar with the celebrant in black vestments. As the liturgy gave precedence to that day's feast of the anniversary of the cathedral's consecration, hopeful white was prescribed. The diocesan administrator, (Bishop) Mgr Fox was celebrant; the master of ceremonies was (Bishop) Fr Moran; Archbishop Mannix presided from the episcopal throne, and Coadjutor-Archbishop Simonds, and thirty priests assisted. Of Wren's family, only John Francis, Joseph and Angela were present. Nellie was ill, Margaret and Mary were overseas. The pall-bearers included Arthur Calwell, deputy leader of the federal parliamentary Labor Party; Sir Gilbert Dyett, federal president of what is now the Returned Services League; and a committeeman of the Victoria Racing Club, H. G. Raymond. Among the thousand or so mourners were politicians (Labor) and representatives of the law, the various sports Wren had promoted and the religious establishments he had assisted. Several hundred looked on behind the railings around the cathedral courtyard. Nonetheless, the master of ceremonies, Sir Gilbert Dyett, remarked haughtily that there were many people absent who should have been there. In three years, *Power Without Glory* had done its work. Still, the wreaths required two floral cars. Boys from Xavier College Preparatory School, which was to acquire Studley House one day, provided a guard of honour. On the way to Boroondara Cemetery in Kew the cortège deviated past Studley House, where an ailing Nellie Wren watched from the window. The two archbishops went to the graveside.[3]

The Catholic *Advocate* praised Wren for his charity and concern for freedom, recalling his efforts on behalf of Fr Jerger. The *Sporting Globe* over four weekly issues published complimentary memoirs under the by-line of the noted sportswriter Merv Williams.[4] Other obituaries were not effusive and on the whole drew attention to Wren's being 'a mystery financier' somehow influential in public affairs. The *Argus* and the

Sydney *Daily Telegraph* spoke of 'a fabulous empire of wealth and power'. The *Bulletin*, under more conservative ownership than in 1906, simply published a letter, prominently, from a correspondent who claimed to have patronised the Tote as an 'urchin' and regarded it as 'the evil fount and origin' of Wren's 'empire'. He had made Labor 'racing-mad'. The communist *Guardian* highlighted an 'Obituary in four lines', which had been received by a not very modest Frank Hardy:

> Born in the slums—shame—where evils breed
> He rose by trading in despair and greed;
> Bought governments and press, as money can,
> And died defeated by a common man.

On the other hand, the Lord Mayor Robert Solly, son of Wren's deceased friend, reminded Melburnians that John Wren 'delighted to do good by stealth and no one will ever know the extent of his benefactions and the hundreds of people he helped attain security'.[5]

At the Pleasant Sunday Afternoon at Wesley Church, where W. H. Judkins features in knightly guise in a stained glass window, Rev. Sir Irving Benson was disinclined to let Wren rest without a last rebuke:

> Wren never forgot … and never forgave the closure of the Collingwood Tote and had worked ceaselessly and untiringly for a legalised lottery … no name has been more frequently mentioned on this platform during a period of years. His death recalls the valiant fight for righteousness and clean politics led by such champions as the Reverends T. S. B. Woodfull, Henry Worrall and [not Rev.] W. H. Judkins …

More deprecation followed from Benson, who obviously never forgot nor forgave, and recalled with an unacknowledged quotation Monty Grover's stricture in the *Lone Hand*:

> It was remarked that Mr Wren was seldom seen in the precincts of Parliament House, but the crack of his whip was frequently heard in its corridors. Someone will write an objective study of this controversial figure who started behind scratch and came to such astounding power.[6]

Reckoning

This biography has attempted to probe the substance and extent of Wren's alleged wrongdoing. It does not claim to be exhaustive. There is a challenge here for those who feel there is more to be weighed on the debit side of Wren's moral ledger. There is also more to be discovered about Wren's activities in New South Wales and even South Australia, for example, but several discussions with scholars in these fields discouraged me from making what looked likely to be unrewarded efforts.[7] Perhaps documents will turn up one day, as they did with the Wren–Evatt relationship, to throw light on issues only adumbrated here. However, assuming that Wren is entitled to the right not to be pilloried by unsustainable (rather than just unproved) accusations, we can come to some conclusions.

Wren was not a gangster in the American (Al Capone) sense: that is, a social marauder with a 'machine' that was prepared to kill, rob and terrorise his fellow citizens. It should be evident from the Smythe case (Chapter 4) and Chapter 12 that Hardy's accusations of involvement in homicide are groundless and malignant. For the fourteen years that he ran the illegal Tote, Wren did rely on toughs to protect it, and to deter hooligan elements on his pony tracks. But there is no evidence that, on Wren's behalf, they were engaged in gangland activities. In any case his interests did not make it necessary for him to do so. And, contrary to Rev. Benson's charge, far from not forgiving the closure of his Tote, Wren was after 1907 well rid of it.

Wren was not a racketeer involved in protection levies, prostitution, drugs, bootlegging, rack-renting, etc. One can understand that some moralists would regard gambling as a 'racket' even when 'honestly' conducted, especially in the socio-economic conditions of the late nineteenth and early twentieth century However, 'wowsers' deserve their disparaging appellation. They tolerated gambling for 'gentlemen' in elite clubs. They were oppressive and class-conscious and, when triumphant, responsible for such squalid features of social life as ubiquitous back-lane betting and, after the First World War, the infamous six-o'clock swill. Their attitude was punitive: if the lower classes must gamble and drink, let them do it in degrading circumstances.

The Tote was illegal, and it would be naive to believe that because Wren payouts to an already corrupt police force were not proven, they did not occur, and that witnesses and jurors were not nobbled as required. Before the Tote was closed in January 1907, this was hardly a contribution to Collingwood law and order. Wren was no saint. On the other hand, accusations by Hardy that Wren bribed high officials like Mr Justice Hood, for example, can be dismissed out of hand.

Charges that Wren rigged or corrupted major sports events have not been sustained. In the case of Murmur's Caulfield Cup, it is quite clear that, as even Grover suggested, the rumours were false. Wrestling and perhaps motor-pacing were not honestly contested and became, as elsewhere, entertainments rather than genuine sport. Moreover, Wren cannot be blamed for all actions of his employees and associates, particularly those as irrepressible as Sugar Roberts. Nor can he be blamed for the perseverance of obsolescent institutions such as proprietary horse racing. More to the point, Wren gave a boost to a number of sports, including racing. In his history of Victoria, Geoffrey Blainey refers to Wren as 'making a fortune out of gambling and the shadowy side of sport' but, like others, casts no light on these 'shadows'.[8]

In his business dealings, Wren's reputation was one of fair dealing and integrity, as is evidenced by those who associated with him. This is not to say that he did not drive hard bargains and take advantage of whatever legality allowed. As Arthur Calwell said:

> he observed the principles of commercial morality, and to those of my political persuasion commercial morality leaves much to be desired; but he still had a sense of morality that wealthy men often ignore … In the belief that John Wren was a better Australian than his detractors, which I sincerely hold, I asked to be a pall-bearer at his funeral.[9]

In politics, there is no doubt that Wren used his wealth to influence pre-selection ballots, that he paid the electoral (and other) expenses of some candidates and that he expected and often received support for his interests in return. But he did not cut off those who did not respond. Much has been made of Wren's attempt to get Frank Anstey to resign for Tom Ryan in 1919, but nothing of the fact that he continued to support the ardent socialist when he would not co-operate. In Australia, backstairs support for politicians is hardly a rare blight on a generally well-functioning democratic system. Was the performance of those politicians we suspect of taking Wren's money worse than that of others? We have seen how that notable 'fixer' and Labor 'numbers man' (Senator) Pat Kennelly, had to solicit a small repayable loan from Wren to buy a house. It is typical of Hardy to state that Kennelly was a multiple property owner as a result of taking a slice of Wren's donations to the Labor Party for himself. This was a deliberate lie, as was his attempt to frame Kennelly as a 'scab'. If Kennelly was in Wren's 'pocket', why did Wren not simply give him the whole sum? In old age, Kennelly, in a position to know, maintained that Wren did not corrupt the Labor Party and suggests that Wren understood its culture:

> I got on with him all right. He never asked me to do anything I wouldn't have done. He was Labor. He wanted Labor. He told me more than once he didn't know why he supported them. He said: 'I get more off Menzies than I get from you people.' There was never one penny of Wren's money that went into the office of the Labor Party. While it's true he supported candidates.[10]

If Colin Bednall's anecdote in Chapter 10 suggests that Wren could peremptorily call in his debtors in the Labor Party, yet in the same period his loss of control over trotting shows the contrary. At the very least, Kennelly's statement cautions against exaggeration. A parade of reputable persons, such as Calwell, and those with talent but not without taint like E. G. Theodore, did not shun association with Wren. They were in a position to know what went on behind the scenes. There was no political 'octopus'; there were machinations, yes, but not enough to make a 'machine'.

Wren was not a political theorist nor a man of progressive ideas. The Australian status quo suited his interests. Aside from protecting them, as a capitalist would, it can be believed that, in supporting Labor, he simply wanted to promote, as he put it, the welfare of 'the class from which [he] sprang', a role that was not devoid of vanity and even sentimentality. His critics seem unable to explain his popularity with unionists or their preparedness to use his patronage. While he contributed to the torpor of Victorian politics from 1920 to 1950, he was not responsible for it—nor for a Labor phenomenon like Ted Theodore, whom he obviously supported in Brisbane, Sydney and Canberra. The groans, if genuine, of Anstey and Tunnecliffe that Wren had deprived them of their ideals through his largesse should be seen as pitiful, but have been taken seriously. What should be explored is whether, at the time, our system of politics had positive uses for catalysts (and wire-pullers) like Wren—and scholars might look for others of lesser note but certainly operative. That radical hero, Dr H. V. Evatt, obviously thought Wren most useful—part of the 'system', in fact.

Wren maintained allegiance to the British social democratic state and, in spite of many years of doubt and non-attendance, to the Catholic Church. Unlike Herbert Brookes, some leading members of the Protestant Federation and supporters of the Nationalist, United Australia, and Country parties, Wren did not conspire with organisers of 'secret armies'—the ultimate subversion of the political process. In no sense a crusader, he saw no incompatibility between Catholicism and the secular state of his day, was anti-sectarian and saw the advent of the Santamaria Movement as fatal to unity in the Labor Party. His ultimate support of Menzies was a natural development for a pragmatic wealthy man once the Chifley government espoused socialist policies.

Arguably, Wren was Australia's leading promoter of public entertainment in the first half of the twentieth century. He was not just fleecing the gullible, as is believed by many. He was also a productive investor, not a parasite on the stock exchange.

One has the impression from the currency of words like 'shady', 'shadowy'and 'mysterious', that were continually applied to Wren that he had no public personality. One reason for this book giving lengthy quotations—with reference, for example, to the Building Workers' strike of 1906, Sinn Fein of 1917, Fr Jerger's extradition in 1920, and so on—is to give him a voice. Wren had been on display often enough before the Hardy trial of 1950. Images of him in the film *Ireland Shall Be Free* (1920) suggest not a political arachnid but, when it suited him, a self-assured, gregarious, eloquent man of affairs. Wren's lack, in general, of ostentation was misconstrued. He preferred to belong to the populist Collingwood Football Club rather than climb into the exclusive Melbourne Club.

Finally, Wren's philanthropy was genuine and beneficent, most of it delivered without fanfare, and should need no explication.

In refuting or insisting on proof of vicious allegations against Wren, I may have presented him as a better man than he was. An historian can work only with the evidence before him. Wren was literate, but far from an effusive correspondent. His management style was hands-on, with responsibility delegated to trusted and, it would seem, generally trustworthy if not competent lieutenants. There must surely have been correspondence between family members during the drama of 1950–1, but if so it is not known to survive. Just as the Evatt–Wren and other letters so recently discovered should make some difference to an assessment of Wren, there may be finds in the future which incline more to an unfavourable view of him. Until then, and afterwards, one should bear in mind the maxim of Manning Clark's son, Andrew, when expressing justifiable outrage at slanders against his father:

> People are not entitled in a civil society to pursue a malicious campaign of character assassination based on a big lie.[11]

It is unfortunate that the celebrated historian and parroting scribes did not consider this before accepting Frank Hardy as an authority on John Wren.

Notes

Introduction [pp 1–5]

1 Calil and Toibin (comps), *The Modern Library*, 73.
2 Lockwood, 'No redress for Hardy's victims', 18–19.
3 Simons, 'Evatt–Wren link surprises Hardy', *Sunday Age*, 9 August 1992.
4 All Clark quotations from Clark, *A History of Australia*, V, 273-4, 298.
5 Simons, 'Evatt–Wren link surprises Hardy', *Sunday Age*, 9 August 1992.
6 Sorrenti, 'Monumental as anything', Good Weekend magazine, *Sydney Morning Herald*, 11 April 1992, 33-4.
7 I am thinking of personal friends and acquaintances. JG
8 Davison, Hirst and Macintyre (eds), *The Oxford Companion to Australian History*, 702.
9 Cain, *On with the Show*, 162.

Chapter One [pp 6–34]

1 Compare with Hardy's *Power Without Glory*, 28.
2 It was the custom in Catholic Ireland to baptise a child soon after birth in case of an early death. It was believed that without the sacrament its soul could not enter heaven.
3 J. F. Wren interview, June 1986; Wren to Scullin, 22 November 1941, Wren papers.
4 Criminal Trial Briefs, Regina v Meredith and Others, 25 February–1 March 1889, VPRS 30/817/15 Central Register of Male Prisoners VPRS 521/41/23036; Petition of John Wren and Margaret Wren to Governor of Victoria, Law Department, 13 July 1891, VPRS 264/18, Supreme Court, Capital Case Files; *Age*, 26, 27, 28 February 1889; *Observer*, 3, 31 January, 1 March 1889; *Argus*, 26, 28 February, 8 March 1889; *Age*, 26 February 1889.
5 Victorian Probates, No. 280/007, E. A. Wren, 31 July 1936.
6 *Argus*, 27 July 1935; *Australian Leather Journal, Boot and Shoe Recorder*, 15 August 1935, 85; *Australasian Footwear*, 31 July 1935, 207.
7 In *Power Without Glory*, Hardy portrays Arthur as a glum, unregenerate homicide, the gangster consort of the notorious criminals Squizzy Taylor and Richard Buckley.
8 Army Records, John F. Wren, Department of Defence, 239/4/2/57 13/8/1915, AIF, Attention Paper of Persons Enlisted for Service Abroad (ANA).
9 Hardy, *Power Without Glory*, 31.
10 Quoted in Pearl, *Wild Men of Sydney*, 205.
11 J. F. Wren interview.
12 *Australian*, 28 August 1976.
13 Phelan, *ADB, 11*, 212-13.

14 Letters to his sister in Hackett papers.
15 Derriman, 'John Wren: the family breaks its silence', *Sydney Morning Herald*, 24 December 1987.
16 Postcards from Ellen Wren in Wren papers.
17 J. F. Wren interview.
18 'Studley House', photocopies from Historic Buildings Council, Victoria file: 6006486, documents presented at registration hearing, 15 March 1989; *Age*, 10 March 1970.
19 Norris papers.
20 Ibid.
21 *Herald*, 31 January 1977.
22 Clark, *A History of Australia*, V, 274.
23 J. F. Wren interview.
24 Ibid.
25 *Sun*, 1, 3 September 1934.
26 Personal communication from Dr E. Ryan, former president of the Old Xaverian's Association, April 1997.
27 Wren papers.
28 Peter Norris was a principal of the legal firm Corr & Corr, and a close friend of Wren's youngest son, Joseph. Norris papers.
29 J. F. Wren interview; White, in Arnold and Morris, *Monash Biographical Dictionary*; Wren papers.
30 Wren papers.
31 Nora Wren to Joseph Wren, December 1953 to September 1956, Wren papers.
32 *Mercury* (Hobart), 19 October 1953; *Examiner* (Launceston), 20 October 1953.
33 Information by telephone from C. Koch, 15 May 2002.
34 Howells, *Against the Stream*, 92-3, 123.
35 P. Kelly, *Sporting Globe*, 8 November 1953.
36 Barnes interview, Browne research notes (copy held by J. Griffin).
37 Ross, *These Things Shall Be!*, 127; correspondence with E. Ross, 18, 22, 26 July 1989; A Turner research notes (copy held by J. Griffin).
38 Letter from Margaret Andreas, Wren papers.
39 Macintyre, *The Reds*, 65; Wren papers; Norris papers; information from C. J. Wren.
40 *Herald*, 18 May 1942; *Sun*, 19 May 1942; Bennison, *Memories Rekindled.*
41 Page, *Bradman*, 329; O'Reilly, '*Tiger*', 198; *Sporting Globe*, 18 November 1953.
42 *Advocate*, 6 September 1919.
43 Hackett papers; Mullins letter to Wren family, nd, *c.* 1976, Wren papers.
44 Newman College file and Hackett letters, Jesuit Archives.
45 Norris papers.
46 Ibid.
47 N. Brennan papers.
48 Wren papers.
49 Buckley et al., *Doc Evatt*, 215: 'He anticipated benefits in return for his money—in the case of the church, a cynic would say, that Wren aimed to buy his way into heaven through his close association with Archbishop Mannix'.
50 *Age*, 25 July 1913; *Truth*, 26 July 1913; A. A. Kay in Norris papers.
51 Buggy, *The Real John Wren*, 138.
52 Wren to Theodore, 4 October 1949, Wren papers.
53 Fitzgerald, '*Red Ted*', 409-1.

54 Letter, *Eureka Street,* November 1992.

Chapter Two [pp 35–58]

1 Don, *ADB, 3,* 82.
2 Serle, *The Rush to be Rich,* 183; Moorhouse, *ADB, 5,* 281–3.
3 Kiddle, *Caroline Chisholm,* 81–4.
4 Vaughan et al., 'Catholic education', 56-7.
5 *Argus,* 17 November 1913.
6 Inglis, *The Australian Colonists,* 90.
7 Goold, *ADB, 4,* 266.
8 Wren to James Scullin, 22 November 1941, Wren papers.
9 McKernan, *Australian Churches at War,* 113.
10 Leeper, *ADB, 9,* 54–7.
11 Copy supplied to author by the late Dr A. G. Serle.
12 Briggs, *Victorian Cities,* 278.
13 Serle, *The Rush to be Rich,* 158–60.
14 Crowley, *A Documentary History of Australia,* vol. 3, 268–70; McCaughey et al., *Victoria's Colonial Governors,* 296–7.
15 Clark, *A History of Australia, V,* opposite 304.
16 Cannon, *The Land Boomers,* 157–64.
17 Ibid., 140.
18 Ibid., 131–8; Baillieu, *ADB, 7,* 140.
19 Cannon, *The Land Boomers,* 64.
20 D. McRae to N. Brennan, 13 April 1968, courtesy N. Brennan.
21 Cannon, *The Land Boomers,* 36.
22 Davison, *The Rise and Fall of Marvellous Melbourne,* 249.
23 Quoted in N. Brennan, *John Wren, Gambler,* 23.
24 Quoted in Barrett, *The Inner Suburbs,* vii.
25 Davison, *The Rise and Fall of Marvellous Melbourne,* 208.
26 '1901 Census', *Victorian Parliamentary Papers,* 1902–3, vol. 2, no. 25, cited in Hibbins, *A Short History of Collingwood,* 35.
27 Davison, *The Rise and Fall of Marvellous Melbourne,* 181.
28 Barrett, *The Inner Suburbs,* 61.
29 Ibid., 41.
30 3 May 1866.
31 Davison, *The Rise and Fall of Marvellous Melbourne,* 172; Hearn (Senyard), Collingwood Values, 5, 7; N. Brennan, *John Wren, Gambler,* 205–16.
32 1 May 1907.
33 Clark, *Select Documents in Australian History 1851–1900,* 685, 604.
34 8 January 1881.
35 Davison, *The Rise and Fall of Marvellous Melbourne,* 201; Hearn (Senyard), Collingwood Values, 5, 7.
36 Standish, *ADB, 6,* 172–3; de Serville, *Pounds and Pedigrees,* 42–76.
37 O'Callaghan, *ADB, 11,* 49; Haldane, *The People's Force,* 122–31.
38 1 February 1909, 450–4; 1 April 1909, 688–90.
39 *Lone Hand,* 1 May 1907.
40 4 October 1906.
41 Cameron Royal Commission, cited in *Lone Hand,* 1 May 1907.
42 *Gisborne Gazette,* 5 March 1926.

43 *Gisborne Gazette*, 5 March 1926.
44 Dow (ed.), *Trollope's Australia*, 168.
45 Blainey, *Our Side of the Country.*
46 Vamplew et al. (eds), *The Oxford Companion to Australian Sport*, 292, 310.
47 Dow (ed.), *Trollope's Australia*, 168.
48 Inglis, 'Gambling and culture in Australia', 12–13.
49 McCaughey et al. (eds), *Victoria's Colonial Governors*, 264.
50 Corrigan, *ADB*, *3*, 466.
51 Twain, *Mark Twain in Australia and New Zealand*, 161–4.
52 'Characteristics of Australian gambling', in Caldwell et al. (eds), *Gambling in Australia*, 27.
53 Adams, *ADB*, *3*, 15.
54 O'Hara, *A Mug's Game*, 95-6.
55 Vamplew, 'From sport to business', 23–4.
56 Charlton, *Two Flies Up A Wall*, 130–8.
57 Pacini, *A Century Galloped By*, 138.
58 Julius, *ADB*, *9*, 528–9.
59 Pacini, *A Century Galloped By*, 261–5.
60 *Common Weal* (Sydney), 1918.
61 Costello and Millar, *Wannabet?*, 8–10.

Chapter Three [pp 59–76]

1 Buggy, *The Real John* Wren; *ADB*, 7, 477–8, records how 'even in his last years he was able to recall all Victorian League grand final scores, as well as the results (with innings totals) of all Australia–England Test cricket matches.
2 Buggy, *The Real John Wren*, 2.
3 Ibid., 9.
4 Ahern, *A Century of Winners*, 87–91.
5 Buggy, *The Real John Wren*, 8–11.
6 Stremski, *Kill for Collingwood*, 59.
7 *Lone Hand*, 83.
8 Buggy, *The Real John Wren*, 17–19.
9 *Lone Hand*, 85.
10 *Advocate*, 12 December 1896.
11 McConville, 'John Wren', 55.
12 N. Brennan, *John Wren, Gambler*, 40.
13 Quoted from *Argus* in Buggy, *The Real John Wren*, 17.
14 19 November 1903.
15 Stremski, *Kill for Collingwood*, 297 n.9.
16 *Mercury*, 25 May 1893, quoted in Stremski, *Kill for Collingwood.*
17 Buggy, *The Real John Wren*, 25.
18 *Mercury*, 16 November 1893; N. Brennan, *John Wren, Gambler*, 38.
19 *Lone Hand*, 82.
20 Gaunson, *ADB*, *4*, 238; McConville, 'John Wren', 66.
21 *Mercury*, 28 June 1994, quoted in Stremski.
22 *Mercury*, 25 July 1995, quoted in Stremski.
23 21 November 1895, quoted in Stremski.
24 31 October 1895, quoted in Stremski.
25 17 October 1895, quoted in Stremski.

26 Buggy, *The Real John Wren*, 17; Stremski, *Kill for Collingwood*, 297 n.9.
27 Buggy, *The Real John Wren*, 17.
28 14 November 1903.
29 *Lone Hand*, 83; Bevan, *ADB*, *7*, 283–5.
30 Browne research notes (copy held by J. Griffin).
31 *Lone Hand*, 83.
32 Chief Commissioner of Police Correspondence, cited in McConville, "John Wren', 55 n.31
33 *Victorian Parliamentary Debates* (Legislative Assembly), 16 December 1998.
34 Hardy, *Power Without Glory*, 121–30.
35 *Lone Hand*, 84.
36 Proceedings are reported in *Leader*, 11, 18 March, 29 April 1899; *Age*, 14, 26, 28, 29 April 1899; *Argus*, 28, 29 April 1899.
37 6 May 1899.
38 Proceedings continued in *Age*, 18 May 1899; *Argus*, 18 May 1899; *Herald*, 10 May, 3 July 1899; *Leader*, 1 July 1899.
39 *Age*, 14 April 1899.
40 *Herald*, 6 November 1899.
41 *Lone Hand*, 84.
42 Records of Conduct of Service, Victoria Police, Registers nos 3060 and 4361, Victorian Police Historical Unit, Melbourne.
43 Death certificate 1223, 14 February 1939, Registry of Births, Deaths and Marriages, Melbourne.
44 Hardy, *Power Without Glory*, 123.
45 Hood, *ADB*, *9*, 358–9; Forde, *The Story of the Bar in Victoria*; Jacobs, *Judges of Yesterday*, 35–6; obit., *Argus*, 30 January 1922; Cannon, *The Land Boomers*, passim.

Chapter Four [pp 77–99]

1 *Argus*, 10 November 1905.
2 O'Donnell, *ADB*, *11*, 60; Buggy, *The Real John Wren*, 40–1.
3 *Gisborne Gazette*, 2, 9 October 1925; photocopied extracts of O'Donnell's memoirs, courtesy G. Browne.
4 *Gisborne Gazette*, 9 April 1926.
5 8 January 1906.
6 *Gisborne Gazette*, 26 February 1926.
7 *Gisborne Gazette*, 9 October 1925.
8 12 November 1906.
9 7 November 1903.
10 Buggy, *The Real John Wren*, 43.
11 Dunstan, *Wowsers*, 224.
12 Buggy, *The Real John Wren*, 44.
13 *Argus*, 18 January 1904.
14 *Herald*, 17 February 1904, quoted in Dunstan, *Wowsers*, 226.
15 6 July 1905.
16 Buggy, *The Real John Wren*, 32.
17 *Lone Hand*, 1 May 1907, 86–7.
18 Buggy, *The Real John Wren*, 32; *ADB*, *9*, 94.
19 28 June 1905.
20 1 May 1907, 87.

21 28, 29 June 1905.
22 29 June 1905.
23 City of Melbourne, VPRS Rate Books 1853–1975 Unit 42, 1906, La Trobe Ward, nos 746 and 749.
24 Fitzgerald, *Seven Days to Remember.*
25 *Lone Hand*, 1 May 1907, 87; Buggy, *The Real John Wren*, 32; *Australasian Typographical Journal*, 1 November 1904.
26 28 June 1905.
27 City of Melbourne, VPRS 932, Unit 3943, City Tattersalls Ltd, Memorandum and Articles of Association, 9 August 1905; and Statutory Report of Meeting to be held on 18 September 1905.
28 Grover says: there 'was probably an erroneous rather than a groundless suspicion. The horse personally achieved an honourable success by three lengths,' *Lone Hand*, 1 May 1907, 86.
29 Green, *ADB*, 9, 91–2; Jensen, *Dan Green.*
30 24 May 1906.
31 Database of Illegal Gambling Cases in Victoria, June–December 1905, unpublished, not exhaustive, based on *Argus* crime and law reports, compiled by D. Cash (copy held by J. Griffin).
32 *Argus*, 9, 12, 30 September, 7, 13, 27, 28 October 1905; *Truth*, 16 September, 7 October 1905.
33 *Argus*, 13 October 1905.
34 Record of Conduct and Service of Cornelius Crowe, Victoria Police Archives, 29 May 1897; Crowe, *The Inquiry Agent*, 53.
35 Crowe, *Serious Tampering with the Course of Justice.*
36 *Argus*, 23, 24, 25 November 1905.
37 Cf *Lone Hand*, 1 May 1907.
38 *Argus*, 30 November 1905.
39 Ibid; Crowe, *The Inquiry Agent*, 62, 71–5.
40 *Truth*, 11 December 1915; *Argus*, 25 March 1916.
41 *Gisborne Gazette*, 2 April 1926.
42 *Age*, *Argus*, 8 January 1906.
43 *Argus*, 8 January 1906.
44 *Argus*, 8 January 1906.
45 *Herald*,10 January 1906.
46 *Herald*, 11 January 1906.
47 *Argus*, 11 January 1906.
48 *Argus*, 10 January 1906.
49 12 January 1906.
50 N. Brennan, *John Wren, Gambler*, 81.
51 *Gisborne Gazette*, 9, 16 April 1926.
52 Anderson, *Larrikin Crook*, 15–24.
53 N. Brennan, *John Wren, Gambler*, 86.
54 18 January 1906.

Chapter Five [pp 100–128]

1 Cyril Pearl's phrase in *Wild Men of Sydney*, 206. Savanarola in the 1490s denounced corruption and immorality in Florentine society and in the Catholic Church, and was burnt at the stake.

2 Legend attributes the invention of 'wowser' to John Norton who derived it from 'We Only Want Social Evils Remedied'. In his *The Australian Language*, Sydney, 1978, 136–7, Sidney Baker opines: 'Moral and social philistinism ... had endowed us with the brand of clerical mind that battens on mild and normal pleasures and exaggerates them into orgiastic lusts'. The *OED* defines 'wowser' as an Australianism meaning 'a puritanical enthusiast or fanatic'.
3 1 July 1906.
4 Fysh, who was twice premier of Tasmania (1877–8, 1887–92), and Federal Post-Master General (1903–4), supported the transfer of Tattersall's Lottery to Tasmania.
5 *Review of Reviews*, 1 July 1906, 30.
6 *Truth*, 23 June 1906.
7 McKernan, 'An incident of social reform in Melbourne, 1906', 71.
8 Pacini, *A Century Galloped By*, 179, 187–90.
9 Judkins, *ADB*, *9*, 527.
10 Quotations from McKernan, 'An incident of social reform in Melbourne, 1906', 73–8.
11 *Truth*, 21 July 1906; Buggy, *The Real John Wren*, 108–10; Dunstan, *Wowsers*, 240.
12 *Table Talk*, 20 July 1906, cited in Dunstan, *Wowsers*, 241; Worrall, *ADB*, *12*, 574–5.
13 Dunstan, *Wowsers*, 238–45; McKernan, 'An incident of social reform in Melbourne, 1906', 80; Buggy, *The Real John Wren*, 112; *Truth*, 4 August 1906.
14 Bongiorno, *The People's Party*, 179.
15 Dunstan, *Wowsers*, 254–7; *Punch*, 14 June 1906; Smith, *ADB*, *11*, 670–1; *Lone Hand*, 1 May 1907, 88.
16 *Age*, 25, 27 September 1906; verse quoted in Buggy, *The Real John Wren*, 97–8; for Fitchett, see *ADB*, *8*, 511–13.
17 Buggy, *The Real John Wren*, 118–22.
18 *Truth*, 1, 8, 15 December 1906; Pearl, *Wild Men of Sydney*, 207; Bongiorno, *The People's Party*, 80.
19 *Lone Hand*, 1 May 1907, 88; Clark, *A History of Australia*, *V*, 273–4.
20 Reproduced in Crowe, *One Big Crime*, 42.
21 Cannon, *The Land Boomers*, 164 and passim.
22 Crowe, *One Big Crime*, 45.
23 Cited in *Spectator*, 18 August 1911.
24 7 September 1912.
25 Clark, *A History of Australia*, *V*, 359.
26 Martin, *Robert Menzies*, vol. 1, 15.
27 Osborn, 'A full day's work: a life of the Rev. T. S. B. Woodfull', *Proceedings of the Uniting Church Historical Society*, 2, 1, 1995, 3–35.
28 King, 'The tarring and the feathering of J. K. McDougall', *Labour History*, 45, 1983, 54–67.
29 McKernan, *Australian Churches at War*, 170.

Chapter Six [pp 129–148]

1 McConville, 'John Wren'.
2 [Judkins], 'The gambling demons in Australia', 30.
3 Moloney, *ADB*, *10*, 542.
4 Kennelly to Wren, 15 July 1940, Wren papers.

5 Crisp, *The Australian Federal Labour Party, 1901–1951*, 78.
6 Murray, *The Split*, 39–40.
7 McMullin, *The Light on the Hill*, 254.
8 Jones, *ADB*, *9*, 516.
9 Liston, *ADB*, *10*, 117–18.
10 Jungwirth, Autobiography.
11 Ford, *Cardinal Moran and the ALP*, 276.
12 Hughes and Graham, *A Handbook of Australian Government and Politics 1890–1964*, 285–305, 443–5, 410–11.
13 Ford, *Cardinal Moran and the ALP*, 237.
14 Sawer, *Australian Federal Politics and Law, 1901–1929*, 52; Bongiorno, *The People's Party*, 168; *Lone Hand*, 1 May 1907.
15 Bongiorno, *The People's Party*, 34, 172.
16 Bongiorno, *The People's Party*, 172–3; McCalman, *Struggletown*, 39; *Commonwealth Parliamentary Handbook*, 1918, 416; *Bulletin*, 1 December 1904.
17 Crowe, *The Inquiry Agent*, 45; *Vigilant*, 1 July 1920.
18 Findley, *ADB*, *8*, 496–7; McMullin, *The Light on the Hill*, 53–4.
19 *Argus*, 19 June 1908; *Australian Sentinel*, 6 July 1908.
20 Solly, *ADB*, *12*, 10.
21 McCalman, *Struggletown*, 37–8; Bongiorno, *The People's Party*, 185.
22 Childe, *How Labour Governs*, vi–vii.
23 Best, *History of the Federated Tobacco Workers' Union of Australia, Victorian Branch, 1884–1968*, 128; Solly, *ADB*, *12*, 10.
24 Bongiorno, *The People's Party*, 174.
25 Calwell, *Be Just and Fear Not*, 41; McMullin, *The Light on the Hill*, 142; Prendergast, *ADB*, *11*, 280–2; the late G. Serle, personal communication, 1987.
26 Bongiorno, *The People's Party*, 137, 183–4; *Herald*, 5 January 1907; *Bulletin*, 6 December 1906.
27 Wren to Scullin, Wren papers.
28 Bongiorno, *The People's Party*, 185–6; F. Brennan, *ADB*, *7*, 400–2; Hardy to K. Ryan, F Brennan papers.

Chapter Seven [pp 149–173]

1 Fitzpatrick, 'The spectrum of Australian bicycle racing; 1890–1900', in Cashman and McKernan (eds), *Sport in History*, 330–4.
2 1 May 1907, 86.
3 *Argus*, 16 December 1901.
4 *Argus*, 20 December 1901; *Australasian*, 28 December 1901.
5 *Argus*, 18, 19, 30 December 1905.
6 *Lone Hand*, 1 May 1907, 86.
7 Opperman, *Pedals, Politics and People*, 69–70.
8 *Lone Hand*, 1 May 1907, 86.
9 *Notable Australians: The Pictorial Who's Who*, first edition, West Australia, 1978, 962.
10 Opperman, *Pedals, Politics and People*, 69–70.
11 Ibid., 71.
12 Ibid., 154.
13 Ibid., 494.
14 Some remarks by a contemporary champion jockey, Darren Beadman, in the

Sydney Morning Herald (20 October 2000) confirm this generally accepted opinion. He calls the Cup 'the toughest test of stamina in the Australian racing calendar ... when the gates fly open it is on for young and old. These are not two-year-olds sizzling over 1,200 metres [in the Golden Slipper]. These are seasoned, hard, tough campaigners ... You don't get to rest in this Cup ... it is twice as far as the juvenile scamper ... This isn't a midweek staying contest for amblers ... This is competition at its finest. The pressure is on from the moment the colours go on ... you need a good on-pace runner that is tough. One that will get out of the machine and get mobile without going beserk ... no doubt fast stayers win the race.

15 *Lone Hand*, 1 May 1907, 86.

16 Clark, *A History of Australia*, V, 273.

17 Cavanough, *The Caulfield Cup*, 'I have detailed ... contemporary accounts ... those people who understand horse racing will appreciate that the running showed no signs of malpractice' (102–7); Buggy, *The Real John Wren*, 47–52.

18 'Musgrave galloped openly and vigorously at Caulfield', Cavanough, *The Caulfield Cup*, 103. NB. The weight (8 stone 12 pounds) attributed to Murmur in *Miller's Guide*, 1987, is incorrect.

19 Buggy, *The Real John Wren*, 50.

20 Cavanough, *The Caulfield Cup*, 103.

21 Pollard, *The Pictorial History of Australian Horse Racing*, 144.

22 Ibid., 105; *Miller's Guide*, 1987, passim.

23 Quoted in Cavanough, *The Caulfield Cup*, 105.

24 Ahern, *A Century of Winners*, 133.

25 Ibid., 107; Buggy, *The Real John Wren*, 52.

26 Cavanough, *The Caulfield Cup*. 107; Buggy, *The Real John Wren*, 52.

27 *The Australian Turf Register*, Melbourne, August 1901, 837.

28 *Victorian Parliamentary Debates*, 13 September 1906, 1777 .

29 Quoted in Buggy, *The Real John Wren*, 79.

30 Agnew, *Australia's Trotting Heritage*, 80–1.

31 27 September 1905.

32 Rubinstein, 'The changing demographic and socio-economic status of the Jewish community of Victoria, 1870–1980', 228.

33 But not listed in Main and Holmesbury, *The Encyclopedia of League Footballers*, 24–5.

34 Lemon and Freedman, *The History of Australian Thoroughbred Racing*, vol. 2, 387.

35 Clark and Sagazio, *The Story of Rippon Lea*, 24–5.

36 *Argus*, 27 July 1935.

37 A galloway is a small, strong horse originating in Galloway, Scotland.

38 Buggy, *The Real John Wren*, 80.

39 Eggleston, 'Confidential Notes'.

40 *Lone Hand*, 1 May 1907, 82.

41 Pacini, *A Century Galloped By*, 187–9.

42 Buggy, *The Real John Wren*, 142.

43 2, 16 December 1905.

44 Buggy, *The Real John Wren*, 145–6.

45 Ibid., 144–5.

46 Ibid., 80.

47 Pacini, *A Century Galloped By*, 196.
48 *Power Without Glory*, 162–5.
49 *New Zealand Turf Register*, 1903–4; *Truth*, 28 November 1903; *Australian Trotting Stud Book Mares' Index*, vols 1–9, Melbourne, 1970s, 79–80, 210–11, 236; Brown, *One Hundred Years of Trotting*, 60, 61; Beckett, *ADB*, *7*, 239–40.
50 Agnew, *Silks and Sulkies*, 64–5.
51 Quoted in ibid., 65.
52 Ibid.; *Australia's Trotting Heritage*, 85–7; 'Our most controversial official', *Harness World*, April 1980, 22–5.
53 Agnew, *Australia's Trotting Heritage*, 99–100.
54 Ibid., 94–6.
55 Ibid., 100–3.
56 Buggy, *The Real John Wren*, 157–8.
57 Ibid., 160.
58 Ibid., 160–1; *Brisbane Courier*, 24 April 1923; Noud, *Courses for Horses.*
59 Lemon and Freedman, *The History of Australian Thoroughbred Racing*, vol. 2, 435.
60 'Report of Joint Select Committee ... Horse Racing in Western Australia', *Western Australian Parliamentary Papers*, 1915, vol 2, paper A3, 46–8.
61 11 May 1912.
62 24 August 1912.
63 28 December 1912.
64 Lemon and Freedman, *The History of Australian Thoroughbred Racing*, vol. 2, 35.
65 'Report of Joint Select Committee ... Horse Racing in Western Australia', *Western Australian Parliamentary Papers*, 1915, vol. 2, paper A3, 66.
66 4 January 1913.
67 Lemon and Freedman, *The History of Australian Thoroughbred Racing*, vol. 2, 435; *Australasian*, 8, 15 June 1912, 1 May 1915.
68 'Report of Joint Select Committee ... Horse Racing in Western Australia', *Western Australian Parliamentary Papers*, 1915, vol. 2, paper A3, 66.
69 Tomlinson, *Born Winners, Born Losers*, 48–9.
70 4 January 1913.
71 *Australasian*, 19, 26 April 1913.
72 'Report of Joint Select Committee ... Horse Racing in Western Australia', *Western Australian Parliamentary Papers*, 1915, vol. 2, paper A3, 24.

Chapter Eight [pp 174–187]

1 Buggy, *The Real John Wren*,153–4.
2 Ibid., 151.
3 Notices sighted in *Argus*, 25 July, 29 August, 6, 29 September, 5, 30 October 1908; Brisbane, *Entertaining Australia*, 157 (by courtesy of Mimi Colligan, Melbourne).
4 *Advocate*, 4 July, 5, 26 September 1908.
5 *Advocate*, 11 September 1909.
6 Personal communication, May 2002.
7 Amadio, *ADB*, *7*, 49–50; Austral, *ADB*, *7*, 124–5.
8 Buggy, *The Real John Wren*, 153–4.
9 *Table Talk*, 12 September 1927 for profile of Talbot. Obits in *Argus*, *Sun*, 18 July 1949.

10 Buggy, *The Real John Wren*, 155.

11 Pratt (ed.), *The National Products Handbook of Australia's Industries*, 336.

12 Cain, *On with the Show*, 166.

13 Information from Richard Lean Jnr, Bonbeach, Melbourne.

14 VPRS, 932/12991, Richard Lean Pty Ltd, PROV; Wren papers.

15 Sullivan, Corbett, Fitzsimons, and Jeffries were successively world champion heavyweight boxers between 1885 and 1905. Peter Jackson was born in the West Indies, was 'adopted' as an Australian, won the Australian heavyweight title and was unbeaten in 28 fights overseas. Sullivan drew the 'colour line' to avoid fighting him. 'Young Griffo' (Arthur Griffiths) was unacknowledged world featherweight champion.

16 Buggy, *The Real John Wren*, 124–5.

17 Ibid., 125–6; see 'Boxing' in *The Australian Encyclopaedia*, 2, Sydney, 1958, 84–7.

18 Clark, *A History of Australia*, V, 273.

19 Buggy, *The Real John Wren*, 130.

20 The Canadian Tommy Burns, world heavyweight boxing champion 1906–8, is not to be confused with the popular welterweight champion of Australia with the same name who flourished in the immediate post-war period.

21 Buggy, *The Real John Wren*, 134-7.

22 Ibid., 131–2.

23 Ibid., 136.

24 Clark, *A History of Australia*, V, 271.

25 Quoted in Corris, *Lords of the Ring*, 95.

26 Quoted in Gordon, *An Eyewitness Account of Australia*, 182.

27 Corris, *Lords of the Ring*, 95–6.

28 D. Cash 'Stadiums Ltd (1914–37) and Stadiums Pty Ltd (1937–83): A Guide to Records in the University of Melbourne Archives', copy held by author.

29 Ibid.

30 Broome, 'Boxing' in Vamplew et al. (eds), *The Oxford Companion to Australian Sport*, 69.

31 What was called 'Boxers and Wrestlers Proportion' compared to 'Gross Takings' was as follows:
(1920) £20,723 out of £43,406
(1925) £34,136 out of £92,089
(1930) £34,590 out of £61,955
(1940) £41,295 out of £88,020
(1950) £60,377 out of £155,144
See Cash, 'Stadiums Ltd (1914–37) and Stadiums Pty Ltd (1937–83): A Guide to Records in the University of Melbourne Archives', copy held by author.

32 Corris, *Lords of the Ring, passim.*

33 Park and Champion, *Home Before Dark*, 81.

34 Minutes, 23 August, 6 September, 1 November 1916.

35 Corris, *Lords of the Ring*, 189.

36 To Fred Kay (in unidentified press interview by J. M. Rohan), Wren said, when he saw how unprepossessing Kay was, 'The fact that your mother and grandmother [Mrs Eliza Foster] were great friends of mine are no reason why I should endanger your life'. Tommy Burns, noted welterweight champion of Australia in the 1940s, wrote to Wren (2 February 1952) thanking him for advising him to quit. However, Burns did 'come back' as late as 1954 in spite of commenting that

no rational man enjoys boxing professionally (letter in Wren papers).

37 Hardy, *Power Without Glory*, 661; Corris, *Lords of the Ring*, 160.
38 Hearn, 'Collingwood values'.
39 *Truth*, 14 December 1907.
40 Cain, *On with the Show*, 165.
41 Quoted in York, 'No holds barred', 7.
42 Gordon, *An Eyewitness Account of Australia*, 239–40.

Chapter Nine [pp 189–195]

1 Stremski, *Kill for Collingwood*, 1–5.
2 Hutchinson and Ross (eds), *The Clubs*, 84.
3 Richards with Phillips, *The Kiss of Death*, 1–2, 22.
4 Stremski, *Kill for Collingwood*, 61, 80–1.
5 Sandercock and Turner, *Up Where Cazaly?*, 57.
6 Cf. Ibid., 59: 'It was accepted that players would get a 'hand-out' from their club after each game. The money either came under the lap from wealthy patrons [one of the allegations against John Wren] or was disguised in the club's balance sheet as legitimate expenses'.
7 Ross (ed.), *100 Years of Football*, 32.
8 Stremski, *Kill for Collingwood*, 124, 306–7.
9 Interview with R. Rose, Melbourne, November 2001.
10 Richards with Phillips, *The Kiss of Death*, 76.
11 Hutchinson and Ross, *The Clubs*, 86.
12 Stremski, *Kill for Collingwood*, 115–16.
13 Ibid., 109.
14 Ibid., 309 n.44.
15 Ibid., 146.
16 Ibid., 147.
17 Ibid., 309 n.56.
18 Hansen, *The Magpies, 1892–1992*, 122; Stremski, *Kill for Collingwood*, 170.
19 Stremski, *Kill for Collingwood*, 167–70.
20 Woods obit, *Age*, 11 February 2002.
21 Macintyre, 'Football weathers the storms of war', 91.
22 Griffin, 'A big lie'.
23 *Australian*, 8 January 2001.
24 Stremski, *Kill for Collingwood*, 173.
25 Hansen, *The Jack Dyer Story*, 122–3. Compare Dyer's story 'I felt hate', in *Herald-Sun*, 1 October 1992, where he says Jack Regan, champion Collingwood full-back, not Rippon, told him to contact Wren.

Chapter Ten [pp 196–208]

1 Alfred Harmsworth, later Baron Northcliffe, established a prototype penny tabloid, the *Daily Mail*, in 1896 in London. It was highly influential, particularly during the First World War. Northcliffe eventually purchased the prestigious *Times*.
2 Wilde et al (eds), *Oxford Companion to Australian Literature*, 119; Whyte, *ADB*, *12*, 480–1; Buggy, *The Real John Wren*, 228.
3 Fitzgerald, *'Red Ted'*, 72; N Brennan, *John Wren, Gambler*,159.
4 Fitzgerald, *'Red Ted'*, *passim;* Theodore, *ADB*, *12*, 197–202.

5 Wren papers.
6 Ibid.
7 Quoted from *Daily Mail* in Fitzgerald, *'Red Ted'*, 82.
8 *Daily Mail*, 27 October 1916.
9 *Bulletin*, 11 May 1916.
10 *Daily Mail*, 23, 25 October, 10 November 1916.
11 *Daily Mail*, 30 November 1917.
12 Fihelly, *ADB*, *8*, 495.
13 *Labor Daily*, 9 July 1935; Lemon and Freedman, *The History of Australian Thoroughbred Racing*, vol. 2, 418–19; *Argus*, 23 October 1929; *Courier-Mail*, 10 July 1935.
14 Guyatt, 'The publicists', 247.
15 Weller (ed.), *Caucus Minutes 1901–1945*, vol. 1, 1901–17, 442. For confusion on that day, see Fitzhardinge, *The Little Digger*, 225–7. Sharpe may have been the member who 'actually left the room but not knowing where the rest had gone, returned to the Party room'.
16 *Argus*, 19 August 1916, 28 March 1917; *Brisbane Courier*, 28 March 1917.
17 Copy of letter, pp. 2-4, held by author (p. 1 missing).
18 'Mr Norman White with John Wren' , 16 January 1919, in Wren papers.
19 Buggy, *The Real John Wren*, 228.
20 Murdoch, *ADB*, *10*, 624–5.
21 Zwar, *In Search of Keith Murdoch*, 81.
22 Norris papers.
23 Zwar, *In Search of Keith Murdoch*, 81.
24 Norris papers.
25 Bednall, *ADB*, *13*, 149–50. In 1965 Bednall was appointed to UNESCO's Committee of 20 on Space Communications. Later, appalled by the poverty he saw in Asia, he joined the Australian Labor Party and stood unsuccessfully against (Sir) Philip Lynch in the 1972 and 1974 federal elections. He became media consultant to prime minister Gough Whitlam.
26 Bednall in Norris papers.
27 Ibid.
28 Ibid.
29 Norris papers.
30 See under Bridget Partridge, *ADB*, *11*, 151–2.
31 Nairn, *'The Big Fella'*, 65.

Chapter Eleven [pp 209–219]

1 *Australasian*, 10 April 1915.
2 Grant, *Jacka VC*, 164.
3 Robson, *First AIF*, 49; Jacka, *ADB*, *9*, 452–3.
4 VA 679, Registrar General and Office of Titles 1887–1960, VPRS 932, Defunct Trading Company Files, Unit 6982, Jacka Edmonds & Company Pty Ltd, 8 December 1919, PROV.
5 Grant, *Jacka VC*, 166.
6 Ibid., 170–1.
7 VPRS 932, Unit 369, Item 6982, 25 October 1932, PROV.
8 Grant, *Jacka VC*, 170.
9 Dening, *Xavier*, 148.

10 Longmire, *History of St Kilda*, vol. 3, 32.
11 Grant, *Jacka VC*, 173–4.
12 Clark, *A History of Australia, VI*, 345; Macintyre, *Oxford History of Australia*, vol. 4, 285–6.
13 Grant, *Jacka VC*, 185.
14 Ibid., 25
15 Rule, 'Jacka's mob'.
16 Longmire, *History of St Kilda*, vol. 3, 25, 300.
17 Grant, *Jacka VC*, 164.
18 Garden, *Victoria, a History*, 311.
19 26 August 1915.
20 19 August 1915.
21 19 August 1915.
22 21 August 1915.
23 'Detailed Medical History of an Invalid', John Wren, 20 November 1915, CRS B2455, Personal Dossiers for AIF ex-service members, ANA, Canberra.
24 Butler, *Official History of the Australian Medical Services*, vol. 1, 79; vol. 2, 472–3, 502, 568; vol. 3, 642, 696–7, 946, 976.
25 Garden, *Victoria, a History*, 311.
26 For further discussion see Griffin, 'The choice of Achilles?', 52–5.
27 *Sporting Globe*, 11 November 1953.

Chapter Twelve [pp 220–231]

1 Buggy, *The Real John Wren*, 242.
2 Ibid., 185–7.
3 Hardy, *Power Without Glory*, 108–10.
4 Ibid., 276.
5 Anderson, *Larrikin Crook*, 220. Henry Stokes, Anderson says, was considered a possible agent in Taylor's killing.
6 Hardy, *Power Without Glory*, 399; Buggy, *The Real John Wren*, 229.
7 Buggy, *The Real John Wren*, 231.
8 Hardy, *Power Without Glory*, 283.
9 Buggy, *The Real John Wren*, 182.
10 Anderson, *Larrikin Crook*, 15–16.
11 Buggy, *The Real John Wren*, 181.
12 Buggy, *The Real John Wren*, 181, 187; Buggy to N. Brennan, 23 August 1967 (copy in author's possession).
13 Hardy-Rix and Stavely, *True Blue Stories of Bravery from Victorian Police*, 57–60.
14 Hardy, *Power Without Glory*, 310, 341, 343, 357.
15 *Referee*, 22, 29 March 1917.
16 Hardy, *Power Without Glory*, 396–400.
17 Buggy, *The Real John Wren*, 237
18 Anderson, *Larrikin Crook*, 128–40.
19 Ibid., 183–4.
20 Buggy, *The Real John Wren*, 238
21 Anderson, *Larrikin Crook*, 185.
22 Ibid., 25.
23 Hardy, *Power Without Glory*, 456–61.
24 Anderson, *Larrikin Crook*, 219. For the reports of Clyde Palmer and Tom Kilynak

in the *Sun* and *Herald* respectively, 28 October 1927, see Gordon, *An Eyewitness Account of Australia*, 228–31. Palmer had been tipped off that 'something' would happen at Cutmore's house, and was close by.

25 Anderson, *Larrikin Crook*, 186.

26 1 October 1930.

27 4, 11 October 1930.

28 For Buckley's trial etc., see *Argus*, 26–9 November, 10–12 December 1930.

29 *Truth*, 28 December 1946.

30 Buggy, *The Real John Wren*, 244.

31 26 December 1946.

32 Lynn and Armstrong, *From Pentonville to Pentridge.*

33 *Age*, 26 December 1946.

34 Minutes of Executive Council, Victoria, July–September 1946 (vol. 180) and October–December 1946 (vol. 181), VPRS 1080, Units 140–1, PROV.

35 VPRS 10374, Units 27–29, vol. 27, 1944, vol. 28, 1945, vol. 29, 1946, PROV.

36 18 September 1953.

37 19 September 1953.

Chapter Thirteen [pp 232–255]

1 McConville, 'John Wren', 60.

2 *Advocate*, 21 October 1911; Buggy, *The Real John Wren*, 196.

3 Fred Johns, *Fred Johns Annual (Australia's Prominent People)*, London, 1914, 139: Mannix is 'one of the most brilliant scholars in the Roman Catholic Church'.

4 *Advocate*, 23 September 1916; Phelan, *ADB*, *11*, 212–13.

5 Hoare, *ADB*, 9, 314–15; Brennan, *ADB*, *7*, 402; Heydon, *ADB*, *9*, 277–8; Hughes, *ADB*, *9*, 392–3; Madden, *ADB*, *10*, 370–3.

6 Rentoul, *ADB*, *11*, 363–4; Leeper, *ADB*, *10*, 54–7; Snowball *ADB*, *12*, 7.

7 Quoted in Ebsworth, *Archbishop Mannix*, 188–9.

8 *Advocate*, 10 September 1917.

9 Ebsworth, *Archbishop Mannix*, 192.

10 Phelan, *ADB*, *11*, 212–13.

11 Rivett, *Australian Citizen, Herbert Brookes 1867–1963*, 58–77.

12 Kiernan, *ADB*, *9*, 589–90; Tudor, *ADB*, *12*, 281–2.

13 30 July 1919.

14 2 August 1919.

15 9 September 1919.

16 Beckett, *ADB*, *7*, 239.

17 *Advocate*, 6 September 1919.

18 Murphy, *T. J. Ryan*, 336, 469.

19 Quoted in Ebsworth, *Archbishop Mannix*, 215.

20 *Commonwealth Parliamentary Handbook 1918*, 413.

21 Murphy, *T. J. Ryan*, 463.

22 Fitzhardinge, *The Little Digger*, vol. 2, 262.

23 Rivett, *Australian Citizen, Herbert Brookes 1867–1963*, 62; McKernan, *Australian Churches at War*, 157–8.

24 Cronin and Adair, *The Wearing of the Green*, 119.

25 McKernan, *Australian Churches at War*, 120.

26 *Argus*, 11 March 1920.

27 Ibid., 13 March 1920.

28 Buggy, *The Real John Wren*, 162.
29 13 March 1920.
30 Ibid.
31 *Advocate*, 25 March 1921.
32 Ibid.
33 Cronin and Adair, *The Wearing of the Green*, 123.
34 N. Brennan, *John Wren, Gambler*, 128–30.
35 Kwan, 'The Australian Flag, the Irish Republic and *Ireland Will Be* Free …', seminar paper, 1993, 10.
36 Ibid., 11
37 *Advocate*, 25 March 1921.
38 Buggy, *The Real John Wren*, 205.
39 Henderson, 'The deportation of Charles Jerger', 61–78.
40 *Advocate*, 5 August 1982.
41 21 July 1920.
42 Fitzhardinge, *The Little Digger*, vol. 2, 452–6.
43 23 July 1920, quoted in Henderson, 'The deportation of Charles Jerger', 77.
44 *Advocate*, 25 November 1920.
45 Hannan, *ADB*, *9*, 187–8.
46 Castles, *ADB*, *7*, 588–9; Parer, *ADB*, *11*, 133–4.
47 *Advocate*, 18 December 1920.
48 Ibid., 23 July 1921.
49 O'Farrell, *The Catholic Church and Community in Australia*, 344–6.

Chapter Fourteen [pp 256–279]

1 Wren papers.
2 Fitzhardinge, *'Red Ted'*, 279.
3 Wren papers.
4 McMullin, *The Light on the Hill*, 148.
5 Macintyre, *The Oxford History of Australia*, vol. 4, 253; Kennedy, *The Mungana Affair*.
6 2 July 1928, Wren papers.
7 Young, *Theodore, his Life and Times*, 85.
8 Personal communication.
9 McMullin, *The Light on the Hill*, 149.
10 Quoted in Edwards, *Bruce of Melbourne*, 191.
11 McCalman, *Struggletown*,116.
12 Ibid.; see also Anderson, *Larrikin Crook*.
13 Robertson, *J. H. Scullin*, 123.
14 Lang, *The Great Bust*, 315, 329.
15 Ibid., 329.
16 Ibid, 156.
17 Calwell, *Be Just and Fear Not*, 47.
18 Souter, *Acts of Parliament*, 237.
19 Brennan, *ADB*, *7*, 400–2.
20 Maloney, *ADB*, *10*, 389–90.
21 Fenton, *ADB*, *8*, 482–4.
22 Author interview with J. F. Wren.
23 Drakeford, *ADB*, *14*, 35–6.

24 Hannan, *ADB*, *9*, 187–8.
25 Day, *John Curtin*, 334–5.
26 Murray, *The Split*, 278.
27 *Herald*, 9 October 1926, 17 January, 1 November 1927.
28 VPRS, 932/12767, Upper Watut Gold Mining Company Pty Ltd, PROV.
29 5 April 1930.
30 *Age*, 2 November 1940.
31 Day, *John Curtin*, 335.
32 Ibid., 47.
33 Scarfe, *No Taste for Carnage, Alex Sheppard*, 15.
34 Cook, 'Frank Anstey and Memoirs of the Scullin Government 1929–1932', 366.
35 Mishael, Lend Me Your Ears, part 1, 9.
36 *Labor Call*, 7 November 1940; Anstey, *ADB*, *7*, 80.
37 McMullin, *The Light on the Hill*, 142.
38 Reproduced in Agnew, *Silks and Sulkies.*
39 28 October 1953.
40 Smith, J. J., *ADB*, *11*, 650–1; Donohoe, *ADB*, *8*, 321–2.
41 McMullin, *The Light on the Hill*, 128-9, 142.
42 Nairn, *The 'Big Fella'*, 54.
43 Lang, *The Great Bust*, 307.
44 Tennant, *Evatt, Politics and Justice*, 62.
45 Edwards, *ADB*, *8*, 415–16*;* Edgar, 'King of the West End'.
46 Sir Otto Niemeyer, a director of the Bank of England, came to Australia in mid-1930 at the invitation of the federal government to conduct an enquiry into Australia's public finances. He advised that Australia's living standards were too high and that expenditures and wages had to be reduced.
47 Daly, *ADB*, *8*, 201.
48 McGillick, *Comrade No More*, 12, 34–5.
49 Lang, *The Great Bust*, 106, 145.
50 *Commonwealth Parliamentary Debates*, 1929, vol. 122, 1238–9.
51 McMullin, *The Light on the Hill*, 158.
52 Young, *Theodore, his Life and Times*, 86.
53 McMullin, *The Light on the Hill*, 158.
54 *Commonwealth Parliamentary Debates*, 1929, vol. 122, 290.
55 Ibid., 679.
56 Weller (ed.), *Caucus Minutes 1901–1941*, vol. 2, 1917–1931, 428.
57 Schedvin, *Australia and the Great Depression*, 143.
58 *Commonwealth Parliamentary Debates*, 1931, vol. 132, 881–2.
59 *Argus*, 12 December 1921.
60 *Commonwealth Parliamentary Debates*, 1931, vol. 132, 882.
61 Ibid., 886.
62 Forde in ibid., 883.
63 Ross, *John Curtin*, 66.
64 Wren papers.
65 Crisp, *Ben Chifley*, 158.
66 Author's interviews with Keon and Loughnan, June 1986.
67 Wren papers.
68 Wren to Scullin, 11 April 1947, Wren papers.
69 Wren papers.

70 Martin, *Robert Menzies*, vol. 1, 89 n.59.

71 Ibid., 90 n.60. Dixon wrote in his diary on 16 April 1952: 'I had lunch at the Aust. Club and talked to [Mr Justice] Starke who spoke about Latham's appointment as a job with Lyons in exchange for his making way for the latter as P.M.' See also Murdoch, *ADB*, *10*, 625.

72 Fricke, *Judges of the High Court*, 68; Whitlam, *The Whitlam Government 1972–1975*, 138, 164; Ayres, *Owen Dixon*, 61–4.

73 Nairn, *The 'Big Fella'*, 235.

74 Brown, *ADB*, *7*, 442; Brett, 'Stanley Melbourne Bruce', 137 ('the contrast with its [Bruce Government's] pursuit of unions for breaches of industrial relations was glaring').

75 Knox, *ADB*, *9*, 626.

76 Cowen, *Sir John Latham and Other Papers*, 28.

77 Latham, *ADB*, *10*, 4–5. Macintyre lamely exculpates Latham on the basis that the chain of events was merely 'predicted', not organised. There are clearly differing standards of critical 'analysis' here in comparison to the general treatment of Wren's conduct.

78 Lloyd, 'Not peace but a sword! The High Court under J. G. Latham', 175–202.

79 Whitlam, *The Whitlam Government 1972–1975*, 164. Interestingly, Mr Justice Sir Hayden Starke put off retirement from the High Court until January 1950, when he was almost seventy-nine. By holding back, Starke prevented the Labor government making a less conservative appointment to replace him. Starke behaved towards justices Evatt and McTiernan, Labor appointees in 1930, 'with an undisguised hostility'. Before the bank nationalisation case hearing in 1948 'he rebuffed a suggestion that he should not sit because his wife had a small shareholding in one of the banks' (*ADB 12*, 53). Mr Justice Sir George Rich, who was first appointed in 1913, resigned only in June 1950 aged eighty-seven. The bench, needless to say, remained conservative.

Chapter Fifteen [pp 280–296]

1 Clark, *A History of Australia*, *VI*, 497.

2 Ibid., *V*, 298.

3 Tennant, *Evatt, Politics and Justice*, 39–41.

4 Ibid., 39–41.

5 Ibid., 59–60.

6 Lang, *The Great Bust*, 315–16.

7 Calwell, *Be Just and Fear Not*, 194.

8 *Argus*, 18 April 1935.

9 Rich, *ADB*, *11*, 372.

10 Tennant, *Evatt, Politics and Justice*, 117.

11 Crockett, *Evatt, a Life*, 92–5; Hasluck, *The Government and the People, 1939–1941*, 366–7.

12 Hasluck, *The Government and the People, 1939–1941*, 280.

13 Tennant, *Evatt, Politics and Justice*, 127.

14 Day, *John Curtin, a Life*, 406–7.

15 Lang, *The Turbulent Years*, 194.

16 Dalziel, *Evatt the Enigma*, 19.

17 Ibid., 19–20.

18 *Commonwealth Parliamentary Debates*, 167, 174

19 Ibid., 5 November 1941, 187, 70.
20 Renouf, *Let Justice Be Done*, 245.
21 *Daily Telegraph*, 4 October 1946.
22 McMullin, *The Light on the Hill*, 238.
23 Tennant, *Evatt, Politics and Justice*, vii, 26.
24 Buckley et al., *Doc Evatt*, 216.
25 Letters, *Australian Book Review*, August 2001, 6-7.
26 Buckley et al., *Doc Evatt*, 215.

Chapter Sixteen [pp 297–318]

1 McConville, 'John Wren', 54.
2 Ibid., 54 n.34, 56.
3 McCalman, *Struggletown*, 36–7.
4 Ibid., 36–70.
5 Carringbush Regional Library, *Copping it Sweet*, 80.
6 Ibid., 237.
7 5 March 1935.
8 Hibbins, *A Short History of Collingwood*, 45.
9 Scarfe, *No Taste for Carnage, Alex Sheppard*, 22–4.
10 See Sheppard (ed.), *Catholic Action and Australian Labor*.
11 Hibbins, *A Short History of Collingwood*, 45.
12 Hardy, *The Hard Way*, 53–8.
13 McCalman, *Struggletown*, 116–19, 177–9.
14 Hardy, *The Hard Way*, 53–4.
15 *Age*, 4 March 1954; see also *Herald*, 3–5 March 1954; *Sun*, 4–6 March 1954.
16 'Confidential Notes', Menzies Library.
17 McCalman, *Struggletown*, 38.
18 Ibid., 101.
19 Local option is a process whereby the residents of a locality vote on whether alcoholic drinks should be sold.
20 Victorian ALP Central Executive Minutes (part of DLP papers, La Trobe Library), Special Meetings, 14 October, 9 December 1927.
21 Ibid.
22 Blackburn, *ADB*, 7, 310–2; McMullin, *The Light on the Hill*, 143; N. Brennan, *John Wren, Gambler*, 152–5.
23 McManus questionnaire in N. Brennan papers; Holt, 'A Lifetime of Service'.
24 McMullin, *The Light on the Hill*, 248–65.
25 Letter, *Eureka Street*, November 1992.
26 Tunnecliffe, *ADB*, *12*, 284–5; *Table Talk*, 18 August 1927.
27 Hogan, *ADB*, *9*, 323–5; White, *John Cain*, 76.
28 Calwell, *Be Just and Fear Not*, 44.
29 Jungwirth, Autobiography.
30 White, *John Cain*, 57–8.
31 Quoted in *Advocate*, 15 November 1928.
32 The main features of the Premiers' Plan were: 'reduced government expenditure, increased taxation, reduction of interest rates on the deposits and advances by banks and the conversions of the government debt on the basis of a $22\frac{1}{2}$ per cent reduction'. Cotter, 'War, boom and depression', 267.
33 McMullin, *The Light on the Hill*, 179–80; White, *John Cain*, 70; Garden, *Victoria*,

a History, 374; Tunnecliffe, *ADB*, *12*, 285.
34 Calwell, *Be Just and Fear Not*, 41–4; Calwell, *ADB*, *13*, 341–5.
35 *Argus*, cutting dated 25 April 1939.
36 Duncan, *Crusaders or Conspiracy?*, 183–4.
37 McManus, *The Tumult and the Shouting*, 24–5.
38 Quoted in White, *John Cain*, 98.
39 Kiernan, *ADB*, *8*, 589–90.
40 The *Guardian* mentioned forthcoming legislation with approval on 19 August 1939, and on 26 August had a headline, 'Big Dairies Grab Huge Profits', which referred also to the mergers by big companies and the reduction of 284 retail dairies in the past three years.
41 White, *John Cain*, 100.
42 Barry, *ADB*, *13*, 121–3; Barry papers.
43 Personal information.
44 Bell, *ADB*, *13*, 159; McCalman, *Struggletown*, 115.

Chapter Seventeen [pp 319–339]

1 Kent, *The Solomon Islands*, 118.
2 *Argus*, 23, 25 March 1918; *Table Talk*, 28 March 1918; *Australasian*, 30 March; *Leader*, 30 March 1918; *Australian Encyclopaedia*, 8, 1958, 382.
3 *Table Talk*, 6 November 1913.
4 VA 679, Registrar-General and Office of Titles, VPRS 932, Unit 9021, PROV.
5 *Argus*, 17 September, 22 November, 5, 6, 12 December 1924.
6 *Argus*, 12, 13, 18, 19 December 1924; 6, 8, 9, 10, 14, 15, 16 January 1925.
7 Cain, *On with the Show*, 169.
8 *Argus*, 12 January, 27 November, 7 December 1925; 25 July, 21 November 1927; 19 March 1930; 31 January, 7 February 1931; 18, 19 January 1932.
9 *Argus*, 3 May 1933.
10 *Argus*, 18 April, 22, 24, 29 December 1932.
11 Stremski, *Kill for Collingwood*, 101–2, 303.
12 *Argus*, 18 April, 22, 24, 29 December 1932; 4 February, 5, 6, 10, 13, 20 April, 9, 11 May, 8 December 1933; 27 May 1934.
13 *Argus*, 27 November 1934.
14 *Argus*, 1 April, 24, 27, 30 September, 29 November, 5 December 1935; 31 January, 12, 13 February 1936.
15 *Argus*, May, June, July, 1, 7 August 1936, passim; *Truth*, 1 August 1936; Richmond *Guardian*, 1 August 1936; *Victorian Parliamentary Debates*, Session 1936, vol. 199, 28, 30, 214, 215, 248.
16 *Argus*, 31 July 1936.
17 Emmerson, 'George Beavis, the pioneering years of midgets'.
18 Hardy, *Power Without Glory*, 569–70.
19 Dunstan (ed.), 'Racing and Politics', 363–9, *Argus*, 23 February 1939.
20 *Argus*, 12 August 1933.
21 Dunstan, 'Racing and Politics', 366–8.
22 *Argus*, 4 March 1939.
23 *Argus*, 14 March 1939.
24 Armstrong, *Frank Hardy and* Power Without Glory, 50.
25 *Argus*, 7 February 1928.
26 Armstrong, *Frank Hardy and* Power Without Glory, 50.

27 Donaldson, *ADB*, *8*, 318–19.
28 *Sporting Globe*, 19 November 1932.
29 14 March 1935.
30 Dyett, *ADB*, *8*, 394.
31 *Harness World*, April 1980, 25.
32 *Vigilant*, 15 August 1938.
33 *Victorian Parliamentary Debate* (*Legislative Council*), Session 1928, 109–60.
34 *Victorian Parliamentary Debates* (*Legislative Assembly*), Session 1929, vol. 179, 1189.
35 Ibid., vol. 180, 4 September 1929, 1357.
36 Ibid., 1 October 1929, 1932–4.
37 Ibid., 24 September 1929, 1782–96 (and 1 October 1929, 1927).
38 Ibid., 15 October 1929, 2218.
39 Ibid., 16 October 1929, 2231–5.
40 Pacini, *A Century Galloped By*, 324–6.
41 Ibid., 330.
42 Argus, 5 March 1918.
43 *Argus*, 13 June 1918.
44 *Royal Commission on Racing in Queensland 1929*, 2 vols, 23 October 1929.
45 D. O'Mara to H. W. Austin, 9 October 1953, Wren papers.
46 Deed of sale, 24 June 1954, Wren papers; Noud, *Courses for Horses*, 2–3, 21.
47 *National Times*, 3–9 January 1982.
48 Connolly, *ADB*, *8*, 89–90.
49 Ahern, *A Century of Winners*, 177; Buggy, *The Real John Wren*, 54.
50 Buggy, *The Real John Wren*, 53; personal communication, A. Sleigh.
51 Buggy, *The Real John Wren*, 54.
52 *Sporting Globe*, 4 November 1953; Buggy, *The Real John Wren*, 55.
53 Ahern, *A Century of Winners*, 196.
54 Cash, John Wren and Racing, 70–1.

Chapter Eighteen [pp 340–350]

1 O'Farrell, *The Catholic Church and Community in Australia*, 337.
2 N. Brennan, *John Wren, Gambler*, 132, 215.
3 It would be interesting to know if Murphy (1948) was published after the attack by leading Catholic Actionist, S. M. Keon, on Wren in July 1948.
4 Ebsworth, *Archbishop Mannix*, 434.
5 Murphy, Daniel Mannix, (1948) 72, (1972) 64.
6 N. Brennan, *John Wren, Gambler*, 132.
7 Garden, *Victoria, a History*, 296.
8 N. Brennan, *John Wren, Gambler*, 132.
9 Garden, *Victoria, a History*, 348; author interview with J. F. Wren.
10 Ebsworth, *Archbishop Mannix*, 196–7.
11 Santamaria, *Daniel Mannix*, 53.
12 Carr, *ADB*, *7*, 569–70; Phelan, *ADB*, *11*, 212–13 ; Kenny, *ADB*, *9*, 569–70; N. O'Donnell, *ADB*, *11*, 60–1; T. Brennan, *ADB*, *7*, 402.
13 Hardy, *The Hard Way*, 60.
14 Archer, *The Treasure House*, 23.
15 *Advocate*, 9 May 1929.
16 Gregory, *Church and State*, 203.

17 *Victorian Parliamentary Debates*, 1941, vol. 212, 2190.
18 Ibid.
19 N. Brennan, *John Wren, Gambler*, 215–16.
20 Ebsworth, *Archbishop Mannix*, 434; personal communication with C. Wren.
21 Hackett, *ADB, 9*, 153–4; letters to his sister, in Hackett papers.
22 Duhig, *ADB, 8*, 356–9; Boland, *James Duhig*, passim.
23 Wren to Duhig, 31 January 1930, Brisbane Diocesan Archives.
24 Boland, *James Duhig*, 257.
25 Duhig to Wren, 2 June 1952, Brisbane Diocesan Archives.
26 Wren to Duhig, 9 February 1929, Brisbane Diocesan Archives.
27 Wren to Duhig, 7 August 1946, 4 June 1948, Brisbane Diocesan Archives.
28 Duhig to Wren, 17 May 1950, Brisbane Diocesan Archives.
29 Duhig to Wren, 24 September 1953, Brisbane Diocesan Archives.
30 Duhig to Mrs [Ellen] Wren, 10 November 1953, Brisbane Diocesan Archives.

Chapter Nineteen [pp 351–363]

1 18 August 1927.
2 White, *John Cain & Victorian Labor, 1917–1957*, passim.
3 Duncan, *Crusaders or Conspiracy?*, 117.
4 Browne, Stan Keon; McCalman, *Struggletown*, 226–41.
5 McMullin, *The Light on the Hill*, 248, 265; White, *John Cain & Victorian Labor, 1917–1957*, 128–41.
6 Duncan, *Crusaders or Conspiracy?*, 117.
7 Murray, *The Split*, 93.
8 Ibid., 92.
9 *Sun*, 28, 30 July 1948; *Age*, *Argus*, 29 July 1948 *et seq.*
10 Murray, *The Split*, 93.
11 Ibid., 67.
12 Author interview with Keon, June 1986.
13 'Keon' in Carringbush Regional Library, *Copping It Sweet*, 166, 237–41.
14 Crisp, *Australian National Government*, 188.
15 E. G. Theodore in *Labor Daily*, 25 May 1925.
16 N. Brennan, *John Wren, Gambler*, 196.
17 Wren to Scullin, 22 November 1941, in Wren papers.
18 Personal information.
19 *Bulletin*, 25 December 1976; see also Meeking to Brennan, 30 March 1968, copy in author's possession courtesy N. Brennan.
20 *Bulletin*, 25 December 1976.

Chapter Twenty [pp 364–384]

1 Author interview with J. F. Wren; P. Freeman, *Age*, 9 January 1982.
2 Author interview with J. F. Wren.
3 *Sporting Globe*, 28 October 1953.
4 Blainey, *Mines in the Spinifex*, 83–4; Hore-Lacy, *Broken Hill to Mt Isa*, 188–9.
5 VPRS 932/12767, Upper Watut Gold Mining Co Pty Ltd, PROV.
6 Author interview with Ray Betts, Melbourne, 29 April 2002.
7 VPRS 567/779/9570, Roma Mooga Oilfields NL, PROV.
8 Boland, *James Duhig, passim.*
9 Jensen, *ADB, 9*, 480–1.

10 Wilkinson, *A Thirst for Burning*, 9–15.

11 VA679, Register General, Office of Titles, VPRS567, Defunct Mining Company Files 1871–1958, Unit 779, Item 9570, Roma Mooga Oilfields NL. Notice in *Victorian Government Gazette*, 24 October 1928, 2857 and Memorial of Registration, PROV.

12 VPRS 567/779/950, Roma Mooga Oilfields NL. Statement and balance sheet, directors' statements at AGM, 24 April 1930, PROV.

13 Ibid., balance sheet at 30 April 1932 and 31 October 1933.

14 Blainey, *The Rush That Never Ended*, 311–12.

15 Adamson, *A Century of Change*, 142.

16 Australian Securities Commission, CO 148198; Stock Exchange of Melbourne, *Official Report*, August 1932.

17 Stock Exchange of Melbourne, *Official Report*, March 1933.

18 Blainey, *The Rush That Never Ended*, 312, estimates £800,000 by 1939.

19 Boland, *James Duhig*, 271.

20 'Dead at 84, Bill Borthwick, discoverer of gold field in Fiji', *Pacific Islands Monthly*, July 1994, 8.

21 K. Kennedy on Theodore in Appleyard and Schedvin, *Australian Financiers: Biographical Essays*, 301.

22 Salisbury and Sweeney, *The Bull, the Bear and the Kangaro*, 247–8.

23 Fitzgerald, *'Red Ted'*, 345–6.

24 Stock Exchange of Melbourne, *Official Report*, January 1935, 10.

25 VPRS 567/816/10039, Loloma Gold Mines NL, PROV.

26 O'Brien, *The Weekly*, 13; Whitington, *Sir Frank*, 125, 130; Barry, *The Rise and Fall of Kerry Packer*, 36.

27 Stock Exchange of Melbourne, *Official Report*, July 1935, 327.

28 Ibid., September 1935, 432.

29 *Wild Cat Monthly*, 13 January 1940, 38.

30 K. Kennedy on Theodore in Appleyard and Schedvin, *Australian Financiers: Biographical Essays*, 301.

31 VPRS 567/817/10048, PROV; Stock Exchange of Melbourne, *Official Report*, April 1938; *Wild Cat Monthly*, 7 May 1938.

32 Wheelwright, *Ownership and Control of Australian Companies*, 204.

33 VPRS 932/1997, PROV.

34 Freeman, 'The John Wren Legacy', *Age*, 9 January 1982.

35 Norris papers.

36 Return of Directors, 4 October 1961, VPRS 932/7597, Great Boulder Mines Ltd, PROV.

37 *The Times* (London), 23 September 1940; Richardson, 'The origins and development of the Collins House Group 1915–1951', 3–20; Tsokhas, 'A touch of Midas', 132–49; Appleyard and Davies, 'Financiers of Western Australia's goldfields'; Blainey, *The Rush That Never Ended*, 314–16; L. G. Clark, *Built on Gold*; Reid, *A History of Exploration within Western Mining.*

38 VPRS 932/24542, PROV.

39 *War Assets Proprietary Ltd v. Federal Commissioner of Taxation, Commonwealth Law Report*, 91 [1954], 53–98; *Age*, 4 March 1954.

40 Priest, *The Thiess Story*.

41 Peter Freeman in the *Age*, 9 January 1982, calls it 'South Moroco'. Buggy, *The Real John Wren*, 224, says it was purchased on the advice of R. Lean for £54,000. Wren

had never seen the property until he thought of selling: 'Having looked his property over, Wren decided not to sell'.

42 Murray Shire Council, *Galleries of Pink Galahs*, 326.

43 Jo Randall to Joseph Wren, 28 August 1976, Wren papers.

44 J. F. Wren as told to P. Freeman, *Age*, 9 January 1982, and to the author in 1986.

45 Norris papers; auction brochure, 13 December 1984, Baillieu Justin Seward, Perth, in Wren papers. On Commonwealth resumption of a second portion of Spring Hill, there is a letter from the Property and Survey Branch, Department of Interior, Perth, to Manager, West Australian Trustee, Executor and Agency Company Ltd, St George's Terrace, Perth, 43/768, 22 July 1946, and a protest letter setting out arguments against resumption by H. Crosthwaite , Spring Hill, 17 August 1946 to Messrs Buckley, Collins House, Melbourne—apparently to no effect.

46 Norris papers.

47 Buggy, *The Real John Wren*, 56.

48 *Age*, 9 January 1982; Buckley & Hughes to Joseph Wren, 8 April 1954, Wren papers.

49 *Age*, Centenary Supplement, 6 September 1934, 22.

50 VPRS 932/9616, Federal Distilleries Pty Ltd, PROV.

51 Cain, *On with the Show*, 160–1.

52 Author interview with J. F. Wren,1986.

53 VPRS 932/5326, Maize Products Ltd, PROV.

54 Pratt, (ed.), *The National Products Handbook of Australia's Industries*, 268–80.

55 Robertson, *ADB*, *11*, 418–19.

56 VPRS 932/13551, Effront Yeast Pty Ltd, Yeast Company of Australia Pty Ltd, Victorian Yeast Co Pty Ltd, PROV.

57 *Age*, January 1982.

58 Report by P. A. Trouchet on AFEX affairs in West Australia, 20 April 1949, Norris papers; information from R. Betts, Melbourne, 28 April 2002.

59 VPRS 932/25828, Australian Food Exporters Pty Ltd, PROV.

60 VPRS 932/13807, The Realistic Company of Australia Pty Ltd; Lancome Marigny (Aust) Pty Ltd, PROV.

61 *Sydney Morning Herald*, 24, 26 December, 1983.

62 Statement procured courtesy G. Browne.

63 VPRS 932/15373, Clunes Underwear Mills Pty Ltd, PROV.

64 Author interview with Ray Betts, 28 April 2000.

Chapter Twenty-one [pp 385–411]

1 Hackett papers.

2 See pp. 242–3; also *Advocate*, 25 November, 26 August 1920, 19 January 1922.

3 Armstrong, *Frank Hardy and* Power Without Glory, 31–4, 37, 46; Browne, interview with Les Barnes.

4 *Brunswick Sentinel*, 21 February 1994.

5 Gray, 'The truth on Hardy', *Herald-Sun*, 3 May 1994.

6 *Overland*, no. 161, 2000, 72. The publication referred to is Adams and Lee (eds), *Frank Hardy and the Literature of Commitment.*

7 Jack Lindsay's preface to the 1968 edition of *Power Without Glory*, 9–21.

8 For example, my mother, when an adolescent, assisted the midwife at Frank Hardy's birth at Yangery in 1917. She was to be the oldest of eleven children of a dairy share-farmer, generally an impoverished class. She and my grandfather

confirmed the status of Tom Hardy as one of the 'bosses', not workers.

9 Hardy, *The Hard Way*, 39.

10 Armstrong, *Frank Hardy and* Power Without Glory, 2.

11 *Herald-Sun*, 3 May 1994.

12 Armstrong, *Frank Hardy and* Power Without Glory, 6.

13 *Australian Magazine*, 23–4 May 1992.

14 Armstrong, *Frank Hardy and* Power Without Glory, 6–7.

15 Armstrong, *Frank Hardy and* Power Without Glory, 8. Paul Adams says 'Frank worked as a bush labourer picking tobacco and experienced bush life in a depression' (Adams, *The Stranger from Melbourne*, 4). There is no source for this statement. If Hardy was the source, it is worthless.)

16 Hardy, *The Hard Way*, 31.

17 Armstrong, *Frank Hardy and* Power Without Glory, 150.

18 Ibid., 11–15.

19 Ibid., 16–17; cf. Paul Adams, who says that 'when Germany attacked Russia in 1941 he [Hardy] joined the army' (Adams, *The Stranger from Melbourne*, 16). Thus Adams believes Hardy became 'a patriot'.

20 Obituary, *Australian*, 5 February 1994.

21 Quoted by Armstrong, *Frank Hardy and* Power Without Glory, 75.

22 Dick Lean Jnr in Cain, *On with the Show*, 162.

23 Quoted in Adams, *The Stranger from Melbourne*, 76.

24 Author interview with John F. Wren, June 1986.

25 McLaren, *Writing in Hope and Fear*, 3.

26 Author interview with John F. Wren, June 1986.

27 McLaren, *Writing in Hope and Fear*, 3.

28 Armstrong, *Frank Hardy and* Power Without Glory, 44–5.

29 Ibid., 84–5; McLaren, *Writing in Hope and Fear*, 7.

30 *Australian*, 13 April 1985.

31 Rivett, *Australian Citizen, Herbert Brookes 1876–1963*, 71.

32 Albiston, *ADB*, *7*, 29.

33 Rivett, *Australian Citizen, Herbert Brookes 1876–1963*, 71.

34 *Vigilant*, 1 July 1920.

35 Ibid., 12 July 1923.

36 Ruth, *ADB*, *11*, 486.

37 McLaren, *Writing in Hope and Fear*, 7.

38 Armstrong, *Frank Hardy and* Power Without Glory, 78.

39 Ibid.

40 Ibid., 84, 85.

41 Monash University, proceedings of 'Seminar on *Power Without Glory*'.

42 C. Brennan, 'Perfect case that had to fail', 345.

43 Armstrong, *Frank Hardy and* Power Without Glory, 90.

44 Norris papers.

45 Gray, 'The truth on Hardy', *Herald-Sun*, 3 May 1994.

46 Faine, *Taken on Oath*, 35–6, 39.

47 Armstrong, *Frank Hardy and* Power Without Glory, 127.

48 *Australian*, *Sydney Morning Herald*, 8 December 1992.

49 Accounts of the Hardy trial are to be found in contemporary newspapers, in Hardy, *The Hard Way*, 176–244, and in Armstrong, *Frank Hardy and* Power Without Glory, 125–40; copy of transcripts of the trial in the author's possession.

50 Wren, *ADB*, *12*, 583.
51 Faine, *Taken on Oath*, 45–6.
52 *Age*, 29 November 1976.
53 C. Brennan, 'Perfect case that had to fail', 345.
54 *Australian*, 8 December 1992.
55 *Sydney Morning Herald*, 8 December 1992.
56 *Australian*, 8 December 1992.
57 C. Brennan, 'Perfect case that had to fail', 345.
58 Hardy, *Who Shot George Kirkland?*, 77
59 *Sydney Morning Herald*, 17 April 1992.
60 Hardy, *Power Without Glory*, 564–6; Hardy, *Who Shot George Kirkland?*, e.g. 169.
61 Hardy dubiously claimed in the *Sunday Age*, 19 April 1992, that 'Hall first worked for the Commonwealth Investigation Service and then joined ASIO in 1949', its foundation year.
62 *Sydney Morning Herald*, 17 April 1992.
63 Hardy, *Power Without Glory*, 266.
64 Hardy, *The Hard Way*, 147–8.
65 Ibid., 148.
66 *Sydney Morning Herald*, 21 March, 17 April 1992; *Sunday Age*, 22 March, 19 April 1992.
67 Quoted in Armstrong, *Frank Hardy and* Power Without Glory, 184-8.
68 Ibid., 187.
69 Hardy, 'Tall Tales',74.
70 *Sunday Age*, 19 April 1992.
71 Hardy, *Who Shot George Kirkland?*, 85.
72 Ibid., 143; Armstrong, *Frank Hardy and* Power Without Glory, 188.
73 Hardy, *Who Shot George Kirkland?*, 178.
74 K. Brass, interview with Hardy, *Australian Woman's Weekly*, 3 December 1980, 6–7; Armstrong, *Frank Hardy and* Power Without Glory, 184.
75 Simons, 'Evatt–Wren link surprises Hardy'; McNicoll, 'Hardy's libel escape without glory', *Australian*, 8 December 1992.
76 Armstrong, *Frank Hardy and* Power Without Glory, 187; *Argus*, 26 January, 3 March 1923.
77 Hardy, *Who Shot George Kirkland?*, 141.
78 Lindsay wrote a preface to some editions of *Power Without Glory*.
79 Beasley, *Red Letter Days*, 55–91; Lockwood, *Annals Australia*, April–May 1994.
80 *Overland*, no. 161, 2000, 76.
81 Ibid., 72.
82 Ibid., 73–5.
83 Hardy, *Power Without Glory*, 325, 570.
84 *Overland*, no. 161, 2000, 76.
85 Beasley, *Red Letter Days*, 75.
86 *Annals Australia*, April–May 1994.
87 Beasley, *Red Letter Days*, 77.
88 *Age*, *Australian*, 5 February 1994.

Conclusion [pp 412–419]

1 Norris note, 22 May 1990, Norris papers.
2 *Age*, *Argus*, *Sun*, 28 October 1953.

3 Other pall-bearers were Bernard Nolan, M. J. Cody, Bill Beckett, H. Glowrey, H. W. Austin, N. E. Nilsen and W. Donohoe. Others present included E. J. Hogan (former premier), Senator Kennelly, Jack Cremean MHR, Parker Moloney (former federal minister), four current state ministers (Messsrs Barry, Fraser, Galbally, Coleman), J. O'Carroll MLA, P Jones MLC, N. H. Connolly (president of the Licensed Victuallers' Association), Dame Mary Daly (Catholic Womens' Organisation), Percy Page (former secretary of Melbourne and Richmond football clubs), Dick Lean, Lou Richards (Collingwood football captain), Sid and Gordon Coventry (former Collingwood 'greats'), Bill and Mick Twomey and Jack Hamilton (current premiership stars), Billy Cook (Sydney jockey), A. Lopes (Wren's current horse trainer) and Fred Kay (Granny Foster's grandson and champion boxer).

4 The captions were: 'The real John Wren—he had a heart of gold'; 'Never pull my horses—Wren to trainer'; 'Millionaire Wren was once left £20,000' (a reference to Wren's rejection of Granny Foster's legacy); 'Wren rewarded deeds'. Williams had been a professional boxer in the 1920s and later a referee and a journalist of integrity. (*ADB*, *16*, 554).

5 Obits, 27, 28, 29 October, 4, 5 November 1953.

6 Quoted in N. Brennan, *John Wren, Gambler*, 243.

7 An obit in the *Sydney Morning Herald*, 27 October 1953, states that Wren once had a pony track in Sydney 'which went out of existence when the Sydney Turf Club was formed'. I discovered this too late for a follow up. The *Australian Encyclopedia*, vol. 4, 539, says that the Sydney Turf Club Act was proclaimed in August 1943.

8 Blainey, *Our Side of the Country*, 194.

9 Buggy, *The Real John Wren*, xii.

10 Armstrong, *Frank Hardy and* Power Without Glory, 69; *Age*, 20 August 1979.

11 *Age* 1996, newspaper cutting, detail of date illegible.

Abbreviations

MHR	Member of the House of Representatives
MLA	Member of the Legislative Assembly
MLC	Member of the Legislative Council
MP	Member of Parliament
PROV	Public Record Office Victoria

Conversions

1 inch	2.54 centimetres
1 foot	0.30 metre
1 mile	1.61 kilometres
1 furlong (220 yards)	201.17 metres
1 acre	0.4 hectare
1 ounce	28.35 grams
1 pound (lb)	0.45 kilogram
1 gallon	4.55 litres
1 acre	0.40 hectare

On 14 February 1966, Australian currency changed from pounds, shillings and pence (£, s, d) to dollars and cents at the rate of £1 to $2. Twelve pence made up one shilling, and twenty shillings made up one pound. A guinea was a pound plus a shilling.

Sources

Archival collections

Australian Securities Commission records, Melbourne
John Vincent Barry papers (National Library of Australia, Canberra)
Frank Brennan papers (National Library of Australia, Canberra)
Brisbane Diocesan Archives
Defunct Trading Company files, Victoria
Historic Buildings Council, Victoria, file for Studley House (Melbourne Diocesan Historical Commission)
Melbourne, City of, rate-books and other records
Melbourne Trading Company files
Mines and Petroleum Company files
Peter Norris papers (Melbourne Diocesan Historical Commission)
Society of Jesus (Jesuit) Archives, Melbourne
Victoria, Executive Council, minutes
Victoria, Premier's Office, correspondence files
Wren papers (held by Christopher J. Wren, Melbourne)

Books, articles and manuscripts

Adams, Paul, *The Stranger from Melbourne: Frank Hardy—a Literary Biography 1944–1975*, Perth, 1999.

Adams, P. and C. Lee (eds), *Frank Hardy and the Literature of Commitment*, Melbourne, 2003.

Adamson, Graeme, *A Century of Change: the First Hundred Years of the Stock Exchange in Melbourne*, Melbourne, 1984.

Agnew, Max, *Australia's Trotting Heritage*, Melbourne, 1977.

——'Our most controversial official', *Harness World*, April 1980.

——*Silks and Sulkies: the Complete Book of Australian and New Zealand Harness Racing*, Sydney, 1986.

Ahern, Bill, *A Century of Winners: the Saga of 121 Melbourne Cups*, Brisbane, 1982.

——*A Century of Winners: the Saga of 27 Melbourne Cups*, Brisbane, 1988.

Anderson, Hugh, *Larrikin Crook: the Rise and Fall of Squizzy Taylor*, Brisbane, [1971].

Appleyard, R. T., and Mel Davies, 'Financiers of Western Australia's goldfields', in R. T. Appleyard and C. B. Schedvin (eds), *Australian Financiers: Biographical Essays*, Sydney, 1988.

Archer, Fred, *The Treasure House*, self-published, Melbourne, nd [1974].

Armstrong, Pauline, *Frank Hardy and the Making of* Power Without Glory, Melbourne, 2000.

Arnold, John and Deirdre Morris, *Monash Biographical Dictionary of 20th Century Australians*, Melbourne, 1994.

Ayres, Philip, *Owen Dixon*, Melbourne, 2003.

Barrett, Bernard, *The Inner Suburbs: the Evolution of an Industrial Area*, Melbourne, nd [1971].

Barry, Paul, *The Rise and Fall of Kerry Packer*, Sydney, 1993.

Beasley, Jack, *Red Letter Days: Notes from Inside an Era*, Sydney, 1979.

Bennett, Bruce and Jennifer Strauss (eds), *The Oxford Literary History of Australia*, Melbourne, 1998.

Bennison, Ben, *Memories Rekindled*, London, nd, c.1942 (extracts in Norris papers).

Best, Alleyn, *History of the Federated Tobacco Workers' Union in Australia, Victorian Branch, 1884–1968*, Melbourne, 1989.

Blainey, Geoffrey, *Mines in the Spinifex: the Story of Mount Isa Mines*, Sydney, 1960.

——The *Rush That Never Ended: A History of Australian Mining*, Melbourne, 1963.

——*Our Side of the Country: the Story of Victoria*, Sydney, 1984.

——*A Shorter History of Australia*, Melbourne, 1994.

Boland, T. P., *James Duhig*, Brisbane, 1986.

Bongiorno, Frank, *The People's Party: Victorian Labor and the Radical Tradition 1875–1914*, Melbourne, 1996.

Brass, Ken , 'The doubt that inspired Frank Hardy's new book', *Australian Women's Weekly*, 3 December 1990.

Brennan, Colm, 'Perfect case that had to fail', *Law Institute Journal*, May 1994, 344–5.

Brennan, Niall, *John Wren: Gambler, His Life and Times*, Melbourne, 1971.

Brett, Judith, 'Stanley Melbourne Bruce', in Michelle Grattan, (ed.), *Australian Prime Ministers*, Sydney, 2000.

Briggs, Asa, *Victorian Cities*, Melbourne, 1968 (first edition London, 1963).

Brisbane, Katherine, *Entertaining Australia*, Sydney, 1991 (copies by courtesy of Mimi Colligan, Melbourne).

Broome, Richard, 'Boxing' in Wray Vamplew et al. (eds), *The Oxford Companion to Australian Sport*, Melbourne, 1992.

Brown, Greg, *One Hundred Years of Trotting*, Sydney, 1881.

Browne, Geoffrey, John Wren, his Tote and the Police, manuscript, nd (held by its author, Melbourne).

——*Biographical Register of the Victorian Parliament, 1900–84*, Melbourne, 1985.

——interview with Les Barnes, Brunswick Public Library, 21 December 1989 (copy held by J. Griffin).

——Stan Keon, manuscript,1994 (held by its author, Melbourne).

Buckley, Ken, Barbara Dale and Wayne Reynolds, *Doc Evatt: Patriot, Internationalist, Fighter and Scholar*, Melbourne, 1994.

Buggy, Hugh, *The Real John Wren*, Melbourne, 1977.

Butler, A. G., *Official History of the Australian Medical Services in the War 1914–18*, vol. 1, *Gallipoli and Palestine*, Melbourne, 1930; vol. 2, *The Western Front*, Canberra, 1940; vol. 3, *Special Problems and Services*, Canberra, 1943.

Cahill, A. E., 'Catholics and Federation', *Australian Catholic Historical Society Journal*, vol. 22, 9–30.

Cain, John, *On with the Show: a Glimpse Behind the Scenes of Entertainment in Australia*, Melbourne, 1998.

Caldwell, Geoffrey, 'Characteristics of Australian gambling', in G. Caldwell et al. (eds), *Gambling in Australia*, Sydney, nd (c.1985).

Calil, Carmen and Colin Tobin (compilers), *The Modern Library: the Two Hundred Best Novels in English since 1950*, London, 2000.

Calwell, A. A., *Be Just and Fear Not*, Melbourne, 1972.

Cannon, Michael, *The Land Boomers*, Melbourne, 1966.

Cannon, Michael (ed.), *Hold Page One: Memoirs of Monty Grover, Editor*, Main Ridge, Vic., 1993.

Carringbush Regional Library, *Copping it Sweet: Shared Memories of Richmond*, Melbourne, 1988.

Cash, Damian, John Wren and Racing, manuscript, nd.

——Stadiums Ltd (1914–37) and Stadiums Pty Ltd (1937–83), A Guide to the Records in the University of Melbourne Archives, manuscript (copy held by J. Griffin).

——Database of Illegal Gambling Cases in Victoria June–December 1905, manuscript and not exhaustive, based on *Argus* crime and law reports (held by its author, Melbourne).

——John Wren's world of racing', in G. Hutchinson (ed.), *They're Racing*, Melbourne, 1999.

Cavanough, Maurice, *The Caulfield Cup*, Sydney, 1976.

Charlton, Peter, *Two Flies up a Wall: the Australian Passion for Gambling*, Sydney, 1987.

Childe, V. Gordon, *How Labour Governs: a Study of Workers' Representation in Australia*, London, 1923 (Melbourne, 1964), with a foreword by F. B. Smith.

Clark, Lindesay G., *Built on Gold: Recollections of Western Mining*, Melbourne, 1983.

Clark, Manning [C. M. H.], *Select Documents in Australian History 1851–1900*, Sydney, 1955.

——*A History of Australia*, vol. I, *From the Earliest Time to the Age of Macquarie*, Melbourne, 1962; vol. V, *The People Make Laws 1888–1915*, Melbourne, 1981; vol. VI, *'the old dead tree and the young tree green' 1916–1935*, Melbourne, 1987.

Clark, Mary Ryllis and Celestina Sagazio, *The Story of Rippon Lea*, Melbourne, 1995.

Colligan, Mimi, *Canvas Documentaries: Panoramic Entertainment in Nineteenth-Century Australia and New Zealand*, Melbourne, 2002.

Cook, P., 'Frank Anstey and Memoirs of the Scullin Government 1929–1932', *Historical Studies*, no. 18, 72, April 1979.

Corris, Peter, *Lords of the Ring*, Sydney, 1980.

Costello, Tim and Royce Millar, *Wannabet? Winners and Losers in Gambling's Luck Myth*, Sydney, 2000.

Cotter, Richard, 'War, boom and depression' in James Griffin (ed.), *Essays in Economic History*, Melbourne, 2002.

Cowen, Zelman, *Sir John Latham and Other Papers*, Melbourne, 1965.

Crisp, L. F., *The Australian Federal Labor Party 1901–1951*, Melbourne, 1955.

——*Ben Chifley: a Biography*, Melbourne, 1960.

——*Australian National Government*, Melbourne, 1965.

Crockett, Peter, *Evatt, a Life*, Melbourne, 1993.

Cronin, Mike and Daryl Adair, *The Wearing of the Green: a History of St Patrick's Day*, London, 2002.

Crowe, Cornelius, *Serious Tampering with the Course of Justice*, Melbourne, nd [1907].

——*The Inquiry Agent: a Drama of Real Life etc.*, Melbourne, 1909.

——*One Big Crime*, Melbourne, 1920.

Crowley, Frank K., *Modern Australia in Documents*, 2 vols, Melbourne, 1973.

——*A Documentary History of Australia*, vol. 3, *Colonial Australia 1875–1900*, Melbourne, 1980.

Dalziel, Allan, *Evatt the Enigma*, Melbourne, 1970.

Davies, Lloyd, *In Defence of My Family*, Perth, 1987.

Davison, Graeme, *The Rise and Fall of Marvellous Melbourne*, Melbourne, 1978.

Davison, Graeme, John Hirst and Stuart Macintyre, *The Oxford Companion to Australian History*, Melbourne, 2001.

Day, David, *John Curtin, a Life*, Sydney, 1999.

de Serville, Paul, *Pounds and Pedigrees: the Upper Class in Victoria, 1850–80*, Melbourne, 1991.

Dening, Greg, *Xavier, a Centenary Portrait*, Melbourne, 1978.

Derriman, P., 'John Wren: the family breaks its silence', *Sydney Morning Herald*, 24 December 1987.

Dow, Hume (ed.), *Trollope's Australia*, Melbourne, 1966.

Duncan, Bruce, *Crusaders or Conspiracy? Catholics and the Anti-Communist Struggle in Australia*, Sydney, 2001.

Dunstan, David (ed.), 'Racing and politics', in his *Victorian Icon: The Royal Exhibition Building*, with Mimi Colligan, Melbourne, 1996.

Dunstan, Keith, *Wowsers: being an Account of the Prudery Exhibited by Certain Australian Men and Women in such Matters as Drinking, Smoking, Prostitution, Censorship and Gambling*, Melbourne, 1968.

Ebsworth, Walter A., *Archbishop Mannix*, Melbourne, 1977.

Edgar, S., 'King of the West End', *National Times*, 2–8 May 1982, 12–14.

Edwards, Cecil, *Bruce of Melbourne: Man of Two Worlds*, London, 1965.

Eggleston, Frederic, Confidential Notes: the Victorian Parliament as I Knew it, manuscript (Australian National University Library).

Emmerson, K., 'George Beavis, the pioneering years of midgets', *Speedway Net*, 9 April 2002.

Ferrier, Carole (ed.), *Point of Departure: the Autobiography of Jean Devanny*, Brisbane, 1986.

Fitzgerald, Ross, *'Red Ted': The Life of E. G. Theodore*, Brisbane, 1994.

——*Seven Days to Remember: the World's First Labor Government*, Brisbane, 1999.

Fitzhardinge, L. F., *The Little Digger: William Morris Hughes, a Political Biography*, vol. 2, Sydney, 1979.

Fitzpatrick, J. 'The spectrum of Australian bicycle racing 1890–1900' in Richard Cashman and Michael McKernan (eds), *Sport in History*, Brisbane, 1979.

Ford, Patrick, *Cardinal Moran and the ALP: a Study in the Encounter between Moran and Socialism 1890–1907, its Effects upon the Australian Labor Party, and the Foundation of Catholic Social Thought and Action in Modern Australia*, Melbourne, 1966.

Forde, John Leonard, *The Story of the Bar in Victoria: from its Foundation to the Amalgamation of the Two Branches of the Legal Profession 1839–1891*, Melbourne, 1913.

Freeman, Peter, 'The John Wren legacy', *Age*, 9 January 1982.

Fricke, Graham, *Judges of the High Court*, Melbourne, 1986.

Garden, Don, *Victoria, a History*, Melbourne, 1984.
Gibson, Ralph, *My Years with the Communist Party*, Melbourne, 1966.
Gilchrist, Michael, *Daniel Mannix: Priest & Patriot*, Melbourne, c.1982.
Glass, Margaret, *Tommy Bent: Bent by Name and Bent by Nature*, Melbourne, 1993.
Gordon, Harry, *An Eyewitness Account of Australia*, Melbourne, 1976.
Gray, Paul, 'The truth on Hardy', *Herald-Sun*, 3 May 1994.
Grant, Ian, *Jacka VC: Australia's Finest Fighting Soldier*, Melbourne, 1989.
Gregory, J., *Church and State*, Melbourne, 1973.
Griffin, James, 'Daniel Mannix and the cult of personality', in O. Macdonagh and W. Mandel (eds), *Ireland and Irish History*, London, 1986.
——letters section, *Australian Book Review*, April 2001.
——'The choice of Achilles? What did happen to Albert Jacka?', *Quadrant*, February 2002.
——articles on Wren, Evatt etc., *Eureka Street*, August–October 1992.
Griffin, James and Geoffrey Browne, 'Some light in shady places', in P. Bull *et al.* (eds), *Irish-Australian Studies*, 1991.
Guyatt, B. J., 'The publicists: the Labour press, 1886–1915', in D. J. Murphy, R. B. Joyce and Colin A. Hughes (eds), *Prelude to Power: the Rise of the Labour Party in Queensland, 1885–1915*, Brisbane, 1970.
Haldane, Robert, *The People's Force: a History of the Victorian Police Force*, Melbourne, 1986.
Hannaford, C. H., *Index to the* Lone Hand, *1907–13* (first series), vol. 1 no. 1, May 1907 to vol. 13, 7 November 1913, Adelaide, 1967.
Hansen, B, *The Magpies, 1892–1992*, Melbourne, 1992.
——*The Jack Dyer Story: the Legend of Captain Blood*, Melbourne, 1996.
Hardy, Frank J., *Power Without Glory: a Novel*, Sydney and Melbourne, 1975 (first edition, 1950).
——*Journey into the Future*, Melbourne, 1952.
——*The Hard Way: the Story Behind* Power Without Glory, Melbourne, 1992 (first edition, London, 1961).
——*But the Dead are Many: a Novel in Fugue Form*, St Albans, Herts, UK, 1976 (first edition, London, 1975).
——*Who Shot George Kirkland?: a Novel about the Nature of Truth*, Sydney, 1981.
——'Tall tales' in K. Childs, *A Month of Lunches*, Melbourne, 1984.
Hardy-Rix, Shirley and Ralph Stavely, *True Blue Stories of Bravery from Victorian Police*, Melbourne, 1997.
Hasluck, Paul, *The Government and the People, 1939–1941*, Canberra, 1952.
Hearn (Senyard), June, Collingwood Values, seminar papers on *Power Without Glory*: its Historical Significance, 1976, tapes held in Council of Adult Education Library, Melbourne.

Henderson, G., 'The deportation of Charles Jerger', *Labour History*, no. 31, 1976.

Hewett, D., letter in *Australian Book Review*, April 2001.

Hibbins, G. M., *A Short History of Collingwood*, Melbourne, 1997.

Hocking, Jenny, 'Marketing Frank Hardy: the revival of biography as scandal', *Journal of Australian Studies*, vol. 68, 2001.

Holt, Stephen, 'A lifetime of service', *National Library of Australia News*, December 2002.

Hore-Lacy, Ian (ed.), *Broken Hill to Mount Isa: the Mining Odyssey of W.H. Corbould*, Melbourne, 1981.

Howells, A. F., *Against the Stream: Memories of a Philosophical Anarchist 1927*–1939, Melbourne, 1983.

Hughes, Colin A. and B. D. Graham, *A Handbook of Australian Government and Politics, 1890–1964*, Canberra, 1968.

Hutchinson, Garrie (ed.), *They're Racing: the Complete Story of Australian Racing*, Melbourne, 1999.

Hutchinson, G. and J. Ross (eds), *The Clubs*, Melbourne, 1998.

Inglis, K. S., *The Australian Colonists: an Exploration of Social History*, Melbourne, 1974.

——'Gambling and culture in Australia', in Geoffrey Caldwell *et al.* (eds), *Gambling in Australia*, Sydney, c.1985.

Jacobs, Philip A., *Judges of Yesterday*, Melbourne, 1924.

Jensen, H. I., *Dan Green: Mystery Man*, Brisbane, 1948.

[Judkins, H.], 'The gambling demons in Australia', *Review of Reviews*, 1 July 1906.

Jungwirth, J., Autobiography (copy of galley proof pages 2 and 17 held by J. Griffin, by courtesy Geoff Browne, Melbourne).

Kennedy, K. H., *The Mungana Affair: State Mining and Political Corruption in the 1920s*, Brisbane, 1978.

——on Theodore, in R. T. Appleyard and C. B. Schedvin (eds), *Australian Financiers: Biographical Essays*, Melbourne 1988.

Kent, J., *The Solomon Islands*, Melbourne 1972, 1973.

Kiddle, Margaret, *Caroline Chisholm*, Melbourne, 1957.

King, T, 'The tarring and feathering of J. K. McDougall', *Labour History*, no. 45, 1983, 54–67.

Koch, Christopher, *The Boys in the Island*, Sydney, 1990 (first edition 1958).

Kwan, E., 'The Australian Flag, the Irish Republic and *Ireland Will Be Free*, a Forgotten Australian Film of 1920, seminar paper, Department of History, Research School of Social Sciences, Australian National University, April 1993.

Lang, J. T., *The Great Bust: the Depression of the Thirties*, Sydney, 1932.

——*The Turbulent Years*, Sydney,1970.

Lemon, Andrew and Harold Freedman, *The History of Australian Thoroughbred Racing*, vol. 2, *The Golden Years from 1862 to 1939*, Melbourne, 1990.

Lindsay, Jack, Preface to the 1968 edition of Frank Hardy, *Power Without Glory*.

Lloyd, Clem, 'Not peace but a sword: the High Court under J. G. Latham', *Adelaide Law Review*, vol. 2, no. 2, 1987.

Lockwood, R., 'No redress for Hardy's victims', *Annals Australia*, April–May 1994, 18-19.

Longmire, Anne, *St Kilda: the Show Goes On, History of St Kilda*, vol. 3, Melbourne, 1989.

Lynn, Peter and George Armstrong, *From Pentonville to Pentridge: a History of Prisons in Victoria*, Melbourne, 1996.

McCalman, Janet, *Struggletown: Public and Private Life in Richmond, 1900–1965*, Melbourne, 1984.

McCaughey, Davis, Naomi Perkins and Angus Trumble, *Victoria's Colonial Governors*, Melbourne, 1983.

McConville, Chris, 'John Wren: machine boss, Irish chieftain or meddling millionaire?', *Labour History*, May 1981.

McGillick, T., *Comrade no More*, Perth, 1980.

Macintyre, Stuart, *The Oxford History of Australia* (G. Bolton, general editor), vol. 4, *1901–19, The Succeeding Age*, Melbourne, 1993.

——'Football weathers the storms of war' in J. Ross (ed.), *100 Years of Football*, Melbourne, 1996.

——*The Reds: the Communist Party of Australia from Origins to Illegality*, Sydney, 1998.

McKernan, Michael, 'An incident of social reform in Melbourne, 1906', *Journal of Religious History*, vol. 10, no. 1, 1978.

——*Australian Churches at War: Attitude and Activities of the Major Churches, 1914–1918*, Sydney, 1980.

McLaren, John, *Writing in Hope and Fear: Literature as Politics in Postwar Australia*, Melbourne, 1996.

McManus, Frank, *The Tumult and the Shouting*, Adelaide, 1977.

McMullin, Ross, *The Light on the Hill: the Australian Labor Party, 1891–1991*, Melbourne, 1991.

McNicoll, D., 'Hardy's libel escapes without glory', *Australian*, 8 December 1992.

Main, Jim and Russell Holmesbury, *The Encyclopedia of League Footballers*, Melbourne, 1992.

Marshall,Vance, *Jail from Within*, Sydney, 1918.

——*World of the Living Dead*, Sydney, 1919.

Martin, A. W., *Robert Menzies: a Life*, vol. 1, *1894–1943*, Melbourne, 1993.

Meudell, George D., *The Pleasant Career of a Spendthrift*, London, 1929.

Mishael, H. Lend Me Your Ears, part 1, autobiography, manuscript, LaTrobe Library, Melbourne, courtesy G Browne, Melbourne.

Monash University, proceedings of 'Seminar on *Power Without Glory*', typescript, 1976 (copy held by J. Griffin).

Moorhead, Alan, *A Late Education: Episodes in a Life*, London, 1933.

Murphy, Dennis, *T. J. Ryan: a Political Biography*, Brisbane, 1975.

——(ed.), *Labor in Politics: the State Labor Parties in Australia 1880–1920*, Brisbane, 1975.

Murphy, D. J., R. B. Joyce and Colin A. Hughes (eds), *Prelude to Power: the Rise of the Labour Party in Queensland 1885–1915*, Brisbane, 1970.

Murphy, Frank, *Daniel Mannix*, Melbourne, 1948 (new edition 1972).

Murray, Robert, *The Split: Australian Labor in the Fifties*, Melbourne, 1970.

Murray Shire Council, *Galleries of Pink Galahs: History of Murray Shire*, 1973.

Nairn, Bede, *The 'Big Fella': Jack Lang and the Australian Labor Party 1891–1949*, Melbourne, 1986.

Noud, Ken, *Courses for Horses*, Brisbane, 1989.

O'Brien, Denis, *The Weekly: a Lively and Nostalgic Celebration of Australia through Fifty Years*, Melbourne, 1982.

O'Farrell, Patrick, *The Catholic Church and Community in Australia: a History*, Melbourne, 1977.

O'Hara, John, *A Mug's Game: a History of Gaming and Betting in Australia*, Sydney, 1988.

O'Leary, M. A., *Till the Shadows Lengthen: Caritas Christi Hospice, Kew, 1938–1988*, Melbourne, 1988.

O'Leary, Zoe, *The Desolate Market: Biography of Eric Lambert*, Sydney, 1974.

Opperman, H. F., *Pedals, Politics and People*, Sydney, 1977.

O'Reilly, Bill, *'Tiger': 60 Years of Cricket*, Sydney, 1965.

Osborn, L. 'A full day's work: a life of the Rev. T. S. B. Woodfull', *Uniting Church Historical Society*, vol. 2, no. 1, 1995.

Pacini, John, *A Century Galloped By: the First Hundred Years of the Victoria Racing Club*, Melbourne, 1988.

Page, Michael, *Bradman: the Illustrated Biography*, Melbourne, 1983.

Park, Ruth and Rafe Champion, *Home Before Dark*, Melbourne, 1995.

Pearl, Cyril, *Wild Men of Sydney*, Melbourne, 1958.

Pollard, Jack, *The Pictorial History of Australian Horse Racing*, Sydney, 1971.

Pratt, Ambrose (ed.), with Edward Leeson, *The National Products Handbook of Australia's Industries*, Melbourne, 1934.

Reid, D., *A History of Exploration within Western Mining*, Perth, 1981.

Renouf, Alan, *Let Justice Be Done: the Foreign Policy of Dr H. V. Evatt*, Brisbane, 1983.

Richards, Lou with Stephen Phillips, *The Kiss of Death: Memoirs of a Sporting Legend*, Melbourne, 1989.

Richardson, P., 'The origins and development of the Collins House Group 1915–1951', *Australian Economic History Review*, vol. 27, March 1987.

Rivett, Rohan, *Australian Citizen, Herbert Brookes 1867–1963*, Melbourne, 1965.

Robertson, John, *J. H. Scullin: a Political Biography*, Perth, 1974.

Robson, Lloyd L., *The First AIF: a Study of its Recruitment*, Melbourne, 1970.

Ross, Edgar, *These Things Shall Be! Bob Ross, Socialist Pioneer, His Life and Times*, Sydney, 1988.

Ross, J. (ed.), *100 Years of Football*, Melbourne, 1996.

Ross, Lloyd, *John Curtin: a Biography*, Melbourne, 1977.

Rubinstein, W. D., 'The changing demographic and socio-economic status of the Jewish community of Victoria, 1870–1980', in H. L. Rubinstein, *The Jews in Victoria, 1835–1985*, Sydney, 1988.

Rule, E. J., 'Jacka's mob', *Reveille*, 1 January 1939.

Salisbury, Stephen and Kay Sweeney, *The Bull, the Bear and the Kangaroo: the History of the Sydney Stock Exchange*, Sydney, 1988.

Sandercock, Leonie and Ian Turner, *Up Where Cazaly?: the Great Australian Game*, Sydney, 1981.

Santamaria, B. A., *Against the Tide*, Melbourne 1981.

——*Daniel Mannix: the Quality of Leadership*, Melbourne, 1984.

Sawer, G., *Australian Federal Politics and Law, 1909–1929*, Melbourne, 1956.

Scarfe, Wendy and Allen, *No Taste for Carnage, Alex Sheppard: a Portrait 1913–1997*, Melbourne, 1997.

Schedvin, C. B., *Australia and the Great Depression: a Study of Economic Development and Policy in the 1920s and 1930s*, Sydney, 1976.

Semmler, Clem, 'The most Australian rebel spun class yarns', *Australian*, 5 February 1994.

Senyard, June, *see* Hearn, June

Serle, Geoffrey, *The Rush to be Rich*, Melbourne, 1971.

Sheppard, A. W. (ed.), *Catholic Action and Australian Labor*, Sydney, 1953.

Simons, Margaret, 'Evatt–Wren link surprises Hardy', *Sunday Age*, 9 August 1992.

Sorrenti, V., 'Monumental as anything', *Good Weekend* magazine, *Sydney Morning Herald*, 11 April 1992.

Souter, Gavin, *Acts of Parliament*, Melbourne, 1988.

Spann, R. N., 'The Catholic vote in Australia' in H. Mayer, *Catholics and the Free Society*, Sydney, 1961.

Stivens, Dal, *Jimmy Brockett, Portrait of a Notable Australian*, London, 1951.

Stremski, Richard, *Kill for Collingwood*, Sydney, 1986.

Sugden, E. H. and F. W. Eggleston, *George Swinburne*, Sydney, 1931.

Syson, Ian, '50 years of *Power Without Glory*', *Overland*, no. 161, 2000, 72–8.

Taylor, Kit, *A History with Indexes of the* Lone Hand*: a Biography of the Australian Monthly*, Melbourne, 1977.

Tennant, Kylie, *Evatt, Politics and Justice*, Sydney, 1970.

Thiess, Joan, *The Thiess Story*, Brisbane, 1981.

Tomlinson, Jenny, *Born Winners, Born Losers: a History of Thoroughbred Breeding and Racing in Western Australia since 1833*, Perth, c.1990.

Tsokhas, K., 'A touch of Midas: the rise of Western Mining Corporation', *Australian Economic History Review*, March 1984.

Twain, Mark, *Mark Twain in Australia and New Zealand*, Melbourne, 1973.

Vamplew, Wray *et al.* (eds), 'From sport to business: first seventy-five years of horse racing in South Australia', *Journal of the Historical Society of South Australia*, vol. 11, 1983.

——*The Oxford Companion to Australian Sport*, Melbourne, 1992.

Vaughan, R. B. *et al.*, Catholic Education: A Pastoral Letter of the Archbishop and Bishops Exercising Jurisdiction in New South Wales, Sydney, 1879, *see* 'Seedplots of immorality' in Frank Crowley, *A Documentary History of Australia*, vol. 3, *Colonial Australia, 1875–1900*, Melbourne, 1980, 56–7.

Weller, Patrick (ed.) with Beverley Lloyd, *Caucus Minutes 1901–1941*, vol. 1, *1901–17*, Melbourne, 1975; vol. 2, *1917–33*, Melbourne 1975.

Wheelwright, E. L., *Ownership and Control of Australian Companies: a Study of 102 of the Largest Public Companies and Corporations Incorporated in Australia*, Sydney, 1957.

White, Kate, *John Cain & Victorian Labor, 1917–1957*, Sydney, c.1982.

Whitington, Don, *Ring the Bells: a Dictionary of Australian Federal Politics*, Melbourne, 1956.

Whitington, R. S., *Sir Frank: the Sir Frank Packer Story*, Melbourne, 1971.

Whitlam, Gough, *The Whitlam Government 1972–1975*, Melbourne, 1985.

Wilde, William H., Joy Hooton and Barry Andrew (eds), *Oxford Companion to Australian Literature*, Melbourne, 1985.

Wilkinson, Rick, *A Thirst for Burning: the Story of Australia's Oil Industry*, Sydney, 1983.

York, Barry, 'No holds barred', *National Library News*, June 1997.

——'Thomas John Ley, politician and murderer', *National Library News*, July 2001.

Young, Irwin Edward, *Theodore, his Life and Times*, Sydney, 1971.

Zwar, Desmond, *In Search of Keith Murdoch*, Melbourne, 1980.

Index